The
Biblical
Times

The
Biblical
Times

Edited by
Derek Williams

BakerBooks
A Division of Baker Book House Co
Grand Rapids, Michigan 49516

© 1997 by Inter Publishing Service (IPS) Ltd.

First published in the USA
by Baker Books
a division of Baker Book House Company
P.O. Box 6287, Grand Rapids, MI 49516-6287
ISBN: 0-8010-1155-8

First published in the UK
by Eagle
an imprint of Inter Publishing Services (IPS) Ltd.
St. Nicholas House
14 The Mount
Guildford
Surrey GU2 5HN
ISBN: 0-86347-183-3

Library of Congress Cataloging-in-Publication Data. A record for *The Biblical Times* is available from the Library of Congress.

Printed in Spain by Grafichromo

For information about all new releases available from Baker Book House, visit our web site:

http://www.bakerbooks.com

Contributors

The Biblical Times is the result of teamwork. The principal team members are:

MANAGING EDITOR
David Wavre, Inter Publishing Service Limited

GENERAL EDITOR AND AUTHOR
Derek Williams

ARCHITECTURAL DIAGRAMS
Howard Birchmore

COPY EDITOR
Susan Wavre, Inter Publishing Service Limited

EDITORIAL CONSULTANTS
Dr Carl Armerding, Professor, History of the Old Testament, Regent
College, Vancouver, Canada
Dr John Bimson, Librarian and Lecturer in Old Testament and Hebrew,
Trinity Theological College, Bristol
Gordon McConville, Professor, Old Testament, Wycliffe Hall, Oxford
David Wenham, Professor, New Testament, Wycliffe Hall, Oxford

ILLUSTRATOR
Jane Taylor, Genus Art.

LAYOUT AND DESIGN
Sally Hiller, Inter Publishing Service Limited

MAPS
Sally Maltby

PHOTOGRAPHY
Jon Arnold

PROJECT COORDINATOR
Lynne Barratt, Inter Publishing Service Limited

PICTURE RESEARCH
Holly Whitelaw, Inter Publishing Service Limited

RESEARCHER
Ricarda Leask

WRITERS
Mike Fearon
David Porter

Contents

The Biblical Times has been arranged chronologically throughout.

It starts with the creation, and a number of other pages out of chronological sequence. The Introduction explains the principles involved due principally to uncertainty amongst scholars of the dating of certain events. The detailed index provides the best way to finding particular events, places or people.

The principal headings are as follow.

Introduction

The Bible is set in, and throws light on, a wide context of world affairs. Egypt, Assyria, Babylon, Persia, Greece, Rome – great empires ebbed and flowed while the people of Israel prospered or suffered; the background kept changing as the drama was played out in Palestine. And beyond it, other civilisations grew and flourished at the same time. These had little or no reference to the Near East, yet in their own way set the scene for the world societies of today.

The purpose of this book is to enable you to see the biblical drama clearly in its wider cultural context. At the same time, we have attempted to present that drama in a fresh way. It is written as if each event has just happened and is being reported by an eyewitness. Into the biblical material is drawn local information known from other sources, and set alongside it are stories of other events going on nearby or further afield at the time.

Wherever possible we have used genuine artefacts and remains to illustrate the text, together with artists' impressions based on archaeological research, and a few photographs of contemporary sites where once-significant acts in the drama took place.

To achieve a degree of consistency and coherence, we have had to make a few decisions about events over which scholars disagree. Many of the dates are prefaced by 'c.' (circa) meaning 'about', because with different calendars in use in ancient times exact dating is sometimes impossible, and minor variations may be seen in other reference books.

This is true especially for the life of Christ, in which the precise dates and order of events and teachings cannot be deduced completely from the Gospels.

Some events can, however, be dated quite differently with apparently equal scholarly support. Two of these affect us especially. One is the date of the Exodus, the hurried departure of the Israelites from Egypt. We have opted for an early date, c. 1400 BC; many scholars would place it later, around 1280 BC.

The other concerns some of the New Testament events and letters, especially those associated with Paul's letter to the Galatians. We have opted for the earliest date possible for Galatians (c. AD 49) and have dated Paul's activities accordingly. Some scholars would give a later date and a different order of events.

In all such cases where similar decisions have been taken, the choice is that of the authors. But the scholarly disagreements do not materially affect the overall teaching and message of the biblical documents.

One other period has of necessity been a matter of considerable conjecture, and that is the 'pre-history' – from the dawn of creation to the time of Abraham and the patriarchs. A book which places the Bible in its world historical context cannot ignore this period, but the biblical material itself is so scanty and perhaps poetic in nature that we have drawn heavily on other material and allowed a greater degree of poetic licence in the retelling of the biblical narrative.

Inevitably we also concentrate more on the narrative parts of the Bible. The 'teaching' books are dealt with as far as possible in the context of the events which gave rise to them. Where the biblical events are packed closely together in a relatively short space of time, as in the New Testament, the proportion of other world events reported becomes rather less; where there are wide gaps in the biblical record, there is more material from elsewhere.

Modern place names are used whenever this would be helpful, even if they would have been unknown at the time of the events. Where this is impossible or intrusive, some indication of a location is usually included within the text so that it can be identified on a map. And as this is a book which is as likely to be used for reference as it is to be read through steadily, titles and names are usually explained or briefly put into their context whenever they appear, rather than being explained only on their first occurrence.

As the story unfolds, some explanation of it is given. The authors write from a deep respect for the integrity and message of the Bible, and have tried to allow the Bible to explain itself. They have sought to avoid any denominational over-emphases of specific issues.

It is our hope that all readers of whatever church allegiance (if any) will find in these pages, not only clear illumination of the facts (which do not appear in chronological order in the Bible itself), but will through those facts receive fresh encouragement to find in the Bible not only a catalogue of history but also the source of inspiration for life today.

When time began

It was beyond human imagination. One moment there was nothing, only someone – God. Then there was something. In an explosion of creative energy, matter as we know it began its slow process of formation and development.

Exactly how it formed, and why it began when it did, are secrets known only to its creator. Every generation has its own explanations, couched in the terms of reference which its culture uses to frame a working philosophy of life.

The biblical account, believed by many to reach back into the recesses of the corporate human memory and to have been implanted there by God himself, suggests that it followed a simple sequence. Each step in the sequence is directed by the divine choreographer, and is called a 'day'; biblical writers use the same word for both a 24-hour day and an indefinable period of time and allow the context to indicate which is meant.

Christians differ over which use of the term is intended in Genesis 1, but the overall message is that history and time had a definite beginning within the will and purpose of God. The sequence given is:

• At the command of God, light appeared. God separated light and darkness. He named them 'day' and 'night', and the first day dawned.
History had begun.

• On the second day, God created the sky. He called it good.

• On the third day, he created dry ground. He made plants and trees, to bear fruit and produce seeds. History was already inventing a future. God called it good.

• On the fourth day, God made the sun and the moon and the vast carpet of heavenly objects. He called them good.

• On the fifth day, God made living creatures that teemed in the seas, and birds that flew in the skies. He called them good also.

Sunrise over clouds.

• On the sixth day, God first made living creatures to roam the land and produce young. God called them good.

• On the sixth day, God also made human beings, bearing the stamp of his own likeness. He created them as man and woman, installed them in his newly-created world, and gave them the responsibility of ruling and caring for all that he had made.
God surveyed everything that he had made, and pronounced it very good.

• On the seventh day he rested from his work of creation; and that is why the seventh day, throughout history, has always been held to be holy.

(Genesis 1:1–2:3; cf. 2:4–7)

The meaning it always holds

The first three chapters of Genesis form a foundation to the whole biblical narrative. Written as a succinct account, they depict in simple terms theological truths which can be understood in every generation and culture:

• God is the controller both of the initial act of creation and the on-going creative life of the world. The rose blossoms each year because God wills that it should. There is no biblical basis for a belief in 'Nature' or in 'Providence' as a blind benevolent force.

• The world was created in a sequence, the crowning act of which was the creation of human beings. There is a broad correlation between the biblical sequence and generally accepted scientific chronology.

• Human beings are not the dominant earth-species by a freak of natural selection, but by the deliberate choice of God who has created men and women in his own image.

So although the dolphin, for example, has intelligence and abilities we are only now beginning to recognise, dolphins can never be considered the peak of creation, for they are not made in the image of God. That image separates us from the animals.

• The world, as first created, was a good creation: God so describes it, no less than six times.

• His deliberate choice of making human beings able to respond to him and with an inherent responsibility for the environment gives a sense of meaning and purpose to human life and society. We exist to reflect the creator's character and concerns and to find in his good purposes the fulfilment which all people desire.

• His specific choice of two people points to his desire to be known and to live in close relationship with human beings. The biblical saga shows the dogged determination of God to maintain those close links with at least some people, despite the rejection of him and his purposes by many.

• That rejection is pictured in the account of Adam and Eve's 'fall'. It has cataclysmic effects on the whole race, affecting every member of the human community and every fibre of society. It is seen as the root of all evil and suffering which quickly becomes endemic. It seems to magnify the weaknesses and limitations of all created things, so that Paul in the New Testament can speak of creation's 'frustration'.

(Romans 8:20)

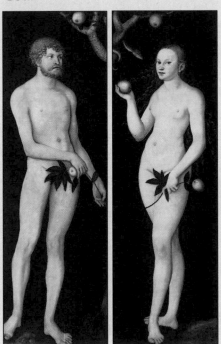

God – represented in many ways, but maybe portrayed most of all as the Creator, by Michelangelo, Sistine Chapel.

God – the universe's one and only constant factor

The existence of God is assumed in the biblical narrative, and no attempt is made to prove him. Rather it sets out to describe what he is like, how he acts and what he requires of human beings. God is himself uncreated; until he made the physical order of time and space there was no time or space, and as these dimensions form the only reference points we have to understand and describe anything, the ultimate nature of God is therefore beyond our comprehension.

The biblical narrative is believed by Christians to contain the basic revelation of this God, which was made not in a set of presuppositions but through the sometimes painfully drawn-out saga of real-time and often imperfect events. Among the principles it implies are:

• He is complete in himself. His creation of the world and its inhabitants is an act of love, not of loneliness. He desires to share his goodness because it is good.

• He is a community in himself. The New Testament revelation of God as a tri-unity – one God expressed and experienced as three genuinely distinct 'persons' – baffles human understanding. But it points to a divine 'community' of relationships of which all human relationships are but a pale reflection.

• He is separate from his creation. There is no biblical ground for the belief that all humans are part of the Godhead, that everything is God, or that the universe itself is part of the being of God (such beliefs are called 'pantheism' and 'panentheism'). God is not a part of his creation.

• He is the one and only God. In a world where primitive societies worshipped celestial objects, pieces of rock and fearsome natural forces, the first verses of the Old Testament describe a cosmos in which all these, and every part of the world, are created by the one God.

First humans to know God placed in ideal location

The man and the woman created by God and called to live in harmony with him were placed in a garden in Eden. They were given basic instructions about survival and responsibility to look after their home.

The garden contained beautiful trees, and those that yield nourishing fruit. In the centre were two trees: the tree of life, and the tree of the knowledge of good and evil. The garden was irrigated by a stream which on leaving Eden divided into four flowing through neighbouring territories.

God gave the man – whose name 'Adam', appropriately meant 'man' in Hebrew – the responsibility of tending this idyllic garden and enjoying it. All its fruits were his to enjoy, with the sole exception of the fruit of one tree at its centre.

One of Adam's tasks was to give names to every living creature. God brought them to him one by one, and he decided what they should be called. But none were suitable as companions and helpers for Adam. God therefore created 'woman', from Adam's own bones.

Living in perfect simplicity, naked and unashamed, the two human beings were supremely happy. They had each other, they had satisfying work to do, they lived in an idyllic environment, and a close relationship with God.

(Genesis 2:8–25)

Adam and Eve as seen by Lucas Cranach, one of the many paintings from the late Middle Ages.

Where was the Garden of Eden?

Paradise garden lost

Adam and Eve in the Garden of Eden, by Jan Brueghal the Elder, 1568–1625.

The location of the Garden of Eden is unknown, though two of the four rivers mentioned in Genesis 2 – the Tigris and Euphrates – are well known today.

There have been many attempts to determine the site of the garden, and the biblical region of Eden, from the clues that appear in Genesis. For example:

• The land of Havilah may refer to the region between the Black and Caspian Seas, where gold and precious stones are to be found.

• The River Pishon may be the same as one that the ancient Greeks called the River Phasis, which flows into the Black Sea. The legend of Jason and the Golden Fleece refers to this region, and it has been suggested that the fleece may be a reference to the skins used as sieves by gold prospectors.

• Although Mesopotamia is often thought to be the cradle of humanity, there are other possible clues to a location in the Iranian highlands.

• There are plenty of red herrings. For example 'Cush' (2:13) may not necessarily be the same city as the Ethiopian 'Cush' mentioned later on in the Old Testament – there were several places of that name. And the existence of an ancient city in Mesopotamia called 'Enoch' does not necessarily mean that it is the 'Enoch' mentioned in Genesis 4.

But all theories about the precise location of mankind's first home are speculative. A catastrophe such as the great flood described in Genesis 6–8, would have modified the landscape, and transformed, if not wiped out, many remains.

The cradle of civilisation and the Garden of Eden have often been associated with the upper reaches of the Euphrates.

Adam and his partner disobeyed the law of Eden and were banned for ever from it.

The tragedy occurred after a conversation between the woman and a serpent, who appears to have entered the garden from outside. The serpent blatantly questioned the fairness and integrity of God. When he suggested that God was simply lying when he said that eating fruit from the tree of knowledge would bring death, she picked some and shared it with Adam.

Immediately, they were overcome with guilt and embarrassment and sought to clothe themselves with leaves. When God came that evening to talk with them, they hid among the trees. But he knew they

were there, and summoned them into his presence.

Adam blamed the woman; the woman blamed the serpent. But God recognised that each was guilty.

The woman would discover that childbearing will be painful, and that the perfect relationship between man and woman is damaged.

Adam would find work a drudgery, where once it was a pleasure. The earth would be hard to cultivate. And death entered the world, making the passage back into God's presence fearful, and severing their intimate contact with him on earth.

God also cursed the serpent: one day a descendant of the woman would destroy its power and treachery for ever. It seemed as if God was speaking not to the serpent directly but to some evil power that had been directing it.

God now clothed them properly with garments made of animal skins. And at least part of his reason for driving them out of the garden was a concern that they should not now eat of the tree of life and be doomed to live for ever in their fallen state.

(Genesis 3)

The spirit world – a parallel creation

Mediaeval picture of demons – horns, forked tail, pitchfork etc, painted by Hans Memling.

The Bible takes for granted that God created spiritual beings as well as physical creatures. It does not say when the **angels** were created, but they were already present as witnesses to the creation of the natural world (Job 38:7), and are courtiers in God's eternal presence (Job 1:6, Isaiah 6:2–4). They are God's servants and praise him (Psalm 103, 148). But their powers and status are finite: Jesus is far greater than the angels (Hebrew 1:4–14), and the angels will one day be judged by human beings (1 Corinthians 6:3).

There are different types of angels, and different ranks: countless numbers of them surround the throne of God (Daniel 7:10), and God uses angels throughout the Bible as his agents and messengers.

The New Testament describes a rebellion in which some angels chose to reject their God-given position. Their leader is Satan, the devil (Matthew 25:41), and there are a number of references to their punishment (e.g. 2 Peter 2:4).

Demons are rarely mentioned in the Bible, except in the Gospels which describe a period when demonic activity was unusually widespread. The prince of the demons is Baal-zebub – Satan (Matthew 12:26–28).

Satan (Hebrew: 'adversary') is described as a personal being in the Bible. He is called the serpent, the devil, 'the accuser of the brethren' and 'the ruler of the kingdom of the air'. The word 'devil' means 'somebody who slanders' or 'the accuser'.

Satan's fall was due to pride and jealousy (1 Timothy 3:6; Isaiah 14:12–15 is sometimes taken to be a reference to the fall of Satan). In the New Testament he is portrayed as a personal, powerful destructive force in the world. But he is not infinite, and is the loser in all his biblical encounters with Jesus in the Gospels.

At the end of history, Satan will be finally defeated and thrown into a lake of fire where he will suffer unending destruction (Revelation 20)

Everyone for himself leads to murder

The first recorded murder in the biblical narrative took place when Abel, son of Adam, was killed in a fit of religious jealousy by his brother Cain.

The expulsion from the garden had spoiled man's relationship with God but not destroyed it: offerings were made to him.

Cain, the older, was a cultivator of the land, and his brother Abel a keeper of animals. Cain gave to God the firstfruits of his harvest. Abel gave the choicest meat from the firstborn of his flocks. God rejected Cain's sacrifice and accepted Abel's, perhaps because the former was an offering of surplus rather than sacrifice. In anger, Cain killed Abel.

He was doomed to be a wanderer on the earth, never more to see a harvest from fields he had tended. But Cain bore God's sign as well as his curse to protect him from human vengeance and to inhibit a floodtide of violence.

The family of Adam spread, for example in the line of Lamech, a descendant of Cain. Jabal was regarded as a patriarchal figure among nomads and livestock breeders and his brother Jubal invented human music. Their half-brother Tubal-Cain founded a school of metal-working, making bronze and iron tools.

But disobedience and sinfulness spread throughout the world. People began worshipping gods of their own making. Images of bulls and fertility gods became common in many cultures; at Jericho even human skulls were used in rituals. Some ancient folk myths suggest the social disintegration made the gods angry because the riotous behaviour of humanity disturbed their rest.

(Genesis 4, 5)

An early representaion of Adam and Eve. from a Fourth century Roman catacomb.

What a wonderful world!

The universe: 8,000 million galaxies and more, stretching beyond the reach of sophisticated radio-telescopes.

The milky way: one galaxy, 100,000 light years across, containing perhaps 100,000 million stars and countless planets.

The solar system: one star (the sun), 15 million degrees Celsius at its core, 6,000 degrees on its surface, is a giant nuclear power station radiating heat and light to its nine orbiting planets.

The earth: a ball of rock over 12,500 km (7,800 miles) in diameter with a molten centre of iron and nickel about 4,500 degrees Celsius. It contains 525 million cubic km (325 million cubic miles) of water covering 70 per cent of the surface. Above it is a delicate mix of life-sustaining oxygen and nitrogen stretching about 640 km (400 miles) into space.

The ecosystem: contains about 300,000 named species of plant and 1.2 million named species of animal. There are many varieties within each species; in South America there are 100 different kinds of mosquito! In a single gram of soil there are several hundred million microscopic bacteria.

Adam starts the human race

Adam and Eve are presented in the Bible as the first truly human people, that is people who God specifically made aware of his existence and purposes. In biblical language, they were made 'in the image of God'. Christians differ in their detailed beliefs as to whether the narrative also implies that the pair were literally the first ever modern humans created specially by God without any evolutionary ancestors, or if God took existing creatures and upgraded them by an additional creative act. It has also been suggested that God chose Adam and Eve as representatives of

A celestial map of the planets. This is a mediaeval reproduction of the Roman original according to Ptolemy, c. AD 150.

the emergent human race, giving them the responsibility of knowing God and his will and sharing it with others. However the account, which is written in a highly stylised and compressed form, is interpreted there are some pointers to a factual basis behind it.

• Some genetic research on the male chromosome suggests that there was a concentrated group of modern human ancestors about 270,000 years ago; others dispute the size of the group and claim it was large, however.

• The Fertile Crescent across Iran and Iraq into Syria, where the biblical Eden was apparently located, is known to have been an early cradle of civilisation.

• There are parallels in the development of neolithic (New Stone Age) man c. 15,000–10,000 BC and the developments noted in the early chapters of Genesis, including the beginnings of settled agricul-

ture, the use of metal, and the development of artistic and religious culture.

• Many cultures have their own creation stories which include accounts of the first people (and later of a catastrophic flood) similar to the biblical narrative. Although the biblical account is sometimes read as just another ancient myth, the similarities of the accounts may point to a common memory which has been packaged in different cultural and religious terms. In that case, Christians would suggest that the Genesis account has been filtered through the specific cultural form which God chose as the vehicle for conveying his detailed revelation to mankind. As such it preserves within an accurate historical framework an authoritative theo-logical introduction to the saga of God's dealings with a community he singled out for a special purpose.

The story of life

Every generation has its explanation of how life originated and developed, and vigorously defends that explanation against all previous ones. Some Christians argue that any estimated chronology based on current scientific knowledge which ignores the biblical account is fatally flawed. Others suggest that Genesis is a timeless explanation of why (not how) the world came into existence, forming a preface to the story of God's dealings with humankind, and therefore not in conflict with science. The chart illustrates the general scientific belief at the end of the twentieth century.

4500m BC	Creation of the universe (4500m BC)
4000m BC	First primitive life forms (4000m BC)
3,000m BC	First known fossils (algae)(3500m *BC*) First oxygen-producing plant organisms (3000m *BC*)
2,000m BC	Atmosphere has become oxygen-rich (2000m BC)
1000m BC	First one-celled organisms (1700m BC) First one-celled sexual organisms (1100m BC) First multi-celled seaweeds (800m BC)
500m BC	First animals (600m BC) 'Explosion' of life forms in Cambrian period(550m BC)
200m BC	First dinosaurs (225m BC)
100m BC	Dinosaurs become extinct (60m BC) Australopithecus (man-like ape) (4.5m BC) African 'Lucy' (man-like ape) (3m BC) Homo Habilis (man-like ape) (2m BC Homo Erectus (first fully upright man-like creatures) (1.5m BC)
50m BC	Neanderthal man (75000 BC) First appearance of modern man) (homo sapiens)(50000 BC) Many cave paintings in Africa and Europe (30000 BC)
1m BC	Time of Adam and Eve? (1500 BC)

What a person!

The human body: 206 bones mobilised into intricate action by 600 muscles, aereated by 300 million air sacs in the lungs, warmed and enlivened by 6.5 litres (10 pints) of blood circulated 1,000 times a day through blood vessels together stretching for tens of thousands of kilometres.

The human brain: A gelatinous blob about 1.4 kg (3 lb) in weight, divided into two hemispheres and containing billions of neurons which each carries millions of electrical impulses along thousands of nerves between the brain

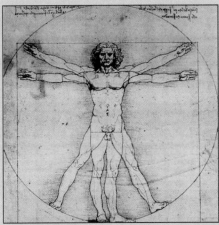

Leonardo da Vinci's famous sketch of an idealised man.

and the body. More complex than the biggest-yet computer, the brain is the seat of consciousness which can not only act instinctively and reason, but which can also communicate rationally with others and spiritually with its creator, and create and appreciate beauty and art.

The human genome: The double helix of DNA (deoxyribonucleic acid) in each cell of the body has yet to be fully mapped, but it contains all the genetic information necessary to determine the shape, growth, functions and individual characteristics of the entire person. Over 100,000 genes are spread across the 46 chromosomes in DNA; over 3,000 of them control the brain, 2,000 control the liver, and 1,100 the heart.

Noah's wet weather forecast gets frosty reception

One old man reported to be taking a stand against the current decline in public behaviour, was Noah, who seemed to have gone mad.

He claimed that God was very angry because human beings are completely wicked, and that God told him to build a ship and to load it with his entire family, and a breeding pair of every bird, animal and land creature in the world. Noah's responsibility was to make sure there was enough food for them.

God would destroy the world and all its inhabitants. It would rain solidly for 40 days and 40 nights. Everybody would die except Noah and his family who would be safe inside the boat.

In a society where most people blatantly boast of their immoral deeds and glory in their ability to cheat the system and look after number one, nobody could point a finger at Noah. His piety, his reverence for God and his integrity, were a byword, though he was often humiliated and mocked by his neighbours.

Going down to Noah's yard for a good laugh would have been a popular pastime. The shape of his huge boat loomed over what few trees still stood nearby. Built to what Noah claimed was a precise blueprint from God, the vessel would not win any design awards but was certainly seaworthy. Its 137 m (450 ft) hull resembled a huge box 14 m (45 ft) high, laboriously coated in pitch inside and out. In the interior there were hundreds of compartments, which Noah and his family were fitting out ready for the animals they were convinced would come aboard.

(Genesis 6)

Landfall on Mount Ararat

Noah's ark starts floating off as the wicked desperately seek survival, Michaelangelo, Sistine Chapel.

The torrential rain continued 40 days and nights just as God had foretold. The flood lasted a total of 150 days and then Noah and his precious living cargo were back on land. Noah realised the waters were receding when a dove sent out from the ark returned with a freshly-plucked olive leaf in its beak.

Before the rain began, a steady stream of animals and birds came to the boat. Possibly some of the bystanders considered asking Noah to let them in too, but events moved too quickly. As the last animal entered, the great wooden door of the boat silently swung shut. At the same moment, torrential rain began to fall.

Attempts to persuade Noah to open the door were unsuccessful.

Many fled to the hills, leaving their possessions behind, but were overwhelmed by the waters.

The ark came to rest on Mount Ararat. There was an emotional scene on the mountain as Noah led his family in worship and sacrifice to God. And God promised Noah and his sons that he would never destroy all living creatures nor curse the ground again on account of human wickedness. He made a covenant with Noah, that the new world is a resource for humanity.

In the immediate context of the massive death-toll of the flood, there was a sombre note to the covenant. Noah could eat animal flesh, but carcasses must be drained of blood. Human blood too was declared precious, and any who spill it would be answerable to God.

But it was a covenant of life, not of death. The command was to be fruitful and to fill the earth. The world would never perish again by water. As a sign of the covenant, God appointed the rainbow to be a reminder for all time of his promise.

(Genesis 7–9)

The nations in early Genesis

The early chapters of Genesis have occasionally been interpreted to teach the inferiority of the Hamite races (which include the coloured peoples of the world). This is not only bad theology but bad anthropology, for the various studies of the Genesis account of ethnic and racial origins indicate that the Hamite peoples have contributed so overwhelmingly to the world's technological advances that they might reasonably be described as the founders of civilisation itself.

(Genesis 10)

The Flood: a universal tradition

Legends of a great flood are found in many world cultures, often with significant details that echo the account in Genesis. There are about 150 flood traditions currently known, and many of them are quite independent of each other. Some examples:

• In the Indian sub-continent, there are stories of a deluge 'sweeping away all mankind' and of the construction of 'a great ship' in which 'beasts of the field, the birds of the air and ... the family' were saved.

• A coin struck at Apamea in Macedonia depicts a chest floating on the water, people coming out of it, and a bird bearing an olive branch. On the front are the letters NOE.

• The Babylonian historian Berosus wrote that 'a great flood took place ... Kronos appeared to him [Xisuthros] in a vision and told him that on the 50th day of Dasius there would be a flood in which mankind would be destroyed ...

He must build a boat and enter it with his friends and relations, and put on board provisions, together with birds and quadrupeds. After the flood had come and abated, Xisuthros sent out birds from the vessel.' Berosus also gives a list of 10 antediluvian 'kings' which corresponds closely with the 10 patriarchs from Adam to Noah.

• In Greek legend, Zeus flooded the earth on account of human wickedness. One man, Deukalion, was saved.

Those traditions found in countries near to the Middle East tend to emphasise human wickedness as the cause of God sending the flood; those further away tend to suggest more arbitrary causes. Many traditions mention misconduct by giants, which might be a memory of Genesis 6:4.

It has been suggested that some of these accounts incorporate memories handed down from Noah himself by oral tradition. Many details have the stamp of eye-witness accounts. For example the Babylonian *Epic of Gilgamesh*, states that the gods are said to have gathered round Noah's altar 'like flies' – but with so many human and animal corpses around, the altar may well have been surrounded by real flies.

A careful reading of the biblical account will solve at least some disagreements over the nature of the flood. What few details are given, and the Hebrew words that are used, allow for the possibility that there were catastrophic rainstorms in the Middle East and similar regions, and snowstorms on higher ground and colder areas such as Siberia. This hypothesis certainly permits the reconciliation of the biblical flood and the geological Ice Age, and explains such matters as the preservation of mammoths. Some relics of the antediluvian culture would remain.

Christians differ over whether the account suggests a worldwide flood, or one which covered the area in which the biblical nations lived.

Tongue tied

It is now clear that the lessons of history are not learnt by successive generations. The moral and religious free-for-all before the flood continued after it.

God is said to have been so displeased with the human arrogance and self-sufficiency which ignored his loving care that he caused the scattered nations to develop their own individual languages. International and even inter-tribal communication became difficult as each culture fostered its unique vocabulary and grammar.

The last straw had been the attempt by the people of Babel (Babylon) to build a self-sufficient city with the world's tallest building, symbolising their rejection of God the Creator and the belief in their own superiority over other peoples.

(Genesis 11:1–9)

A table of nations

According to tradition, Noah's three sons spread out, Japheth claiming Greece and western Turkey, Shem colonising Mesopotamia and Ham moving into North Africa. These territories were then further divided amongst their descendants. However, tradition is often hard to pin down to exact geographic features.

Hardy people have religious hearts

Worldwide, c. 10000–8000 BC

Human beings who have replaced the Neanderthals as the dominant species on earth, have a strong sense that life continues in some form after death.

Even Neanderthals buried their dead with some care, placing alongside the corpses everyday objects such as weapons and food. But Late Stone Age humans have more elaborate practices suggesting that they believe that the life to come is some form of continuation of this one.

At Grimaldi on the north Mediterranean coast, for example, an old woman and a young man have been buried together, placed in a crouching position and decorated with crowns and bracelets. The youth may have been sacrificed on the tomb. Nearby, a young boy has been buried with his head pointing north and shells, stags' teeth and ornaments beside him.

Life is hard for the people who are sparsely scattered across the globe. Food, mostly reindeer, horses and wild boars, is hunted down with slings and stones, and more recently with bows and arrows. Hunters sometimes disguise themselves in animal skins in order to get close to their quarry and remain undetected. Fish are plucked from the waters with barbed bone fishhooks or harpoons. Fruit, berries, honey and vegetables are collected from the wild as a supplement to the diet.

People wear coarse clothes made from animal skins sewn together with dried gut or horsehair thread. For tools, they use flint axes, awls and scrapers. Those who do not live in caves make shelters from tree branches. Fire provides warmth and protection.

But there is time for leisure, perhaps also with religious overtones. Paintings of animals and humans on cave walls portray hunting and gathering scenes, and the mating of horses (perhaps associated with fertility rites). Sometimes animals are shown already captured, and these paintings may be part of a pre-hunt ritual to provoke success.

Many caves, particularly in France and Spain, contain numerous Stone Age paintings. The cave in Lascaux, in France, is covered with hundreds of impressive paintings executed with wood ash and other natural pigments, which testify to great artistic skill.

Fast Facts 6000–4500 BC

Tassili, north Africa, c. 6000 BC: Rock paintings at this Sahara-edge site are highly stylised and depict hunting, gathering, and some human figures with terrifying poses, perhaps as religious symbols.

Mehrgarh, south Asia, c. 6000 BC: Mud-brick storehouses are being built by the people of this village on a terrace of the River Bolan on the Kachhi Plain. The stores suggest a developing social structure and trading system. Rich grave goods are placed with the dead.

Anatolia, Turkey, c. 6000 BC: The settlement of Catal Huyuk is one of the world's most advanced communities. Its unfortified 13 hectares (32 acres) contain a group of rectangular dwellings built so close together that they can be entered only through holes in the roofs. The people are primarily cattle ranchers and have their own domestic religious shrines rather than a central place of worship. They trade with other centres in volcanic glass (used in tool and weapon making) and ornaments.

Jarmu, Iraq, c. 5000 BC: The people of this settlement about 160 km (100 miles) east of Asshur live in square houses with several rooms, built of pressed mud. They eat with bone spoons and sew with bone needles, weaving wool and flax on stone spindles. Their tools are made of flint or limestone. They cultivate wheat and barley, rear sheep, cattle and pigs, and wear clay and stone necklaces. They bury their dead under the floor of their houses, and worship a pregnant goddess.

Hassuna, Iraq, c. 4500 BC: Children get a better deal after death than adults at this village on the Tigris River some 80 km (50 miles) north of Asshur. Their bones are kept in a large jar in the house, and they are given small pots and cups for refreshment. Adult bones are unceremoniously piled up in a corner. The largest houses may have up to seven rooms arranged in two blocks around a courtyard.

People start doing what God told them to do

Worldwide, c. 8000–6000 BC

The responsibility given by God to the human race to become stewards of the earth's resources is at last being applied. Since the ice cap finally began to recede c. 11000 BC there has been an explosion of human creativity in many places.

Cereal crops (barley, wheat and millet) are being grown deliberately for food, whereas before only wild grasses were gathered and ground into coarse meal. Animals are being taken from the wild, kept in separate enclosures, and so herded for their food and skins. Domesticated cattle, sheep, goats, pigs and horses have joined the ubiquitous

Black Hill in Devon is typical of prehistoric burial mounds to be found throughout Europe. These were often simply piles of stones heaped over a shallow grave.

dog, which has been man's friend for many centuries. People are also making pottery containers – some of them decorated – and weaving rushes or reeds into baskets.

The change from hunter-gatherer to cultivator-herdsman has enabled small semi-nomadic groups to settle down and to congregate in stable communities. Indeed, agriculture and community go hand in hand because the new skills require some collaborative activity between

Stone rules over Europe

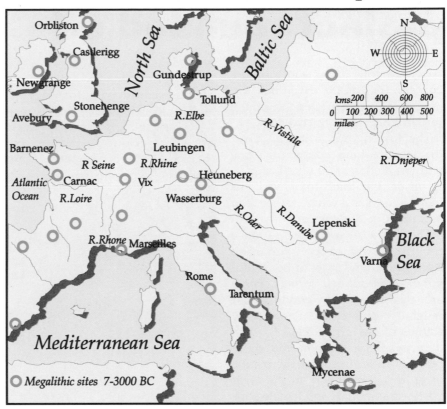

Megalithic sites 7-3000 BC

Megalithic sites seem well spread out throughout Europe, though certain regions, such as Brittany, seem to have been more heavily populated. Most sites combine burial grounds with centres of religious significance – though the exact nature of the sites involved can often only be guessed at.

different families. People live in small villages, often near watercourses, and the population is increasing rapidly. Tools have improved although wall painting is less in evidence.

Funerary rituals continue, however. In some European areas the flesh is stripped from the dead and only the skeleton buried. Weapons and food are no longer always buried, and in some places

have been replaced by religious objects, perhaps suggesting that the hereafter is now considered to be rather different to the present world.

There is some uncertainty as to whether these changes have arisen spontaneously in different areas or if they have spread from what is generally regarded as the cradle of civilisation, the Middle East. The latter is considered most likely.

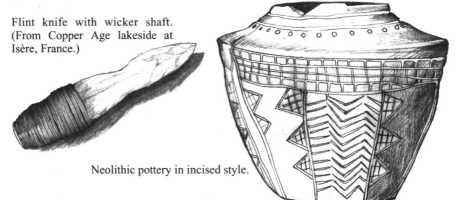

Flint knife with wicker shaft. (From Copper Age lakeside at Isère, France.)

Neolithic pottery in incised style.

Jericho building project rounded off

Jericho, c. 6000 BC

A round stone tower and rounded corners to private dwellings are giving the town of Jericho in the Jordan Valley a distinctive look.

The tower, over 8 m (27 ft) in diameter, is built entirely of stone and has a staircase on the inside. It is inside the thick town wall, so may be used as a refuge rather than as a first line of defence.

The houses, which were once round with domed roofs and made from brick, tend now to be rectangular with rounded corners. There are also two cultic buildings for religious ceremonies. They house statues of the gods, one of which depicts a man, woman and child, perhaps indicating that the people of Jericho, like others in the Near East, worship male and female gods who have a divine child.

The inhabitants are domesticating animals for food and clothing, as well as continuing to hunt them in the forests of the lush river valley. They are also cultivating cereal and fruit crops on the rich sedimentary soil outside the town walls.

This massive tower of ancient Jericho is 9 m (30 ft) in diameter. Situated inside the thick town wall, it could have been used as a refuge or store.

Middle East goes potty

Canaan, c. 5000 BC

It used to be child's play, but now it's a burgeoning industry. Pouring water onto mud and moulding it into shapes has been a well-known dirty trick of every child since creation. Parents have now realised that by more careful moulding and by hardening the clay in an oven rather than under the midday sun it has more practical uses than simply making building bricks.

Pottery, as it is called, is now being used widely for food storage and liquid containers, replacing the more traditional skin, wooden and reed vessels. The art of making pottery is not new, however, and has been imported into Canaan by settlers from Syria and Anatolia to the north.

Some containers are simple bowls, but others are shaped more carefully with handles and rims. They are sometimes decorated with geometric shapes either painted on or sculpted into the clay before it is fired at a relatively low temperature. The pottery is often dark coloured and usually glazed, and straw is frequently chopped and added to the clay to make it more malleable. This does however tend to weaken the larger pots.

The villagers in southern Turkey today, still live in houses reminiscent of the older, beehive structures in the area.

Busy bees

Khabur Basin, c. 4300 BC

People along the Khabur River between Syria and Assyria are building mysterious beehive-shaped structures on circular stone foundations. They range from 4–9 m (13–32 ft) in diameter and are made from sundried mud bricks. They have rectangular antechambers but their use is unclear; they may be temples or town halls.

The settlements are certainly developing a municipal organisation; streets are being cobbled by joint community effort. But the people make sure that their personal possessions do not fall into the wrong hands by stamping clay pots with a pendant or disk which they carry around their necks.

The pots are being given intricate woven patterns of black, red and white over a cream- or peach-coloured base. The designs include triangles, squares, scallops and small circles as well as birds, flowers and gazelles, although the most popular seem to be double axes and bulls heads, believed to have religious significance.

What certainly are of religious significance are the talismans – terracotta figures of doves and women in labour – used against the dangers of childbirth. Stone amulets are also made featuring bulls' heads and hooves.

Hot, dry Sumer ushers in new settled way of life

Sumer, c. 4200 BC

The light-skinned, dark-haired people of Sumer are slowly transforming the landscape between the Tigris and Euphrates rivers. They have broken the ancient cycle of hunting and gathering, and have domesticated goats and sheep and cultivated good strains of wheat and barley.

Mesopotamia ('The Land Between the Rivers') is inhospitable country, where the scorching sun burns down from cloudless skies and shrivels all but the hardiest, most sheltered plants. But a few scattered tribes are now wresting an existence from the two great rivers. Small towns are beginning to appear along their banks, with fields of grain spreading in wide semi-circles around them. Groups of date-palms hug walls that encircle proud palaces and temples – and the humbler dwellings of the common people.

Nobody knows where the Sumerians came from. They are probably migrants from Asia Minor, possibly from the old city of Catal Huyuk, the recent descendants of Stone-Age farmers who clung to the perimeters of reedy swampland close to the Persian Gulf. Sumerian legends suggest that they were village dwellers as long as 4,000 years ago, though at that time they would have lived in

Mud houses by the river bank, surrounded by palm trees.

the hills near the rivers' sources, where rain falls more frequently.

Europe's first farmers won't go it alone

Central Europe, c. 4100 BC

A new breed of farmers is settling into the thickly-forested expanse of Europe, where civilisation is not moving so quickly as in the lands of the fertile crescent. Villages only gradually establish themselves and communities often die out.

This is no country for the isolated pioneer. Organised communities are the only effective way of gaining safety for the people and increased productivity.

Residents of one village of about 30 wooden longhouses located some 120 km (75 miles) north-west of Warsaw are changing the ecosystem by cattle grazing and cultivation, extensive timber cutting and land clearance. It is a ruinous policy that could exhaust

A woman grinding corn on a saddle quern, with typical conical huts from Bronze Age Britain.

the land and deforest and depopulate the village and its environs. But there are not many economic resources in the area, and there is fierce competition for what there is. Hence the village's defences – a ditch and palisade system.

The villagers believe in an after life. They bury objects with their dead, such as a bow and a quiver of arrows, which they consider to be essential tools in the next world. Some of the first metalwork seen in Europe is to be found in the graves, including copper tools and attractively decorated diadems. The latter probably indicates status within the social hierarchy.

Fast Facts c. 4000 BC

Britain: Farmers are clearing trees and planting crops on Salisbury Plain in southern England. The climate is warm and dry, the soil chalky and light. Some of the farmers have emigrated from continental Europe where competition for land is fiercer.

Europe: Wild horses have been harnessed by people on the plains of eastern Europe. Leather thongs attached to a piece of antler across the horse's mouth provide a means of controlling the horse's head, and thus the direction in which the horse will run. Bareback riding is spreading fast.

Africa: On the rolling, vast savannah grasslands nomadic peoples clad in animal skins eke out a primitive existence, sheltering in caves or building portable lean-to's. They depend for food on the movements of roving herds. Their origins are unknown, though they may be the descendants of Put – the only offspring of Ham of whom the Bible is silent.

Ur totally devastated by flooding

Sumer, 4000 BC

The murderous Euphrates has burst its banks with ferocious savagery. The silence of the desert now broods over the ruined city of Ur. As in many other Sumerian towns and villages, desolation has claimed its proud houses and temples, and its once-busy streets are deserted. The earliest civilisation to have been built on this spot lies under a thick stratum of mud more than three metres (10 ft) thick, already hardening into clay.

Similar scenes are repeated over the entire plain between the Tigris and Euphrates rivers. The two rivers have become a single massive flood basin with often interconnecting tributaries. The course of the two rivers changes often.

Elsewhere the devastation has been less severe. The town of Kish, for example, has been left under less than 500 cm (18 in) of mud. But the Kishites are hardly rejoicing in their good fortune. This is a natural disaster worse than anyone can remember, and some are making comparisons with the great flood of Noah's time, stories of which have been handed down by word of mouth through generations. But God has kept the promise he made then. Though an area 700 km long by about 170 km wide (435 miles by 105 miles) has been affected, the world has not been destroyed.

Nevertheless the rivers have permanently changed their courses. The northern tip of the Persian Gulf has been reclaimed from the sea, with sediment from the twin rivers. Now, the two rivers merge a few kilometres before reaching the Gulf. The region is of great strategic importance: known as the cradle of civilisation, it contains some of the oldest and most advanced settlements known.

Mesopotamia: the cradle of civilisation

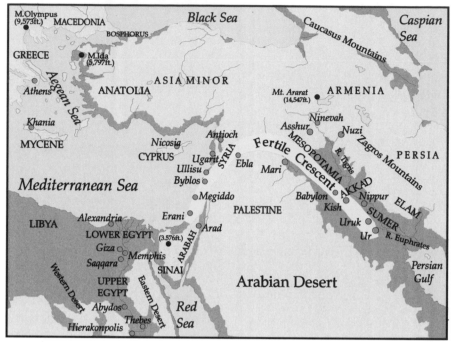

The area stretching from Egypt through to Syria and down the Euphrates to the Persian Gulf has been called the cradle of civilisation. Society developed early due to the favourable climatic conditions of the area, nowhere more so than in the so-called Fertile Crescent benefiting from the regular water supply of the Rivers Tigris and Euphrates.

Hot metal

Near East, c. 4000 BC:

Copper ore is being dug from the ground east of the Jordan, and in Anatolia and Armenia. The metal runs out of the rock when heated and is used for manufacturing axe heads, awls and similar implements. The development has given the present era its pet name, Chalcolithic, from chalcos (copper) and lithos (stone).

Rocky outcrops such as these found near Petra in Jordan are high in copper, which was extracted in the area.

Life's too short to notice the smell

Avebury, Britain, c. 3750 BC

Fancy a new suit of clothes? First, of course, you must catch and kill an animal, then get its skin off. But the skin is too hard and coarse for human covering so you must soften and tan it first.

To do this you soak it in urine, and then scrape off the fat with a flint and comb out the coarse hairs. Then you hang the skin in animal dung until it swells. Next, soak it in a sweeter-smelling oak resin before rubbing it with animal brains until it is soft and supple enough to sew into garments.

With such occupations to while away the days, it may not be surprising that the longest life expectancy of people in this new western England settlement is 36 years for men and 30 for women. Half the children die before their first birthday, often from malnutrition or ricketts, and up to 40 per cent of the people are dead by the age of 20.

If the smell of their clothes is not enough to suffocate them, then there is always tetanus, polio, TB, sinusitis and malaria to carry them off. Arthritis, broken bones and dental decay and abcesses add to the everyday pains.

And if you want to avoid being cut off in your prime by accident, then you will not go out at night. Wolves, brown bears, wild boars and deadly vipers are unwelcome

Avebury stone circle, surrounded by a ditch, which was undoubtedly part of the early fortifications, still comprises over 50 upright stones today spread over 50 acres.

and usually lethal creatures to meet in the dark, which is when they go hunting for tasty flesh. Unfortunately, fellow humans when angry can sometimes inflict a deadly blow in daylight, especially with a well-aimed arrow.

With such hazards to contend with it is hardly surprising that the people are superstitious. They see little difference between the natural and the supernatural, and witch doctors attempt to work out the causes of disasters. Sacrifices and

rituals are performed to avoid dangers. Young naked girls mark out the first furrows with a plough in order to ensure a good harvest, and the last sheaf to be reaped is offered back to the earth in an act of contrition for having taken its produce.

As more forest space is cleared, so the dead are beginning to be buried in mounds. The carcase is exposed first, however, until the flesh has decomposed. This is to allow the spirit to get free. Only then are the bones gathered together in a wooden building which is then earthed over.

The people here have moved in from Salisbury Plain, each family claiming its own territory and adopting a self-sufficiency lifestyle. They have built rectangular timber houses for shelter, and keep cattle and other animals, although they rely on crops for their main food supplies. Cattle are kept stalled for most of the year and fed elm and ivy leaves, largely because there is little grassland in the forest-covered terrain.

During the summer however, the people often move out with their animals to open-air camps and fresh grazing on hills such as Bishops Cannings Down and Overton Hill. They generally stay in one area for about 20 years until the soil is exhausted. By which time, of course, they are too.

Fast Facts c. 3500–3200 BC

Eridu, Iraq, c. 3500: This Mesopotamian centre southwest of Ur is believed to be the earthly home of Enki, the god of the subterranean waters. A unique temple with a single square room containing an altar opposite the entrance has been built. The walls are made from mud bricks and decorated with deep thumb prints.

Britain, c. 3500 BC: Windmill Hill near Avebury has become a centre for both trade and religion. Pottery from Abingdon in the upper Thames valley near Oxford and from the Cotswold hills is marketed here. Objects associated with death and fertility are also made here. Figures are carved from chalk with prominent genitals but no heads for use in religious rituals.

Europe, c. 3500 BC: In Europe agriculture is being revolutionised as animals replace humans as the principal means of driving ploughs, and pulling farm carts built with solid wheels hewn from tree trunks. Oxen have proved more

than equal to the task, and animal-power is now more prevalent than man-power as a means of traction. Pulling power has now become an important new criteria – alongside meat and milk yield – by which to judge the worth of livestock. Horses are also being harnessed for agricultural purposes – not just for riding.

Canaan, c. 3500 BC: Small towns are protected by massive fortifications, and mud-brick houses have plastered, polished and often painted walls, with reed mats on the floor. A fertility cult is

practised. The dead are often buried under the floors of houses – minus the head, upon which features are reconstructed in clay with shells for eyes. These effigies are used for cultic purposes, probably ancestor worship.

Crete, c. 3200: Settlers have been arriving here from Asia Minor and the Dodecanese. They have brought with them Anatolian customs and art, including stone maces and squatting figurines similar to those used in mother goddess cults in Anatolia.

Settlers come and go

Canaan, c. 3500 BC

Some people are born under a wandering star and never settle anywhere for long. Others pine for a sweet place called home and never budge from it for life. As if to prove that there's 'nowt so queer as folks', both sorts are living side by side in Canaan.

The settling sort are typified by the Ghassulians, whose permanent villages in the Jordan valley boast rectangular brick houses with stone foundations. A main room opens onto various courtyards and the houses are huddled together with only narrow alleys between them. There are no fortifications round the settlements.

Ghassulians grow grain, dates and olives and store some of their produce in pits (silos) dug into the ground. They make their own distinctive pottery including a horn-shaped drinking vessel with short handles. They use copper for implements, and have decorated the walls of their houses with animal and mythical figures.

Other people in southern Canaan tend to wander between temporary settlements, herding animals to fresh pastures and hawking home-made craftware. Their focal point seems to be a temple such as the one at En-Gedi in the desert, to which they travel from time to time. A 20-m-long (65-ft) but very narrow room has a platform for a statue of the god and benches for the worshippers. Outside is a pool for ritual washings. Animals are offered as sacrifices.

Ivory figurine of a woman. The eyes are inlaid with lapis lazuli, a much prized semi-precious stone. Early predynastic period.

Village fired up

Bulgaria, c. 3100 BC

The fate of a village in the Serdica area of northwest Bulgaria is typical of the ferment going on in central Europe at the present time. Having been settled by the Yamnaya immigrants, it was attacked by the Baden people.

In one of the houses a potter's kiln was broken into while it was still burning. Some of the pots were destroyed, but the rest had their firing completed by the conflagration which engulfed the village.

The Yamnaya are a nomadic shepherd-people who moved about 500 years ago from beyond the Volga when the climate grew worse. They brought with them two-wheeled ox-drawn carts. As they spread into the Balkans they were welcomed for their new skills and wealth.

But the massive migrations now taking place are overloading the resources of the region and land conflicts are now commonplace. Previously wealthy settlements on both sides of the Danube have been destroyed by the pressure of refugees and by raids from the Yamnaya. Now the Baden people, who have pushed eastwards into Transylvania and northwest Bulgaria, are challenging the Yamnaya supremacy throughout the region.

High tech replaces sticks and buckets

Sumer, c. 3300 BC

Modern labour-saving techniques are replacing old-fashioned and difficult ploughing methods. Agriculture and animal husbandry, previously different activities, are now being combined as farmers find ingenious ways of tending the earth.

Today's ploughs are pulled by oxen harnessed to sophisticated new implements made out of copper. The ore is dug from the ground and smelted in simple furnaces. The process is a far cry from the old method whereby a crooked branch was dragged by hand to make furrows for planting.

The old way of watering seedlings during the rainless summer months was by drawing water from the river in small pots. This laborious process has now been largely automated. Narrow breaches are being made into the natural levees that have built up over the centuries, allowing river water to flow into artificial canals and water basins. From these the precious liquid is transferred into irrigation ditches with the aid of a shaduf – a bailing bucket suspended on the end of a long counterweighted pole.

Gradually, fields further away from the river are being cultivated, with the aid of river water routed along newly dug canals, some of which extend several kilometres from the river. Control over water rights is becoming crucial.

The rich alluvial soil is each year topped with a fresh layer of mineral-rich silt deposited by the spring floods. This replenishes the ground and enables crops of barley, wheat and vegetables to be grown year after year.

Merchants take up writing

Merchants have taken to writing and keeping records in a big way. They are also subsidising the first schools: such as this nineteenth century print of an early arab school.

Sumer, 3200 BC

The Sumerians have developed a series of special signs which can be carved in stone, clay or slate to communicate numbers, objects or ideas.

Priests use reed pens to make these strange marks or 'picto grams' on clay tablets, which can then be understood by others who have previously learned the significance of each sign or symbol.

This so-called 'writing' has become hugely popular with merchants who have enthusiastically adopted the idea to record business transactions.

Distinctive tokens of various shapes have been used by farmers since 8000 BC to keep an inventory of their commodities. These tokens have gradually come to be used as bills of lading, or delivery notes, to accompany goods bought and sold; currently the tokens are sealed in bullae, or clay balls. The merchant usually scratches a symbol on the outside of the bullae to indicate how many tokens each contains. But even this method is now being superseded by markings on clay tablets. In this easier and more elegant system, a picture of the token is drawn on the tablet. The pictogram system appears to be flexible enough to describe any object that can be expressed in spoken words.

The system is being copied and improved by other civilisations. The nearby city of Susa, in Elam, has developed the basic idea of crude object-outlines into a set of wedge-shaped or 'cuneiform' marks which represent sounds and can be combined to make complex words. This is so clearly superior to pictograms (which can express only a single concept) that it is already recognised as the system of the future and its use is spreading rapidly.

Drinks trade changes minds

Near East, c. 3500 BC

Intoxicating effects have been detected in certain rotting fruits. Dates, figs and grapes that have been left in jars and pots have been found to ferment as the fruit decomposes, producing a juice with a stronger flavour and often strong mind-altering, and pleasurable, properties.

Alcoholic drinks are now being produced deliberately. Malted cereals have been found to be the most economical raw produce with which to produce them, though grapes are also a strong contender.

Trojan heart

Troy, c. 3000 BC

A new city has been built for a king on the Aegean coast south of the Hellespont. Called Troy, it has a heart-shaped human face carved into one of the limestone towers on the entrance gate. It has holes drilled around its ears and is the first such decoration to have been made anywhere.

The four metre-thick (13 ft) walls protect a settlement of rectangular brick houses, some of which are roofed with slate. It has been founded by settlers from Thrace, which lies between northern Greece and the Black Sea.

Although the city has no port, it is in a strategic position to command the Hellespont Straits.

Statue of a king/priest, from Uruk, Southern Mesopotamia, 25 cm tall.

Meat by the barrow-load

Britain, c. 3500 BC

Meat is on the menu when a new barrow (burial mound) is begun. First, the axis of the barrow is marked out with piles of soil. Then the celebrations begin.

In Wessex, the people usually eat oxen, but in Yorkshire they prefer roast pork. Some tribes relish geese. Animals are sacrificed in religious offerings, although in times of crisis humans are sacrificed.

Many gods make hard work for Sumerians

Sumer, c. 3000 BC

There are over 3,000 gods, each believed to control some aspect of nature or human life, according to Sumerian cosmology evolved by the priests.

In addition, each village has its local deity. Even ploughs and mounds of building materials are believed to possess their own gods!

Not all the gods have equal power. A special quartet of gods is believed to control the main natural spheres: earth, air, water and heaven. An, the ruler of heaven, was once deemed to be the most powerful; but his place has now been usurped by Enlil, the lord of the air.

The priests claim that the gods experience the same range of emotions as their worshippers: they eat, drink, love and marry. They have the same needs as humanity. The gods are not silent but communicate through the priesthood, with signs and omens, such as the shape of the liver found in a sacrificial sheep. Superstition is rampant.

The Sumerians believe that people have been carved from clay by the gods, in order to serve as their slaves and failure to worship the deities can lead to catastrophic floods, pestilence and drought.

To placate the gods, temples have been built on elaborate platforms raised above the ground – perhaps to elevate them closer to heaven, or maybe just to lift them above the flood waters during the rain season. When these simple buildings collapse, the ruins are used as the foundation for a more imposing structure.

The sequence of new buildings rising from the ruins of the old is beginning to resemble a series of gigantic steps. These magnificent 'ziggurats' are adorned with exquisite sculptures and colourful frescoes, depicting bare-chested men with long hair and beads wearing kilt-like garments.

The Sumerian city-states are flourishing economically. Trade with the peoples of Syria, Asia Minor and the Persian Gulf has promoted the growth of Lagesh and Uruk (or Erech) into the most powerful city-states.

Symbolic figure of a goat about to nibble a tree, and made from shell, lapis-lazuli and gold. This Sumerian artefact was found in Ur, stands 46cm tall and dates from c. 2500 BC. its function is unknown.

The big men take the lead

Sumer, 2900 BC

'Big men' are taking on big roles and building personal dynasties in Sumer.

Until now, important decisions have been made by councils of aristocrats and elders. In crises, the council has usually appointed a 'big man' (or 'lugal') to lead and to make speedy decisions for the duration of the emergency, after which he would return to his former occupation.

Today, the lugals are increasing their range of powers from the purely military to include the civic functions of the councils which appointed them.

One reason is the increased frequency of disputes over water rights which is causing periods of inter-city hostility. The proliferation of canals which divert part of the flow of the Tigris or Euphrates is reducing the amount of water available further down-stream.

The development means that what was a democratic republic is becoming a traditional monarchy. The rights of the citizens appear to be eroding daily, all too often like the local canal banks.

It is estimated that each of the country's dozen or so major cities has several thousand inhabitants, each increasing rapidly. The world has never seen such rapid or comprehensive urbanisation.

Traveller in mountain tragedy

Austro-Italian border, c. 3000 BC

A man from northern Italy has died while crossing the Alps. He appears to have taken shelter from the blizzards in a depression in the ground and died of exposure. His body was frozen in the permanent snows of the high mountains.

He was tattooed, and his belongings included an impressive axe with a copper head bound to a yew handle. He was also carrying a deerskin quiver with fourteen flint-tipped arrows, a flint knife, leather leggings, a rain-cloak of woven grass, and a fur cap with a leather strap. His equipment made superb use of fourteen different woods and demonstrates a far more developed Alpine society than was assumed.

Menes creates united Egypt

Egypt, c. 2950 BC

Menes has become ruler of a unified Egypt, though whether the unification was his achievement or that of his predecessor, Narmer, is not certain. The various territories on the Nile are now under a single administrative system.

The so-called 'god-king' has successfully extended his rule to embrace Lower Egypt where land reclamation schemes are beginning to force back the swamplands. Menes has founded the Thinite dynasty, and is ruling from Memphis in Upper Egypt, close to the Nile Delta, on land already rescued from the swamps.

This white-walled city gleams resplendent under the hot tropical sun. Other prosperous Egyptian cities include Elephantine, Hierakonpolis and Abydos. The dynasty, harassed on several borders by nomadic tribes, may well choose to expand its lands further to the south, where Nubia is a tempting prospect.

Many glorious feats are attributed to Menes. But many of them were probably the achievements of his

The first capital of united Egypt was Memphis. The first two dynasties lasted until c. 2685 BC, with the third dynasty seeing the start of pyramid building.

Settlements of varying importance abound in Egypt, virtually exclusively along either bank of the Nile. Earlier Bronze Age settlements appear to have been confined to the Nile Delta region, with up-river sites following later.

As rulers and dynasties changed, so did the capital.

immediate forebears. Not much is known about them, but they are named as Narmer and Aha on contemporary carvings.

Sahara dries

Africa, c. 3000 BC

The good weather which made the North African hinterland hospitable after the last Ice Age, some 6,500 years ago, is changing radically. The vast lakes are drying up, and grazing savannahs around the edge of the Sahara are retreating fast. The vast mountain woodlands are also receding.

The lions, elephants, hippopotamuses and rhinoceroses that roam the Sahara are having to search further afield for feeding grounds as the level of the Sahara's lakes drops rapidly, and the land begins to revert to desert.

Great dust storms blow furiously and with increasing frequency turning this once fertile area into a huge dust bowl in which only the hardiest can survive. The slow but constant spread of the desert seems irreversible.

A mirage caused by the heat in the Sahara Desert.

Sumerian scholars produce epic achievements in better writing

Sumer, 2750–2550 BC

Epic poems and myths are now being recorded for posterity in the new cuneiform (wedge-shaped) script using improved writing techniques.

The earlier practice of etching an unsightly series of bumps and ridges in vertical columns starting at the top right hand corner has been abandoned. Scribes often smudged previous characters with their hands.

Instead, reed writing tools are being made with a sharp triangular point which can be pressed into the clay writing tablet making a neat wedge-shaped impression. And rows of characters are now written in horizontal rows from left to right.

Learning to read and write demands years of rigorous training in the edubba, or 'tablet house', which is probably the first formal school. It is often an annexe to a palace or temple. Students pay tuition fees to the ummia, or headmaster, to learn reading, writing and arithmetic.

Sumerian mathematics is based on the number 60. As this is divisible by 12 other integers, it is useful for measuring food or land. It is also useful for recording time, though not with great accuracy.

Among the epics being written in the new style is the popular 3,500-line *Epic of Gilgamesh*. It tells of King Gilgamesh's heroic exploits, including his encounter with the elderly Utnapishitim who is said to have survived a major flood by building a floating ark for his family and livestock. It is one of several versions of a flood myth which circulate in the area and echo the famous story of Noah.

This inscribed clay tablet is a seventh-century copy of the *Epic of Gilgamesh*, and features the account of the flood.

They moved the earth in uphill task

Silbury, Britain, c. 2600 BC

As if there were not already enough hills in western Britain, the intrepid natives have built their very own. It has taken over a century to complete, and is 40 m (130 ft) high with a flat top 30 m (98 ft) across. It is 165 m (540 ft) wide at the base.

The earth-moving project is estimated to have taken 18 million man-hours. Some 35 million basket-loads of rubble were used to build it, being passed along a human chain which slowly spiralled up the growing hillside. It is said to contain a quarter of a million cubic metres of chalk.

It is the largest-ever man-made hill, surpassing those already built at nearby Marlborough and at Hatfield. There are also some in Yorkshire. They may act as territorial markers, or as watchtowers or astronomical observatories. The one at Silbury is on a low-lying and wet site. The building project has done much to unify the local population through the careful centralised planning needed to see such a large civil engineering project through to completion.

Fast Facts 3000–2500 BC

Europe: Copper axe-heads are being used as the earliest metal tools made in Europe.

Western Europe: Huge megalithic monuments are being constructed upon many European sites. They feature avenues of standing stones, whose brooding presence seems to instil an atmosphere of mystery and awe. Many are known to have purposes other than funerary, such as astronomical observation.

India: Farmers in the Indus Valley are now making extensive use of the plough.

Egypt: Resplendent in the burning sun, Egypt is near to the height of its early prosperity and power. The country is indisputably at the centre of the world's stage, with enormous influence and political power. It has recently dispatched quarrying and mining expeditions to Nubia.

Sumer, c. 3000 BC: A ziggurat has been built at Erech, the first of its kind. It consists of a high terrace of trodden clay and mudbrick which acts as a base for a temple, reached by a stairway.

Egypt, c. 2558 BC: A second pyramid at Giza has been built by King Chephren using local limestone. The walls are veneered with red granite brought from the Aswan quarries about 965 km (600 miles) away. It looks taller than his father's pyramid, although it is in fact shorter but is built on higher ground.

Crete, c. 2500 BC: The island is being infiltrated by people from Anatolia and Syria. Most on the island still live in caves, although some have moved into houses. Pottery skills have developed, with black, grey, red and yellow vessels. They are decorated on the outside, although wide bowls are often left plain. Cretans are good at making clay figurines, and squatting females, often with fat hips and thighs, are popular.

Britain, c. 2500 BC: Work has begun to enclose the Avebury stone circles with massive earthworks (a henge) consisting of a tall mound and a ditch which is some 15 m (50 ft) deep. Four gaps have been left for entrances. According to some observers, the Avebury builders are megalomaniacs who aim simply to have the biggest and best religious and trade centre in the land.

Near East, c. 2500 BC: People in many places are using seals to identify their belongings. The seals, which are pressed into soft clay, come in a variety of shapes. In Mesopotamia there are cylinder seals, in Syria there are stamp seals, and beetle-shaped stones are used to make seals in Egypt. In Hatti land and Anatolia the latest craze is seals made into signet rings.

Egyptians obsessed by death

Egypt, c. 2600 BC

Egypt is obsessed with death. As each king's mud-brick mastaba (burial chamber) has become increasingly sophisticated, ordinary people are now taking steps to have their own remains preserved.

Each king is believed to become one with the god Isis after death as a natural part of the cosmic order. Burial chambers may now consist of as many as 70 rooms up to 5 m (16 ft) high. The chambers are filled with treasures and household items – a temptation for burglars.

Their bodies are mummified by being immersed in preservatives and filled with aromatic substances before being tightly bandaged.

By contrast, ordinary villagers are now burying their dead in sand to preserve them.

The elaborate ceremonies are related to the religion of the land. Egyptian kings now claim to rule the land of the Nile as the heirs or even incarnations of Horus, the son of Osiris. Osiris is believed to have been a former ruler of Egypt who was brutally murdered and decapitated by his jealous brother, Seth.

In popular mythology, Seth scattered Osiris' mortal remains across Egypt. But the dead king's loyal sister-wife Isis joined his body together again and resurrected him from the dead. Osiris now lives as lord of the afterlife. The story encourages Egyptian kings to arrange for the careful preservation of their own bodies and of the most faithful of their courtiers.

Horus (often depicted as a falcon) is said to have fought his uncle, Seth (a ferocious beast with a long snout), managing to castrate him, but losing an eye in the process. The earth god Geb declared Horus the winner and appointed him as Osiris' successor.

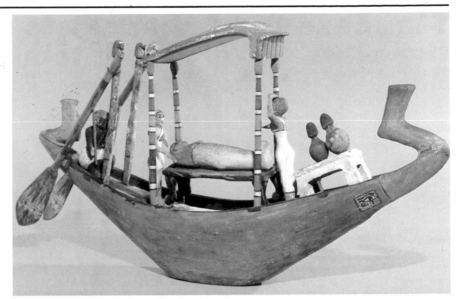

This painted wooden boat, c.1900 BC represents a re-enactment of the journey of a dead man's soul to Abydos, the sacred city of the god Osiris, the lord of the afterlife.

Builders stoned out of their minds?

Avebury, Britain, c. 2800 BC

The people of this prominent west country settlement have begun to build a massive stone circle using huge sarsens (natural stones) from the Marlborough Downs to the north. The colossal task is enough to make a grown man go weak at the knees even thinking about it.

To begin with, the very first sarsen, chosen to stand in the middle of the ring, weighed about 50 tonnes; others are light by comparison, weighing in at about 20 tonnes. They are levered out of the soil with tree trunks, and lowered onto a sledge made from elm and oak which itself weighs about a tonne. The sledge is dragged along a track of logs laid in front of it.

To secure the stone on the sledge and to pull it along, tough ropes 15 cm (6 in) thick are made from thongs of leather. A hundred cow hides are needed to make the 20-m (65-ft) ropes required to move a single stone. Fifty pairs of men push and pull the sledge for the 6.5 km (4 mile) journey to the Avebury site, which takes about four days. For the uphill parts, more men are drafted in.

Once on site, there are several days' more work to get the stone upright. A hole is dug for it, and it is levered off the sledge and propped up by tree trunks. Raising it to a vertical position requires the continuous strength of the 100 men following orders exactly. Once upright, the sarsen is held straight by joists, and clay is packed around the base.

There are 30 stones in the southern ring, and another 12 in the inner ring, circling the central obelisk. A second ring to the north has 27 stones with a 3-stone cove in the centre. It is believed that the two rings are for religious ceremonies at different times of the year.

The sarsens are naturally-occurring sandstones which originated in the gravel beds laid down when the region was covered by the sea. The drizzle and damp of the Ice Age (the area just to the north was ice-bound) caused the under-lying chalk to soften and the sandstone beds slipped down the hills, often splitting into pillars or diamond-shapes as they did so.

Staircase to the stars

Egypt, c. 2620 BC

Egyptian king Zoser will be laid to rest in the most spectacular tomb ever built. One sacred text explains that the purpose of the tomb, which resembles a Sumerian ziggurat, is to provide the king with a staircase so that he might climb up to heaven.

Chief architect Imhotep (who is also a doctor and an author) was responsible for the design of the six-stage stepped pyramid, 62 m (204 ft) high on a base 125 by 109 m (411 by 358 ft) at Saqqura. A compound of other buildings surrounds the pyramid to serve the dead king's needs. The whole complex, which is enclosed by a 10 m (33 ft) high wall, is over 1.6 km (1 mile) wide.

The tomb began as a traditional mastaba, a box-like structure of mud-brick and built on top of an underground tomb. It reflects the belief that preservation of the physical body is essential to the afterlife.

The first mastabas were divided into several compartments, one for the body and the others for the dead person's treasures. There were also compartments for food and drink. A wooden boat was buried nearby for the dead person to use in the afterlife. A mound of sand cased in bricks arranged in stepped form was placed inside the mastaba, which signified the creation which emanated from the god Atum while he sat on a primeval hill.

Imhotep's pyramid is an image of Atum's primeval hill, a symbol of the source, sustenance and continuation of life. It has a complex system of shafts, tunnels and chambers in the underground tomb, which includes space for other members of the royal family. The ingenuity lies in the extension of the mastaba to become the lowest of six stages with sides of successively smaller length. The whole structure is faced with very fine dressed limestone, to enable it to survive the rigours of time.

Cheops gets biggest ever pyramid tomb at Giza

The Great Pyramid of Cheops, with the mysterious Sphynx in the foreground.

Giza, Egypt, c. 2600 BC

The greatest pyramid ever has been built for King Cheops at Giza. Standing about 146 m (481 ft) high, its base area is 13 acres, and its 230 m (756 ft) sides are orientated almost exactly east to west and north to south. The entire pyramid is faced with shining white Tura limestone, which was laid from the top downwards.

Other buildings around provide for the dead king's needs, including tombs for the king's courtiers who hope to serve him after death. East of the pyramid is a funerary temple, and a false door in the pyramid has been built to allow the dead king to get there.

A roofed trench near the pyramid houses full-sized wooden boats, one of which is 44 m (143 ft) long and includes a sizeable cabin and a full complement of oars.

About 2,300,000 separate blocks were used to build it, each weighing about 2.5 tonnes. Most came from nearby quarries. Unskilled labourers were employed seasonally according to the demands of their own agricultural jobs. About 4,000 skilled stone masons were also used and special accommodation was built for them to live on site.

During the construction, which took at least three years, rations were issued for the work forces, and surgeons were on hand for accidents while scribes wrote down exactly what was happening.

The king's architect, Hemon, changed his plans twice during construction. Instead of a burial chamber underneath the surface of the plateau, a small chamber was built within the pyramid. He also added a grand gallery, 7.5 m (25 ft) high and enclosed by a corbelled roof, which leads to the King's Chamber at the centre of the pyramid. The king's own sarcophagus, cut from a single block of granite, is placed at the west end of the chamber.

Egypt has never had it so good

Egypt, c. 2580 BC

Egypt now has an elaborate tax system, which operates according to each taxpayer's land holding. Land which is regularly covered with flood water is taxed at a higher rate than more arid land further from the Nile. Cattle and wares are also taxable, and crop quotas are assigned according to the expected high-water mark on the Nile at Elephantine each spring.

In this fertile land, irrigated by canals and reservoirs, barley and a type of wheat called emmer are the chief bounties of the verdant countryside. Vegetable gardens and orchards line the lush riverside, providing lettuces, chickpeas, cucumbers, broad beans and lentils enough for all. Vineyards are a common sight, though beer – rather than fermented grapes – is the staple drink, consumed by all.

Outside their mud-brick houses, the peasants keep their sheep, goats and pigs. Pairs of oxen stand ready to plough the land. Fish, whether fresh or dried, remains a common source of protein for the well-to-do; but, along with meat, it is a rare luxury for the poorer people. They subsist mainly on bread and beer.

Irrigation channel, with traditional earthen banks, near Aswan.

Classes divided by work

Professional musicians play at a funerary banquet.

Egypt, c. 2500 BC

Favourite courtiers live in opulent homes, with many rooms surrounding a large open court-yard. Chairs are linen-covered and even game boards are inlaid with ivory. The wealthy wear white linen and braided black wigs to feast on goose, dates, figs and bread, while being entertained by harpists.

The poor who wait at table wear simple loin cloths. Many are prisoners of war, or slaves.

The work cycle of the middle classes' revolves around three seasons: the Nile flood (the inundation), the sowing season (the emergence), and harvest (the drought). Part of the harvest is paid in tribute to the king.

During the inundation, when farming is not possible, field workers are often conscripted by the king for tomb-building.

The well-bred Egyptian is educated at papyrus school, and taught to master the reed brush, ink palette and erasing stone to perfect his use of the 700 signs. Whippings are frequent in this school, where the teachers are the priests. Egyptian writing goes back as far as 3100 BC. It is a conservative picture language. Stylised characters represent everyday objects, ideas or sounds. It does not have the potential subtlety of the Sumerian script. Egyptian scribes use a paper-like material made from papyrus reeds for their elaborate record keeping.

Doctors use plants instead of traditional magic spells

Sumer, c. 2500 BC

Trained physicians are moving into the Sumerian cities to provide a radical alternative to traditional exorcists in the treatment of sickness.

The new doctors, who record their prescriptions on clay tablets, use plants and minerals for their remedies instead of spells and incantations. Their often disgusting-tasting potions are sweetened by ale. One remedy requires ale to be boiled over resin and then mixed with bitumen oil.

Salves are obtained from minerals high in natural fat and mixed with soda ash. Saltpetre is used as an astringent to stem blood flows, and salt is rubbed into wounds as an antiseptic.

However, the average life span of 40 years does not seem to have been lengthened substantially by these remedies. When the rich die they are interred in brick-built vaults beneath their houses, whilst the poor are wrapped in reed matting and placed in freshly-dug graves outside cities.

Consumerism reaches Europe

Europe, 2500 BC

With new population mobility, new commodities are appearing.

Copper is beginning to replace stone for the blades of daggers and axes. While this metal allows a sharper edge than could otherwise be honed with a neolithic implement, the new substance is not as sturdy as stone. Progress is being made in honing and refining and the search for stronger metals.

Drinking cups shaped like upturned bells are thought to have been first developed in the low countries. They are often beautifully decorated, and frequently used for alcoholic beverages. Some drinking vessels have longer necks added to the basic bell design. These are regarded as prestigious artefacts and often buried with their deceased owners.

Brave new civilisation

Indus Valley, 2500 BC

People have started building in the Indus Valley in Pakistan. Their history is unknown, not least because of the difficulty of understanding their unique pictographic script.

They may have been nomads from Baluchistan to the west, coming to the fertile valley in search of grazing for their sheep and goats. During the heat of the summer, they migrate to the cooler heights of the Himalayan foothills.

Cultivation is greatly assisted by the region's annual floods but these can be dangerously unpredictable; and the river often changes its course in spite of the levees and irrigation systems that have been set up. Plains and whole villages are often submerged.

The area also has fine forests which provide ample supplies of timber. Leopards and tigers prowl them, while the savannah grasslands are home to elephants, rhinoceroses, graceful antelopes and wild hogs, providing ample fresh meat.

Priests and traders grow fat on land

Sumer, 2500 BC

Priests are now profit-makers as they cultivate and rent out their extensive lands, and give gifts of land to curry favour and influence with the civil government.

And traders venturing into the east are bringing back expensive luxury goods which can be sold for large sums.

Priestly power has grown along with the temples. Peasants are asked to give a proportion of their harvest to the priests in order to please the gods and bring good fortune. Not all is hoarded in the guarded granaries, however; some is given by the priests to widows, orphans and other poor.

Full-time career opportunities are available in temple administration. Finance and building managers are sought to free the priests for their religious duties.

The temples increasingly look like miniature cities, as singers and musicians, cooks, maids, cleaners and weavers augment the priests and administrators. Slaves toil in the temple fields, while craftspeople such as carpenters and ceramic artists set up business in the precincts.

Traders venturing in sailing boats beyond the Persian Gulf to the Indus Valley and around the southern Arabian Peninsular have brought back exotic ivory combs from the Indus and carnelian beads from Elam.

Those happy to trade in more conventional goods are lashing timber and stone acquired in the north onto rafts and transporting it down river, using inflated animal skins to increase the rafts' buoyancy. Traditional heavily-laden donkey caravans continue to trek through Syria to the Mediterranean coast and eastwards through the Zagros mountains into Elamite territory.

This inlaid plaque from Ur depicts the Sumerian army going into battle.

Jericho's walls come tumbling down

Jericho, c. 2300 BC

The palm city of Jericho, a major city for 6,000 years on the edge of the Jordan Valley, has been ransacked by invaders who are now reported to be settling back into its lower slopes. They were probably nomads who resented Jericho's monopoly of fertile land.

Set in a rich food-producing area, Jericho has been a leading centre for Canaanite culture almost since people emerged from caves to build houses.

For the past 1,000 years it has been a fine walled city with stone towers and a strong defensive wall surrounding the city to protect it. Life for its people has no longer been a matter of survival; arts and crafts have flourished there.

Well-developed pottery, often red glazed, and wooden tables, stools and beds filled the houses. Small boxes have been inlaid with ivory, and there was a temple serving the people living in their rectangular houses.

Caravans seek new pasture

Mesopotamia, c. 2050 BC

Middle Bronze Age Mesopotamia looks something like a seething anthill or beehive as its peoples constantly move from place to place in search of fresh pasture for their livestock. Camel caravans usually avoid the large cities of the coastal plain and take the higher roads in the hill country.

One family on the move is that of Terah, a name associated with the commonly-worshipped moon god. He and his son Abram and their dependants have moved almost 965 km (600 miles) up the Euphrates River from Ur in the deep south to Haran in the north-west. Both cities are noted caravan centres.

It is a prosperous region. Ur has an imposing temple tower and ziggurat. There has been a city on the site from about 4000 BC, and past dynasties have left imposing relics, such as the royal tombs. At nearby Mari the royal palace covers eight acres and has all the latest luxuries; there is also a splendid library of over 25,000 cuneiform tablets.

(Genesis 11:27–32)

Cities become states

Sumer, 2500 BC

The population of the nation of Sumer is believed to have reached the half million mark. And 80 per cent of the people live in city-states.

One such city-state is Uruk. It has a 10 km (6 mile) wall surrounding it, which is described in the *Gilgamesh Epic* as glistening 'with the brilliance of copper'. The wall provides an essential defence against barbarian invaders who find the easy terrain no barrier to their attacks. Outside the wall 76 villages are embraced by the city-state. Civil wars are increasingly common as city-states battle with each other for water rights.

A beautiful inlaid Sumerian games board. The game looks intricate, and highly decorative. It appears to be a game of strategy, an early cross between chess and draughts.

Travelling on a promise from God

Haran, c. 2010 BC

A risky gamble has prompted one of Haran's long-established families to move out on a journey to an unknown land. Although Abram, son of Terah (who died in the city not long ago) has no children by his wife Sarai, he has been telling friends in Haran that God has promised him that he will be the founder of a great nation. On the basis of his fertility so far, the gamble is a huge one.

The family is originally from Ur. They came to Haran after the death of Abram's brother, also called Haran. Abram settled here with his wife, father and Lot, his nephew. He is now 75 years old, and while this is not yet old age it is late in life for the kind of adventure on which he is embarking. Especially when the stakes are so improbable.

(Genesis 12:1–5)

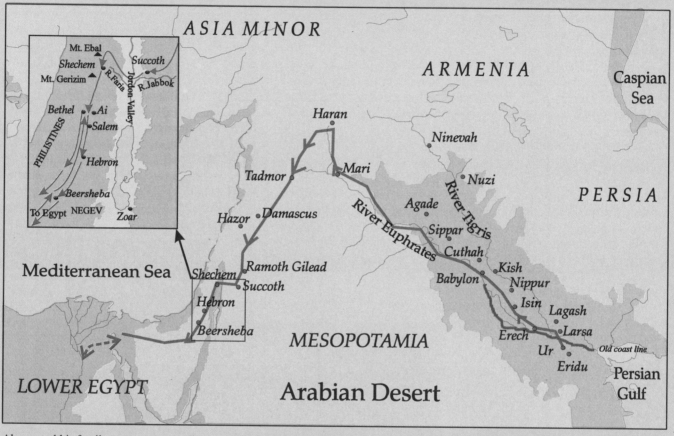

Abram and his family were great travellers, covering over 2,000 miles in all during their travels.

Abram takes his God to Canaanite towns

Canaan, c. 2000 BC

Abram has risked offending people in the Shechem area by building an altar to Yahweh at the site of earlier Canaanite shrines.

The prosperous nomad, whose extensive caravan consists of numerous servants, flocks and herds, claims that God has told him that he will give the land of Canaan to Abram's offspring who will apparently be a numerous as the stars or the sands on the sea shore.

Abram has since moved on from Shechem towards Bethel, where he repeated his religious action in the hills to the east of the town. The local people's reaction to his actions and prophecies is not known.

What is known is that the 'promised land' is spewing out its inhabitants by refusing to sustain them. Abram is joining the growing number of nomads moving south due to famine.

(Genesis 12:6–8)

Alabaster statue of Ebih-II, overseer of Mari, a town near Haran.

Abram's narrow escape with wife and life

Egypt, c. 1995 BC

Semi-nomad Abram, one of many Semites to have emigrated to Egypt from famine-stricken Canaan, has escaped the Pharaoh's court with no more than a royal rebuke for a potentially disastrous deception.

Abram, knowing that travelling women are liable to be conscripted into unwelcome service in the royal harem, told his stunningly beautiful wife Sarai to act as if she was his sister. He feared that he would be killed by jealous courtiers if he confessed to being her husband.

The Egyptians, overwhelmed by her beauty, reported her arrival to the Pharaoh. Sarai was taken to his court, and Abram and his family were given preferential treatment with gifts of livestock and servants.

For Abram, it was an ethical nightmare. And it turned into a

The hills around Bethel still provide stony pasture-land today.

medical and spiritual nightmare for the Pharaoh. No sooner had Sarai entered the royal household than it was plagued by a series of serious illnesses. The Pharaoh did not need his astrologers and magicians to tell him the reason. He knew instinctively that Sarai was married and Abram's God was displeased.

Pharaoh merely banished Abram and his family from the land, taking none of his property as a fine for the deception. Abram seems to lead a charmed life; having survived physical famine and Pharaonic fury, he appears wealthier than ever.

(Genesis 12:10–13:2)

The Lot is cast in family feud

Canaan, c. 1990 BC

Abram's family has been rocked by a personality clash that has resulted in the caravan splitting up.

The crisis was provoked by Abram's new Egyptian wealth. He and Lot both have livestock, but Abram's increasing flocks have created a water shortage around the camp sites. Abram, who has brought the caravan back to Bethel where he has been worshipping God at the altar he built there previously, is having his meditations disturbed by furious wrangling at the wells between his herdsmen and those of Lot.

Abram, as family patriarch, has been remarkably accommodating to his nephew. Having suggested a parting of the ways he gave Lot the first choice of territory. Lot had the easy decision of whether to take the fertile territory watered by the Jordan, or the less attractive grazing in the Canaanite uplands. He chose the former, and the two have parted.

Though Lot has a much better agricultural situation, he may find living in the low lands a testing time spiritually. The Canaanites are notorious for their wickedness and depravity, and the cities of the plain

are likely to be a great temptation in many ways.

Following the split, Abram claims to have received a fresh vision from his God Yahweh promising that all the land that Abram could see is to be given to his offspring who will be as numerous and as uncountable as the dust in the desert and the stars in the sky.

If this promise is God's reward to Abram for his faith, it will take a good deal more faith to believe it. Neither Abram nor Sarai is getting any younger, and there is no sign of offspring yet.

(Genesis 13)

Fast Facts 2000 BC

Iraq: The Third Dynasty in Abram's old city of Ur is, under Shulgi, completing the superb administrative infrastructure begun by his father, Urnammu. Roads and canals are being built. An extensive police force is maintaining law and order, and government inspectors ensure that all goes according to plan.

Turkey: A mighty empire is beginning in Asia Minor. Settlers there have taken the name 'Hittites' after the original inhabitants of the area. Tidal, a member of the coalition against the cities of the plain is a Hittite.

Egypt: Pharaoh Mentuhop II has succeeded in uniting the country. However, he is finding it difficult to control the nomads of the Nile Delta. They may present a threat to the unity of the kingdom.

Crete: Society is changing, as urban explosion creates new cities at Knossos and Phaistos, each with a splendid palace and crowded streets. A new road network and a new written language complete what promises to be a revolution in Cretan life.

Troy, c. 2100 BC: The city has been destroyed by fire. Its walls and fortifications, which engineers have been improving and strengthening for decades, could not protect the city against the inferno. The magnificent hall, filled with gold, copper and bronze vessels which demonstrated the wealth of the Trojans is now a pile of ash. Plans have already been laid to rebuild the city.

Abram honours his God

Canaan, c. 1990 BC

The powerful tribal patriach, Abram, has confirmed his allegiance to the little-known God Yahweh in a magnanimous act of personal sacrifice.

Returning from the battle of the four kings, Abram was met in the plain by the king of Sodom and the priest-king of Jerusalem, Melchizedek, who pronounced a traditional blessing upon him.

Abram responded by giving him a tenth of his battle-spoils. Bystanders understood the significance of this, for Abram was acknowledging that giving a tithe to a priest was the same as offering thanks to Yahweh for the victory.

The king of Sodom then urged Abram to keep Sodom's possessions as his reward and merely return the people whom Chedorlaomer's coalition had captured. But Abram declined, and called God as his witness that he had vowed to make no profit from the people he had rescued: no human being would ever be able to say, 'I made Abram rich'.

He agreed to accept only food to replenish his army's supplies consumed during the battle, and the share of the booty that was appropriate to his contribution to the fighting. His decision avoided setting up subtle power-structures and establishing Abram's subservience to the king. But the principal effect has been to make Abram's commitment to Yahweh clear beyond doubt to all his neighbours.

The political situation in the region is now highly unstable following the destruction of the cities of the plain, the economic havoc wreaked by Chedorlaomer and the disappearance of Chedorlaomer from the scene.

(Genesis 14:17–23)

Fortune lost and found in war

Canaan, c. 1990 BC

The Semite adventurer Lot has lost all his wealth in a bitter war of liberation only to get it all back again following a dramatic intervention by his even more powerful uncle, Abram.

Sodom, Gomorrah, Admah, Zeboiim and Zoar – cities of the Canaanite Plain – had been subjects of King Kedorlaomer, ruler of the super-power Elam, for 12 years.

Canaan. A coalition of the kings of Babylon, Ellasar and Goiim under Chedorlaomer crushed the insurgents.

Their strategy was simple but effective. First the invaders conquered all the territory to the north of the cities, depriving the rebels of military support. Then they advanced south against the cities of the plain.

The rebels made a desperate

Emaq Ha Ela (the Elah Valley) emphasises today the lushness of the valley with the barren nature of the surrounding hills.

Elam held them for exactly the same reason that Lot chose to live there. They are prosperous cities surrounded by fertile, well-watered land.

But an alliance of the heads of each city assembled an army to fight for their freedom.

In response a draconian military force of Elamites swept through

stand against the Babylonian coalition in the Valley of the Dead. They were routed, and Sodom and Gomorrah were sacked and pillaged, losing goods and food supplies. Lot was taken prisoner, and lost everything he owned.

But a survivor reached Abram and reported what had happened. He immediately called the 318 trained men of his household (being wealthy he has a private army) and went to his nephew's aid. He pursued the victorious invaders for 240 km (150 miles) north to Dan, where he attacked them by night.

He divided his small force, leaving the Babylonians to defend on what seemed several fronts. He pursued the retreating and disorganised army beyond Damascus and recovered the stolen property. Lot recovered everything he had lost.

(Genesis 14:1–16)

War for all

In wartime every able-bodied male in Palestinian households is liable for conscription, and he returns to normal work afterwards. There are no professional soldiers. 'Armies' are usually small war-bands, and alliances are common between peoples who have a common enemy or who want to share the spoils of a common attack. This explains Abram's success with a small (318) force but directed with brilliant military tactics.

Abram's promised child will shatter his servant's hopes

Mamre, c. 1985 BC

Old men dream dreams. Old Abram has visions – or illusions. According to his latest spiritual revelation his long years without a male heir are numbered. He has entered into an extraordinary religious contract here with his God Yahweh.

Under the agreement or covenant Abram and Sarai will become natural parents of a son and subsequent generations from him will be 'as uncountable as the stars in the sky'. They are also to possess the land of Canaan where Abram currently resides.

The news has come as a great disappointment to Abram's chief servant, Eliezer of Damascus. Although he has been employed by Abram for a relatively short time, he had been adopted as his heir. In the event of a natural son being born, Eliezer would forfeit his right to the estate.

This is the latest in a series of undertakings given to Abram by Yahweh. The new covenant follows the pattern established in the two which Yahweh made with Noah. In those, Noah was placed under obligation towards God, who responded to his obedience with promises of favour and protection.

The terms of the covenant, however, are expressed in language quite different from that of civil contracts, in which the parties have equal obligation to each other. The covenant with Noah, and the latest with Abram, are more similar to the many covenants that establish treaty relationships between kings (or gods) and their peoples, dating back as far as 3000 BC.

Surprisingly, Abram, whose wife is barren, seems to have accepted the promise of descendants quite

Satellite photo of the land of Israel

readily, but though he is extremely wealthy he asked God for some kind of guarantee to the promise of land. God therefore ratified his covenant by accepting a ceremonial animal sacrifice from Abram. Subsequently he elaborated his promise to him in a dream.

In the covenant God undertakes that:

• Abram will live out his life to a good age and die in peace.

• He will have many descendants, and they will be enslaved exiles for 400 years.

• They will emerge from the experience as a wealthy people.

• The exact area being given to Abram's descendants stretches from the Nile to the Euphrates.

(Genesis 15)

Family splits over slave's surrogate pregnancy

Mamre, c. 1985 BC

Abram has become a dad at the ripe old age of 86, ten years after God's momentous promise that he would.

But the birth has split the family, because the child's mother is not Abram's wife, but her maid.

It is customary that if a wife has no children she gives a slave girl to her husband, to have a child by him for her. This is meant to ensure the all-important birth of an heir.

After 10 fruitless years Sarai could not believe the dream-message that was given to her husband. And, in a hot-tempered confrontation with Abram she accused Yahweh of deliberately making her infertile. She demanded that Abram begin a sexual relationship with her Egyptian servant, Hagar, to found a family.

But when Hagar became pregnant she began to taunt Sarai with her barrenness. The furious Sarai began to ill-treat Hagar who, although heavily pregnant, ran away.

But she returned days later to beg Sarai's forgiveness. Sitting by a well on the desert road out to Shur, she was met by the angel of the Lord who commanded her to return and submit to Sarai. She returned in hope, not despair. Hagar the handmaid, like Abram the millionaire, had also been given promises by God:

• Her descendants will be too many to count.

• Her baby would be a boy and he is to be named Ishmael (which means 'God hears').

• He will be a rebellious, difficult boy who will live at odds with his brothers.

Hagar has called the well Beer Lahai Roi – 'I have seen the One who sees me'.

(Genesis 16)

It's a sore deal!

Mamre, c. 1980 BC

The male members of wealthy semi-nomadic Abram's extensive household are pretty sore about the old man's latest vision of God.

As part of his deal with Yahweh, they've had their penis foreskins cut off as a sign that if they break the covenant they and their descendants will be cut off from God's promises.

In return, God has reiterated his former promises that Abram will found a dynasty, that his descendants will possess Canaan (where he is now living as an immigrant), and that God will be the God of Abram and his descendants for ever. As a further sign he is no longer to be called Abram (which means 'Exalted Father' and is a tribute to God), but 'Abraham' ('Father of Many').

Every male born in the future, whether sons of Abraham's line, slaves bought from foreign countries, or any other member of the household, is also to be circumcised.

Sarai too is to have a new name, Sarah, signifying that from her will be descended nations and kings.

Abraham has found these promises hard to believe. He is almost 100 years old, Sarah at 90 is well past child-bearing age. He challenged the bizarre promise, offering Ishmael, the 13-year-old son he fathered with his servant Hagar, as the most logical recipient of God's blessing. But God insisted that although Ishmael will be blessed and become the father of a nation, it is the child of Sarah – to be called Isaac – with whom God's covenant will be established.

Perhaps because he recognises that the name Isaac, which means 'He laughs', is a mild rebuke from God for his own failure to take the

Old oak tree at Tabor.

promises seriously, Abraham has carried the latest command to the letter. The males in Abraham's household, including himself and Ishmael, are now recovering from their minor operation. The covenant relationship with God has suddenly become more prominent in their thinking.

(Genesis 17)

Two cities destroyed in explosive disaster

Jordanian Plain, c. 1975 BC

The cities of Sodom and Gomorrah have been totally destroyed in a major natural disaster. The surrounding Jordanian Plain has

Salt flats, Dead Sea — the area where Sodom and Gomorrah are reputed to have been destroyed.

also been extensively damaged. There are three known survivors.

While some people are suggesting a supernatural explanation, it is likely that an earthquake or other tectonic movement on the geological fault which runs through the area from east Africa to Mount Hermon set off a chain reaction.

Gases released from the earth's interior may have been ignited by domestic fires. Fuelled by the rich oil and bitumen deposits which lie close to the surface, the initial conflagration would have spread rapidly through the region.

However, divine vengeance is not being ruled out as a primary cause. Both cities were notorious for their complacency, blatant immorality and blasphemy. Sodom has become a byword for sexual perversion. Few regions so materially prosperous have been so spiritually corrupt.

Eyewitnesses spoke of seeing clouds of burning sulphur, bitumen and mineral salts being thrown high into the air and raining down mercilessly on the cities and covering them entirely.

One victim was engulfed by a suffocating storm of mineral dust. As her husband, Lot, and his two daughters – the only survivors – watched helplessly, she was literally turned into a pillar of salt. She had paused briefly behind her fleeing family to watch the pall of smoke and debris rising from the carnage.

Lot came to the fertile lands of Sodom after a family dispute with his uncle, Abram, which resulted in the older man undertaking to restrict his animals' grazing to the less attractive Canaanite uplands. It looks as if Abram had the better of the deal. It could be centuries before the plain is fertile and habitable again.

(Genesis 19)

Lot tells of 'supernatural' visitors

Canaan, c. 1975 BC

One of the survivors from Sodom claims that the disaster was a direct punishment from his God on the city's evil lifestyle.

He says he was warned of the catastrophe by two angelic visitors. His uncle, who lives in Canaan, says he too had the same message from the same angels.

According to Lot, the two strangers had arrived in the city the previous evening and he persuaded them to stay with him. The house was later surrounded by a gang of men demanding that the strangers be handed over to be sexually abused. But they were struck by mass blindness, and in the ensuing confusion the strangers advised Lot to leave the city.

Although they warned that Sodom was about to be destroyed, Lot was only able to persuade his wife and daughters to leave. The rest of his family is presumed dead.

The strangers disappeared shortly after leading Lot and his daughters to safety. They have not been identified. Lot insists that they were 'angels' – messengers of the God Yahweh, who could tolerate the wickedness of Sodom no longer. He quotes them as saying, 'The outcry to the Lord against its people is so great he has sent us to destroy it.'

Recently his uncle, Abraham, provided traditional Eastern hospitality to three strangers without at first realising, he claimed, that they too were angels.

The strangers arrived without warning at Abraham's tent, pitched under the great trees of Mamre. Over a meal of roast calf, freshly-cooked bread and milk dishes, they said they were going to Sodom to find out whether the city was as sinful as its reputation.

In an astonishing bout of bartering, Abraham pleaded with God to spare the city if righteous people existed there; it would be unjust to destroy the city, he argued, if that were so. The Lord finally agreed to spare the city if just ten righteous people could be found there.

One of them also commented that in a year's time Sarah, his wife, would have a son. Sarah, listening at the tent-flap, laughed aloud.

'Why did she laugh?' asked the stranger. 'Is anything too hard for the Lord?'

(Genesis 18:1–19:20)

Sede desert near the Dead Sea.

Art demands high price

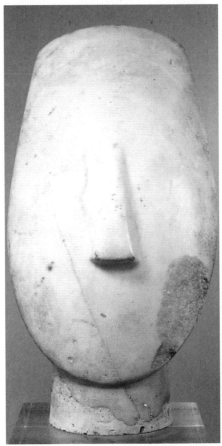

A marble stylised woman's head, from Amorgos, Crete.

Crete, c. 2000 BC

The Minoan civilisation has an enviable reputation for beautiful works of art. Minoan traders bring blue paste beads and ornaments from Egypt and ivory from Syria. Her jewellers create wonderful gold trinkets. And Minoan vases in characteristic grained marble are becoming sought after by wealthy connoisseurs.

Fail-safe

Gerar, c. 1974 BC

The centenarian semi-nomad, Abraham, who believes he will have a child by his wife almost gave her away when he moved into town. For the second time in his life his faith failed him and he passed off his wife Sarah as his sister, believing otherwise he might be killed because of her.

The incident took place in Gerar, in the Negev, a region very susceptible to drought. Nestling in the fertile coastal plain and well watered by Mediterranean rainfall, Gerar is a favourite place of many nomadic people. The local king, Abimelech, took the 90-year-old but still beautiful Sarah as his wife, but before he could consummate the marriage God confronted him in a dream and threatened to kill him.

Abimelech protested that he could hardly be blamed and at a public meeting faced Abraham with his duplicity. It made Abimelech look the more God-fearing man. Abraham has been taught a hard lesson about trusting God. When he had tried the same trick in Egypt it also ended in shameful rebuke – and a handsome pay-off of royal land and goods to appease the gods.

(Genesis 20; cf. Genesis 12:14–20)

Desert-ed by a cruel step-mother

Gerar, c. 1967 BC

A middle-aged mother and her teenage son are tonight wandering alone among the scattered nomads of the southern desert, homeless and friendless. And all because their guardian matron loved her own son more.

Lady's maid, Hagar, had worked for years for Sarah, the wife of wealthy semi-nomad, Abraham. She had even consented to letting Abraham get her pregnant, because Sarah was infertile, thinking that he would inherit the family fortune and secure her future.

But when Sarah at last gave birth to Isaac three years ago, she had little time for her adopted son Ishmael and his mother. The last straw came when she caught the spotty teenager laughing at the sight of the wrinkly Sarah – who at 90-plus is old enough to be his great-grandmother – pampering the toddler at his weaning party.

In a fit of rage Sarah ordered the pair off the premises, despite the protests of Ishmael's father, Abraham. He may be the clan patriarch, but she most definitely rules the roost.

Abraham is quoted as saying he believes that despite the great hardship the pair will suffer, his God will care for them and raise a future nation from them. Reports from the desert suggest that the old man might be right again.

When Hagar and Ishmael collapsed in the wasteland from exhaustion and dehydration, they opened their eyes to find that they had stopped close by a well. Hagar herself is said to believe the assurances given by God to Abraham.

(Genesis 21:1–21)

Kind friends

Beersheba, c. 1965 BC

Wealthy but aging patriach, Abraham, and the king of the Gerar region (known by his dynastic title of Abimelech) have signed a friendship treaty. Abraham, who has lodged in the area for some years, is obliged to show the same hospitality and kindness to the Philistine peoples as they have shown to him. The treaty is binding on both men's descendants.

(Genesis 21:22–34)

The stone-strewn landscape of the Jordan Valley near the Dead Sea.

Egypt's Middle Kingdom survives death of monarch

Memphis, 1962 BC

Amenemhet, king of Egypt, is dead, after reigning in peace and further uniting his country. Rumours are rife that he was assassinated.

Amenemhet moved the Egyptian capital to Memphis. Under him Thebes has declined in importance, although the Theban god, Amon, has become a prominent Egyptian deity. He established a sophisticated civil service, used media propaganda to enhance his regal image, and created an effective modern state. For the past ten years his son Sesostris was co-regent; Sesostris will now accede to the throne.

Egypt was first unified under the great Mentuhotep II who acceded in 2134 BC and ruled for 50 years, inaugurating the Middle Kingdom. He built on the achievements of his predecessors, curbed the independent power of the nomarchs (local rulers), and ruled from his capital, Thebes. Mentuhotep was a patron of traditional and folk art. Like all the Theban kings, he sponsored cultural progress; art, literature, jewellery and architecture all thrived in what is widely considered to have been a golden age.

Fast Facts c. 1950 BC

Wales: Copper is being mined on Parys Mountain, Anglesey.

Northern Europe: Stone circles and monuments are to be seen in many places, sometimes as isolated monuments, more often as large ordered sites: e.g. Caracanet, France, and Avebury in England.

Byblos in Lebanon has become a major timber-exporting port, as the durable qualities of cedar are becoming widely recognised

Egypt has given up domesticating antelopes and oryx and is turning to hunting and fishing to supplement agriculture. Beef and dairy husbandry is common throughout the Near East. Increasing agricultural sophistication is evident in many areas. Africans are growing water melons, Indians are growing tea and bananas, and Arabians are growing figs.

Phylakopi a once insignificant village on the island of Melos, Greece, is now exporting obsidian.

Phoenician and Cretan ships are being made with square sails; and up to three masts.

Babylon has replaced Sumer as the leading Middle Eastern power. The decimal system is being used for the first time in its accounts.

France: There has been a large volcanic eruption in the Massif Central.

Child saved from sacrificial pyre

Beersheba, c. 1960 BC

A young boy has been saved in the nick of time from the pyre on which he was about to be burned by his father as a human sacrifice to God.

He was already tied up and lying on the wood, and was about to have his throat cut before the fire was lit. But his father heard a noise on the otherwise deserted mountainside. He found a ram was caught in a thornbush, which provided a providential last-minute substitute for the boy on the makeshift altar.

Although not unheard-of, human sacrifice in Canaan is rare. Animal sacrifices for religious purposes are made frequently by many tribespeople. This was even more unusual in that the boy, Isaac, was the only son and heir of elderly parents Abraham and Sarah, from Beersheba on the edge of the southern desert, who had been childless for decades until his eventual birth.

The incident occurred on Mount Moriah (now identified with Jerusalem) in central Canaan, a rocky and, at present, uninhabited hill about three days' journey north from Beersheba. Two servants with pack animals accompanied the pair to the valley below the hill but did not witness the scene of this unusual sacrifice.

Abraham claimed later that he had set out knowing that Isaac was the intended victim, but naturally without telling the boy. He believed that his God was calling him to kill the one person in whom all his hopes for a future dynasty lay.

When questioned by Isaac on the journey about the intended sacrifice, the old man would say only that 'God will provide the lamb'. He says he believed that God could, if necessary, raise Isaac from the dead.

As a result of his unquestioning obedience he claims that Yahweh has confirmed the promise that his descendants will be 'as numerous as the stars' and that many nations will be blessed by God through him.

It had been a supreme test of faith for one whose trust in God has faltered spectacularly at times in his life. It suggested to him that God is to be trusted beyond all human considerations, even with the things or people that his followers love most and pin their hopes on.

The incident also sets a precedent ruling out the possibility of any religious murders or ritual killings of people by the members of Abraham's tribe in the future. Yahweh appears to be a God who values all human life and who accepts sincerely-offered animal sacrifices both as emblems of devotion and as substitutionary means of atoning for wrongdoing once and for all.

(Genesis 22:1–19 cf. Hebrews 11:17–19)

The Sacrifice of Isaac, as illustrated by Rembrandt.

His first real estate is a graveyard

Old Jewish graveyard in the valley of Hinnom, outside Jerusalem.

Mamre, c. 1950 BC

Abraham's beloved wife, Sarah, is dead, at the age of 127 years.

Her grieving husband, having completed the official mourning, has negotiated with the Hittites to purchase a place to bury her. As a nomad with no permanent residence, and himself a foreigner in the land, he had no other option.

Though he was offered any of the Hittite tombs, he asked instead to purchase the Cave of Machpelah near Mamre. He insisted on paying the full market price when its owner offered it to him as a gift.

He has buried Sarah there, and the cave has become a legally-established burial site for Abraham's people; the first piece of the promised land Abraham believes his descendants will possess.

Its present inhabitants have occupied the land for at least a thousand years. They live in large city-states of which one of the most impressive is Jericho.

The region is of great strategic importance; highways between Africa, Asia and Europe criss-cross Canaan and its environs. Consequently, neighbouring powers often threaten its security.

(Genesis 23)

41

Chain of coincidence links two families

Beersheba, c. 1945 BC

A chain of coincidences at the end of a 650 km (400 mile) journey into the unknown has linked two related families in a new and loving marriage.

It was the romantic adventure of which young dreams are made. A trusted servant sets off laden with gifts to find a bride for his employer's son. Alone in a foreign land he prays to his master's God with the risky request that the first woman who offers to water his camels will be the one.

And lo and behold, the password is spoken to the letter by a girl who is beautiful, unmarried, and a member of the right clan. What's even more surprising, she and her family agree readily to the match.

'What could we say?' commented an amazed Laban, the girl's brother and family spokesman. 'This was all Yahweh's doing. You can't argue with a God who arranges things like that.'

The chain of events was set in motion by the elderly Abraham, a semi-nomad living in Beersheba but who originates from Haran near the Euphrates headwaters in north-western Mesopotamia. He was determined that his only son Isaac should marry within the clan, but all his relatives lived up north.

So he despatched his chief steward to seek out a wife on Isaac's behalf. Arranged marriages of this kind are common among many tribespeople today. But this time, the arranging seems to have been done in heaven, and no one on the ground had the heart to haggle over the bride price.

Abraham, whose often wild-sounding prophecies in the past have generated at least private disbelief among his family and staff, has been proved right again. His parting words to his servant were that Yahweh would send his angel to accompany him and make his quest a success.

Isaac and his bride, Rebekah, are certainly not arguing with that as they bed down together in their new tent.

(Genesis 24)

Wait for me!

Beersheba, c. 1850 BC

Twin boys born to golden oldies, Isaac and Rebekah, couldn't wait to get into the world. Said Rebekah, already well into her 50s, 'They've been kicking each other and me to bits for the past nine months!'

And although little Jacob got beaten to the light by his red-haired brother, Esau, he emerged from the womb clinging to Esau's heel as if afraid of being left behind – or trying to stop him being first.

The happy couple had thought they were doomed to be childless and had prayed for a son. But old-age births run in the family. Isaac himself was born when his father was 100. Esau has been nicknamed 'Edom' (red) because of his colouring. Jacob's name means 'heel grabber' or 'deceiver'.

(Genesis 25:21–26)

Well at Tell Arad, near Beersheba.

Same old story, fresh new stars

Gerar, Philistia, c. 1870 BC

The scriptwriter of history seems to be running short of plots. In a re-run of his father's comic capers, Semitic semi-nomad, Isaac from Hebron, has stepped into the role of cowardly husband.

And even the hapless stooge who fell victim to the straightman's near-tragic farce had the same name as his counterpart in the earlier production.

Twice in his long life Isaac's father, Abraham, had passed his wife Sarah off as his sister to avoid unwelcome critical attention from jealous rivals who might stage an accident to get rid of him.

Well-rehearsed in the family's dramatic arts, Isaac played it by the book when he moved south-west to Gerar on the Philistine border because food supplies had run out in Canaan. He persuaded his attractive wife, Rebekah, to play the part of his sister.

But he couldn't keep his hands off her, and in a rash moment of backstage passion he was spotted in the wings by the king of Gerar, known by the generations-long title or family name of Abimelech. A previous Abimelech had caught Abraham in the same act, having been warned in a dream. An earlier incident had taken place in Egypt.

Hauling Isaac in front of the footlights, the enraged king waxed eloquent on the scenes of divine wrath which such a deception risked. If Rebekah had been carried off by an amorous Geraran, the gods could have rung down the curtain on the nation's performance.

But it all ended happily in a spectacular finale as Abimelech gave the prosperous Isaac and his wife the full protection of the royal court, to ensure that his own line enjoyed a long run.

(Genesis 26:1–11)

Esau in a stew as Jacob cooks the books again

Canaan, c. 1800 BC

Isaac's sons, Jacob and Esau, have twice fallen out over a pot of stew. Now they are locked in bitter resentment which has ended in a death threat.

Esau, a distinctive figure with long red hair and beard and limbs as hairy as a young goat's, is the elder twin by a matter of seconds and legally entitled to the significant blessing of his father. Isaac is known to prefer the outdoor hunter Esau to the more domesticated Jacob, for whom their mother Rebekah has a very soft spot.

Their ageing father, Isaac, afraid that he might die without having given the traditional patriarchal blessing to his elder son, asked Esau to hunt some wild game for him and cook him his favourite meal. Then he would bestow the blessing.

But at the instigation of their mother, Rebekah, Jacob impersonated his brother to Isaac whose sight had almost gone and so received his brother's blessing. To overcome the problem that the difference between Esau's hairy skin and his own smooth flesh could hardly escape even the blind Isaac, Rebekah covered Jacob's arms in goat-hair.

After some initial uncertainty Isaac pronounced the blessing on Jacob. This binding, legal enactment transmitts' God's covenant promise from one generation to the next. Once given, it cannot be withdrawn, and it cannot be given again to another. Jacob was promised that he would be honoured by nations and served by his brethren: 'Those who curse you

Bedouin cooking round a fire in the open.

will be cursed,' pronounced Isaac, 'Those who bless you will be blessed.'

When Esau returned to find his blessing stolen from him, he begged his father for one too, and received the lesser, ominous message: 'You will live by the sword and you will serve your brother. But when you grow restless, you will throw his yoke from off your neck.'

On a previous occasion, returning ravenously hungry from a foraging expedition in the country, Esau had found Jacob preparing a bubbling pot of rich lentil stew, and demanded to be given some. Jacob coolly offered to sell a helping of stew in return for his brother's rights as elder son. Esau, more interested in preserving his life than in keeping his birthright, agreed.

Jacob might have expected Esau to change his mind. But having eaten, Esau simply got up and left. He is known to value his inheritance lightly, even though he stands to inherit considerable wealth. He also thinks little of the covenant God made with his father, because he has married two pagan Hittite women.

Nevertheless, following the latest and more serious deception, Esau tells anyone who will listen that 'Jacob stole my birthright'. The relationship between the two, which has never been close, has now deteriorated irreparably. Jacob seems to have truly earned his name 'the deceiver'.

Jacob has fled to Haran where Rebekah has urged him to find a wife from among his uncle Laban's daughters in the family's home country of northern Mesopotamia.

(Genesis 25:27–34; 27:1–28:9)

Water fights dry up

Beersheba, c. 1850 BC

The disputes over water between Isaac and Abimelech are over. The two men have signed a peace agreement and are content to live 32 km (20 miles) apart. And to cap it, Isaac's servants discovered a new source of water the day the agreement was drawn up.

Isaac had grazed sheep and goats in the drought-prone hill country around Abimelech's city of Gerar, but as the number of his animals increased so did pressure on the restricted water supplies. There had been increasing fights between both men's staff at the wells.

The native Philistines, jealous of Isaac's prosperity, had filled in the wells he used in an attempt to drive

him away, even after Isaac had moved from the immediate vicinity of Gerar at Abimelech's request.

Abimelech has publicly recognised the blessing of Isaac's God on his family since the patriarch moved to the region, and suggested the treaty. The newly-discovered well has been called appropriately Beersheba, the well of the oath.

The area receives an average of less than 25 cm (10 in) of rainfall a year, and there is little surface water apart from intermittent streams which flow in the rainy season. Most water is carried in underground streams which are tapped by deep, laboriously-dug and often deep bore-holes.

(Genesis 26:12–33)

Fugitive passes God on stairs

An awestruck dignitary pays his respects. This beautiful statue is made of gold and bronze.

Bethel, Canaan, c. 1790 BC

Jacob, son of Isaac, claims that while running fast from the murderous reach of his brother, Esau, he ran straight into the arms of Yahweh his God.

The upstart confidence trickster who twice cheated Esau out of his inheritance and status is not renowned for his piety. But he has set up a stone pillar to his God as the foundation of a future shrine for when he returns to his homeland. He has also vowed to give a tenth of his possessions to Yahweh.

He claims that he dreamed of a staircase like that up the side of a ziggurat which reached into heaven. Angels were climbing up and down it. God was standing at the top and reiterated the promise given to his grandfather, Abraham, that their numerous descendants would occupy Canaan and enjoy Yahweh's protection. God also promised that he would remain present with Jacob wherever he went, and would return the fugitive to Canaan.

Awestruck at the unsolicited visitation on someone who even he might regard as beyond God's favour, Jacob pledged his allegiance to Yahweh.

Jacob was travelling north from Beersheba in the Negev towards Haran, a city controlled by the Mitanni on the headwaters of the Euphrates, where his relatives live. Bethel, or Luz, is a prosperous city about 20 km (12 miles) north-west of Jericho. Abraham also worshipped God there.

(Genesis 28:10–22)

Married at last – to the wrong sister!

Haran, c. 1780 BC

Seven years hard labour came to a blissful end when Jacob climbed into bed with the bride he'd worked for out of sheer love. But when her veil was drawn aside, he found he'd been mismatched with her older sister.

Jacob, son of Isaac, an immigrant from southern Canaan, has been working as a herdsman without wages for his uncle Laban. His labour was to be in lieu of the traditional mohar (bride-price) for Laban's younger daughter, Rachel, which the penniless Romeo could not otherwise afford.

It had been love at first sight when Jacob, fleeing from his vengeful brother, had arrived in Mitanni and met Rachel in what Jacob might have described as a 'divine appointment'. As he stopped at a well to ask directions, his cousin turned up with her sheep. She fell for him as he broke with local tradition, opened up the well and watered her sheep before all the neighbourhood flocks had gathered.

A colourful scene, with women jostling at a well in eastern dress, painted in the late nineteenth century AD.

'The past seven years have seemed like only a few days,' said the love-struck groom at his wedding feast. But the honeymoon was short-lived when he discovered that he had slept with Rachel's older sister, Leah, whose plain looks had never attracted him. But in keeping with local custom – which the locals hadn't told him about – the older girl had to be married first.

Enraged at having been deceived, the only compensation he could exact from Laban was the promise of Rachel as a second wife. The price was the same – seven more years work – but as a concession he was able to buy now and pay later. Within a few weeks, he had his second bride.

In the complex web of relationships in this scattered Semite tribe, Laban is the sister of Jacob's mother, Rebekah and also a descendant of Nahor, the brother of Jacob's paternal grandfather, Abraham.

(Genesis 29:1–30)

False witnesses to face death penalty in new laws

Susa, Elam, c. 1760 BC

Witnesses who falsely accuse others of capital offences such as murder, burglars and people who receive goods stolen from temples or the state, are to be executed according to the recently-codified legal judgements of King Hammurabi of Babylon.

To safeguard property and people's innocence, the judgements specify that proper contracts are to be drawn up for the loan or safe-keeping of valuables. The person who has temporary custody of another's property is liable to pay double its value in compensation to the owner if it is stolen while in his care.

Hammurabi, king of Babylon since 1792, has erected a 2.5 m (8 ft) obelisk engraved with these and many of his other legal judgements at Susa in the Elamite region some 320 km (200 miles) east of Babylon. Other similar obelisks are believed to be under construction elsewhere.

The obelisk, hewn from hard-wearing diorite (greenstone), a volcanic rock, depicts Hammurabi being given tokens of power – a sceptre and a ring – from the sun-god, Shamash. It is inscribed in Akkadian script in vertical columns.

It covers a wide but not complete range of legal judgements. Homicide, both culpable and accidental, is omitted except in the case of violence done to a female citizen causing miscarriage, which is subject to a fine of ten silver shekels, or half a mina if she dies.

Several pronouncements relate to marriage and sexual conduct. Drowning is prescribed for adultery, but permission is given for the husband of a barren priest-ess to take a votaress (woman in religious orders) as a concubine in order to have children.

Minor crimes or wilfully-inflicted injuries are to be punished in

Hammurabi's obelisk setting out his laws. Hammurabi, himself, is shown seated.

proportion to the offence. A son who hits his father is to have his hand cut off, and a person who breaks a citizen's bone shall have one of his bones broken. However, in accordance with the strong social caste system of Babylonia, offences against slaves or peasants warrant less heavy punishment than if committed against citizens.

Hammurabi's empire now extends from the Mediterranean coast to the eastern lands beyond the Tigris and Euphrates rivers. He has built a strong centralised government, and has taken personal interest in the development of fine waterways and irrigation systems, and agriculture. He has revitalised the economy with an efficient tax system, and has erected many fine public buildings – and chronicled his achievements in literary tributes.

Mari hammered by Hammurabi

Babylonia, 1757 BC

The great city of Mari, founded at the beginning of the third millennium BC on the west of the Euphrates, has been destroyed by Hammurabi of Babylon. The palace of its deposed ruler, Zimri-Lim, lies in ruins, the magnificent columns of the upper stories reduced to rubble among the ground-floor rooms.

Mari's huge library is buried somewhere under the ruins. Its 20,000 clay tablets documented every aspect of palace life, including the endless round of sieges, chariot wars and incursions from nomadic warbands.

Some of the more personal royal correspondence has reached a wider audience than intended. One Mari ruler wrote to his unruly son, 'How long do we have to keep an eye on you? You're so young! Your brother is leading armies. Can't you even run your own household?' To which the prince replied, 'How can you call me young when you promoted me? You know that though you are my Daddy, there's always been a servant or some other underling you cared for more than me. I'm coming to see you to have this matter out once and for all, Daddy.'

The Mari kings are not the first to have had problem children. The city, which lies over 320 km (200 miles) north-west of Babylon, gained its fabulous wealth from trade passing along the Euphrates Merchants travelled to and from Cyprus, Crete and turkey, carrying wine, oil, grain and wool.

Among its many great buildings was the 300 room palace which incorporated stores, offices and school rooms as well as living quarters with an advanced drainage system. It was a cultic centre, housing many prophets.

It is derelict now, and what treasures could be retrieved from the ruins have been carried away by its conquerors.

Childless wives hire surrogate mothers

Haran, c. 1750 BC

The maternal instinct proved stronger even than the security of being loved by a doting husband for Rachel wife of Jacob.

His first love but his second wife, Rachel was devastated by being unable to bear him any children, while her rival and older sister, Leah, had presented Jacob with four strapping sons. So she gave her maid, Bilhah, to Jacob to act as a surrogate mother.

The practice is common in many areas of high infant mortality. The offspring of such semi-official unions have full family status and the concubine is protected legally and financially.

After Bilhah successfully produced two sons, Leah appeared to have reached the menopause. So, not to be outdone, she gave Jacob her maid, Zilpah, as well. Zilpah also bore two sons, before Leah's fertility returned and she gave birth to two more sons and a daughter.

But the baby boom wasn't over yet. Surrounded by her husband's prolific progeny, Rachel eventually conceived and gave birth to Jacob's eleventh son, Joseph. With Rachel cooing 'God's taken away my disgrace' over the only child of Jacob's first love and the baby of the family, Joseph seems all set to be thoroughly spoiled.

(Genesis 29:31–30:24)

'I want to go home'

Haran, c. 1750 BC

Jacob son of Isaac, whose wealth now exceeds that of his father-in-law and uncle, Laban, for whom he has worked for two decades, is to retrace his grandfather Abraham's footsteps and migrate south to Canaan. His decision follows growing rifts and allegations of fraud within the family.

'I've been cheated time and time again,' he exploded recently. 'And my adoptive family have turned against me. But my God has made me prosper more than them.'

Counter-accusations have been levelled against Jacob, who arrived in Haran as a fugitive from the consequences of his own duplicity. They include having genetically engineered his wealth by a programme of selective breeding which ensured that his employer's flocks remained weak while his were strong and productive.

Laban had attempted to thwart Jacob's obvious ambition from the beginning by driving the animals his son-in-law had chosen for his wages – the patterned-fleeced 'Jacob's sheep' – out of his reach before Jacob could round them up. But the wily Canaanite soon learned how to breed replacements.

Relationships have ebbed to an all-time low. When Jacob first asked to go home Laban consulted his divining cups and read in the movement of the wine that Jacob's God Yahweh was the cause of both the men's prosperity, and persuaded him to stay on.

Now, even Jacob's wives, Leah and Rachel, who have never travelled further than the end of the city, are ganging up on their father. They accuse him of spending illegally the bride price Jacob had paid through his work and later his wages. They are already packing for the 650 km (400 miles) walk to Jacob's birthplace.

(Genesis 30:25–31:18)

Jacob and his retinue settled over a wide area of the hill country from Shechem (which was to become Samaria) in the middle of the country, to Gilead (on the eastern bank of the Jordan), down to sites previously associated with Abraham, such as Mamre and Beersheba in the Judean desert.

'Stop thief!'

Gilead, c. 1750 BC

Laban of Haran has chased a thief for over 480 km (300 miles) – and then failed to find the evidence he was looking for.

He was convinced that his household idols, considered essential for his spiritual and material well being, had been stolen by a member of his family who has emigrated with his nephew and son-in-law Jacob back to Jacob's homeland.

But despite a thorough search of the extensive retinue, the objects were not found. Jacob's family and servants co-operated fully with the enquiries, except for his wife Rachel who declared herself ritually unclean and refused to get up from her bed. Jacob himself follows a religion which disdains idols and representations of gods.

Tired of the continuing animosity between them, the two men – each reputed to be as devious as the other – erected a memorial cairn in the hill country of Gilead east of the Jordan, as a boundary stone between their tribes and as a sign of peace.

(Genesis 31:22–55)

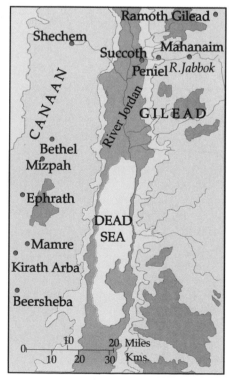

Limping Jacob quietly slips out of trouble

Shechem, Canaan, c. 1745 BC

He's more religious than he used to be. He's older, wiser and less impetuous. He's even got a new name. But the wily old Jacob is still as slippery as ever.

The son of Isaac, a confidence trickster turned devoted husband and prosperous semi-nomad, has come home to roost after two decades on the run. He steered his small townful of relatives, servants and animals all the way from Haran, and landed on his feet near the hill country town of Shechem where he has bought land to live on.

On the way he had survived an apparent assassination attempt and slipped out of an awkward reunion with his brother.

His new settlement is about a day's journey from Bethel, where God had given him a farewell promise that one day he would return. And God figured so prominently on the long slow journey back that Jacob's first act after pitching his tent was to build an altar to the God he is now calling, in typically extravagant terms, 'the mighty God of Israel'.

'Israel' is the new name he claims was given him after a titanic struggle with an angelic figure who attempted to kill him at the Jabbok fords east of the Jordan. He fought off his attacker even after suffering a dislocated hip which has left him with a permanent limp.

But Jacob turned from victim to aggressor as he recognised the divine nature of his opponent. Knowing that only God could help him over the biggest hurdle of his life – meeting his brother, Esau, who he had ruthlessly tricked out of his rights – Jacob clung to his assailant demanding a blessing. The new name given in the blessing means 'he who struggles with God'.

It was his second religious experience on the journey. Some miles to the east at Mahanaim, he had a fresh dream of angels which

The considerable and solid foundations of the East Gate to the fortified town of Shechem.

suggested to him that he was entering God's camp. Following that, the normally self-sufficient fixer prayed that Yahweh would fix the meeting with Esau to his advantage.

In the event, Jacob did his own share of fixing. He sent an embassy of servants ahead with a massive gift of 400 goats, 220 sheep, 30 camels, 40 cows and 10 bulls, and 30 donkeys; whether as a bribe or as conscience money he did not say. He also split his entourage into two, doubling the family's chances of survival if attacked.

Esau, who now lives in the deep south in the Seir region, and is father of the Edomite tribe, took 400 men to meet Jacob's retinue which local intelligence clearly had interpreted as a threat.

However, Esau was in no mood for a fight and extended a tearful welcome to his long-lost prodigal brother.

Nonetheless Jacob was taking no chances. Having agreed to follow Esau back into Seir at the speed of the slowest child in the family, he turned west to Succoth instead, where he stayed for some time before crossing the Jordan and moving further west to Shechem. Distance, he must have thought, is a great defence even when you do have God on your side.

(Genesis 32:1–33:20)

Rape seeds savage plot

Shechem, c. 1740 BC

The impulsive rape of one woman by one man has resulted in the brutal massacre of the entire male population of this strategic town in central Canaan.

Dinah, only daughter of the powerful semi-nomad, Jacob, who settled in the area recently, was raped by Shechem, the son of Hamor who is the area chieftain. Following the incident he asked to do the honourable thing and marry her – out of love rather than duty.

Jacob's sons took a leaf out of their father's book and schemed revenge. They agreed to the match on condition that all the men in Shechem should be circumcised to conform with Israel's tribal religious custom. It seemed a small price for the Shechemites to pay to gain influence over their rich and potentially threatening neighbour.

But the minor operation left the men militarily impotent and vulnerable. Jacob's sons took full advantage of their temporary discomfort and returned to cut off far more than custom required. The town is now mourning its loss, and old Jacob is not amused either. He fears reprisals from other tribes.

(Genesis 34)

Dreamy teenager given the boot by brothers

Canaan, c. 1733 BC

A teenage boy, who incurred his older brothers' wrath for his arrogant dreams and monopoly of their father's affection, has survived an attempt on his life and has been sold into slavery.

Joseph and his magnificent coat by Henri Vernet (1789–1863).

Joseph, just 17 and wearing the expensive and highly decorated robe given him by his doting father, Jacob, was seized by his jealous brothers when he visited them at work. The semi-nomadic sheep farmers were grazing their flocks when the grassland near Shechem, some 21 km (13 miles) to the south, became exhausted.

The second youngest of 12 boys, Joseph is said to have had dreams which he interpreted as portents of his future supremacy over the whole family. Among his fantasies he saw the sheaves of corn, being gathered by his brothers, bowing down to his, and the planets representing his parents and brothers bowing to him in the sky.

Far from home, the 'pampered pet' was easy prey to his siblings. One of them, Reuben, persuaded them to take the conscience-easing route of abandoning the boy in an underground storage cistern where he would starve to death, rather than actively knifing him.

But when a caravan of Midianite traders passed by, the lure of money proved stronger than the lust for revenge, and they agreed with Judah to sell Joseph as a slave. It has been suggested that Reuben intended to rescue Joseph from the cistern, but he was away from the others when the deal was struck.

To explain Joseph's disappearance to their father, they killed a goat and stained Joseph's unique coat of many colours with its blood, to look as though he had been 'mauled to death by a lion or bear'.

Jacob is said to be inconsolable, believing that the boy is dead. Joseph was especially close to him because he was the first child born to Jacob's second wife, Rachel.

Meanwhile, the traders, who were carrying luxury goods including spices, medicinal and cosmetic preparations from the east to sell to the rich elite of Egypt, are reported to have sold the good-looking Joseph at a tidy profit to Potiphar, a senior military official in the Pharaoh's court.

The teenager's brothers appear to have sworn an oath of secrecy to cover their guilt, and none appears willing to reveal the truth to their aging father.

(Genesis 37)

Newcomers to test Egyptian state unity

Egypt, c. 1700 BC

Building on the gains of the last century, Egypt is continuing an aggressive policy of land reclamation and canal building. Sesostris III (1878–1843 BC) added strong military forces and defences, and centralised the government in three administrative regions. More recent kings of this 'thirteenth dynasty' continued and consolidated the reforms. By 1720 BC Egypt stood as high as it had ever stood in domestic and international prestige.

But increasing immigration in recent decades began to alter Egyptian society. Many Palestinians have come to Egypt, and Asiatic immigrants have settled in the eastern delta, changing what had been an ethnic Egyptian community into a mixed one. Some of these new people groups now want independent administration and even local armies.

Egypt is now a country where several dynasties hold power, as some of the foreign arrivals have established local kingships. The major upheaval, however, has been caused by the Hyksos. They came from Asia and have set up large and powerful communities in the north of Egypt.

The Hyksos, who have introduced the Egyptians to horses as means of speedy transport and formidable accessories in battle, are building forts along the Horus Road between Egypt and Canaan. The forts have barracks for soldiers, and are equipped with footbaths filled with soothing oils.

The Hyksos are a Semitic people whose name means 'foreign rulers'. They have commercial and political influence throughout Palestine and Syria. They are reported to have burned down some Egyptian cities and demolished temples. They worship the Canaanite god Baal, who Egyptians identify with Seth.

Magician pulls off kingdom's top job

Egypt, c. 1720 BC

A 30-year-old Semite from Canaan who was drafted into the Pharaoh's team of magicians and soothsayers, has landed the newly-created job of Minister of Agriculture and Food Supplies due to his predictions.

A wooden statue of the chancellor Nakhti, who occupied a position similar to Joseph's, albeit a few hundred years earlier, c. 1950 BC.

Joseph arrived in Egypt when he was 17 and, until recently, was in prison for attempted rape – a charge he vehemently denies. He has proved to be a far more sophisticated interpreter of the Pharaoh's troubled dreams than any of the experts. He is also so good-looking that half the women in the court claim to be in love with him.

Pharaoh had dreamed of seven thin cows eating seven fat cows, and then even more surreally, seven thin ears of corn gobbling up seven fat ears. The quirky images baffled the brightest mind-readers, and became the talk of the court.

After one of his routine poison-testing but mind-clearing sips of Pharaonic wine, the chief cupbearer remembered having met Joseph in prison, and that the young Semite had interpreted dreams accurately when they shared a cell together. He also remembered that he had not kept his promise to try to influence Joseph's release, and remedied the omission immediately. Joseph, having modestly claimed that the interpretation would come from his God, not from his own insights, declared that the current prosperity Egypt was enjoying would last for seven years. It would then be followed by seven years of hardship and famine.

The best way of dealing with this situation, he suggested, was to appoint an executive to govern Egypt, who would be responsible for building storehouses to stockpile resources while they were plentiful, and for organising food rationing schemes well before the famine.

Pharaoh responded by giving the job to Joseph himself, on the grounds that God had endowed him with unparalleled discernment and wisdom.

He invested him at a ceremony during which the young man was presented with fine robes, a gold chain of office, and his own chariot and driver as symbols of royal approval. The Pharaoh has declared him second in command of the nation.

(Genesis 41)

FLOOD AND FAMINE
Egypt's cycle of life

Rainfall in Egypt is infrequent. At the base of the Delta, for example, approximately 3 mm (1 in) falls every year. Egypt's crops are irrigated, and its animals watered, by the great Nile River which floods every year. In the Egyptian calendar, the period from July to November is called the Inundation.

Water overflows the Nile banks into walled fields giving them a deposit of river silt, rich in organic waste and minerals, as well as the life-giving water. This prepares the ground for the next season (November to March) which is called the Emergence. This is when the bulk of Egypt's crop farming is carried out; for the remaining season from March to July (the Drought) the Nile almost disappears virtually reduced to a trickle along its parched channel.

Joseph's prophecy to Pharaoh predicts a period of unusually generous annual flooding, after which seven years are to follow in which the waters will fail, leaving spoiled crops, hungry animals and starving people in a land seemingly encroached upon by the surrounding desert.

These paintings from the tomb of Onson, in Thebes, show work in the field as the harvest is brought in and the fields are ploughed. Grain is then baled and loaded on board ship – to be taken down river, either for storage or to be sold.

1700–1600 BC

Wealthy Semites accused of spying

Egypt, c. 1715 BC

Ten wealthy Semites carrying bags of silver on the pretext of buying grain for their famine-smitten family in Canaan, have been charged with spying by Supplies Minister Joseph.

He has imprisoned one of them, Simeon, as surety and ordered them to return to Egypt with their young-est brother, Benjamin, in order to confirm their *bona fides*. He has threatened to kill Simeon if not.

The Semites are among many seeking corn in Egypt as the worst famine in living memory holds much of the Near East in its grip. The reserves stored up at Joseph's command during the previous seven good harvests are likely to meet demands, and to make a good profit for the state granaries.

Many of the foreign food-seekers are interviewed by Joseph before he signs the export orders. Observers report that when the 10 brothers bowed before him he became harsher than usual and immediately accused them of being military spies looking for weak points in Egypt's national defences.

He jailed all of them for three days, despite their protestations of innocence and threatened to hold all except one in custody until their young brother could be fetched to confirm the truth of their story.

However, lacking firm evidence of their evil intentions, he allowed all but Simeon to go, and granted them their grain supplies.

It is believed that they came from the same region and perhaps the same tribe as Joseph himself. During one of the interviews, aides say that he appeared to understand their language without the aid of an interpreter, and that he left the room hastily with tear-filled eyes as if suddenly suffering a bout of home-sickness.

(Genesis 42)

'My dreams have come true at last!'

Egypt, c. 1712 BC

Joseph, the Pharaoh's minister in charge of agriculture and food supplies, has come face to face with his brothers who once plotted to kill him – and has forgiven them.

In a series of dramatic encounters in which he withheld his true identity from them, Joseph made his own dreams come true.

As a teenager he had dreamed his jealous brothers would bow to his authority. Now they have, and they now also depend on him for vital grain supplies in famine-stricken Canaan.

This wall painting from the tomb of Sebekhotep in Thebes shows Semitic envoys presenting tribute, 1420 BC.

Yet 15 years ago they plotted to kill him as the pampered pet of his doting, aging parents. Only the chance passing of a Midianite trade caravan saved his life as they sold the hapless youth into slavery instead of slitting his throat.

Two years ago his 10 half-brothers came to Egypt to buy grain. Joseph recognised them, and accused them of spying as a ploy to hold one of them, Simeon, hostage to ensure they all returned with his own blood-brother, Benjamin. To compound their obligation and to test their honesty, he returned their money secretly in their grain bags.

Their father, Jacob, refused to allow them to bring Benjamin to Egypt. But when their grain ran out they had no choice. It was his life at risk of an Egyptian tyrant, or theirs at risk of starvation. They loaded their mules with gifts for the minister, and brought back the silver coins he had returned to their bags.

Again the cunning second-in-command of all Egypt withheld his identity. He even lied about God having given them their money back. And again he sent them home with the grain and money but he also hid his personal silver drinking cup in their baggage. This time, he ordered his guards to chase them and to arrest the 'thief' – who was Benjamin.

That had them really grovelling as he offered to release all but Benjamin. They knew the loss would kill their father; Benjamin was the sole surviving son of his union with his beloved wife Rachel. But Joseph, believed dead, came from the same union and after playing out the charade for as long as he could, he finally broke down and revealed the truth about himself.

'You meant to harm me,' he said, 'but God took hold of the situation for good and here I am in a privileged position not even I could have dreamed of!'

As the reunited brothers feasted together, Pharaoh ordered the whole clan to be brought to Egypt, where they would remain in security without fear of hunger. Which was more than they'd dreamed of.

(Genesis 43–45)

Grand old man finds son at last

Goshen, Egypt, c. 1710 BC

A 130-year-old man has travelled some 480 km (300 miles) from Canaan to Egypt to be reunited with the son he gave up for dead over two decades ago.

The emotional reunion took place in Goshen, in north-eastern Egypt, as Jacob embraced his long-lost son Joseph, Egypt's Minister of Agriculture and Food Supplies.

During the long journey, accompanied by 66 members of his family and staff, together with their considerable possessions and livestock, the old man paused at Beersheba in southern Canaan to worship his God. His forebears, Abraham and Isaac, had also offered animal sacrifices to God there.

Jacob claims that his small clan will one day become numerous and will return to Canaan, which he believes God has promised shall be their homeland.

At Goshen, in the fertile Delta region of Lower Egypt, Joseph drove out to meet the family, and escorted them to their new home. The Pharaoh had offered them the choice of location, and they chose Goshen because of its pasture land. Although shepherds and goatherds are looked down on by the more sophisticated arable farmers of Egypt, the Pharaoh has ordered them to be given the best area and has offered royal employment to their most skilled people.

(Genesis 46, 47)

This painted stone statuette is a good illustration of realistic Egyptian art.

Foreign father given state funeral

Hebron, Canaan, c. 1700 BC

Jacob, the father of Zaphenath-Paneah (also known as Joseph), Egypt's chief minister, has been given the funeral honours normally reserved for a Pharaoh. He was believed to have been 147 years old.

Pharaoh declared 70 days of mourning, just two short of the traditional number for a head of state, in Jacob's honour. A solemn procession accompanied the body to his homeland to be buried, as he had requested, with his grandparents, Abraham and Sarah, and his father, Isaac, at Mamre, north of Hebron.

The cortege included senior officials and nobles of Egypt, with a guard of honour as well as Jacob's numerous family.

Once across the Jordan, the emotional Semites ordered a seven-day rest period as they re-entered the territory which they believe their God has promised they will one day inhabit.

The final burial was in a cave. The Semites do not believe in building special mausoleums or pyramids, nor do they normally embalm bodies to preserve them for the next life, on which they seem to have hazy ideas. However, Jacob's body had been embalmed for the journey, but by Egyptian doctors rather than the usual cultic funeral directors, perhaps out of respect for his religious views. The process was completed in about a month, almost half the normal time.

One of Jacob's last acts from his death bed was to pronounce prophetic blessings on his 12 sons, and to adopt as his own, Joseph's sons Ephraim and Manasseh, who had been born before Jacob emigrated to Egypt (see box).

(Genesis 49:29–50:14)

A family affair

As he peered into the gloom of the fast-approaching after-life, Jacob – also known as Israel – pronounced a traditional blessing on his family foretelling in general terms what their fortunes would be. Already the heads of sizeable clans who inhabit the pasturelands of Goshen in the Lower Delta region, the 11 sons emigrated to Egypt to join their brother, Joseph, and to escape famine almost two decades ago. They were given these predictions by their dying father:

Reuben: The firstborn will forfeit his status because of his relationship with Bilhah, his father's mistress.
Simeon, Levi: Two angry young men whose violence will lead to their descendants being scattered among other tribes.
Judah: Nicknamed the lion, he is predicted to be the founder of 'Israel's' head tribe, from which will come a future great leader.
Issachar: A scrawny donkey for whom the grass is always greener on the other side; his tribe will trade its freedom for possessions.
Dan: Called to produce judges, but his tribe could become unjust and venomous.
Gad: His descendants will live in a buffeted border country but will not be overrun.
Asher: Agriculturalists and traders from this prosperous tribe will feed kings of the future.
Naphtahli: A beautiful people who will stay true to their religious roots.
Joseph: The young outcast made good, Egypt's great leader has become an example and a mediator of God's patient care.
Benjamin: The youngest son will have a warrior's streak of bravado.

(Genesis 49:1–28)

No vendetta, says Minister

Goshen, Egypt, c. 1700 BC

Egypt's most powerful Minister of State is to allow his double-crossing brothers to live in peace. Although they once tried to kill him, he has promised not to return the threat, despite recent suggestions that they coldly exploited their father's death-bed piety by claiming falsely that he had requested Joseph to forgive them.

It is not even certain that the old man knew the full truth of their duplicity which resulted in Joseph being sold as a slave to Midianite traders who sold him on in Egypt. After a spell in prison there, he rose to high office because of his skill in interpreting dreams.

The brothers' fear of reprisals had grown after the death of their father, who they saw as the last remaining restraint on Joseph's vengeance.

(Genesis 50:15–21)

Hippo-potty!

Egypt, c. 1580 BC

A herd of pet hippos have driven the Hyksos ruler of Egypt potty. The hippopotami belonged to puppet king, Seqenenre, down south in No (Thebes) but his boss Apophis couldn't stand the noise they make – even though he lives 644 km (400 miles) away in Avaris in the Delta region.

The row escalated so badly that the two cities declared war on each other. The Egyptians in Thebes reckoned the complaint was just another provocative insult from their Hyksos overlords. But it ended in tragedy.

King Seqenenre died of injuries sustained in the battle. He was struck repeatedly on the back of the head, leading to speculation that he was taken by surprise, when fleeing. Some wonder if he might have been killed by courtiers keen to gain favour with the Hyskos.

The banks of the River Nile at Luxor.

China grows despite unrest

China, c. 1700 BC

A new civilisation is developing in the Far East.

There have been people in China for thousands of years. Most of them have concentrated in the northern, fertile and well-watered region of the great Yellow River, the Hwang He. As with the developing cultures of the Middle East, Chinese settlers have progressed from hunting to herding. Relics of those early civilisations include houses built half underground and pottery that some believe bear marks of an early Chinese alphabet.

China is now experiencing a renewed burst of development. Agriculture is becoming well established. Nomadic tribespeople are becoming settled farmers. The Xia dynasty, now appearing to be in its death-throes as it faces massive internal unrest, still presides over what is becoming a very high order of civilisation.

Most other great civilisations have also grown up along rivers. The Indus in India has nurtured a valley dynasty, the Tigris and Euphrates saw the first settlements of what was to become the great Mesopotamian culture, and the long Nile River has brought life and sustenance to Egypt.

State feeds on taxing famine

Egypt, c. 1710 BC

As drought and famine tighten their grip on Egypt and Canaan, the Egyptian state machine is growing fat by gobbling up ordinary people's assets.

Under the direction of Food and Supplies Minister Joseph, people whose money has already run out are handing over to the state their remaining livestock and their ancestral land to pay for vital grain. And although they receive free handouts of seed corn for planting, they are obliged to pay back one fifth of their crops to the government.

The only exceptions to the rule are the priests, who, because they already receive an allowance from the state for their sacred functions, are allowed to retain their lands. The population is now in effect a workforce employed by the state in a so-far benign form of slavery.

(Genesis 47:13–27)

Medicine is food from the gods

Egypt, c. 1550 BC

Doctors get their powers to heal from the god, Thoth, and their herbal prescriptions for illnesses sometimes include magic spells or are claimed to be revelations from the gods, according to a papyrus scroll recently compiled from older writings.

Running to over 870 paragraphs, the papyrus is preoccupied with removing evil from the body, often using laxatives including magnesia and senna pods. One prescription to clean out the digestive system consists of 25 measures of milk with eight each of honey and figs, boiled, strained and to be taken daily for four days.

Other prescriptions contain urine or dung, which evil spirits are believed to find obnoxious and will therefore leave the patient who takes the potion. While some illness is believed to be sent by the gods as a punishment, other causes such as worm infestations are recognised.

Contraceptive advice includes a woollen suppository soaked in a mixture of honey, acacia leaves and other herbs. Grey hair can be prevented by taking medicine made from black substances, and baldness can be cured by rubbing into the head a mixture of oil and the ashes of burned hedgehog spines.

Other documents in the Egyptian physician's library include treatises on surgery for physical injuries and fractures. Doctors use stitches, adhesive plasters, bandages and splints. Cancers are sometimes burned out. Physicians also double as dentists, using the time-honoured methods of brute force and pliers to extract decayed teeth. Gum disease is a more common problem than caries, however.

Women's diseases are sometimes treated by a form of fumigation. The doctor asks the patient what smell she perceives (in her mind), and the prescription is for a real smell – say of roast meat – to be given to her. Among the tests available to determine whether or not a woman can conceive a baby are an examination of her breasts (if they are firm it is believed she will conceive) and also the placing a clove of garlic in her vagina. Apparently, if her breath smells 24 hours later, she is considered likely to conceive.

Whatever remedy is given, it is accompanied with the appropriate incantation which attributes to it a power of its own derived from the spirit world.

Detail from a Book of the Dead, well preserved on papyrus, showing the soul of the deceased being weighed.

Fast Facts 1750–1550 BC

Ephrah, c. 1730 BC: Semi-nomad, Jacob, has returned to live with his elderly father, Isaac, following the death of his favourite wife, Rachel. She had become pregnant again, but the delivery proved too great a strain for her ageing body. She was buried in Bethlehem. The baby, who has been named Benjamin, survived. (Genesis 35:16–20)

Mamre, c. 1725 BC: Isaac the son of Abraham, who was once almost offered as a child sacrifice, has died aged 180. He was the father of Jacob and Esau, who buried him. It is believed to have been the first time the twins have met since their brief encounter on Jacob's return to Canaan. (Genesis 35:27–29)

Aegean, c. 1700 BC: The ruined palace at Knossos has been rebuilt as a splendid and imposing building, a fitting monument to the Minoan people whose maritime empire maintains trading links with major centres in the eastern Mediterranean and as far west as Sicily.

Egypt, c. 1700 BC: A Semitic immigrant slave has been jailed for the attempted rape of the wife of top military commander Potiphar. She claims that when he approached her, she screamed and he fled, leaving his cloak behind. In his defence he pleased that she had sought to entice him, and he had wriggled out of his cloak in order to escape her. Although he was not believed, he is proving to be a trustworthy prisoner and has been given responsibilities and privileges by the warder. (Genesis 39)

Pakistan, c. 1700 BC: The Bronze Age city of Harappa has been abandoned by its inhabitants. It has been populated since 2500 BC, and is a landmark of the Indus Valley. Situated on the Ravi river, the city included fortifications and accommodation for the many labourers who worked there. It had a prosperous food industry, and its many granaries and food handling buildings now lie deserted. Built mainly from mud bricks, Harappa occupied a man-made mound which reinforced the extensive defences.

Western Pacific, c. 1700 BC: Traders are moving out from the Bismarck Archipelago, near New Guinea, to settle in south-west Pacific islands including the Solomon Islands and Fiji. They practise the same agriculture there as they did in their home islands. They are also versatile craftsmen; items made of volcanic glass are often offered for trade. They also appear to be good navigators.

Egypt, c. 1668 BC: The horse has arrived in Egypt, drawing the chariots of the Hyksos, the Semitic people who have invaded and are now ruling the nation.

Eastern Europe, c. 1650 BC: Rye is becoming a popular grain crop in Eastern Europe, especially in the north where summer is short. Rye is ready for harvest much sooner after planting than wheat.

Hyksos rule is broken

Thebes, c. 1570 BC

King Ahmose of Thebes has reunited Egypt and inaugurated the 'New Kingdom'. He has completed the expulsion of the foreign Hyksos kings, who have ruled Egypt since c. 1674. He has also recaptured Northern Nubia (Sudan) and made inroads into Palestine.

The generally benevolent Hyksos rulers had brought peace and affluence to Egypt and treated the indigenous population fairly. They allowed the Egyptian way of life to continue, and did not attempt to eradicate the native language in administration and commerce. Egyptians had even been allowed to hold government office.

But the Hyksos, who were urban Semites from Palestine, have always been 'foreign kings' in Egyptian eyes. Even the Pharaoh who is remembered for his wise appointment of Joseph, steering the country through seven years of famine, was not loved by all.

Though Joseph's achievement is still admired, some Egyptian nationalists suggest that he was merely helping his fellow-alien to rob the country. Others point out that although the drought resulted in an almost total transfer of private land to crown ownership, the people survived and the system that was set up afterwards was hardly exploitative.

The alien presence in Egypt had grown strong under the Hyksos, especially in the Semite centres of population in the Nile Delta, of which the most flourishing is that of Joseph's descendants.

The Hyksos ruled in two simultaneous dynasties, the more dominant one holding power over vassal kings. They established their power by using horses and chariots in battle, but these, and their alliance with Nubia, were not enough to prevent their eventual overthrow by the army of king Ahmose.

Hittite king struck down

Babylon, c. 1595 BC

Mursili I, the Hittite king and raider of Babylon, has been assassinated. He had pursued an aggressive policy of expansion.

The Hittites, who seemed a major force in the making, are now beginning to disintegrate in civil unrest. Their borders are looking increasingly vulnerable.

Nobody knows where the Hittites came from. Their home territory is Hatti, on the Turkish plain, from which their name is derived. They arrived there c. 1900 BC, bringing with them a language of the same Indo-European family to which most other European languages belong. The local people were forced to accept the invaders' culture and language. About 1800 BC they captured Hattusha, and made it their capital in c. 1680 BC when the Hittite leader, Labarna, founded the Old Hittite Kingdom.

Mum's the word behind the throne

Egypt, c. 1500 BC

Queen Hatshepsut is staking her claim to power following the death of her husband, Tuthmosis II, and the accession of her young stepson-nephew, Thutmosis III. She rules the roost at court as regent and many believe she is seeking to

Detail from a wall painting of a banquet.

undermine the new king's position.

She has begun building a magnificent mortuary temple in a bay of the cliffs at Deir el-Bahari, which is aligned with the great temple of Amun across the River Nile at

Karnack. It is unique in Egyptian architecture, as it rises in three colonnade-fronted terraces to a central rock-cut sanctuary.

It includes a relief on the middle terrace which depicts her birth (complete with the royal official's false beard) and implies that she was conceived and chosen to be Pharaoh by the god, Amun. The relief also shows her coronation in the presence of the gods. She is now asking to be called Khnemetamun Hatshepsut, 'She who embraces Amun, the foremost of women'.

Hatshepsut's association of the god Amun with her own fortunes follows a pattern set by previous New Kingdom rulers. Her adviser (and according to some, her lover) Senenmut has erected on her behalf two red granite obelisks to Amun in the temple at Karnak. Quarried at Aswan, they were transported down the river on rafts over 90 m (300 ft) long.

Stonehenge completed

The great stone circle at Stonehenge.

South-west Britain, c. 1490 BC

A monument constructed from huge stones has been completed some 1,500 years after it was begun. Stonehenge, on the Salisbury Plain in south-west Britain, consists of a circle of 40 sarsen (limestone) stones topped by 35 lintels surrounding an older circle of bluestones.

The original circle, which was quarried in the Presili Hills of south Wales, had once been dismantled and erected elsewhere, but has now been returned to Stonehenge. Inside this inner circle is a new horseshoe of five triliths (two pillars capped by a lintel) aligned with the midsummer sunrise. This in turn surrounds a smaller horseshoe of bluestones.

The sarsen has been brought from the Marlborough Downs, about 24 km (15 miles) north of Stonehenge. The stones were transported using wheels, pulleys, canoes and rollers. The lintels have sockets which fit onto projections on the uprights, and the lintels of the main circle have tongued and grooved links with each other.

Stonehenge has long been a centre of worship, with an annual ritual at the summer solstice. It also enables observers to observe the sun and moon and to predict eclipses. A similar but smaller stone circle has been built recently at Scone, in Perthshire in Scotland.

A whole new ball game

Mexico, c. 1500 BC

They play to win in Mexico's latest craze. And it doesn't pay to be a loser. Defeated players – or at least the team captains – in the ball game called tlachtli are beheaded.

A new court for the game has just been built in the south-east of the country near the Guatemala border. It consists of an alley about 7 m (22 ft) wide between high sloping banks. Players propel a solid rubber ball from end to end using only their hips, thighs and elbows. The ball is then bounced off the sides of the alley at high speed, the slope making its trajectory erratic and unpredictable.

Teams usually consist of four or five players, although they play in pairs on smaller courts. In keeping with the serious nature of the sport, teams probably represent clans or aristocrats vying for power through their chosen competitors. The results of the games unify the winning communities and reinforce the leaders' authority.

Fast Facts 1600–1450 BC

Greece, 1600 BC: The Greek language, once a conglomeration of loosely connected language groups and dialects, is at last unified. The earliest Greek spoken was 'proto-Greek', the language of the first migrants into the Greek peninsula at the beginning of the second millennium BC.

Crete, c. 1550 BC: A magnificent summer villa has been built at a small village, connected by a paved road with the palace at Phaestos on the south coast. The village, once a small collection of houses, has been extended to meet the needs of the villa. Gypsum veneering has been used throughout and the frescoes are amongst the finest ever seen.

Egypt, c. 1518 BC: The teenage king Tuthmosis II has married his half-sister Hatshepsut, the elder daughter of the late king and queen. The marriage makes his position stronger because he was the son of a minor royal wife. He became heir to the throne after the deaths some time ago of his two elder brothers.

Egypt, c. 1483 BC: Tuthmosis III, sole regent at last after the death of his stepmother-aunt, Hatshepsut, has set about expunging her memory from all monuments. He has destroyed many of the reliefs at the temple of Deir el-Bahari and has smashed her statues into a nearby quarry. He has attacked the tombs of her courtiers and walled up her red-granite obelisks at Karnak. He has dedicated a shrine at Deir to the cow-goddess Hathor.

Phoenicia, c. 1460 BC: The port of Joppa has been captured by the Egyptian general Djehuty who smuggled 200 of his men into the city in baskets purporting to contain booty captured by the prince of Joppa. The soldiers emerged after dark and opened the city gates to allow the army in.

Wessex, Britain, c. 1450 BC: Powerful warlords have organised a trade network on an unprecedented scale. They reach as far north as the Orkney Islands with gold sun discs and amber objects, and to Argyll in Scotland with jet necklaces. Overseas trade includes various amber objects to Brittany, Scandinavia, Egypt and Mycenae, copper objects to Czechoslovakia, and raw materials and gold to Ireland. Trade seems often to be conducted through middle-men situated on the European mainland.

Queen barges into Punt

Egypt, c. 1500 BC

Queen Hatshepsut has sent an expeditionary force of five sailing ships down the Red Sea to Punt (Somalia) in order to acquire myrrh trees for in the temple of Amun. Myrrh has not been grown in Egypt before.

When the Egyptians landed they met with a friendly local chief who welcomed them and loaded the ships with myrrh trees (their roots protected by sacking), myrhh resin, ebony, ivory, cinnamon wood, panther skins, monkeys and slaves. In return the Egyptians gave away beads, axes, daggers and bracelets. The explorers saw Punt villages built of domed huts on stilts.

Trade is also developing with Nubia (Sudan) via the Nile River. Local fishermen in the region of the First Cataract are now responsible for keeping clear a navigable waterway which was first built around the rocks and rapids in about 2300 BC. Oil, honey and clothing are commonly bartered for Nubian ivory, ebony and panther skins.

The Red Sea coast.

Mighty Megiddo falls at last

Canaan, c. 1481 BC

The Canaanite city of Megiddo has fallen to Egypt after a seven-month seige. The forces had failed to take it earlier when it was wide open. Led by Tuthmosis III, the army had already marched successfully through Canaan conquering Gaza and Yehem.

Tuthmosis had approached the city through a risky pass wide enough only for one pack horse at a time, despite the reservations of his commanders who were afraid of being ambushed and anxious that part of the army would be fighting while the rest was still queuing. But the king's faith that the god, Amun, was on their side seemed confirmed when they surprised the Canaanites.

In the battle which followed, the Canaanites were routed and fled to their city. But the Egyptians paused along the way to collect loot, giving the people of Megiddo time to fortify their position and necessitating the seige.

The victory gives Pharaoh Tuthmosis III a solid base for controlling the many tribes in Canaan. It follows several attempts to consolidate his power there.

Megiddo is situated in the Carmel Mountains 30 km (19 miles) south and east of Haifa, and has been occupied for centuries. Its architecture has been influenced by Egyptian styles, and during the relative peace of recent years an impressive palace, temple and gateway have been built. The city has also been influenced by culture from the north. The people are great art-lovers and prize carved ivory which they have acquired from Phoenician craftsmen.

The remains of the city of Megiddo.

Fast Facts 1450–1400 BC

Egypt, c. 1447 BC: Seven captive princes from Nubia have been sacrificed to the god Amun by King Amenhotep II. In traditional style, he first smote them with his mace and hung them upside down on the prow of his ship. Six were then hung on the enclosure wall of the temple at Thebes, and the seventh was returned to Nubia and hung from the walls of Napata so that 'the king's victorious might may be seen for ever'.

Egypt, c. 1419 BC: The new king Tuthmosis IV, who succeeds his father, Amenhotep II, who reigned for 34 years, is using propaganda to secure his position now and in the afterlife. A long inscription on a tall stone between the paws of a sphinx at Giza tells how the young prince went hunting in the desert and fell asleep in the shadow of the sphinx. The sun god embodied in it appeared to him in a dream and promised that if the sand engulfing the great limestone body of the sphinx was cleared the boy would be king.

France, c. 1400 BC: A large dolmen or megalithic tomb, has been built at St Georges de Levezac. It contains impressive stone walls and ceilings, and is covered by earth. But megalith building is literally a dying art; the once common activity is becoming rare throughout Europe.

Crete devastated by volcano

Crete, c. 1470 BC

A massive volcanic eruption on the small Greek island of Thera has caused thousands of deaths and widespread damage. Much of Crete, some 90 km (60 miles) to the south has been destroyed, as have the islands of Karpathos and

and poisonous fumes fill the air. Most of the island's palaces and stately homes have been reduced to rubble. Tidal waves estimated at over 30 m (100 ft) high have swept through the region and sea levels on the eastern Mediterranean have fallen as a result.

a similar disaster some 300–400 years ago. Governed by kings, Crete is a largely peaceful island with a civilisation rivalling those of Egypt and Mesopotamia. It boasts two-floored palaces built around central courts and possessing toilets connected to an efficient sewage disposal system.

Volcanic eruptions have always held people in dread. The Mediterranean still contains a number of active volcanoes. This painting shows Vesuvius in 1810.

Rhodes. Parts of the Asia Minor coast are also affected.

Five centimetres of ash cover Crete, damaging arable farmland,

It is not the first time that Crete has been devastated by natural disaster. The palaces of Knossos and Phaestos had been rebuilt after

Cretan art includes frescoes painted on the plaster walls of the larger houses, and fine gem engraving and jewellery.

A new form of linear writing has recently replaced the older pictographic style, in which 90 signs represent syllables and ideograms represent objects.

Its religion centres on goddesses to whom male deities are subordinate. Ceremonies include the unique bull-leaping in which young people of both sexes perform somersaults and handstands over the back of a bull which is later sacrificed. Men mix freely with unveiled women in a liberal social structure.

It is a thriving trading nation with its own sea-going ships. It grows its own wheat, barley, olives and grapes, with a variety of vegetables and fruits. Animals are not widely eaten, but fish and shellfish are.

Warrior-king reigns 50 years

Egypt, c. 1450 BC

The mummified body of Tuthmosis III of Egypt has been entombed in the Valley of the Kings with great ceremony. He was a warrior who greatly expanded Egypt's empire.

After succeeding his father, Tuthmosis II, in c. 1504 BC, he took some time before emerging from the shadow of his domineering aunt Hatshepsut.

He led 17 victorious campaigns, and over 350 cities fell to Egypt under his command. He defeated the Syrians at Jezreel and later at Megiddo. He also attacked the kingdom of Mitanni, which was attempting to destabilise Egyptian supremacy and captured several of its cities. He never succeeded in

conquering the whole kingdom, however and had to abandon his ultimate territorial objectives in Mesopotamia.

Under Tuthmosis the Egyptian empire reached as far as the Euphrates river, and he increased the power of Egypt in Nubia, building a provincial capital at Napta.

A deeply religious man, he financed temples from his battles, and undertook major public works in Karnak, Heliopolis, Memphis, Abydos and Aswan. He is succeeded by his son, Amenhotep II, who is already a champion oarsman said to be able to row six times as fast as his nearest rival.

An unidentified mummy with features of his face painted on to his shroud.

Danish hasty?

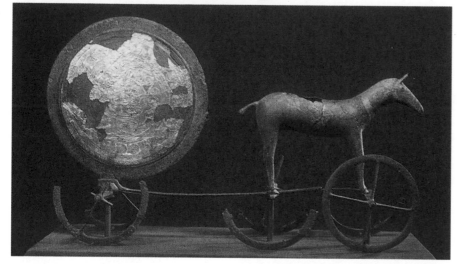

Denmark, c. 1400 BC

Danish women have taken to wearing on their abdomens a disc of engraved bronze armed with a spike to keep over-ardent admirers at bay. Their skirts remain short, however, made from woollen

The Trundholm sun chariot. The model, found in a grave, is 60 cm (2 ft) long, and the sun is made from beaten gold.

bands hanging from a belt, topped with half-sleeved jumpers and tailed with short woollen socks.

By contrast, men wear hooded coats over a belted skirt (peplum). They have also devised protective skullcaps made from several layers of material and sometimes fixed to a wooden framework. The Danes make their clothes from black wool which is pulled from the sheep in summer and woven on large wooden looms. The wool is supplemented by flax, leather and some fish skins.

One young woman in her 20s, fashionably attired complete with spike, has been buried alongside the ashes of a child, possibly her own. Most Danes are buried in coffins made from hollowed-out tree-trunks (they are split first, then re-joined after being hollowed), which are then placed in tumuli which may be 4 m (13 ft) high and 20 m (65 ft) in diameter. Only children are cremated.

Little is buried with them. Occasionally they are given a drink made from bilberries, wheat and honey, and they may wear ornaments or have small objects such as hair ribbons and awls beside them.

Bronze Age costume based on preserved examples excavated from peat bogs in Denmark.

Catalogue of confusion

Akhetaten (Amarna), c. 1360 BC

Canaan is falling into confusion as its city-states grow more powerful and refuse to submit to Egyptian rule, according to some 400 letters which have been filed away at Akhetaten. Half the letters were sent from Canaan and Syria. The signatories include leaders of Megiddo, Shechem, Gezer, Tyre, Hazor and Jerusalem, who pledge loyalty to Egypt but in some cases may be feathering their own nests.

In one letter, Abdiheba, the governor of Jerusalem, appeals for archers to be sent to maintain order. He explains that a caravan of silver and gifts from the province intended for the Pharaoh had been hijacked near Aijalon.

Amenophis IV was Pharaoh around 1360 BC. This impressive, though damaged, statue was originally painted.

In a later letter Abdiheba complains that 'the land of the king is lost; all of it is taken away from me ... I am made like a ship in the middle of the sea,' he adds, graphically describing the disorder which surrounds him.

He and other writers often refer to the Habiru, a derisory term applied to wandering bands of gypsies who seem to live by raiding settlements. Despite the similarity of the name, they are not believed to be related to the Hebrews, many of whom are slaves in Egypt but whose ancestors lived in Canaan.

Mitanni falls to Hittites

Mitanni, c. 1370 BC

Mitanni, ruled since c. 1500 BC by the Aryans, has fallen to the Hittites, newly re-established under Suppululiumas.

Mitanni includes most of Syria and much of Mesopotamia. It extends from Kirkuk westwards to the Mediterranean. It has always been a desirable prize for Egypt and the Hittites.

Suppululiumas became king c. 1380 BC in uncertain circumstances, although he was one of the sons of the previous king, Tudhaliyas III. After some years strengthening the kingdom internally, he began looking to counter-attack Hatti-land's many enemies, chief of which were the Mitanni to the south-east (north of Assyria).

Having experienced major losses recently in Aram (Syria), he has now led a well-planned expedition across the upper Euphrates to attack the Mitanni from the rear. He made treaties with tribes en route across difficult terrain. He sacked the Mitanni capital of Wassukkanni and then turned west into Syria whose princes, lacking Mitanni support, submitted to him without a fight. Halab (Aleppo) in northern Syria fell to Hittite control, although Carchemish to the north remained hostile.

In the fifteenth century an Egyptian–Hittite alliance had driven the Mitanni out of Syria, but later the Egyptians changed sides and supported them. Mitanni even provided a woman from the royal family for the Egyptian harem. The Egyptians continue to be Mitanni's allies against the Hittites.

Mitanni's territories are now divided between the Hittites and the newly independent Assyria. Its army has not been annihilated, however, and remains a force which might need to be reckoned with in the future.

Buried in their boots

Haguenau Forest, Alsace, c. 1400 BC

The Europeans of this region have abandoned the custom of burying their dead in the embryo position and instead are laying corpses on their backs. They are also developing a unique brand of decorative leggings made from twisted bronze spirals.

The spiral leggings are mostly worn by women to draw attention to their shapely legs, but are also used as shin-protectors by men. Once fashioned from twisted bronze wire, the leggings are now made from a richly-decorated broad bronze band edged with wire; the spiral may have up to a dozen turns.

The dead are often aligned with their heads towards the rising sun, and animal offerings are placed in the graves. The head of one girl has been placed on the head of a pig, recalling her occupation as a swineherd and providing her with a symbolic meal for the after-life. Among other objects buried with the dead are pottery pitchers, cups and bowls, often decorated with a simple zig-zag motif, and a selection of metal weapons and ornaments mainly made out of bronze.

The new rulers of the Mitanni demanded gifts and obsequious politeness. This golden statue (63 cm [2 ft] tall) shows a man offering a sheep.

Fast Facts 1400–1350 BC

Egypt, c. 1400 BC: King Amenophis III has established a marine police force to patrol the Delta area to deal with pirates (who often capture ships to make slaves of their occupants) and smugglers who evade customs duties on imported goods.

Britain, c. 1400 BC: The weather, Britain's favourite talking point, is getting colder and wetter. While the production of peat is encouraged by the climatic changes, arable farming is not. This seems to have caused the people to get more warlike; hillforts are common as communities are forced to protect themselves from others who are close to starvation.

Britain, c. 1350 BC: A major improvement in food supplies has occurred through the discovery of winter sowing. Most of the barley now used (which makes up 80 per cent of the total grain grown) is hulled and can be sown all year round. The population is increasing as a result of increased supplies. Fields are more irregular and cross-ploughing is used.

Egypt, c. 1377 BC: King Amenhotep III has had a 1.5 km (1 mile) long pleasure lake dug for his wife Queen Tiy to sail on. It is near his Malkata palace to the south of Medinet Habu on the west bank at Thebes. The couple celebrated its opening by sailing in the royal barge *The Aten Gleams* complete with its retinue of sailors, servants, musicians and cooks and courtiers.

Crackdown on families of foreign workers

A daughter of Pharaoh Akhenaton, 1350 BC.

Egypt c. 1350 BC

The eighteenth dynasty is continuing its crackdown on foreigners living in Egypt. The regime which ousted the Hyksos in the 1550s has now moved against the Israelites because of their prosperity and the potential security threat posed by their large numbers.

The Pharaoh has ordered that midwives called to attend to Israelite women in labour must ensure that no Hebrew boy survives. However, many midwives are believed to be disobeying the injunction and are claiming that the Hebrew women, made tough and strong by their life of unremitting toil, give birth so quickly after crouching on the birthstool that the midwife arrives too late to fake a still-birth.

Pharaoh has responded by ordering that all male Hebrews born must now be thrown into the Nile. Female children will probably end up as slaves and be absorbed into Egyptian culture.

Years of ethnic tension have brought the Israelites, once the darlings of the Hyksos pharaohs, into slavery. As a small clan they emigrated to Egypt from Canaan some 400 years ago, when one of them, Joseph, rose to become chief minister of state.

But fears that this prosperous and widespread people-group might come to dominate native Egyptians or even fight against them if the country were to be invaded have led to the Israelite settlements in Goshen, near the Wadi Tumilat, being turned into labour camps. In the popular mind, they are lumped with the Habiru and other gypsy-like groups of semi-nomadic and independent peoples.

But persecution seems to have made them thrive even more. Even the strenuous construction and agricultural work they are forced to do has not crushed them.

Coloured glass vase in the shape of a fish, c 1850 BC. Found in El-Armarna.

Princess adopts abandoned baby

Nile Delta, c. 1350 BC

An Egyptian princess, identified by some sources as Tharmuth, has adopted a baby she found abandoned in the shallows of the river Nile. Believed to be about three months old, the male Hebrew child had been left in a papyrus basket caulked with pitch.

Osiris, the god of the underworld, seen here seated and being attended. From the *Book of the Dead of Hunefer*, c. 1310 BC.

Current Egyptian law requires males born to Hebrews to be drowned in the Nile at birth, but abandoning them is a preferred method of disposal by mothers who hope their children will survive. The shallow reed beds offer protection from the sun and from predatory crocodiles.

Tharmuth has called the child Moses, a common Egyptian name-ending but which in Hebrew also means 'pull out'. She will not bring him up on her own. She has employed a Hebrew wet-nurse, Jochebed, to wean him. Rumours in the Israelite camps suggest that Jochebed is in fact the baby's natural mother.

(Exodus 2:1–10; cf. 6:20)

King makes the sun god shine brightly

Akhetaten, Egypt, c. 1345 BC

King Akhenaten (formerly known as Amenhotep IV) has built a new capital dedicated to the sun god Aten after whom he has named himself, and has declared Aten-worship the official religion of Egypt. The new capital, Akhetaten (Amarna), is midway between Thebes and Memphis.

He made the decision when it became clear that the cults of Amun and Aten could not co-exist peacefully. Amun worship has now been banned, its temples closed and its assets seized. And as the king is still widely recognised as a god, the large priesthood of Amun is now unemployed and unemployable: prayers to Aten are now offered through the king alone.

However, the move has not won popular support. The Aten, technically the sun itself as an incarnation of the god Re, has been venerated for centuries but never before worshipped in its own right. Many Egyptians can see no reason why the gods should not be worshipped equally. They are even banned from praying to Osiris to see them through the afterworld.

According to a special hymn written by the king and carved on a wall in Amarna, Aten is the creator and sustainer of the universe, concerned as much for other lands as he is for Egypt, but is only known personally to the king. Aten controls day and night, gives life and water to all and numbers each person's days. Everyone and everything was made for him:

*'Thou does set each man in his place
and supply his needs;
Each one has his food, and his lifetime
is reckoned. ...
How excellent are thy plans, thou
Lord of eternity!'*

The king's new capital is ringed by a natural amphitheatre of cliffs on both sides of the Nile. It is marked off by a series of 15 large upright stones (steles) with reliefs showing the king and his family adoring Aten. The linear development stretches along the east bank,

Pharaoh Akhenaten and Queen Nefertiti. An unusual painted stone statuette.

and the ends of the city are linked by a wide Royal Avenue flanked by official buildings, the palace andtemple. Upper-class houses are built on spacious estates and furnished with gardens and pools.

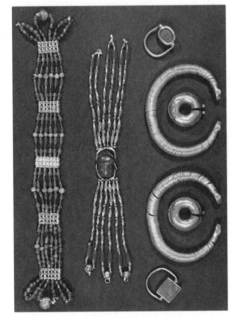

Egyptian jewellry from c. 1350–1300, worn by a princess or high-ranking courtisan.

Queen loses two young suitors

Egypt, c. 1326 BC

Queen Ankhesenanum has lost her potential second young husband only weeks after the death of her first, the 17-year-old Tutankhamun. She had contacted the Hittites asking for a prince to marry, and King Suppiluliuma sent her Prince Zannanza.

But he was murdered at the border, almost certainly on the orders of Horemheb, the army chief and close ally of Ay, an elderly civil servant who queen Ankhesenanum has now been forced to marry and who therefore succeeds Tutankhamun.

The boy king died of unknown causes and has been buried in the Valley of the Kings. His mummy has been placed in a solid gold coffin securely encased in two wooden coffins each overlaid with gold. His face is covered with a gold funerary mask and over 170 grave goods accompany the body into the afterlife.

The burial chamber is the only room of his tomb to be decorated. The walls have been painted with scenes from his funeral and his acceptance by Osiris into the underworld. Also buried in his tomb are the still-born foetuses of his daughters. One had been aborted, probably spontaneously, at five months, and the other at eight or nine months. They have also been embalmed and mummified.

Tutankhamun was not buried in the tomb intended for him close to Amenhotep III, because there had not been time to make it ready. Instead, he was buried in a tomb intended for Ay, now his successor. Even his wooden coffins had been intended for someone else; the name Smenkhare has been erased and the king's inscribed over it.

Murderer flees the country

East Delta, Egypt, c. 1320 BC

One of the Pharaoh's courtiers, Moses, has fled into the Arabian desert after murdering a slave-gang overseer.

He had attacked the overseer who he found beating a Hebrew slave working on a building site.

Although adopted and educated in the Egyptian royal court, Moses is believed to have Semitic parentage.

However, while he may regard the slaves as his own people, they clearly regard him as a quisling. The day after the murder he revisited the area and intervened in a fight between two Israelites. The aggressor revealed that Moses' identity and crime were well known, even though he had attempted to keep it secret. He fled at once, and an order for his arrest and execution has been made.

(Exodus 2:11–15)

Students beaten by keen teachers

Egypt, c. 1325 BC

The murderer Moses would have had his first introduction to the art of physical punishment at school. The prevailing philosophy of education in Egypt is that 'a lad's ear is on his back and he listens when he's beaten'.

The chief academic pursuits are languages and writing, both vital in a nation which has wide international influence and trading agreements. The language of international commerce is Akkadian cuneiform (wedge-shaped) script, although Moses as a Semite would have learned the simpler Canaanite linear alphabet and Egyptian hieroglyphs as well.

Children (mostly boys) from as young as four are taught in open-air schools and begin writing practice on potsherds (broken clay) and shards of limestone. After four

years of elementary schooling they proceed to more advanced work which may include composition of official documents and learning ancient history by chanting it aloud in chorus.

Students use red and black pigments applied with a reed brush, and slabs of sycamore wood skimmed with gypsum plaster are used (and re-used) as formal writing boards. Papyrus is expensive and generally used in scrolls only by expert scribes.

The excavation of a Caananite mortuary temple at Tell el Dab'a in Goshen has produced evidence of Semitic presence in the Nile Delta region at the time of the biblical account.

Education is highly developed in the court. Children of the palace harem, the hub of the court's domestic life in which Moses was raised, are generally educated by the harem overseer. Princes are given further education by personal tutors, usually retired court officials or army officers.

Robbers swarm to beehives

Mycenae, Greece, c. 1300 BC

The living and the dead are being stung by grave robbers who are swarming to the beehive tombs which have recently become a hallmark of Mycenaean civilisation. The domed structures are easily broken into.

The circles of masonry narrow upwards and the final hole is covered by a slab. The structure is prevented from collapse by the lateral pressure of the stones. The largest beehive tomb is some 13 m (43 ft) high by 14.5 m (47 ft) in

diameter. It is driven into the hillside and approached by a roofless passage. The lintel over the door is 8.5 m (26 ft) wide and weighs 120 tonnes.

Among the treasures waiting for grave robbers are ivory carvings, golden eating and drinking utensils, and duck-shaped bowls carved from rock crystal, besides gold ornaments and brooches. Weapons are also buried with their owners, and one royal tomb containing three bodies has some 90 swords in it.

Egyptian writing boards and implements.

Phoenicia gets rich on international trade

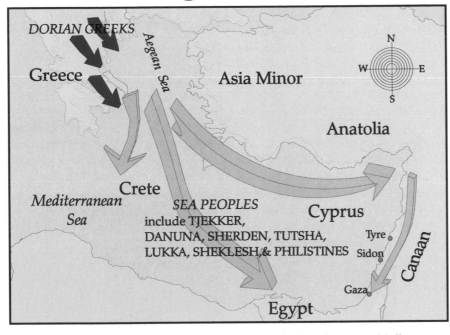

The Sea Peoples were a varied group of tribes, who arrived on the eastern Mediterranean coast in successive waves over many hundreds of years. Some originated in Greece, moved through the Greek islands and spread to Cyprus, the Phonecian coast and Egypt. Others may have originated in Asia Minor or Anatolia. Their main area of integration and conquest lies along the coastal regions from Tyre to Gaza, though they appear never to have ventured far inland.

Phoenicia was successfully invaded by Egypt, of whose empire it has been a valuable part; there has been considerable trade between the two countries, particularly in ships and art objects. Arvad, a Phoenician city, was one of the conquests claimed by Thutmose III.

But in 1400 BC the Phoenicians took advantage of Hittite pressure against Egypt to begin a campaign of rebellion to achieve independence.

Phoenician coast from Rosh Ma Nigra extending north.

Phoenicia, c. 1300 BC

A strip of land 320 km (200 miles) long and 24 km (15 miles) at its widest between the Lebanese mountains and the Mediterranean coast is becoming a major trunk route for international trade.

Phoenicia is a collection of city kingdoms. The chief settlement Sidon gives the area its common name of Sidonia. Other important cities include Tyre, Tripoli and Acre. The country is also often called Canaan on account of the large Canaanite population there. Over the centuries they have established ports in easily defended harbours, and local populations are subject to them.

Phoenicia's inhabitants are Semites and are thought to have first settled there around 2500 BC. They have been culturally influenced by Babylonia. In 1800 BC

Fast Facts c. 1330–1300 BC

Egypt, c. 1332 BC: The new boy-king has changed his name to Tutankhamun, signifying a return to the worship of Amun which was banned by his predecessor. Old temples are being re-opened and new ones being built. The king has initiated extensive building projects at Karnak and Luxor.

Hatti-land, c. 1325 BC: The Hittite king Murshilish is praying to the gods to deliver his people from an outbreak of bubonic plague or typhus. The outbreak has been so severe that the country's defences have been weakened and tribes on the northern fringes are beginning to attack it. In the past there have been warnings to people who eat scavenging dogs and pigs to ensure that the meat is well cooked, to avoid contamination with sometimes lethal worms. Rats tend to feed on waste food in the streets and are believed to spread disease.

Egypt, c. 1321 BC: The elderly King Ay has died after only four years on the throne, and his successor Horemheb, formerly commander-in-chief of the army, has set about completing the reinstatement of the cult of Amun. He is appointing priests from the army, whose loyalty he can rely on, and has demolished the temple of Aten. He has strengthened his position by marrying the sister of Queen Nefertiti, Akhenaten's beautiful wife.

Leubingen, Saxony, c. 1300 BC: A 15-year-old girl has been sacrificed after the death of an old man who was possibly a prince. It is believed that he insisted on taking her with him to give him pleasure in the after life. It is not known if she died willingly. Their bodies have been arranged in a cross-shape, the girl above the man, in a tumulus 4 m (11 ft) long by 8 m (22 ft) high.

Ugarit, c. 1300 BC: The vassal king of this Aramean city has been accused by his Hittite overlords of business corruption. The city is the main trade terminal on the Syrian coast from which lapis lazuli is exported. The king has allegedly been exporting pebbles and passing them off as the semi-precious stones. He has admitted that the supply of lapis lazuli has dried up.

God given new name

Sinai Peninsular, c. 1279 BC

In a world where many gods are worshipped, one who changes his image might seem to make little difference. But according to Moses, the aging son-in-law of a Midianite priest, the ancient God followed by the clan of Abraham – many of whose descendants are now slaves in Egypt – is stirring himself after centuries of apparent inactivity.

From now on he is to be called Yahweh, a name previously known but little used. It means 'the one who is' or 'the one who makes things happen'. And in keeping with this new image of liveliness he will rescue his people from slavery and restore them to Canaan, the land Abraham adopted over 600 years ago, claims Moses.

The desert in parts of the Sinai and Negev is surprisingly covered in dry, mainly thorny, stunted vegetation.

A shepherd among the semi-nomadic Midianites who sheltered him and gave him a wife some 40 years ago, Moses says Yahweh appeared to him at a holy bush in the southern desert while he was leading his sheep to grazing grounds in the mountains.

At first he was sceptical of the vision when he felt Yahweh calling him to return to Egypt and to negiotiate the release of the Israelites. Although bi-lingual and well educated in Egypt he is out of touch with his own blood relatives, and Moses pleaded personal inadequacy and inappropriateness as a reason for turning down the commission.

But he says that Yahweh gave him signs to perform before both the Israelite and Egyptian leaders as proof of his authenticity. His shepherd's staff turned into a snake, and he contracted and was healed from a skin disease in the space of minutes.

And as a concession, Yahweh agreed to allow Moses' brother Aaron to act as public spokesman. It is believed that the two men recently made contact after decades of separation following the news that Pharaoh Seti had died and that Moses was no longer on the wanted list for a murder he committed as a young man and for which he has never stood trial.

The new name of God remains only a partially-explained mystery. It declares him to be ever-alive, and the plural of majesty, the 'royal we', which he used implies his total supremacy. The appearance of what seemed to be a flaming but unscorched bush suggest a combination of holiness and compassion.

But Yahweh has not declared himself as a God of war, fertility, the elements, or of any other matter of human concern, in the manner of other gods. Moses, no doubt, is praying that Yahweh will be all of them as he sets out on what promises to be a hopeless task at an age when most men would be looking for an easier way of making a living.

(Exodus 3:1–4:17)

Trendy city profits from pots and pans

Mycenae, c. 1280 BC

After a hard day's sport or hunting, it's time to change into the latest fashions for an evening's feasting and dancing in the city that has become one of the wealthiest places in the world.

Mycenaean pottery.

Mycenae in Greece dominates trade routes with the Greek mainland and is taking advantage of Egypt's recent weakened hold on the Levantine ports. It has established trading posts at the Canaanite port of Ugarit and at several places in Asia Minor. It has an important ivory carving industry and produces what is reputed to be some of the world's best pottery and bronze weapons.

The people claim that it was founded by the hero, Perseus, and that they are descended from tribes which settled in Greece during the great European migrations of 2000 BC. They speak a Greek dialect and have developed a script handwriting. Their conquest of Knossos in Crete established them as leaders of the Aegean civilisation.

Mycenaean architecture includes massive city walls and a Lion Gateway that has become a well-known landmark. The surrounding region is prospering, and at neighbouring Tiryns a new citadel has been designed which its builders believe will be impregnable.

Holiday plans spoilt by extra work

Nile Delta, c. 1277 BC

Plans for a three-day public holiday by the Israelite slaves working on Pharaoh Rameses' civic building projects have been rejected, and their working practices tightened. The slave camps are brimming with anger at their leaders for having orchestrated the confrontation.

The slave leaders, Moses and Aaron, with the agreement of the Israelite elders, went to Pharaoh to request that the Hebrews be allowed to hold a festival to their God in the desert. As it would involve sacrifices of cattle, which are sacred in Egyptian religion, they felt it would be insensitive to hold the festival on Egyptian soil.

Pharaoh not only refused but also cut off the supply of chopped straw used to reinforce and stabilise the bricks they were making. But despite the consequent rise in breakages and longer hours in moulding the mud, the quotas must

Making bricks in Egypt today, following age-old methods.

Wooden model of workers making bricks.

still be maintained. A deputation of Hebrew foremen protested to Pharaoh, but he simply accused them of laziness.

His refusal drew an angry response from the Hebrews who regard Moses as an outside trouble-maker. They claim that his interference has put the whole community at risk. Although demoralised, Moses says he has had further visions and messages from God reinforcing his divine appointment as leader. He claims that Yahweh has told him that he will act with great power over the oppression of Egypt. But it is a message which the Israelites are in no mood to listen to.

The once-flourishing Hebrew community, based in Goshen to the east of the Delta, has been exploited by several pharaohs. They are working mostly on Pithom, 'the mansion of the divine Athum', situated near the eastern tributaries of the Delta, west of Lake Timsah, and on Rameses which is being built on what is believed to be the site of the ancient Avaris, the former capital of the Hyksos rulers of Egypt some 400 years ago. Rising in splendour is a complex of palaces, official residences and a glaze factory.

(Exodus 4:29–6:12)

Fast Facts 1300–1270 BC

Britain, c. 1300 BC: Cremation rather than burial is beginning to be used. The ashes of the dead are placed in large, rather crude, urns with rolled edges and thick decorated rims.

Sardinia, c. 1300 BC: The people on this island have begun building conical towers, or nuraghi, as sanctuaries and defensive towers. They have platforms on the top and step-like tiers around the sides. There are a few narrow openings and a narrow corridor leading to a chamber. Villages are springing up around them, with low round huts built of dry stone walls and thatch.

France, c. 1290: BC: The people of Brittany are exporting their distinctive weaponry to Holland. It includes bronze spearheads, rapiers with bronze hilts and ceremonial blades some of which weigh as much as 2 kg (4 lb). Ceremonial weapons are exchanged when pacts are made.

Ireland, c. 1290 BC: Twisted ropes of gold up to a metre (1 yd) long are being exported from here, mainly to France. The ropes are entwined spirally and worn around the neck.

Egypt, c. 1279 BC: Pharaoh Seti I of Egypt has died. His campaigns against Syria, his conquest of Palestine, his successful confrontations with Libya in the west and his battles against the Philistines (culminating in a peace treaty) have made him a much-admired monarch. His major architectural achievements include the temple at Abydos (still under construction) and his own magnificent tomb near Thebes in the Valley of the Kings. His son Rameses II now reigns from the royal city of Rameses.

Rephidim, Sinai Desert, c. 1270 BC: A desert skirmish over the most fertile oasis for miles has been won decisively by the Israelites under the leadership of a young general, Joshua. The semi-nomadic Amalekites who range over the Sinai Peninsular had tried unsuccessfully to rout the newcomers. To celebrate, Moses erected an altar dedicated to Yahweh the Banner. Throughout the battle Israel had the edge whenever Moses held his hands up in prayer. (Exodus 17:8–15)

Egypt battered by unnatural disasters

The River Nile turns to blood: a scene from the film *The Ten Commandments*.

Delta region, c. 1275 BC

The people of the Nile Delta are battling with the aftermath of nine successive natural disasters which have occurred over the past few months. A battle of wills between Pharaoh Rameses II and rebel slave leader Moses is being seen as a battle of the gods which has brought unprecedented suffering.

The titanic clash stems from Moses' previously-rejected request for a public holiday to celebrate a religious festival. His catchphrase has become, 'Let my people go!'

The bargaining began as a tussle of cult magic but quickly turned into something more sinister. When Moses and Aaron came before Pharaoh he challenged them to prove their powers by performing a miracle. Moses threw his staff on the ground and it turned into a snake. The feat was matched by the court sorcerers, although Moses' reptile proved to be the more life-like by cannibalising the rest.

Early one August morning, when Pharaoh went for his daily dip in the flooding river, Moses directed Aaron to strike the water with his staff. The water went blood-red, probably polluted by poisonous algae and red soil washed down by heavy spring rains in the African mountains. The fish died and the people had no drinking water.

But Pharaoh did not change his mind; he ordered his sorcerers to duplicate the miracle, and announced himself unimpressed – although they appeared unable to reverse the trick and sterilise the water. A frustrating game followed as Pharaoh first agreed to Moses' terms to get the plagues lifted then immediately went back on his word with devastating results.

Each plague affected the Nile River, the life-giving artery that feeds and irrigates Egypt. A plague of frogs, was followed by plagues of mosquitoes and flies thriving on the rotting wildlife and stagnant water and spreading disease. It is believed that insect-born anthrax then caused a huge loss of livestock, and that insect-borne disease was also responsible for the plague of open sores which affected most people.

However, from the flies onwards, the area of Goshen where the Israelites live remained unaffected. Then in February/March hail and thunderstorms funnelled up the Nile basin, following familiar regional weather patterns, and destroyed the early flax and barley harvests. That caused a large increase in the locust population, and a few weeks later hordes of destructive insects were blown by the south-east wind down the Nile valley eating every green leaf.

Finally, a thick, tangible darkness which lasted for three days was created by a heavy dust-storm which, because of local geography, once again left the Hebrew territories unaffected.

At this, Pharaoh almost submitted, but his attempts to haggle with Moses over detail quickly led to a stalemate. In the end he ejected Moses and threatened that if he ever saw the slave leader again, he would kill him. Moses responded with his own threat: there will be no more attempts to negotiate; the matter is now wholly in the hands of the God of the Israelites.

(Exodus 7–10)

Hatti pins hope on treaty

Egypt, c. 1280 BC

A treaty made between Rameses II of Egypt and the king of the Hittites (Hatti-land), Hattushilish, has been carved on the walls of two Egyptian buildings and written in Akkadian and cuneiform texts in Boghazkoi in eastern Turkey.

Both versions record an everlasting peace treaty between the two superpowers who face each other across the Mediterranean Sea. The treaty states that neither country should trespass across the borders of the other and that they should assist each other in times of attack. On the death of either ruler, the other country should support the accession of his son, sending military force to assist him if necessary.

This far-reaching treaty also includes an extradition agreement. Anyone who flees to Hatti-land from Egypt will not be allowed to settle there, and refugees from Hatti cannot stay in Egypt.

This was their darkest hour

Nile Delta, c. 1275 BC

Egypt is today a grieving and devastated nation. Every family is in deepest mourning. In one terrifying night the firstborn of every family has been killed.

The pick of the animals has also been slaughtered. Even the royal palace, protected by soldiers and sorcerers, has not escaped. Pharaoh's eldest son is among those who have died. The ecological disasters of the plagues were as nothing compared to this.

While the sound of wailing fills the land, a vast river of people, animals and luggage is moving out of Egypt, as purposeful and inexorable as the great Nile itself.

After over 400 years in Egypt the Israelites are on the march, following the dreams and visions of their forefathers and the claims of their 80-year-old leader Moses that their God has a new and better land for them to go to, somewhere in Canaan where their ancestor Abraham once settled.

Through long years of slavery and suffering the story of the promised exodus has been handed down from generation to generation. Now it is actually happening. To a bystander these footsore and tired people might seem like refugees; but ask them, and they will tell you they are going home.

They alone of the people of the Nile Delta escaped the hand of the angel of death. But only just, by virtue, they say, of a hastily-prepared sacrifice and ceremony which marked them out from the rest of the population. It was a nail-biting climax to months of dashed hopes and deep suffering.

Yesterday each Israelite family slaughtered an unblemished lamb, painted its blood on the lintel of their house, and ate the meat with herbs and unleavened bread. Every part of the carcass was consumed or burnt, and the meal eaten by the family dressed in travelling clothes. Dubbed the Passover, because it was eaten on the night that the avenging Lord passed over their homes, the ceremonial meal is intended to be an annual event.

It was still night when the broken and despairing Pharaoh summoned Moses and Aaron and begged them to leave Egypt with their people. The slaves have been loaded with valuables and provisions by their former taskmasters partly because the people are now terrified of the God of the Israelites, and partly because a supernatural change of heart seems to have taken place.

At the head of this huge procession are the two brothers, Moses and Aaron, whose long battle with Pharaoh ended with the national tragedy of the plague of the firstborn. They are leading about 600,000 Israelite men as well as women and children. A number of sympathetic Egyptians accompany them with their families.

(Exodus 11–12)

Gold pendant inlaid with precious stones bearing the royal insignia of Rameses II.

Kadesh conflict declared a draw

Kadesh, Syria, c. 1274 BC

A battle between Pharaoh Rameses II of Egypt and the Hittite leader, Muwatalli, has ended with both sides claiming victory. Though Egypt has declared itself military victor, the Battle of Kadesh, fought on Syrian soil, has not resulted in the Hittites losing their grip on the region.

Since the great Suppiluliuma I died in 1346 BC the Hittites have increased the power he gained for them, though they have had to fight many wars to keep it. In particular, Assyria is rapidly consolidating its new independence and is laying claim to substantial territory.

The Hittites' main enemy remains Egypt, however, which badly wants Syria for itself and is not prepared to see another major power in the region expanding its borders and its sphere of influence. But the Hittite possessions have extended out to the Aegean in the west, to Armenia in the east, and down into Mesopotamia and Syria as far south as Lebanon.

It is likely that the two empires will now have to live with each other, as the constant warfare is draining both economies and causing much domestic unrest.

c. 1275–1270 BC

Stuck-in-the-mud army watches slaves walk on water to freedom

Nile Delta, c. 1275 BC

Israelite slaves walk on water. And their God's presence can be seen with the naked eye. By comparison, Egypt's army has become a force of literal stick-in-the-muds.

In an episode which Egyptian historians will want to erase from the national memory out of sheer embarrassment, the Pharaoh's crack chariot unit has sunk in the marshes east of the Delta while the workforce of Israelite brickmakers and builders walked across them following what could only be described as an unearthly glowing cloud which they said was the manifestation of their God's presence.

The escaping Hebrews had camped by the Sea of Reeds, having doubled back towards the Mediterranean coast. Despite protests, their leader Moses claimed he was following precise directions from Yahweh. The Pharaoh concluded that they were going round in circles and made one last desperate attempt to get them back.

He set out with a force of 600 battle chariots backed up by other divisions, trapping the Israelites by the marshes at nightfall. The panicking slaves turned on their leader, who assured them Yahweh would rescue them and struck the waters symbolically with his staff.

The Egyptian army overwhelmed by the sea, as depicted in the film *The Ten Commandments*.

No Israelite slept that night. A violent east wind from the desert beat down on the water, shrieking blasts whistled through the reeds and the sound of rushing water made the animals bellow in protest. But while it was still dark the people crept from their sodden tents and saw in the light of their glowing cloud that a narrow causeway of dry ground had opened up across the marshes.

They grabbed their belongings and with the cloud illuminating their path stepped gingerly across, while the pursuing army stumbled in the twilight. In the still-damp ground many chariots lost their wheels or became bogged down, the army panicked and tried to retreat as Moses stretched his arm over the marshes again and the causeway became covered in water once more.

The Israelites are making for the waterless wastes of the Sinai Desert, where they will clearly need all the help their God can give. They are travelling south-eastwards, despite their stated objective being Canaan in the north-east, because they believe Yahweh has told them to avoid the coast road through Philistia.

As they prepared to move on to their new life, they had consecrated each firstborn male to Yahweh. And they solemnly agreed to eat the Passover meal every year on the anniversary of this exodus from Egypt. Among the treasures they are carrying are the venerated bones of Joseph, one of their forefathers, whose family emigrated to Egypt during a famine some 400 years ago.

To celebrate their remarkable escape, Moses and his sister Miriam composed a song of triumph which echoed through the desert: 'Sing to Yahweh, for he's the greatest; the horse and its rider he's flung in the sea!'

(Exodus 13:1–15:21)

Was Rameses II the Pharaoh Moses and the Israelites had to contend with? Most authorities identify him as the Pharaoh who changed his mind. Rameses II was also a great builder: this monumental head of a statue lies in the temple he built at Luxor.

'God gives us each day our daily bread!'

The mountainous range of the Sinai Peninsular seems to extend for ever.

Zin Desert, Sinai, c. 1274 BC

The Israelite God seems to have an inexhaustible supply of resources. He also seems to have an inexhaustible supply of patience. No sooner does he meet one request than the refugees are grumbling about something else.

On arrival at Marah in the Shur Desert to the north of the Sinai Peninsular, they complained at the inevitable bitterness of the artesian well-water laden, as it always is, with dissolved salts. Moses, their leader, laced the well with an aromatic shrub in what he claims was a moment of divine inspiration.

Now the Israelites, probably the biggest single group of all the migratory peoples who are wandering the world at present, understandably have grown tired of their staple diet of milk, cheese and mutton supplemented by whatever cereals and vegetables they can find along the way, which is not a lot in this sparsely-peopled scrubland. They are staying near the coast of the Gulf of Suez.

As they pined for the admittedly-rare beef stews of Egypt, an exhausted flock of migrating quail

Peak of Mount Sinai.

dropped from their regular flight-path into the camp, to be hungrily caught, killed and plucked by the Israelites before the desert vultures had time to zero in on the unexpected spread. Better than beef, the quails had been a gourmet's delicacy and a slave's dream back among the pyramids. Put it down to Yahweh, said Moses.

As if that was not enough, the next morning they woke to what looked like snow on the ground until they discovered that it tasted like honey-baked wafer bread. Stuck for a name they called it 'manna', which sounds better kept in their own language than translated into anyone else's because the word is simply the scatterbrain's 'thingamy' or 'what's-its-name'. Literary culture is not their strongest point.

This, claimed Moses, is to be their daily bread substitute for the duration of their journey to their new land. It is to be seen as a sign of Yahweh's continued care, for which they should be truly thankful, he said.

Miraculously, there was enough on the ground for everyone to have enough. It was not to be hoarded, Moses said, and those who disagreed soon found their storage jars had turned into maggot nests. Except on Fridays, when they are told to collect a double portion and store it overnight for use on their weekly Sabbath, a day in which no travelling, food gathering or other work is allowed.

It is a hand-to-mouth existence. Their God, who still demonstrates his presence in a cloud in the normally cloudless sky, clearly means to keep them on their toes.

(Exodus 15:22–16:36)

Yahweh bulldozed by impatient worshippers

Sinai Peninsular, c. 1274 BC

When Moses left the Israelite camp for a conference with Yahweh six weeks ago the crowd of perhaps a million people fell silent. As he climbed into the holy mountain, a sense of God's presence and majesty covered the area and filled them with awe.

When Moses returned to the camp, the crowds fell silent again. Only this time it was the shame-filled and embarrassed silence which might fall on a funeral wake when the supposedly-dead person walks in to find his relatives prematurely celebrating his death.

In that short space of time they had shoved aside Yahweh, who they once regarded as the supreme and unrepresentable God, and replaced him with an image of a bull calf. It was a return to the Canaanite religion their forefathers had left centuries ago, and not dissimilar to the worship of Apis in Egypt who is incarnated in a live bull and of Hathor the goddess portrayed as a heifer.

It cost them dear. In order to make the image they have melted down many of the valuable gold trinkets they had been given when they left Egypt.

They have also lost some 3,000 of their own people executed on Moses' command, and countless others have died in an outbreak of disease which is being interpreted as Yahweh's punishment for their idolatry.

The whole episode was a study in contrasts. Before he left for his conference, Moses had gathered the elders together and, on the basis of a previous revelation from Yahweh, warned them of God's holy nature and strict requirements. He called on them to renew the covenant by which Yahweh contracts to be their God in return for their obedience and undivided devotion. It had been a solemn religious festival in which all had seem to take part with great sincerity.

The octogenarian leader returned to a festival of a very different kind as the elders, led by his own brother Aaron, partied under the shadow of the golden statue to the chant, 'This is your god'.

The greatest contrast of all was between the reaction of Moses and the reasoning of Aaron. In a fit of anger Moses smashed the monumental stones on which were inscribed the core commandments of Yahweh. The first was 'You shall have no other gods apart from me' and the second was 'You shall not make any image to represent me'.

Aaron excused his action on the grounds that public opinion demanded visible gods and that Moses, missing on a storm-covered mountain, was presumed dead. With the lame but conscience-stricken plea of a toddler caught in an act of vandalism, he said, 'I just told people to throw their jewellery into the fire, and it sort of formed into this calf!' He made no mention of the skilled craftsmen who had cast the mould.

Moses called a camp meeting, invited those who wished to stay faithful to Yahweh to join him, and next day went back on to the mountain, despite his previously long ordeal, to pray that Yahweh would forgive them. In an exemplary act of mass capital punishment the Levites, who had not taken part in the idolatry, executed some 3,000 unrepentant worshippers. Disease has stricken many more.

The Israelites are unique in contemporary culture in forbidding the physical representation of the gods. The choice of a bull-calf, which represents fertility, was appropriate even if misguided in an area of low rainfall and harsh living conditions.

(Exodus 19; 24; 32)

Leader weathers storms of discontent

Sinai Peninsular, c. 1273 BC

When a leader delegates responsibility in the interests of justice, he is opening the door to opposition. That is one of the hard lessons being learned in the desert of Sinai by the emerging nation of Israel.

The former slaves have struggled to organise themselves into a cohesive unit while living as semi-nomads. Moses accepted the advice of his father-in-law, Jethro, a

The bronze bull from the kingdom of Sheba testifies to widespread bull worship throughout Arabia. Its eyes were originally inlaid with precious stones and it was covered in gold plate.

Midianite priest who follows a different god and who occasionally visits his extended family in the desert, to appoint elders to arbitrate in disputes. For some time Moses had heard all complaints, however trivial.

In an unusual initiation ceremony, the 70 elders were taken to the Tent of Meeting, Israel's shrine, where the Spirit of Yahweh so touched them that they began spontaneously to speak inspired words of praise and encouragement. Their experience has not been repeated since, although it was shared at the same time by two elders who had been unable to attend the meeting.

But such demonstrations of spiritual and organisational unity have been rare. The camp is regularly split by controversy and complaint, especially over the privations of desert life. Signifying both his justice and his mercy, Yahweh is said to have reacted to the complaints by a fire which damaged tents on the edge of the camp, and by once again providing a generous helping of stranded quail.

The most serious revolt came from the leadership team itself. Moses' sister Miriam and his brother Aaron made an issue out of the leader's apparent inconsistency in serving Yahweh yet having married a foreign wife. They also felt that he was getting more credit than they were for being a mouthpiece of Yahweh.

Such an attack from a source so close to the man who single-handedly engineered the exodus of the slaves from Egypt has surprised many.

Moses is known as a self-effacing person who finds public speaking and high-profile leadership difficult, and who if pressed would probably say he wished he could have remained a shepherd in Midian. He is also unique in that he is said to have had several direct encounters with Yahweh the God who keeps others at bay with awesome signs of his holiness.

It was God who apparently resolved the family dispute by inflicting Miriam with a skin complaint. Moses, caring as ever and without a trace of bitterness, prayed for her healing which occurred after an irritating week's wait.

The Israelite leader is a remarkable man of patience. Many others would have resigned after half the number of no-confidence votes he has had to endure.

Yet when it comes to crises the man who has steered them through many dangers and moulded their religious and social life still commands respect. Through him Israel is gaining a sense of nationhood parallel to that of any other people-group.

(Exodus 18; Numbers 11, 12)

Doomed to die in the merciless desert

Kadesh Barnea, c. 1273 BC

The tribes of Israelites poised on the verge of entering Canaan, the land of Yahweh's promise where their ancestor Abraham once lived, have turned back into the Sinai Desert in disappointment.

According to Moses, God has doomed all but a handful to die in the desert. Their children, however, will be allowed to enter what they are already calling 'the land flowing with milk and honey'.

The sudden reversal occurred after a reconaissance party representing each of the 12 tribes returned from Canaan carrying a huge bunch of grapes and baskets of pomegranates and figs as samples of what awaited the nomadic slaves who long to settle in freedom.

But the small print of their report revealed that the existing occupants of Canaan have built fortified city-states. And among them are the

Desert rocks in the midday sun.

unusually tall and powerfully-built descendants of the legendary giant, Anak, who occupy Hebron. Wild but unsubstantiated rumours quickly swept the camp that the Anakim are the half-spirit, half-

Frieze of large grapes, Capernaum.

human Nephilim believed to have lived before Noah.

The baskets of fruit were not enough to sweeten the bitter verdict that the Israelites, lacking a well-trained and equipped army, would be annihilated if they attempted to cross the border. It was a major reversal of their former confidence that Yahweh would give them living space.

And it was because of their lack of confidence in him that his verdict was pronounced. The God who had seen them through the Red Sea north of the Gulf of Suez despite the close attentions of Pharaoh's army, who had provided water from dry rocks and meat and bread from thin air, had promised to see them into their new homes. But they opted for the known deprivations rather than the unknown risks, and Yahweh, it seems, has taken them at their word and dumped them in the desert.

A minority report from two of the 12 explorers, Joshua, Moses' young personal assistant, and Caleb, suggested that the odds were not insuperable. For their faith they have been promised a place in Canaan. The waiting period for them is going to seem interminable.

(Numbers 13, 14)

71

The law of Yahweh

The laws given by Yahweh to Moses cover four areas of human life: the moral, social, religious ceremonial, and religious sacrifices. The ten commandments form a timeless core to the whole law, setting out a framework of belief and behaviour which other laws amplify. They show that God is to be at the centre of both personal and community life. The other laws vary enormously and are not recorded in a systematic form. Here are some samples of the other laws which Moses claims were also given to him by Yahweh.

On servants

Hebrew servants are to be freed after six years, and they do not have to pay for their freedom. However, if a servant has been given a wife by his employer, she must remain in service. The servant can opt to remain in service also, but if he does it is a lifelong commitment.

Exodus 21:2–11

On injuring others

Murderers are to be executed. People who kill others unintentionally will be directed to safe places where they can claim sanctuary from revenge killing. Kidnappers and people who curse their parents are also to be executed. A person who injures another in a fight must compensate him for his time off work. Servants who are maimed by their employer must be set free at once. A bull which gores people must be killed, and so must its owner if it has a history of attacking people and has not been properly tethered.

(Exodus 21:12–35)

On caring for property

Animal thieves must pay back four or five times what they stole if the animals have been killed, double if the animals are found alive and well. If thieves are bankrupt, they are to be sold into service. Someone who starts a fire which spreads to a neighbour's property must pay compensation. If property is stolen while it is being looked after by a third party, the latter must go to court and satisfy the judges that he did not steal it himself.

(Exodus 22:1–15)

On being good neighbours

A man who seduces an unmarried woman shall marry her and pay the appropriate bride-price to her family. Widows and orphans are not to be taken advantage of but cared for, as are strangers who live in the land. Anyone who lends money and takes a person's cloak as a pledge must return it in the evening so that the borrower will not be cold in the night. False reports are not to be spread, bribes are not to be taken, favouritism is not to be shown in court either to rich or poor, and justice is not to be denied to the poor. If an enemy is seen to be in need of practical assistance, he is to be given it.

(Exodus 22:16–23:9)

The ten commandments

1. I am the God who has delivered you from Egypt and you must worship no other.
2. You must not manufacture any image or representation with the intention of worshipping it.
3. You must not treat the name of Yahweh lightly or abuse it.
4. You must keep the Sabbath as a day apart, dedicated to rest, in recognition that God also rested on the seventh day of creation.
5. You must respect and honour your parents.
6. You must not commit murder.
7. You must not commit adultery.
8. You must not steal.
9. You must not tell lies about your neighbour or perjure him in court.
10. You must not be covetous about anything that belongs to your neighbour.

(Exodus 20:1–17)

The tabernacle was housed inside a tent-like structure, itself surrounded by a larger 'courtyard' formed by a protective canvas wall. Precise measurements and instructions were given by Yahweh for the manufacture of all the items associated with his worship.

Israelite feasts

Unlike the religious feasts of other nations, which are usually times when the gods are thought to sit at table with human beings and eat with them, the Israelite feasts are times of celebration and acknowledgement of God's goodness and provision. Honouring God is not to be associated with fear and deprivation, though the nature of the festivals underlines his greatness, his infinite power and authority.

Similarly, though confession of sin is a necessary part of a feast, there is no counterpart to the mortification, self-wounding or other expressions of expiation common in many religions. Indeed, that is the whole point: feasts celebrate the fact that even the sin that makes the sinner (and God) grieve is taken away by his mercy. Though repentance is a prerequisite for someone to be accepted by Yahweh, the just punishment is laid on a substitute animal.

Here are some of the common feasts which Moses says were commanded by Yahweh. Several of them will only become appropriate when the Israelites settle into their own land.

The Passover Festival (March/April)

This great festival is a memorial of the night of deliverance from Egypt. It copies the meal that was eaten then. It is followed by the **Feast of the Unleavened Bread** (instituted as a reminder of the hasty last meal eaten in Egypt). For a whole week no bread made with yeast is eaten and no work done. On the first and last days of the festival, sacrifices are offered at religious assemblies, and on the last day the first sheaf of barley to be reaped is to be offered to God. Both feasts were instituted on the night of the exodus and are to be repeated annually.

(Exodus 12:1–28, 43–49; Numbers 28:16–25)

The Feast of Harvest

Also known as the Feast of Weeks (or Pentecost) it is to be held in May/June, 50 days after the Passover Sabbath. It is marked by sacrifices and a religious assembly, and is to be a celebration of the grain harvest.

(Exodus 23:16; Numbers 28:26–31; cf. Leviticus 23:15–21; Deuteronomy 16:9–12)

The Feast of Ingathering, or Tabernacles (Booths)

Held at the time of the autumn rains and the ploughing seasons, it celebrates the final gathering of fruit. The people are to make small tents (tabernacles or booths) out of tree branches, and live in them for seven days. It is to be a reminder of the time that the Israelites are spending in the desert. (Exodus 23:16; 34:22; Numbers 29:12–40)

The Day of Trumpets

Another autumn festival (held in the seventh month, Tishri, mid September), it celebrates the Sabbath. No hard labour is to be done, and sacrifices are to be offered.

(Leviticus 23:23-25; Numbers 29:1–6)

The Day of Atonement

A solemn festival on the tenth day of the seventh month during which the blood of the atoning sin offering is to be sacrificed to God, and the people confess their sins. The removal of sin from them is illustrated by the scapegoat which has their sins laid on it by a symbolic act and is then led out into the desert never to return. Only on this day will the chief priest enter the holiest part of the worship tent.

(Numbers 29:7–11; cf. Leviticus 16:2–34)

The Sabbath

Although not regarded as a major festival, the weekly Sabbath, or day of rest, is an important feature of Israelite life. Its main purpose is to focus attention on God as the giver of all things, and to recognise afresh human dependancy on him; God can never be worked out of a job. Food can be prepared the night before, fires are to be kept in overnight, and servants and animals are to get time out too. Once every seven years the whole land is to be given a sabbath, a fallow period for soil recovery.

(Exodus 23:10–12; 31:12–17; 35:1–3)

Moses and the tablets of the law. Taken from the film *Exodus*.

Where on earth is Canaan?

Potential conquerors of the Mediterranean's eastern coastal districts could be forgiven for getting lost here. The signposts keep changing and no one can tell you exactly where 'Cannan' is.

The name derives from Noah's grandson, and describes both a people and a land. The Canaanites are a Semitic people, closely related to the Phoenicians, and the land they occupy mostly lies within Phoenicia. Generally 'Canaan' refers to the land and people of the Syro-Phoenician coast, though it can also include the area stretching inland to the Dead Sea. The Egyptians often use the name Canaan to mean their entire Syro-Phoenician territories.

Canaan is also used more widely to describe the coastal plain and a hinterland of hills. A number of

The Bezet Valley on the north coast is a rich, lush area.

races live there, many of whom – the Hittites, Jebusites, Amorites, Hivites and others – are believed to be descendants of the original Canaan, son of Ham, son of Noah.

To add to the confusion, the 'Amorites', a people living in the Jordanian hill region of Canaan who allied with Abraham to rout the four kings, is also used as a synonym for 'Canaanites'. Ethnic Amorites form such a strong part of the population that their name can logically stand for the whole area.

However, a stretch of the Phoenician coast containing a number of Canaanite (Phoenician) seaports has been conquered in recent years by the Amorite kingdom of Amurru from the Lebanese mountains overlooking Canaan, connecting 'Amorite' with a specific location.

A region full of contrasts

Canaan, which is roughly 200 km (125 miles) north to south and about 65 km (40 miles) east to west, packs a wide variety of contrasting natural regions into its small area. The Israelites' first sight of it was from the arid sandstone mountains of Transjordan, east of the River Jordan which is reckoned as the region's boundary.

They looked down on the lush vegetation of the river valley where wild animals roam. It is part of a rift valley which runs from Galilee down into east Africa. Almost sub-tropical, it is stifling hot in summer with daytime temperatures regularly topping 38°C (100°F). In winter temperatures rarely fall below 18°C (65°F).

Rising above the river valley to the west are the limestone Judean uplands where there are pockets of good grazing near the springs. The area is pitted with valleys and not easy to travel or conquer. The annual rainfall of 20–30 cm (8–12 in) is low.

Further to the west is the coastal

plain, a narrow and flat area colonised by the Phoenicians. Its mild Mediterranean climate enjoys 40–70 cm of rain (16–27 in) each year. To the south, from the Dead Sea into Arabia, is the Negev, a dry and rocky desert where there are few settlements.

Several major trade routes cross the region from north to south. The Way of the Sea runs up the coast from Egypt before turning inland to

Galilee and then on to Damascus in Syria (Aram). Also running to the same destination is the King's Highway which begins at the Gulf of Aqabah and skirts the edge of the hills east of the Jordan.

A third route runs up the west bank of the Jordan linking major settlements such as Jerusalem and Megiddo. The region is a strategic buffer between the tribes of northern Mesopotamia and Asia Minor, and those in Egypt, Arabia and North Africa.

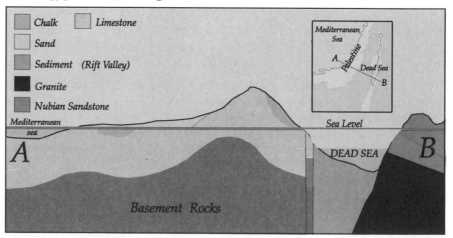

The land of Canaan, seen in cross section, showing the geological formation and the deep trough of the Dead Sea well below sea level.

A Who's Who of Israel's enemies

Canaan, c. 1200

These are the major threats to Israel:

• The **Ammonites** occupy an area to the east of the River Jabbok. They are already conducting skirmishes. The Ammonites are descended from Lot's son Ben-Ammi, and in Moses' time the Israelites were commanded to treat them kindly. Their allies include the Moabites.

• The **Amorites** were themselves displaced by the Philistine settlers, and are currently scattered on both sides of the Jordon: Amorite kings ruled most of the Transjordon at the time of the conquest and were among the first targets of Joshua's.

• The **Aramaeans** (Aramites) are in the northern region. Both Isaac and Jacob had Aramaean wives; often, and wrongly, the Aramaeans have been called 'Syrians'.

• The **Hazorites.** Hazor in the north of Canaan was destroyed by Joshua but was never occupied by him. It is now rebuilt by Canaanites, though as yet unfortified.

• The **Hittites** are probably related to the now defunct Hittite empire which extended from Asia Minor to Syria. They are strong around Hebron.

• The **Hivites** are based in the Lebanese mountains. Their history is obscure, though some think that they are the same people as the Horites, often mentioned earlier.

• The **Jebusites** were the original inhabitants of Jerusalem, which they call Jebus. The city was destroyed in the Judah campaigns of the early conquest but the Jebusites are determined to regain it.

• The **Midianites** chiefly threaten Manasseh in central Canaan. There are five Midianite families, tracing their descent back to Abraham through Midian his son. Moses' wife was a Midianite. Their army is the first ever recorded as using camels in warfare.

• The **Moabites** live in the plateau east of the Dead Sea. They are descended from Lot, and the region was well populated before Lot settled there. Moabite incursions into Israelite territory have reached Jericho.

• The **Perizzites** are indigenous hill-dwellers. Very little is known about them.

• The **Philistines** occupy the southern coastal plain and are beginning to make incursions inland.

• The **Sidonians** are Canaanites living in the area around Sidon. Their strength is such that they represent a significant threat to the Israelites, and several military incursions have been attempted.

75

King-size statues adorn magnificent new temple

The Great Temple at Abu Simbel, built by Rameses II.

Egypt, c. 1240 BC

Visitors to Egypt are unfailingly impressed by Rameses II's new Great Temple at Abu Simbel on the west bank of the Nile. Its facade, cut out of rock, measures 30 m (98 ft) high and 35 m (115 ft) wide, and displays four statues of the king.

Each shows the sovereign (whose people regard as divine) seated with members of the royal family in a much smaller scale at his feet. Eight further statues of the king form the eight pillars of the Great Hall. Twice a year the rising sun shines at the appropriate angle to illuminate four more statues in a niche at the back of the temple. Three of them are of Egyptian gods, the fourth is of the king. The temple is decorated with scenes from the king's battle victories and portrayals of the king enacting sacred rites.

A small temple nearby is a scaled-down version and includes statues and decorations of the queen.

Empire booked up to date

Nippur, c. 1230 BC

A vast economics library of 12,000 tablets records most of the significant points in what has been an unusually prosperous century for the Kassites. Quite apart from their other accomplishments the Kassites are notable literary enthusiasts.

The library, located at Nippur the religious capital, has established a new scribal tradition using innovative systems of dating its archives which has played a major part in standardising Akkadian and Sumerian written texts.

The region is also the centre of an influential literary movement; many ancient tales are being freshly retold and rediscovered by a new generation.

New sounds of music

Europe, c. 1250 BC

Europe is humming to new sounds of music as the technology of instrument manufacture becomes more finely-tuned.

In Denmark, for example, the old cattle horns have been transposed into lurs, huge bronze trumpets which require serious practice to be played well. They are made in various keys, mostly C, D and F, and the most sophisticated models will play 22 tones over four octaves.

Lurs are used to accompany religious worship and vary in shape. Some have a short curved tube like a hunting horn, and are often fitted with a chain running from the bell to the mouthpiece so that the musician can hold them steady.

They are cast by the 'lost wax' method in which a wax model is stuffed and surrounded by clay. When molten brass is poured into it, the wax melts and runs out of the bottom. Lurs are cast in several sections so that they can be transported easily, but the casting and assembly needs to be accurate because a defect will ruin the pitch of the instrument.

On the western fringes of Europe the Irish are making bronze horns in several keys (C, C sharp, D and D sharp) but they are more limited than lurs. They usually have only a couple of notes per octave, and the mouthpiece can be at the side or the end.

The Irish also make crotals for percussion; they are hollow bronze balls with pieces of bronze inside.

Across Europe metal is used to make rattle pendants for horse harnesses. But some things never change. Drums are still made out of skins stretched over large pots.

Silver lyre with an inlaid front, found in the royal burial pit of Ur in Babylonia.

Royal divorce hits the headlines

The principal room, possibly the audience chamber, of the royal palace at Ugarit.

Ugarit, c. 1250 BC

Amistamru, king of Ugarit in northern Syria, has left his wife who is the daughter of the king of Amurru, a neighbouring state. The Hittite king, Tudhaliya IV, has been hearing the case in court on behalf of the royal plaintifs.

His wife has been ordered to take all her belongings and never to return to Amistamru's house. The couple's eldest son Utri-sharruma, who is the crown prince of Ugarit, is permitted to go with his mother if he wishes, but in so doing will forfeit his right to the throne.

The other children of the marriage are deemed to belong to Amistamru and his former wife is not allowed any claim to them. Nor is she permitted to return to them after her husband's death.

Trade drives on amber

Northern Europe, c. 1250 BC

In the Baltic countries, amber means go. The naturally occurring resin is the gold of the north, being used as a unit of exchange for a wide variety of goods, and as an export commodity in its own right.

There are two main amber trade routes from the Baltic to the Mediterranean. One runs to the northern Adriatic via the Alpine passes, and then down the Dalmatian coast to Greece. The other starts in northern Russia via the Danube to the Adriatic. There is also a sea route from Brittany.

The Nordic world has no mineable deposits of tin or copper, which are needed for the manufacture of weapons. Tin is imported from Brittany, Cornwall and Bohemia, and copper from the Alps, using amber and livestock as payment.

Stone warriors to get new defensive role

Corsica, c. 1250 BC

Granite menhirs, imposing 2-m (6-ft)-high statues of warriors are being broken up by the island's new rulers and the materials are being recycled into defensive watchtowers.

The new structures, called torres, serve to defend villages and sometimes also double as places of worship. Sited on easily-defensible heights such as hill tops, spurs or rocky escarpments, torres have a central tower usually linked to the wall defending the village.

They have false corbelled roofs and are entered along a passage which may be open to the elements or covered with stone slabs. They are often small inside; one is only 10 m (33 ft) long by 2 m (6 ft) wide. Some have side chambers, benches and niches.

Fast Facts c. 1250 BC

Mycenae, c. 1250 BC: The Mycenaeans have built massive fortifications around their chief citadel, which include walls made from large irregular blocks of stone. The improvements reflect a growing sense of unease among the rulers, despite the eminence of Mycenaean civilisation.

Minorca, c. 1250 BC: The peoples of this island are building spectacular stone altars called taulas in the centre of their villages. Huge rectangular pillars 4m (13 ft) high and almost 3m (9 ft) wide support rectangular tables in an engineering miracle. Their purpose is uncertain; it is rumoured that they are used for human sacrifice, although they may be for the exposure of corpses.

Peschiera, northern Italy, c. 1250 BC: The people here have invented a safety pin which is proving far more practical for holding clothes in place than the traditional straight pins. They have also invented a metal razor for shaving.

Swiss Alps, c. 1250 BC: Workshops here are becoming expert in knife-making. The early curved blades with wooden handles are being developed into fine specimens with flanged hilts covered with thin sheets of horn. Some are now made entirely of bronze with baroque shapes and a ring to hang them by.

Counted out

Moab plains, c. 1230 BC

Only three survivors of Israel's exodus from Egypt over 40 years ago remain, yet according to a recent census, the population has remained virtually the same size as it was then.

The census is part of the tribal confederacy's preparation to leave the desert and to divide the 'promised land' of Canaan among themselves. It recorded 601,730 men, a fall of less than 2,000 on the number who left Egypt.

Four of the 12 tribes showed a small decline. Reuben was 3,000 down, Gad 5,000, Ephraim and Naphtali both 8,000. Simeon recorded a huge 37,000 decline from its 59,300 in Egypt. The other seven tribes all recorded increases.

The three survivors are Moses, the leader, and the two spies, Joshua and Caleb, who produced a minority report recommending immediate advance into Canaan within months of entering the desert. Joshua has been commissioned publicly as successor to Moses who is now very old and has been told he will not himself enter the land. (Numbers 26; 27:12–23; Deuteronomy 31:1–8)

Bedouin tents outside Jerusalem in 1850. Such scenes of nomadic life are rare today.

So near, yet so far

Moab plains, c. 1225 BC

Moses, the charismatic leader of the Israelites for some 50 years, has died. He has been buried in an unmarked grave on a mountain in

An altar, made of roughly hewn stone.

Moab, just miles short of the Jordan River and the land of Canaan to which he was leading his people.

He will go down in history as one of the all-time greats, who was never corrupted by the immense power he wielded. Almost single-handedly he moulded a hoard of disaffected slaves into a united confederation of 12 tribes which has grown and prospered despite being forced to live as semi-nomads in the inhospitable Desert of Zin for a generation. One of his last acts was to pronounce a blessing on each tribe.

Born a Hebrew but educated in the Egyptian court, Moses spent what many would consider their most creative years as an obscure shepherd in Midian. Called by Yahweh to lead the Israelites out of slavery, he demurred because of his age and his dislike of being upfront. Aaron, his brother, was appointed spokesman as a concession.

His humility never left him, despite occasional lapses due largely to anger and frustration at the barrage of complaints and opposition he encountered from some of his own people. Ironically it was one of these which robbed him of the privilege of completing his own journey to Canaan.

Known as a man of prayer who was closer to Yahweh than anyone else, he fulfilled God's instructions in political, legal and social as well as religious matters. He formulated a complex set of social laws, patterns of worship and a basic theology. Through him Yahweh demonstrated his power and presence with signs the like of which had never been seen before.

He married Zipporah and had two sons by her, Gershom and Eliezer. He is to be succeeded by his personal assistant Joshua, however, rather than by a family dynasty.

(Deuteronomy 33, 34)

Israel pours into Canaan at last

Jordan Valley, c. 1220 BC

They have done it again. A million or more people from the tribes of Israel have crossed a stretch of water on foot without getting a drop into their sandals let alone their baggage. Their long-promised invasion of Canaan has begun.

History repeated itself as the River Jordan, swollen and flowing fast because of the spring rains in the northern uplands, suddenly dried up near Adam, about 25 km (15 miles) north of the crossing point opposite Jericho. It is believed that a landslide temporarily dammed the river in an area where loose soil is frequently washed into the valley by torrential rain coursing down intermittent wadis.

About half a century ago the Israelites escaped from slavery in Egypt across the Sea of Reeds which had been given a timely blow-dry by strong winds. They regard both events as major interventions by Yahweh, fulfilling his promise to make them a mighty nation established in Canaan.

The crossing had been prepared carefully for a week. People had been ordered to prepare food for the journey and to pack their belongings. A small reconnaissance party had been sent ahead and the 12 tribes moved from their campsite in the eastern uplands near Moab into the Jordan Valley where they waited for three days.

On D-day itself there was no sign of any transport to ship the hordes

The valley of the Jordan River.

across the turbulent water. Although not wide, it represents a significant barrier at this time of the year when it is well over 3 m (10 ft) deep and flooding beyond its normal width of about 30 m (100 ft).

But the people broke camp as ordered, and the priests lifted onto their shoulders the ark of the covenant, the symbol of Yahweh's presence, and waded into the water. It was then that the level began to drop dramatically until the stony riverbed was clearly visible. The priests stood with the ark in the middle to reassure the crowds who hurriedly picked their way across. Even the fainthearted believed that Yahweh would not allow the ark to be swept away.

A small group of families belonging to the tribes of Reuben, Gad and Manasseh remained on the east bank. In the occupation strategy they have been allocated territory to the east of the Jordan. However,

their men of military age have crossed into Canaan to support the invasion forces.

When the crossing was completed, 12 stones – one for each tribe – were removed from the spot where the priests had stood to make a memorial cairn on the west bank. Not long after the water rose again.

Further religious rituals have been enacted since, adding to the tension felt by the inhabitants of the region as they face the possibility of being totally inundated by the invaders. The Israelites seem in no hurry to attack, but display an unnerving confidence in Yahweh as they bide their time.

They ritually circumcised all the males who had been born during the desert wanderings, and celebrated the Passover, a re-enactment of the exodus from Egypt.

(Joshua 3–5; cf. 1:10–18; 2:8–12)

Fast Facts 1250–1200 BC

Negev, c. 1235 BC: Aaron, the co-leader of the Israelites and brother of Moses, has died on a desert mountain. He became the spokesman for the nation in Egypt under Moses' direction, and the founder of the order of priests who offer incense and sacrifices. His priestly robes have been passed to his son Eleazar. A 30-day period of mourning has been observed. (Numbers 20:22–29)

Anatolia, 1220 BC: Worshippers in the Hittite capital, Hattusas, congregate in the grotto outside the city walls. Carved portraits of Hittite deities, headed by the sun goddess Arinna and her husband, the weather god Hatti, preside over the frequent religious services. Religion is a very important matter for the royal family, which includes a number of priests among its members, and religious festivals take precedence over all other matters including military campaigns.

Greece c. 1200: The great Mycenaean palaces lie in ruins, large areas have been evacuated, and a demoralised population is seeking shelter in the debris. The palaces were constructed of wood and rubble-cored walls, making them vulnerable both to earthquake and fire from the oil lamps. The Mycenaean culture had been a shadow of its earlier glory, and the palaces had become administrative centres and storehouses.

China, c. 1200 BC: The country's first light chariots are being manufactured. They have between 18 and 26 spokes per wheel and sparkle with polished bronze. The prestigious vehicles, which are intended mostly for hunting, are believed to have been copied from a Caucasian design which has been brought to China via central Asia and the northern steppe.

All fall down in city!

Jericho, c. 1220 BC

Flesh and stones have one thing in common: they both crumble at the approach of the Israelites.

The peoples of eastern Canaan go weak at the knees as they observe the invaders roaming like locusts across the Jordan Valley and threatening to consume all obstacles in

Gold, silver and metal objects have been looted and placed in their religious sanctuary.

Only one family has been spared, ironically that of a woman whose profession – prostitution – would normally render her liable to instant execution under Israelite law. But Rahab had hidden the Israelites'

The exact site of the Jericho destroyed by Joshua is unknown. Archaeologists have found evidence of fortified settlements and violent destructions at the site, but the dates of the remains do not so far appear to tally with those of Joshua's invasion. The biblical record does not claim that the city was large or heavily fortified, however. The walls which fell down could have been the remains of previous fortifications or a ring of houses forming a protective barrier around the settlement. It is also possible that a nearby site had taken on the name of Jericho at this time. For the biblical writers, the significance of its destruction was that the victory came through an 'act of God' and not by military muscle.

their path. Even the walls and houses of Jericho have collapsed before them, as if in obeisance to their superiority – or to their God.

In their first major offensive since crossing into Canaan, the Israelites under the command of Joshua circled the settlement and marched their army around it every day for six days, led by their priests trumpeting a haunting wail through ram's horns. On the seventh day they marched round seven times in silence, and the weakened foundations gave way at the sound of their one triumphal shout.

The settlement has been destroyed and its inhabitants killed.

reconnaissance party some weeks before, and a pre-arranged signal of a red band fluttering from her house ensured that the attackers left it alone. She is said to have recognised that Yahweh was unstoppable, and was prepared to assist him and live rather than resist him and die.

Following the attack, Joshua laid a curse on anyone who should attempt to rebuild the settlement. That did nothing to improve the confidence of the leaders of other city-states who are now wondering who will be next to face the Israelite foe – and if they will be left standing afterwards.

(Joshua 2; 6)

Oath proves stronger than fiction

Judean uplands, c. 1210 BC

Yahweh is a God who keeps his promises even when he – or his people – have been deceived into making them. That startling truth has been discovered, to their great relief, by the people of Gibeon.

They have been given a permanent guarantee of safety by the Israelites who they tricked into signing a treaty. Most other nations would have torn it up and massacred its authors when the deception became public, but not Israel.

The Gibeonites, occupying a settlement a short distance north of Jerusalem, had allied with several city-states to oppose the invaders. But before resorting to brute force they tried a little guile first.

A delegation posed as travellers from a distant country, complete with travel-worn clothes and mouldy provisions. Their proposal for a peace treaty was accepted. Although the Israelites are forbidden to make treaties with people in Canaan, they have no instructions about dealing with people from further afield, and they did not think to ask their priests to enquire of Yahweh for some.

When they uncovered the scam they considered that vengeance was the greater of two evils. The more honourable solution was to keep the treaty, allow the Gibeonites to live, but to conscript them as domestic servants in perpetuity. Part of their new role will be to supply Israel with water from the major cistern (reservoir) which until now the Gibeonites have controlled.

Asked to explain their deception, the leaders of Gibeon said they had heard of Israel's plan to wipe out all the people of Canaan. 'We were scared of losing our lives,' they explained. 'Slavery seemed preferable to death.'

(Joshua 9)

Invaders are not invincible

Judean uplands, c. 1220 BC

A temporary set-back inflicted on the Israelites by the defenders of Ai has shown up the weak spot in the invaders' armoury.

An initial attack on this easy target was repelled by determined Canaanites. The defeat which cost Israel 36 lives was attributed to the withdrawal of Yahweh's support following a breach of religious laws by a handful of their people.

During an inquiry into the defeat, the Israelites used their unique system of casting lots to identify the lawbreakers. The chief priest carries a pair of dice called Urim and Thummin which are thrown according to a strict procedure so as to determine guilt or innocence.

The leaders worked through the tribes, and then the families of the selected tribe, until the culprit was found. He was named as Achan, from the tribe of Judah. He had kept for himself a robe and about 3 kg (over 6 lb) of gold and silver which had been taken from Jericho and dedicated solely for the use of Yahweh.

His collection of souvenirs was regarded as having been stolen from God himself, and the punish-

Ai was a short distance to the south-east of Bethel. The name Ai means 'ruin': it may have been an already ruined settlement used as a fortress outpost, a first line of defence, by the people of Bethel.

ment – death by stoning – was implemented swiftly.

The fortress of Ai, an outpost of Bethel in the hill country about 25 km (15 miles) north-west of Jericho (see picture caption) represents a strategic foothold for Joshua. After dealing with the internal corruption, he captured it at the second attempt. Its defenders were lured to a battle line outside it and an ambush squad at the rear simply walked into the undefended fort

and set it on fire.

The initial defeat of the 12-tribe confederacy for the sin of one person in one tribe reveals the close unity which has been established by them and the absolute loyalty to Yahweh and to each other which is expected. Human nature being what it is, other Canaanites may now be hoping that Israelites will prove to be their own worst enemies.

(Joshua 7; 8)

A long day's fight beats five cities

Gibeon, c. 1210 BC

Time seemed to stand still as a powerful confederation of five city-states which had attacked Gibeon were destroyed and their inhabitants executed by the Israelites. The victors had come to the aid of Gibeon, with whom they recently made a treaty.

The massacre followed an astonishing feat of endurance and determination by the Israelites under the leadership of their general, Joshua. This was accompanied by phenomena which can only be put down as acts of God.

For the Israelites, it began with an exhausting all-night march to Gibeon from Gilgal, a distance of

some 32 km (20 miles), most of it uphill. Instead of pitching their camp and resting, they immediately pitched into battle, and routed the confederation. A severe hailstorm wreaked havoc among the fleeing soldiers, the giant stones claiming more casualties than the swords.

It is understood that Joshua had prayed to Yahweh for extended time to finish the battle. To the victors that entailed super-efficiency; to the vanquished night could not fall soon enough. The cloudy sky after the storm may have kept the temperature cool enough for him to continue to fight without a midday break. The Israelites

certainly seem to have been endowed with superhuman strength to have achieved so much in a single day.

A poet's chronicle suggests that both sun and moon were stopped in their tracks for the whole morning thus lengthing the day. To the Canaanites who were astrologically-minded this would have been a bad omen and contributed to their sudden flight.

The next day Joshua captured the five kings and hung their bodies on trees as a sign of their disgrace. Their cities of Jerusalem, Hebron, Jarmuth, Lachish and Debir have been ransacked by the Israelites.

(Joshua 10:1–28)

Israel's unique battle plan

In many respects the Israelite confederacy is no different from any of the tribes and city-states vying for *lebensraum* in Canaan through what they regard as holy wars ordered by their gods. Indeed, it seems remarkable that Yahweh, who by the Israelites' own accounts is a God of justice who welcomes aliens and strangers, should continue to support such an aggressive and at times ruthless people. They frequently slaughter anything that moves when they take over a settlement.

In a highly unusual spiritual experience, as the Israelites set out on their conquest, Joshua is reported to have been confronted by an angel of God who had taken the guise of a heavenly warrior. In reply to Joshua's question as to which side the angel was on, he said simply, 'neither'.

(Joshua 5:13–15)

Ordering Joshua to remove his shoes as a sign of subservience in Yahweh's presence, the angel implied that God's purposes are far greater than tribal ambitions and human skirmishes, even if his purposes somehow incorporate such things into the overall plan.

It almost looks as if he has accepted Israel warts and all with the intention of slowly bringing them round to his point of view. According to one source Yahweh chose them not because they were numerous or powerful, but simply because he loved them and was keeping his bargain with Abraham

(Deuteronomy 7:7,8).

That may help to explain their commitment to wholesale destruction, and their adoption of unusual methods. Their total war policy – shared by many tribes – focuses on the religious 'ban' in which enemy peoples and goods are given over wholly to Yahweh by being destroyed. Valuables such as gold and silver are normally saved to adorn the national shrine. Souvenir hunting, treaties and intermarriage

Theatre of war

Most nations including the Israelites use bows and arrows with a range of some 300 m (330 yd). For closer fighting, wooden-shafted spears with bronze heads, curved swords and short axes are wielded with deadly effect. The Israelites have no trained standing army; men of fighting age are called up as and when needed from all the tribes.

Many Canaanite city-states are fortified with thick walls built against a steep bank, with a deep ditch in front. The walls are topped with walkways and battlements to protect defenders. A smooth curved slope rising from the ditch protects the lower part of the wall. The walls at Hazor are about 15 m (50 ft) high, with a moat as deep and some 80 m (260 ft) wide.

The earthen fortifications and walls of Hazor, strategically situated on a hilltop. Mount Hermon can be seen in the distance.

with conquered tribes are strictly forbidden.

(cf. Deuteronomy 7:1–6)

The policy is not consistent, however. At Ai the people were allowed to plunder livestock and possessions, perhaps as a concession to their humanity following Achan's fall into temptation (Joshua 8:1–2, 26–29). The dominant concept in any conflict is that of fighting for Yahweh, not for personal or national gain.

That leads them into unusual methods, the processing around Jericho being one (Joshua 6). Another was during the northern campaign when Joshua destroyed

Hazor. Instead of killing or taking his opponents' horses – valuable war machines – he lamed them so that they could never again be used in conflict. He also burned the chariots, which any other commander would have seen as a priceless asset for future battles.

(Joshua 11:6–9)

The Israelites, it seems, are being encouraged in these small ways not to ape their neighbours slavishly. Instead, they are to rely on relatively simple weapons, which in turn increases their dependence on Yahweh. It is this which seems to dominate his strategy, although not always his people's.

Occupiers hold the forts

Canaan, c. 1200 BC

Pockets of indigenous Canaanite peoples continue to live in uneasy tension with their warlike Israelite and Philistine neighbours. But the tidal wave of conquest which has swept over this small land for some 20 years appears to have abated. For the time being, people of all cultures are picking up the pieces of normal life again.

Israel now effectively controls the whole of Canaan from Kadesh and Hazor in the north above Galilee, to Lachish and Hebron deep in the Negev to the west of the Dead Sea. The five Philistine cities of Gaza, Ashdod, Ashkelon, Gath and Ekron remain fiercely independent, and in the north-west the Phoenicians remain largely in control and few Israelite expeditions have penetrated their defences.

The land has been parcelled out among the 12 tribes of the occupying confederacy, 3 of whom are now settling back on the eastern side of the Jordan. Settlements throughout the region have been given to the Levites, the sanctuary attendants who do not qualify for specific territory.

An additional six sites have been designated 'cities of refuge', safe havens for people accused of unintentional manslaughter where revenge killings are prohibited.

(Joshua 10:29–22:34)

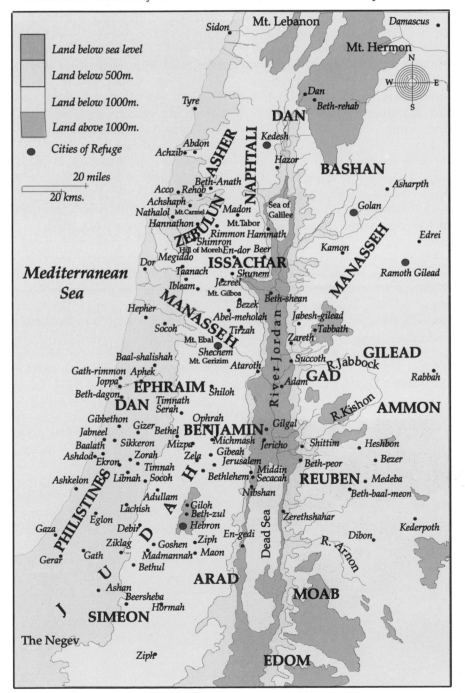

Hittites have collapsed

Anatolia, c. 1200 BC

The mighty Hittite empire has collapsed only a few decades since it dominated near eastern culture. The final agents of its destruction are said to be the marauding sea peoples flooding across the region.

The Hittites have been under pressure for some years. Harvests have failed and grain has been imported from as far away as Egypt to stave off famine. Politically, Assyria has been pressing them from the east and the vassal states in Syria have not been paying their taxes. The Gasga people have been menacing the northern borders too.

It had looked for a while as though King Suppiluliumas II had succeeded in halting the decline. He defeated the Assyrians and regained control of the Isuwan copper mines. He was also recovering support from Syrian vassals and had won an important sea battle off Cyprus.

But all was in vain. The Sea Peoples first cut off the northwestern trade route, and conquered Cilicia and Cyprus to cut off the copper supplies. When northern Syria fell to them, Anatolia was left weak and relatively defenceless.

The Hittites have dominated the region for 250 years, maintaining power by controlling trade routes through which they received essential raw materials.

c. 1200 BC

We'll stick to Yahweh say Israelites

Shechem, c. 1200 BC

Joshua, the aging military and spiritual leader of the Israelite confederacy, has led the 12 tribes in a solemn renewal of their covenant with Yahweh in which they have pledged to serve him alone.

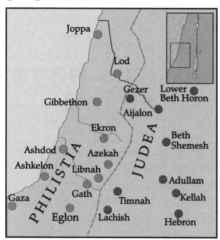

A formidable array of well-defended towns presented Israel with a virtually impenetrable barrier towards the sea. Philistine entrenchments were well dug in.

In what Joshua himself conceded may be his last major speech, he reminded a national assembly of the great and mighty acts of God which had brought them to the 'Promised Land', and urged them to remain faithful to the Yahweh who had stuck by them through bad times and good.

He warned them that disobedience could have disastrous effects, however. The indigenous peoples would then become Israel's conquerors and regain the land, he said.

His stirring message ended with a challenge to choose this day whom you will serve: 'Yahweh or the gods of other nations.' The people made a resounding response: 'We will serve Yahweh,' they shouted back. Following the familiar pattern of contemporary treaties, which base rules on a historical overview, Joshua declared the assembly to be the statutory witnesses to the document.

It was the second covenant renewal during Joshua's leadership. A similar gathering took place on the mountains Ebal and Gerizim near Shechem some years ago, and included animal sacrifices and public reading of the Law of Moses.

The choice of Shechem on both occasions was probably intended to reinforce the Israelites' sense of being in the stream of history controlled by Yahweh. It was here that their ancestor Abraham had set up the first-ever altar to him in Canaan.

(Joshua 23; 24; cf. 8:30–35; Genesis 12:6,7)

Waves of Sea Peoples flood region

Near East, c. 1200 BC

They come in ships. They come in wagons. Tall warriors wearing feathered headdresses and accompanied by their families and their belongings are pouring over the whole region, taking over settlements and killing their opponents, in seemingly endless waves.

No one knows where these Sea Peoples have come from. Like primordial creatures emerging from the deep they seem to be washed up on the shores of the eastern and southern Mediterranean to forage on land. Some say they come from the island of Crete. Others, perhaps unrelated in anything except ambition, are said to come from Turkey, Libya and even Asia.

And among the deadly flotsam they have brought with them is a new metal called iron with which they make devastating weapons, far more technologically advanced than anything known so far.

Nowhere from Ugarit in the north to Egypt in the south is undrenched by their destructive surf. They are reportedly responsible for washing away the final remains of the mighty Hittite empire. They have flushed out the inhabitants of Sidon who have taken refuge in nearby Tyre. And they have cascaded through southern Canaan in an orgy of destruction.

The only beneficial effect so far seen by the Canaanites is that the invaders – who in this area are often known as Philistines, but who have other names elsewhere – have become a military moat to keep the Egyptians at bay. But there is always the risk that the moat will overflow and flood a region already reeling under the invasion of the Israelites.

The solid stones of the foundations of the East Gate to the city of Shechem.

Joint ventures fund risky trade

Ugarit, c. 1200 BC

Merchants are clubbing together to fund overseas trading ventures. In one recent agreement four merchant venturers amassed 1,000 shekels of silver to finance an expedition to Egypt.

It is not always a safe bet. Many merchants lose their lives in the pursuit of wealth, usually at the hands of bandits for whom merchandise is of higher value than human life. Townspeople in Ugarit are responsible for the safety of foreign merchants and must pay compensation if one is murdered and the killer is not caught. But not every city-state is so humanitarian.

The richest merchants form a class of their own in Ugarit, known as the mariannu, a title granted by the king which bestows a status second only to that of the royal family. Some are hugely wealthy; one is reported to own several estates and to have been given whole villages by the king.

Ugarit has become the chief trading post in northern Syria, a position it has held unchallenged for 200 years despite its relatively minor political significance. It is a terminal for land routes from Anatolia, Syria and Mesopotamia, and is also a thriving sea port.

The goods which pass through it range widely from all the basic foodstuffs including grain, fruit, oil, cheese and wine; fabrics and yarn including flax, linen and its own speciality of purple dyed wool; metals of all kinds; and livestock from cattle to geese.

Among the more exotic items marketed here are myrrh from Arabia, lapis lazuli from northern Afghanistan and ebony from central Africa.

A bearded trader bearing what seems to be a gift of gold. From Susa in northern Syria.

Israel faces tough opponents

Canaan, c. 1200 BC

The twelve tribes of Israel are settling into their Promised Land. Every tribe has been given its own territory. But the Israelites will have to secure Canaan against numerous threats before they can consider their conquest complete.

Watching with ominous interest are many people-groups. Some, like the Philistines, possess military might and fortified cities; others threaten Canaan from terrain that is easily defended and almost impossible to attack.

Mighty neighbours are only part of Israel's problems. The conquerors are at risk from inside their new borders as well. There are pockets of resistance that must now be eradicated – a task for which the Israelite soldiers will need to develop new, guerrilla skills.

Both Israel's strength and weakness lie in the high ground that forms most of its territory. Though the hills and plateaux of Canaan are a natural defence against attacking armies, they are criss-crossed by valleys and interrupted by plains. These offer shelter to resistance fighters and also divide Israelite territory into separate areas, making it difficult for the occupying army to co-ordinate its response to military threats. The Israelites have at least one major advantage. They have developed highly efficient water-storage systems.

All change in Mexico

Mexico, c. 1200–1000 BC

Dramatic changes are taking place in Mexican social structures.

Originally nomadic, the people have been living in agricultural villages since c. 3000, but now the beginnings of urban society are appearing as many of the people begin to leave the villages and build cities.

This long-established people-group, who were hunting big game in the region as long ago as c. 9000, has begun to erect monumental buildings, displaying the characteristically horizontal design that is a feature of Mexican architecture at this period. Unusual clay figurines are also to be seen.

A Moabite warrior, from Rediom-al-Aabed in Jordan, c. 1200 BC.

Philistia holds world in iron grip

Canaan, c. 1190 BC

The Philistines are holding the rest of Palestine (or Canaan, which is now being named after them) in an iron grip – literally – as they refuse to reveal details of their new metal technology. And every nation in the world would like to know the secret.

It's believed that the Philistines brought it from Cyprus, where Greek settlers were pioneering the use of metals. Today iron-working is a closely-guarded monopoly in Philistia and neighbouring peoples have to pay a heavy premium for access to Philistine skills – if, that is, the Philistines decide to co-operate.

Iron gives any army an overwhelming advantage in battle. For example, a sortie from the hills of Judah into the Philistine plains during the southern Canaan campaigns had to be abandoned in the face of Philistine iron chariots and weapons. So by choosing who is denied access to the new technology the Philistines are guaranteed military domination of the plains.

The Philistines came to the region

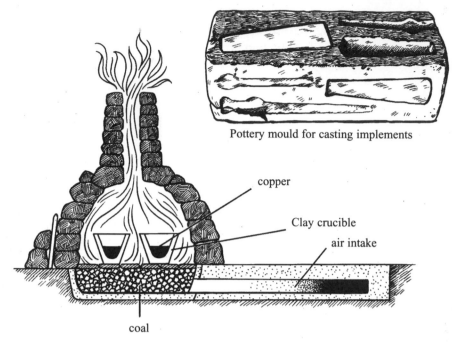

Pottery mould for casting implements

copper

Clay crucible

air intake

coal

A reconstructed copper-smelting furnace found in the eleventh-century level of Tell Qasile in Philistia. Two clay crucibles containing the remains of smelted copper were also found.

as part of the mass movement of Sea Peoples in the early twelfth century. Large groups only settled there shortly before the Israelites' arrival in Canaan. The five Philistine cities (Gaza, Ashkelon, Ashdod, Ekron and Gath) control the adjacent Mediterranean waters so completely that they are known as the Philistine Sea.

Forgetful Israelites choose the bad old days

Canaan, c. 1180 BC

It seems that the Israelites will never learn. They are once again turning away from their God, Yahweh, and are flirting with the religions of their neighbours. They are intermarrying with Canaanites and even serving Canaanite gods; Israelites are regularly seen among the worshippers at Canaanite shrines and sacred places, bowing down before the pagan idols, the most widely worshipped of which seems to be Baal.

Since the death of Joshua the nation has passed through troubled times. There is a sense of being leaderless, despite Judah's successful campaigns against the Philistines, the taking of three of

their strongholds and the sacking of the Canaanite city of Jerusalem. Yet the days of Moses and Joshua are well remembered, and few nations have as much cause to be grateful to their god. This makes the Israelites' frequent apostasy all the more perplexing.

The Israelites seem locked into a pattern of apostasy followed by remorse and forgiveness. Against that background the judges have risen to occupy a key role in national leadership. Established under Moses originally as community arbitrators, the Israelite judges are today a major force in political life, though the Book of the Law remains in the keeping of the priests.

Othniel is victorious

Canaan, c. 1180 BC

Judge Othniel has led the Israelites to victory against their cruel oppressors, the Aramaeans, whose subjects they have been for eight long years. The defeat of King Cushan-Rishathaim today marks the end of a period that many have interpreted as the God of Israel punishing his people for their flagrant rejection of him.

Israelites claim that their God led them out of slavery in Egypt and guided them through the desert to Canaan. But he seems to have stood aside as they suffered under the Aramaeans. Othniel's rapid rise to power coincided with a time of national repentance.

(Judges 3:7–11)

He stooped to conquer

Canaan, c. 1190 BC

People everywhere share the ambition to accomplish what they perceive to be their life's work before they die or become too old. Few will rest as contentedly in their graves as Joshua the son of Nun. He led the tribes of Israel into Canaan after 40 years of desert nomadism, directed their military conquests, and marshalled them into their designated tribal territories.

The centenarian has been buried in the hill country of Ephraim, his own tribal region. All Israel looks back with gratitude to a hero who overcame his natural fears through a deep dependence on Yahweh. He was one of that rare breed of leaders who are not afraid to admit their need of spiritual succour.

Joshua was in his early teens when Moses led the Israelite slaves out of Egypt into the Sinai Desert. As the young man grew, his spiritual qualities and leadership gifts quickly emerged. Recognised as someone on whom Yahweh's Spirit rested, Joshua was appointed as Moses' personal assistant. His long apprenticeship gave him first-hand experience of the joys and frustrations of public life.

On his appointment Moses changed his name from Hoshea (salvation) to Joshua (God saves), perhaps in prophetic anticipation of his future role. Later commissioned to be Moses' successor, Joshua continued in his subservient role until the old man died.

Facing the future alone and with some trepidation, he is said to have been encouraged by a message from Yahweh which told him to 'be strong and very courageous, for I have commanded you to lead these people into the land I have promised them. As I was with Moses, so I shall be with you'. He might have been forgiven for thinking that such courage was easier commanded than practised, but Yahweh also instructed him to meditate day and night on the Israelite law which his predecessor had written down. It became a source of constant strength and inspiration for him.

His faithfulness to God dated back to his youth. He and his friend Caleb voiced dissent at the pessimistic report of their fellow spies after a fact-finding tour of the Promised Land shortly after the exodus from Egypt. Out of faith, more than youthful brashness, they recommended advance but were outvoted. But only they lived to eat the fruit of Canaan.

The countryside of central Canaan today, near Sebaste.

Joshua has left no obvious successor. The Israelites, who claim that their 'king' is Yahweh, are likely to depend on national leaders who emerge as needed for specific tasks, rather than on a permanent central court and civil service. Each of the twelve tribes is semi-autonomous and has its own leadership and disciplinary arrangements. It is an ideal form of government which can only survive for as long as the tribes remain true to the religious faith and law which unites them in a common life and purpose.

(cf. Exodus 24:13; 32:17; 33:11; Numbers 13:16; 14:6–38; 27:18–23; Deuteronomy 31:1–8; Joshua 1; 24)

Fast Facts
1200–1170 BC

Crete, c. 1200 BC: Refugees from Mycenaean Greece are pouring into Crete as they flee the troubles at home. A new society built on a combination of Minoan and Mycenaean cultures is being developed on the island.

Britain, c. 1200 BC: The weather is definitely getting worse. Average annual rainfall has increased considerably. Some settlements have been flooded out of existence and some farmlands are turning into bogs. The population is falling, probably because of plagues spread in the damp conditions, and available farmland has been reduced due to over-cultivation as well as to the floods.

China, c. 1200 BC: A regional ruler has been buried in one of the most elaborate tombs ever built, at Dayangzhou in the Jiangxi province near the Yangtze River. It contains 356 pottery vessels, 50 bronze vessels, over 400 bronze weapons and tools, and 150 carved jades. Some of the bronzes are large, including a half-metre-long tiger with a bird perched on its back. One of the jades is of a bird-man. The tomb reveals that the Shang dynasty's culture has spread far from the Yellow River.

Peloponnesia, 1190 BC: Reports from Egypt mention that 'the northerners are being disturbed in their isles'. This refers to the arrival of Mycenaean colonists in Peloponnesia and Kephallenia. They come in peace and the colourful, quirky artwork that instantly identifies their pottery is beginning to be seen around the region, especially in Cyprus.

Egypt, 1187 BC: Rameses III has successfully repulsed an attempted invasion by the Sea Peoples, and is pursuing his defeated enemies deep into Palestine and Syria. Rameses, who made defeat of the Sea Peoples a policy matter when crowned in 1198, conducted a brilliant military operation. The invaders were well into the Nile before Rameses' fleet, which had been lying in wait, struck. The Egyptians' treatment of the invaders was decisive and savage, sending an unmistakable message to any other Mediterranean bandits who might contemplate attacking Egypt.

Canaan, c. 1175 BC: Shamgar the Israelite has killed 600 Philistines with an ox goad. His non-Israelite name has led some to suspect that he is the product of one of the mixed marriages between Israelites and local people which is believed to have provoked the wrath of God on the nation. But Shamgar's exploits have saved Israel from the Philistine threat, at least for the forseeable future. (Judges 3:31)

87

Ehud delivers back-hander to Moabites

Gilgal, c. 1180 BC

Ehud the Judge has sent King Eglon of Moab on his way to the next life with a single thrust of a home-made sword. All Israel is cheering both his bravery and his cunning.

Ehud was heading a delegation to deliver tribute tax to Eglon, whose legendary girth matched his enormous wealth. But he also carried a surprise back-hander. At the Moabite court he persuaded Eglon that he had a personal message for him from God, to be delivered in private.

Alone with the tyrant in the royal chambers, he grabbed his hidden sword and killed the king. Eglon probably never saw the weapon: Ehud moved quickly as the sword vanished deep into the folds of Eglon's huge belly.

Ehud made his escape, locking the doors after him. The servants assumed their master was using the lavatory, only becoming concerned when he did not reappear. Eventually they broke down the doors and found the king dead.

The Israelite's success was due to his left-handedness, considered by his fellow-countrymen to be a serious handicap. The sword was strapped to his right thigh, where no security guard would bother to look for a weapon.

Ehud meanwhile summoned the Israelites to a pre-emptive attack, and is reported to have destroyed 10,000 Moabites. There is now every prospect of a peaceful future for the twelve tribes.

The Moabite oppression had lasted for 18 years. After the death of Othniel the nation turned away from Yahweh. In what was taken to be punishment from God, Eglon captured Jericho, a show-piece of the newly-established Israel. Some went so far as to describe Eglon, and his allies as 'God's instruments'.

The Moabites had ruled in the area at least half a century before the Israelites arrived, and treated the usurpers with contempt, imposing punishing taxes.

(Judges 3:12–30)

The foundations of storehouses and of some of the city walls are all that remain of the once proud city of Hazor.

City rises from ashes

Hazor, c. 1170 BC

The Canaanites have rebuilt Hazor, their old stronghold 24 km (15 miles) north of Galilee, to become almost three times the size of Jericho. The Israelites face a new and powerful threat.

Always a strategic gateway between Egypt and Asia, Hazor was an obvious target for Canaanite re-occupation. Ironically, this area was decisively conquered by Joshua but now oppresses Israel – a fact taken by many as a sign of God's displeasure at Israel's continuing apostasy.

Even in ruins Hazor was an impressive sight. Forty thousand people lived there, in a city extending for 121,000 sq m (30 acres) overlooking a lower plateau of 708,000 sq m (175 acres). Around the plateau mighty earthworks and a dry moat completed a virtually impregnable defensive ring that forced invaders to scale a rampart approximately 30 m (100 ft) high. Joshua left Hazor as a pile of ash and rubble, a visible reminder of his genius as leader and the greatness of Israel's God.

The Hazorite leader Jabin is known as a king of Canaan, and Sisera, who commands the Hazorite army, is a local dignitary in his own right. Heavily armed and equipped with a massive force of 900 iron chariots, the Hazorites now represent the most serious threat to Israel since the conquest.

(Joshua 11:1–11; Judges 4:1–3)

Fast Facts 1170–1150 BC

Egypt, c. 1170 BC: The royal funerary temples and graveyards of Thebes have seen the first workers' strike. In protest at not being paid on time, builders stopped work until their demands were met.

Egypt, c. 1160 BC: Economic problems continue to plague the Pharaohs. A combination of food shortage (caused partly by lower than anticipated Nile flooding), a rising powerful and corrupt priestly elite, industrial unrest in the royal mortuary and a growing crime rate all combine to place the people under strain.

Babylon, c. 1158 BC: After an unprecedented 576 years, the Kassite dynasty has ended with the death of its last king, Enlil-nadin-ahi. In recent years it had been raided by Assyrians and Elamites (Persians) and effectively ruled by the Elamites despite strong internal resistance. Many treasures and statues have been taken to the Elamite capital, Susa, including the laws of Hammurabi and the national statue of the god Marduk.

Britain, c. 1150 BC: Hill forts are becoming more common. Some are surrounded by sophisticated ramparts of clay and rubble, similar to those built by the Urnfield people in mainland Europe. British warriors now carry leaf-shaped bronze swords, spears with their heads fastened by a pin, and shields of leather, wood, or (for ceremonial purposes only) bronze. Bronze razors for shaving are however in common useage.

Jael strikes blow for women's liberation

Ephraim, c. 1170 BC
Women strode in where men feared to tread and liberated Israel from the Canaanites led by General Sisera.

The view from Mount Carmel onto the Kishon Valley.

Plain of Esdraelon, usually firm ground favouring Israel's enemies, became a field of mud. Sisera's chariots became a liability that ensured defeat.

Judge Deborah, a head of state involved in daily adjudication of civil cases, told Barak the warrior that God had chosen him to lead an army of 10,000 against Sisera, commander of King Jabin's army.

She even predicted the location of Sisera's defeat – the Kishon River which runs from the hill country to the Mediterranean, north of Carmel. But Barak refused to fight unless Deborah accompanied him. She agreed to do so but assured Barak that because of his timidity the honour of defeating Sisera would belong to a woman.

Though the Israelite forces were slender they received supernatural help: the Kishon was suddenly flooded by freak rains, and the

The fleeing army was pursued through a narrow valley which restricted Sisera's ability to regroup. His retreat was further hampered by flash floods caused by the swollen rivers from the hills.

Sisera abandoned his doomed and shattered army and attempted to make his way on foot back to Hazor.

He sought overnight shelter in the tent of Heber the Kenite, whose wife, Jael – a secret sympathiser with the Israelites – split his head with a tent peg as he slept.

Later she handed the corpse over to Barak, who had proof of the victory he wanted (and for which he had fought with personal courage and brilliant leadership), but had been robbed of the glory of slaying the oppressor himself.

The Israelites believe that this marks a decisive turning point in the struggle against King Jabin.

Deborah's chant of victory could hardly contrast more strongly with the initial timidity of Barak. It was a pouring out of praise to the God in whom Barak had been unable to trust; emphasising, as he could not, that no armed force in the world could withstand a people who enjoyed the protection of Israel's God.

She took the opportunity, however, of reminding those who were celebrating with her that the nation – even including herself and Barak – had had to be woken from their pessimism and truly believe that God could bring victory; and while she led the cheering crowds in celebrating the tribes of Israel who had fought in the battle, she had some stern words for the tribes who had not.

Indeed, the victory song might well be construed as a manifesto of national unity to be built on trust and obedience to God.

(Judges 4, 5)

Girl bought for mixed bag

Egypt, c. 1150 BC
Despite increased trade between Egypt and Crete, the standard medium of exchange – silver – is often substituted for mixed goods.

In one recent deal, a slave girl's price was fixed in silver but paid for by clothes and bronze vessels, each priced separately but the total equivalent to her silver value. The purchaser called in the bronze from neighbours who already owed him credit.

Major foreign trade is carefully controlled by the state, but sandals, textiles, other minor items and foodstuffs are often sold to individuals in waterfront shops near to the ports.

Gideon: modest man of faith

Ophrah, c. 1150 BC

Sombre crowds gathered today at Ophrah of the Abiezrites (part of the tribe of Manasseh) for the burial of Gideon. His long career as Israel's fifth judge was marked by brilliant military victories and a strong commitment to national dependence on Yahweh.

He was buried within sight of the altar that he had erected as a young man, to mark the place where the angel of the Lord had appeared to him. For Gideon, Ophrah was the place where Yahweh gave him his life's work. He was to liberate the Israelites from the Midianites, the latest in a long list of hostile nations oppressing Israel. Like those others, it is claimed, the Midianites were permitted by Israel's God to be instruments of his punishment for rejecting him. In this case the rejection had lasted for seven years.

His first test of military skill came when, in response to a Midianite-Amalekite offensive, he called up the armies of Manasseh, Asher, Zebulun and Naphtali. He asked God to confirm his leadership. He laid a woollen fleece out overnight and asked God to allow only the fleece to be soaked by dew. Still fearful and uncertain, he asked that the next night the fleece should remain dry while the ground was soaked.

Most old soldiers at the funeral remembered the army's perplexity when Gideon, operating under direct orders from God, sent most of the men home. With 300 men out of the original 32,000 he went on to rout the enemy in a surprise night attack.

He showed considerable diplomatic skills when his allies the Ephraimites took umbrage at a late appeal for help against the Midianites. He played down his own victory and gave them credit for theirs. His determination was displayed when he and his exhausted men pursued the kings

A shepherd carrying his sheep over his shoulder in the traditional manner.

Holiness begins at home

Gideon's nickname, Jerub-baal ('Let Baal deal with him'), was given to him early in his career, and the name stuck.

It dates from what Gideon regarded as his first mission from Yahweh – to tear down an altar to Baal which his own father, Joash, had built. God had already commanded the Israelites to destroy all heathen shrines and altars in their midst. It was perhaps fitting that the man who was to be God's instrument against the nations should start by putting things right in his own family.

Gideon carried out the task with the help of ten men. It was a strongly Baal-worshipping district, so they worked under cover of darkness.

The next morning the local community found the altar destroyed, and with it the sacred pole that had stood nearby. A new altar had been built in their place, on which a bullock had been sacrificed. Among the ashes of the fire in which it had been burnt, the horrified Ophrahites could still make out charred fragments of the sacred pole. It was a typical sacrifice to Yahweh.

The townspeople easily tracked down Gideon and his helpers. They confronted Joash and demanded the death penalty for his son.

But Joash stood firm. He pointed out that if Baal was as powerful as they believed, he was quite capable of executing his enemies himself. To take that privilege away from him was a supreme insult to Baal. So it was that Gideon acquired a new name – 'Jerub-baal' – and Joash, some say, made the first steps to repentance and reconciliation with God.

(Judges 6:25–32)

Zebah and Zalmunna, who had slain his brothers. He executed the kings and punished the towns that sheltered them from justice.

He refused to found a royal dynasty, telling the Israelites, 'The Lord will rule over you.' The only trophy he took from his conquered foes was their golden earrings, which he used to make a religious image in Ophrah. It was an act of indulgence which backfired; despite his own loyalty to Yahweh the image became an object of devotion for others.

The presence of many of Gideon's 70 sons among the mourners was a reminder that his legacy may be an uneasy one. His prosperous old age, his many wives, and the birth of a son Abimelech by a concubine, all contrast – not entirely happily – with the young warrior whose exploits are now distant history.

(Judges 6–8)

Tragic story ends happily ever after

Judah, c. 1150 BC

Wealthy farmer Boaz and his new bride, Ruth the Moabite, have crowned a fairy-tale romance with the wedding of the year.

It was all smiles as family and friends toasted the happy couple – a very different situation to the

The corn was separated from the husk with a large seive-like basket. A fork was used to gather up the straw.

desperate plight of Ruth and her mother-in-law Naomi only a year ago. Add to this romance the ingredients of a chance meeting, an extraordinary coincidence and a nail-biting legal cliff-hanger, and you have an epic which proves that real life is stranger than fiction. ...

The story began many years ago in Judah. Naomi was married to Elimelech, both Ephrathites from Bethlehem, Judah. They had two sons. Famine was raging in Judah; Moab was a land of fertile plains and well-stocked pastures. Elimelech took his family there, but tragedy followed tragedy. First Elimelech, then both their sons died, leaving three lonely widows.

One of Naomi's daughters-in-law, Orpah, stayed in Moab in the hope of a second marriage; the other, Ruth, gave up any chance of remarriage to look after Naomi in her old age. 'Where you go I will go. ... Your people will be my people and your God my God,' she announced in what must be one of the most remarkable undertakings ever made by a Moabitess to a Judahite woman.

Even more remarkable was the

coincidence that found Ruth gleaning in the field of wealthy farmer Boaz under the Levirate law allowing foreigners to pick up any grain dropped by the harvesters. When Boaz was told her name he assured her that he had heard of her concern for her mother-in-law and was greatly touched.

Boaz gave his labourers secret orders to deliberately drop more plentiful gleanings than usual. It was only when Ruth arrived home with a huge load of barley and told Naomi of Boaz's generosity that she discovered who her benefactor really was: a close relative of her dead father-in-law, Elimelech.

Naomi instantly realised that here was a literally heaven-sent solution to the problem of Ruth's future. Under Levirate law, a man is bound to marry the widow of a kinsman who dies without an heir, and the obligation extends to the next-of-kin. Naomi urged her daughter to ask Boaz to marry her. Boaz gladly agreed. It was a considerable undertaking, for it involved not only marrying Ruth but purchasing the family land from Naomi, thus taking on all Elimelech's responsibilities.

There was one more obstacle to be overcome in this extraordinary courtship. The law states that if a relative is to act as a 'kinsman-

redeemer' (as the lawyers call it), the closest relative to the dead man must be given the first opportunity to exercise his right to marry the widow. It happened that one of Boaz's neighbours was in fact more closely related to Elimelech than he was. But after tense deliberations the neighbour decided that he could not afford to purchase the land and look after Ruth as well. With all legal requirements now satisfied, Boaz and Ruth were free to marry.

Local lawyers have pointed out that Levirate law has been vindicated. Campaigners for moral values have pointed out that what attracted Boaz was Ruth's exemplary care for her mother-in-law. The priests are putting yet another slant on the story, emphasising Boaz's well-known piety, his godly business practices and his respect for religious traditions.

But this is a story in which everybody lives happily ever after. Boaz now has a wonderful marriage (their first son was born recently). Ruth has a husband, a home, a son and a bright future in her adopted country. Naomi can look forward to an old age which, far from being lonely and impoverished, will be gladdened by her new family, including the grandson who, the local women have prophesied, will 'renew her life'.

(Ruth 1–4)

In many parts of the world the traditional method of winnowing is still used.

Civil war ends king's short reign

Shechem, c. 1150 BC

Abimelech's attempt to become a king in Israel has ended after just three years. Bitter in-fighting among rivals for power has left the city of Shechem a smouldering ruin.

The pretender was a child of Israel's former judge Gideon and a woman from Shechem. He had massacred his 70 brothers before being crowned king by the people who had financed his coup by hiring mercenaries.

One of Gideon's sons, Jotham, escaped the massacre, and put up a spirited verbal opposition before fleeing to exile. He likened Abimelech to a thornbush inviting people to shelter in safety under it. He cursed the people of Shechem for betraying Gideon and his family.

Abimelech was soon opposed by a newcomer to the city, Gaal, who won widespread popular support. But his rash abuse of the leader prompted Abimelech to call his bluff by sending in the army to fight it out. The citizens of Shechem, who locked themselves in its inner fortress, were burned to death.

But when the people of Thebez resorted to the same defence, a woman pushed a millstone off the top of the tower. It fell on Abimelech, who asked his servant to put him out of his agony and the shame of being killed by a woman.

The incident has ended Israel's brief flirtation with kingship. The model of city-states held its attractions, but their own model of a theocratic confederacy ruled by Yahweh is still ingrained.

(Judges 9)

This model of a cultic Canaanite site dates from c. 1100 BC. Was this scale model used in a home or did it serve some other purpose?

Honour is regained at daughter's expense

Gilead, c. 1140 BC

Family tragedy has dogged the steps of Jephthah, Israel's latest military deliverer, who has succeeded in beating back the Ammonite incursions. Having been rejected as illegitimate by his family because of his birth to a non-Israelite prostitute, he was recalled by his tribe of Gilead to lead them in battle.

But in a rash moment of exultation at having his honour restored, he vowed that if he was victorious he would make a human sacrifice of the first person to greet him on his return home. The hapless victim was his daughter, an only child.

The vow was unusual for an Israelite, whose law prohibits human sacrifice which is also relatively rare among the other tribes of Canaan. Despite the widespread belief that he was motivated and empowered by Yahweh for his superhuman military role, his religious education seemed to be somewhat lacking.

His commitment to fulfilling the vow remained total, although he did allow his daughter two months to enjoy her friends and to prepare for her untimely death.

His victory over the Ammonites, in which he destroyed 20 towns, was followed by an inter-tribal feud with the Ephraimites sparked by a trade of insults. Once more Jephthah found himself fighting for his honour. He is reported to have slaughtered 42,000 people, including refugees who were hacked down after failing a simple test of dialect to determine their tribal loyalty. Anyone who mispronounced the word shibboleth (meaning flood) was deemed an Ephraimite, whose accent gave the word a distinctive turn.

(Judges 10–12)

Fast Facts 1150–1100 BC

Egypt, c. 1139 BC: Considerable concern has been expressed over the prospects for national growth and security now that the great Pharaoh Rameses III has died. The priests of Amun are looking increasingly likely to step into what may well become a political vacuum.

Babylon, c. 1120: Nebuchadnezzar I has successfully attacked the Elamites, who in 1158 defeated Babylon's ruling Kassite dynasty. He has retrieved important archives and the statue of the Babylonian god, Marduk. Nebuchadnezzar is an Isin prince from the settlers who moved into Babylon when the Elamites abandoned the city. His midsummer attack was unexpected and dust clouds from the battle darkened the sky.

Sardinia, c. 1100 BC: Sardinia's traditional nuraghi dwellings are developing into a fine architectural form. The tower is shaped like a cone with the top sliced off. It is built with large, carefully dressed stones, with a platform on top and tiers arranged like steps around the tower. There are a few narrow openings and a small corridor leading to the inner chamber. Recent enhancements have included corbelled ceilings to the chambers and internal access. Some ambitious builders are even incorporating secondary towers.

Cities of refuge span the country

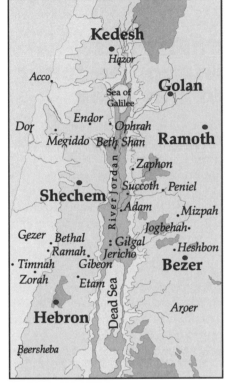

The Cities of Refuge under the Judges.

Canaan, c. 1100 BC

Justice and mercy are entwined in Israelite law and nothing expresses that so clearly as the city of refuge.

Six cities, each belonging to the Levites, were designated by Joshua as sanctuaries for people who had killed someone unintentionally and who were too far from the altar at the central shine, the traditional place of sanctuary in many cultures.

While in the city, the man-slayer cannot be killed by the victim's family, as would happen if the murder was intentional. But he must stay there in exile until the death of the current high priest, perhaps as a form of imprisonment emphasising the gravity of even accidental homicide, and to give his exile a specific time limit.

(Joshua 20:1–9; Numbers 35:6–34)

Greece is born again

Ruined temples, the warm sea and countless islands represent the typical stereotype of Greece throughout the ages. The temple of Poseidon on Cape Sunium near Athens.

Greece, 1100 BC

Currently in a cultural dark age after the collapse of the splendid Mycenaean civilisation, Greece is experiencing the first stirrings of rebirth.

The various migrations in the region during this period have resulted in the spreading of Greek dialects: for example Dorian, Aeolic and Ionian. In Arcadia, Pindar and other regions of Greece a variety of ancient dialogues continue to be spoken. But in Athens, the Attic dialect (a version of Ionian) is still spoken. And the enduring Atticism of the Athenians is a matter of great pride for them. Attica itself is a territory of 2,600 sq km (1,000 sq miles) and much larger than most Greek states; a fitting centre for a renaissance.

Writing has virtually disappeared with the collapse of the Mycenaean palaces. The palaces themselves lie in ruins. Yet there are plenty of indicators that art, literature and creativity have not died: for example, beautifully-decorated pottery, stirring epic poems that are declaimed from memory and handed on orally from generation to generation, and ingenious artefacts making use of the newly-discovered technology of iron.

A jug with a spout in the shape of a griffin's head.

Samson's wedding not made in heaven

Zorah, Canaan, c. 1120 BC
Samson, the long-haired muscleman from Zorah, has shocked family and neighbours by announcing his intention to take a bride from the Philistine nation currently ruling over his own people.

Most shocked of all are his parents, who say that Samson's birth was foretold by God himself who appeared to them as the Angel of the Lord. He told them that their son (then not even conceived) was to be set apart for God's service and would be a national deliverer.

His long hair and beard are the result of Nazirite vows, a religious vocation established in Moses' time. Samson is not a typical Nazirite: he was dedicated before birth (the vows are normally voluntary) and his dedication is for life (see box).

His impressive physique and growing pride in his national heritage persuaded sceptics that Samson's parents were telling the truth about God's promises, but the engagement has cast new doubt on whether Samson is the man to deliver Israel.

He is certainly strong. On his first visit to Timnah, where his fiancée lives, possessed by the Spirit of the Yahweh, he tore a young lion apart bare-handed.

But his parents are reported to be very unhappy about the relationship. Quite apart from the fact that it is the parents' job, not the son's, to choose a bride, they are deeply hurt by the fact that the woman is a Philistine. Samson's lack of respect towards his father is as nothing by comparison with the scorn with which Samson appears to be treating God's directives against mixed marriages.

(Judges 13:1–14:7)

The Nazirite Vow

Nazirites promise to set themselves apart for God for a specified period of time. Their vows (which are listed in the Book of Numbers 6:2–21) include:
- To be teetotal, abstaining from wine and wine products;
- Not to eat grapes or raisins, or drink grape juice;
- Never to shave or cut their hair;
- To avoid going near corpses (even those of close relatives).

Nazirite long hair is an unmistakable symbol of consecration to God, so much so that the principal ritual that marks the end of the period of Nazirite vows is shaving the head and burning the cut hair. Sacrifices to God and a holy meal follow, after which the ex-Nazirite may once again drink wine and is freed from his dietary vows.

Samson's downfall was his predeliction for pretty women. The subject has inspired many artists, in this case Rubens.

Philistines trump the joker of the pack

Timnah, Philistia, c. 1120 BC
The fact that Samson is tipped as Israel's next leader is a big joke to the Philistines who have wiped the smile off the eccentric Nazirite's face. But he had the last laugh, if killing 30 people can ever be funny.

Samson was on his way to his wedding when he found that a swarm of bees had made a honeycomb in the carcase of the lion he had killed earlier with his bare hands. Ignoring the Nazirite prohibition on touching corpses, he helped himself to the honey.

During the traditional bridegroom's feast Samson made a rash bet. He challenged his 30 Philistine wedding companions to solve a riddle within a week, the stake being 30 linen garments and 30 suits of clothes – a costly prize.

The riddle was based on a reference to the honey incident, and after four days nobody had solved it. The Philistines were furious and forced Samson's wife to persuade him to tell her the answer.

Then Samson, gripped with fury against his wife and the Philistines, promptly slew 30 inhabitants of Ashkelon, about 37 km (23 miles) away, and presented the 30 conspirators with the dead men's clothes. Then he left his new wife and went back to his father's house.

The Philistines, who were not exactly amused, had the last laugh when they handed Samson's bride to his best man.

(Judges 14:8–20)

Samson ass-assinates his enemies with a jawbone

Philistia, c. 1120 BC

In a fearsome display of raw power and divine assistance, Samson has slaughtered 1,000 Philistines single-handedly – with only an ass's jawbone as a weapon.

The carnage is the latest in a bloody tit-for-tat feud that has been building up ever since Samson stormed out of his wedding feast. Though widely interpreted by the in the fields of the Philistines, there was massive destruction not only of grain but of vineyards and olive groves.

The Philistine counter-revenge was swift. In brutal retaliation they burned to death Samson's bride and her father.

Samson, mad with grief, went on a wild killing rampage, eventually hiding in a cave near his home. It is

The Blinding of Sampson by Rembrandt. Sampson's prowess provoked the jealousy and anger of the Philistines who were to avenge themselves most cruelly (see next page).

Philistines as a divorce *de facto*, Samson's absence lasted only until harvest time when he returned, bearing gifts and clearly anxious to repair the rift.

He arrived to find his wife given in marriage to his best man. Her parents had been convinced Samson would not be back. Faced now with a very angry son-in-law they offered to give him their younger daughter as bride in recognition of the arrangements that had already been made.

He refused, and planned a bitter revenge against the Philistines. He tied 300 jackals in pairs and fastened a flaming torch to each pair. When he let the animals loose some indication of the fear that this massively strong Israelite strikes into his enemies, that when the Philistines came looking for him it was with an army of at least 1,000 men. The people of Judah, horrified at the prospect of a local feud provoking all-out war with their oppressors, insisted that he must be handed over to his accusers.

Samson allowed himself to be tied up with new ropes, but he used his super-natural strength to snap them when he faced the Philistines. Seizing the jawbone of a recently-killed donkey, he wielded it just like a harvester's scythe, cutting a hugh swathe through his enemies.

(Judges 15)

End of term for Mycenaean men

Greece, c. 1120 BC

The palaces and citadels at Mycenae, Pylos, Tiryns and Thebes have all been destroyed and their kings killed in battle. Mycenaean civilisation is finished.

It is widely believed that the so-called sons of Heracles were responsible. The rough Greek-speaking Dorians from the north claim to be descended from Heracles and say the land is rightfully theirs.

The attack did not come out of the blue. Over the past decades the Mycenaeans have strengthened their fortifications and built a wall across the Corinthian isthmus. But despite walls of up to 12 m (40 ft) high and between 4 and 14 m (12—45 ft) thick, all four citadels fell like matchsticks.

The destruction brings to an end a civilisation which has been in decline since the turn of the century. Rumours of murders in the royal family and revolts among the lower classes aided a gradual weakening of the state and a breakdown in law and order which had already forced many people to emigrate. Some survivors are, however, creeping back into the ruined palaces.

The palaces were built from rubble masonry to a design which dates back to New Stone Age times. Each had a megaron, a rectangular roofed structure with one of its short sides opening on to a court-yard. There was a portico, vestibule and main room with a low circular hearth. Other rooms included guest rooms and bathrooms carefully decorated with frescoes depicting warriors.

Culturally the Dorians are inferior to the Mycenaeans. Apart from the iron slashing sword and long bronze clothing pin, they have contributed little to the world so far.

Eyeless in Gaza – but he brings the house down

Gaza, c. 1110 BC

Samson, the Israelite judge with a giant's strength, has died as he lived. Compromised by his moral weakness, blind and helpless, he has turned the tables on his Philistine tormentors and destroyed them and himself in one final spectacular feat of strength.

The Temple of Bacchus in Baalbeck of which little remains, is faced with huge columns. It is easy to see how the whole structure could be undermined through the removal of a couple of key supports.

Not for the first time, a woman was his downfall. Despite 20 years as Israel's judge, Samson's roving eye and his casual attitude to his Nazirite vows have never left him. Passing through the southern city of Gaza, he visited a prostitute, forgetting that his long hair and notorious physique made him instantly recognisable.

Predictably, the local people ambushed him at the city gate, but he surprised them by leaving before the night was gone by simply tearing the gates out of the ground and carrying them on his shoulders.

Many have wished to know the secret of Samson's strength. However, it was his abiding weakness – women – that finally made him give the secret away. He fell in love with another Philistine, Delilah. She was immediately instructed to find Samson's secret, and willingly agreed. He successfully fooled her three times, but then gave way. The secret, he explained, was in his long hair, the symbol of the Nazirite vow.

That night, Delilah woke Samson, shouting that the Philistines were about to attack him. He leaped up sure that his great strength was enough to deal with any threat. But he found the house surrounded by Philistines and his head shaved bare. His strength had left him, and the Spirit of Yahweh had been withdrawn from him. The Philistines blinded him and put him to slave duties in the Gaza prison.

But the tragedy was yet to turn into triumph. In the murky prison, nobody noticed that Samson's hair was growing back. When some time later his captors dragged him from his cell to entertain a drunken feast in honour of the god Dagon, the blind and manacled Samson's request to lean against the temple pillars was granted.

His wasted muscles once more flexing with the old mighty power, it was the work of a moment to push the pillars out of their mountings and bring the whole temple crashing down on the huge crowd. It is estimated that well over a thousand people died in the collapse, including Samson himself.

(Judges 16)

Canaanite and Philistine gods

It is likely that the Philistines brought their own gods with them to Palestine and amalgamated them with local Canaanite religion. The only information about the Philistine religion comes from the Hebrews but references to Canaanite deities are frequent in contemporary writings.

Dagon (Dagan)

Worshipped throughout Mesopotamia since the middle of the third millennium BC, Dagon is a chief god of the Philistines: Gaza is a centre of Dagon-worship. The Israelites also call him Dagan ('grain'), which may well link him to the gods of vegetation and grain, though his exact identity is somewhat vague. He is also commemorated in various place names and personal names in the region.

Ashtoreth (Ashtoroth)

The Philistines' mother goddess incorporates elements of fertility ritual, love and war; she is widely worshipped throughout the Middle East. Representations of naked women are to be found in many places and a significant number are images of Ashtoreth. Ashtoreth-worship is a depraved and immoral practice. It is a powerful attraction to the Israelites in Canaan, where Ashtoreth-worship was well-established, however.

Baal

The name 'Baal' has been a source of confusion among Israelites, for its meaning is 'master' or 'husband', and in that sense has sometimes been applied with good intentions to Yahweh. But the indigenous Canaanite culture is the setting for flourishing Baal cults, centred round the storm-god, Hadad, who is known as 'Baal' to his worshippers. Called the son of Dagon and the consort of Ashtoreth, Baal is a god who triumphs over death and floods and is a symbol of fertility. He is regarded as the greatest of all Canaanite gods.

More home comforts

Reconstructed early Israelite house, Eretz Israel Museum, Tel Aviv.

Canaan, c. 1100 BC

The tribes of Israel, after making-do for decades, are finally building comfortable homes for themselves. Quality lifestyle was not a priority in their first years of conquest.

Many families lived in crowded quarters in what was left of the old fortified Canaanite hill-cities they had conquered, often sharing their cramped space with sheep and goats.

Some Israelites, unable to make the transition easily from a nomadic existence in the desert, preferred to live in tents on the edge of town. In fact their first purpose-built houses – circular with a beehive-like roof – looked rather like tents themselves.

Today's superior houses are square and their single entrance faces north. They have few windows so the house remains cool. And as each house has its own small yard in front, Israelites no longer have to live in the same room as their animals!

There is still room for improvement, however. The houses are built of mud (the Israelites learned their skills as slaves in Egypt), and they leak. Also they are small: it is fortunate that the climate is mild, as most daily activities take place in the yard. On the other hand, these houses can easily be expanded: the flat clay roof is strong enough to allow temporary second-floor accommodation during the summer months and a simple ladder serves as staircase.

Dan dares

Laish (Dan), c. 1110 BC

Israelites from the tribe of Dan have taken this northern Canaan city and renamed it after their ancestor. It was chosen because of its remoteness from other centres which might have come to its aid, and is the furthest north the Israelite confederacy has penetrated.

The Danites, who until now have remained semi-nomads since entering Canaan, are a blustering almost loutish people whose motto seems to be 'who dares, wins'. While exploring the region, the advance party commandeered the household idols of a wealthy man named Micah, and bribed his personal priest, Jonathan, to service their religious rituals.

Both the aggression and the fact that the silver shrine, although dedicated to Yahweh, contravenes Israelite law, suggest that despite the succession of God-fearing judges who have pulled them from the spiritual and military abyss, the Israelites continue to wander far from the ideals laid down by their first leader Moses.the spiritual and military abyss, the Israelites continue to wander far from the ideals laid down by their first leader Moses.

(Judges 17, 18)

Sling out

Canaan, c. 1100 BC

A new weapon is having a major effect on battles. The 'sling', when used by skilled operators, is both accurate and powerful. Missiles weighing as much as 450 grammes (1 lb) are capable of being hurled at up to 140 km per hour (90 mph).

The weapon is a leather strap, shaped in the middle to hold the missile – usually a round or egg-shaped stone. The ends of the strap are whirled around with the left hand above the slingster's head.

A young boy with a sling.

One end is then released allowing the stone to fly to its target.

Among the Israelite forces the Benjamites have a particular reputation as slingsters. They are ambidextrous, so can use the sling in either hand – no mean feat with such a difficult weapon.

(cf. Judges 20:16)

Chou! Wu-wang shanghais dynasty

China, c. 1110 BC

Wu-wang of the Chou kingdom has overthrown the Shang dynasty, a hegemony of semi-independent states which had grown progressively weaker in recent years.

The roofs of an old Buddhist temple in Kangding, Sichuan seem to have little changed since time immemorial.

A bronze standing figure, 260 cm (8 ft 6 in) tall, c. 1100 BC. Excavated in Sichuan.

However, the defeated states are still a force to be reckoned with and the Chou leaders have only established weak control from their capital near Sian. They plan to formalise the loose Shang feudal structure, but some municipalities are already trying to break away. There is particular pressure from nomadic tribes in the north and northwest, on the outer fringes of the territory.

The Chous have taken three generations to defeat the Shang. Wu-wang's grandfather moulded them into the most formidable power west of the Shang, who had been split by rivalries and moral decay.

According to popular belief the first major dynasty was established in 2300 BC by Yu, the Chinese Noah, who drained away floods to make China habitable. The Shangs took over in 1500 and their well-established succession of 30 kings did much to develop Chinese culture.

They were gifted people who lived in large houses and had a mature agricultural economy which used cowrie shells as a medium of exchange. The Shangs were skilled in jade and bronze work, making delicate ornaments as well as magnificent urns, large statues and weapons.

The Chou see themselves as consolidators rather than innovators, and have readily accepted many of the Shang achievements. They intend to continue the bronze, textile and pottery industries, and will base their economy on the seemingly bountiful agricultural produce of the peasant class.

A bronze ritual vessel c. 1200 BC with two extremely life-like rams on each side of the vessel. It is unusual for Chinese artefacts of the period to be so true to life.

Corrupt priests carve up gifts

Shiloh, c. 1100 BC

The corrupt sons of an elderly and God-fearing priest are carving up worshipper's gifts for their own use, and are treating cult servants as their personal prostitutes.

Traditionally, priests are entitled to a share of the meat for the sacrifice offerings. But Eli's sons have abused the privilege, demanding the choicest cuts for themselves before the sacrifice has even been offered to Yahweh.

Such depravity smacks of the Canaanite cultic religions which the Israelites are supposed to have eradicated. And their father Eli is powerless to do anything about his wayward sons. Indeed, a prophet has pronounced a curse upon them and their descendants and prophesied that both sons will die on the same day, but nothing changes.

Shiloh is the centre of worship for all Israel. It is the place where the ark of God is kept, where Joshua set up the tabernacle. It is in the hill country of central Canaan, about 14 km (9 miles) north of Bethel.

(1 Samuel 2:12–36)

Time flies in short days

Egypt, c. 1100 BC

The Egyptians have produced a text giving the hours of daylight and darkness for each month. Each day is always 24 hours long, but as the division between daylight and darkness varies according to the season, it has not yet been possible to produce hours of equal length.

It is not the first Egyptian time machine. Star clock charts date back to before 2000 BC. A civil calendar with 12 months was divided into 36 ten-day weeks plus five additional days.

Suitable stars or constellations were chosen so that there was one which rose heliacally (moments before the sun rises and obliterates the stars) on the first day of each week. By looking at the stars and consulting the chart, the observer could work out the time of night.

Then came shadow clocks. A base had four marks supporting a crossbar at one end. It was set up to face east, and as the sun moved up and round, the shadow of the crossbar shortened and moved across the marks, creating four daytime divisions.

Water clocks were invented to enable people to tell the time during the hours of darkness. A vessel was filled with water at the onset of darkness, which then trickled out through a small hole. Calibrations on the inside of the container showed how many divisions of the night had passed. The night, whatever its length, was divided into 12 equal periods and so there were separate scales for each of the 12 lunar months.

Gang rape avenged by mass murder

Gibeah, c. 1110 BC

Up to 65,000 soldiers are believed dead, and numerous towns destroyed and their civilian populations slaughtered, during a brief bout of bitter civil war among Israelite tribesmen. The action began in response to news of a gang rape which had shaken the nation.

A travelling Levite and his concubine (additional wife) had lodged in Gibeah, a settlement held by the tribe of Benjamin in southern Canaan. A crowd of bullish lager louts hammered at the door demanding homosexual activity with the visitor. Instead he offered them his female companion instead, who was then repeatedly raped and then killed.

Grieved and shaken, the Levite cut her body into 12 segments and sent the gruesome remains with a covering explanation to each of the confederacy's tribal heads. Public revulsion was widespread and a national assembly was held at Mizpah. After hearing the Levite recount his story, an army was raised to punish Gibeah's culprits. War broke out when the Benjaminites refused to hand them over.

The initial attacks on Benjamin were repulsed and some 40,000 Israelites were reported killed. But an ambush turned the tide and 25,000 Benjamites were killed and their tribe beaten into submission.

The bitterness has not continued once the score was settled. The tribes agreed that Benjamin should be allowed to reconstruct itself. A force was sent to Jabesh Gilead, which had not supported the alliance, and all virgin women were abducted to become wives for the survivors and to ensure the continuation of the tribe. Similarly, women were also abducted, without further bloodshed, from Shiloh.

(Judges 19–21

This stele shows two priests, a father and son, entering into a solemn agreement, recorded in detail on the stele.

Invaders repelled

Assyria, c. 1100 BC

Tiglath-Pileser I, emperor of Assyria is engaged in an armed struggle against the Ahlamu, a tribe of Semitic barbarians.

They come from the desert steppes to the east of the Euphrates, and are sometimes called Aramaeans. They have already made significant conquests in Syria and there is an Aramaean king in Babylon. Their language, Aramaic, is already spoken over a wide area.

Tiglath-Pileser has also staged battles against the Muski and Gasga, tribes which have spread across central Anatolia since the fall of the Hittites. They had taken control of old trade routes and river crossings.

Tiglath-Pileser has led Assyria since 1112 and the nation is back to its former glory. His reign is marked by the same brutality as that of his predecessors.

The savage punishments inflicted on law-breakers are notorious. They include amputation of ears, fingers and lips; castration; and coating criminal's faces in boiling pitch. The arrival of Hittite blacksmiths around 1200 and the Assyrian control of the iron-ore deposits of Asia Minor have enabled the creation of a fearsome army with chariots, infantry and heavily-armoured assault forces.

New judge was child prodigy

Ramah, c. 1070 BC

There can be little doubt that in the case of Samuel, the itinerant judge whose word is law for the Israelites, the child was father of the man.

For the first time in decades the Israelites have a single figure to whom they may refer disputes. Unlike previous judges, however, he is not also a military commander.

Essentially a man of peace, Samuel also has a gift of prophecy, speaking out Yahweh's messages to the people. He learned that art as a child in what was perhaps the sternest test he has faced.

He was dedicated by his mother to service at the religious sanctuary because she believed that his birth was an answer to her prayers. As he attended the priest Eli, he claims to have heard Yahweh calling to him one night. Thinking it was Eli, he went to the old man who assumed the boy was dreaming. But when it happened a third time, he advised Samuel to reply, 'Speak Lord, for your servant is listening'.

When he did, he was told to give the priest a telling off in the name of Yahweh, who was not pleased with his failure to control his lawless sons who were abusing their priestly position. Graciously, Eli accepted the word and the boy prophet did not get beaten for hearing things.

Samuel has now returned to his family home in Ramah, in the hill country about 8 km (5 miles) north of Jerusalem. A disciplined man, he makes a regular circuit to visit the Israelite centres where he sits as judge.

The circuit links Bethel, a shrine commemorating Jacob's meeting with Yahweh; Gilgal, where a cairn marks the entry of the Israelites into Canaan; and Mizpah. Samuel also administers at Ramah, where he has set up an altar to Yahweh.

(1 Samuel 1–3; cf. 7:15–17)

Stolen ark proves too hot to handle for its captors

Kiriath Jearim, c. 1060 BC

The ark of the covenant is back in Israel, and there is a mood of heartfelt relief throughout the nation.

The ark of the covenant. A first-century stone carving from Capernaum.

The holy box containing relics of Israel's relationship with Yahweh and the tablets of the Law had been captured by Philistine raiders. It is the most prized possession of the people.

It symbolises the ancient covenant made between them and God and represents a point of meeting between sinful human beings and a perfectly righteous God; it is the emblem of the presence of Yahweh and the assurance of victory in battle.

The loss of this treasured artefact, some argue, was the result of treating it like a lucky charm. Following defeat by the Philistines, the Israelite elders decided that the ark should go with the soldiers into battle. Hophni and Phinehas brought it into the camp, where it was received with rapturous excitement.

The tumult in the Israelite camp, however, had the unintended effect of inspiring the frightened Philistines to new efforts. They slaughtered the Israelite infantry, captured the ark, and killed the priests Phinehas and Hophni. On hearing the news, their father Eli collapsed and died.

Such a fate had been predicted by Israel's judge Samuel some years ago, as Yahweh's judgement on their profligate lifestyle.

The Philistines carried their prize off to Ashdod, but soon found that it brought only trouble. Lodging the ark in the temple of Dagon, they found the statue of the god flat on its face the next morning. When this happened a second time they moved the ark to Gath, but there the population was suddenly afflicted with tumours. Popular belief that the God of Israel was avenging the capture of the ark turned to panic when the ark was transferred to Ekron and disease broke out there too.

Seven months after the capture, the inhabitants of the Judahite town of Beth Shemesh were surprised to see a large party of Philistine dignitaries arriving. They handed over the ark, laden with placatory gifts of golden images of the plagues it had brought them.

The Israelites, despite the Philistine's apology, have had to learn hard lessons from this experience. The thank-offerings at Beth Shemesh were marred by the deaths of about 70 local people who let curiosity get the better of them and treated the ark as an intriguing curiosity.

Deciding, like the Philistines, that the ark was not a tourist attraction, the Beth Shemeshites took it to Abinadab's house in Kiriath Jearim, about 24 km (15 miles) to the north where proper provision could be made for its safe keeping. Eleazar, son of Abinadab, was consecrated as guardian of the holy treasure.

(1 Samuel 4:1–7:1)

Heartfelt change brings success against enemies

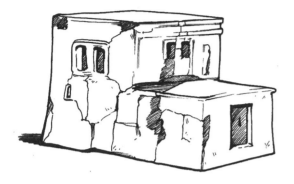

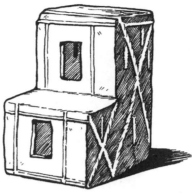

Ramah, c. 1050 BC

Go into the average Israelite community today and you will find a new attitude among the people. The nation has turned back to Yahweh.

Samuel has initiated a national campaign to eradicate all traces of foreign religions. The people have followed him wholeheartedly.

Religious commentators have not been slow to point out that disaster ensued when the Israelites fell away from God; but he is blessing them now they are serving him.

At Mizpah, for example, a Philistine foray threatened to disrupt a ceremony of national repentance and consecration. But after the people had prayed fervently, and Samuel had offered a burnt sacrifice, a sudden violent thunderstorm threw the Philistines into disarray. For the first time in decades, the Israelites routed them.

(1 Samuel 7:2–12)

These model houses, made out of baked clay, were found in southern Syria, and date from c. 1000 BC. They served as altars for household rites, but give a good idea of domestic architecture of the period.

Iron grip

Canaan, c. 1040 BC

Israel's war machine is severely hampered by the Philistine monopoly on iron. It means that besides the Philistines' huge advantage of iron chariots, Saul's infantry have neither swords nor spears. The only ones in the whole army are those belonging to Saul and Jonathan themselves.

Blacksmiths are unknown in Israel, a deliberate strategy of the Philistines who want to prevent other nations arming themselves and to preserve their monopoly. For the same reason, they charge extortionate fees for sharpening iron-edged implements.

(1 Samuel 13:16–22)

Give us a king!

Ramah, c. 1050 BC

Growing popular demand for a centralised monarchy has become so strong in Israel that a delegation of leaders from all 12 tribes has presented an official request for one to Samuel.

The demand stems partly from a sense of déjà-vu which is troubling many in Israel today.

Samuel is now elderly, and has nominated his sons as his successors as judge. But like Eli before him, Samuel has the sadness of knowing that his sons are corrupt and far from honouring Yahweh.

Future-watchers with a sense of history are remembering the bad old days when Israel had no central leadership of any kind. Some suggest that nations with kings do better in battle.

Samuel sees the request as a rejection of all he has done for the people. But he is more grieved that the people are rejecting Yahweh as their King and leader, in preference for a human monarch.

He has warned the elders that God says that a human king will rule harshly, will over-tax his people, will restrict their liberty, extort, oppress them and not listen to their pleas for relief.

But they are in no mood to listen. Strangely, Yahweh appears to be sympathetic despite the evident rejection of the ideal of theocracy, a state ruled by religious agreement. It is rumoured that he has authorised Samuel to appoint a king.

(1 Samuel 8)

Fast Facts 1105–1083 BC

China, c. 1100 BC: Remarkable sculptures may be seen in China. The first efforts appear to have been produced in the An-Yang period but sculpture has also been a feature of both the Shang and Chou dynasties. In all cases the work is primarily decorative: the An-Yang pieces are of marble and are highly stylised representations of human beings and animals, made to be bases for columns. Shang and Chou sculptors have created small heads and animal figurines, used to decorate bronze artefacts.

Assyria, c. 1100 BC: Tiglath-Pileser has extended his country's domination to the Lebanon. When he arrived there, the Egyptian king sent him a gift of a crocodile – whether as a veiled warning to proceed no further south is uncertain.

Babylon, c. 1105 BC: Nebuchadnezzar of Baby-lon has staged a disastrous attack on Elam in an attempt to avenge the Elamite sack of Babylon c. 1158. His troops were struck down with plague and almost killed him in their panic retreat.

Egypt, c. 1100 BC: Two thousand Libyans have been taken prisoner and are being forced to speak Egyptian. Prisoners of war are normally settled in their captor's homeland but in time they may acquire full citizens' rights.

Babylon, c. 1083 BC: A terrible famine has struck the nation. People in the cities are reduced to eating human flesh and it is reported that the king Marduk-nadin-ahhe has disappeared.

New king chosen at the national lottery

Mizpah, c. 1045 BC

If the Israelites ever want to hold a talent-spotting competition, they could hardly devise an entertainment as full of suspense as the one they used to choose their first king. Nor could they have found a more unsuspecting and bewildered star.

But he is one of the most impressive young Israelites of his generation: Saul, son of Kish, stands at least a head higher than anybody else.

Saul, a man whose interest in national and spiritual affairs was so sketchy that he did not even know who Samuel the Judge was, found himself near Ramah in pursuit of donkeys that had strayed from his father's herd. His servant suggested consulting the local seer – Samuel.

Samuel was expecting him, having been forewarned by Yahweh that a man was shortly arriving who was to be the king of Israel. Samuel convinced the reluctant Saul that he was God's choice as leader, and anointed him with oil. He foretold events that would authenticate his claims, and told Saul that the Spirit of God would transform him into a different person.

Saul returned home but did not tell his father what had happened. And then the real drama began. At a national assembly Samuel used Israel's time-honoured method of determining Yahweh's choice – casting religious dice.

The talent contest became a national lottery. Slowly tribes were eliminated then clans and families were chosen. Finally Saul hit the jackpot but he had locked himself in the baggage room out of fear.

The popularity of the choice and the feeling of national unity that has surrounded the appointment is a good omen for the beginning of an entirely new phase in Israel's history.

Donkeys are still useful beasts of burden in the Middle East today. This photo shows a Palestinian riding his donkey near Ramah.

Saul has meanwhile returned home to Gibeah. His style of leadership is not to found a court but to respond to needs like the judges before him.

(1 Samuel 9, 10)

Brine of Britain savours beef

Britain, c. 1050 BC

Demand for a different kind of food preservation has led to the setting up of a salt-recovery industry at Walton-on-the-Naze in Essex.

Sea water is evaporated in large open pans, and the residue of concentrated brine is further reduced by boiling in crude vessels. Like all the equipment used in the process, the vessels are ceramic. The new industry depends on warm weather to facilitate evaporation and therefore only operates in summer.

This is a growth industry. More and more British are farming cattle. Salt is needed to preserve meat, and is also an essential dietary supplement for livestock.

Saul takes charge

Gilgal, c. 1040 BC

Saul's reign as king has been confirmed following a spectacular military victory in which he delivered the Gileadites who had been besieged by the Ammonites.

At a national assembly at Gilgal in which he handed over full leadership to Saul, the elderly judge and prophet Samuel issued a stern warning. He reminded them of his own unblemished record as their leader and of their national history as the chosen people of Yahweh. The king they had just crowned had been chosen in preference to God, and their choice might yet rebound against them, he said.

Warning them of the power of God to punish disobedience, he provided a dramatic illustration by calling on Yahweh to send thunder and rain; the weather promptly changed. The people, confronted with the spectacle of storms in the dry harvest season, acknowledged their sin in asking for a king and pleaded with Samuel to intercede with God on their behalf.

The old prophet assured them that though they had made a mistake in desiring a king, if they promised to serve Yahweh and obey him, then he would not reject his own people.

The ceremony included religious peace offerings in what amounted almost to a covenant renewal.

(1 Samuel 11, 12)

The Jezreel Plain seen from the heights of Mount Gilboa.

Ten per cent interest after regal inflation hits army

Bitter end to hero's sweet interlude

Michmash, c. 1035 BC

Israelite soldiers have won a reprieve for King Saul's son Jonathan after their hero faced the death sentence for eating sweets on duty.

Saul had placed his men under an oath not to eat until evening. The men were soon weak from hunger. Jonathan, who before he heard of the ban, ate some wild honey, considered it a bad decree. The risk of revolt if Saul carried out his threat to kill any culprit dissuaded the king from executing his son. Further rows over food followed.

A mixed herd of sheep and goats on the West Bank.

asked for and only 600 regrouped at Gibeah, a nearby Israelite-held town.

While waiting for the delayed Samuel, Saul offered animal sacrifices to appease Yahweh, a task which his contract of office explicitly excludes. The elderly prophet predicted that as a result of his presumption, Saul's kingdom would not pass on to his immediate family.

(1 Samuel 13:1–15)

Rock-cut pool and spiral stairway excavated in El-Jib, ancient Gibeah. It has 79 steps leading to water 25 m (80 ft) below the surface.

Gibeah, c. 1030 BC

Saul's army has been reduced to 10 per cent of its original strength after most of its 6,000 men went home when they were humiliated by the Philistines.

Saul's reputation has also dived to an all-time low since he deputised for the absent Samuel in a religious ceremony. The action was interpreted by the judge as, at best, a misguided act of panic and, at worst, a bad case of royal pride.

Led by Saul's son Jonathan, Israel had taken the initiative by attacking the Philistine outpost at Geba in rugged country a short distance north of Jerusalem and ideal for guerrilla tactics. But Philistine reinforcements, well-equipped with chariots, were quickly on the scene and scattered the Israelite army. Most gave up a fight they had not

Panic attack

Michmash, c. 1035 BC

Jonathan is a hero in the Israelite camps tonight after a daring exploit turned the course of the war against the Philistines.

With only his armour-bearer, he approached a Philistine outpost and used the defenders' abuse and invitation to a fight as a sign that Yahweh would protect them.

They had killed 20 or so, when an earthquake shook the ground and threw the Philistines into utter panic. The Israelites then attributed the earthquake to God's special providence, and descended on the fleeing soldiers.

(1 Samuel 14:1–23)

In the evening the soldiers, faint with hunger after a day's fierce battle, butchered cattle and sheep from the day's plunder and devoured them. But they failed to prepare the meat according to religious requirements.

Saul attempted to deal with it by offering sacrifices to Yahweh, and built an altar. There followed a confused attempt to ascertain the will of God by casting lots, which resulted in no clear guidance as to the next stage in the campaign.

As a result, the campaign against the Philistines is, for the present, at an end. The Philistines have withdrawn to their own territory, to regroup, re-arm and fight another day.

(1 Samuel 14:24–48)

103

Egyptians make better mummies now

Egypt, c. 1050 BC

If you die today in Egypt you could end up looking better than you ever did in life.

Egyptian embalmers, masters of the art of mummification since 3000 BC, have developed new skills that make the corpse look plump and life-like. The technique involves inserting linen packs of sawdust under the skin. Artificial eyes are now also used, and bedsores concealed by leather patches.

The old method, by which internal organs were stored separately and the body wrapped in resin-soaked bandages (from which the word 'mummy' is derived), has

Even cats were mummified by the Egyptians. They were domestic animals as well as being one of their gods.

been abandoned. Today's bandages are soaked in a bitumen-like substance and the body no longer decays inside.

All of which is good news for devout Egyptians. The whole point of the exercise (which takes, including rituals, about 70 days) is to make the corpse look as good as possible for the afterlife. They believe that appearance is all-important, so artificial eyes and sawdust intestines are no problem – provided they are convincing. And if the head looks life-like it doesn't matter that the embalmers have extracted the brain (usually with a probe through the nostrils).

Everything in the tomb is designed to give the deceased an easy passage into immortality. Texts are painted on the walls claiming that he or she lived a good life – a useful revision-aid when the deceased is cross-examined by the gods, though once again it doesn't matter if the answers are false.

There are also paintings of houses, trees, gardens, servants and other possessions. It is believed that they will be present in the next world. An entire industry has developed making funeral jewellery and furniture.

Birds, fish and animals have also been embalmed, for Egyptian

religion associates animals with the gods. Some embalmers have even been called on to mummify shrews. But only the wealthiest and most important humans can benefit from their skills, for this is the art of preserving the bodies of the aristocratic dead.

Mummy and decorated coffin of an unnamed priestess from Thebes, c. 1050 BC.

Saul's future in doubt

Southern Canaan, c. 1030 BC

The career of Saul as king of Israel looks bleak after reports that the favour of Yahweh and the backing of Samuel have both been withdrawn.

Samuel had told Saul that Yahweh intended to punish the Amalekites for their ill-treatment of Israel. Saul must attack them and completely destroy every human being and animal.

Saul mustered a huge army and set up an ambush to trap the Amalekites but he decided to spare some and to take their king captive and to confiscate the fattest animals

rather than kill them.

Samuel went to see Saul, heard the noise of the animals and realised immediately what had happened. Challenged with the evidence of his disobedience, Saul tried to justify himself but Samuel refused to accept his excuses.

He warned Saul that he was now rejected as king. In a final act of penitence, Saul persuaded Samuel to lead the worship of God one last time in his presence. Then Samuel himself executed King Agag, as Saul ought to have done.

The two men parted shortly afterwards. Saul has gone back to

his home in Gibeah, and Samuel has returned to Ramah. It is reported that Samuel is deeply grieved by what has happened, and intends never to visit Saul again.

(1 Samuel 15)

The hill country south of Bethlehem provides excellent pasture.

Samuel announces new king-in-waiting

Bethlehem, c. 1035 BC

Another unknown young man from a small tribe is being tipped as a future king of Israel after being anointed by Samuel in a secret ceremony in Bethlehem, 8 km (5 miles) south of Jerusalem.

Samuel's official reason for going to Bethlehem was to offer a sacrifice to God. But he arrived depressed and appeared anxious not to increase Saul's antagonism towards him.

Samuel invited local resident Jesse and his sons to the sacrifice. Jesse arrived with seven of his sons, all tall and good-looking. Samuel, however, demanded whether there were any more, commenting that Yahweh is more impressed by inner spiritual strength than by outward physical qualities. The eighth, David, was summoned from his duties as shepherd.

In an impromptu ceremony the prophet anointed the youngster with oil and in front of his father and brothers announced that David has been chosen by God as the true king of Israel.

David is already being spoken of as filled with the Spirit of God, as was Saul when he was crowned. But God's Spirit is now widely believed to have departed from the king, whose irrational behaviour has led some to suggest that he is actually under the influence of a demon.

(1 Samuel 16:1–13)

Giant killer David!

Socoh, Judah, c. 1025 BC

The headless body of Philistine giant Goliath lies abandoned on a battlefield at Socoh tonight, a gory reminder of one of the most astonishing turnarounds in the history of Israelite–Philistine feuding.

His conqueror David – already a favourite at Saul's court, where his harp-playing has done wonders to soothe the king's depression – has been proclaimed a national hero.

Jesse's sons are drastically revising their opinion of their younger brother. He came to Socoh, 24 km (15 miles) west of Bethlehem,

The unexpected victory of the boy David, very much the under-dog, over the mocking giant presents a powerful image of the triumph of good over evil.

on the Philistine border, where the Israelite army has been confronting a massed Philistine force. David's errand was to take food from Jesse and bring him back news of his sons.

He found a demoralised army cowering before a 3-m (10-ft) giant Goliath, who twice daily for over a month has been challenging Israelite soldiers to single combat. This colossus, heavily armoured in bronze, carried a massive spear tipped with the finest Philistine iron.

The Israelites had been unable to produce a champion to respond, despite the huge rewards that Saul has been promising – wealth, exemption from taxes and marriage to his daughter. The sight of the giant, whose plumed headdress tops a mountain of armoured muscle, has been enough to keep prudent men inside their tents. David made no attempt to conceal his contempt at his kinsmen's cowardice.

The young man offered to fight Goliath himself, citing his exploits against lions and bears while protecting his sheep. When Saul offered him the use of his personal armour, David declined.

'He went out there in just his shepherd's tunic, with his sling and five pebbles,' explained Eliab, his older brother. 'Goliath couldn't believe it. But David just stood his

David presenting Goliath's head to Saul.

ground and said that he had come to fight in the name of the God whom Goliath and the Philistines despised.'

As Goliath stepped purposefully forward, the frightened Israelites saw David calmly fit a pebble into his sling. His aim was unerring. Goliath was probably dead before his huge body crashed to the ground. David finished the job with the giant's own sword.

The Israelites, now cheering, seized the initiative and pressed forward. The region tonight is littered with Philistine corpses, all the way back to their home cities.

(1 Samuel 17)

Skinny bride

Gibeah, c. 1025 BC

It was a challenge of which legends are made. Kill 200 enemies and you can marry the king's daughter. And giant-killer David rose to the task. Having turned down marriage to Princess Merab – his entitlement for slaying Goliath – he was equally reluctant even to marry her sister, Michal, who was infatuated with him, largely because he could not afford a princess's bride-price.

So potential father-in-law, Saul, proposed a bizarre, bloody alternative: 200 penis foreskins cut from Philistine corpses. David obliged, counting out the skins personally in front of Saul.

It is suggested that Saul secretly hoped that David would be killed in the attempt. But all he achieved is married bliss and popular acclaim for his rival. The king's jealousy is now said to be at fever pitch.

(1 Samuel 18:17–30)

Jealousy strikes a discordant note

Gibeah, c. 1025 BC

Music may be the food of love, and on the spirit gently lie, but for once its charms failed to bring harmony to the king's troubled mind. Instead, it roused such discord that he flung his spear at the music maker, narrowly missing him.

And so giant-killer, David, brought regularly into court to serenade the king, lives to fight and play another day.

The incident occurred the day after the army returned from the Socoh campaign to a rapturous reception from the women of Israel. Their songs and dances made it very clear they regarded David as the real hero of the war. Saul – jealous because his own exploits were being played down – sank into a bout of depression. When David was summoned to play his harp in Saul's quarters the king seized the opportunity to rid himself of the youth.

Saul is beginning to realise that the newcomer might be a credible challenge to his authority. Matters are not helped by the close friendship that has developed between David and the king's son, Jonathan.

In an effort to contain the challenge, Saul has made David commander of more than a thousand troops. This has backfired however, as the battalion has been a conspicuous success in campaigns.

(1 Samuel 18:1–16)

David on the run as Saul issues death warrant

Southern Canaan, c. 1020 BC

David the giant-slayer, king's son-in-law, and master musician, is tonight an outlaw on the run somewhere in the southern deserts. His crime is his popularity.

But not all of Saul's household supports the king's vendetta. His daughter Michal – David's wife – helped the fugitive escape and covered his tracks. And her brother Jonathan, a close friend of David, had given him advance warning of Saul's death threat.

David first fled north to Ramah, where he took refuge with Samuel in the prophets' district. When Saul caught up with them, there were extraordinary scenes as first local prophets, then Saul's men, and finally Saul himself were overcome by ecstatic experiences as prophecy poured from their lips.

David went next to the village of Nob near Jerusalem. Weaponless and hungry, he asked the priest Ahimelech for help. He lied to explain why he was unarmed: he was, he said, on urgent business for Saul.

Ahimelech told him to take Goliath's sword, which was kept in the village. There was no food except the consecrated bread of the sanctuary, but the priest allowed him to eat it on the grounds that David and his followers were ceremonially clean.

He then travelled west into Philistia, where he lodged incognito in Gath with King Achish; thus he carried Goliath's sword into Goliath's home town. He was soon recognised, and escaped by pretending to be insane, clawing at the woodwork and dribbling down his beard.

He was next seen at the cave of Adullam in Judah, in the western hills near the Philistine border. Four hundred discontented men have joined his mercenry band. Further sightings include one in Mizpah in Moab, east of the Dead Sea, where David arranged safe lodgings for his parents; had they remained at Bethlehem they would have been at the mercy of Saul.

It was a wise move. Not everyone is friendly to the fugitive, and David's movements were betrayed by Doeg the Edomite. Saul launched a revenge attack on the people who had helped David. He ordered a massacre of the priests of Nob and the local population.

It was the act of a desperate and deranged monarch who recognises a serious threat to his throne, and who knows that he has lost not only the approval of the people but also of Yahweh.

(1 Samuel 19–22)

David had to flee for his life often in the extremely rough terrain of the Judean desert approaching the coast of the Dead Sea. Seen here is an eroded cliff face near the Dead Sea.

Royal feud gets temporary relief

En Gedi, c. 1020 BC

King Saul got double relief when fugitive David caught him with his trousers down in the En Gedi Desert.

He used a cave as a convenient loo stop, unaware that his enemy was lurking in the dark behind him. But David opted to embarrass the king instead of killing him.

The oasis of En Gedi, in the Negev Desert, features this impressive waterfall and cooling pool of fresh water.

While Saul attended to his personal needs, David cut off a piece of the king's robe. Even that small gesture threw him into anguished remorse, for, as he told his men, he had laid hands on 'the Lord's anointed'.

When Saul left the cave David followed and made an emotional plea. He pointed out how easily he could have cut the king's throat instead of his robe, and he begged Saul to accept the gesture as evidence of good faith.

Realising how near he had been to death, Saul broke down and wept. He acknowledged that the kingdom was destined to pass to David, and implored him to treat the present royal family kindly when that happened.

The episode comes as the climax of a cat-and-mouse game that has spanned many miles of desert. Both David and Saul have been warily watching each other's movements and also fighting the Philistines.

Hearing that the Philistines were raiding Keilah, one of the towns in the low-lying region between the Philistine coast and the hills of Judah, David went to its aid. When his men protested that they were not at battle readiness, David assured them that he had prayed and that Yahweh had promised success. They saved the city.

It was news of this victory that had brought Saul hot-foot to Keilah to besiege the city and capture David. But David took to the desert with his small army, now 600-strong, and Saul could not find him.

Though some desert tribespeople had been feeding information on David's whereabouts to Saul, he has remained free. The unscheduled cave stop took place on one of many desert forays Saul has been making in search of David.

But despite David's generous act, there seems little hope of relief for him from Saul's obsessive hunt.

(1 Samuel 23, 24)

Saul asks witch way

Jezreel, c. 1010 BC

The increasingly desperate king of Israel has turned to the occultists he once banished from the land to bring him spiritual advice in the face of Philistine aggression.

As part of his zeal for Yahweh, the younger Saul outlawed spiritualist mediums. But now years later he has consulted one because the normal channels of communication with Yahweh appear to have broken down.

The medium conjured up an apparition of the late judge Samuel, to her own surprise as well as to Saul's. Samuel did not seem pleased to be disturbed and had no comfort for the troubled king. He reiterated the message of doom he had pronounced when alive.

Saul now faces a massive Philistine army which has penetrated deep into northern Canaan without any spiritual reassurance of national victory, and with a prophecy concerning his own death ringing in his ears.

Due to the durability of folk religion the medium had continued to operate despite the ban, and her presence was openly acknowledged when Saul's officials made enquiries. It also says something about her arts that she was unable to recognise the disguised king and that she did not appear to expect a genuine materialisation of Samuel.

The incident, which occurred at the village of Endor, 9 km (6 miles) north of Shunem in the northern region of Jezreel, has puzzled observers. As orthodox Israelite thought does not believe the dead can communicate with the living, other options are suggested. It may have been a God-guided projection from the woman's evident telepathic powers, or a demonic spirit which for once spoke the truth. But perhaps also Yahweh allowed a breach of his own rules to make a telling point.

(1 Samuel 28)

Brand new husband for wise wife

Judean desert, c. 1020 BC

Wealth and wisdom are not always combined. Nabal, a landowner in Carmel, a village deep in the scrubland of southern Judah, had plenty of the former but little of the latter. The discrepancy cost him the one thing money could never buy back – his life.

A highly intricate, decorated saddle would have been of great value to David.

When the band of brigands led by outlaw David asked him for protection money in return for assisting his servants, Nabal – whose name means 'fool' – told them to get lost in the desert.

Fortunately his wife Abigail had more sense, loaded up a caravan of goodies, and bought off the bandits before they could finish off her husband. But when the rich man heard of his narrow escape, he collapsed with a heart attack and died.

David, impressed by Abigail's worldly wisdom as well as her good looks, has invited her to become his third wife. She is some compensation to him for having lost Michal, Saul's daughter, in a *de facto* divorce ordered by the king after David's sudden abandonment of court life. The fugitive has also married Ahinoam of Jezreel, another village in the deep south; Michal, meanwhile, has been married off by her father to someone else.

(1 Samuel 25)

Second chance

Desert of Ziph, c. 1020 BC

For the second time in a matter of months David has refused to exploit a chance to kill King Saul. Led to the rebel leader's hide-out by information from the same desert people who betrayed David before, Saul brought a 3,000-strong force into the desert in search of his rival.

But David found Saul first. As the heat of the desert evening cooled into night, he crept in to where Saul was sleeping, his spear close at hand. One of David's companions offered to kill the king with the king's own spear. But once again David insisted that he would not harm Yahweh's anointed. Saul would die in God's time, either by natural causes or in battle, he said, leaving as quietly as he had come.

When Saul and his camp awoke from what some think was a supernaturally-induced sleep, he found David taunting his body-guards from a nearby hill-top, displaying Saul's spear and water-jug. Saul once again made an emotional speech of gratitude for David's mercy, prophesied great things for him and went home humbled, and probably frustrated at yet another failure to capture the outlaw.

(1 Samuel 26)

Double, double cross

The city of Gath was positioned on the crest of this hill.

Judean desert, c. 1010 BC

Rebel leader David has a charmed life. He has crossed sides to join the Philistines, his old enemies, but has been using their protection to wage a secret guerrilla war against them, pretending to his hosts that he was hassling the Israelites.

And when he faced the real possibility of marching into battle with the Philistines against Israel, the generals overruled the king and decided that he was too great a risk. He retreated home gratefully, with a suitable show of contrived regret and offended honour.

David had first settled into Gath, one of the five main Philistine cities and home town of the giant warrior Goliath who he slew as a young man. His reported exploits so pleased the city's ruler, Achish, that he gave David the nearby settlement of Ziklag for his own use.

But the Amalekites, another marauding nomadic tribe which has proved a thorn in the sides of both Philistia and Israel, destroyed it while he was away and kidnapped the women including David's wives. In a raid of extreme courage and determination, David, heavily outnumbered with only 400 fit men and 200 left behind exhausted, recovered all the plunder and women, and killed many of the Amalekites.

(1 Samuel 27; 29–30)

Saul is dead and Israel is defeated

Northern Canaan, c. 1010 BC

King Saul is dead. He has committed suicide on Mount Gilboa, at the close of a day of disasters.

Having been seriously wounded by an arrow, he fell on his own sword rather than be finished off by his enemies. His three sons have also fallen in battle.

And in a touching final act of kindness, the men of Jabesh Gilead have made the dangerous journey by night through Philistine lines to retrieve the bodies of Saul and his sons. Saul's first victory as king was the liberation of their town; and it is there, where his reign began with such bright promise, that Saul has been laid to rest amidst weeping and fasting.

In the end it was not David – who has twice spared his sovereign's life – who killed him.

On the battlefield, Israelite corpses lay where they fell on Mount Gilboa, including David's much-loved friend Jonathan. Saul, cowering and bloodstained from fatal arrow-wounds, had ordered his armour-bearer to kill him. But the armour-bearer refused and so both he and Saul fell on their own swords.

One zealous Israelite who brought the news of the defeat to David, who is likely to succeed to the throne, claimed to have killed Saul himself as an act of mercy. David was so incensed at his presumption that he had him summarily executed.

David has gone into a period of mourning and composed a personal lament. 'Tell it not in Gath,' he sang, 'lest the uncircumcised rejoice. Weep for Saul, daughters of Jerusalem. How the mighty have fallen.'

Tonight numerous Israelite towns in the Jordan Valley are deserted and lines of homeless refugees are making their way into the Israelite

Mount Gilboa and the plains of northern Canaan.

hinterland. They are racing against time, for the victorious Philistines are pouring into the valley and occupying large tracts of land.

(1 Samuel 31; 2 Samuel 1)

Rival kings

Canaan, c. 1010 BC

The 12 tribes of Israel have elected two rival kings. The men of Judah have anointed David, fulfilling a long-standing prophecy.

He has promised to reward the people of Jabesh Gilead who retrieved and tended Saul's body, but he warned that they must be strong and brave; for Judah is only one of 12 tribes, and laying claim to the kingship of the whole nation will be difficult.

In Manahaim east of Jordan, Abner, Saul's commander, has made Saul's son Ish-Bosheth king over the 11 tribes of Israel that have not accepted David's kingship. Ish-Bosheth's title is purely nominal, as much that is west of Jordan is now under Philistine control.

(2 Samuel 2:1–11)

The Philistine city of Gath once straddled this hill.

Why me?

Babylon, c. 1010 BC

A poet has complained that though he has lived an exemplary life he has been abandoned by the king and by the gods. How, he demands, can any human being know what will please the gods?

He catalogues a series of woes and disasters that have befallen him, and describes how the god Marduk was in the end merciful and restored him to his former well-being.

The *Poem of the Righteous Sufferer* rejects the view that good and evil are divine reward and punishment. The poet remains agnostic concerning the moral demands of the gods, and concludes that all one can do is have faith that in the end the gods will be merciful.

In the poem, that is indeed his experience and his wealth is restored. The account resembles an Israelite story about Job, a God-fearing person who suffers horribly.

Another piece of Babylonian literature, *The Theodicy*, takes the form of a dialogue between a sufferer and his friend. In this, the friend tries to convince the sufferer that the gods do in the end reward good and punish evil. The key to prosperity is piety. The sufferer rejects this view, but the argument clearly rises above the crude mythic fatalism of the Righteous Sufferer poem.

Tragedy and intrigue leave David angry but victorious

Gibeon, c. 1008 BC

A show duel that went tragically wrong began a bloody chain of events that has ended with the death of Ish-Bosheth, king of most of Israel.

The contest was proposed by Abner, Ish-Bosheth's aide, in a transparent attempt to limit David's growing influence. Joab, who is increasingly recognised as one of the hardest soldiers in David's army, accepted.

Twelve men from each army were chosen to fight as representatives of the rest. It was a humane alternative to huge casualties. But each pair of soldiers killed each other, leaving the matter entirely unresolved.

A fierce battle followed which David won. In the fighting, Abner was pursued by Joab and his brothers, and killed one of them in self-defence. But he placated his pursuers with an impassioned speech. From that time on, his influence grew with Ish-Bosheth.

But relations soured when Ish-Bosheth accused Abner of sleeping with one of the royal concubines as a way of claiming the throne for himself. Furious at the allegation, he switched sides and undertook to bring all Israel under David's rule.

David – whose standing in the nation has been mounting as the House of Saul has declined – was in a buyer's market. He drove a hard bargain, insisting that if Abner wanted to change sides he must bring with him Michal, the first love of David's life, given by Saul to another man during David's exile. He did so, and Michal joined the royal household in Hebron with David's other wives and the sons that had been born to them.

Abner immediately embarked on several rounds of diplomacy with the other tribes, persuading them to shift their allegiance from his former employer to David.

It was a short-lived triumph for Abner. Joab, still smarting at his brother's death, murdered him. But David, outraged at his death, commanded public mourning and publically dissociated himself from the murder.

News of the death demoralised Ish-Bosheth and his men. Abner was the strategist and architect of Ish-Bosheth's bid for the crown; but Ish-Bosheth's popularity had been waning. At this low point in his fortunes he fell to two assassins from the tribe of Benjamin.

His killers hoped to be rewarded by David, but they should have considered his attitude on hearing of Saul's death. Predictably, David declared himself outraged by the murder and had the assassins executed.

(2 Samuel 2:12–4:12)

Return of the ark brings new life

Jerusalem, c. 1000 BC

The triumphant return of the ark of Yahweh to Jerusalem from storage in the city of Kiriath Jearim marks a new direction in Israelite fortunes.

Crowds of cheering, singing spectators watched as the holy box was carried carefully by oxen through the city gates and into its streets. Musicians and dancers celebrated its return, stolen by the Philistines over 20 years ago. No more powerful symbol of David's victory can be imagined.

His own exuberance was plain to see. He stripped off his royal clothes and wore a religious robe as he danced without inhibition at the head of the procession. Only Michal, his wife, considered the exhibition 'undignified'. The celebrations concluded with traditional animal sacrifices.

But those who were dancing ecstatically in the streets took care not to go too near the ark, which is regarded as the most sacred object in Israelite religion. This was proved horrifically true when a bystander, Uzzah, attempted to steady it with his hand when the oxen stumbled, and instantly died.

But nothing can spoil the mood of rejoicing in Jerusalem for long. Following the death of Ish-Bosheth, Israel has finally united under David, who at the age of 30 becomes king over the whole nation. He has ruled the tribe of Judah for seven-and-a-half years.

He has lost none of his military genius; during that time he has easily defeated two attempted pre-emptive strikes by the Philistines in the Valley of Rephaim close by Jerusalem. That was followed by a major victory over the Jebusites at Jerusalem, which he has now made the royal city.

The return of the ark to Jerusalem was an event which outshone even David's coronation over all Israel at

The return of the ark was celebrated by spontaneous dancing in the streets.

Hebron after Ish-Bosheth's death. The action speaks volumes about his continuing devotion to Yahweh.

(2 Samuel 5–7)

David has repaid an old debt to friend

Jerusalem, c. 995 BC

Loyalty and promise-keeping are high on King David's list of human virtues. So he has found a way to commemorate his friendship with Saul's son Jonathan.

After considerable searching, he located a surviving son of Jonathan, a cripple called Mephibosheth, and he has arranged for him to be brought to the royal palace.

Mephibosheth, whose disability meant he could never succeed to the crown and also made him a laughing stock all his life, thought he was going to his execution. But not all old scores in Jerusalem today are being settled in blood.

Jonathan's son has leaped from living off hand-outs in Lo-Debar to being a man of prosperity and importance. All the former possessions of the house of Saul are now his, and David has ordered Ziba, Saul's servant, to manage Mephibosheth's new estates – a necessary delegation, since the new favourite lives in Jerusalem, where he is honoured at court and eats at the king's high table.

(2 Samuel 9)

Warrior king forbidden to build holy temple for God

Jerusalem, c. 990 BC

Favourite sons can often get away with murder. But not if their 'father' is Yahweh.

King David, whose blood-stained hands have brought hitherto unknown freedom to Israel, has had his plans to build a temple to Yahweh thwarted by God himself.

David's citadel in Jerusalem.

David is aware of the contrast between his splendid palace and the worship tent in which the ark is being kept. As he begins to gain victory over his enemies, he is adamant that proper provision should be made for an appropriate home for the ark of the Lord.

Nathan the prophet, who acts as court chaplain, was at first enthusiastic. But that night Yahweh spoke to him and rebuked him. Nathan then had the awkward task of explaining to the king that he is not allowed to build a house for God. Instead, Yahweh decreed that his temple will be built by a son still to be born, who will rule in quietness.

David is extremely disappointed that his cherished project will not now take place. But Nathan also brought a promise from God: David's son, though he will not always do what is right, will never be rejected in the way that Saul was. The House of David will be established 'for ever'.

When he heard this David was overwhelmed. He is said to have spent hours in prayer, thanking Yahweh not only for the promise but also for his gracious protection and preservation of his people.

(2 Samuel 7)

Fast Facts c. 1000 BC

Assyria: Human sacrifice is dying out in the Middle East but the Assyrians still practise it. If the omens show the king to be threatened with great danger, a substitute king is appointed who reigns while the danger continues. If he and his consort are still alive when the danger has passed, they are ritually put to death. Other places where human sacrifice still persists are Palestine Phoenicia and North Africa.

China: The Shang dynasty has refined its methods of divination, following a period when diviners were consulted on numerous topics and daily concerns. Now the practice of divination is restricted to sacrifices, the coming ten days, the coming night, and hunting. Animal bones are used, hollowed out and subjected to intense heat. The stress cracks thus produced are interpreted to predict a lucky or unlucky outcome. Mostly the interpretation is an optimistic one, perhaps because full details of the prediction and who made it are afterwards carved into the surface of the bone.

Cyprus: One result of the growing commerce between countries is that wherever you go there is usually somebody who speaks your language. Wen-Amon, an Egyptian trader travelling to the Lebanon to buy timber, escaped pirates by taking refuge in Cyprus. Making his way to the house of the town leader, he asked, 'Is there anybody here who speaks Egyptian?' There was.

Britain and Europe: As horses are used more and more, the first harnesses are appearing. They comprise cheek pieces made of antler horn or bronze, and strip fittings of bronze. There are also nave bands, pendants and bronze phalera – all of which are much used in European horse riding.

Ramah, Canaan: Samuel, the last great judge of Israel, has died at his home. A gifted prophet, he guided the 12 tribes through their transition from a loose confederation to a united nation under the headship of their first king, Saul. (1 Samuel 25:1)

Bronze Britons burn dead

Britain, c. 1000 BC

The Bronze Age in Britain is entering its maturity. It began 900 years ago when invaders in the south and east brought with them a tradition of war-making, skill with bows, and daggers of bronze.

All of which made their defeat of the Late Stone Age Britons an easy matter. The megalithic burial monuments and long barrows (earthen mounds in which the dead were buried) gave way to round barrows. The earlier practice of burying the dead together with all the needs and trappings of daily life has given way to a more spiritualised concept of death. Cremation is now common; the mound, empty of ornaments and artefacts, being raised over the ashes. Cremation is also becoming the norm from the Aegean to Central (and in some cases Northern) Europe.

In Dorset, the Deverel-Rimbury people have been burying their dead in characteristic urns in unmarked cemeteries. They also dispose of their dead in specially constructed barrows, or in the sides of existing mounds. It is believed that these people have been influenced by continental burial practices.

Another feature of the Late Bronze Age landscape in Britain (and a consequence of the invaders' influence) is the stone or wooden circle. They are centres of religious life, and some, such as the circle at Avebury, were completed early in the Bronze Age; others, most notably the splendid structure at Stonehenge, have been added to and refined over a millennium.

Throughout the Bronze Age, the use of metal has been extended in many ways. It is a sign of the times that more bronze is used in weaponry today than in agriculture or other domestic applications.

Agriculture is changing too. Barley now makes up 80 per cent of the grain harvest, and emmer wheat the rest. A major breakthrough has

Silbury hill near Avebury is the largest man-made burial mound in Europe, standing over 40m (130 ft) high.

been the discovery of winter sowing. Seventy per cent of the barley is the hulled variety, which can be sown in winter and so ensures a steady food supply all year. Fields are now cultivated by cross-ploughing.

The increase in crops and food is causing a population boom.

On the move

India, c. 1000 BC

The Vedic culture of India is moving into a new phase: historians have pronounced the 'Early Vedic' period to be at an end.

The Vedic period began when the Aryans migrated from the north-western region and settled in the Ganges valley. Equipped with chariots, and militarily sophisticated, they displaced the native Dravidians and farmed the area.

Now the Aryans are on the move again, expanding their territory and also warring between themselves. Their sacred book the *Rigveda* directs worship to an impersonal force of truth (Rita), to individual named gods, and also to natural forces such as fire and the sun. Indian religion encompasses a priesthood, a highly developed sacrificial system (including the soma sacrifice which employs intoxicating drugs), and a stress on the need for salvation and for union with the infinite reality.

Rulers get big heads

Mexico, c. 1000 BC

The Olmec people have built a large ceremonial centre at San Lorenzo in Southern Veracruz. Among the monuments are eight colossal basalt sculpted heads, the largest more than 2.85 m (9 ft) high, portraying Olmec rulers. Several massive basalt altars have niches in the front containing figures of the rulers. The centre is also equipped with a stone drainage system.

The basalt comes from quarries in the Tuxtla Mountains, which means that it was brought at least 80 km (50 miles). First the stones were dragged to navigable streams and loaded onto balsa rafts, then they were floated down to the Gulf of Mexico and up the Coatzacoalcos

The snarling jaguar featured on this ceremonial axe head proclaims its power to cleave open the realms of the spirit world.

River. From there, rollers were probably used to help in the final haul up the San Lorenzo plateau.

The Olmec eat mainly meat and have cannibal tendencies. They are thought to use hallucinogenic drugs extracted from poisonous marine toads. Their mythology includes the legend that long ago a race of were-jaguars were produced from the union of a woman and a jaguar; the offspring are sexless and have cleft heads. The figurines in the altar niches are usually holding either a were-jaguar baby or a rope with which to bind captives.

Israel tops the league of nations

Canaan, c. 990 BC

The Israelites under their new king David seem invincible as tribe after tribe falls to their military might.

They scored a major victory against the Philistines at Megeth Ammah. As a result, Philistia is now a subdued force.

A convincing defeat of the Moabites (the people who had looked after David's parents when he was in exile) resulted in two-thirds of their soldiers being culled after capture. The Moabites are now subject to David.

A battle against the king of Zobah, on the northern border of Israel, resulted in a thousand captured chariots being added to Israel's armoury. David lamed all but a handful of the captured war-horses, however. Charioteering is not a method of war favoured by the Israelites.

Further north in Aram (Syria) he won a dramatic victory against Damascus and to the east a victory over 18,000 Edomites in the Valley of Salt further spread his fame as a commander, and established his rule over the Edomites.

He is not an addicted conqueror with an insatiable lust for blood, however. But he is a formidable opponent if he is insulted, as the Ammonites found to their cost. They rejected a message of sympathy from David when their king died, and humiliated his messengers. In two subsequent battles he killed 40,000 of them and their Aramean allies.

David's attitude to war is in marked contrast to that of Saul. His trophies are all brought back to Jerusalem where they are dedicated to Yahweh, as with all his plunder.

(2 Samuel 8,10)

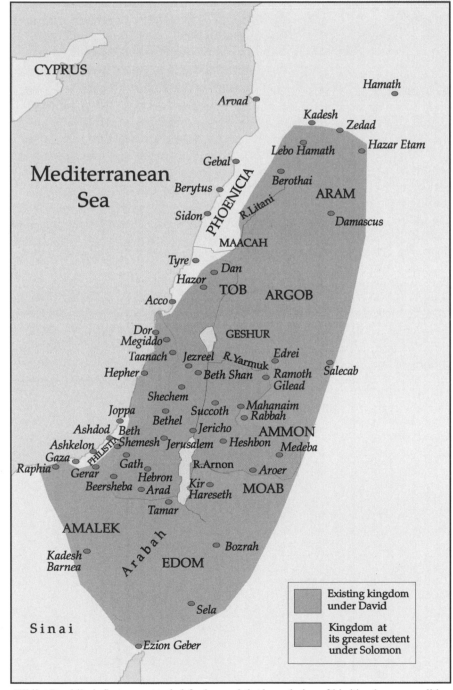

Whilst David's influence extended far beyond the boundaries of his kingdom, consolidation of the extention of his influence would have to wait until Solomon.

Hot iron

Middle East, c. 1000 BC

Iron is the hot substance of the age as metallurgists learn to use the new metal which some predict will replace bronze. Iron knives already outnumber those made from bronze in Cyprus and Syria, and the two substances are used in equal quantities in Greece.

Until recently, iron has been used only for decorative purposes and has been regarded as a precious metal. It may have been discovered by accident, as a by-product of copper smelting. The melting point for iron is higher than copper or bronze. When it is first forged, iron is malleable and quite soft. But if it is reheated in a furnace with carboniferous materials and then quickly cooled by being quenched in water, it becomes extremely hard and is usually called steel. It is valued in the making of weapons.

Jerusalem, the city of David

There has been a city called Jerusalem on the present site in the hills of Judah since at least the third millennium. Egyptian and other ancient documents mention Jerusalem. The name probably means 'foundation of peace'.

Originally it was probably a hill fortress, controlled by Egypt. Later, it is almost certainly the 'Salem' ruled by Melchizedek (Genesis 14).

By the time the Israelites entered the Promised Land it was ruled by the Jebusites, whose king Adonizedek was the loser in one of Joshua's more famous victories.

But the superb natural defences of the city made it impossible for Joshua to seize it; the Jebusites, in fact, boasted that even a force of blind men and cripples could defend the city (2 Samuel 5:6). It was strongly fortified on a steep-sided hill.

As 'Jebus', it remained a Jebusite city, its occupants secure behind their strong walls. However, the tribe of Benjamin took the area of the city immediately outside the

fortifications, creating in effect a divided city.

It boasted an ingenious water system, in which a spring outside the city was channelled beneath it in a tunnel, and accessed by a deep well. It is likely that David's commando force took the city by climbing the well and then opening the gates.

There were a number of reasons why he chose Jerusalem as his capital. One was the reason that had made it desirable to so many people in the past: its strategic location. Also, the taking of Jerusalem would help to establish good relationships between the Judahites and the Benjamites.

Model of Jerusalem as it might have looked in David's day.

The city of Jerusalem was little more than a fortified village astride a small hill to begin with under David. King Solomon then greatly increased its area and built the temple.

The walls of Jerusalem here follow the lines of the original wall erected by David.

David has built his palace there. Its ornately carved timbers and delicately carved stonework, and most of the skilled craftsmen who worked on the building, were sent from Hiram, king of Tyre, as a gift to the new monarch.

Many people have seen this prosperity as a sign that God really is with David, though the increasing numbers of wives and concubines in David's household has made others fear that David, too, might have moral weaknesses that threaten the long-term stability of the monarchy.

(cf. 2 Samuel 5:9–12)

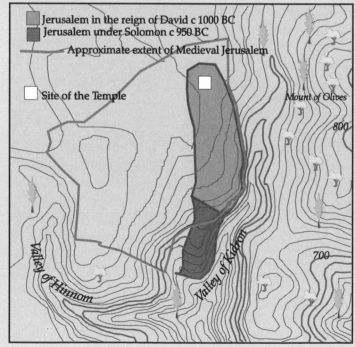

Jerusalem in the reign of David c 1000 BC
Jerusalem under Solomon c 950 BC
Approximate extent of Medieval Jerusalem

Site of the Temple

Mount of Olives

800

Valley of Hinnom

Valley of Kidron

700

David's glorious reign celebrated in verse

The Israelite hymnbook is expanding rapidly, for King David is proving to be a gifted psalm-writer.

David, though his reign has been marked by tragedy and human error, has always given honour to Yahweh and acknowledged that all his achievements as king have been made possible only by God. He is recognised as a man of genuine, if flawed, piety.

His psalms are well known all over the nation, both those written for congregational singing and the profound meditations with which he tends to commemorate the great moments of his life. Here are some quotations from the king's psalm-book.

When hiding from Saul in a cave:
> Listen to my cry,
>   for I am in desperate need;
> rescue me from those who pursue me,
>   for they are too strong for me.
> Set me free from my prison,
>   that I may praise your name ...
> (Psalm 142:6–7)

After defeating the Edomites:
> Give us aid against the enemy,
>   for the help of man is worthless.
> With God we shall gain the victory,
>   and he will trample down our enemies ...
> (Psalm 60:11–12)

During Absalom's rebellion:
> I lie down and sleep;

> I wake again, because the LORD sustains me.
> I will not fear the tens of thousands drawn up against me on every side
> (Psalm 3:5–6)

One of the most beautiful of his psalms, which makes a fitting note as he nears the end of his life, is the song of praise he sang to the Lord after one of his great victories:

> The LORD is my rock, my fortress and my deliverer;
>   my God is my rock, in whom I take refuge,
>   my shield and the horn [= strength] of my salvation.
> He is my stronghold, my refuge and my saviour —
> from violent men you save me.
> I call to the LORD, who is worthy of praise,
>   and I am saved from my enemies.
> (2 Samuel 22:2–4)

He has set down his final thoughts on his reign in poetry that has the

Palm trees in an oasis in the South Sinai Desert. David would often have taken refuge in such a place.

assurance of a man who, though his life has known defeat and disgrace as well as glory and honour, has utter faith that his God will be perfectly just and perfectly loving:

> The Spirit of the LORD spoke through me;
>   his word was on my tongue ...
> Is not my house right with God?
> Has he not made with me an everlasting covenant, arranged and secured in every part?
> Will he not bring to fruition my salvation
> and grant me my every desire?
> (2 Samuel 23:2, 5)

The humility and piety of all David's poetry makes a telling contrast to the pronouncements of Saul.

Fast Facts c. 1000 BC

**old, Wales:** A cape has been made from a single sheet of gold. It is a 'pectoral' or shoulder cape, and its surface is richly decorated in such a way that when worn, the cape seems to have folds like cloth. It is backed with leather and has bronze strips sewn on for strength. The gold from which it is made comes from Ireland. Such an artefact has been seen nowhere else except in ancient Egypt, but the growing number of gold-beaters in Europe suggests a new decorative industry might be starting.

Switzerland, Alps: Swiss hunting knives are acquiring an impressive reputation. Early models had curved backs and wooden handles. Later knives had flanged hilts, were lap-jointed and were fitted with thin sheets of sharp horn. But today's all-bronze product is the finest yet, with intricate decoration and a ring to hang the knife from one's belt.

France: New schools of metalwork are opening all over Europe, with several in France. At Medoc, massive laterally-flanged axes are forged for export throughout the country. In Brittany the coastal peoples make distinctive spearheads and rapiers with bronzed hilts which are exported to Holland. There is another active production centre in nearby Normandy.

Sardinia: The traditional nuraghi defensive towers are being developed into a fine architectural form. The cone-shaped tower built with large, carefully-dressed stones, has a platform on the top and step-like tiers around it. Chambers with corbelled roofs, and a second storey accessed by an internal staircase, are now being included. Villages growing under the shadow of these towers have huts with low, circular drystone walls.

Wales: The region on the western fringe of Britain has been the scene of some horrific child sacrifices. It is believed that the earbones of children were removed, which could only be done by removing the brain as well. The earbones may have served as symbols of the brain, and both may have been eaten. Some women have also been buried alive alongside their deceased husbands.

115

Royal affair is uncovered

Jerusalem, c. 985 BC

A royal love affair with a married woman, initially covered up by the carefully-planned murder of her husband, has been exposed by court prophet Nathan.

King David has admitted to what is an extraordinary lapse by a man who once refused to lay a finger on Saul to gain the greater prize of national leadership, and who has always put great emphasis on both human and spiritual loyalty.

If David had been carrying out his military duties the disaster would never have happened. But having dispatched his commander, Joab, to what has turned out to be a successful campaign against the Ammonites, lounging one evening on the roof of the palace he saw a beautiful woman bathing.

It was Bathsheba, the wife of Uriah, one of his generals who was away fighting. He sent for her and slept with her. As a result she became pregnant.

David immediately summoned Uriah back from the war and tried to persuade him to spend the night at home with Bathsheba; when the child was born, he calculated, it would appear that it had been conceived that night.

But Uriah refused, citing the battleground rule that serving soldiers must abstain from sexual intercourse. So David gave him a letter to take to Joab. Uriah never knew he was carrying his own death warrant: it instructed Joab to put Uriah in the front line during the next battle, where he died.

When Bathsheba's mourning was completed, David lost no time in moving her into the royal palace as his wife, where the baby was born – a boy.

It looked as if he had got away with it, until Nathan the prophet turned up one morning with a touching tale.

A poor man had a young ewe lamb, his prized possession, he said. He lavished love and care on it. But a rich neighbour with a huge flock of sheep chose to seize the poor man's lamb and slaughter it, instead of one of his own, to feed a visitor.

David was outraged, but Nathan pointed out that he was merely describing the king's behaviour. He pressed the point home: Yahweh was angry because by his adultery David has despised everything that he received from him.

And as a result, warned Nathan, the sword will now never depart from David's house. Calamity will befall it. The royal harem will be given to another man. The king has sinned in secret, but his punishment will be all too public.

Cconscience-stricken, David instantly repented. Nathan assured him that he would not die for his crime. But the son born out of the adultery would die. And as soon as the prophet left the court, the baby became sick and died in a few days.

It has been a shattering experience for David, whose repentance is clearly expressed in the psalm he has composed:

Cleanse me with hyssop, and I shall be clean;
wash me, and I shall be whiter than snow.
Let me hear joy and gladness;
let the bones you have crushed rejoice.
Hide your face from my sins
and blot out all my iniquity.
Create in me a pure heart, O God,
and renew a steadfast spirit within me.
(2 Samuel 11, 12; cf. Psalm 51)

David hears Nathan out – as seen by Rembrandt.

Young royals flee as rape and murder split family

Jerusalem, c. 980 BC

Rape and murder committed by two of the king's sons has tarnished with scandal a royal household once held in high esteem. Now, it seems, David's family life is about as convoluted as any commoner's, and he appears unable to do anything about it.

David's son Ammon not only raped his half-sister Tamar, but also abandoned her afterwards. He has consistently refused to take any responsibility for her, and she is now living in her brother Absalom's home, a broken woman.

King David, a notoriously lenient father, has made no attempt to punish Ammon, and his anger seems to have had no practical effect. Absalom has refused to speak to Ammon for two years and his bitter hatred of him has been obvious.

Matters came to a bloodthirsty head when Absalom invited his royal brothers to a sheep-shearing feast. He ordered his men to get Ammon drunk and then murder him. The other brothers fled in panic. By the time they returned home rumours were spreading like wildfire: some said that all the brothers had been massacred.

Absalom fled to exile, seeking asylum with his maternal grandfather north of the Sea of Galilee.

According to Israelite law, Ammon's murder should be avenged by his next-of-kin. That means David should put Absalom to death. But he grieves more for Absalom's exile than he did for Ammon's death; Absalom, the tall handsome prince with the flawless skin and luxurious hair, is the son closest to his father's heart.

(2 Samuel 13)

King flees Jerusalem

Jerusalem, c. 980 BC
King David has been forced out of his own capital by the threat of his son Absalom to stage a coup.

Absalom was brought back into royal favour after a ruse by Joab convinced the king to forgive him, and a two-year stand-off allowed tempers to cool.

But the king wants his son Solomon to succeed to the throne, even though Absalom is legally next in line.

So for the past four years, Absalom has acquired a prestigious chariot and a small force of 50 retainers. He has carefully built up his influence and popularity among the people, and has promised greater access to justice should he ever become king. He has made it his business to flatter as many disgruntled people as he can, and he looks every inch a plausible successor.

Leaving court on the pretext of wanting to worship Yahweh at nearby Hebron – he claimed to have vowed to do so· while he was in exile – he has proclaimed himself king there. He has already gained considerable popular support, and has even persuaded Ahithophel, one of David's trusted aides, to join him. His faction is growing in strength daily.

David made the instinctive response of the seasoned desert

The eastern approach to Jerusalem: David fled through this valley.

guerrilla fighter. He left Jerusalem, thus preventing its destruction, and refused to carry the ark of Yahweh with him.

There were emotional scenes as he took the road out of the city over the Mount of Olives. Soldiers and faithful servants who were with him were weeping openly.

As Absalom advanced, David went north-east on the Jericho road, little more than 16 km (10 miles) away from his son's advancing army. He was met on the road by Ziba, Mephibosheth's servant, bringing provisions. When Ziba said that his master was still in Jerusalem, David feared the worst. Mephibosheth, grandson of Saul, hoped he too might become king.

At Bahurim, just outside Jerusalem, a member of the House of Saul, called Shimei, insulted him and pelted him with stones. The king's response was characteristically gracious, though his mind must have been in turmoil as he left the royal city behind and headed on into the desert.

But he has left one friend there. Hushai the Arkite has been charged to enter Absalom's service, and as an 'agent in place' to subvert the advice of Ahithophel.

(2 Samuel 15:1–16:14)

Absalom blunders in

Jerusalem, c. 975 BC
Absalom has entered Jerusalem, while allowing weak King David to escape. This could well be the turning point in the campaign.

Ahithophel, a revered counsellor at David's court who has joined Absalom, had warned that attacking cities would only provoke a civil war despite strong support for Absalom's claim to the throne.

He also recommended that Absalom should take for himself the harem that David had left as caretakers of the palace. The shame of the insult to the king would be so devastating that David would never be able to come back.

Absalom sought a second opinion from Hushai, a friend of David and still secretly loyal to him. He promptly advised a search-and-destroy policy, laying waste any city that might harbour David and his men. The prospect of glamorous further conquests appealed to Absalom's vanity.

Ahithophel knew that Absalom had thrown away his chance of victory. Taking Jerusalem was mere time-wasting. David knew the desert intimately. If he could get to his old allies in time, occupy his old strongholds and regather his strength, David would be unstoppable. Ahithophel coolly assessed Absalom's likely action, returned to his home town, put his affairs in order, and committed suicide.

Meanwhile, Hushai sent a message to David, telling him what he had advised Absalom to do and urging him to cross the Jordan immediately, in case Absalom changed his mind. David went on to Mahanaim, where as Hushai had anticipated he has been able to regroup, organise his army, and enjoy the hospitality of the local people. Absalom now has to face a king who is rested, refreshed, and ready to fight.

(2 Samuel 16:15–17:29)

117

The rebellion is over

Ephraim, c. 975 BC

The king's rebel son Absalom is one of 20,000 dead fighters as David's army finally put down the rebellion in the forests of Ephraim.

Many died in the dangerous forest terrain, as well as in battle; David's men had the advantage of experience in rough wooded terrain.

As Absalom was riding through the forest he encountered a detachment of David's men. In the confusion, his head became tangled with a tree, his mule bolted, and he was left hanging in mid-air by his

The hill country of Ephraim is both remote and inhospitable.

long hair.

The men reported this to Joab, who was furious that they had not taken advantage of Absalom's helplessness. Although David had specifically commanded Joab in their hearing to be gentle with Absalom, he ignored the command and killed Absalom himself.

When David heard the news, his wild lamenting shocked the troops by its intensity and Joab prevented a major breakdown of morale by demanding that David pull himself together and address his men. Otherwise, Joab pointed out, it would seem that the life of the rebellious Absalom mattered more than the lives of David's loyal warriors, who had just been fighting and dying for him.

It is a sad end to a well-conceived and strategically accomplished campaign. But his weakness as a father, his inability to discipline his sons and his failure to realise that Absalom's death was the quickest way to end a potentially open-ended and bloody conflict, all diminish this, perhaps David's greatest victory.

(2 Samuel 18:1–19:8)

Plague averted

Jerusalem, c. 975 BC

An outbreak of plague has been averted after King David built an altar to Yahweh and repented of his presumption in holding a military census. The plague was interpreted as Yahweh's judgement on David's pride in his fighting machine.

He paid the market price for the land on which he built the altar even though its owner, Araunah the Jebusite, offered to donate it free of charge. Offerings to God should not cost nothing, David said.

The old king is now forbidden by his advisers to go into battle, and it may have been his frustrated fighting spirit which prompted him to count the number of men of military age in the nation. For once even Joab, not known for his religious scruples, opposed the idea although he did not hinder its execution.

In Yahweh's eyes the numbers may not count for much, but for human strategists the fact that 500,000 were reported to have registered in Judah alone, and 800,000 in the other tribes, will make other nations think twice before launching any sudden attacks. Yet despite the strength of forces and David's victories in years past, there have been an increasing number of skirmishes with the Philistines again recently.

(2 Samuel 21:15–22; 24:1–25)

Reconciliation as king returns

Jerusalem, c. 975 BC

David is back in Jerusalem. His grieving for Absalom is completed.

Crowds turned out to welcome him home. Cheering and singing, they lined the same roads along which David fled as a refugee not long ago.

Magnanimous in victory, David has forgiven Shimei, who cursed the king as he fled from the city. Shimei had met David and begged for forgiveness. He received even more: a guarantee of his safety by his personal oath.

He has also forgiven Ziba, who tried to make his fortune by letting David think that Mephibosheth had personal ambitions to steal the throne. But instead of punishing the servant, he ordered that Mephibosheth's estates – previously transferred to Ziba – be divided equally between them. Saul's grandson responded with even greater magnanimity and donated them all to Ziba out of joy that David was safe.

The king has shown his gratitude to those who cared for him at Mahanaim, too.

Only one person has been left out. Joab, who killed Absalom against the king's express orders, has not been forgiven. His job as military commander has been given to Absalom's chief commander, Amasa. Joab has been singled out for the king's resentment.

(2 Samuel 19:8–40)

Rumblings of discontent

Canaan, c. 975 BC

The storm of Absalom's rebellion may have passed, but the discontent in Israel rumbles on like distant thunder.

For a short time David's kingdom has returned to its original single tribe of Judah which he ruled immediately after the death of Saul. The other 11 tribes split off after a Benjaminite, Sheba, objected to the Judeans' exclusive protection of David during the rebellion.

David despatched Joab to deal with the situation, and the ruthless army commander pursued Sheba to Abel Beth Maacah in Dan, north of Galilee, where he had sought refuge. The city was saved from destruction by a woman who organised Sheba's execution inside the city and threw his head over the wall to Joab. He called off the siege and returned to Jerusalem.

Joab had already had his ration of blood for the week. On the way north he had murdered David's messenger and Joab's rival commander Amasa for taking too long to call out the Judean army to defend the king. His own position as number two in the kingdom has once more become as secure as David's position as number one.

(2 Samuel 19:41–20:26)

King David dies after settling succession

Jerusalem, c. 970 BC

King David is dead, and one of the most significant chapters in Israelite history has closed. Characteristically, he tied up some loose ends and displayed to the last his native wit and ingenuity.

In his final years he enjoyed the companionship of Abishag, a beautiful young woman who acted as nursemaid but avoided sexual intimacy with him.

As he has grown increasingly old and frail his sons have been looking beyond him to a throne that would soon be vacant. Adonijah, his oldest surviving son, set his heart on succeeding his father.

A charismatic, handsome man who was always able to persuade his father to let him do whatever he wanted, Adonijah's plan to succeed culminated in a great festive sacrifice attended by some of his brothers, Joab, and other members of the court. Solomon was among those who did not receive an invitation. At the festival, Adonijah was virtually proclaimed king.

But King David and the prophet Nathan reassured Bathsheba that the promise made to her that her son should be king would be fulfilled, David appointed Solomon as co-regent, and Nathan performed the anointing at a splendid coronation that won the hearts of the people. Adonijah's supporters have fallen away, and he has pleaded with Solomon to spare his life.

David made a death-bed speech to Solomon, charging him to follow Yahweh and keep his commandments. He warned Solomon about individuals at court and in the army who needed to be watched closely, and others who needed to be cherished and protected.

Now David is dead, buried in the holy city with his forefathers. He reigned for about 40 years. He succeeded a spiritually bankrupt king, and his own reign was not without scandal. But there will never be another as great as David.

(1 Kings 1:1–2:11)

Wise guy gains

Gibeon, c. 970 BC

Solomon is proving one of those pious kings whose big ideas are tempered by a genuine humility. After offering a thousand sacrifices to God, he was given the fairy-tale offer: to ask for whatever he wanted.

Whereas many would have been tempted to ask for health, wealth and happiness, Solomon acknowledged his own inexperience and the enormity of the task ahead. He asked that Yahweh would confirm his promises to his father David concerning the future, and for the wisdom and knowledge which he regarded as indispensable for ruling the kingdom.

According to Solomon, God so approved the request that he promised to give him not only wisdom, but also wealth and honour beyond any other monarch.

(1 Kings 3:4–15; 2 Chronicles 1:2–13)

Jerusalem: the lasting tribute to King David, who made it his capital city 3,000 years ago, seen here from Mount Scopus.

Rivals removed in court purge

Jerusalem, c. 970 BC

Three of Solomon's closest rivals have been removed as the king consolidates his position as David's legitimate successor. Adonijah, the oldest surviving son of David, and Joab, David's former army commander, have been executed, and the priest, Abiathar, has been sent to internal exile.

Matters came to a head when Adonijah, claiming to accept Solomon's authority, asked permission to marry Abishag, the Shunammite concubine who had nursed David in his old age. Solomon regarded this as another devious attempt by his half-brother to seize the throne by claiming direct links with King David.

Solomon decide to remove him, and ordered his execution.

Joab, who had previously conspired with Abiathar in Adonijah's attempted coup before David's death, sought sanctuary in the shrine of Yahweh. But as his crimes of murder had been premeditated, he was not entitled to claim protection as set out in the Law of Moses, and was executed beside the altar.

Abiathar the priest was treated more leniently. Because he had once carried the ark of the covenant, Israel's sacred casket, he was allowed to live in Anathoth, 6 km (4 miles) north of Jerusalem. Another opponent of David, Shimei, was also spared and ordered to stay within the confines of Jerusalem.

(1 Kings 2:13–38)

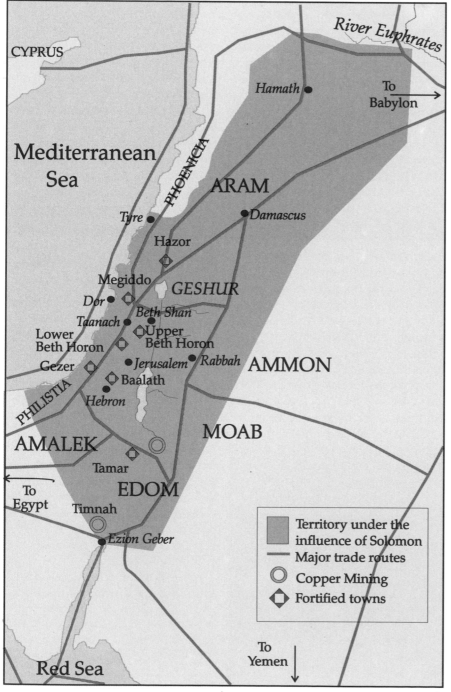

The full extent of King Solomon's kingdom at its height.

North American building mounds

Ohio, c. 960 BC

The people of the Adena culture are building huge and richly-furnished burial mounds up to 20 m (65 ft) high in several sites in present-day Ohio, Indiana, Kentucky, Pennsylvania and West Virginia.

The grave goods include strings of freshwater pearls, copper plaques, tubular tobacco pipes and polished stone tools. Upper-class people are buried in log tombs, which are then burned, before being covered by a mound.

The living Adena occupy round huts with conical roofs. A framework of upright posts is walled in with wattle, and a central smokehole in the skin-covered roof provides ventilation for the central hearth.

Solomon establishes trading links with Tyre

Jerusalem, c. 966 BC

A trading connection between Israel and Phoenicia, dating back to the early years of David's reign, has been revived by King Solomon as part of his ambitious temple building project.

Under the agreement, King Hiram of Tyre, whose kingdom is rich in cedar forests and stone quarries, is providing the materials and much of the labour force, as he did for the building of David's

Huge centuries-old cedars covered the mountains and hills of Lebanon and were its richest and most reknowned resource.

palace. Solomon is paying the market rate for both.

Such arrangements help Tyre as much as Israel. Tyre, between the sea and the magnificent cedar forests of Lebanon, is principally a ship-building power. But people cannot eat wood, and although Hiram's expressions of delight that another godly king has come to the throne of Israel are probably genuine, he is not giving charity.

Solomon is paying him 440 kilolitres (97,000 gallons) of pressed olive oil and 4,400 kilolitres (121,000 bushels) of grain in exchange for timber and skills. Hiram's ships also continue to ply precious stones and exotic timbers into Solomon's warehouses.

Other nations are making alliances and trading links with bourgeoning Israel. Solomon has married the daughter of the Egyptian Pharaoh which brings together two important nations. It also gives Solomon the town of Gezer as his bride's dowry, currently a burned-out ruin but an important trading centre located between Jerusalem and Egypt.

(1 Kings 3:1; 5:1–18; 2 Chronicles 2:1–18)

Major festival cancelled again

Babylon, c. 960 BC

For the ninth year running, the New Year Festival has not been celebrated in Babylon because of poor security in the nation.

The festival is the means by which the Babylonians receive their god Marduk's blessing for the year ahead, and it is seen as essential to the nation's well-being. To be unable to celebrate it bodes ill.

Normally, the festival lasts several days. There are ceremonial cleansings and prayers until the fourth day, when the *Epic of Creation* is recited and acted out. The king then has all symbols of his

royalty removed by the high priest and is ceremonially slapped around the face and ears. He kneels before Marduk and swears that he has committed no sins, nor neglected his duties.

The high priest returns his royal garments, and he is slapped around the face again, as hard as possible – if the pain brings the king to tears, it shows that Marduk is pleased. In the evening a white bull is sacrificed. Later in the festival, the king takes the hand of Marduk's image and leads him down the Processional Way and through the Ishtar Gate.

Gilt edged city points to God

Jerusalem, c. 957 BC

Jerusalem has become a boom city in which silver and gold are as common as stones, and rich cedar wood is an everyday building material. The temple is a wonder of the world. And the new Palace of the Forest of Lebanon is a vast structure built largely of cedar and high-quality rose-tinted limestone.

Included in King Solomon's lavish building programme is a Hall of Justice and a palace for the king's wife, the daughter of Pharaoh.

Huge royal stables house 1,400 chariots and 12,000 horses, and his bloodstock is imported from top breeding nations like Egypt and Cilicia. Israel is even exporting horses and chariots to the Hittites and Arameans.

The sheer prosperity of the nation speaks of its new glory. The king's unique throne is inlaid with ivory and plated with the finest gold. Its decorations include six steps flanked by carved lions, with two more lions standing at the armrests. Solomon has also had 200 large and 300 small golden shields made, not for battle but for display in the palace. Other symbols of greatness include the golden goblets in the royal household, and the royal merchant fleet.

The wealth and splendour of Israel often makes visitors realise how great Israel's God is. The Queen of Sheba in the Yemen came to test Solomon's fabled wisdom by asking him some hard questions. But she was as impressed by his wealth as by his wisdom and declared that everything she had seen and heard had convinced her that Yahweh was blessing Israel, and that Solomon's accession was a sign of God's eternal love.

She brought tribute of gold, spices and precious stones, and Solomon gave her gifts from the royal treasury.

(1 Kings 10; 2 Chronicles 9)

Solomon's temple: celebration as massive project is completed

Jerusalem, c. 970 BC

Solomon's magnificent temple has been dedicated to Yahweh with a huge 14-day celebration in which 22,000 cattle and 120,000 sheep and goats were sacrificed. Burnt, grain and fellowship offerings were made in the courtyard before the temple.

It is reported that God has appeared to Solomon and declared himself pleased with the work. He promised again that if Solomon followed his father's example and lived in faithful obedience to Yahweh, then the royal line of David would sit on the throne of Israel for ever. But if Solomon or his sons should turn away from God by failing to honour his commands or by following other gods, he would remove Israel from the land he had given them and would reject the temple.

The temple that Solomon built, fulfilling his father David's great desire, is both a shrine to house the ark of the covenant and a constitutional building at the centre of the nation's life. It bears some similarities to the desert tabernacle, the mobile worship-tent which accom-panied Israel through the desert and into Canaan.

The sanctuary is strongly reminiscent of the tabernacle, but it has an added entry porch and three rooms inside. Alongside the middle chamber (the Holy Place) and the Most Holy Place are storage rooms. Some aspects of the design have been influenced by the Phoenician workmen sent by Hiram, king of Tyre.

The temple is modest in size – (about 27 m (87 ft) long by 9 m (30 ft) wide – and is not intended to hold a large congregation. It is seen as the house of God, where he promised he would dwell among his people. It has taken seven years to build, however, using a large task force of labourers. All heavy tool work was done away from the site, which was regarded as holy. The stone was cut and dressed at the quarry, probably underground to ensure that the noise did not carry, and when brought to the site was worked on in silence.

Constructed from Lebanese cedar and local limestone, it has small windows set high in the roof. Its inner walls are clad with cedar planking, and gold covers almost every surface to create an unforgettable sight. But only a few selected priests will ever enter the Holy Place and fewer still will pass through the gold-plated olive-wood doors into the Most Holy Place.

The temple furnishings have been made by Hiram, a craftsman from Tyre, working under Solomon's direction. They include bronze pillars, chains, pomegranate decorations, and lily-shaped trims. He made, among many other items, a huge bronze basin for washing, supported by 12 bulls, which stands in the courtyard.

The entry chamber is unfurnished. In the Holy Place there are golden tables holding the Bread of the Presence, five pairs of golden lampstands, and the altar of incense. In the Most Holy Place is the ark of the covenant. There are intricate decorations on walls and doors, using motifs from plant life and representations of angelic beings. Some seem to be purely decorative, with no obvious symbolic function.

As part of the opening ceremonies, Solomon brought valuable artefacts which David had consecrated to God and placed them in the Temple storage rooms.

(1 Kings 5:1–9:9; 2 Chronicles 2:1–7:22)

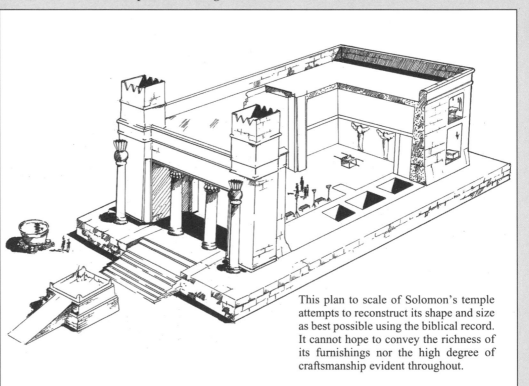

This plan to scale of Solomon's temple attempts to reconstruct its shape and size as best possible using the biblical record. It cannot hope to convey the richness of its furnishings nor the high degree of craftsmanship evident throughout.

Solomon's wisdom: first among equals

Solomon's wisdom is now a byword, and his intellect and breadth of knowledge are extraordinary. He is acknowledged by the academic world as a brilliant scholar. He has devised 3,000 proverbs and over 1,000 songs, is a perceptive scientist, and a specialist in flora and fauna. Students come from all over the world to sit at his feet.

His wisdom is best displayed in his legal judgements, where his razor-sharp mind goes to the issues at the heart of the most complex cases. In a famous hearing, two prostitutes both claimed to be the mother of the same baby. One said that the other had stolen the infant from her because her own child had died. Solomon ignored the legal pleading and sent for a sword to cut the child in half and give half to each woman.

One woman agreed to the plan, vowing that neither of them should have the child. The other begged him to let the child live, even if it meant losing it to the other woman. Solomon promptly awarded the child to the second woman, who was clearly its mother.

The king stands in a long tradition of wisdom which spans the cultures. Babylon and Egypt are equally famed for their books of wisdom, and Phoenicia and Israel have their own class of wise men and women who advise governments and arbitrate in disputes.

Many of the sayings consist of practical commonsense advice on daily living, especially in maintaining harmonious relationships and keeping out of trouble.

The Teaching of Amenemope, written in Egypt not long ago, contains many striking parallels to collections of Israelite wisdom-sayings in both style and content. 'Guard yourself against robbing the wretched,' it warns. 'Don't remove landmarks. Don't run after riches. If you get rich by robbery, your ill-gotten gains will soon disappear. Don't associate with hot-headed people. You're better off with bread and contentment than with wealth and contention.'

The Babylonian Theodicy which dates from at least a century ago, is a treatise written by a priest on the problem of suffering. The hero debates with his friend as to why the many gods allow or cause people to suffer. The similarity to the Israelite story of Job ends there, however.

Solomon is also credited with writing a superb love poem in which a man courts a woman. The couple speak of their love and hunger for each other, and a chorus adds comment and advice.

(1 Kings 3:16–28; 4:29–34; cf. 2 Samuel 14:2; 1 Chronicles 27:32)

This miniature shrine of King Tutankhamun was a glory in gold. Solomon's temple was also covered in gold – but built to a monumental size.

Solomon's judgement seen by an unknown Dutch master. This story best exemplifies King Solomon's wisdom and has been popular throughout the ages.

Solomon's Poetry

I have come into my garden, my sister,
my bride;
I have gathered my myrrh with my
spice.
I have eaten my honeycomb and my
honey;
I have drunk my wine and my milk
(Song of Songs 5:1)

Solomon's Philosophy

There is a time for everything,
and a season for every activity under
heaven
a time to be born and a time to die,
a time to plant and a time to uproot,
a time to kill and a time to heal,
a time to tear down and a time to build,
a time to weep and a time to laugh,
a time to mourn and a time to dance .
(Ecclesiastes 3:1–4)

Solomon's Proverbs

Wisdom is supreme; therefore get wisdom.
Though it cost you all you have, get
understanding.
(Proverbs 4:7)

Like one who seizes a dog by the ears is a
passer-by who meddles in a quarrel not
his own.
(Proverbs 26:17)

Dorian nomads settle old scores

Sparta, c. 950 BC

Dorian nomads, the last of the groups which have invaded Greece from the north, are settling in villages in Peloponnese Laconia (southern Greece). At least four of them have formed a political union under two kings.

Laconia, which is south of Argolis and Arcadia and east of Messenia, was once prosperous and well-populated but has been largely deserted since the Dorians destroyed the Mycenaean civilisation there 200 years ago.

where the River Eurotas emerges from the Arcadian mountains. It has the most fertile soil of the area, although it is better suited to fruit trees and vines than to grain, due to its stony nature.

It also has a port at Gytheum, some 45 km (28 miles) south of the town on the Laconian Gulf. Through its small harbour it is developing contact with both the Aegean and the Mediterranean.

The Dorians are developing a new style of pottery. It resembles the 'protogeometric' style that

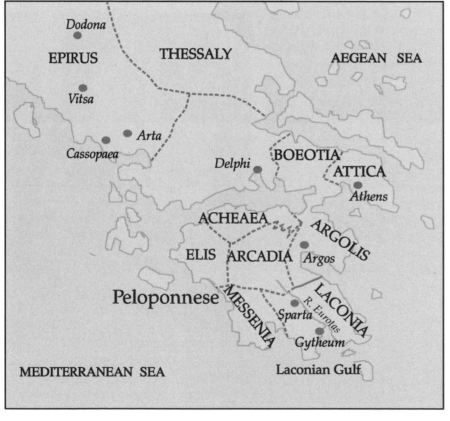

The principal states and cities of ancient Greece.

The remaining Mycenaean occupants of the area are now forced to become slaves, and many are emigrating in search of a better life. They often become pirates and head for Asia Minor, Thrace, Macedonia, Italy and eastern Sicily.

One of the new villages is Sparta, which sprawls over a group of low hills at the head of an alluvial plain

evolved in the last century in central Greece, but has clearly been influenced by the west and northwest rather than by Argos or Athens. It marks a step forward in Dorian culture, because apart from widespread chaos and destruction, all they have so far invented is iron slashing-swords and long bronze clothing pins.

Shepherds go up in the world

Vitsa, Epirus c. 950 BC

Wandering Balkan shepherds have established a summer village at Vitsa, in Epirus in north-west Greece, 1,030 m (3,375 ft) above sea level. Situated in a small trough sloping down from a ridge, the place is uninhabitable in winter, because of snow and the gales which blow down the trough.

Vitsa has about 12 houses, built from small stone slabs and having straight sides. Most Balkan homes are circular, made from poles and thatch. When a house falls down, another is erected on the rubble.

Nomadic shepherds are common in Epirus. They have a patriarchal leadership system, and each leader is well armed to protect his people and flocks against sheep-robbers and wild animals. Agriculture and fishing are also part of the local economy.

Despite their frequent travelling, the people keep religious links with the places they have lived in. Epirus boasts many famous oracles. There is one of Zeus at Dodona, and another at Trampya. There is a shrine of Hecate at Oricum, and one of the Nymphs near Arta. Pan worship is common too.

So the Aenianes, a tribe from Dodona who now live in the upper valley of the Sperchus, send men and maidens to worship Zeus in Cassopaea in southern Epirus, as well as worshipping him at home. They also keep a cult of Achilles' son Neoptolemus in Delphi. The Boeoti tribe send envoys to Dodona every year, dressed in special garments, to worship Zeus.

The 60 inhabitants of Vitsa bury their dead in simple trenches in a cemetery which adjoins the lowest house. The bodies are closely packed together in layers, two to five deep, and the top layer is close to the surface. They mark each site with a row of white stones. A small retaining wall on the downward slope stops the sites rolling away.

Rhyme time of year

Hebrew Calendar and Selected Events

Hebrew Name	Modern Equivalent	Agriculture	Feasts
Abib; Nisan	Mar-April	Spring (later) rains; barley and flax harvest begins	Passover; Unleavened Bread; First Fruits
Ziv (Iyyar)	April-May	Barley harvest; dry season begins	
Sivan	May-June	Wheat harvest	Pentecost (Weeks)
Tammuz	June-July	Tending vines	
Ab	July-Aug	Ripening of grapes, figs and olives	
Elul	Aug-Sept	Processing grapes, figs and olives	
Ethanim (Tishri)	Sept-Oct	Autumn (early) rains begin; ploughing	Trumpets; Atonement; Tabernacles (Booths)
Bul (Marcheshvan)	Oct-Nov	Sowing of wheat and barley	
Kislev	Nov-Dec	Winter rains begin (snow in some areas)	Hanukkah (Dedication)
Tebeth	Dec-Jan		
Shebat	Jan-Feb		
Adar	Feb-March	Almond trees bloom; citrus fruit harvest	Purim
Adar Sheni	(This intercalary month was added about every three years so the lunar calendar would correspond to the solar year.)		

Gezer, c. 950 BC
Children are using the 'farmer's year ditty' as a writing exercise which also helps them to remember the months of the year. The calendar follows the order of the civil year but marks off the months according to the dominant agricultural activity.

One youngster, typical of many, has scratched his copy in Hebrew script onto a soft piece of limestone 11 cm high and 7 cm wide (4.25 in by 2.75 in). It has a hook-hole so that he can hang it up on the wall at home. The ditty runs:

Two months of ingathering [oil and wine].
Two months of sowing.
Two months of spring growing.
One month of flax pulling.
One month of barley harvesting.
One month of wheat harvesting.
Two months of pruning [vines].
One month of summer fruiting.

Slave race division is made official

Jerusalem, c. 950 BC
People of non-Israelite racial origin but living within the nation's borders have been declared officially to be slaves. thousands of able-bodied men have been conscripted into gangs working on King Solomon's numerous building projects around the country.

So far, however, no Israelites have been enslaved although the system of temporary forced labour as a means of taxation is still in force. The racial groups affected are the Amorites, Hittites, Perizzites, Hivites and the original inhabitants of the capital, the Jebusites. All are descendants of the Canaanites who occupied the regions which Israel invaded under Joshua some three centuries ago.

The first 20 years of Solomon's reign have been dominated by a massive building programme. While much attention has been focussed on the royal palace and the temple, he is now rebuilding, restoring and resettling numerous villages. He is also fortifying cities in militarily sensitive regions of the kingdom, particularly those controlling trade routes. Among those to have been rebuilt is Gezer, the queen's dowry, which was burned down by her father the king of Egypt.

(1 Kings 9:15–24; 2 Chronicles 8:3–16)

This small stone calendar, found in Gezer and inscribed by a schoolboy, lists a farmer's tasks for the different seasons of the year.

Fast Facts 979 BC

Babylon, 979 BC: Babylon's new king Nabu-mukin-apli has been denied his coronation celebrations. The country is so weakened by half a century of political instability that the traditional New Year Festival (at which kings take the throne) had to be cancelled. However, there is more than injured pride at stake. The festival is the main religious event of the year, at which the king ceremonially 'takes the hand of Marduk'. Marduk is the chief god, whose blessing is considered to be vital if the country is to prosper.

Babylon, 979 BC: The theft of the statue of Marduk by Assyrian raiders has caused further problems for Babylon. His worshippers believe that his statue guarantees his presence, and to lose the statue is a grave insult to the god. The statue is a central element of the New Year Festival, and without it worshippers have no opportunity to gain Marduk's favour by bringing offerings of fruit and playing music to the statue. Babylon's enemies are aware of the statue's significance which has often been carried away as a war trophy.

Trouble and strife for king of many wives

Jerusalem, c. 935 BC

Israel's most successful king is beginning to make mistakes, according to prophets who are pronouncing Yahweh's displeasure on Solomon's sensual lifestyle. Their warnings are apparently endorsed by a series of revolts within the hitherto peaceful kingdom.

Foreign women, always Solomon's pleasure, are proving his downfall. His harem now numbers 700 wives and 300 concubines from many nations, including Moab, Ammon, Edom, Sidon and the Hittite empire, with which Yahweh has forbidden intermarriage on the grounds that they would entice Israelites from him.

Polygamy is not forbidden in Israelite law, and is regulated so that it is a form of secondary marriage, rather than multiple adultery, with basic rights for concubines who, if they are taken at all, are supposed to be Israelites. But meaningful relationships with the husband must be impossible in a harem of 1,000 women.

Solomon has also become more interested in foreign deities as he has become older. He now shares his religious affections with idols including Molech, whose worshippers practise child sacrifice, and Ashtoreth who is the focus of a grotesque fertility cult. He has erected shrines and altars to some of these foreign idols, claiming that his wives need to worship them.

According to sources at court, Yahweh has pronounced judgement on Solomon. A prophecy is circulating which suggests that the kingdom will be wrenched apart, and one of Solomon's underlings will be king after Solomon dies.

As if God were endorsing their warnings, Solomon recently has faced several potential revolts. Relations with his closest ally, Hiram of Tyre, have cooled since

Solomon gave him 20 cities as collateral for a loan. Hiram claims with some justification that the cities have been largely depopulated and the surrounding area stripped of resources, and has not hidden his displeasure.

Hadad, an Edomite prince who escaped the slaughter of Edomites under David and Joab, has returned from exile in Egypt where he has been living since he was a teenager, and appears intent on making as much trouble for Solomon as possible.

In the north, Rezon, another refugee from David's victories (this time at Zobah near Damascus) is also causing trouble and looks like being a thorn in Solomon's side for the foreseeable future. He has

The coastline north of Sharon.

seized Damascus, which was David's northern headquarters, with serious consequences for Solomon's control in the north.

(1 Kings 11:1–25)

Splitting image for coup

Jerusalem, c. 935 BC

An attempted coup to overthrow King Solomon, which threatened to split the nation, has been defeated. Its leader Jeroboam has sought political asylum in Egypt. The coup had received prophetic endorsement as discontent grows over the king's heavy taxation and forced labour on state projects.

Jeroboam, who has no royal family connections, had been a promising civil servant who first attracted Solomon's attention for his efficiency and industriousness while landscaping Jerusalem's defensive terraces. He was later put in charge of the porters from the tribe of Joseph, effectively controlling the state transport machine, a very significant responsibility in a growing, commercial empire.

But his loyalty to the king was surpassed by his loyalty to his tribe Ephraim, whose territory to the north of Jerusalem was threatened by the capital's expansion and economic domination.

Jeroboam launched the coup after

a newcomer to the prophetic bands attached to the court, Ahijah, split his cloak into 12 pieces as an image to foretell the future division of the nation, due to Yahweh's anger at Solomon's religious apostasy. He gave 10 pieces to Jeroboam, signifying the 10 tribes he will lead. The other two tribes will continue to have a king from David's line, Ahijah predicted.

The prophet also warned that the event would not take place until after Solomon's natural death, but Jeroboam chose to work to his own timescale. The rebellion was quickly crushed and a death warrant issued for its leader.

Ahijah comes from Shiloh, 32 km (20 miles) north of Jerusalem. It was the former seat of government and religion for the federation of tribes led by the pre-monarchy 'judges'. He is probably one of many who are losing sympathy for Solomon's suffocating centralised bureaucracy and the king's tolerance of the gods of other nations.

(1 Kings 11:26–40)

New king's policies divide nation

Shechem, 930 BC

Ten of Israel's twelve tribes have declared independence from the house of David following the decision of the new king Rehoboam to pursue even more vigorously his father Solomon's policies of state ownership and centralised government.

The kingdoms of Judah and Israel. Their changing fortunes after the collapse of Solomon's kingdom can be seen in the decreasing territory controlled by them.

Speaking to an assembly of tribal leaders, he promised that while his father's policies had felt like a horse-whip on their backs, his would sting them like a studded punishment-whip.

The northern tribes responded by murdering the chief of staff sent to enforce Rehoboam's rule, and have called the former rebel leader Jeroboam to be their king. He had only just returned from political exile in Egypt. His leadership had been predicted by a prophet.

Rehoboam had travelled to Shechem for the formal ratification of his kingship following Solomon's death. It was at this central Israelite city some 400 years ago that Joshua had renewed the nation's covenant with Yahweh as the tribes of Israel claimed Canaan for their own, and Rehoboam was no doubt hoping for a similar show of national unity and fervour.

But instead, a delegation from the northern tribes demanded lower taxes and shorter hours for enforced state work in return for continued loyalty.

The former advisers to Solomon counselled Rehoboam to make concessions, but his contemporaries, enjoying their first flush of power after years in the political wilderness, urged him to take a tough line.

When Rehoboam's harsh policies were announced after three days of intensive consultations the northern delegation walked out of the ceremonies. Rehoboam sent Adoniram, his chief of staff responsible for forced labour, to enforce his authority, but the angry mob stoned him to death.

The division of the kingdom also saw a resurgence in the worship of other gods. This is a small architectural model of a Canaanite shrine dating from the time.

Rehoboam fled in his chariot to the safety of Jerusalem, where the two southern tribes of Benjamin and Judah have pledged allegiance to him. A further attempt to crush the rebels by sending a fighting force of 180,000 men was abandoned on the instructions of a prophet, Shemaiah, who claimed that Yahweh did not wish for a civil war.

The northern tribes reconvened to make Jeroboam their king. The division may strengthen the hold on the area of Shishak, king of Egypt, who sheltered Jeroboam, and will make the weakened tribes vulnerable to attack.

(1 Kings 12:1–24; 2 Chronicles 10:1–11:4; cf. Joshua 24)

Fast Facts c. 950 BC

Africa, c. 950: Hunting dogs are being used for the first time in the Cape of Good Hope area. They are domestic animals that have been specially trained for the task.

Lebanon, c. 950 BC: The dense forest of Lebanon, fed by ample rainfall and well irrigated by numerous water courses, is providing wood for ships and building projects across a wide area. As well as the legendary cedar groves, olives are also grown in Lebanon alongside grapes, mulberries, figs, apples, apricots and walnuts.

Middle East, c. 950 BC: Iron ploughs, sickles and cutting tools are now in common use; iron has become much more available since the fall of the Hittite kingdom, although in some regions the strong Philistine presence still holds the monopoly of iron founding.

Europe, c. 950 BC: Tin mining is becoming a major industry. The mineral is found around small granite deposits. It is sometimes at ground level but often is buried. In Britain a new metal alloy, lead-bronze, is being developed.

Somerset, Britain, c. 950 BC: People of this western area are building a major track from brushwood, held in place with pegs. Where the ground is very wet, they use extra planking.

Priests stampede as bull gods are sent in

The funerary god Ptah-Sokaris-Osiris represented as a bull in front of a mountain, Egypt, c. 950 BC. The practice of venerating bulls was widespread at the time.

Shechem, c. 928 BC
The ten tribes of northern Israel have gone to the gods by order of King Jeroboam. The state-financed erection of bull idols has caused a stampede of priests of Yahweh anxious to leave the country.

Lacking the unifying effect of a central religious shrine since the tribes split from their southern cousins clustered around Jerusalem, Israel has built two worship centres, at Dan in the far north and at Bethel near the southern border. They are dominated by giant golden statues of bull calves which Jeroboam has decreed shall be Israel's gods.

Such images are strictly forbidden by traditional Israelite religious laws. Jeroboam is said to be justifying them as merely the earthly pedestals on which the invisible and unrepresentable Yahweh rests, as are the cherubim in Solomon's temple in Jerusalem.

But critics point out that the bull is worshipped in local Canaanite religions as a fertility symbol. And it is at least coincidental that the bull cult at Memphis has profoundly influenced religious thought throughout Egypt where Jeroboam was a political refugee for several years.

The new shrines, together with numerous 'high places' for goat and bull worship, are serviced by newly-recruited priests who are not restricted to the tra-ditional priestly tribe of Levi. As a result, many priests loyal to Yahweh are leaving the north and returning to Jerusalem, finding a spiritual oasis in what to them is a political and tribal wilderness.

Jeroboam celebrated the opening of the shrines by inaugurating a new festival designed to coincide with the southern Feast of Tabernacles, offering animal sacrifices at both centres.

(1 Kings 12:25–33;
2 Chronicles 11:14–16)

Capital fortified

Shechem, c. 927 BC
In a further bid to unify his new breakaway nation, King Jeroboam of Israel has designated this strategic site as his new capital, and has begun to fortify it.

Shechem, in the hill country occupied by the tribe of Manasseh, lies in a valley between the towering peaks of Mounts Ebal and Gerizim. Although not a specially fertile area, there are ample freshwater springs emerging from the limestone hills, and the city stands at a crossroads of trade routes.

It is steeped in Israelite history. It was occupied by the patriarch Abraham, who offered his first-recorded sacrifice to Yahweh there. Later, his grandson Jacob camped there on his return to Canaan, and it is where the invading Israelites under Joshua ratified their covenant with Yahweh.

Jereboam has also strengthened the fortifications of Dan, his northernmost city, where he has

The old walls of Dan.

built the largest gateway so far seen in the land. Peniel, to the east of the Jordan and also associated with Jacob, is another development area.

(1 Kings 12:25)

Preacher falls for the lion's share

Bethel, c. 927 BC

A successful preacher who fell to the sin of gluttony has been pronounced tasteless by a hungry lion.

The prophet, who has not been named, had spectacularly opposed King Jeroboam at his new shrine in Bethel. He foretold that a king named Josiah would rule in Jerusalem and make human sacrifices of the apostate priests on the Bethel altar. As a sign, he predicted that the altar stone would split.

When Jeroboam gestured regally to order the prophet's arrest, his arm became paralysed, possibly by a minor stroke or blocked artery. Then, when cold water was used to quench the burnt sacrifice, the altar stone cracked.

The signs achieved what the words could not. The king asked the prophet to pray for his healing, the prayer was answered and the king's arm restored. Jeroboam then offered the prophet food and drink, which he refused on the grounds that God had told him to fast until he returned to his own land.

But as he left, he was followed by an elderly prophet who enticed him home to supper by claiming that God had changed his mind and ordered that they should eat together. The confused but hungry preacher agreed, but while they ate the old man condemned him for disobeying the original command.

The preacher's body was later found on the road to Judah, apparently having been mauled by one of the Asiatic lions which prowl in the hill country of central Canaan. Unusually, however, the body had not been eaten and the preacher's donkey was found wandering nearby, unharmed.

He was buried by the old prophet who re-wrote his will to ensure that he was buried alongside him 'because his message will certainly come true'. King Jeroboam does not seem worried, however; once his initial scare had worn off, it was business as usual at the shrines.

(1 Kings 13)

The holy of holies: from the ruins of a small temple in Arad, Israel. We assume that the shrine and altar at Bethel would have had a similar layout.

All the king's family is wiped out

Tirzah, c. 908 BC

A rebel leader has overthrown the king of Israel and murdered his entire family. Baasha, from the Issachar tribe south-west of the Sea of Galilee, killed King Nadab while he was fighting a campaign against the Philistines in Gibbethon, in the south of Israel.

Having seized the throne, Baasha systematically killed all the remaining family of Israel's first king – and Nadab's father – Jeroboam. Although a common insurance policy taken out by usurping monarchs in the political turmoil of many near-eastern tribes, the brutal action was also a grim fulfilment of an old prophecy that Jeroboam's house would be destroyed.

Nadab had been king for less than two years, following his father's death from old age.

(1 Kings 14:19, 20; 15:25–31; cf. 14:14)

Fast Facts 930–924 BC

Jerusalem, 930 BC: King Solomon has died, aged about 60. He had reigned for some 40 years and will be remembered as a wise man. His crowning achievement was the erection of the temple to Yahweh, but his double-mindedness proved to be his downfall. He was buried in Jerusalem.

Jerusalem, c. 927 BC: King Rehoboam has increased the chances of survival of his two small southern tribes against incursions from Egypt, Moab and Philistia by building a horseshoe of fortifications around his eastern, southern and western flanks. He has not fortified the north, however, perhaps hoping for eventual reunion with the 10 breakaway tribes of Israel. (2 Chronicles 11:5–12)

Egypt, c. 924 BC: King Shishak (Sheshonq) has died and his mummy, encased in coffins of silver and wood, with falcon heads of the god Horus engraved on them, has been buried in the royal tombs at Tanis. Shishak came from a Libyan family in Bubastis in the eastern Delta. He was previously commander-in-chief of the armies, and will be remembered as a strong king who united Egypt by bringing together the factions of Thebes and Tanis, largely by giving positions of authority to his own sons. He is succeeded by another son, Osorkon I.

Egyptian army sweeps up Judah and Israel as far as Megiddo

Thebes, 925 BC

A massive Egyptian task force has returned to base victorious after sweeping through Judah and Israel. Over 150 settlements have been destroyed or badly damaged, palace and temple treasures have been looted, and heavy fines imposed on the rulers.

The Egyptians are giving praise to Amun after their most significant campaign since the days of Rameses III (1182–1151) and his celebrated battles against the Sea Peoples. According to some estimates, 1,200 chariots and 60,000 Lybian and Nubian troops were deployed, together with a force of auxiliaries, in simultaneous assaults on different targets.

The operation, directed by Pharaoh Shishak (Sheshonq), was initially to punish foreigners for

north of Jerusalem. Its threatening presence was enough to extract from Judah's king Rehoboam the gold and treasures from Solomon's lavish palace and temple. Thus compensated, the Egyptians decided not attack the capital but continued to strike on through Judah, destroying and looting settlements on the way.

They then drove into Israel despite its king Jeroboam's friendship towards Egypt. Shishak set up his northern field headquarters near Megiddo, from where raiding parties harassed the Galilee region. In an emotionally charged ceremony, he erected a victory stele detailing his conquests in the place where, 500 years ago, Tuthmosis III conquered the Canaanites.

Shishak's military success is to be recorded for posterity on the walls

doubtful if the nation will be able to consolidate its gains from this hit-and-run war. Despite its success in foreign affairs, Shishak's administration has a weak hold on home affairs.

After the invasion, the defeated kings licked their wounds. Rehoboam ordered bronze replicas of the lost golden shields from the temple. Encouraged by the prophets, he thanked God that Jerusalem had been spared worse things. An act of national repentance appears to have appeased Yahweh's immediate anger at Judah's open apostasy.

(1 Kings 14:25–28;
2 Chronicles 12:1–12)

Crown prince's death seen

Tirzah, c. 926 BC

The death of crown prince Abijah, firstborn son of Jeroboam, from an undisclosed illness has been described by an elderly respected prophet as a portent of the future disintegration of Israel.

The prophet Ahijah, now blind and living in Shiloh, was consulted by Jeroboam's wife who had approached him anonymously for advice. Ahijah had foretold Jeroboam's rise to kingship over the ten northern tribes.

But his sharp inner sight made up for his disability and he saw through her disguise. She had offered only the standard fee for peasants, not nobles, who consult prophets – 10 loaves of bread. He greeted her by name and warned her that Abijah would die as soon as she returned home.

It was a sign, he said, of Yahweh's displeasure at her husband's performance. He claimed God was saying to Jeroboam, 'I tore the kingdom away from David's house

Pharaoh Shishak's bracelets. Were they made from temple gold?

killing a handful of Egyptians in a border incident near the Bitter Lakes. But it has also provided an opportunity for Egypt to stamp its authority once more on its strategically-placed neighbours.

Once into Canaan, the force divided. One arm neutralised the southern trading posts and forts along the desert fringes of the Negev. It also attacked the Red Sea port and copper-smelting centre of Ezion Geber.

The main force swept up the centre to Gibeon, a short distance

of the temple of Amun at Karnak. A new court is to be built by the Second Pylon, and its south outer wall will be decorated with a relief of Shishak victorious through the grace and strength of Amun, with captives falling around him, and detailing the settlements he had destroyed or plundered. The sandstone quarries at Gebel el-Silsila have been re-opened to provide building material.

However, following the withdrawal of the expeditionary force back into Egypt, it is considered to give you. But instead of following David's example and obeying me, you've made your own gods and pushed me out.

'Therefore I shall cut your family off from Israel. Your son is the first to go. And the nation itself will become as weak as a reed swaying in the current of a river,' the prophet Abijah concluded.

The royal family recently moved from Shechem to Tirzah, some 10 km (6 miles) north. An attractive settlement at the head of the Wadi Farah, it has been inhabited for some 2,000 years and was captured by Joshua in the early days of the Israelite invasion.

(1 Kings 14)

A view of the area around Tirzah, near Shiloh, Samaria.

Judah crushes sacred cows

Ephraim, c. 913 BC
The army of Judah has crushed the sacred cows of its more powerful cousin Israel. It routed the Israelite army, which carried its bull gods as lucky mascots, and captured the shrine of Bethel.

Both states have been belligerent towards each other, though the fight was probably sparked off by Israelite aggression. When the armies faced each other near Mount Ephraim, it was King Abijah of Judah, outnumbered two to one, who took the initiative.

In a powerful speech appealing to Israel's deeply-ingrained religious sentiments, he accused its king Jeroboam of deserting the Yahweh both states once worshipped, and of overthrowing the legitimate successor of King David, Rehoboam, who Abijah – his son – described as 'weak and easily influenced'.

While Judah had remained true to Yahweh, offering the daily sacrifices in Jerusalem with punctillious rituals, Israel had replaced Yahweh with bull-calf gods and the traditional tribe of priests with anyone who could afford the cult's membership fee, he claimed. If Israel persisted with its attack, it would be fighting God himself.

The rhetoric did not impress Jeroboam, who planted an ambush to the rear of Judah while his rival was making his speech. Surprised and alarmed, the Judeans prayed to their God and their priests blew their trumpets. In an unexpected reversal, they defeated the more numerous Israelites and inflicted heavy casualties.

Judah captured Bethel, near the battlefield, and also the towns of Ephron and Jeshanah. It is the first time either side has gained significant ground from the other since they ceased to be one nation.

Religious leaders in Judah are hailing the victory as a sign that Yahweh has declared the tribe to be a shining lamp in the darkness of civil war and religious apostasy.

(1 Kings 15:1–8; 2 Chronicles 13:1–19)

Fast Facts 920–900 BC

Jerusalem, c. 913 BC: Rehoboam, first monarch of the southern kingdom of Judah, has died of natural causes aged 57. His 17-year reign was marred by continual skirmishes with Israel to the north, and with the establishment of foreign gods in the country. He leaves 18 wives, 60 concubines and 34 children. (1 Kings 14:21–31; 2 Chronicles 11:18–21)

Assyria, 912 BC: Ashur-Dan II has died after a reign of 22 years. He was the first king for over a century to have conducted regular military campaigns. His main concern was with regaining territory that had been seized by the Arameans. He also invaded Kadmukhu on the Upper Tigris. He brought back and resettled people who had fled Assyria due to hunger and poverty, and he also began construction work on the craftsman's gate and the New Palace at Ashur. He is succeeded by his son, Adad-Nirari II.

Macedonia, Greece, c. 900 BC: Bronze ornaments consisting of two spiralling coils linked by a loop are becoming increasingly fashionable in the prosperous town of Vergina as are the so-called 'spectacle' fibulae which spiral around a figure-of-eight centre. Vergina trades with southern Yugoslavia and beyond, selling a variety of metal goods, woven materials and some dairy produce.

Poland, c. 900 BC: Europeans are increasingly building fortifications around both hills and low lands. Recent designs in Poland have replaced earlier ramparts, ditches and wooden fences with a series of wooden frames with stone facings, rubble infill and a sloping bank. Covered gateways may also act as lookout points. In south-west Germany, forts built along river valleys at 10–15 km intervals are used by locals as refuges.

Drinking their health

Peru, c. 900 BC

Ritual drunkenness is part of the daily life of the people of Peru. They brew chicha, or maize beer, which has a three per cent alcohol content. The fermented, nutritious drink is made from sprouted maize kernels, which are ground, added to water and heated.

Big chicha drinking bowls are made from gourds, and drinkers pour a few drops of beer on the ground each time for Mother Earth. Since 1800 BC, the cultivation of maize, which is associated with both religion and fertility, has been a major part of their mainly horticultural economy. It depends on a complex system of irrigation, and wild bushes are cleared regularly to create bigger fields watered by new canals.

An Olmec ceremonial adze.

Peruvians in the desert coastal settlements, the Sierra and the rain forests trade with each other. The cultivation of maize, together with peanuts, cotton and hot peppers originated in the rain forests. One of the coastal peoples' big trading advantages is salt, which they extract from pans near the sea.

They build houses of stone, bamboo, wood or sun-dried bricks. They also use a wattle and daub type mixture of bamboo and mud-plaster, or else tie mats woven from split bamboo onto a pole frame.

Since 1400, the Chavin culture has spread over Peru, with its distinctive style of abstract, finely exe-cuted stonework with symbolic carvings of eagles, the alligator-like cayman and cats. It has similarities to the Olmec culture of Mexico. The people worship stone images of sky, earth and water deities, and have a priesthood that exercises great power in the secular world.

Metalworking, especially in gold, has spread to Peru from Colombia. Golden rings, crowns, pendants, pins and spoons are among the artefacts fashioned by craftsmen.

Massive rout in Canaan from Asa to Zerah

Mareshah, c. 896 BC

An Egyptian and African invasion force has been chased out of Canaan by Judean defenders.

Led by Zerah from Cush (Sudan), who is believed to have been acting on the direct orders of Pharaoh Osorkon I, the invaders lined up in a valley near this southern town east of the Philistine border on the road to the Judean foothills.

But inspired by a prayer offered by their king Asa, the Judeans tore the invaders apart and then plundered several Philistine towns and nomadic camps nearby.

Asa, who succeeded his father Abijah in 910, is a devout believer in Yahweh, to whom the victory is being attributed. In his prayer, he said, 'We rely on you, and in your name we go. May no man stand against you.'

(2 Chronicles 14:9–15)

Sacrificial altar at Tel Dan, Golan heights.

Queen mum drops from pole position

Jerusalem, c. 895 BC

Maacah, the Judean queen mother, has been sacked from her honorific but powerful political position in a religious shake-up ordered by her grandson, King Asa. In a final symbolic act, her private Asherah pole was chopped down and burned on the city's Kidron Valley garbage tip.

The inexperienced Asa had relied heavily on the matriarch after he was catapulted onto the throne by his father Abijah's premature death. Abijah had reigned for less than three years.

But he was influenced even more by the prophets of Yahweh. One of them, Azariah, urged Asa to make Yahweh the sole God of the Judeans, as he used to be. 'Yahweh is always with you when you seek him sincerely,' Azariah said. 'But if you leave him, he will leave you.'

The prophet reminded Asa of his nation's history of defeat when it abandoned its religious laws and rituals. 'Be strong and keep going,' he urged the young king, whose father had been a devout worshipper of Yahweh. 'You will get God's reward if you work for him.'

Asa responded by cleaning up the Judeans' religious act. He repaired Yahweh's altar and restored the temple treasures. He ordered the images of other gods to be destroyed, although their hilltop shrines have not been ploughed up.

At a mass rally in the city this spring the nation's covenant with Yahweh was ratified by the sacrifice of 700 cattle and 7,000 sheep and goats. The attendance was swollen by recent immigrants from the northern kingdom of Israel. They have been drawn by Judah's peace and its restoration of Yahweh worship. King Baasha in the north is strongly polytheistic.

(1 Kings 15:9–16:7; 2 Chronicles 15:1–18; cf. 2 Chronicles 14:2–6)

Assyria aims to conquer world

Assyria, c. 894 BC

In an annual ritual display of strength, King Adad-Nirari II has marched through the whole area of Khanigalbat without any resistance, collecting tribute as he goes. He has extended his march along the Khabur River and the Euphrates.

It is Assyrian custom that every spring the king musters his troops 'at the command of Ashur' and leads them through places they have previously subdued. They fight anyone who dares oppose them along the way. Some opponents hide from them, but most bring gifts, embrace the king's feet and promise to pay regular tribute.

Those who fail to keep their promise are tortured, their populations massacred or enslaved, their towns and villages set on fire and their trees and produce uprooted. Such action causes neighbouring chieftains to hasten with their own gifts to swear allegiance, and the

9th century BC relief from Nimrud showing tribute to the king being weighed.

Booty consisting of flocks, human captives and chariots being led away by the conquering Assyrians.

army will return home laden with captives, flocks and herds.

After a recent campaign in the north, the Assyrians marched away with 150 chariots (plus crew and horses), 460 horses, 61 kg (134 lb) of both silver and gold, 3,040 kg (60 cwt) of both lead and copper, 9,117 kg (180 cwt) of iron; 1,000 copper vessels, 2,000 copper pans, bowls and cauldrons, 1,000 brightly coloured woollen and linen garments, many wooden tables and couches made from ivory and overlaid with gold, 2,000 head of cattle, 5,000 sheep; the ruler's sister and the daughters of his nobles and their dowries, and 15,000 subjects.

The local prince was put to death, and an annual tribute of 1,000 sheep, 145,000 litres (4,000 bushels) of grain, 1.2 k (36 oz) of gold and 6.5 k (15 lb) of silver was imposed on his successor .

Assyria's determination to conquer the world is driven by three motives. They want simply to protect their land from hostile neighbours. Secondly, they are naturally acquisitive; and thirdly, their wars have a deep-seated religious motive. They believe that their god, Ashur, is the supreme divinity, and think that the king of Assyria, as Ashur's representative on earth, should therefore hold sway over all other nations.

Fast Facts c. 900 BC

Arad: A new temple to Yahweh has been built at this southern border town in the Judean desert (the Negev). Its design is similar to Solomon's temple in Jerusalem. It has two stone incense altars, two offertory tables, a lampstand and a pedestal for an object similar to the ark of the covenant. In the courtyard there is a sacrificial altar made from uncut stones and topped by a flint slab.

Beersheba: This important city is being restored following its destruction by the Egyptian king Shishak (Sheshonq). The original plan is being followed, with new storehouses built beside a new gate. The old fortification has been replaced with a strong casemate (double-skinned) wall. The palace is being restored and the market square enlarged.

Damascus: The Aramean kingdom based on this city-state is growing steadily in power and wealth under King Rezon (Hezion). It is now flexing its muscles and threatening Israel and Phoenicia politically, militarily and economically.

Europe: Smiths in Britain, Ireland and north-western France are still producing large quantities of high quality weaponry, domestic utensils and ornaments in bronze, even though iron looks set to replace it as a material. Lead is still used very occasionally. In Dover and Belfast goldworking is flourishing.

Cyprus: Plain hemispherical bowls, often used in graves, are being exported from this island to Athens and Rhodes. Cypriots are also exporting bronze tripods and bowls to Crete. Transport is generally provided by the Phoenician fleet.

Prophet gets porridge for bearing truth

Jerusalem, c. 886 BC

The increasingly irascible Asa, king of Judah, has sent a prophet to prison for criticising his foreign policy.

The king had made a foreign treaty with Ben-Hadad, ruler of the Arameans (Syrians) centred on the city-state of Damascus, paying him handsomely in order to turn him against his previous ally Israel.

The Israelites, once joined to Judah by a united monarchy, had been fortifying the border town of Ramah just 8 km (5 miles) north of Asa's capital of Jerusalem. They had intended to blockade trade with Judah and force it into submission. But Baasha, king of Israel, abandoned his plan and retreated to Tirzah when he heard of the new alliance.

The treaty with a foreign power went against Judah's traditional policy of relying solely on their God Yahweh, according to the prophet Hanani. Although Israel had withdrawn its threat, the Arameans now posed a bigger one, he claimed. Military attack and economic sanctions would be equally effective weapons against this small and vulnerable state.

'God's eyes range over all the

The stele of Si Gabbor, priest of the moon god. This monument is representative of Aramaic culture and religion as their influence spreads from Phoenicia to Babylonia.

world and strengthen those who trust him fully,' Hanani told the king. 'You have done a foolish thing.'

It was hardly music to the king's ears, and the prophet was effectively silenced. Asa also ordered Hanani's sympathisers to be harassed. Meanwhile, the Judeans are now de-fortifying Ramah and are recycling the building materials to strengthen the frontier posts at Geba and Mizpah.

(1 Kings 15:17–22; 2 Chronicles 16:1–10)

Two kings after royal bloodbath

Tirzah, c. 885 BC

Having lost three successive kings (Baasha, Elah and Zimri) in two years of bloody power struggles, the ten tribes of Israel now have two rival kings jockeying for position.

Today Omri, who has staged a military coup backed by the army, is firmly in place here in the capital of the northern kingdom. The location of his rival Tibni, who commands widespread popular support but has only a small guerilla force, is uncertain.

The two men laid their claims to the throne following the suicide of Zimri. His accession had been opposed immediately by the army and Omri, its commander, cornered him in his palace. With no exit open to him Zimri, who had been king for only seven days, opted to set fire to the palace and perish in the blaze.

Zimri had taken the throne himself by murdering King Elah, the legitimate but heavy-drinking son and heir of Baasha. Zimri, one of Elah's officials, murdered the drunken king at a party and then killed the rest of his family to prevent reprisals. Elah had reigned for less than two years following the death of his father who had been cursed by a prophet.

(1 Kings 16:8–21)

Fast Facts c. 890–880 BC

Assyria, c. 891 BC: Assyria's king Adad-Nirari has died after a reign of 20 years during which he reasserted the country's territorial claims. He rebuilt the previously abandoned palace at Apqu, on the edge of the Assyrian heartland, and established storage depots to supply the campaigning army.

Assyria, c. 890 BC: A new tactic is being used by the army. Redoubts, temporary fortifications usually square or polygonal, are erected without flanking defences and are used to besiege enemy cities.

Egypt, c. 889 BC: King Osorkon and his co-regent Shishak (Sheshonq) have died within months of each other. They have been buried together at Tanis. The throne is to be taken by Takelot, one of Osorkon's sons. Last year Osorkon gave the chief priesthood of Amun at Karnak to Shishak.

Tirzah, c. 886 BC: Baasha, king of Israel since 908, has died following a prophet's curse which consigned his family to become a dog's dinner. 'Dogs will eat those who die in the city, and birds those who die in the country,' warned Jehu son of Hanani. Baasha had continued to promote foreign religious practices and had eliminated all potential rivals to the throne. (1 Kings 15:33–16:7)

Gibbethon, c. 885 BC: The siege by Israelites of this Philistine city has been lifted following the internal coup staged by army commander Omri. The campaign which involved foot soldiers and charioteers was part of a continuing harassment in border areas by both nations. (1 Kings 16:15)

Assyria, 884 BC: King Tukulti-Ninurta II has died after a reign of six years. He tended to lead his armies into regions already conquered by his predecessors, and then to press only a little beyond them. He carried out significant building work in Nineveh and Ashur, including the temple of Anu and Adad, and the shrine of Enpi at Ashur. He is succeeded by his son, Ashurnasirpal II who is ambitious, vain, energetic, courageous and ruthless, and eager to expand the might of Assyria.

Flayed, skinned, or buried alive – I choose, says chief executioner

The Palace of Nimrud, as seen in a nineteenth-century hand-coloured engraving.

Syria, c. 883 BC

The people of Suru, a vassal Syrian Aramaean city on the banks of the River Khabur, will think twice before attempting again to escape Assyrian dominance. They have been subjected to a punishment beating which will deter all but the most foolhardy rebels in future.

Ashurnasirpal II's chief executioner has been giving details of the standard methods of punishment used in such campaigns. 'I built a pillar over against the city gate and I flayed all the chiefs who had revolted, and I covered the pillar with their skin. Some I walled up within the pillar, some I impaled upon the pillar on stakes, and others I bound to stakes round about the pillar. ...

'I cut the limbs of the officers, of the royal officers who had rebelled. ... Many captives from among them I burned with fire, and many I took as living captives. From some I cut off their noses, their ears and their fingers, of many I put out the eyes. I made one pillar of the living and another of heads, and I bound their heads to tree trunks around the city. Their young men and maidens I

burned in the fire.'

The Khabur region has been submissive to Assyria since the time of Adad-Nirari II, but incited by the neighbouring power of Bit-Adini, the people of Suru assassinated their Assyrian-chosen governor and replaced him with a man

Lioness mauling an African, from a painted ivory carving from the period.

from Bit-Adini. On hearing of their rebellion, Ashurnasirpal immediately marched 320 km (200 miles) in blazing heat to put it down.

Its elders fell at the king's feet as he arrived, saying, 'If you please, slay! If you please, let live! Do whatever your heart desires!' Accordingly, Ashurnasirpal stormed the city and the elders handed over the rebels, including the new governor, who the king has replaced. He has also exacted heavy tribute and punished the guilty parties with customary cruelty.

The king of Babylon, Nabu-apla-iddina, sent troops including his own brother to Suru to back the anti-Assyrian forces. Both Babylon and Assyria have an active interest in Suru, a wealthy state on the middle Euphrates trade route. The Assyrians came out on top, but remarkably relations between the two nations remain cordial.

Mediterranean sea used to wash weapons

Phoenicia, c. 883 BC

In accordance with ancient ritual, Ashurnasirpal washed his weapons in the Mediterranean after a major campaign along the western limits of Assyria in which, once again, Assyria met little resistance.

He took hostages from Carchemish and Patinu, and then crossed the Orontes to reach Lebanon. As the king washed his weapons, he was showered with gifts from the coastal cities of Tyre, Sidon, Byblos and Arvad. The gifts included gold, silver, tin, copper, copper containers, linen garments with multicoloured trimmings, large and small monkeys, ebony, boxwood, and ivory from walrus tusks.

As they offered their gifts they embraced his feet. Then, retracing his steps, he climbed the Amanu mountains, erected a stele, and took local timber back to Assyria for temple-building.

Omri capitalises on strategic hill

Samaria, c. 879 BC

King Omri of Israel has abandoned his predecessor's capital at Tirzah and has moved westwards to build a new headquarters on a previously unfortified hilltop.

Called Samaria, possibly after the site's previous owner Shemer, the 100 m (300 ft) hilltop commands good views over a fertile valley some 11 km (7 miles) north-west of Shechem. It gives better access than Tirzah to the coastal plain trade routes.

Omri paid 70 kilos of silver for the site and is building strong defences around it. He is planning an ornate palace, temples and large water-storage cisterns. He has hired Phoenician craftsmen to supervise the project, who are stamping it with their own distinctive style.

The rich alluvial valley below Samaria is liable to flooding in the rainy season but produces good crops of grain and olives.

(1 Kings 16:23,24)

Samaria, straddling the hill country occupies a strategic position. Founded by King Omri in the heart of the West Bank area it is destined to become a great city.

Ahab finishes his ivory tower

Samaria, c. 870–865 BC

King Ahab has completed the palace begun by his father Omri by decorating it and its furnishings with expensive ivory inlays and carvings.

He has also erected a temple to the storm god Baal-melqart, taking Israel further from its tradition of worshipping Yahweh as the supreme God and incurring the wrath of Yahweh's prophets. Both buildings have tall pillars topped with palm-leaf-shaped decorative capitals. They rank among the most spectacular achievements of Ahab's extensive building programme throughout his kingdom.

He has also strengthened Samaria's defences. The hill-top city is now surrounded by a casemate (double-skinned) wall built from rectangular limestone blocks with smooth faces fitting perfectly together without mortar.

At Megiddo he has filled in Solomon's casemate wall to make it stronger. A governor's palace and three blocks of storehouses have been built over former private houses. Ahab has also sunk a shaft to tap the water which is channelled along a man-made tunnel from a spring outside the city.

Hazor has virtually doubled in size in recent years, making King Solomon's large gateway redundant. Part of the old casemate wall, now inside the city, has been converted into stores using the void between the skins. New stores and a solid wall have been added.

(1 Kings 16:29–34; cf. 22:39; Amos 3:15; 6:4)

The remains of the West Gate into the city of Samaria still stand, though these foundations are of a later date.

Prosperous and stabilising reign ends

Samaria, c. 874 BC

Omri, the king of Israel who restored political stability and economic prosperity to the ten tribes ravaged by internal feuds, has died after a reign of only 12 years.

An astute politician, he inherited a weakened nation which was territorially smaller than in its heyday under its first independent king Jeroboam. But once he became sole ruler in 882, having shared power unwillingly with the upstart rebel leader Tibni who died within four years, Omri restored its fortunes.

He reasserted Israelite authority over Moab to the east, and he built a strong new capital at Samaria. He re-established friendly relations with Judah and made a political treaty with Ethbaal, king of the Phoenician ports of Tyre and Sidon. The treaty was sealed by the marriage of Omri's son Ahab to Ethbaal's daughter Jezebel.

However, he was unable to hold the Arameans at bay and was forced to grant free market concessions to merchants from Damascus who traded in Samaria. He also paid heavy tribute-taxes to the Assyrians who briefly swept through the region.

During his reign the middle and upper classes grew noticeably richer, but the poor did not benefit from the general prosperity and some lost their lands. The religious prophets were constantly opposed to Omri's encouragement of Canaanite shrines and the concessions he increasingly made to their worship. He is succeeded by his son Ahab.

(1 Kings 16:21–28; cf. 20:34; Micah 6:16)

King Ashurnasirpal II in full court dress. This stone bas-relief comes from Nimrud, is over 2.4m (9ft) tall and dates from 875 BC.

Royal banquet inaugurates royal city

Calah, Assyria, c. 877

Ashurnasirpal II has been entertaining 69,574 guests for 10 days to celebrate the opening of Calah, his new capital city. They came from as far away as Iran, Anatolia and Phoenicia. The menu, packed with lavish foods, has been inscribed for posterity on a royal stele.

Calah (Nimrud) is a strategic site some 80 km (50 miles) south of the former royal residence, Nineveh, protected by the River Tigris to the west and by the Upper Zab in the south. Once a small town, it was founded by Shalmaneser I some 500 years ago and then abandoned. Prisoners from the subdued lands have been settled in it.

Everyone under Assyrian dominance was required to give time free of charge to work on the city, and some forced-labour groups were transported to Assyria to complete it. It is surrounded by a wall, and contains orchards and a zoo. A canal has been dug from the Zab to water the surrounding plain.

King Ashurnasirpal is seen here feasting in his garden.

Ashurnasirpal's palace is built from cedar, cypress, juniper, boxwood, mulberry, pistachio-wood and tamarisk. It covers 24,800 sq m (6 acres) and is divided into administrative, ceremonial and domestic quarters. The domestic wing is air-conditioned by wide vents cut in the walls. The stone slabs lining the rooms are carved with reliefs and inscriptions, and statues of wild animals and monsters surround the buildings.

A temple and ziggurat have been built for the local war god Ninurta. Adad and Shala, Sharrat-nipkhi, Ea(-sharru) and Damkina, Gula, Kidmuru, Nabu, the Sibitti, and Sinare are also honoured with temples. Ashurnasirpal has also authorised building work on the Ishtar temple, the Adad temple and the Bit-natkhi at Nineveh. He has repaired the temple of Sin and Shamash at Ashur, and is renovating the palace at Apqu.

The cost of all this may not be recognised as such by the Assyrians. Their cities and populations are rich and civilised only because they have impoverished the tribes and nations they have subdued. The distant subjects of this vast empire are destitute and in constant attempted rebellion. Assyria's income comes by force, and the kingdom's stability is founded on terror.

Jehoshaphat launches a national teaching mission

Elijah's hollow: a small corner of green in the vast wilderness of Mount Sinai is associated with the place in the desert where most probably the prophet Elijah took refuge.

Jerusalem, c. 869 BC

A nationwide religious crusade to teach the basics of faith in Yahweh has been launched by King Jehoshaphat of Judah.

Five civil servants, eight Levites and two priests have been charged with the task of touring the two tribes of Judah and Benjamin to read and explain the Law of Moses on which their worship is based. At the same time, the shrines of other gods are being closed down and male prostitutes associated with them have been banished.

The king has continued the policy of his father Asa by removing Canaanite shrines and discouraging all other religious beliefs and practices. He recently assumed full control of the country after the death of his father with whom he was co-regent for over three years.

Jehoshaphat has also embarked on a widespread building and fortification programme to further strengthen his borders. Some Philistine and Arab leaders to the south-west of Judah are reported to be paying him tribute-taxes in order to discourage him from ransacking their territory by force with his large army.

(2 Chronicles 17:1–19;
cf. 1 Kings 22:46)

King dies of foot rot

Jerusalem, c. 869 BC

King Asa of Judah has been buried after a lavish state funeral. He had been ill for the past two years, probably with an obstruction in his vascular system which led to gangrene in his legs and feet.

A huge bonfire in his honour was lit in the capital of this small state after his body had been embalmed with exotic spices and perfumes. He was buried in a rock tomb he had prepared for himself.

Since 873 he has shared the throne with his son Jehoshaphat, who now succeeds him. Asa reigned for 41 years in all. Despite some lapses of behaviour and compromises of his religious scruples he will be remembered as a godly man who brought stability to Judah.

(1 Kings 15:23,24;
2 Chronicles 16:11–14)

'God's man brought my son to life'

Zarephath, c. 864 BC

A dead man has been restored to life by an Israelite prophet, according to his widowed mother, who also claims that the prophet Elijah has promised that her meagre supply of food will never run out while he stays with her.

The woman, whose name has not been released, said her son had been ill for some time before he collapsed. Distraught, she assumed that she was being punished by the gods for her sins. But Elijah took the young man to his room, prayed to Yahweh, and returned him alive to his mother. 'I believe Elijah's a man of God, the mouthpiece of Yahweh,' she said afterwards.

The prophet is an enigmatic figure in this coastal town governed by Ethbaal of Sidon a few miles to the north. He is a refugee from King Ahab of Israel who he had denounced for condoning the worship in Israel of the god Baal-melqart – who is the chief god of the very area where Elijah is now living. Ethbaal is also the father of Ahab's wife Jezebel, who is destroying altars to Yahweh in Israel and has ordered the execution of his prophets.

Elijah, who thus appears to have run from the frying pan into the fire, was a hermit in hiding before moving to Zarephath. He is believed to have lived in the barren hills near Jericho, overlooking the Jordan river, where he fed off scraps dropped by ravens.

When he met the widow in Zarephath she was about to bake bread from her last supply of flour and oil. Because of her poverty and the famine due to prolonged drought, she had no hope of buying more. How Elijah has managed to provide for her remains a mystery. Or another miracle.

(1 Kings 17:1–24; cf. 18:4, 30)

Worship fired up by act of God

Carmel, c. 864 BC

Yahweh has been re-established as the chief God of the Israelites after a sacrifice burst spontaneously into flames. The phenomenon occurred during a religious contest here and is being interpreted as a direct intervention by Yahweh.

The contest was between 850 priests of Baal-melqart and Asherah, the Phoenician gods promoted by Jezebel the wife of Israel's king Ahab and Elijah, prophet of Yahweh. It was called after Elijah challenged his fellow countrymen to stop worshipping several gods and instead to accept as supreme whichever one set fire supernaturally to the sacrifices being offered.

Following the contest and the public proclamation of Yahweh, a huge downpour ended the three-year-long drought which has caused widespread food shortages. That was seen by local people as a further sign of Yahweh's supremacy over the Phoenician storm god who had failed to bring rain.

But Elijah signed his own death warrant by slaughtering the priests of the other gods at the foot of Mount Carmel, in accordance with the Israelite religious laws laid down by Moses. In her anger, Jezebel ignored the public acclaim being heaped on Elijah, and ordered his execution.

Carmel, a headland on a ridge some 550 m (1,500 ft) high, lies near the Mediterranean coast and is often used as a worship centre.

Baal-melqart was the god of thunder and lightening. This ninth-century stele shows him brandishing a stick representative of thunder and holding a lightening bolt in the shape of a spear.

Close to the border between Israel and Phoenicia it is usually green and wooded, but now is parched by the drought which Elijah claims is Yahweh's punishment on Israel.

Under a cloudless sky and hot sun the priests of Baal had performed their rituals for most of the day. They even mutilated themselves in a frenzied attempt to make Baal send fire on their altar.

The spectacle brought ribald mockery from Elijah. He suggested that Baal was perhaps asleep, sitting on the latrine, or travelling abroad, and he encouraged them to shout louder.

After hours of vain pleading they gave up and Elijah took over. He built an altar to Yahweh with 12 stones representing the tribes of Israel. Then in an extravagant gesture to prove he was no fraud, he poured buckets of water over the tinder-dry wood and the newly-slaughtered bull.

Avoiding all histrionics, he raised his hands to heaven and prayed simple words: 'Yahweh, the God of Abraham, Isaac and Jacob [Israel's ancestors], let it be known that you are truly God, that I am your servant, and that you will turn the hearts of the people back to yourself.'

What happened next was sudden and unexpected. Whether by lightning strike or spontaneous combustion, the soaking altar became a raging fire. The crowds at once began to chant, 'Yahweh is God! Yahweh is God!'

But despite the national revival there was no rest for Elijah. The prophet who has been on the run for the past three years took to his heels again when Jezebel renewed her death threat. He was last reported heading south towards Judah.

(1 Kings 18:1–19:3; cf. Deuteronomy 13:12–18; 17:2–5)

Fast Facts
c. 880–870 BC

Assyria, c. 880 BC: Ashurnasirpal has finally subdued the region of Zamua (southern Kurdistan) after three violent rebellions led by the sheikh Nur-Adad. In the first two campaigns Ashurnasirpal looted and destroyed all Nur-Adad's towns and garrisons, slaughtering and plundering as he went. In this final campaign, he has ravaged Zamru and several other cities, and claims to control the whole of Zamua, which has promised tribute and free labour. The Zamuans will be used to build the new city at Calah. The king added that he had been into places where some of the men dress like women.

Assyria, c. 879 BC: Ashurnasirpal has responded to news of vassal sheikh Amme-baal's assasination by crossing the Tigris to avenge his murder. Amme-baal's forced loyalty for 13 years had provoked anger among his own people. Ashurnasirpal's thirst for vengeance met little resistance and he has returned home with a lavish tribute and several new princesses, plus dowries, for his harem.

Macedonia, c. 870 BC: Twelve slab-lined cist tombs have been dug north of Mount Olympus, half a metre below ground level, with a small tumulus above each one. The corpses inside are smeared with clay and the joints between the slabs are also filled with clay. In some cases, when the corpse has decomposed, the bones are mixed up in a ritual.

Assyria, c. 870 BC: The Assyrian army has used inflated goat skins as rafts to cross the Euphrates. After a bloody battle the army subdued a coalition of rebellious states of Laqu, Khindanu and Sukhu.

Young cocks peck off the laughing hyena!

Samaria, c. 860–857 BC

Conquering Israel's capital looked like being chicken feed for Ben-Hadad II of Damascus. But when he faced the Israelites couped up in Samaria, 232 cocky young officers just marched out of the front door, pecked the smile off his face and made him run for his life.

The Aramean king had gathered a pack of 32 neighbouring kings and their armies to besiege Samaria. He barked out his demands: the silver and gold for protection money, the cream of the women for sex and their children for slavery. Or else Israel's feathers would fly.

King Ahab, whose army was mostly deployed outside the capital, had no choice but to agree. But the hungry hyena demanded more: personally to enter the city and loot it. At this, Ahab squawked 'Foul!' and refused to hand over the golden egg.

'I'll turn you into mincemeat!' Ben-Hadad howled. 'Don't count your chickens before they're hatched!' retorted Ahab.

And while the 32 hyenas were laughing at their lunch prospects over a noonday drink, the 232 young officers strutted from the city, killed the scouts sent to arrest them and, followed by their army, tore into the Aramean ranks.

Ben-Hadad did not have time even to get into his royal chariot. He made an undignified exit on a borrowed horse and galloped to safety. Israelite detachments from the surrounding area converged on the Arameans and inflicted heavy losses.

According to Israelite sources, the strategy was inspired by an unnamed prophet who said that Yahweh their God would achieve victory to prove his supremacy once more. It certainly gave Ahab something to crow about.

(1 Kings 20:1–21)

Babylonian epics written again

As a sign of their continuing recovery from years of Aramaean invasions and battles, the Babylonians are writing literature again. One new production is the *Erra Epic*, about the old days of terror, invasion and plague, and the subsequent regeneration of the nation's grandeur. But many old texts are being re-issued.

The Epic of Creation

Apsu and Tiamat, personifications of the waters under the earth

A Marsh Arab village: conditions have changed little in the Euphrates delta, home of the epics of the flood and the creation.

and sea, gave birth to the gods. When these gods became troublesome Apsu, the father, wanted to destroy them because he couldn't sleep for the noise. His plan was thwarted by Ea, 'the all-wise', who destroyed Apsu.

Then Marduk, 'mightiest from the first', was born, and fought Tiamat, who was seeking revenge for the destruction of Apsu. Marduk won the battle and thus saved all the other gods and became recognised as the supreme deity.

Using the dead body of Tiamat, Marduk then completed the creation of heaven and earth:

> He slit her in two like a fish of the
>   drying yards,
> the one half he positioned and
>   secured as the sky...
> He placed her head in position,
>   heaped the mountains upon it...

made the Euphrates and Tigris to flow through her eyes.

Then Marduk decided to create mankind. The other gods then built the cities of Babylon and Esagila for Marduk, declaring him 'King of the gods of heaven and earth, the King of all the gods'.

The Epic of Gilgamesh

Written on 12 tablets, this tells of the adventures of Gilgamesh, king of Uruk, who was two-thirds god and one-third man. Despite his masterful victories against demons, monsters and even a great bull of heaven who was sent to kill him, he cannot escape a broken heart when his friend and companion, Enkido, dies, and his own search for immortality ends in despair.

The Flood

A story about a man who was warned by the god Ea that the hostile god Enlil was planning to cover the whole earth with water. Ea called out to him, 'Build a ship; forsake wealth, save thy life, bring all seed of life in the ship.'

The man did as he was told, endured the flood, and his boat came to rest on the top of Mount Nisir. He sent out a dove and a swallow, which re-turned, and a crow which didn't, he released the animals and offered sacrifice on the mountain.

King's mission to restore religion in Babylonia

King Nabu-apla-iddina of Babylon has donated a new image of Shamash, sun-god and god of justice, to the people of Sippar, a town in Babylonia, who have held great festivities. The king gave new festival garments for all the statues of the main gods, and banquet food for the priests. The new statue itself was consecrated according to ancient, secret rituals which endow it with life.

The original statue of the god was lost in the Aramaean invasions of previous years, and worship has since been carried out in front of a large sun-disk. Then a small statue of the god was recently found on the banks of the Euphrates from which the new image has been copied.

Sceptics say that the 'discovery' was set up by religious people wanting to restore the cult to its former status. The king, however, has gone on record saying that his action is part of a divine commission to him from the great god Marduk to resettle the old religious centres, set up shrines and re-establish the old rites and offerings to the gods.

Nabu-apla-iddina has also given food endowments for the goddesses Ishtar and Nanaya at Uruk, on the banks of the Euphrates some 40 km (25 miles) north of Ur. And he has donated quantities of aromatics to the Esagila temple of Marduk in Babylon.

Shamash is not one of the most important of Babylonian gods, but he is very popular. At the festival, the worshippers used a hymn to Shamash which includes the lines:

The merchant who practises trickery
* as he holds the corn measure*
who weighs out loads of corn by the
* minimum standard,*
but requires a large quantity in
* repayment,*
the curse of the people will
* overtake him before his time;*

if he demanded repayment before the
* agreed date, there will be guilt upon*
* him.*
His son will not assume control of
* his property, nor will his brothers*
* take over his estate.*
The honest merchant who weighs
* out loads of corn by the maximum*
* standard, thus multiplying kindness,*
it is pleasing to Shamash, and he
* will prolong his life.*
He will enlarge his family, gain
* wealth,*
and like the water of a never-failing
* spring his descendants will never*
* fail.*

Gods are present in their images

The Babylonians, in common with other people in Mesopotamia, believe that people were created to serve the gods. They literally feed, clothe and care for their gods just as they do for their king. The gods are believed to be present within their images, so when the image of a god is carried off in war, the god is considered absent until the image is returned.

Images in the temples are usually made of precious wood, and clothed in gold-plated garments with breast-plates and crowns. They are made in special workshops, and stood on pedestals in their temples. The gods are visited by lesser gods and worshippers and from time to time go out, perhaps to hunt.

They are fed the best food, and they eat behind closed curtains. When they have finished with the food, the dishes are given to the king, and afterwards to members of the king's family or court. The amount of food is often substantial, and may include bread, meat from sheep, lamb, bulls and wild boars, birds and ducks, ostrich eggs, dates,

A protective spirit carrying a goat and an ear of corn. Part of a bas-relief from Nimrud, c. 875 BC.

figs, raisins, beer and wine.

Individuals have their own personal gods. They pray and offer sacrifice to them, and in return their god intercedes for them with the other gods, and protects him or her against evil. People also wear prophylactic amulets to guard against evil spirits. Spirits of people who have died violently are especially feared. Private homes are protected by guardian figures – sometimes of dogs – that are made, consecrated and then buried near the front door.

An old text from sometime between 1570 and 1150 tells of the 'good' man's devotion to his god:

Supplication was my concern,
* sacrifice my rule;*
the day of the worship of the gods
* was my delight,*
the day of my goddess's procession
* was my profit and wealth.*
Veneration of my king was my joy,
and I enjoyed the music in his
* honour.*
I taught my land to observe the
* divine rites,*
to honour the name of the
* goddess I instructed my people.*
The king's majesty I equated to that
* of a god.*

Elijah returns after depression treatment

Damascus, c. 863 BC

The charismatic prophet Elijah has returned to his ministry to the world's power brokers following a period of depression in which he was close to suicide.

The much-travelled and outspoken critic of King Ahab of Israel has hiked 725 km (450 miles) from his desert hideout in Sinai (Arabia) to Damascus in Aramea (Syria) to appoint two future kings and a prophet on what he claims were Yahweh's orders.

Yet only a few months ago Elijah had fled from the political stage at the height of his popularity. Suffering from physical exhaustion and doubts as to his personal effectiveness, he had run in fear of his life following a death threat from Queen Jezebel.

He withdrew into his hermit's shell, shunning human society and praying for a quick death. Sustained by unsolicited gifts of food on his long trek south to Sinai, where the Israelites originally received their laws from Yahweh, Elijah holed-up in a cave where he had fresh visions of God.

He claims that Yahweh questioned why he had gone so far without permission to that lonely spot. Then after experiencing the empty void of God's noticeable absence in natural phenomena – earthquake, hurricane and fire – which are traditionally mediators of his presence, he heard Yahweh again in a murmuring whisper like a gentle summer breeze.

Reassured of God's protection, recommissioned to continue as a prophet, and reminded that he was not alone in worshipping Yahweh despite widespread defection to other gods, Elijah began the long journey back.

He stopped off in Abel-Meholah, close to the River Jordan north of Samaria, where he appointed a young farm-hand, Elisha, as his assistant and future successor. He also anointed Jehu, an army commander, as a future king of Israel and then went on to foreign territory to anoint Hazael a future king of the Arameans here in Damascus.

His actions will prompt speculation about a possible coup by Jehu, and incredulity that Yahweh should apparently approve a potential foreign threat to his own chosen people.

(1 Kings 19:3–21)

Mountains turned into molehills

Golan Heights, c. 860–857 BC

The God of the Israelites has turned mountains into molehills according to the Aramean army of Ben-Hadad II which is smarting after its second defeat in a year inflicted by its southern enemy.

Having been trounced by Israel in the hills around Samaria, where Aramean chariots were less effective than cavalry and foot soldiers, Ben-Hadad's advisers combined theology with strategy to form a new battleplan.

They reasoned that Yahweh was largely restricted to hill country. So if Damascus and its allies attacked in level places, their God would be ineffective.

The Arameans also replaced their surviving generals with new officers to ensure that past mistakes were not repeated.

But on the Golan plateau near Aphek east of the Sea of Galilee, the Israelites were apparently warned of the plan by their second-sighted prophets. They killed the Aramean officers, and then watched as the city walls of Aphek collapsed onto the enemy camp.

Ben-Hadad, trapped inside Aphek, sued for peace, offered free-market trading rights for Israel in Damascus and promised to return to Israel the cities his predecessor had taken. King Ahab agreed and set the prisoner free.

The diplomatic gesture was not applauded by Israelite prophets, however. One, who approached Ahab in disguise pretending to have lost a prisoner of war, had his 'confession' answered with a statutory death sentence. He then revealed his badge of office and pronounced Yahweh's death sentence on Ahab.

(1 Kings 20:22–43)

Ravens are a common bird of prey even in the desert.

Shalmaneser claims victory despite setback

Qarqar, 853 BC

There have been many casualties in a major battle between Assyria and a coalition of 12 countries at Qarqar, on the banks of the Orontes, some 200 km (125 miles) north of Damascus.

The Assyrians were en route to Syria, following their usual course across the Euphrates and southwards. The campaign started auspiciously as Shalmaneser III took time out to offer sacrifices to the storm god Aleppo and then demanded tribute-taxes from tribes on the way.

At Qarqar they were met by a coalition of 12 kings headed up by Ben-Hadad of Damascus and Irkhuleni of Hamath. The coalition also included a large contingent of troops sent by Ahab of Israel, supported by Byblos, Egypt and Arvad. According to Shalmaneser's staff, the coalition mustered 52,900 infantry, 1,900 horsemen, 3,900 chariots and 1,000 camel riders.

The battle was bloody and confusing, but afterwards Shalmaneser claimed, 'I slew 14,000 of their warriors with the sword. I rained destruction on them. ...The plain was too small to let their bodies fall, the wide countryside was used up in burying them. I spanned the Orontes with their corpses like with a bridge.'

However, although the Assyrians continued after the battle to march towards the Mediterranean, Shalmaneser met stiffer opposition than expected. Since neither Hamath nor Damascus were captured, the coalition of states may well cause problems for Assyria in the future.

A procession of prisoners, being led off with their livestock. From the palace of Tiglath-Pileser III, c 730 BC.

King separates state and religion

Jerusalem, c. 853 BC

An attempt to centralise the tribal system of justice in Judah has been enacted by King Jehoshaphat. He has also created an unprecedented distinction between state and religious jurisdiction.

As part of the king's long-term reform policies, he has appointed judges in the fortified cities which fall directly under his control. They are charged with a strict code of honesty and impartiality in their application of the law.

Amariah, the chief priest, is made minister of religious justice, and Zebadiah, a leader of the Judah tribe, is promoted to minister of state justice. It is uncertain whether the system will penetrate as far as the smaller villages where sacred and secular laws are administered without distinction by local elders.

(2 Chronicles 19:4–11)

Soldiers fired

Samaria, c. 853–852 BC

One hundred Israelite soldiers have been burned to death in an apparent act of divine judgement on their king Ahaziah. They had been sent in two divisions of 50 men each to arrest Elijah the prophet who had criticised the injured Ahaziah for consulting the healing shrine of the Philistine god Baal-Zebub at Ekron, some 70 km (45 miles) south of Samaria.

The prophet refused to accompany them and called down divine fire as confirmation of Yahweh's words of judgement. A third division begged for, and received, mercy before the prophet repeated his message in person to Ahaziah.

The king, who had been seriously injured in a fall from a window, has since died as Elijah predicted. He had reigned for less than two years since the death of his father Ahab.

(1 Kings 22:51–2 Kings 1:18)

Fast Facts c. 865–860 BC

Samaria, c. 865 BC: Abnormally dry weather for several years has been forecast by the impressive prophet Elijah. In an audience with Israel's king Ahab, Elijah said the drought was Yahweh's punishment for the nation's preference for Baal-melqart. (1 Kings 16:31–33; 17:1)

Israel, c. 864 BC: One hundred prophets are reported to have been kept hidden in the many caves which pierce the limestone hills of the Carmel area. They were supplied secretly with food by one of King Ahab's closest aides, Obadiah, who oversees Ahab's domestic arrangements and who has remained faithful to Yahweh despite the royal purge in favour of Baal-melqart. Obadiah recently brokered a meeting between Ahab and the prophet Elijah.

Egypt, c. 860 BC: Osorkon has built an enormous red granite hall in the temple of the cat-goddess Bastet at Bubastis, Lower Egypt. The hall is decorated with reliefs of himself and his wife, Queen Karomama, celebrating his jubilee. He has also commissioned buildings in his name at Memphis, Tanis, Thebes and Leontopolis.

Egypt, c. 860 BC: Osorkon has strengthened his position following the death of Harsiese, who declared himself king in the south of Egypt some years ago. Harsiese's kingship was never officially recognised, but it represented Egypt's increasing fragmentation. Osorkon has made one of his sons, Nimlot, high priest of Amun at Thebes, and another son, Sheshonq, high priest of Ptah at Memphis.

'Ruler is not above the law'

Jezreel, c. 855 BC

A ruler who manipulates the laws of his own land has sold himself to the devil, according to the outspoken prophet Elijah. As a result of the prophet's fearless attack, King Ahab of Israel has been forced to admit errors in a property deal.

Ahab had been eyeing next-door's vineyard from his country residence at Jezreel, 35 km (22 miles) north of the capital Samaria. He wanted to create a traditional palace garden where he could relax and enjoy nature's colourful bounty. But its owner Naboth refused to sell what his sons could inherit, and Israelite law forbids compulsory purchase.

The Phoenicians have no such scruples, however, and Queen Jezebel, Ahab's Phoenician wife,

adopted the autocratic style of government to which she is accustomed. Scolding the sulking king for not exerting his power, she arranged a party at which false witnesses accused Naboth, a respected member of the community, of blasphemy and treason.

Both crimes carry the death sentence, and Naboth and his heirs were promptly executed by stoning. But when Ahab took the land, Elijah pronounced Yahweh's displeasure. 'You've sold yourself to evil,' he thundered, 'so you'll die miserably and your heirs won't get your land.'

The shocked king bowed to higher authority and acknowledged his guilt by donning the penitent's and mourner's coarse sackcloth shift and by fasting. In a

Vines were often suspended so that grapes could be plucked from below.

second message from Yahweh through Elijah, Ahab was told that the inevitable disaster would be postponed until a later generation because of his contrition.

(1 Kings 21; cf. 2 Kings 9:21,26)

Arrow gets through monarch's disguise

Ramoth Gilead, c. 853 BC

Israel has failed to recapture its border town of Ramoth Gilead from the Arameans and its king Ahab has been killed in the battle. The armies of both Israel and Judah have been decimated.

Ahab had ridden into the war zone in disguise in order to protect himself from snipers, but he was felled in a hail of arrows fired at random into the advancing line.

The attack was a joint operation between Israel and its southern cousin Judah. The two states have grown closer since the marriage of Judah's king Jehoshaphat to one of Ahab's daughters. It

was during a family get-together in Samaria that the battle alliance was suggested. A previous treaty between Israel and Damascus had not been honoured by the agreed return of cities captured by the Arameans.

Both kings were anxious to follow custom and consult the gods before risking the encounter. The court prophets of Baal-melqart and Ashtaroth in Samaria all forecast a victory for Israel. But Jehoshaphat insisted on receiving confirmation from a prophet of Yahweh. The

Mounted archers could wreak havoc amongst the enemy, as this frieze from Nineveh shows.

only one available, Micaiah, is unpopular in Ahab's court because of his usually negative predictions.

Sarcastically, he mimicked the staff prophets' advice before claiming that they were all gripped by the power of the lie to preserve

their jobs. He went on to warn that Israel's army would be like sheep scattered over the hills without a shepherd to lead them.

Ahab, although openly critical of Micaiah, hedged his bets by wearing soldier's clothes rather than royal robes. Jehoshaphat retained his regalia, however, and acted as an unwitting decoy for Aramean snipers before they recognised him and drew back.

Israel's king was unluckily hit by a stray arrow which pierced the joint of his body armour. He bled to death in his chariot, which was later washed down at the prostitutes' bathing pool in Samaria. It gave local dogs a taste of blue blood which the minority Yahweh worshippers pointed out was a fulfilment of an earlier prophecy by the eccentric Elijah.

(1 Kings 22:1–38; 2 Chronicles 18:1–34; cf. 1 Kings 20:34; 21:19)

Bolognese source of Italian wealth

A large bronze shield over 1m (3 ft 3 in) across, c. 650 BC. Over 40 such shields survive. The bronze was hammered out and the decorations punched with stamps from the back. A handle was attached behind the central boss. Some shields were gilded and typical designs include sphynxes, palmettes, rosettes, lines and cable patterns.

Bologna, Italy, c. 850 BC
The fast-growing city of Bologna is becoming one of Italy's most prosperous centres. The people are skilled in bronze and iron work, and are developing a thriving trade with their neighbours in the south. Copper and iron are imported from Tuscany. They major in farming implements, like chisels and sickles, and jewellery rather than weapons.

The people, in common with many other Italians, increasingly cremate their dead. They collect the charred bones after they have been burnt on a pyre and put them in an urn, which is lowered into a small hole at the bottom of a well. The well is then sealed with a stone slab.

The distinctive urns are made of dark clay, have a broad neck and are decorated with curved patterns. They have only one handle, which makes them difficult to move. The lids are sometimes just an upturned bowl, or a clay model of a helmet. The helmet-urns can be decorated with circles and discs which resemble a very stylised human face.

Some urns are made in the shape of a roofed hut, especially in the Latium area. They are normally oval or rectangular, and often have a door, fastened with a crossbar, to retain the ashes. Windows are painted on the sides, and the roofs have gables with eaves. They are normally made of clay, but very occasionally from bronze with elaborate decoration of birds' heads or boats.

Tumuli recycled

Illyris, Albania, c. 850 BC
Burial mounds (tumuli) for important or wealthy people are being reused many times over in this European region. Some may contain more than 100 burials, and the same tumulus may be used for hundreds of years.

Subsequent burials are made by digging a shaft down into the tumulus and burying bodies at its foot. The shaft is then refilled with soil. In the process, the diggers often disturb earlier buried objects such as bones, iron spears, swords, knives and battle-axes, ornately decorated pottery vases as well as pins, brooches and other jewellery. Oxen are sometimes sacrificed and buried too.

A life-size terracotta mask from Cyprus. These masks were left in tombs to frighten off evil spirits.

Colonists build new temple for Astarte

Kition, Cyprus, c. 850 BC
Phoenicians (Canaanites) from Tyre have built a huge temple on the site of one abandoned 150 years ago, which has the same dimensions but a different internal structure. Kition, on the southern coast of Cyprus, is the Phoenicians' first colony on the island.

Measuring 33.5 m (37 yd) by 22 m (24 yd) it is one of the largest temples the Phoenicians have ever built. It has a rectangular open courtyard in front, with porticoes along the north and south walls. Each portico has a roof supported by two rows of seven pillars.

The entrance to the holy of holies is flanked by two rectangular stone pillars, similar to the Jachin and Boaz pillars in King Solomon's Jerusalem temple, which was also built by Tyrian masons. The temple is dedicated to the Phoenician deity Astarte, and employs a large staff, including guards and servants, bakers, barbers and prostitutes.

As a concession to indigenous Cypriot religious practice, masks, either in the form of human faces or of bulls, are commonly worn in temple worship.

Moab fooled by mirage

Edom, c. 852 BC

Furious generals in Moab are holding an inquest into why their army was lured to defeat by a desert mirage. Their king Mesha has offered his son as a human sacrifice in a desperate attempt to secure the aid of the gods when a revenge mission involving 700 crack soldiers also failed.

The Moabites had been mobilised when a united army from Judah and Israel attacked their relatively weak southern defences near the River Zered south of the Dead Sea.

Heavy rain on the Moabite hills cascaded into the wadi causing a flash flood. The water was spread across the area by irrigation channels hastily dug by the invaders on the advice of their prophet Elisha. The red rocks reflected eerily in the streams under the early morning sun, which the superstitious Moabites interpreted as an omen that the invaders had already shed each others' blood.

Hungry for plunder, the Moabites charged into the attackers' camp only to be met by a highly motivated and well-disciplined force which decimated the poorly-trained and hastily-armed volunteers. Israel went on to destroy not only settlements but also the crops and trees on which the survivors would have depended.

The mountains of Jordan seen from across the Arava Valley.

Mesha and his 700 soldiers attempted a revenge attack on Edom, a vassal state of Judah through which the attackers had marched, but that also failed. Aware that the rout had the marks of divine intervention, he sacrificed his son in the capital Kir Hareseth to appease the gods.

The Israelite attack was prompted by a rebellion by Mesha who for some 50 years has been subject to the ten tribes. Shortly after the death of Israel's king Ahab he had withheld payment of an annual tax of sheep culled from his huge flocks.

Ahab's successor Jehoram allied with Judah's king Jehoshaphat and with Edom for the raid. Prophetic support from Elisha, who is no friend of Israelite kings, was prompted by the presence of Jehoshaphat who is a devoted follower of Yahweh.

The attack had almost ended in disaster before it began when the army ran out of water during the seven days it took to march the 160 km (100 miles) south from Samaria. The flash flood served a dual purpose in refreshing the Israelites as well as deceiving the Moabites.

(2 Kings 3)

Babylonians call for help

Babylon, c. 851 BC

King Marduk-zakir-shumi has called on Assyria to help to deal with a revolt by his younger brother Marduk-bel-usati who is backed by the Arameans. Shalmaneser promptly rose to the occasion and personally led an army to defeat the rebels.

Marduk-bel-usati fled to the mountains, where he was later pursued and defeated by Shalmaneser at Khalman. Afterwards, Shalmaneser toured Babylonia's religious centres at Cutha, Babylon and Borsippa, offering sacrifices in their temples. He has also given food and wine, brightly coloured clothes to wear and many other gifts to inhabitants of Babylon and Borsippa.

A treaty has existed between Babylonia and Assyria for several years as a result of the Aramaean threat to both nations. The exact terms of it are unclear, but it is thought that they include a guarantee of the Babylonians' crown aa well as some form of mutual defence agreement.

A god, emblematically portrayed as a flying bird and hovering over a tree, symbolic of the rich vegetation of Mesapotamia, is flanked by two kings. This symbolic representation seeks to convey the message that the king has power over nature.

Theatre of war stages pure farce

En Gedi, c. 852 BC

What was billed as a battle of epic proportions ended in farce as the star warriors slaughtered each other in sheer confusion.

When the cast of thousands from the combined forces of Moab, Ammon, and the Mount Seir region of Edom invaded the small kingdom of Judah, they staged a series of ambushes intended to catch the Judeans but which only snared their own side. Anyone with a foreign accent was a potential target. Either the fight managers forgot to provide the armies with a common uniform, or rumours of treachery spread through the camp and it became every man for himself.

The audience of Judeans was reduced to tears of laughter and songs of jubilation as the spectacle unfolded. Without firing an arrow in anger they marched into the battlezone to discover the action was over and the desert littered with dead bodies. It took them three days to clear the site of equipment, clothing and other goods dropped by the invaders.

Moab, which has become increas-

Water flows abundantly at the En Gedi spring in the desert.

ingly belligerent under King Mesha, probably saw Judah as a soft target. Moab has been dominated by Judah's larger sister Israel for half a century.

The king of Judah, Jehoshaphat, did not have time to call for Israelite aid as the attackers forded the Dead Sea near its southern end and drove northwards along its western shore. But he did have time to call on his God at a hastily-arranged mass rally in Jerusalem.

In an emotional prayer, he called on Yahweh to act with justice. Moab, he pointed out, had been spared slaughter centuries ago on Yahweh's instructions when the Israelites first invaded Canaan under Joshua. It was hardly fair, therefore, for God to let Moab walk over his people.

Following his prayer, a prophet named Jahaziel predicted that Judah would not have to fight. 'The battle is Yahweh's, not yours,' he declared. 'Take up your positions, stand still, and watch Yahweh win for you.'

They marched to this desert settlement with priestly trumpets sounding a martial beat to keep up their spirits. They staggered home under the weight of plunder to dance music.

(2 Chronicles 20)

Second sight blinds Aram soldiers to their target

Samaria, c. 850 BC

A company of Aramean soldiers sent to capture the Israelite prophet Elisha has been captured – by the prophet Elisha.

The single-handed coup is the latest in a series of spoiling tactics used by the Israelites against Aramean incursions. Using his second sight, Elisha has continually frustrated the Arameans by predicting, like a highly-placed spy, where they will attack, and warning Israel's defences.

According to Elisha's assistant the force was large enough to surround Dothan, where the pair was staying. But surrounding the

army was a force of angels. Elisha, when confronted by the commander, was not recognised, and he persuaded the Arameans that they were in the wrong place.

Afflicted by a mental block if not physical blindness, the Arameans let him guide them only to discover that their destination was the capital Samaria where they immediately became prisoners of war. But having fed them, the Israelites let them go, believing that their embarrassment was punishment enough. No more raids by the Arameans have been reported since.

(2 Kings 6:8–23)

A rocky outcrop near Samaria. Dothan stood on a similar hill.

Rash deal made him an outcast

Samaria, c. 850 BC

Gehazi, the personal assistant to the prophet Elisha, got more than he bargained for when he stopped an Aramean nobleman and asked for payment for services rendered.

Naaman, a senior commander in the Aramean army, had been healed of a skin disease by obeying Elisha's instructions to immerse himself seven times in the River Jordan. The prophet had refused payment, but had allowed the Aramean to take a cartload of Israelite soil on which he could build a shrine to Yahweh in Damascus.

Gehazi, however, thought that a foreigner ought to make a donation to the prophetic community's living expenses. So he made up a story about penniless prophets having just arrived in Samaria and asked for money and clothing, which Naaman gladly gave him.

Elisha instinctively knew what his servant had done. The guilty Gehazi broke out in a rash when he denied any wrongdoing, as Elisha pronounced the punishment: Naaman's disease would now be his.

It is unusual for Arameans to seek help from the Israelite God, but Naaman was prompted to do so by a servant girl who had been captured in Israel during a border raid. The commander followed normal protocol by first approaching King Joram of Israel for healing. The king's expletive was heard by Elisha who took over the case.

(2 Kings 5)

Tax increase bears heavy toll

Ashurbanipal killing a wounded lion: lion hunting was one of his favourite pastimes.

Assyria, c. 859 BC

King Ashurnasirpal II has died after a 27-year reign. He will be remembered for his ruthless ambition for the nation's expansion, and for his many building projects, including the new city of Calah.

He undertook many extravagant building programmes in which he usually had himself represented hunting wild lions and conquering various peoples.

Resistance to Assyria increased in recent years among the subdued nations, largely because of the very heavy tribute, including unpaid labour, that he imposed. He is succeeded by his eldest son, Shalmaneser III.

The River Jordan in the 19th century: the likely site of the ceremonial washing.

Fast Facts
c. 860–850 BC

Assyria, c. 856 BC: Shalmaneser has captured Til-Barsip, the capital city of Syrian Bit-Adini. It has been renamed 'The Quay of Shalmaneser' and populated with Assyrians. They have built a palace on top of a mound overlooking the Euphrates which will serve as a base for operations on the western front. It has taken three major campaigns to achieve and opposition has been severe.

Ezion Geber, c. 852 BC: A fleet of large merchant ships sailing under the joint flags of Israel and Judah has been destroyed before being put into service at this port on the Gulf of Aqabah. The cause of the disaster is unknown, but religious leaders claim it is Yahweh's judgement on Jehoshaphat, king of Judah, for entering an alliance with Ahaziah of Israel. (1 Kings 22:48f, 2 Chronicles 20: 35f)

Egypt, c. 850 BC: Takelot II has succeeded his father as king of Egypt. His half-brother Nimlot, the high priest at Thebes, has married his daughter to the new king, securing relations between north and south and confusing the family tree by becoming his half-brother's father-in-law. Nimlot has also tried to strengthen his own position by putting his son in charge of affairs at Herakleopolis.

Scotland, c. 850 BC: The Scots have discovered that leather shields provide better protection than bronze against swords. They now make beaten bronze shields for ceremonial purposes only.

Athens, c. 850 BC: People are getting richer in Athens, and they're taking their wealth with them to the grave. In a recent cremation, a large model granary and more than 80 pieces of jewellery and pottery were buried with a woman's ashes. Athens, made up of several villages, is an arable farming region with trade contacts with the Aegean islands but not with central Greece itself.

Cannibals turn to vultures

Samaria, c. 850–845 BC

The lifting of the Aramean siege of Samaria came too late for one mother. She and her neighbour had just killed and eaten her son in a nightmare struggle for survival.

But within hours the Israelites were pouring out of their capital city and swooping like vultures on the rich leftovers in the abandoned Aramean camp. They included the woman's cannibal neighbour who had agreed that her son would be next on the hit list – but had then hidden him away.

During the long-running siege by Ben-Hadad II many poorer Israelites had been reduced to acts of barbarism, while for the rich the black market in foods forbidden by their strict dietary regulations flourished. A donkey's head was reported as fetching 80 shekels (about a kilo) of silver.

The end came swiftly as King Joram ran out of patience and threatened to behead the prophet Elisha who he blamed for the siege. The man of God had predicted it as a punishment from Yahweh for Israel's wholesale abandonment of him as their sole God.

The Arameans just left their camp, their equipment and food in a mad hurry after an unfounded rumour of an impending counter-attack by combined forces of Hittites and Egyptians spread like fire through the ranks.

The site was found abandoned by four hungry outcasts with skin diseases who had gone there to surrender themselves in the hope of being made slaves or given charity. Having eaten themselves sick and having stashed away all the booty they could carry to ensure they need never beg again, they informed the authorities in Samaria of the city's good fortune.

A couple of horsemen were sent to check it out before the gates burst open and the vultures descended. An army officer was trampled to death in the rush. Supplies in the camp were so plentiful that the price of food dropped immediately, with fine wheatmeal selling for only about twice the price of common barley. Meanwhile Elisha was reminding observers that he had also predicted the fall in price and the death of the officer.

(2 Kings 6:24–7:20)

Symbolic end to cruel reign

Jerusalem, c. 841 BC

A prolapsed bowel has brought what some describe as a symbolic end to the eight-year reign of a king who gutted his family and nation.

When Jehoram took over the tiny state of Judah he dismembered his family by killing his six brothers who he feared as rivals. Then he re-introduced the shrines of Canaanite deities which his father had cut out believing them to be a cancer eating at the nation's soul.

Later he led a disastrous campaign against Edom which had rebelled against Judah's control, narrowly escaping death himself and seeing his army flee in disarray after an Edomite military pincer-movement. The Philistine border

city of Libnah also seceded and Philistine and Arabic invaders filleted Jehoram's palace of its treasures and enslaved his wives and children.

He had been warned of his likely premature death from intestinal disease in a rare letter written by the elderly and infirm prophet Elijah. Critics saw his end as Yahweh's judgement on his policies. Jehoram, who was 40 years old, was denied burial in the normal kings' tombs, and there was no official mourning period for him. He had married a daughter of Ahab, king of Israel, and is succeeded by his youngest son Ahaziah.

(2 Kings 8:16–24;
2 Chronicles 21:4-20)

Megalith for mega reign

Dibon, c. 840–830 BC

A commemorative monument detailing King Mesha's achievements during his long reign over Moab is to be erected in this city 20 km (12 miles) east of the Dead Sea.

The 1-m (3-ft) piece of black basalt is inscribed in Phoenician script with an account of Mesha's overthrow of Israelite domination after the death of Ahab in 853 BC.

King Omri has also been involved in various forays to try and extend his kingdom – unsuccessfully. This black standing stone was commissioned by Mesha, king of Moab, to celebrate his victory over Omri.

The king attributes his success to his god Chemosh, for whom he built a temple at Qarho.

Mesha claims that Chemosh told him to take Nebo which he attacked at night, killing its 7,000 inhabitants and ransacking its shrine to Yahweh. He also captured the Israelite towns of Ataroth and Jahaz with the god's aid, the monument says.

The stone describes Mesha's building projects in Qarho, which included walls and fortifications, parks, a palace and reservoirs, all built by Israelite prisoners of war. It also records his extension of numerous other towns including Bezer, Medeba and Baal-meon.

Man of bald miracles

If Elijah was Yahweh's fire-raiser, Elisha is his sledgehammer. He is a wild man of action, prone to petulance and of striking appearance: he is one of few men in this region who are bald-headed. Fearing no man but with a heart for the world's unfortunates, he has continued his former master Elijah's tradition of speaking God's words to the rulers of Israel, Judah and Syria (Aram).

A Canaanite shrine near Meggido.

He originates from Abel-Meholah to the east of the Jordan Valley, and as a young man worked as Elijah's assistant before embarking on his own unique ministry leading one of the schools or communities of prophets. He is better known as a popular miracle worker than as a statesman. Here are some of the more spectacular actions attributed to him.

Waterworks
Following the departure from this world of Elijah, which he witnessed, Elisha tested if he had truly inherited Yahweh's Spirit by throwing his cloak on the river Jordan and commanding the waters to part so that he could cross as Elijah (and Joshua) had done before him. Later, in Jericho, he poured salt water into a well which was probably infected by parasites as a symbolic act through which Yahweh purified it. (2 Kings 2:13–22)

Bear truth
Elisha was accosted near the Baal-melqart shrine at Bethel by a mob of teenagers. They jeered at his appearance and mocked his unswerving loyalty to Yahweh. He cursed them in God's name and later they were attacked and killed by a pack of bears from the nearby hills. (2 Kings 2:23–25)

Oil well
One of Elisha's associate prophets died, leaving his widow and two sons in debt. They were liable to be sold into slavery. Elisha told her to borrow all the olive oil jars she could, fill them from her own jar – which never ran out – and sell the oil to pay the debt. (2 Kings 4:1–7)

Child care
A wealthy couple in Shunem 8 km (5 m) north of Jezreel gave Elisha a

The ruins of Ahab's stables, Elisha's key opponent, near present-day Meggido.

room whenever he travelled through the area. They asked for nothing in return but the prophet, wishing to repay their kindness, discovered that they were childless. He foretold that they would have a son. But years later the boy died suddenly, possibly from cerebral malaria or meningitis. The woman, in deep distress, rode to find Elisha who returned with her and raised the boy from the dead. (2 Kings 4:8–37)

Food processor
At Gilgal, near Shiloh in central Israel, the prophets were having a community meal during a food shortage. The chef had included a bitter gourd in the stew which was a powerful purgative. Elisha's symbolic act of adding flour to it made the food edible. On another occasion during a famine Elisha predicted correctly that 20 small barley loaves he had been given would satisfy the whole community. (2 Kings 4:38–44)

Axe-ident
The prophets had outgrown their community centre and wanted to build another. While chopping trees in the Jordan Valley one of them dropped an expensive iron axehead into the water. Having borrowed it, he was obliged to pay for it, which would have enslaved him temporarily. Elisha made the axehead float to recover it. (2 Kings 6:1–6)

All the King's messengers
Among the lesser-known prophets who have confronted kings are:

Ahijah (Jeroboam), 1 Kings 11:29–39; 14:1–18

Shemaiah (Rehoboam), 1 Kings 12:22–24; 2 Chronicles 11:2–4; 12:5–8

Iddo (Ahijah), 2 Chronicles 13:22

Anonymous (Jeroboam), 1 Kings 13

Azariah (Asa), 2 Chronicles 15:1–8

Hanani (Asa), 2 Chronicles 16:7–10

Jehu (Baasha; Jehoshaphat), 1 Kings 16:1–4, 7; 2 Chronicles 19:1–3

Anonymous (Ahab), 1 Kings 20:13–14, 22, 28, 35–43

Micaiah (Ahab & Jehoshaphat), 1 Kings 22; 2 Chronicles 18

Jehaziel (Jehoshaphat), 2 Chronicles 20:14–17

Schools of religious sharks

'Is it you, you troubler of Israel?' The words of King Ahab, meeting Elijah after three years of divinely-ordained and politically crippling famine, sum up the relationship between the kings of Israel and Judah and the prophets they consult or are confronted by.

Prophets in these nations are like hungry sharks circling a crippled ship. They are independent of mind and bold of spirit, ready to snap their spiritual jaws on any political strategy, military tactic, commercial treaty or religious practice which does not meet their strict criteria.

Three words are used for 'prophet' by Hebrew writers. The first is always translated 'prophet', the second 'seer' and the third is translated either 'prophet' or 'seer'.

The first refers to anybody who is called to proclaim God's words to human beings. The prophets who came to meet Saul in 1 Samuel 10:10 are described by this word.

Of the ten times that the word translated 'seer' is used, six refer to Samuel. There are many recorded instances where a prophet is clearly in possession of privileged information about the present or the future; Saul's servant intended to make use of Samuel's gifts to find the missing donkeys, and Samuel's response indicated that this was well within his prophetic powers (1 Samuel 9).

However, the prophets are required to put all such gifts of foresight and prediction primarily to the service of Yahweh.

Fanatical devotees of Yahweh and implacably opposed to other gods and the nations which follow them, the prophets group in schools or communities for mutual support, often around a famous leader such as Samuel, Elijah or Elisha (2 Kings 6:1). They operate as lone messengers, however, when the Spirit of Yahweh prompts them to speak his specific word to a national leader.

Convinced that Yahweh is the supreme ruler of world events as well as of the affairs of Israel and Judah, they are both historians of the past and pilots for the future. Their strong criticisms refer directly or implicitly to actions which have broken the covenant made between Yahweh and Abraham, ratified on several later occasions. Future predictions range from warnings of death to promises of seemingly impossible victories.

Usually they deliver their message verbally and in straight terms, but they have been known to use illustrative symbols. Nathan told a parable to convict David, for example (2 Samuel 12:1–15) and Ahijah tore his coat into 12 pieces to symbolise the division of the tribes (1 Kings 11:29–31).

The traditional test of a true prophet is whether or not his words come true (eg Micaiah's challenge, 1 Kings 22:24–28). How the prophet becomes convinced of the truth of his message is unclear, although Elisha's use of harp music suggests that periods of quiet meditation are vital (2 Kings 3:14–19). In some cases the message is of a 'two plus two equals four' spiritual logic based on Yahweh's ancient commands; if you disobey God like this, disaster will come like that.

At times the prediction is very specific and personal. Ahijah predicted the exact time of death of Jeroboam's son, (1 Kings 14:12,17), and an unnamed prophet directed the successful (but highly unusual) military strategy of Ahab's defeat of Ben-Hadad II (1 Kings 20:13–22).

Their personalities vary widely. There are loners like Elijah, prone to depression, and lively charismatics who earn the title 'madmen' (2 Kings 9:1–3, 11–12). The latter sometimes burst into spontaneous prophesyings, which are more like general proclamations of God's character and truth than specific messages directed at individuals or the nation (eg 1 Samuel 10:5–7). The one thing they all have in common is that they are respected when they speak favourably and despised when they do not.

Fast Facts c. 850–840 BC

China, c. 850–840 BC: The author Fan-Li has published an important new book on fish cultivation. The oppressive King Ii has been replaced by the Kung-Ho ('public harmony') regency.

Jerusalem, c. 848 BC: King Jehoshaphat has divided his wealth and lands among his seven sons, according to his will just published. His eldest son Jehoram, who has been co-regent for the past four years, takes over as king. Jehoshaphat, who was a zealous religious and social reformer, died aged 60 after 25 years on the throne. (2 Chronicles 20:31– 21:3)

Northern Babylonia, c. 843 BC: The Assyrians have defeated the Kassite tribes of Namri in the Zagros foothills. The Kassites were part of Marduk-bel-usati's revolt in 851 and along with the Chaldeans had become an independent and niggling threat to Assyria. King Marduk-mudammiq was not captured, but the Assyrians plundered his palace and harem and took his horses. Shalmaneser plans to install as king of Namri a member of the Kassite-Khabban tribe, Yanzu, who has sworn allegiance to Assyria.

Damascus, c. 843 BC: Ben-Hadad II has been assassinated by a close aide but otherwise unknown pretender Hazael, who has seized the Aramean throne. The king had been ill for some time and had sent Hazael to get a prognosis from the Israelite prophet Elisha. The promise of recovery was followed by a prediction that Hazael would become king and wreak havoc on Israel. The aide seems to have wasted no time in making the prediction come true. (2 Kings 8:7–15)

Calah, Assyria, c. 841 BC: Shalmaneser has built a huge storehouse in the corner of Calah's wall 'for the ordnance of the camp, the maintenance of stallions, chariots, weapons, equipment of war and the spoil of foe of every kind'. Army troops will be assembled, equipped and inspected in three huge courtyards before the annual campaigns. The surrounding rooms are for armouries, stores, stables and officers' lodgings.

Thebes, Egypt, c. 839 BC: A violent rebellion has been crushed by King Takelot II, its leaders killed and their bodies burned (thus denying all hope of life after death). The rebellion was over who should become high priest of Amun after the death of Nimlot.

Military coup ends in bloody purge

Jezreel, c. 841 BC

Two kings, a queen mother and some 70 royal relations have been murdered in a military coup staged by the aggressive Israelite army general Jehu. He has claimed the throne for himself.

Jehu was anointed king during a surprise visit by a messenger from Elisha the prophet; unconfirmed reports suggest the messenger was named Jonah. Jehu wasted no time in fulfilling past predictions that Ahab's dynasty was set for a bloody end.

The general had been leading a joint Israel-Judah campaign against King Hazael of Aram (Syria), seeking to recapture the border town of Ramoth Gilead. The reigning monarch of Israel, Joram, had been wounded in the battle and was convalescing at his country residence in Jezreel, where he was visited by his cousin Ahaziah, newly installed as king of the southern state of Judah.

Ordering his staff to prevent anyone leaving the camp and passing news of the prophetic message to the kings, Jehu rode to Jezreel with a small detachment of soldiers. Messengers who were sent to meet him realised his intention and fell in behind him rather than return to their base.

When Joram himself came out, Jehu claimed there could be no peace in Israel while foreign gods were tolerated, then drew his bow and shot both him and Ahaziah. Entering the city he saw Jezebel, Ahab's widow, and called for his supporters to throw her down from a palace window. She died instantly, and although he ordered her body to be buried, it was consumed by scavenging animals, as the prophet Elijah had predicted years ago.

That was only the beginning of the purge. Jehu sent an ultimatum to Samaria's elders to choose one of Ahab's family as king and then to stand up and fight, or to kill all of Ahab's family and submit. They elected to kill the 70 rather than risk a bigger massacre.

Other members of the royal retinue have since been killed, as have 40 members of Ahaziah's family whose only crime was to be caught visiting their relations in Jezreel during the coup.

By any standards Jehu is a hard and heartless man, a dynamic leader who drives people as furiously as he drives his chariot. He calmly sat down to his evening meal after the killings which for him were all in a day's work. He is also given to extravagant gestures; he ordered Joram's body to be thrown into the field which Ahab had forcibly and illegally taken from Naboth.

He has certainly removed an unjust and despotic regime, and many here believe Ahab's dynasty has got only what it deserved. But others question whether such violence can produce a lasting peace.

(2 Kings 9:1–10:14)

A frieze from Nineveh showing King Shalmaneser on his chariot crossing a stream.

He stoops to conquer

Samaria, c. 841 BC

Bereft of friends in Judah, having killed its king and his relatives; bereft of friends in Phoenicia, having killed the priests of Baal-melqart; and still at war with the ever-troublesome Hazael of Damascus, Jehu, king of Israel, has been forced to hitch his wagon to the Assyrians.

The Black Obelisk of Shalmaneser III records his campaigns during his 31-year reign. A procession of conquered peoples bring their tribute to the Assyrian king.

It cost him his dignity as he was forced to bow low in homage to King Shalmaneser. And it cost him money as he bought continuing Assyrian protection with a heavy tribute-tax.

It has also made Israel vulnerable to total domination by this major power which for a decade has been making regular excursions to the Mediterranean Sea and has taken back treasures and treaties as souvenirs. It would dearly like to rule the whole of Canaan; Jehu may have given it on a plate.

Back in Calah, Shalmaneser has recorded his achievements on a 2m (6ft) high block of black alabaster. Shaped like a pyramid with steps at the top, it is inscribed with summaries of the king's wars and with pictures of foreign nationals, including Jehu, paying him homage and taxes.

Unsuspecting priests massacred in temple

Samaria, c. 841 BC
Hundreds of priests and prophets of Baal-melqart have been hacked down in their own temple by supporters of Jehu, the new king of Israel. They had been lured there for a national celebration.

The king presented them with new robes and joined them in making sacrifices. But he left early, and ordered 80 soldiers to massacre all who were inside.

Jehu was accompanied by Jehonadab, a member of the small and extremist Rechabite sect. The Rechabites claim to be the only true followers of Yahweh and loyal descendants of the Israelites who left Egypt. They live as semi-nomads, rejecting all the trappings of settled life including permanent houses and arable farming.

Since his accession to the throne through a military coup, Jehu has consistently claimed to be a devoted follower of Yahweh. However, his tactics are considered unnecessarily brutal by some, and despite his crusade against Baal-melqart he has not closed the bull-god shrines at Dan and Bethel.

(2 Kings 10:11–33)

Locked in

Damascus, c. 841 BC
The new king, Hazael of Damascus, locked himself in his capital to escape the attacks of Shalmaneser of Assyria. Hazael, a so-called 'son of a nobody', became king after the murder of Ben-Hadad.

Hazael was defeated in battle but then put himself beyond Shalmaneser's reach. Undeterred, the Assyrian ravaged the orchards and gardens around Damascus and plundered cities in the nearby Plain of Hauran. He then left, taking the road to the coast, to receive tribute on Mount Carmel from Tyre, Sidon and King Jehu of Israel. He erected a commemorative stele on Mount Carmel.

Boy king placed on the throne

Jerusalem, c. 835 BC
The sole surviving son of King Ahaziah, whose existence has been kept a closely-guarded secret for seven years, has been anointed and placed on the throne of Judah in a carefully-staged coup. The temporary regent, Queen Athaliah, has been executed.

The baby heir to the throne, Joash, had been hidden in a palace store-room by Ahaziah's sister after the king had been murdered by the Israelite usurper Jehu. Queen Athaliah had begun to murder the royal family in order to retain the throne for herself.

The coup was organised by Jehoiada, a priest loyal to Yahweh and to the blood-line of the kings of Israel dating back to David. He had arranged for the nurture and protection of the infant and will act as regent until the seven-year-old Joash comes of age.

Jehoiada had called the Levites, who organise temple services, and the elders of Judah to a special Sabbath celebration. All leave for the loyal temple guards was cancelled. As a precaution, the guards inside the temple were armed with war trophies stored there, because carrying arms into the temple area would have aroused suspicion.

During the formal ceremony, the seven-year-old was placed on the throne, crowned, and presented with a copy of the covenant or religious law which governs Judah's relationships between God, king and country.

He was then taken to the two giant entrance pillars where he was publicly acclaimed king to the sound of trumpet blasts and loud cheering from the assembled people.

When Athaliah heard the hubbub she vainly summoned army assistance. But she was swiftly arrested and summarily executed for her crimes of murder.

Following the coronation and renewal of the covenant, an organised mob ransacked the temple of Baal which Queen Athaliah had patronised. The building was demolished and its chief priest killed on his altar.

A sense of quiet relief has now settled over what once again is being called 'the city of David'.

(2 Kings 11; 2 Chronicles 22:10– 23:21)

This detail of an early sarcophagus shows a young boy playing a lyre. Since King David's day it appears that playing the lyre was a skill that young men were often trained in.

Assyrian conflict on all fronts intensifies

Assyria, c. 824 BC

With civil war still raging around him, King Shalmaneser has died after a reign of 35 years, 31 of which were devoted to war. He is succeeded by his son Shamshi-Adad who faces the unenviable task of quelling the civil war and maintaining and expanding Assyrian power. The vassal rulers of the north and east have taken advantage of the civil war to withhold their tribute.

Under Shalmaneser, the Assyrian soldiers went further than ever before, setting foot in Armenia, Cilicia, Palestine, the Taurus and Zagros mountains and the shores of the Persian Gulf. Cilicia is the prime source of iron for the Near East and is an important link in maritime trade with Cyprus and Greece.

In southern Babylonia, Shalmaneser faced problems with the Chaldean tribes, and he had to intervene in central Babylonia when there was a Syrian-influenced revolt. Campaigns in the north-east became difficult as peoples of the eastern Taurus, around Lake Van, united into a potentially powerful kingdom in Urartu, with a considerable army.

He followed his father's steps into southern Kurdistan, successfully tackling opposition from the Medes, a nomadic people who posed little threat, and the Persians in north-west Iran.

Assyria's enemies are stronger than they used to be, and although Shalmaneser always claimed victory his campaigns often failed. And the cracks now widening in the nation's central organisation make the future of Assyrian dominance much less certain.

Shalmaneser lived in Nineveh for the first part of his reign. Later, he completed and expanded Calah and moved there. He rarely left it in his twilight years, during which he lost his grip on the nation.

Three years ago one of his sons, Ashur-danin-aplu, revolted along with 27 cities including Assur, Nineveh, Erbil and Arrapha. He entrusted his younger son, Shamshi-Adad, with the task of repressing the rebellion. The revolt was against the structure of the kingdom. The rural nobility and free citizens objected to the power given to provincial governors, who were often rich and insolent.

Phoenician ivory open-work plaque with a sphinx amongst stylised plants. Found in the Assyrian city of Nimrud, it confirms the Assyrians' wide trading and looting.

Managers to sort out chaos of temple finance

Jerusalem, c. 812 BC

A new management team has been appointed by royal command to take charge of temple maintenance after the priests and Levites had failed to supervise adequately the fundraising and repairs. The situation had been allowed to drift for some time before action was finally taken.

According to a survey, the 125-year-old building needs urgent repairs, and there are suggestions that money given for its maintenance has been channelled into other funds. A separate building fund has been opened.

A secure box in the temple is now used to collect the half-shekel weight of silver which each person is obliged to pay towards its upkeep. Many are giving more than the minimum following the assurance that proper accounting methods are now being employed. Donations are counted by a lay official and the high priest, and paid directly to those responsible for materials and wages.

The silver and other goods given as part of the worshippers' regular religious devotions, such as guilt and sin offerings, are still channelled into the personal support of the priests who have no other form of income.

The initiative came directly from Joash who, like many kings in the region, regards himself as the personal custodian of the national shrine. He is a devout follower of Yahweh under the tutelage of the priest Jehoiada, who is virtually the king's adoptive father.

(2 Kings 12:1–16; 2 Chronicles 24:1–14)

Roles are reversed

Calah, c. 820 BC

In a major reversal of roles, Babylonia has helped the king of Assyria to put down rebellion in his land.

The revolt began towards the end of Shalmaneser's reign involving several cities of Assyria and led by one of the late king's sons.

Babylonia's aid has enabled the present king Shamshi-Adad V to keep his throne. The two nations have made a new treaty, and in it Babylonia has made the most of Assyria's weakness. The Assyrian king is not even given a royal title in the records.

The terms of the treaty demand that Assyria surrenders fugitives to Babylonia, and hands over information about anti-Babylonian plots. The treaty oath is sworn by Babylonian gods only.

This small stone shows an Aramean chariot with two men. It comes from Tell Halat, near Aleppo in Syria. The Aramean bully-boys are here seen trampling underfoot an unfortunate adversary. Aramean cavalry and skilled charioteering were no match for their neighbours, such as Israel.

Israelite army shredded

Canaan, c. 812 BC

The bully-boys of Aram (Syria) are taking advantage of Assyria's weakened hold on the western reaches of its empire and are once again sending raiding parties into Israel, Philistia and Judah.

Jehoahaz of Israel is suffering numerous raids which have been attributed to Yahweh's intolerance of other gods promoted by the king who recently succeeded his father Jehu who died of old age. His army has been shredded like processed wheat.

Jehoahaz has barely enough horses even for ceremonial duties, and just 10 chariots for them to pull. He has only a few thousand foot soldiers. He is reported to have led an act of national returning to Yahweh, and there are signs that the oppression may be easing.

Further south, Aram's Hazael recently took control of the Philistine city of Gath and attempted to subdue Jerusalem. He was paid off by Joash its king who handed over considerable wealth from the temple and palace in return for peace.

(2 Kings 12:17,18; 13:1–7)

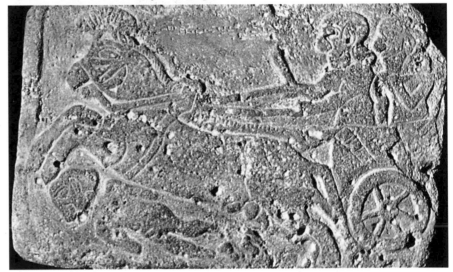

'He was easily led'

Shake-up in Valley of Salt

Jerusalem, c. 796 BC

Some kings are born leaders, while others are led by their advisers. As King Joash of Judah is laid to rest after a violent end to his 40-year reign, his epitaph is simply, 'He was easily led'.

For many years, under the eye of the godly priest Jehoiada, his guardian and surrogate father, Joash led Judah through a period of relative stability. He restored the traditions of Yahweh to the centre of Judean culture.

But following the priest's death, Joash paid more attention to the liberal establishment which lobbied for a relaxing of the strict religious laws. Attendance at temple ceremonies dropped sharply, and Asherah poles were erected as focal points for popular pagan rites despite protests from the prophets of Yahweh.

The low point of Joash's slide from high principles came when Jehoiada's son Zechariah protested at the state of affairs and accused the king of disobeying Yahweh. For that treasonable indiscretion, Zechariah was stoned to death with Joash's approval.

From then on, it was downhill all the way as the Arameans renewed their attacks. In one, the capital's leadership was wiped out by a small force which the defenders easily outnumbered but could not beat off. In another, the invaders were paid off by Joash who handed over to them many of the temple and palace treasures, saving the city but losing face.

Tired of defeat and sickened by the treatment of Zechariah, a group of officials assassinated Joash. According to one account he was killed while in bed, perhaps during a stay at a garrison at the Millo on the east of the city. He is succeeded by his 25-year-old son Amaziah.

(2 Kings 12:19–21;
2 Chronicles 24:17–27)

Dead Sea, c. 790 BC

The nation of Edom (Seir) has been shaken by defeat in the Valley of Salt south of the Dead Sea. Some 20,000 soldiers are reported to have been killed in a ferocious onslaught by neighbouring Judah.

But the victory left an unsavoury taste in the mouth of one Judean prophet who denounced his king, Amaziah, for currying favour with the gods he had defeated. Before submitting to an order to silence his protest, he uttered a dark threat that Amaziah would be destroyed one day.

Amaziah had recruited a large army reported to number 100,000, following a national census. He had also proposed using mercenaries hired from Israel but was warned against them by a prophet who claimed Yahweh would not support an attack which relied on fighters from an apostate country.

Following their dismissal on full pay, the disappointed mercenaries ran amok. They captured the plunder bonus they had expected in

The Dead Sea with the Jordan rift valley beyond.

Edom from Judah instead, leaving 3,000 people dead after a rampage of sheer vandalism through the northern half of the country.

Judah's victory was no less brutal. Half the Edomite casualties had first been taken prisoner, but later were sent to their deaths like lemmings by being driven over a steep cliff. To appease Qos, the understandably offended god of Edom, Amaziah offered sacrifices to its images which he had captured during the raid.

Edom, founded by Esau the rejected twin son of Israelite patriarch Isaac, had been conquered by King David and despite being allowed some autonomy had been subject to Judean domination ever since. However, for the past generation or so it has enjoyed more than usual freedom, and Amaziah's action was intended to bring it back into line.

(2 Kings 14:7;
2 Chronicles 25:5–16)

Modern art is grotesque

Italy, c. 800 BC

When someone at Vetulonia made a candlestick with the figure of a girl on the top, her elongated arms forming a large triangle on each side of her, he illustrated a trend in today's Italian art. It reflects a mixture of the fantastic, the realistic and the grotesque.

suggesting wings. In Tarquinia an artist has made an incense burner with the body of a bird made like a carriage on wheels, with the head of a deer. The body itself is hollow, and closed by a perforated lid which is also in the form of a bird's body with an animal head.

The Apulians attach abstract and

A typical, colourful painting of musicians from the Tomb of the Leopards.

The people of Villanova are making bronze figures that follow the Greek 'geometric' pattern but with distinct Italian differences; the figures, whether animal or human, are grotesque rather than accurate and have abstract circles for eyes and monstrous noses.

Other creations include a creature that is half bird, half ox, with an abstract circular design on its body

often grotesque three-dimensional figures to the handles of brightly painted wide-bodied vessels. Small wheel-like designs often decorate the narrow handles. They export these distinctive vessels, which show no trace of Greek influence, to the rest of Italy and to the west coast of Illyria. Modern art is clearly fantastic, especially if you are a merchant.

Israel king stamps on the Judah 'prickly weed'

Judah, c. 785 BC

Describing Judah as a prickly weed, Jehoash of Israel has stamped his neighbour's army into the ground, blown a gaping hole in Jerusalem's wall and looted what remained of the temple treasures.

Glowing with pride after his victory over Edom, Amaziah of Judah challenged Israel. Jehoash responded with a parable that proved a prediction of the ensuing fight. A thistle proposed marriage between its seedling and a cedar's, he chortled, but it got stamped on by a wild animal. Jehoash accused Amaziah of having an inflated ego, and advised him not to pursue his desire for power over the northern tribes.

Amaziah did not take the hint and continued his provocation. In the battle at Beth Shemesh 24 km (15 miles) west of Jerusalem, his army was blown away like thistledown. The city of Jerusalem was then ransacked before booty and hostages were taken. Amaziah himself was taken as a prisoner of war but released after his capital had been looted.

(2 Kings 14:8–16; 2 Chronicles 25:17–24)

Fast Facts
c. 800–782 BC

Assyria, 800–790 BC: Bars of silver are being stamped in Assyria and Syria (Aram) to guarantee the quality of the metal. Until now, silver used in trade was weighed out at each transaction, but unscrupulous traders could use debased metal or false weights with little danger of detection.

Egypt, 800–790 BC: Many workers have to function in constant pain because hard physical labour causes cartilege damage and arthritis. Many

also suffer back pain. Spondylosis, a hereditary condition caused by stress fractures of vertebral arches, is prevalent among some families in the Cairo area.

Greece, c. 800–790 BC: Villages all over Greece are clubbing together to form poleis, or city-states. Each is ruled by a small group of wealthy landowners who also act as judges over disputes and providers of grain when food is short. Most of the city-states are in the fertile plains and are walled for defence.

Samaria, c. 798 BC: The prophet Elisha has died

after an illness. He is believed to have been over 80 years old. A charismatic extrovert, one of his last actions was to foretell the defeat of Aram (Syria) by Israel at the hand of Jehoash. (2 Kings 13:10–21)

Jerusalem, c. 792 BC: Azariah, or Uzziah as he is more generally known, has been made co-regent by popular demand. He is the 16-year-old son of King Amaziah who has fallen in popularity since his futile attack on Israel, during which he had been taken prisoner. (2 Kings 14:13,21)

Samaria, c. 790 BC: Jehoash has succeeded in recaptur-

ing several border towns from the Arameans since the death of their king Hazael c. 796. (2 Kings 13:24, 25)

Assyria, c. 782 BC: King Adad-nirari III has received 30 tons of copper and bronze and 60 tons of iron as tribute tax from Damascus. He has also procured 100 cedar trees from Lebanon which will be used in his palaces and temples. He has also gathered tribute from Tyre, Sidon, and Joash of Israel. He is attempting to regain control of southern Syria in the face of an ever-increasing threat from the Urartu.

Jonah hooked by fishy argument

Nineveh, c. 760–750 BC

Some people do very odd things in the name of religion. According to Jonah, however, Yahweh is also in the habit of doing things which are at odds with the received wisdom of how he should act. The Israelite prophet is trying to explain to sceptical colleagues how God seems to have rewritten the rules.

Jonah, who normally patrols the corridors of King Jeroboam II's court, claims Yahweh told him to go trawling for converts in foreign waters. From forecasting wealth and peace to Israel he thought he heard God calling him to forecast doom and destruction in Nineveh, 1125 km (700 miles) to the east.

elements. Having picked Jonah, they tried vainly to save the ship before throwing him overboard as a peace offering to the raging powers.

The storm calmed, and the ship survived. Surprisingly, so did Jonah. He claims he was snapped up by a giant fish. As he prayed the prayer of a literally drowning man, the fish decided he was thoroughly indigestible and belched him up in the shallows before the meagre and fetid air supply in its stomach ran out.

Convinced now that Yahweh had been trying to net his obedience, not his credulity, Jonah went to Nineveh where he preached his message with all the conviction of

the creator of all living things – is concerned for all people in danger, even if they are not paid-up Israelites. So now Jonah is returning to Israel to preach the fishy theology about the city which got hooked by Yahweh.

(Jonah 1–4; cf. 2 Kings 14:25)

Seafaring Ways

Sea travel is a risky business, as Jonah discovered; storms are common in the Mediterranean.

The first great seafaring nation was Egypt, which was building seaworthy ships by 3000 BC. It was largely a summer traffic, for the winter storms and harsh weather virtually closed the seas.

Afterwards, the Phoenicians from 1000 BC explored and colonised the Mediterranean, even venturing out into the Atlantic in search of tin; their brave explorations were rewarded with profitable finds in Cornwall. They may have also circumnavigated Africa.

The Israelites have no good harbours and sheltered coasts, so have not become a sailing nation. Solomon's ally King Hiram, however, plied the seas with rich cargoes.

The Greeks, too, use the sea as a highway in preference to land travel which is often hard and difficult.

The ship Jonah took was probably a large one, capable of long voyages, and equipped with banks of oars for use when the wind died. It would have had a rounded prow; warships have protruding prows and are designed for ramming operations, a standard tactic in naval warfare. A merchant ship would have had a deck cover to protect the cargo and perhaps the oarsmen from storms, and it was under such a cover that Jonah would have been sleeping when the storm arose.

Small coastal traders, similar to this typical Mediterranean boat, were the most common form of sea transport for many centuries.

Seeing that the Ninevites had probably never heard of Yahweh and that a mass conversion to the Israelite religion would be the same as a political conversion to Israelite rule, Jonah refused the tempting bait of an expenses-paid business trip and booked for a Mediterranean cruise heading west towards Spain instead, just to make sure he got nowhere near Nineveh.

Yahweh had other ideas. The dream cruise ran into a nightmare tempest and the ship began to sink. The sailors, always among the most superstitious of mortals, drew lots to find out whose god had been so offended as to unleash such angry

an agnostic. To his utter surprise the people and their leaders accepted his warning that the city would be destroyed in six weeks unless it turned from its bad ways, announced a period of national repentance, and averted the catastrophe.

But why Yahweh should care about a pagan city which not long ago was supplying forces to the Assyrian overlords of Jonah's own region, he still could not fathom. To add to his confusion, the bush he sheltered under dried out and left him hot and bothered under the blazing sun.

And that, Jonah now claims, turned the tide in his thinking. Just as the prophet was concerned for his own burning skin, so Yahweh –

Royal city in confused state

Nineveh, c. 760 BC

Nineveh became a second capital of Assyria some 300 years ago, during the reign of Tiglath-Pileser I (c. 1115–1077 BC), who extended it and rebuilt its walls. But for the past few decades Assyria as a whole has been in a state of confusion.

During the reigns of Adad-nirari (809–782) and Shalmaneser IV (781–772) regional governors took an increasing share of responsibilities formerly adminstered by central government. An autonomous action such as that taken by the governor of Nineveh after hearing Jonah has become commonplace.

The current king, Ashur-dan III, has embarked on disastrous campaigns in central Syria, and several cities including Ashur and Guzana have been the scene of extensive revolts. There have been

The site of the great city of Nineveh has now mainly reverted to fields. Its inner wall, seen in the foreground, measured some 12 km/7.5 miles around and could have housed a population of 175,000.

natural disasters, too, with outbreaks of bubonic plague, flooding and famine following the total solar eclipse of 763. They were regarded as portents of the anger of the gods.

Nineveh, which stands at the confluence of the Tigris and one of its tributaries, has a large population estimated by Jonah to be 120,000. A census in Calah, somewhat smaller than Nineveh, in 865 gave its population as 69,574, so he may not be far wrong.

It experiences hot, dry summers from May to October when the land becomes parched. Because the city and its environs are on land higher than the Tigris, large-scale irrigation has so far proved impossible.

A seventh-century Phoenician merchant ship, such as the one Jonah would have travelled on.

Fast Facts
c. 780–770 BC

Assyria, c. 780 BC: Honey bees are now buzzing in the Suru and Mari regions on the middle Euphrates. The governor Shamash-reshusur brought the bees from the mountains of eastern Turkey. The insects, unknown until then in Assyria, are being used to produce honey and wax.

Greece, c. 776 BC: A day of games has been held at Olympia on the River Alpheus in the western Peloponnese in honour of the god Zeus. They took place in the sanctuary of Zeus situated in a wooded valley. The games consisted of running and wrestling, and prizes were garlands of wild olives. It is planned to hold these games every four years. Similar games are said to have been held before in other centres including Corinth.

China, c. 771 BC: The Chou kingdom has been invaded by the neighbouring Jung tribe which came on horseback from the Mongolian steppe. The king, the ninth ruler of Chou, was forced to flee his capital of Hao and set up a new one to the east in Loyang in central Honan. He is slowly losing authority but is still needed to rubber-stamp the power that in reality is wielded by others. His kingdom is fraught with internecine feuds.

Egypt, c. 773 BC: Sheshonq III has died in Tanis after a reign of half a century. During this time Egypt has had two dynasties fighting for control, one based in Leontopolis and one in Tanis, with a powerful priesthood also exercising influence in Thebes. The country is increasingly fragmented. Sheshonq is succeeded by King Pami.

Etruscans with the bit between their teeth gallop to prosperity

Italy, c. 750 BC

It may not seem very significant at first, but the Etruscans recently designed a new kind of horse-bit. It mixes an idea from Iran with a Greek geometric style. It is made of bronze, and the cheek-pieces are cast in the shape of a horse.

The significance is simply that the Etruscans are becoming an inventive and prosperous people. Their economy, based on industry and agriculture, exports fine pottery, bronze and gold work, ironware, vehicles, furniture, leather goods and richly-dyed linen.

Founding an Etruscan city is a complex activity surrounded by rites. When the site has been chosen they dig a pit and throw offerings into it. From there the city walls are marked out. Then the founder takes a plough with a bronze share and yokes a cow and a bull to it. He ploughs a furrow along the line where the walls are to be built, lifting it across the places reserved for gateways. He lays the clods carefully on the inner side of the furrow, making a symbolic moat and wall.

Afterwards, an open space on each side of the walls remains sacred, and no one is allowed to build or plough in it. Etruscans believe that every city must have three gates, three streets and three temples, dedicated to Jupiter, Juno and Minerva. The temples of Venus, Vulcan and Mars must lie outside the city walls.

So must the dead. Like other Italians, the Etruscans have cemeteries outside the towns. Cerveteri

An extraordinary decorative horsebit — which could hardly have had any practical use and must have been used on ceremonial occasions.

house denotes a woman's. The dead often lie on benches in the tombs, sometimes in terracotta coffins, together with personal possessions.

In this life, the Etruscans keep ducks, geese, guinea fowl and chickens, pigs, goats, cattle and sheep. They hunt wild pig, hares, deer and doves, and they fish in the freshwater lakes.

Their major source of metal is on the island of Elba, in the territory of Populonia. Copper, tin, silver lead and iron are mined open-cast. Smelting furnaces, used mainly for copper, have a truncated cone some two metres in diameter at its base. It is lined with refractory tiles, and a perforated partition divides the upper from the lower chamber.

Smelters place the ore with some charcoal in the upper chamber, and light a fire below it. The iron oxide separates out and stays in the upper chamber, while the molten copper flows through the perforations into the lower chamber, where it is collected.

Since the start of regular Olympic games, athletes are being increasingly looked upon as role models and sources for artistic inspiration. This early Greek plate from Athens of a discus-thrower bears the inscription 'Cleomelos is beautiful'.

Their towns are large. Cerveteri (Caere), for example, has a population of about 25,000. It lies on the coast between Tarquinia and Veii and its territory encompasses the Tolfa hills which are rich in metals, the main reason for the city's prosperity and close trading links with Greece.

has one at Sorbo, between the city and the coastal plain. They use both well graves for the burial of ashes in urns, and trench graves for the burial of corpses.

They often build small funerary monuments near the entrance to the tombs. A phallic form denotes a man's grave and a symbol of a

Prophet banned for 'fat cow' remarks

Samaria, c. 760–750 BC

An otherwise unknown prophet from Judah has been banned from the shrine at Bethel for his scathing attack on the social and religious conditions of Israel.

Amos, a herdsman and smalltime farmer from Tekoa, slandered Samaria's rich women socialites by calling them 'fat cows'. They and their families will become as impoverished as the underclasses they exploit, he warned.

The message appears to be as foreign as the messenger to local professional prophets of Yahweh. The prosperity of Israel, whose borders now extend virtually as far as they did during Solomon's reign, is seen by many as a sign of God's blessing.

Under the leadership of King Jeroboam II, the current weakness of Assyria's hold on the western fringes of its empire has been exploited to the full. Trade flows freely, and offers good profits to the merchant class. Market stalls are laden with exotic products. Customs dues fill the national coffers, providing revenue for

The remains of the ancient city of Samaria are on the hill to the left.

extensive public building works and the development of the textiles, armaments and metal industries.

But, claims Amos, it has all been achieved at the cost of social injustice. The leisured upper class women are trampling the working class into the mud with their demands for luxury goods and haute cuisine.

Justice, he says, is denied to those who cannot afford to pay bribes. The landed gentry are gobbling up the fields of small farmers by demanding cut-price grain and then forcing them to sell land after a poor harvest. The nouveau riche lounge on ivory-veneered beds and fritter away their extended holidays at lavish parties and concerts.

Yet at the same time they complain at the restrictive sabbath laws which reduce their potential for profit-making. Indeed, the religious state of the nation is fatally flawed, the prophet argues. Despite high attendance at the shrines, many people are mixing worship of Yahweh with that of other gods. Some shrines, like that at Bethel, are dedicated entirely to foreign gods.

A list of signatories on trade documents lodged at Samaria – the nearest thing Israel has to a residents' directory – shows as many people are named after Baal as after Yahweh. Such tainted devotion is anathema to Yahweh,

Amos claims.

God has no pleasure in correctly-followed rituals when the worshippers are spiritually complacent and ignore the obligations of the covenant, he says. Their agreement requires them to obey God's laws and to care for the underprivileged. Amos' denunciation is tinged with sadness; 'You alone of all the nations have I known,' he laments on God's behalf.

The prophet offers only a little hope. Israel is doomed to be overrun by other nations, he predicts, even though they too are subject to Yahweh's judgements because of their bloodthirsty colonialism. But Amos does call the nation to 'seek God that you may live', suggesting that mercy may yet be offered instead of a cataclysmic 'day of the Lord'. Even if the worst comes to the worst, there will be a restoration of faithful people to the land in the future, he adds.

But there is little hope that Amos himself will be reinstated at Bethel. After an official warning from its priest Amaziah, the prophet was reported to Jeroboam alleging that Amos had predicted the overthrow of the king. Amos, claiming only to be a layman with a message from God, left after forecasting that Amaziah's family would be caught up in scandal and bankruptcy.

(Amos 1–9)

Words of warning from the Book of Amos

Seek the Lord and live, or he will sweep through the house of Joseph like a fire. (5:6)

Hate evil, love good; maintain justice in the courts. Perhaps the LORD God Almighty will have mercy on the remnant of Joseph. (5:15)

Away with the noise of your songs! I will not listen to the music of your harps. But let justice roll on like a river, righteousness like a never-failing stream! (5:23,24)

'An enemy will overrun the land; he will pull down your strongholds and plunder your fortresses.' (3:11)

'I will tear down the winter house along with the summer house; the houses adorned with ivory will be destroyed and the mansions will be demolished,' declares the LORD. (3:15)

Loyal lover woos wayward wife

Israel, c. 750–735 BC

What does a man do when the woman he loves walks out and becomes first a prostitute and then a slave? The answer of Israelite law is to divorce her. But the answer one man has come up with is to buy her back. And he has.

Hosea's wife Gomer presented him with two sons and a daughter before leaving him a single parent. When he found her in the slave market in such a pathetic condition that she was offered at half the going rate, he paid up and took her home.

And that, he claims, is a picture of how Yahweh feels and will act towards his wayward 'spouse' Israel (or Ephraim, as he calls the country). But both for his love life and his equally unorthodox message as a prophet he is 'reckoned a fool and a madman', he admits.

His graphic teachings have portrayed God as a jilted lover, a doting parent and an angry guardian. 'How can I forget you?' he laments. 'I loved you as a child, called you out of Egypt, taught you to walk and healed your wounds. I feel compassion for you. Yet the more I called you, the further from me you went.'

'So one day I'll strip you naked in front of everyone, take away the bridal garments I gave you, and expose you to shame and ridicule.'

As evidence of Israel's drift from Yahweh he cites the high incidence of deceit, fraud, muggings, theft, murder and adultery.

He describes a nation torn apart by political intrigue and numerous lawsuits while its leaders have nothing better to do than to get drunk. He pours scorn on the political hopes placed on alliances with foreign powers which he claims will only sap Israel's strength still further.

On the religious level, the people have given their affections to local gods which are incapable of satisfy-

The hill country of Ephraim, near Samaria.

ing their needs, he says. Hosea mocks the Samarian bull-god. 'It's been crafted by a silver-smith! It's not a real god. And one day it'll be smashed to bits,' he warns, suggesting that Assyria, which is already taxing Israel to the hilt, will soon carry it off into slavery.

Israel has only itself to blame, he adds. It has abandoned the covenant agreement with Yahweh. Yet God cannot break his own commitment to faithfulness, and longs to forgive and redeem his people.

Hosea's marriage of personal experience and prophetic ex-position is most poignant in the names he gives to his children. The eldest son is called Jezreel ('God scatters') in memory of the ill-fated city where Jehu killed Ahab's son and established an ultimately apostate dynasty. His second son is Lo-Ammi ('my people no longer'), born after his daughter Lo-Ruhamah ('loved no more'). (Hosea 1-14)

The divine lover's lament from the Book of Hosea

'I will show my love to the one I called, "Not my loved one". I will say to those called "Not my people", "You are my people"; and they will say, "You are my God".' (2:23)

'There is no faithfulness, no love, no acknowledgement of God in the land. ... they break all bounds and bloodshed follows blood-shed. Be-cause of this the land mourns, and all who live in it waste away; the beasts of the field and the birds of the air and the fish of the sea are dying.' (4:1–3)

'Come, let us return to the LORD. He has torn us to pieces but he will heal us; he has injured us but he will bind up our wounds.' (6:1)

'I desire mercy, not sacrifice, and acknowledgement of God rather than burnt offerings.' (6:6)

'They sow the wind and reap the whirlwind.' (8:7)

'When I found Israel, it was like finding grapes in the desert; ... But when they came to Baal Peor, they consecrated themselves to that shameful idol and became as vile as the thing they loved.' (9:10)

'Take words with you and return to the LORD. Say to him: "Forgive all our sins and receive us graciously, that we may offer the fruit of our lips ... for in you the fatherless find compassion."' (14:2,3)

Lofty vision given for lowly state

Jerusalem, c. 740–735 BC

Women of leisure dripping with jewels and draped in designer clothes make their presence smelt as their expensive perfume wafts down the street behind them. Rich families rise early for champagne breakfasts and settle late after consuming cases of vintage wine at lavish dinner parties serenaded by minstrels.

This deep full-size bronze bath from Ur testifies to an undreamt-of level of luxury and personal hygiene.

For some, the high life of Jerusalem is much to be desired, a taste of-heaven on earth. But for others it is much to be despised for the foundation which underpins it is one of corruption and illegality, according to allegations being voiced by one concerned insider.

Major social and political decisions are made by gullible and selfish youths rather than by mature elders, claims Isaiah son of Amoz, a civil servant with an increasingly prophetic tone. Property developers are building big estates and landowners are buying up smallholdings to create large-scale farms, effectively reducing ordinary people to tenants on their own lands. The most vulnerable people such as widows have little social security, he adds.

Furthermore, freethinkers are challenging traditional values and ethics. Things once considered wrong are no longer censured,

while the strict disciplines of ancient wisdom and faithful religion are exchanged for an easy-going hedonism which suggests that 'a little of what you fancy does you good'.

A deeply sincere follower of Yahweh, Isaiah is highly critical of private religious formalism which is not backed up by public righteousness. God hates the feasts and festivals, finds the dutiful offerings meaningless, and is refusing to listen to people's prayers, he says. Judah, and its northern cousin Israel, is like a vineyard which has been carefully tended by its owner but has produced only inedible fruit.

Eventually, he suggests, Yahweh will plough it up and let the 'wild animals' of other nations trample it into a wasteland where only brambles will grow. On that 'day of the Lord', people will run to the

caves for shelter from invading forces.

But like his contemporaries Amos and Hosea, Isaiah lets shafts of hope brighten his gloomy predictions. 'Come, let us talk together,' he quotes Yahweh as saying, 'though your sins are red as the blood of the innocent which you shed, you can become as pure as white snow.' He looks forward to a time when nations will crowd into Jerusalem to seek God's word. And he claims a 'righteous branch' will be born into the royal line to purge Judah of its sin and restore goodness to the land.

Isaiah claims to have been launched on his prophetic career by a vision of awe-inspiring holiness. In it he saw God 'high and lifted up' in a smoke-filled temple, surrounded by worshipping

Women wearing fine embroidered dresses whilst fetching water from the well. A scene observed in 1850 in Palestine and which had changed little throughout the years.

heavenly beings. Over-whelmed by a sense of his own failings and inadequacy, he felt his lips touched symbolically by the fire of Yahweh's presence, purging him of sin and equipping him to speak divinely-inspired words.

(Isaiah 1–6, 8)

163

Princess burnt out

Salamis, Cyprus, c. 750 BC

A Greek princess who married into the royal family at Salamis has been cremated according to Greek custom. The normal practice at Salamis is inhumation. Her remains have been interred in one of the royal tombs in the necropolis, with a large quantity of Cypriot and Greek pottery, including a set of plates and bowls. Her incinerated skeleton wears a necklace of gold and rock-crystal beads.

Horses are sometimes sacrificed in front of the chamber, dressed for the occasion with bronze front bands, blinkers, breastplates and side ornaments. Some leading people have their slaves sacrificed at their funerals so that they can continue to be served in the next life. One king's tomb is furnished with an ivory and gold throne thought to have been made in a north Syrian workshop.

The unique royal tombs have a small chamber with a flat roof, a facade of large square-cut stone blocks and a cornice along the top. By contrast, ordinary people are buried in plain, rock-cut tombs in another part of the necropolis. A pyre of broken vases, imitation clay jewellery, and some carbonised seeds and fruits is placed with the body. It is customary to offer the first-fruits to the gods at a funeral so as to curry favour for the dead.

Shepherds flock to Tiber

Rome, c. 750 BC

Many new settlements on the banks of the River Tiber have been founded by Latin shepherds and farmers in Italy. The Latins, who occupy the plain of Latium in central Italy, already have a few hilltop settlements on the Tiber which makes a deep, S-shaped valley between 800 and 1,600 m (half a mile to a mile) wide.

The edges of the valley have been formed into cliff-like hills and flat-topped spurs which provide natural protection for the small communities who live there. At one point the Tiber is shallow, dividing at a ford which forms the main route across the river for the Latium people. The mouth of the Tiber has a tendency to silt up and prevent access to the sea. The most important new settlement is being called Rome.

Money can buy power

Samaria, c. 743 BC

Money can't buy love but King Menahem of Israel believes that it can buy power. He has just brokered a deal with Tiglath-Pileser III of Assyria with a mountainous 34 tons of silver. It was collected in a 50-shekel tax imposed on all people of means.

Assyrian sources report that Menahem also handed over large quantities of coloured woollen garments and linen garments as part of the deal. Aramean (Syrian) and Phoenician leaders have also handed over heavy taxes.

Menahem, the 16th king of Israel since it split from its southern sister-state of Judah two centuries ago, was a garrison commander in Tirzah before seizing power in 752. He assassinated Shallum, who had been king for only a month, having himself assassinated Jeroboam's son and heir Zechariah.

The new king immediately went on a bloody rampage in Tipshah (Tappuah), about 16 km (10 miles) south-east of Samaria. The city had refused to recognise him as king and in revenge he sacked it and made a special point of knifing all pregnant women.

Such actions have not endeared him to Israelites, and his alliance with Assyria suggests that internal threats from rival factions are growing. The army commander Pekah is said to have widespread support for an alliance with Damascus against the Assyrians. And the prophet Hosea has declared bluntly that the alliance cannot save Israel from Yahweh's profound anger at its religious apostasy.

(2 Kings 15:1–22; Hosea 5:13; 8:9)

The legend of Romulus and Remus, rescued as infants and suckled by a wolf, appears to have grown up at a later date. According to legend they founded Rome on the spot they were reared by the wolf: this potent symbol became the emblem of Rome.

'Don't blame the gods!'

Greece, c. 750 BC

People all over Greece are reciting the poetry of a blind bard, Homer, whose work is steeped in human actions and emotions set against a background of divine action and a belief that history is in the hands of the gods.

The *Odyssey* tells of the brave and wise Odysseus, king of Ithaca, on his return journey to the island during the Trojan War. On the way he has amorous liaisons with the nymph Calypso and the witch Circe (who turned his companions into above what is fated for them.'

Detail from an early Greek vase depicting heroic acts from the *Iliad*. Hercules is shown leading the mythical multi-headed dog Cerberus.

Detail of the frieze from the Parthenon.

But he also believes that human beings bring their suffering on themselves. In one of the works attributed to him, the *Odyssey*, Zeus says, 'How foolish men are! How unjustly they blame the gods! It is their lot to suffer, but because of their own folly they bring upon themselves sufferings over and

pigs). He evokes famous dead people from the underworld, and encounters monsters such as the one-eyed Cyclops and the sailor-eating sea monster Scylla near the whirlpool Charybdis. Back home, he slays the suitors of his wife Penelope.

Homer's other major work is the *Iliad*, centred on the effects of the anger of the Greek hero Achilles during the Trojan War. Achilles is provoked by the abduction of his mistress Briseis by Agamemnon, commander-in-chief of the Greek forces.

While Achilles is in his tent the Trojans, led by Hector, force the Greeks back to their ships and Achilles' close friend Patroclus is killed in the battle. Filled with grief, Achilles kills Hector under the walls of Troy.

Homer may originate from the Aegean island of Chios. He comes from the class of public workers who include potters, metal workers, seers and doctors as well as poets. His works have not yet been written down but are being transmitted orally.

Fast Facts c. 750–740 BC

Italy, c. 750 BC: A new culture is emerging in Italy. The Este people live in the Veneto, north-west of the Po, and they speak their own language, Venetic. They make bronze buckets called situlae, for holding wine, which like most of their other bronze work are decorated with scenes from their everyday life – hunting, fighting, farming, feasting and making love.

Italy, c. 750 BC: An obscure and isolated people living in the north-west corner of Italy (Liguria) make stone statue menhirs in the shape of human figures. No one seems sure what they are for, but they are continuing a practice begun some 2,000 years ago in other cultures.

Sardinia, c. 750 BC: Phoenicians have been establishing a number of trading colonies on the coasts of Sardinia, attracted by the growing wealth of the island which is rich in mineral resources. The Sardinians still build stone towers (nuraghi), as they have since 1500 BC, but they are becoming more elaborate. Rooms are added to old structures.

Cyprus, c. 750 BC: The Phoenicians are increasingly wielding influence in Cyprus, where they control some copper mines. They export copper and other goods from Cyprus to the Aegean and the Dodecanese. They cut down trees to build ships. Some report that Phoenician perfume makers are working in the Dodecanese, using local potters to make perfume flasks according to Phoenician design.

Egypt, c. 750 BC: At least four people are currently claiming to be king of Egypt. Osorkon IV rules at Tanis, Iuput at Leontopolis, Peftjau-bastet at Herakleopolis and Nimlot at Hermopolis just north of Amarna. Each controls a small parcel of land but has no authority over the whole country.

Babylon, c. 745 BC: Since the accession of King Nabu-nasir in 747, the Babylonians have started to keep accurate records and diaries. Written mostly on hinged boards covered with beeswax, the records also include monthly astronomical observations, trade prices, river levels and weather reports.

Assyria's Pul is no pushover

Jerusalem, c. 732 BC

Months of trauma and bloodshed appear to have ended with Assyria in firm control of Aramea (Syria), Israel and Judah, together with their neighbouring regions of Edom and Philistia.

Tiglath-Pileser III, often known as Pul, has destroyed the Aramean capital of Damascus, killed its king Rezin, and made it a formal province of the empire. He also controls many Israelite cities, has deported contingents of both Israelites and Arameans, and imposed a heavy tribute-tax on Judah.

Pul left behind the clear message that any further rejection of Assyrian authority will be dealt with severely. It was echoed by

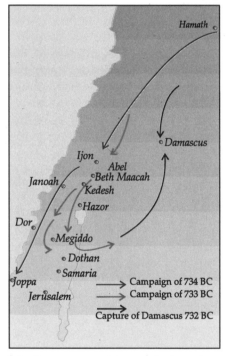

The first two campaigns were both conducted from the north, and ran through Israel.

Isaiah, a prophet of Yahweh attached to the court in Jerusalem, who is predicting wholesale destruction of the southern kingdom if King Ahaz continues his present policies.

The conflict began with an alliance between Rezin and King Pekah of Israel to force Judah to join them in resisting Assyria. Already weakened by border skirmishes

with Edom and Philistia, Ahaz called on Assyria for help. It came swiftly, but at the cost of Judah becoming a vassal state; Pul is a tax collector, not a charitable benefactor.

Fortunately for Judah, Pekah did give some charity. Having killed many Judeans and taken others as prisoners of war, he was rebuked by Oded, another prophet of Yahweh, who urged him to honour God by returning his fellow-countrymen unharmed.

It was an unusual reversal of religious loyalties. According to prophets such as Hosea, Yahweh has transferred his affections from Israel to Judah and has condemned the northern kingdom to extinction. But Judah's Ahaz is far from honouring him exclusively in the traditional way.

In an eloquent statement, Isaiah assured Ahaz that the Syrian–Israelite coalition would not harm him for as long as he 'kept the faith' and took no military or political counter-action. The prophet also warned that association with Assyria would bring only further trouble. He gave Ahaz the opportunity to ask God for a confirming sign, which he refused.

The sign, that Isaiah's young virginal bride-to-be would conceive and have a son, occurred anyway and its significance was probably barbed. The child's nickname 'Immanuel' ('God with us') could signify Yahweh's presence either to

bless or to judge.

Isaiah also predicted that Judah would be humiliated by Assyria and become desolate. People would shave their heads in grief and eat the poor man's diet of curds and honey, he said, giving an ironic twist to the ages-old description of the promised land 'flowing with milk and honey'.

Ahaz, who has closed the temple of Yahweh in Jerusalem and opened street-corner shrines to other gods, would have none of it. The ruthless king who has already sacrificed his own son to the gods in the hellish garbage tip of the Valley of Hinnom is unlikely to exchange weapons for a prayer mat. His main religious act of late has been to build a replica of an altar which caught his eye in Damascus when he travelled there for his interview with Pul.

(2 Kings 15:27–16:18; 2 Chronicles 28; Isaiah 7; cf. Isaiah 17; Hosea 1:6,7)

The final campaign was a brief affair, conducted in a flurry, on many fronts, as the Assyrians finally overcame Judah.

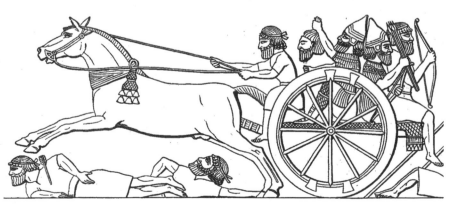

Assyrian warriors riding a captured chariot after a battle.

Post haste for Assyrian revival

Assyria has a new communications network of postal stages across the empire necessitated by the requirement for provincial governors to send regular reports to the king. He has also appointed representatives in the vassal-states to safeguard Assyrian trade and foreign affairs interests.

Vassal states like Judah enjoy protection and support from Assyria, as well as some independence so long as they pay their tribute-taxes and accept Assyrian guidance when necessary. Recent grateful vassals include the Syrian king of Sam'al, 112 km (70 miles) north-west of Aleppo, for whom Tiglath-Pileser suppressed a rebellion, destroying the opposition and reinstating his father in his former position of authority.

Tiglath-Pileser III has decreed that Assyria be governed by a hierarchy of officials appointed by and responsible to himself. Royal inspectors travel round the provinces checking their performance.

Tiglath-Pileser has now pushed the Assyria/Babylonia border to its furthest possible southerly point, along the Diyala from the Zagros mountains to the Tigris. And in another significant victory Assyria has defeated the land of Ullubu north of Nineveh and a Urartu vassal. Some 29 towns have been brought under Assyrian control, and their occupants have been resettled in other parts of the empire.

Further west, Assyria has defeated the state of Arpad, south-west of Carchemish, after two years of repeated sieges. Arpad, which controls important trade routes to the Mediterranean, is being used as a base for dealing with other former vassal states which had joined the Damascus coalition.

The king of this culture which is now spreading like a bush fire across the Near East is regarded almost as divine. He is much less approachable than kings of other states, and visitors must always be blindfolded before entering his presence.

Each sub-court for the royal family members is separately staffed. Society is divided into three classes: citizens who have full rights; slaves who have none; and the lower middle class (including peasants) who are supervised by a master but have some personal

Assyrian stone carving: Elamite musicians celebrate King Ashurbanipal's capture of the town of Madaktu.

rights and may acquire land.

The better-off families live comfortably in large mud-brick houses, some with as many as 12 rooms and an upper floor. They are approached through courtyards lined with storerooms, and some have toilets linked to a drainage system of brick or terracotta pipes.

The economy is based on agriculture. Cows, sheep, goats and poultry are bred for food, and grain and grapes are grown for both home consumption and for export. Mules, donkeys and horses provide overland transport while reed coracles and rafts made from inflated sheep and goatskins tied to a wooden framework ship goods along the rivers.

Women are normally veiled when the leave the house, and tie their hair in plaits. They wear ankle-length gowns. Prostitutes, however, may wear leather jackets and curl their hair. Men, who are heavily bearded and long-haired, wear a knee-length smock. Both sexes adorn themselves with jewellery.

The Assyrians worship a number of gods. Among them are Ashur, the national god; Ishtar, associated with sex and war; Shamach the sun god; Adad the weather god; and Nergal the god of the underworld. Each is believed to be a manifestation of a unified divinity. There are also supernatural forces which influence human affairs, and demons may attack and harm the innocent.

The gods have their earthly homes in temples, usually built in the form of ziggurats. Images are fed and clothed daily, and ceremonies around them conducted, by a variety of temple officials from priests and mus-icians to diviners and exorcists.

Astrology is important too, interpreting the movement of the planets and the weather in terms of omens or portents for the future. Assyrian art often depicts people with large eyes, demonstrating their wonder at the gods.

Keeping the country and its vassal states under control is a large and well-organised standing army which can call on reservists. Chariots and carts give it added speed and mobility, and military intelligence employs spies across the empire. The king often takes a leading part in battles. The inhabitants of lands overrun by Assyria are deported and replaced with refugees from elsewhere, thus weakening ethnic ties and removing a unified opposition.

War over women mars Greek growth

Greece, c. 735 BC

War has broken out in the Peloponnese, at the southern foot of Greece. According to some reports it appears that Sparta has attacked Messenia to the west.

The Spartans claim that some of their young women were molested by Messenians while worshipping at a shrine. When the king of Sparta intervened the Messenians killed him. However, the Messenians say that the Spartan king disguised some boys as girls and ordered them to attack the Messenians.

Impartial observers say that the real reason for the war is that the Spartans want Messenia's richly fertile lands. Whatever the motive, it is not going to be an easy battle; the Messenians have quickly gained a strong defensive position and the Spartans will find it hard to shift them.

The conflict between neighbouring cities reflects the situation elsewhere in Greece where the population is growing and cities are getting crowded. One effect of this is that the poorer people of the cities, finding all the best farming land securely in the hands of the aristocracy, are moving away in search of their own land, forming small outlying villages, and gradually dropping out of city life.

They are called perioikoi, or the 'dwellers around', and less politely as 'sheepskin-wearers' or 'dusty feet' – they cannot afford the smart woven clothes worn by city-dwellers. Some of the villages ask the cities for protection, which gives powerful settlements a ring of dependent, and therefore faithful, allies. Some neighbouring communities are forming leagues to promote regional security and protection.

The aristocrats are becoming more powerful, and the gap between rich and poor is getting wider. The government of a city operates through a council of the 'best men', whose executive officers may be appointed for life, and an assembly of warriors, who rubber-stamp what the council has decided.

Another effect of growth is the founding of colonies abroad. Greeks from the city of Chalcis in Euboea have founded Naxos in Sicily. It is cut off from the rest of the island by rugged territory, but the Greeks have pushed towards Mount Etna, driving the native Sicilians inland, and forming another colony called Leontini.

An early statue, c. 700 BC showing Egyptian influences before the classical Greek style developed.

The Amazons, a race of fearsome women warriors, have become the stuff of legend. How much was based on reality – and how much on warriors' tall stories? This vase depicts Achilles slaying the Amazon Queen Penthesitea. From a black-figured amphora c. 540 BC.

Co-op for food fund

Greece, c. 740 BC

In Crete, Sparta and Carthage communities are eating their meals together, an arrangement called a syssitia. In Sparta, it is financed by each citizen paying a fixed amount towards it; defaulters lose their share in government.

In Crete, there is a common fund. From the crops and cattle produced on the public lands and the tributes paid by the underclass, one part is given to the worship of the gods and the upkeep of public services, and one part to the syssitia. In many cities each person also has to contribute a tithe of his crop to this fund, and serfs pay tribute too. The amounts asked are reasonable, however, and therefore there are very few incidents of serfs revolting against their masters.

Long reign comes to lonely end

Jerusalem, c. 740 BC

Judah's longest-serving and much-loved monarch Uzziah (Azariah) has died after 52 years in charge. Under his leadership the tiny state has grown in power and wealth, suppressing the Philistines, Ammonites and several Edomite and Arab tribes.

Uzziah strengthened the fortifications of Jerusalem and built new border forts in the southern desert. He increased the size of the army which he equipped with advanced weaponry and defensive equipment. A lover of the land, he also developed Judah's agricultural and irrigation systems, to a degree hitherto unimagined.

But his reign, which was shared at each end first with his father Amaziah and then with his son Jotham, was marred by the onset of a major skin disease which sadly forced him to live as a recluse and barred him from the temple services.

It is believed to have broken out when he usurped the priests' authority in the temple and burned incense there to Yahweh. He is not the first king of Judah to discover that temporal power does not bestow a divine right to spiritual ministry, even after a long and successful reign.

(2 Kings 15:1–7; 2 Chronicles 26)

Ammon made an ass

The hill country of Ammon, is today identified with the hills surrounding Amman, capital of Jordan.

Jerusalem, c. 740–735 BC

The once-powerful desert tribe of Ammon has been made literally to look an ass by its neighbour Judah. After a series of attacks, King Jotham of Judah has beaten the Ammonites into submission and has exacted from them 10,000 donkey-loads of grain and over three tons of silver.

The Ammonites live well to the east of the Jordan River beyond Gilead, the Israelite tribal area allocated to Gad and Manasseh. They have never been fully conquered by either Israel or Judah, and historically have been a thorn in both sides. They are the descendants of Abraham's nephew Lot, and have never been part of Israel.

Jotham shared the last 10 years of his father Uzziah's reign before taking full control in 740 BC. He also shares his father's exclusive faith in Yahweh, and has continued the repair of Jerusalem and its temple. He has also further strengthened Judah's southern defences.

(2 Kings 15:32–38; 2 Chronicles 27)

Fast Facts, c. 740–725 BC

Athens, c. 740 BC: Artists are painting scenes of life and death on huge vases, some of which are 1.5 m (5 ft) high. Some depict warships with many oars sometimes in action, with spear-throwing men and corpses drowning in the sea. Others depict funerals, with mourners tearing their hair and beating their breasts. They are used as monuments on rich people's graves, and sometimes they have a hole in the base so that drinks can flow through the earth to quench the corpse's thirst.

China, c. 740 BC: Authors have been writing literature for some time with a stylus on bamboo slabs. The *Book of History*, the *Book of Changes* and the *Odes* are recent additions to literature which is greatly respected by the Chinese people.

Corfu, c. 733 BC: Corfu, an island between Greece and Italy, has been colonised by Eretrians fleeing the war in Greece. Others have moved to Syracuse, on the east coast of Sicily.

Samaria, c. 732 BC: Assyria's Tiglath-Pileser III has recognised Hoshea as king of Israel. Hoshea, who led a faction opposed to Pekah, assassinated the former king and then paid Tiglath-Pileser a fat fee to retain the throne, according to Assyrian sources. (2 Kings 15:30)

Greece, c. 725 BC: Craftsmen in Amyclae have made a pair of terracotta figures. One is of a clean shaven soldier wearing a conical helmet and the other is of a woman with ear-rings and a cap. They both have wide staring eyes and pointed noses, and are designed to be looked at in profile. The eyes, hair, ear-rings and cap are painted.

Assyria conquers Babylon

Babylon, c. 729 BC

For the first time in 400 years, an Assyrian king has been invested with Babylonian kingship. Tiglath-Pileser III 'took the hands of the god Marduk' at the New Year festival in Babylon and was formally accepted as king and representative of the gods by the priesthood before offering sacrifices.

Tiglath-Pileser can now survey an Assyrian empire that extends from the Persian Gulf to the borders of Egypt, up through northern Syria into Cilicia and Anatolia, and controls the Palestine coast as far south as the Gaza Strip.

It has taken the Assyrians three years to reclaim Babylonia from the Chaldeans. When Babylon itself was taken, King Ukinezer was chased to his own capital in southernmost Babylonia (the Iraqi marshes) by the Assyrian army which destroyed his and other Chaldean territory on the way.

Merodach-Baladan, who has long been working undercover for Assyria, had his territory spared, as did the other Chaldean leaders who negotiated a deal with Assyria.

Tiglath-Pileser III, king of Assyria from 744–727 BC, is seen here riding in triumph on a bas-relief from Nimrud.

Defiant Samaria falls

Samaria, c. 721 BC

It was always going to be just a matter of time. But no one could have predicted how long the Assyrian army would have to bombard and blockade Samaria before eventually taking it.

Three years ago Shalmaneser V, newly installed as Assyria's ruler, marched against the city which had stopped paying its tribute-taxes on the death of his predecessor Tiglath-Pileser III. Hoshea, Israel's puppet king, had also made a secret treaty with Egypt against Assyria, for which he was imprisoned by Shalmaneser.

But the walls of the well-fortified city in the centre of Israel resisted all attacks. The water supply and stocks of food were sufficient to maintain the population. After the sudden and mysterious death of Shalmaneser, believed to have been caused by an assassin's sword, his successor Sargon II launched a fresh onslaught on the newly kingless city.

When it fell, he force-marched 27,300 Samaritans to several Assyrian centres, and he is now beginning to repopulate the city with peoples captured in other regions.

The fall of Samaria has been long foretold by the prophets of Yahweh, who see it as symbolising Yahweh's final abandonment of ten of the twelve tribes of Israel which settled in Canaan some 500 years ago. The other two, centred on Jerusalem, are no less vulnerable.

(2 Kings 17)

Flower power blooms

Babylon, c. 721 BC

Merodach-Baladan, a former collaborator with Assyria who collects exotic plants and has built an astronomical observatory, has seized the throne in Babylon. He claims to be descended from an earlier self-sworn king and that the throne is his by right.

Sargon II moved in speedily but was blocked at Der by the Elamites, a forceful tribe from south-west Iran who are backing Merodach-Baladan. Sargon went home, claiming that he had 'smashed the forces of Humbanigash king of Elam' but had decided to leave the rebel king until a later time.

Merodach-Baladan sees himself as Babylonia's saviour, and the means by which the god Marduk will conquer its enemies.

The new plant is likely to wither quickly, however, according to Judah's prophet Isaiah. Babylon will continue to be overrun by other nations, he predicts, and after its brief flowering will become the haunt of jackals and hyenas. And the stars will go out in the king's observatory.

(Isaiah 13)

Lanky Piankhi now strides over Egypt

Egypt, c. 725–720 BC

Egypt has one king again, although probably not the one the people would have elected. Four rival monarchs surrendered in turn to Piankhi, king of Nubia (known as Cush in the Bible) following a battle at Herakleopolis.

Nubia, lying south of Aswan, became independent from Egypt when it created its own capital at Napata a couple of centuries ago.

Devoted to the cult of Amun, Piankhi believes that his authority over Egypt is a gift of the god. On his triumphal march north he stopped at Thebes to celebrate the Festival of Opet when the figure of Amun is carried from Karnak to the temple at Luxor.

Piankhi, who has ruled Nubia for 20 years, has treated the Egyptian kings leniently and made them governors of their areas. An account of his victory has been inscribed on a stele which shows Amun looking on with approval as Piankhi receives the four kings.

He does not appear to have the approval of Yahweh, however. The Judean prophet Isaiah has predicted that the tall and smooth-skinned Nubians will bring tribute to God in Jerusalem. Egypt's civil war will continue, he adds, and worshippers of Yahweh will settle there one day.

(Isaiah 18,19)

A Nubian village near Aswan, and a felucca on the River Nile.

Lambs for the slaughter

Sheep and goats grazing on the hillside near Beersheba.

Jerusalem, c. 715–712 BC

The prosperous wool and mutton producers of Moab have a new market which will ruin their business.

After continuous assaults for several years, Assyria has finally conquered the rolling hills to the east of the River Jordan, destroyed several cities near the River Arnon, and taxed the population in sheep.

The region is in turmoil as grieving people are forced out of their homes 'like fluttering birds pushed from the nest' according to Isaiah from neighbouring Judah. Some have fled the length of the Dead Sea south to Zoar.

Isaiah's counsel is that the devastated country which has often oppressed Israel and Judah, should send sheep to Jerusalem as tribute to Yahweh, as it did when Ahab was king of Israel, in an act of penitence. The defeat is another example of God pricking the bubble of human pride, he says.

(Isaiah 15,16)

Priest has returned to tame lions

Samaria, c. 715 BC

A series of fatal attacks by packs of lions roaming into the former territory of Israel from the Jordan Valley has provided one man with an unexpected return ticket home from an Assyrian refugee camp.

Settlers placed in the area believe the attacks have been provoked by Yahweh, the God of the Israelites, because he is no longer worshipped there. So they called for a priest to be sent back to perform the rituals necessary to tame God and the lions.

Israel has been steadily repopulated by peoples displaced from Syria, Phoenicia and other regions. They have built shrines to the gods they brought with them, including Nergal the Assyrian god of the underworld whose symbol, ironically, is a lion.

(2 Kings 17:24–33)

'Your turn is coming' prophet warns city

Judah, c. 715 BC

Bribery and corruption is as bad in Judah as it was in Israel, and Jerusalem will therefore suffer a similar fate to Samaria, is the claim of the prophet Micah currently circulating here.

Judges are being bribed to give favourable verdicts and prophets are dispensing favourable predictions to anyone who can pay a fat fee, he alleges. Rich landowners are putting smallholders out of business, often by fraudulent means.

Micah, who comes from the southern village of Moresheth-gath, has been a small-time prophet echoing the message of his better-known and more highly-placed contemporary Isaiah for about three decades. He predicted the fall of Samaria before it happened in 721.

He is now suggesting that Jerusalem will suffer a major siege and eventually will be destroyed by the Babylonians. Currently they are well under the Assyrian thumb and his dire warnings have gained little sympathy from the religious establishment.

People who remember Yahweh are as rare as summer fruits gathered after harvest, he says. Instead, everyone behaves like a ruthless hunter. Neither personal friends nor close relatives are to be trusted. 'You'd get torn less by walking through a thorn-hedge than by tangling with even the most considerate people these days,' Micah claims.

But not all is gloom and doom for this champion of the poor and scourge of the rich. He predicts that a ruler 'whose origins are from old' will be born in Bethlehem, south-east of Jerusalem, to 'shepherd his flock in Yahweh's strength'.

Following what he believes is

The hillside surrounding Bethlehem has in parts changed very little over the years.

the inevitable destruction of Judah, a remnant of people will be preserved to start afresh. 'You will go to Babylon; there you will be rescued,' Micah promises. That remnant will grow to become powerful and influential once again, 'like a lion mauling a flock of sheep'. Then Jerusalem will become a world centre for dispensing God's truth, where peace and prosperity will reign.

(Micah 1–7)

Prophetic promises

'I will bring back together the remnant of Israel like sheep in a pen.' (2:12)

'You will cry to God but he won't listen or respond because of your evil ways.' (3:4)

'One day you'll forge your swords into ploughshares, your spears into pruning hooks, and everyone will sit at peace in their own home and garden.' (4:3,4)

'This is how God wants you to live: to act with justice, to love being merciful, and humbly to obey Yahweh.' (6:8)

'There is no God like Yahweh, who forgives our sins. He doesn't vent his anger for ever but loves to show mercy. So he'll drown our sins in the bottom of the sea.' (7:18,19)

Grievous victory

Urartu, c. 714 BC

The king of Urartu died of grief when his army was defeated in a spectacular feat of endurance by Assyrian forces. Sargon II had led his army from Calah through the dangerous Zagros mountains where his soldiers went ahead with bronze picks to cut a path.

Medes bearing tribute to Sargon.

At a pass just south of Tabriz, his exhausted troops, having marched some 480 km (300 miles), became mutinous. In a do-or-die display of strong leadership, he charged against a wing of the Urartian army with his household cavalry, leading in his battle chariot. The surprised enemy gave way, and scattered over the mountains, many dying from cold and exposure. King Rusa of Urartu abandoned his capital at Turushpa and fled into the mountains, where he is said to have died of grief.

On their way home, the Assyrians looted and burned towns, set light to growing crops, left pasture land bare earth, smashed dams so that canals ran to waste in swamps, ruined full granaries, and cut down and burned trees. At Musasir, deep in the mountains, Sargon and his men took precious metals and stones, furniture inlaid with silver and gold, gold, silver and bronze vessels, ceremonial weapons, statues and ornaments.

Stark warning

Ashdod, c. 711 BC

The three-year rebellion against Assyria by this Philistine city-state has been crushed by Sargon II, who has erected a memorial of his victory in the market place. His triumph had been predicted by Judean prophet Isaiah who had appeared regularly in court dressed only in a loin cloth as a symbol of how Assyria would strip the conspirators bare.

Sargon II stands proudly in front of his palace, c. 610 BC.

Ashdod, which lies near the coast about 32 km (20 miles) north of Gaza, had invited neighbouring states including Edom, Moab and Judah to take advantage of Assyria's temporary weakness and refuse to pay tribute-taxes to Sargon. The Egyptians, who would prefer a friendly buffer state between them and Assyria, had promised the conspirators military assistance.

(Isaiah 14:28–32; 20:1–6)

Religious revival has political overtones

Jerusalem, c. 715–712 BC

King Hezekiah is being likened to both David and Solomon for his religious zeal in restoring the temple of Yahweh which his forebears had designed and built over 250 years ago. But just as Solomon created a unified nation centred on the temple and administered by his extensive civil service, so Hezekiah's religious revival is seen as a political rallying point for Judah.

The king, who had shared the throne for some 14 years with his father, assumed full control when Ahaz died in 715. He immediately reversed the policy of promoting multi-faith worship and opened up the temple which Ahaz had bolted and barred.

He also ordered all images and shrines of other gods to be destroyed. They included the bronze snake reputed to have been the one Moses forged in the desert as a sign of Yahweh's healing powers, which had become a venerated relic. Religious taxes, given mostly in kind for the support of the priests, are being restored and storerooms are being built in the temple area to warehouse them.

Hezekiah is also reported to be initiating a royal standard of weights and measures, and to have ordered kilns to produce unified jars bearing his seal for use in commodities trading. But his most overt move to unify the nation was the recently-held Passover celebration. Couriers inviting people to attend travelled far into the region formerly occupied by Israel which despite its decimation by Sargon in 721 still has some devotees of Yahweh living in it.

The response was not as enthusiastic as he might have hoped. Only groups from the tribes of Asher north of Carmel, Zebulun between Carmel and Galilee, and Manasseh (the region around Samaria) made the trip south. Those who did were treated to an elaborate festival which included the slaughter of 1,000 bulls and 7,000 sheep. It had been delayed after the traditional date because of the clean-up.

It followed an equally extravagant opening ceremony for which there were insufficient priests to cope with the ritual slaughters. They were supplemented by Levites. Many had compromised their faith by serving at the altars of other gods, or had simply given up the regular rituals of cleansing and consecration.

The renovation of the temple was organised and executed by teams of priests and Levites after Hezekiah's initial encouragement. In an act of national repentance similar to the traditional Day of Atonement, Judah's sins were confessed over a sacrificial goat.

(2 Chronicles 29–31)

This Assyrian octagonal stone prism describes Sennacherib's dealings with Hezekiah in Jerusalem.

Light work for healing

Jerusalem, c. 703–702 BC

A trick of light has convinced Hezekiah king of Judah not only that his serious illness will be healed but that his life will be long.

Faced with being cut off in his prime by an illness which caused painful swelling, Hezekiah pleaded with Yahweh for an extension of time. The promise that he would live was ratified by an answer to his bizarre request to see the shadow move backwards on the sundial steps. It is suggested that a mirage or an unusual refraction of light caused the phenomenon.

Following his recovery, Hezekiah composed a psalm of thanksgiving in which he promised to 'walk humbly with Yahweh all my years'. But according to Isaiah the prophet, who mediated between God and the king and also prescribed medical treatment for his condition, Hezekiah has already broken his word.

During his illness he was visited by a delegation from Merodach-Baladan, the ruler of Babylon, seeking to enlist his support in an anti-Assyrian coalition. Merodach-Baladan, who ran Babylon from 721 to 710 before being deposed by Sargon II, has recovered a tenuous hold on his former territory.

Although Hezekiah did not promise support, he entertained the delegation with full state honours, a fact which Assyria's spies will no doubt have reported back to Nineveh already. Isaiah said later

The sun stood still for Hezekiah: was this a trick of light or a miracle as he claimed?

that he believed all the temple treasures the delegation had seen would one day be exported to Babylon. It was intended as a rebuke, but the king has taken it as a confirmation that Jerusalem will remain secure during his lifetime.

(2 Kings 20:1–19; Isaiah 38, 39)

Be quiet – you'll win!

Jerusalem, c. 704–703 BC

Judah's latest international treaty with Egypt has been condemned by one of its top advisers. Isaiah, who also functions as a prophet of Yahweh, claims that no political action is required to strengthen the nation against Assyria.

'Your strength is in quietness and trust,' he has told the disbelieving leadership. 'Yahweh longs to show his love to you,' he added, 'but you insisted on arranging foreign cavalry reinforcements.'

The Egyptians are as fallible as anyone else, he warned; 'They're not God.' Assyria, he promised, 'will fall to a divine sword.' Hezekiah is currently strengthening the defences of Jerusalem and the surrounding villages. He is saying publicly that he believes God will help Judah fight its battles.

(Isaiah 30; 31; cf. 2 Chronicles 32:1–8)

Poet is not a-Mused

A typical Arcadian view by Claude Gelee. Artists and poets throughout the ages have been inspired by stories of an earlier bucolic golden age.

Greece, c. 700 BC

A shepherd who claims he was called by the Muses to sing about the gods has published several volumes of poems. One of his first and best known is the *Theogony*, a long work about the origins of the gods and the earth.

Hesiod, who lived in Boeotia, is not an optimistic poet. He comes across as a churlish but reflective farmer who took little joy in life and who felt oppressed by the gods.

His later poem *Works and Days* advises readers how to live honestly and condemns idleness. It uses myth, allegory, parables, proverbs and even threats of divine anger. It also gives practical advice on farming, sea travel (Hesiod's father was a failed sea-trader), and on social and religious conduct.

Lachish left in ashes

Lachish, c. 701 BC

All that remains of this strategic southern city is a layer of ash over a pile of rubble. A deep pit serves as a mass grave for some 1,500 bodies which are covered by the garbage dumped by the city's Assyrian conquerors.

large stones shot from the walls were not enough to beat back the armoured battering rams and the formations of foot soldiers and archers protected by large wicker shields. People attempting to escape the carnage were caught, stripped and impaled on stakes.

The siege of Lachish depicted on a frieze from Sennacherib's palace in Nineveh.

The ruins of Lachish lie today on an abandoned hillside.

Despite its double walls each some 6 m (20 ft) thick, built by Rehoboam 200 years ago, and its heavy gates and well-defended ramparts, Lachish was unable to survive Sennacherib's onslaught. The defenders' burning arrows and

Sennacherib's decisive victory effectively cuts off any hope of military aid being sent from Egypt to assist the beleaguered Judeans and Philistines who are now totally dominated by Assyria. In a lightning strike across the region,

Sennacherib has destroyed 46 cities.

The invasion followed his latest victory over Merodach-Baladan of Babylon and is intended to stamp Assyrian authority across the whole Near East. The western fringes of the empire have been growing restive, and Hezekiah of Judah had defiantly destroyed Assyrian gods. In an attempt to keep the invader at a safe distance, Hezekiah has paid a large tax of a ton of gold and 10 tons of silver, sent with an apology for having offended him.

(2 Kings 18:13–16; Isaiah 36:1)

Fast Facts c. 720–700 BC

Greece, 716 BC: Sparta is celebrating its first victory in the Olympic Games, which has been dominated by its war rival Messenia.

Greece, 715 BC: The 21-year war between Sparta and Messenia is over. Sparta has annexed Messenia and made the population into helots, a status between slave and citizen.

Egypt, c. 715 BC: King Piankhi has insisted that his sister Amenirdis be adopted as the next 'Divine Adoratrice of Amun' at Thebes. The role combines that of wife and chief priestess of the god, and carries

great authority. Although in the past filled by a royal (normally celibate) princess, it has more recently been dominated, and dispensed, by the priesthood.

Assyria, c. 715 BC: Sargon II has moved his capital from Calah to Fort Sargon (Khorsabad) about 19 km (12 miles) north-east of Nineveh. It is closer to Urartu, Assyria's chief enemy, and the move reduces the risks of insurrection by powerfully rich and long-established temple and civic officials in Calah.

Babylon, c. 710 BC: After a three-year campaign, Sargon II has removed Merodach-Baladan from the throne, released prisoners, restored confiscated lands and suppressed highway bandits.

The usurper was besieged in his tribal capital and paid heavy tribute to Sargon for his freedom, including gold, precious stones, exotic woods, brightly dyed clothing, frankincense, sheep and cattle.

Italy, c. 706 BC: Illegitimate Spartans, driven from Greece by the suspicious husbands of their mothers, have settled in Tarentum in the Italian region of Apulia. They were believed to be conspiring against the state. They were conceived during the Messenian war by wives of soldiers who were left alone at home and who persuaded their husbands to let them conceive through younger men to ensure that they bore male children to continue to defend the land. But

the soldiers later rejected them and refused them citizenship, causing deep resentment and the alleged conspiracy.

Assyria, c. 705 BC: Sargon II has died in battle against the Cimmerians, an Indo-European people who have pushed southwards into northern Syria down the east side of the Black Sea. He had reigned for 17 years and is succeeded by his son Sennacherib.

Egypt, c. 702 BC: King Shabaka, who succeeded Piankhi in 715, has died and the throne goes to Shebitku his nephew and son of Piankhi. Shabaka had continued to revive Egypt's traditions and built extensively at Memphis and Thebes.

Jerusalem relieved

Jerusalem, 701 BC

After a turn of events which can only be described as miraculous, the siege by the Assyrians of the capital of Judah has been lifted.

It followed a combination of rumours concerning an impending attack on the siege force by Egypt and an outbreak of disease, probably dysentery, which wiped out a significant number of officers and troops. Sennacherib immediately returned to Nineveh.

Judah had long expected the attack and was well prepared to weather it. Over the past few years King Hezekiah has strengthened Jerusalem's fortifications and modernised its infrastructure. The remarkable feat of engineering which dug a twisting tunnel almost 550 m (600 yd) through solid rock from both ends, with the miners meeting in the middle, had chanelled a steady water supply from the Gihon spring outside the wall into the city.

Hezekiah had also blocked off other water supplies outside the city to deprive invaders, a fact which may have contributed to the outbreak and spread of disease.

Although no shots were fired during the stand-off, there was an intense propaganda war being waged between the two sides. Fresh from his victory at Lachish, Sennacherib sent senior officers to Jerusalem to heap insults on it, its king and its God.

Shouting in Hebrew, the Judean's native language rather than the Aramaic which is the normal lingua franca of diplomacy and trade, the delegation ridiculed the idea of any God withstanding the might of Assyria. Yahweh would go the way of all the others unless the people surrendered, they claimed. And if it came to a prolonged seige, then the inhabitants would be reduced to drinking their own urine and eating

The Siloam tunnel, laboriously hewn out of the rock during Hezekiah's reign, still carries water today as it did then.

their own excrement before very long.

Hezekiah, who in Sennacherib's words was 'shut up in his city like a bird in a cage', took his officials into the temple where they prayed that Yahweh would prove he was the supreme ruler of the world. They also consulted the prophet Isaiah, who issued an eloquent statement declaring that God himself had prompted the rise of Assyria.

He reminded them of the destruction by Assyria of Israel to the north, which he interpreted as Yahweh's punishment for its long-standing apostasy. But this time Yahweh's message was that because of Sennacherib's insolence, 'I'll make him go home. He won't set foot in my city.'

It was a nail-biting climax to Isaiah's long-standing policy of non-violent resistance and of dependence on Yahweh rather than on force of arms or military alliances. When Sennacherib suddenly withdrew, Jerusalem was relieved in more than one sense.

(2 Kings 18:17–19:36; 2 Chronicles 32:1–23; Isaiah 36, 37)

Many towns were besieged by the Assyrians, but few were as lucky as Jerusalem. This stone relief depicts the scene in Lachish as some of King Sennacherib's soldiers carry off booty and prisoners.

Nineveh chosen as new Assyrian capital

Nineveh, c. 700 BC

A major building programme has followed the Assyrian decision to move its capital to Nineveh. Situated on the Tigris River some 130 km (80 miles) north of the previous capital Ashur, it is better placed to control the mighty empire which sweeps across the fertile crescent from Babylonia to Judea.

Nineveh, which has long been regarded as the country's second capital, is also less restricted by the religious traditions of Ashur which have won its citizens wide-ranging exemptions from taxation and labour requirements.

It will now be an 12-km (8-mile) walk round the extended wall, which will be wide enough for three lanes of chariots to drive on. It encloses two civic boroughs covering about 4 sq km (1,000 acres). In places the wall rises to 14 m (45 ft) high, and is pierced by 15 splendid gates.

Inside there are paved streets and squares, private houses, public stores, and a military garrison with stables and a parade ground. Botanical gardens and orchards grow local and exotic plants including myrrh which is said to flourish better in Nineveh than in its native habitat.

To provide water for a population which could exceed 120,000, Sennacherib is building a canal from a dam on the Gomer River 48 km (30 miles) to the north. He is also damming the Khosr River and has built a 275-m (300-yd) aqueduct using 500,000 tons of rock to carry water over a dry wadi bed.

The crowning glory is the royal palace set in an irrigated park. Imported cedar beams support the huge roof which, like the scented-wood doors are decorated with copper overlays. Internally the walls are decorated with ivory and outside they are beautified with glazed bricks and carved cornices. The gates, hung on giant copper pillars resting on cast bronze lions, are approached by a 27-m (90-ft) wide road of white limestone.

Sea attack founders

Assyria, c. 694 BC

Assyrian hopes for defeating Elam by a sea attack foundered when the defenders mounted a land-born counter-attack. The king's son was among the casualties.

Sennacherib ordered ships to be built in Nineveh. They were sailed down the Tigris by Phoenicians, taken overland on rollers to a canal which adjoins the Euphrates and then sailed to the Persian Gulf where Assyrian troops embarked. Elam lies to the east of Babylonia.

When they reached the Gulf of Assyria, the troops took and looted many southern Elamite cities. However, rather than defend their cities in the south, the Elamites went north across the Tigris into Babylonia, capturing and killing the Assyrian puppet king (Sennacherib's son). But when they finally faced the Assyrian army they soon withdrew.

Assyria's attack on Elam was an attempt to stem the growing strength of the Chaldeans in Babylonia. Elam gives them support and provides a place of safety for them.

A reconstruction of one of Nineveh's ancient gateways gives an idea of the scale and magnificence of the ancient capital.

Worth his weight in silver

Babylon, 689 BC

After a siege of 15 months, Babylon has fallen to the Assyrians. The most recent Babylonian king was caught and killed as he tried to escape. Sennacherib gave his captor the dead man's weight in silver.

The Assyrian king then ordered his troops to destroy the city. They robbed the temples, took the holy statues, pulled down houses, temples and walls and destroyed the city's foundations by digging canals across it. Sennacherib has lost all respect for it as a centre of religion because of its years of opposition and because of his personal grief at the murder of his son by the Elamites in 694.

During the siege the price of barley had shot through the roof, the city gates were locked to prevent people leaving, and the streets and squares of the city were filled with corpses because there was no one to bury them.

The sack of Babylon does not have universal support in Assyria. Many have been shocked and appalled at the desecration of a religious centre. Within the royal family factions and divisions have been enlarged by the action. One person who probably is rejoicing is the elderly Judean prophet Isaiah. He had predicted that the city would be devastated by Yahweh 'like Sodom and Gomorrah' and its religious images smashed.

(Isaiah 13:19; 21:9)

Gods saved the new king

Assyria, c. 681 BC

King Sennacherib has been hacked down at a temple entrance by two of his sons. The assassins, Adrammalech and Sharezer, have fled to Hangalbat in Urartu, having apparently failed in their attempt to prevent the throne passing to the designated heir and their younger brother Esarhaddon.

He was abroad at the time of the murder, and as he attempted to re-enter the country was confronted by troops loyal to the coup leaders at Upper Habur. However, they quickly switched allegiance because of general disquiet at the preemptive patricide and the popular belief that Esarhaddon had been chosen by the gods.

Sennacherib had already promoted him in the presence of his brothers and with the support of an oracle from the gods procured by divination. The royal family and civic leadership had sworn allegiance to Esarhaddon at a solemn religious assembly. On his journey home a second oracle confirmed his right to the throne.

(2 Kings 19:37; 2 Chronicles 32:21b; Isaiah 37:38)

Ancient Babylon, on the River Euphrates, with the outline of the great ziggurat clearly visible in the foreground.

The tomb of a dignitary, thought to date from the late eighth century BC and recently excavated in Jerusalem.

Fast Facts c. 700–680 BC

Lydia, c. 700 BC: Croesus of Lydia, a small state in western Anatolia, has introduced a form of currency to replace the barter system. Pieces of electrum, an alloy of gold and silver, stamped with a guaranteed weight and purity, are to be used as a means of exchange. Each coin is of relatively high value. Persia and Greece have quickly followed suit, Greece producing silver and Persia gold coins.

Jerusalem, c. 686 BC: King Hezekiah has died aged 54, a rich and honoured man. He is succeeded by his son Manasseh who has shared the throne for the past 11 years. A devoted follower of Yahweh, he successfully resisted Assyrian advances. (2 Chronicles 32)

China, c. 690 BC: The aggressive kingdom of Ch'u has been invading and annexing the smaller states of the Han Valley. The southern kingdom of Ch'u, situated in the middle of the Yangtze Valley, is becoming one of the strongest in the country. It is different from other states in its language, artistic style and religion, and the people call the ruler 'king', a title only otherwise given to the king of Chou. Yet the people write Chinese script and make bronze vessels in the traditional style.

China, c. 680 BC: As royal authority declines, a new system of overlordship is developing. The rulers of powerful estates are becoming known as hegemons. The first to be recognised is Duke Huan of Ch'i whose territory in western Shantung extends to the sea. He is the only leader with the power to repel the aggressive kingdom of Ch'u as it attempts to invade the north.

Vetulonia, Italy, c. 680 BC: A new technique has been developed by jewellers, called granulation. Grains of gold are pressed into the surface of metal to create a matt area which contrasts with the glossy smooth surface surrounding it. Wiry bronze ornaments of humans and animals are also a local speciality.

Pillar of the faith dies

Jerusalem, c. 681 BC

There are two kinds of strength. One is the physical strength of kings and commanders who rely on the force of arms and the politics of fear. The other is the inner strength of visionaries drawn from superhuman resources to swim against the tides of political expedience and social conformity.

Isaiah son of Amoz belonged to this second group. His recent death after a career spanning the chequered reigns of four kings removes from Judah an astute

A fine, burnished small jug, from about 700 BC appears to have been specially made for use in a shrine, possibly of a wealthy landowner. It was found in Jerusalem.

observer, a wise counsellor and a fearless critic. His message and faith, however, will surely live on, for it reflected eternal verities.

Born into a noble family, Isaiah lived and worked all his life in Jerusalem. He began as a court prophet after a striking vision following the death of King Uzziah whose long reign and great political and spiritual stature had brought renewed prosperity to Judah. As an uncertain future loomed ahead, Isaiah stood transfixed in Solomon's temple and soared into the presence of an unchanging Almighty.

The earthly shapes of altars, fires and decorations sprang into life and became a spectacular kaleidoscope of heavenly sights and divine sounds. Crushed by the weight of glorious holiness he fell limply to the ground, from where he heard Yahweh commissioning him to preach and warning him of the unfavourable response he would provoke.

Only once did Isaiah waver from his task, and he claimed that even that was on Yahweh's instruction. After Ahaz's point-blank refusal to heed his advice, he withdrew from public life for a short while. Towards the end of his life, when the rule of Manasseh took Judah further than ever from God's rule, he also became less active and less consulted. He used his semi-retirement to write his prophecies and chronicle the stories of kings he had served.

Many of his wise words related to specific events. He was especially close to Hezekiah and guided him almost as a mentor through the tense siege of Jerusalem. But throughout his life he received insights which appeared to be more general descriptions of Yahweh's eternal character and purposes.

Indeed, Isaiah was a theologian as much as a predictive prophet. His majestic command of language and his poetic allusions opened a perspective on God which contrasted sharply with the staid, stereotyped and functional beliefs of his contemporaries.

For him, Yahweh was 'the Rock eternal' who will 'keep in perfect peace the person with a steadfast faith' (26:3,4). His God was one to be desired. 'My soul longs for you in the night and in the morning,' he sighed (26:9). He prepares 'a feast of rich food for everyone, a banquet of mellow wine' (25:6).

But Isaiah could also use powerful invective against the social inequality and injustice perpetrated by his own privileged neighbours in the rich suburbs of the lower city. He saw God coming 'with burning anger and clouds of

Old foundations to the walls of Jerusalem dating from this period have recently been excavated.

smoke; his lips are full of wrath and his tongue a consuming fire' (30:27).

Despite his righteous anger, God in Isaiah's perception also offers hope and encouragement. 'Water will gush forth in the wilderness and streams in the desert. The burning sand will become a pool, the thirsty ground bubbling springs. In the haunts where jackals once lay, grass and reeds and papyrus will grow.' And there will be a 'highway of holiness' along which 'the ransomed of the Lord' will walk in safe pilgrimage to the holy city where all sadness 'will flee away' (35:6–10).

Isaiah's death is the subject of some mystery. Unconfirmed reports say that the old man was sawn in two by order, or with the knowledge, of King Manasseh. It is believed that he left a corpus of other writings with the group of prophets who had gathered around him, and among whom his wife was numbered in her own right. He had two sons by her.

(Isaiah 1–39; cf. 2 Chronicles 32:32)

Sparta gets into a state

The countryside surrounding Sparta.

Sparta, Greece, c. 675 BC
The city of Sparta has become the first true state in Greece. It has published a constitution giving its citizens formal rights and creating an elected governing council.

The constitution is the brainchild of one Lycurgus, whose identity is obscure. Unconfirmed reports suggest he received an oracle called 'the great word' at Delphi which instructed him to found a shrine to Zeus and Athena, organise the people into administrative units, establish a council of 30 leaders, and to hold occasional national assemblies.

Sparta has two kings, claiming to be descended from the twin sons of Heracles. Both are priests of Zeus, are provided for from the common purse and hold office for life. They sit on the council which is elected by the 9,000 citizens (or 'equals'). A smaller number of chief magistrates ('ephors') are to be elected annually and will have executive, judicial and disciplinary powers.

People qualify as citizens if they have been educated in the state system and contribute to communal meals from their own estates. Land can be acquired only by inheritance or gift, and the civic status of all but the firstborn sons of citizens remains ill-defined. Sparta is also home to many helots, bonded to estates but not to the owners. They are often ethnic minorities from conquered areas.

Hoplites close in

Greece, c. 680 BC
A new order of infantry has emerged which specialises in close hand to hand fighting. Hoplites, or citizen soldiers, advance in a tight rank (phalanx) eight lines deep to break the enemy line by the weight of their charge.

Each warrior protects his left side with a small round and heavy bronze shield. He wears a helmet with nasal and cheekpieces, a corslet (protecting his trunk) and shin-guards. Each carries a short straight iron sword and a 3-m (9-ft) thrusting spear. They are sometimes supported by lighter-armed archers, slingers and javelin-throwers.

Every citizen who can afford the armour is required to serve as a hoplite. It requires lengthy training and discipline, because hoplites have to function as a single body; individual acts of valour are no longer encouraged.

Enemy plattered

Assyria, c. 653 BC
Main dishes at banquets are normally tasteful delicacies, but there was nothing tasteful or delicate about the one presented on a plate to Ashurbanipal during a dinner celebrating victory over Elam. In fact, the king slashed it with a knife and then spat on it.

But he did not fire the chef, because the offending object was the severed head of his arch enemy Teumman, king of Elam. He had been fleeing Assyrian troops after an unsuccessful attack when he was involved in a chariot accident, arrested and executed.

The Elamites have been a constant irritant to Assyria in recent years despite Ashurbanipal's generous humanitarian aid given in the 60s during a widespread famine. He set up refugee camps for people who had fled across the border into Assyria, and sent grain consignments into Elam itself.

The country is frequently unsettled by the fact that its kings habitually die when young. It is believed that they suffer from congenital defects, which are not helped by the habit of royal males marrying their sisters. And as succession passes through the mother, not the father, Assyrian diplomats monitoring the country are often confused as to who is a legitimate king and who is a usurper.

Different types of goats and sheep are led away. Flocks denoted great wealth and their capture was often documented with more detail and accuracy than that of their former masters.

For the (brief) record, Teumman was a usurper, who attempted to secure the throne by assassinating his predecessor's sons. But he was as bad a shot as he was a driver, and they escaped to Assyria.

Binary code answers sum

Babylon, c. 680 BC

A numerical leap of faith has given Assyria's Esarhaddon the theological confidence to rebuild the devastated city of Babylon.

Following its destruction by his father Sennacherib, the gods had allegedly placed it under a 70-year curse preventing any redevelopment.

But as the figure 70 in Babylonian script becomes 11 when it is transposed, the priests have decreed that the god Marduk had switched the numerals and so modified the curse. Conveniently, the 11 years were up in 680, the year of Esarhaddon's succession.

He cut down the forest of weeds that had grown over the city, then diverted the canals. He personally made bricks to rebuild the city walls and the temple of Marduk. He has resettled the citizens, gave back their privileges and tax-exemptions, and re-established the temple offices and cultic offerings all over the country.

This is not all altruism, however. It serves Assyria's interests to favour Babylonia, and gradually to fill it with vassal chiefs. Good relations are helped by the fact that the king's wife is a Babylonian.

Flautists become literati

An Etruscan vessel with four cups each to hold a different food. Was its use domestic, religious or ceremonial?

Caere, Italy, c. 650 BC

Traders in this oldest of Etruscan cities in northern Italy have adapted the Greek alphabet to their own language and are using it to record their transactions. The idea has been copied, with local modifications, in nearby Veii and Marsiliana. The records are written left to right on waxed wooden tablets using a sharp stylus.

Although modern literacy has come late to the Etruscans, they are already famed for their music and especially for their flutes. Flautists accompany religious festivals, military ceremonies, games, banquets and hunting parties. According to one Greek wit, Etruscans even knead bread, box, and whip their slaves to the sound of the flute.

Twin-piped instruments are most common, but single piped flutes and pan pipes are also played, often accompanied by a seven-stringed lyre. People in the region grow a variety of fruits and vegetables and farm pigs, goats, cows and sheep, but make a mediocre wine from their local grapes. Women wear ankle-length belted tunics and men, who are clean shaven, wear long cloaks.

A fine solid gold Etruscan pendant of Achelus from around 600 BC.

Fast Facts
c. 680–660 BC

Assyria, c. 672 BC: The crown prince Ashurbanipal is being educated in archery, javelin, chariot driving royal etiquette and mathematics. He claims to be able to solve complex mathematical reciprocals and to read abstruse Sumerian and Akkadian texts.

Egypt, c. 671 BC: Esarhaddon of Assyria has declared himself king of Upper and Lower Egypt and Ethiopia, having defeated the Egyptians in a second battle at Ashkelon. It was a long haul for the Assyrians, whose journey to battle took over a month. They travelled by camels lent to them by their desert allies for 15 days through sand dunes, two days through a region of two-headed snakes – and then they were not even halfway. But they won in the end.

Phoenicia, c. 670 BC: The Phoenician city of Sidon made a big mistake in rebelling against Assyrian control. It has been sacked and made into an Assyrian province. Assyrian control now reaches beyond north Syria and Cilicia into Asia Minor. The king of Tyre, neighbour to seaside Sidon, has stayed loyal to Assyria and some outlying villages around Sidon have been given to him.

Byzantium, c. 668 BC: A new city has been founded opposite Chalcedon by the people of Megara. Byzantium is on the southern banks of the Bosporus, the strait that joins the Black Sea with the Sea of Marmora and the Mediterranean, dividing Asia and Europe. The Bosporus is famous for its fish, and Byzantium is in a good position to benefit both from them and from imposing tolls on passing ships.

Sparta, Greece, c. 665 BC: A new 'Festival of naked youths' has been instituted. There are several days of singing, dancing and gymnastics competitions between three teams: boys, young men and older men, held in the blazing heat at the end of July.

Egypt, c. 663 BC: Pharaoh Necho has died, and Assyria has appointed Psammetichus as king of all Egypt.

Sparta, Greece, c. 676 BC: For the first time there has been a musical contest at the Karnea, or festival of Apollo Karneios. A prize was won by poet and musician Terpander, from the Aeolian island of Lesbos. The talented Terpander is already famed for musical innovation. He has invented a seven-stringed lyre and composes music to accompany both his own poetry and that of others, including Homer. The Karnea takes place in August, to mark the grape harvest.

Let off the hook!

Jerusalem, c. 648 BC

A major reversal of domestic policy has occurred following the return of King Manasseh to Jerusalem after being taken hostage by Assyrian King Ashurbanipal.

Manasseh, who was led away in typical Assyrian style like a horse with a hook through his nose, claims to have experienced a religious conversion while abroad. He is now dismantling many of the shrines he has erected over the past 40 years and ordering that only Yahweh be worshipped.

The 52-year-old king had become co-regent with his father Hezekiah as soon as his bar-mitzvah (coming of age) celebrations were over. Following Hezekiah's death in 686 he has transformed the social and religious landscape of Judah. The country has been swept by a merciless wave of violence and oppression from the top downwards, and the king's promotion of crass superstition provoked an outcry from prophets and fundamentalist groups such as the Rechabites.

Astral cults and an image of Baal were given floor space in the temple of Yahweh. Fortune tellers, spiritualist mediums and even witches were allowed to set up their roadside booths with royal approval and were accepted in court on a par with the traditional prophets.

Manasseh personally initiated his sons into a fire cult in the Valley of Hinnom although probably stopped short of sacrificing them to death in the flames as had at first been rumoured. Prophetic protests fell on deaf ears, and public opinion was firmly on the side of tolerance and pluralism.

Judah had been made a vassal state in 671 during one of Esarhaddon's many excursions into Palestine, but Manasseh seized the opportunity to rebel by associating with the Babylonian uprising led by Shamash Shum Ukin, Ashur-banipal's brother, and backed by the Elamites in 652. Manasseh was quickly arrested and abducted to witness personally the protracted four-year siege of Babylon.

It recently ended when Shamash Shum Ukin died in a palace fire thought to have been started deliberately. Conditions in the city were so bad that some Babylonians were reported to have eaten their children. Following the collapse of the rebellion, Ashurbanipal ordered his brother to be buried decently but all other conspirators were to be fed 'to the dogs, pigs, wolves,

A grotesque stone carving of a demon from Babylon.

vultures and fish'.

Quite why Manasseh was let off the hook is unclear, but it is likely that he entered a plea of contrition and vowed allegiance to Assyria. As Egypt has also been kicking against its eastern overlord, Ashurbanipal probably decided that a tame Manasseh in the buffer state of Judah would help maintain Assyrian sovereignty in the region.

Manasseh himself claims to have come to know Yahweh during his captivity and that he now regrets his early enthusiasm for all things

A little child shall lead them

Jerusalem, 640 BC

It was one of the late prophet Isaiah's more enigmatic sayings that 'a little child shall lead them', but if it was ever intended as a literal prediction then it has had a clear fulfilment. An eight-year-old boy has been crowned king of Judah after a popular uprising.

King Amon had been assassinated by his own officials after barely two years in power. But the people rejected the possibility of a military dictatorship or new dynasty. The beleaguered assassins were lynched by the mob and Amon's young son Josiah was led to the throne.

In terms of normal life expectancy the child king offers Judah the hope of a return to relative stability following a period of turbulence since the death in 642 of Manasseh after 55 years on the throne, the longest-ever reign in the history of either Judah or Israel. But whether it fulfils the rest of Isaiah's prophecy of a period of such peace that wolves will lie down with lambs and the earth shall be filled with the knowledge of Yahweh remains to be seen.

Amon had reinstated the religious pluralism for which Manasseh was famed in his early years but which he later turned away from. The precise reasons for the conspiracy against him are unclear.

(2 Kings 21:19–26; 2 Chronicles 33:21–25; cf. Isaiah 11:6–9)

occult. But his dismantling of shrines has not met with great public support. Sacrifices continue at hilltop shrines, although officially only to Yahweh.

(2 Kings 21; 2 Chronicles 33)

Books to preserve the soul

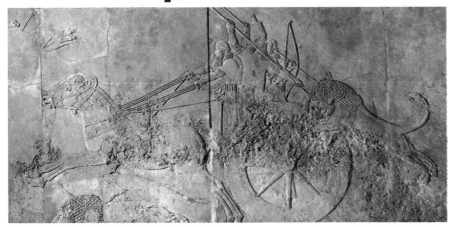

Nineveh, c. 635 BC

The national library at Nineveh has become the largest ever in Assyria, and now contains over 1,000 volumes. King Ashurbanipal has taken a keen personal interest in the project and has ordered the world to be scoured for more texts to add to the collection.

His chief interest is in omens and their interpretation which account for a quarter of all the volumes. The library also contains hymns, descriptions of rituals, prayers, incantations, word lists, grammatical and legal textbooks, and records of Babylonian and Assyrian discoveries in mathematics, astronomy and chemistry.

Though Ashurbanipal was highly literate, his favourite pass time was hunting lions from the relative safety of his chariot.

Most are written in Akkadian.

Ashurbanipal says he collects books both for posterity and also 'for my life, for the guarding of my soul, that I may not have illness and that the foundation of my royal throne may remain secure'.

As a result, he may be careful where he pours his waste water. One of the omens states that if someone pours water at the door of a house and it takes the form of a snake, he will experience evil. But he will know his onions; one incantation requires an onion to be peeled into a fire as the words are recited, so that 'the illness that is in my body may be peeled away like this onion and consumed in the fire this day'.

New ideas imported by Cyprus

Cyprus, c. 640 BC

The decline of Assyrian influence has opened the Mediterranean island of Cyprus to new cultural and religious influences, especially from the Greeks who are fascinated by Cypriot terracotta figures and limestone statues.

The new religious ideas are confined mostly to the cities. Zeus is worshipped in Salamis, Apollo at Kourion, Artemis at Kition and Athena at several places.

In the rural areas, there are gods of healing, weather and war, but the most commonly worshipped are fertility gods, often symbolised by the bull. Sanctuaries centre on an altar where the symbol is placed, often enclosed by sacred trees and an inner and outer courtyard.

At Ayia Irini, where the fertility god is worshipped, there are clay models of bulls, and bisexual centaurs as the demons accompanying the divinity. As it is also a god of war, there are clay models of war chariots and people in armour. The figures are arranged in concentric circles around the altar.

Cyprus is now home to people from many cultures: the Phoenicians in Cyprus worship Astarte, and the Egyptian god Bes has been worshipped here for centuries.

Fast Facts c. 660–650 BC

Corinth, Greece, c. 657 BC: The people of Corinth have a new style of government. The oligarchy of aristocratic Bacchiads has been overthrown by Cypselus ('Chest') who with the support of the priests at Delphi and many non-Bacchiad Corinthians, has set himself up as a 'tyrant' or ruler. The Bacchiads are a narrow faction who pass on power among themselves, and are not even allowed to marry outside the clan. They made an exception for the mother of Cypselus, Ladba, because she was lame. A statement from the oracle at Delphi states that at his birth the Bacchiads tried to kill him but his mother hid him in a chest, implying that his career has divine approval.

Egypt, c. 651 BC: Psammetichus has betrayed the trust put in him by the Assyrians. With the help of King Gyges of Lydia he has expelled the invaders. The country is now fully under Egyptian control again.

Sparta, c. 650 BC: Spartan soldiers currently fighting the Messenians have their spirits boosted and resolves strengthened by chanting the war poems of Tyrtaeus. He exhorts them to obey the kings because they are the closest in the line of succession and to respect and revere the sacred established order. Tyrtaeus goes on to say that military valour is worth more than any other quality and urges soldiers to fight with agression, 'regarding life as their enemy and black death as dear as the rays of the sun'.

Mexico, c. 650 BC: Mexican artists are sculpting two-headed creatures, thought to reflect a growing religious concept of dualism. Clay figurines are also used in worship.

Egypt, c. 660 BC: Thebes, the so-called jewel of Amun, has been sacked by the Assyrians and all the contents of its temple treasury have been laid to waste. The Nubian king of Egypt, Tanutamun, fled to his capital at Napata on the arrival of the Assyrians who had responded speedily to Egypt's recent run of success in regaining its lost cities. Assyria now holds Egypt as far as the border at Aswan.

Royals in line for axe

Jerusalem, c. 630 BC

A member of the Judean royal family has launched a scathing attack on conditions prevailing in the country following the disastrous 55-year reign of Manasseh. In a series of prophetic utterances currently circulating in the capital, Zephaniah, a fourth-generation descendant of King Hezekiah, warns that the country will be destroyed by unnamed invaders unless it seeks 'righteousness and humility'.

him one who 'dispenses justice each morning' and who 'never does wrong'. He will restore Jerusalem to its former glory on a day when people 'will do no wrong and tell no lies'. This God 'is with you, is powerful to save and will delight in you', he adds. 'He will quieten you down with his love.'

The prophet also predicts that the same judgement will fall on other countries. Perhaps with an eye on the growing Scythian threat, he claims that major Philistine cities such as Gaza, Ashkelon and Ashdod will be ruined, that Moab and Amon will become just as deserted and infertile as salt pans, and that the well-irrigated city of Nineveh, the pride of Assyria, will revert back to desert.

(Zephaniah 1–3)

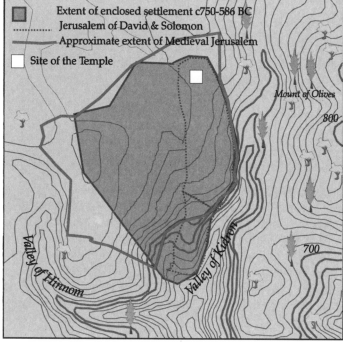

Map of Jerusalem at the time of the invasion.

He singles out the royals and the merchant classes who have the wealth to buy expensive imported clothes and the leisure to follow foreign religions and cults. They will be the first to be axed in the cataclysmic 'Day of the Lord', he says.

Zephaniah also lampoons the wealthy agnostics who consider God irrelevant to their daily lives of getting (by fair means or foul) and spending (lavishly). With poetic licence he describes the high-level state corruption in terms of wild animals stripping a carcase bare.

Although he sees Yahweh as unleashing his anger, he also sees in

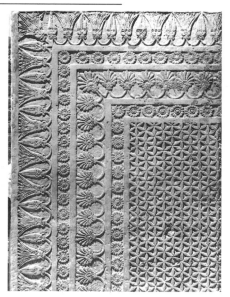

World ruler firmly denounced as 'evil'

Judah, c. 630 BC

Power and wealth are nothing to Judean prophets, especially when they are exercised against their own land. The latest denunciation of Assyria comes from a little-known preacher, Nahum, who lives in the obscure village of Elkosh.

Ashurbanipal, the Assyrian overlord, is condemned as an evil man who plots against Yahweh. And Nineveh, Assyria's capital since about 700 BC, is dismissed as vile and cruel. It is about to get from an unspecified nation the destructive treatment Assyria meted out to Egypt's Thebes 30 years ago.

Writing in a vivid poetic style, Nahum claims that Nineveh breeds lies and lures people to it by the offer of wealth and free sex. It has enslaved innocent people and has other nations in an economic stranglehold.

But the time is coming, he warns, when the dykes will be breached, the city flooded and its fine buildings destroyed. Foreign soldiers will kill everything that moves and loot everything which doesn't. But first, those who Nineveh believes are its friends – rich merchants and city officials – will strip its assets and then flee like a swarm of locusts as the invader approaches.

Nahum attributes the tribulation to his God, who promises vengeance on all who oppress his people. Yahweh, he says, can dry up seas and make the earth quake. He is a good God who cares for his people and is a refuge in bad times. Though slow to express his anger, express it he will and Nineveh will be trodden into the desert.

(Nahum 1–3)

The rich city of Nineveh never ceased to amaze visitors. This superb bas-relief of an early Persian carpet covered a palace wall.

Identical twins, identical sins

Judah, c. 620 BC

Judah and Israel are identical twins with identical sins, according to the young prophet Jeremiah. The southern state of Judah has not learned the lesson of its now-decimated northern twin and will shortly also be destroyed, he claims.

Using the graphic and potentially offensive parallel of prostitution, Jeremiah says that Judah has deserted its divine spouse Yahweh and ravished the gods of other nations without. Moral standards once considered important are now regarded as trivial. Sexual immorality has reached epidemic proportions with each man 'neighing for his neighbour's wife like a lusty stallion', he claims.

Jeremiah denounces the official religious leaders for being as guilty as the civic authorities. Prophets and priests who should know better behave the same as everyone else. 'God would save you if he could find one decent person,' he says.

Jeremiah warns that a cruel army will ravage Jerusalem and show no mercy. The nation stands at a crossroads and should seek out ancient paths of spiritual obedience and social compassion. He looks forward to a day when their descendants will return to make a fresh start in their homeland, shepherded by faithful leaders.

(Jeremiah 1–7)

Reformist whirlwind blows Baals away

Jerusalem, c. 620 BC

In a region often swept by desert gales and whirling dust-devils, there is no wind so feared as the twice-yearly sirocco. Hot, dry and dusty, the easterly gales can reach speeds of over 100 kph (60 mph). They irritate throats and fray tempers, dry out wood and shrink

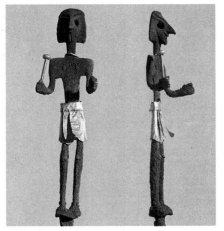

A bronze and gold statue of Baal from Alepo in Syria.

drapes, and mercilessly sweep away anything loose in their path.

But now a new wind of change has scorched the region more dramatically than the worst sirocco, and shows no sign of slowing. It has been descending from the king's throne-room for several years. According to the prophet Nahum, it is the hot breath of a God 'whose way is in the whirlwind'.

Zealous for Yahweh and antagonistic to all other religions, King Josiah has ordered all images of Baal-melqart and his consort Ashtoreth to be removed from the temple in Jerusalem. Along with gods such as Chemosh and Molech, and artefacts of astral cults, they are to be burned in the Hinnom Valley.

All shrines outside the capital have been pulverised. As an act of desecration the ashes of burnt images have been scattered over graves. The luckiest cult prostitutes, priests and spiritualist mediums have been sacked; the unluckiest have been executed.

The reformist wind is also blowing far beyond Judah's boundaries in its former sister state of Israel. The shrine at Bethel, second only in antiquity to the temple in Jerusalem, has been demolished and human bones burnt on it to make it unclean.

Josiah, who became king when he was eight years old, was nurtured in the traditional faith by his childhood advisers. He claims to have embraced Yahwism personally when he was 15 years old, and began his reforms in earnest when he was 20. He began serious repairs to the temple in his mid-20s, at a time when the threat of repercussions from Assyria had faded.

(2 Kings 23:4–25; 2 Chron 34:3–8)

Fast Facts
c. 645–635 BC

Elam, c. 645 BC: Ashurbanipal of Assyria has finally lost patience with Elam. In a policy U-turn he has desecrated the whole country which borders on the north coast of the Persian Gulf, taking leaders prisoner and forcing the Elamite army to merge with his own forces. Even royal tombs were dug up to ensure that dead kings would suffer. Said Ashurbanipal, 'I left the fields empty of people's voices, the tread of sheep and cattle, and the merry songs of harvest home.' But waiting in the wings are the nearby Persians who are poised to occupy the ravaged Elam.

Western Britain, c. 645 BC: Continental-style rectangular houses are replacing the traditional circular timber dwellings in Gloucestershire. At Crickley Hill, rectangular homes flank the street leading to the hill fort, following a pattern of town planning common in Europe.

China, c. 638 BC: The hegemony of Sung has been defeated by the southern kingdom of Ch'u in the centre of the Yangtze Valley. The new leader, the Duke of Tsin (Shansi) is able and resolute. He needs to hold his own state together where three families are contending for supremacy. He is also holding in check the ambitious new state of Ch'in whose peoples are widely considered to be uncultured and uncouth.

Germany, c. 650 BC: Although they still make sheet-bronze buckets, German metalworkers are now fashioning small bowls with handles made of a continuous loop. Hemispherical bowls have twin loop handles attached by cross-shaped bronze plates. Larger hemispherical cauldrons with in-turned rims have loose ring handles. Short spherical pottery jars with conical necks and bowls with dimple bases are common.

Bohemia, c. 650 BC: Wagons are being buried in the graves of rich people. In one recent funeral, a warrior was laid to rest in a four-wheeled hearse with more than 40 accessory vessels.

Reformation played by the book

Jerusalem, c. 622 BC

National unity and religious reform received a shot in the arm when an ancient book was unearthed during restoration work on the temple of Yahweh. Its content caused Judah's king Josiah to lead an immediate act of national repentance and to redouble his promotion of Yahweh as the focus of national unity.

Although an overtly religious act, it has political overtones but occurs at a time when Assyria is unlikely to respond with hostility. It also coincides with a widespread sense of doom and a returning to the gods which has been felt for the past decade in places as far apart as Egypt and Assyria.

The dusty and apparently forgotten 'Book of the Law' was found by Hilkiah, who as high priest is the only person allowed into the inner sanctuary of the temple. He reported the find to the king's secretary Shaphan during a routine meeting to discuss the repair budget.

It dates from the time of Moses who emancipated the Israelites from slavery in Egypt some 600 years ago. It was deposited, like many divine law codes, next to the central shrine, an ornate gold box known as the ark of the covenant.

When he heard the unchanging curses of Yahweh on practices which have become commonplace in Judah, the devout king tore his regal robes as a sign of repentance. He sent a delegation to the prophetess Huldah, believed to be the aunt by marriage of the outspoken young prophet Jeremiah.

The best she could divine was a postponement of the inevitable judgement on Judah. The nation's sins have been found out, she said, and Yahweh's justice must be seen to be done. But Josiah's repentance has been noted in the divine council, she added, and the punishment would not be imposed until after his death.

Following the pronouncement, Josiah led the nation in renewing the covenant with Yahweh and committing it to keeping the Book of the Law. The elders of all villages in Judah were summoned to attend.

There has also been what is claimed as the biggest celebration of the Passover festival since the time of Samuel some 400 years ago. Some 30,000 sheep and goats were ritually slaughtered and 3,000 cattle sacrificed as burnt offerings. During Hezekiah's reform a century ago, just 3,000 sheep and 1,000 bulls were killed.

The priests and Levites played the ceremony strictly by the book, following its instructions to the

A pectoral decoration of a flying falcon, from Egypt, c. 600 BC. This golden jewel, inlaid with coloured glass, was worn by a priest.

letter. As a further demonstration of revived national unity, the sacrifices were provided from the king's stock and were slaughtered and cooked centrally rather than in the traditional family gatherings.

(2 Kings 22:1–23:25; 2 Chronicles 34:8–35:19)

Fast Facts
c. 626–620 BC

South Babylon, c. 626 BC: Nabopolassar has made himself king of the southern marshlands and is attempting to take the whole of Babylonia. He is gaining outside allies including the Elamites to whom he returned the gods which Assyria had looted in the 640s. Some strong cities in the area, including Nippur and Erech, are still held by Assyria, however.

Rome, c. 625 BC: The swampy land between the Palatine, Esquiline and Caelian hills is being drained to form a meeting place (the Forum). The people of the surrounding villages have been joining with those of the Quirinal and Viminal Hills to form a single community. A large drain using Etruscan ideas has been built. A bridge across the Tiber has also been built, providing the first link between the Campanian settlements in the south and Etruria in the north.

Rome, c. 625 BC: The Romans have wiped out the prosperous town of Politorium on the banks of the Tiber 16 km (10 miles) south of Rome. They are anxious to establish a settlement at Ostia, at the mouth of the Tiber, and are competing with the people of Veii for control of the salt pans.

Athens, c. 632 BC: Cylon, a nobleman and Olympic prizewinner, has failed in his attempt to seize the Acropolis and start a tyranny. He is married to the daughter of Theogenes, who became tyrant of Megara by slaughtering the flocks and herds of the wealthy. But Cylon was not supported by the masses and was besieged. He escaped, but friends working with him surrendered and were killed.

Nineveh, c. 630 BC: An Arab king who defected from supporting Assyria has been pursued and caught by Ashurbanipal. As punishment, he was brought back to Nineveh and tied up in a kennel with a collar.

Nineveh, c. 627 BC: Ashurbanipal has died after a reign of 42 years. He was one of the most vindictive of Assyrian kings and not a gifted politician or strategist. He will be remembered both for his malice and his library at Nineveh. He is succeeded by his son Ashur-etillu-ili, who has been co-regent for some years. His death has provoked a series of power struggles in Assyria and Babylonia.

Divine laws given human face

The Book of the Law found by Hilkiah was a version of Deuteronomy, which sometimes refers to itself by that title (eg. 30:10). It is not a legal textbook, however, but a series of three expositions given by Moses and based on the laws of Yahweh.

The main teaching is contained in chapters 5–30, preceded by a historical resumé of Israelite life in the desert after the exodus from Egypt (1–4) and rounded off by further narratives and psalms. Above all, it focuses on the covenant relationship of Yahweh with his people, reaching a climax in a series of curses and blessings to which the assembled Israelites publicly assented (27:9–28:68).

Although the expected harshness is evident – parents are to arrange for the execution of wayward sons (21:18–21) – a softer tone settles over the book as a whole. It testifies

to a humane God who takes the side of widows and orphans, of foreign settlers and the poor, and who commands a similar loving concern to characterise his people.

For example, people are not to turn a blind eye when they see

Archives were of vital importance to many civilisations. This is the archive chamber at Kouyunyuk, as discovered by Layard in the mid-nineteenth century.

someone else's animals straying, but to round them up and even look after them until the owner can collect them (22:1–4). Food growing in a field may be freely plucked by travellers but not carried away, which would be theft (23:24,25). At harvest time some should be left deliberately around the sides for the poor and landless (24:19–22).

Poor people hired for work should be paid promptly. Their outer garments must not be taken as pledges for loans (24:14–18). Indeed, interest on loans is not to be charged to fellow-countrymen at all (23:19,20), and every seventh year all outstanding debts should be cancelled (15:1–6).

A person asked for a loan the year before the general amnesty is not to be tight-fisted even though he knows there is little chance of seeing his money again (15:7–11).

He is also to collect pledges sensitively by not entering homes like a bailiff, and by returning a person's overcoat/blanket each night (24:10–13).

Kings are not to extend their wealth deliberately, nor use their power and influence to gain many wives. Their coronation is to include a public affirmation of the law (17:14–20). Traders are to use honest measures, and not light weights for selling and heavy ones for buying (25:13,14).

Even the grim business of waging war is given a gloss of compassion. Engaged or recently married men are exempt from military service, as are those who have recently inherited property (20:5–9; 24:5). Peace and forced labour is to be offered before cities are attacked and destroyed; the fruit trees outside cities are not to be felled for making siegeworks or fires (20:10–20).

Not unexpectedly, there are strict sexual laws and severe punishments for miscreants. All adulterers are to be executed (22:22–24) but engaged women raped in desolate areas where they could not summon help are spared; only the man dies (22:25–27). The rape of an unbetrothed woman is punishable by marriage (22:28–29). Divorce is permitted (24:1–4) but cross-dressing is not (22:5).

Much of Deuteronomy focuses on the conduct of religious worship. It looks forward to the day when there will be one central shrine (12) and there are stern warnings against following other gods (13). The sanctuaries of other gods are to be destroyed (7:5,6). The religious feasts and offerings are summarised, and readers are reminded of which foods to avoid (14,16).

The book follows the pattern of many similar law codes and treaties known to have existed in the period 1500–1000 BC, and bears Moses' hallmarks. However, its content has probably been edited since.

'God loves you'

The nature of God in Deuteronomy

He is the creator of all things, and the only God capable of taking one nation out of another with signs and wonders (4:32–34)

There is only one Yahweh. So love him with all your heart, soul and strength (6:4)

Yahweh didn't choose you because you were stronger or more numerous than others. In fact, you were small and insignificant. But he loved you, so he helped you (7:7,8)

He is faithful, keeping his covenant of love for ever with those who serve him, and destroying those who reject him (7:9,10)

Yahweh is God of gods, Lord of lords, great, powerful and holy. He is impartial and cannot be bullied (10:17)

When you enjoy all the good things of this life, don't forget that God has given them to you – you haven't earned them for yourself. And don't forget all the great things he has done to bring you to this point (8:10–18).

Assyria in confusion: Nineveh collapses

Nineveh, 612 BC
Confusion reigns in Assyria now that its capital city Nineveh has been destroyed. According to Babylonian sources the Scythians allied with the Medes and the Babylonian leader Nabopolassar laid siege to it. After only three months, despite its mighty defences, the city fell.

The attackers were helped by the flooding of the River Khosr, a tributary of the Tigris, which swept away some of the city's defences. Survivors have fled to Harran in the west, where Ashur-uballit, a member of the Assyrian royal dynasty, has been proclaimed king. He plans to organise his troops there and to call on Egypt, which had sided with Assyria against Babylon four years ago, for further help.

The Medes and the Scythians have since pulled out of the alliance, however, and Nabopolassar is hurrying to strengthen his position. He currently occupies Assyria as far west as Nisbin.

The collapse had been predicted by several Judean prophets. Jonah's preaching some decades ago apparently caused a temporary change for the better in the city's infamous wickedness, and earned a temporary postponement of Yahweh's promised judgement.

More recently, Nahum predicted the flooding and Zephaniah said Nineveh would become a mound on which sheep would graze.

It had been made capital of Assyria by Sennacherib about 700 BC, who extended an already prosperous settlement.
(cf. Nahum 2:6–10; Zephaniah 2:13–15)

Ambitious plans fail

Megiddo, c. 609 BC
An attempt by King Josiah to ensure that Judah remains an independent force to be reckoned with in Near Eastern politics has ended in failure and cost him his life.

Egypt's Pharaoh Neco II was marching northwards up the coast to assist the beleaguered Assyrians against the Babylonians. Josiah gathered his troops at the Iyron Pass near Megiddo where a narrow valley between gently-rolling hills leads into open country, to pick off the invaders as they emerged.

But they sent their archers ahead, who concentrated their fire on the leading chariots where Josiah stood in disguise but in command. He fell under a hail of arrows. Without its king, Judah was already defeated.

It was a sad end to a long and distinguished reign, not least because politically it was unnecessary. Neco had already offered to respect Judah's neutrality in return for safe passage. And he too failed in his objective to save Harran from the Babylonians, arriving there after the city had been taken. Jehoahaz has now succeeded his father as king over Judah.
(2 Kings 23:29–30; 2 Chronicles 35:20–36:1)

The Plain of Jezreel, seen from Meggido.

Fast Facts c. 613–609 BC

Assyria, c. 613 BC: For reasons which are not clear, the Medes have withdrawn from Assyria having invaded it only last year when they took Ashur and Tarbisu. They also made a treaty with Nabopolassar of Babylon, believed to have been ratified by the marriage of his son Nebuchadnezzar to Amyitis the granddaughter of the Median king. The Scythians, who recently moved into Anatolia and north-west Iran and who are friendly to Assyria, may have threatened the Medes.

Egypt, c. 610 BC: After a reign of 54 years, Pharaoh Psammetichus has died. During his tenure, Egypt returned to many of its old religious values and the country has become more stable. Art and trade have flourished, and the country is now a major economy. He is succeeded by his son, Necho II.

Judah, c. 609 BC: Egypt has deposed the lawful king Jehoahaz after he had reigned for only three months, and banished him in chains from the capital. Neco II has replaced him with another of Josiah's sons, Eliakim, whose name has been changed to Jehoiakim as a sign of his subservience. Heavy taxes have been imposed on Jerusalem. (2 Kings 23:31–35; 2 Chronicles. 36:2–4)

Athens, c. 620 BC: An Athenian lawyer, Draco, has introduced 'draconian' new laws for Athens which for the first time have been written down. Most offences are punishable by death. Asked why he is so severe, Draco said that small offences deserved death and he could think of no harsher penalty for greater ones.

Southern Greece, c. 620 BC: After 11 years of besieging the stronghold of Eira, the Spartans have finally defeated the Messenians. Angered and weakened by repeated guerrilla raids by their opponents, the Spartans enslaved the survivors and made Messenia part of the Spartan state.

Preacher's reprieve won by force of argument

Jerusalem, c. 608 BC

The well-known prophet Jeremiah has been saved from death by the force of argument, but it was not strong enough to protect one of his lesser-known colleagues.

Jeremiah, for almost two decades the scourge of the religious establishment, had been hauled before city officials after delivering in the temple precincts his oft-repeated warning that Jerusalem is to be destroyed. The arrival of the officials, who had heard the uproar from their offices in the royal palace, probably saved him from a summary lynching for treason.

Several senior officials argued, however, that someone speaking in the name of Yahweh should be listened to, however shocking his message. They were supported by elders (local lawyers) who pointed to the precedent set during Hezekiah's reign a century ago when Micah was not executed for making a similar prediction.

The argument did not greatly impress King Jehoiakim, who has recently executed Uriah of Kireath-jearim, some 16 km (10 miles) west of Jerusalem, for making similar claims. It is not Jeremiah's first encounter with hostility. His own townsfolk from Anathoth, a Levite city an hour's walk north-east of Jerusalem, plotted his murder some years ago. The prophet claims Yahweh revealed the plot to him so that he could take evasive action. Since Josiah's death last year Jeremiah has been increasingly critical of what he regards as a repressive regime.

(Jeremiah 26; cf. 11:18–23)

The barbarians who so often threatened Jerusalem were often a highly sophisticated military machine. Seen here is a battering ram, looking like a modern day tank, at work against the walls of nearby Lachish.

What's your game, God?

Judah, c. 605 BC

If God is good and just, how can he actively sponsor a team of barbarians who break all the rules of goodness and justice to win power and wealth as a result of his coaching? The age-old question of why a good God allows evil has been given a theological twist by a professional prophet working in the mainstream of Judean religious life.

Habakkuk, whose style and concerns resemble those of his more widely-known contemporary, Jeremiah, claims to have found an answer, but it still remains a matter of faith. Surveying the social and political corruption of Jerusalem, he asks if God is asleep or impotent. To the standard response that Yahweh will use a foreign power to punish his own people, Habakkuk asks how he can encourage punishment which is worse than the crime.

'You are too pure even to look on evil,' he murmurs. 'Yet you stand by and watch while invaders get a perverse thrill out of butchering people.' The answer, he suggests, is that the barbarians will themselves be locked in Yahweh's sin bin for their vicious tackling.

'Those who build empires on blood will be relegated to the bottom division,' he claims Yahweh is saying. 'What they've done to others will eventually be done back to them.' But that does not help anyone now, claims Habakkuk: God's people suffer, and justice is not seen. To which comes the reply that it will be sorted out even if Habakkuk and his contemporaries are substituted before the final whistle brings the game of history to an end.

'My people will be kept safe by their faith in me,' Yahweh tells him. 'And one day the earth will be filled with the knowledge of God just as the waters cover the sea. I am a holy God, so keep quiet and trust me.'

In response, Habakkuk writes a prayer in which he pleads for Yahweh to repeat his awesome matchplays of the past. Then he takes his seat in the stands to watch patiently as Yahweh works out the moves of what perhaps is more like a long chess match than an afternoon's ball game.

(Habakkuk 1–3)

Dream ticket for sage who knows his onions

Babylon, 604 BC

A young Jewish nobleman has won a dream ticket to stardom in his adoptive country. He has been made provincial ruler of Babylon with special responsibility for the stargazers and sages.

And they have every reason to welcome the foreign upstart. He has just saved them from execution through his astute insight into the nocturnal ramblings of King Nebuchadnezzar's mind.

The nobleman, named Belteshazzar by the king but known to his fellow Jews as Daniel, was among those deported from Jerusalem last year as part of Nebuchadnezzar's attempt to sudue the rebellious western city. He was chosen for his good looks, bright intellect and high birth.

Nebuchadnezzar had presented his astrologers with the impossible task of telling him both the content and meaning of a dream which was troubling him, or else face execution. He believed that only someone who divined the content could be trusted to give an unbiased interpretation. Daniel claimed to have received both from Yahweh.

He suggested that a statue made of mixed materials and partially destroyed by a rock represented a succession of kingdoms which will ultimately replace Babylon. All will be smashed by the everlasting kingdom Yahweh will establish, he said.

Following his meteoric rise to power, Daniel requested that three other Jewish exiles, Shadrach, Meshach and Abednego be appointed as assistant administrators so that he could remain at the royal court. In his elation, Nebuchadnezzar probably would have granted a lot more.

But the modest young man is characterised by abstemiousness. He and his companions have consistently refused the rich royal food, perhaps because of its association with religious acts of which they disapprove, but they have outshone their Babylonian counterparts in growth and intellect.

(Daniel 1,2)

Smoking prophecy puffs on

Jerusalem, c. 605 BC

Standing by helplessly while your life's work goes up in smoke must surely rank among the most disheartening of life's tragedies.

But for the prophet Jeremiah, a quarter of a century of prophesying will have to be written up all over again after his only copy was deliberately thrown into the fire by King Jehoiakim. Fortunately, in Judah's oral culture where reading is largely restricted to bills in the market and sacred texts in the temple, he will have memorised his message.

The ink was hardly dry on the long scroll of warnings and predictions when Jeremiah's secretary Baruch read them in the temple during a day of fasting called because of the Babylonian threat.

The incident was reported to the king and the scroll found its way to Jehoiakim who was so incensed that he chopped off each paragraph as it was read and fed it to his brazier. Officials are said to have advised him against the action. He ignored them and ordered the arrest of Jeremiah and Baruch, who have gone into hiding.

Jeremiah later dictated the prophecies, not in chronological order, onto a fresh scroll. And when Baruch complained of writer's cramp, he was given a fresh personal message from Yahweh telling him not to seek great things for himself but to be content with God's promise of safe-keeping.

The prophet began his work some 23 years ago and has been pointing that out in his latest round of messages. His argument has been consistent over that time, he says – and so has Judah's ignoring of it. Now he warns that the nation will serve Babylon for 70 years. With Nebuchadnezzar almost knocking at the city gates, the future must look bleak even to a layman.

(Jeremiah 25:1–14; 36; 45)

Fast Facts
c. 605–600 BC

Jerusalem, c. 605 BC: King Jehoiakim has submitted to the overlordship of Nebuchadnezzar of Babylon, having been placed on the throne by Neco II of Egypt. He has paid a heavy tax penalty and some of his leading citizens have been deported. (Daniel 1:1,2)

Mediterranean Sea, c. 600 BC: The sea is boiling with rival merchant fleets vying for trade. Etruscan metals and pottery are selling well across the sea in African Carthage off ships from the Etruscan port of Caere in Italy despite the jealousy of the Carthaginian navy. Ionian Greeks have established trading posts at Marseilles in southern France and Alalia on the east coast of Corsica; the latter dominates the route to Spain and to Etruscan ports.

Rome, c. 600 BC: The people of Rome have conquered the region of Latium, which includes the ancient city of Alba Longa, between Rome and Campania. It controls a main trade route to southern Italy and its people speak Latin, but it requires considerable draining. In their own city, Romans are now using stone foundations for substantial dwellings and although heavily influenced by Etruscan culture have retained their independence and the Latin language.

Pompeii, c. 600 BC: The Oscan people from the Campania area of Italy have founded the city of Pompeii. It is on a volcanic hill on the west coast, a few miles south-east of Mount Vesuvius.

Egypt, c. 600 BC: Pharaoh Neco II has built a navy using Greek refugees. This unprecedented action is viewed with suspicion by Egyptians who generally avoid sea travel, but is justified by the economic need to play a full part in international trade. Neco has also built a canal between the Nile and the Red Sea.

Socialist poet elected president

The Athenian agora (market place) – the centre of political activity in the town.

Athens, 594 BC

Athenians have made the poet Solon chief magistrate in a desperate attempt to solve the ever-deepening social, economic and political crisis. Discontent is especially acute among the countless small farmers who could be sold into slavery if they fail to pay mounting debts to wealthy landowners.

Poorer people also feel powerless because government is solely in the hands of the aristocrats who have a birthright into the corridors of power.

Solon, who is recognised by many as wise, just and honest, is a socialist at heart. He claims trouble stems from the greed and injustice which destroy political life and personal freedom.

Among his proposed reforms are the cancellation of all debts for which land is a security, and the introduction of a new coinage and matching system of weights and measures approximating to the Euboic standard used elsewhere in western Greece.

All citizens are to be divided into four classes according to their annual production of corn, oil and wine and are to be admitted to the Assembly with an elected executive council of 400 members for which all but commoners are eligible. People will now qualify for inclusion in the council of the Areopagus according to their property holdings rather than by birth.

And all Draco's laws except those relating to homicide are to be replaced by a more humane code of justice.

Solon, the great crusading Athenian reformer.

Reaction to Solon's reforms is mixed. In trying to please all he has succeeded in pleasing none, but he has relieved, if not abolished, a lot of distress. His reforms have also opened the way for the expansion of trade and industry. He, however, having instituted his reforms, has laid aside all public duties and gone travelling.

'Heifer' felled by 'gadfly'

Carchemish, 605 BC

In the poetic language of the prophet Jeremiah, a beautiful heifer has been felled by an ugly gadfly.

In more prosaic terms, the Egyptian army has been comprehensively defeated by the Babylonians at the city of Carchemish on the Euphrates. The victors are now marching southwest into Syria and Judah.

Alluding perhaps to Egyptian gods depicted as cows, Jeremiah describes the country as a 'beautiful heifer'. Egypt had been the only serious challenger to Babylon's ambition to gain control of the former Assyrian empire.

Pharaoh Neco II had already ensured compliance from Judah by deposing its new king Jehoahaz and replacing him with Jehoiakim. But having been defeated at Carchemish, Neco was pushed 225 km (140 miles) south by Nebuchadnezzar and routed again at Hamath.

The only hindrance so far to further conquests across the near east has been the minor delay caused by Nebuchadnezzar's sudden return to Babylon to receive the throne after the death of his father, Nabopolassar.

(2 Kings 23:31–35; 2 Chronicles 36:2–4; Jeremiah 46)

Broken heart weeps for his 'broken pot'

Jerusalem, 597 BC

Judah's capital city is flooded with tears as families are split, homes destroyed and possessions taken by Nebuchadnezzar's pillaging troops. King Jehoiakim, described by Jeremiah, as 'a broken pot which no one wants', has been taken captive to Babylon.

This small sixth-century clay tablet (reproduced life-size) comes from the Babylonian Chronicle, for the years 605–594 BC. Amongst other events it records the crowning of King Nebuchadnezzar II and the defeat of Judah in 597 BC, following the appointment of Zedekiah as puppet-king in Jerusalem.

None weeps more loudly than the prophet who predicted the disaster and vainly urged his fellow-countrymen to take steps to avert it. 'Everywhere I go in the rural areas I see bodies of people hacked down,' he reports. 'In the city streets are all the sights and sounds of famine. And many priests and leaders have been rounded up like animals and herded off to Babylon.'

The grieving spokesman for Yahweh pleads that his God will not break his side of the covenant treaty and that somehow he will bring hope out of sorrow.

For three months Nebuchadnezzar's forces have been camped in the hills, since the teenage Jehoiachin succeeded to the throne following his father Jehoiakim's death from natural causes. Despite the long-standing threat from Babylon and repeated warnings from Jeremiah and other prophets, the royal family has continued its extravagant lifestyle and moral complacency.

'Having a big house does not make you a king,' Jeremiah once said. 'Josiah contented himself with basic comforts and gave himself to social justice. It saved him, and it could save you,' he told Jehoiachin whose inherited administration was split by internal corruption. 'Come off your throne of pride before your people are scattered to the wind like chaff,' he pleaded.

Among the 10,000 men, women and children reported to be trekking into exile is believed to be Pashhur, a priest who had personally imprisoned Jeremiah for his predictions of defeat. Pashhur had been told that his reward for jailing the preacher would be exile for himself and his family.

The people will join a small number who were deported when Nebuchadnezzar rampaged through Hatti-land (Syria-Palestine) in 605. He has taken camel-loads of valuables from the temple and placed Mattaniah, a son of Josiah, on the throne, changing his name to Zedekiah as a sign of his subjection.

(2 Kings 24:8–17; 2 Chronicles 36:9–10; Jeremiah 13:15–27; 14:17–22; 20:1–6; 22:1–30; cf. 52:28)

A larger than life-size glazed brick relief of a soldier in ceremonial dress, from Sargon's palace. This is one from a monumental frieze lined up all around the walls of Sargon's audience chamber. The military might and splendour of Babylon was beyond belief for most of those who had occasion to visit the capital.

Esau in a stew again

Judah, c. 600 BC

Esau will get into a stew again, according to a short but familiar message from a little-known prophet, Obadiah. The descendants of Isaac's son who sold his birthright to Jacob for a bowl of lentil stew now occupy Edom to the south-east of the Dead Sea.

They are going to receive in violence what they have meted out to others, especially to Jacob's descendants in Israel and Judah, claims Obadiah. Their apparently invincible canyons and high plateaux will be penetrated and their settlements destroyed.

The prophet is echoing words of his more famous contemporary, Jeremiah, and it is believed that both are drawing on a common theme in prophetic circles. Edom's antipathy extends back to patriarchal times, and it has often been a vassal of its neighbours. It has frequently rebelled, and is now said to be gloating over Babylon's current oppression of Judah.

(Obadiah; Jeremiah 49:7–22)

Egged on to take the yoke

Jerusalem, c. 593 BC

The whole of Hatti-land (Syria-Palestine) is being egged on by the Judean prophet Jeremiah to submit to the yoke of Babylon like an ox harnessed to a plough. He has even made a milkmaid's shoulder-yoke to carry around the streets as an advertisement for a message many consider to be treasonable.

In his latest outburst, the prophet claims that Yahweh, as the creator of all things, will hand over to Nebuchadnezzar the nations of Edom, Moab, Ammon, Tyre and Sidon as well as Judah. Anyone who tries to resist the coming conqueror will end up with a land looking like scrambled eggs!

Jeremiah's message is opposed by most of the professional prophets of Yahweh and by the mediums and sorcerers of other religions. Characteristically, he claims they are all deceived. In one dual of words two months ago, an incensed Hananiah pulled the yoke from Jeremiah's shoulders and snapped it in two, claiming that Babylon would be broken within two years.

This small tablet details the eclipses of the sun and the moon over 60 years.

'I wish it were so!' exclaimed Jeremiah. 'But as the test of a prophet is whether or not his words come true, we'll have to wait and see who's right. I predict you'll be dead within a year!' For once, Yahweh was not slow in fulfilling his word. Hananiah died today.
(Jeremiah 27; 28)

'Make yourselves at home'

Jerusalem, c. 593 BC

Thousands of Jewish exiles now settling into their new surroundings in Babylon have been told to make themselves at home and not to expect a quick return. They are to build houses, take jobs, have families and even pray for the welfare of their captors, says the prophet Jeremiah.

It will be 70 years before any of their descendants will return, he predicts. Throughout history, the people of Judah and Israel have thought of their corporate destiny in terms of future generations rather than immediate personal circumstances, and the prophet confirms this is to be no exception.

Yahweh has 'good plans for you, plans to prosper you rather than to harm you, to give you a future and a hope,' he says. 'You will find God again when you seek him with all your heart. Then he will bring you home.'

The message is contained in a letter sent to the exiles in Babylon

This exquisite golden chariot stands only about 6 cm (2.5 in) high. The charioteer may be a dwarf, and he is driving an official in an elegant long-sleeved robe.

but is not the only communication he has posted across the desert. It summarises a longer prophecy he despatched to the Babylonian high command predicting its eventual downfall. The nation's proud gods will be humbled by the Chaldeans, who currently occupy land well to the east of Babylon, he says. His colleague Habakkuk also predicted Babylon's fall a decade ago.
(Jeremiah 29; 50–51)

Babylon extends its empire

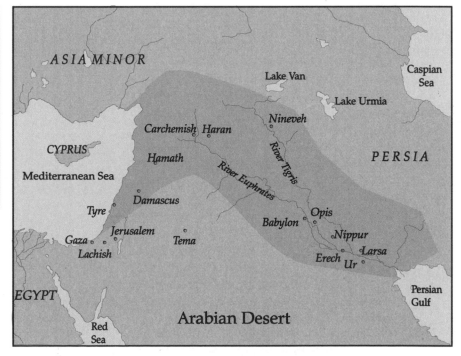

The Babylonian empire reached from the Persian Gulf to the Mediterranean. The most up-to-date iron smelting technology coupled with brilliant military prowess and an utter ruthlessness towards conquered peoples ensured the spread and prosperity of Babylon.

Model judgement passed against nationalist exiles

Babylon, September 592 BC

Every day a Jewish priest goes to the same spot on the suburban roadside where he has built a mud model of Jerusalem, and lies down on his side. At regular intervals he gets up to take grain, beans and oil from storage jars and bakes bread over a cow-dung fire.

Ezekiel is treated with mild humour by many of his fellow exiles now camped along the Chebar canal which diverts Euphrates water into the city. He has been enacting his ritual for a year, having recently turned over to lie on his right side. It is a symbol, he explains, of Yahweh's punishment of Jerusalem.

But now he has introduced a new drama into his eccentric repertoire. He has packed his bags and from inside his model he digs a hole through the wall, then walks away with his pack. That, he says, is the fate of the folks back home. They will be brought to Babylon to join exiled King Jehoiachin.

The priest, who claims he was called to be a prophet after he arrived with the first batch of exiles, is adamant that the Jews' stay in Babylon will be a long one and that Jerusalem will be devastated.

He is echoing the message of Jeremiah who remains in Judah, quenching the defiant nationalism which expects an early return. Even if Noah and Job were alive and joined with Daniel to pray for the nation, they would only succeed in saving themselves, says Ezekiel the prophet.

Ezekiel uses vivid word pictures, often with a surreal, dream-like quality, to reinforce his actions and his gloomy preaching. Judah is like a newborn infant abandoned by its parents but saved from the tip by a kindly patron, he says. But when it grew up it became a prostitute and will be handed over to its lovers – the gods of other lands – to be abused by them.

(Ezekiel 1–19. Siege model: 4:1–5:17; packed bags: 12:1–28; prostitute: 16:1–63)

'Adulterers are to be stripped'

Babylon, August 591 BC

A polished sword glinting in the light of God's glory is poised to fall on Judah, and there is no hope of reprieve, Jewish elders here have been told.

An enquiry by the leaders of the expatriot community to their resident prophet Ezekiel concerning the future of their homeland brought a characteristically forthright reply in which he repeated his regular condemnation of the nation's spiritual 'adultery'.

Judah and Israel behaved like a couple of whores, he told them in a sometimes explicit allegory. They had bedded down with foreigners 'whose genitals were as big as donkeys' and whose ejaculation was as voluminous as a horse's'. Yahweh's response will be to strip them bare, rip off their breasts and crush them to bits, he added.

(Ezekiel 20–23)

Jewish faith is legalised

Babylon, c. 590 BC

King Nebuchadnezzar has declared legal the religion of the Jews, one of several groups of exiles now living in the Babylon region. He has imposed the death penalty for anyone found slandering their God.

The decision reverses his recent attempt to impose political loyalty through religious unity at the dedication ceremony of a new 27-m (90-ft) gold-plated statue of Nabu, his protector god. It follows the apparently miraculous escape of three Jewish dissenters from the furnace to which they had been consigned for blasphemy.

The three Jews, Shadrach, Meshach and Abednego, are all regional governors and had been commanded to attend the dedication. But they refused, and their absence was reported by local leaders jealous of the emigrés' swift promotion. They protested that they could never bow to any god other than their own, who is never represented by an image.

Nebuchadnezzar consigned them to the white-hot flames but claims to have seen a vision of an angel in the furnace who was able to protect the three young men. They were released unharmed and given further promotion.

(Daniel 3)

The three young men in the fire: a poignant illustration fom the Christian catacombs under Rome. Painted at a time when Christians were severely persecuted and for whom the peril of being burnt to death was all too often the grim reality. From the Priscilla Catacomb, Rome, c. AD 220.

King's treble treason trouble

Jerusalem and Babylon, 15 January 588 BC

An attempted alliance with his old enemy and new-found ally, Pharaoh Hophra of Egypt, has backfired on King Zedekiah of Judah who is now facing three charges of treason.

Nebuchadnezzar, who had given him the kingship in return for the promise of good behaviour, has responded to the political treason by marching swiftly to Jerusalem, and tonight has it blockaded. Inside the capital, the outspoken critic, Jeremiah, is repeating his conviction that all alliances and strategies of opposition to Babylon are doomed.

But he is also condemning Zedekiah for his reversal of an earlier policy to release all Hebrew slaves in accordance with the Book of the Law which his father Josiah had discovered. The emancipated slaves had been pressed back into service, which Jeremiah described as a social treason.

And across in Babylon the exiled priest Ezekiel has condemned as spiritual treason Zedekiah's failure to keep his word to Nebuchadnezzar. The oath of allegiance was made in the name of Yahweh. One of the Jews' commandments is that God's name should not be used lightly. To break such an oath to a man is to break it to Yahweh himself, he said.

(2 Chronicles 36:13; Jeremiah 34:8–22; 52:3; Ezekiel 17:11–24; cf. Jeremiah 24:8)

Babylon the great

Blockade is lifted

Jerusalem, 588 BC

Rumours of an invasion force marching up from Egypt have eased the siege of Jerusalem, enabling its residents to return to a semblance of normal life. But the reprieve will only be temporary, according to the prophet Jeremiah whose gloom and doom predictions have a habit of coming true.

He was also among the first to take advantage of the freedom to walk out of the city's front gate. He claims he wanted to sort out the affairs of his family estate at Anathoth, a short distance north of the capital.

But as a known sympathiser of the Babylonians he was arrested by guards on suspicion of desertion. After a thorough beating he was consigned to a dungeon without trial.

According to Egyptian sources, the mission to aid Judah followed a plea for help from a high-ranking Judean army officer. The siege of Jerusalem was itself a result of Zedekiah's political alliance with his southern neighbour.

(Jeremiah 37:1–16)

This aerial photograph of ancient Babylon shows in the foreground the remains of Nebuchadnezzar's palace with many other buildings stretching into the distance.

195

Secret passages

Jerusalem, 588 BC

Details are emerging of secret talks between King Zedekiah and the prophet Jeremiah in the wake of pressures being put on the king by opposing factions.

Zedekiah is said to have admitted frankly to his fear of being tortured by the pro-Babylonian Jews should he capitulate to Nebuchadnezzar; they are aggrieved at the unecessary suffering caused by the lengthy siege. But he is also known to be afraid of the pro-resistance groups to which most of his army officers are loyal.

During a private interview, Jeremiah not only reiterated his advice to surrender quietly but also reassured the king that in surrendering both he and his family would be spared future suffering. If he resisted, however, neither he nor his dependants would escape unscathed.

It was not the first time the king had summoned the prophet for advice. On at least two occasions palace officials have been sent to hear Yahweh's oracle through Jeremiah. And after an earlier private meeting Zedekiah personally ordered that the prophet, who was currently serving a prison sentence, should be kept in more humane conditions under house arrest and be fed at the Crown's expense.

That order was ignored by some, who complained to Zedekiah of Jeremiah's 'treason' and, with royal knowledge if not approval, had him condemned to a slow death in a disused underground storage cistern half-filled with sticky mud. However, the king then backed a sympathiser of the prophet who organised a rescue party.

Zedekiah will go down in history as having made more U-turns than a learner-driver breaking in wild chariot horses.

(Jeremiah 21; 34; 37; 38; cf. 39)

Hope is a long-term investment now

Jerusalem, spring 587 BC

There is something surreal about this 'siege' which has started again. The Babylonian camp, marked by fluttering flags and the smoke for ever rising from the mess tents, can be seen clearly from the walls of Jerusalem.

Against those walls the invader's engineers are building huge ramps of rock and earth. Up them soldiers will climb, manoeuvring their huge battering-rams shielded by canopies from the hail of rocks and arrows which will be launched from the ramparts by desperate defenders. The scene is predictable, a re-run of countless others which have been played out against different scenery.

A shard of pottery from the ruins of the gatehouse of Lachish. Inscribed on it is a letter from a Judean soldier to his commanding officer, from the final days of the Babylonian advance throughout the land.

And yet the city is not so much besieged as blockaded. From tall wooden watchtowers around it, Babylonian guards warn off any daring traders who would try to make megabucks by selling fresh food. Nothing is allowed in, and food supplies are running low. Starvation is Nebuchadnezzar's strongest weapon; weak people cannot fight, however well fortified is their city.

But individuals can come and go, none the less. No doubt they manage to smuggle past the guards a few precious loaves or fresh vegetables from the country villages, although many outlying settlements have also been devastated by the invaders, much as if a swarm of locusts had swept across the region. In that sense, life goes on as normal.

One man who has made use of it is Jeremiah, the pro-Babylonian prophetic adviser to King Zedekiah. Although under permanent house arrest in the barrack area, he is allowed to have visitors. One has been his cousin Hanamel from the village of Anathoth, and the two have just completed a deal to transfer the deeds of family land to Jeremiah in accordance with Judah's strict inheritance laws.

The prophet is jubilant. This, he claims, is a sign from Yahweh that one day, in this place, fields will once again be bought and sold and the fortunes of the people will be revived. On that day God will raise up a righteous leader from the royal line of David.

But for those whose hopes of another reprieve from suffering are rising, he adds, 'But not yet. The city will be destroyed first.' Prophetic hope is clearly a long-term investment with no short-term interest payments.

(2 Kings 25:1–3; Jeremiah 32; 33; 37:17–21; 39:15–18; 52:4–6)

Most villages were defenceless and simply built like Siwan near Jerusalem today.

Holed and sinking fast

Jerusalem, July 587 BC

Like a ship holed on a reef and listing badly, the city of Jerusalem tonight drifts helplessly without a king at the helm as waves of Babylonian soldiers pour over her.

Nothing can now prevent the flagship city of Judah from sinking under the tide of Babylonian domination. Its northern walls have been breached to let in the attackers, and the city's military defenders and civic leaders have hastily abandoned their positions and escaped through the southern wall via the king's garden near the Pool of Siloam.

A Babylonian military council now occupies the strategic Middle Gate area from where it is directing the final mopping-up of pockets of resistance. Detachments are pursuing the fleeing King Zedekiah across the southern desert and rounding up the scattered Judean army.

The 18-month siege began after an abortive attempt by Zedekiah to enlist Egyptian aid against Babylon.
(2 Kings 25:4–7; Jeremiah 39:1–7; 52:6–8)

Holy smoke: Jerusalem's the ultimate burnt offering

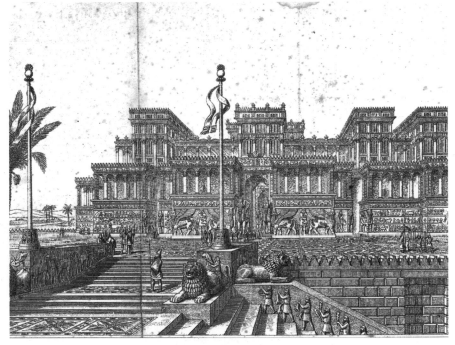

The north-eastern facade and grand entrance to the Great Palace on the River Euphrates. This nineteenth-century drawing is based upon Layard's excavations.

Jerusalem and Babylon, late August 587 BC

Smoke is a familiar sight at the Jerusalem temple: the sweet smoke of incense when prayers are offered; the acrid smoke of burning flesh from animal sacrifices.

But the thick, dark pall of ash and soot which hangs in the still air over the desolate city today is all that remains of Judah's capital. Jerusalem, its royal palace, its private houses and its holy temple, have all become one huge burnt offering to the might of Babylon.

It has taken a month for the invading forces under the day-to-day command of Nebuzaradan to secure the city and bring resistance to an end, although there has never been any doubt of their supremacy. Several thousand leading citizens have been rounded up and chained together to trek the 1,450 km (900 miles) to Babylon where they will join their fellow countrymen already taken into exile.

Among them is King Zedekiah, recaptured after a short burst of freedom and tried for treason before Nebuchadnezzar at his western headquarters in Riblah some 100 km (60 miles) north of Damascus. The last thing Zedekiah saw before he was blinded for life was the execution of his two sons.

But not among them is Jeremiah, who at Nebuchadnezzar's personal request was granted freedom. In a bureaucratic blunder he was in fact temporarily chained to the human crocodile but later released with diplomatic apologies and an imperial pension as compensation. He has elected to stay in Judah.

Before the city was torched, all valuables including the temple furniture were removed. They will swell the treasury and grace the palaces, temples and museums of Nebuchadnezzar's sumptious capital on the River Euphrates.
(2 Kings 25:8–21; 2 Chronicles 36:15–20; Jeremiah 39:5–14; 40:1–6; 52:12–30)

The successive campaigns of the Assyrians demonstrate their unwavering intent to capture Jerusalem and annexe the whole of Judah into their empire.

Map:

Megiddo
Samaria
Shechem
Mizpah · Shiloh · Jericho
Gibeon
Ramah
Jerusalem
Azekah
Lachish → Hebron

0 — Miles 20
Kms 30

Main Babylonian Army 597 BC
Raids by allies
Destruction of Jerusalem 586 BC

Ultimate irony for weeping prophet

Tahpanhes, 585 BC

Life is unfair, and it sometimes reaches its cruellest depths when injustice is wrapped in irony. And today the Judean prophet Jeremiah who has worn his sensitive heart on his sleeve for 40 thankless years, must be reflecting ruefully on the latest and probably last ironic twist to his painful life.

He has been kidnapped by his own people and taken to Egypt, the land from which Yahweh rescued his people 700 years ago. And Jeremiah's message has consistently stressed the futility of any alliance with Egypt in the present. It is the fourth time in his career that he has been held against his will.

Jeremiah is one of those preachers who is emotionally involved in his message and its reception. His insights affect every fibre of his being. 'Oh, my anguish, my anguish! I writhe in pain. Oh, the agony of my heart! My heart pounds within me,' he cried as the inevitable fall of Jerusalem became clear to him (4:19).

Often he turned to Yahweh for comfort in the very anguish to which Yahweh had exposed him: 'O my Comforter in sorrow, my heart is faint within me. ... Since my people are crushed, I am crushed; I mourn and horror grips me. Is there no balm in Gilead?' (8:18, 21–22).

He thought nothing of arguing with God. On one occasion, he spoke of having eaten God's words which 'were my joy and my heart's delight'. He had never colluded with the wicked, so 'why is my pain unending and my wound grievous and incurable? Will you be to me like a deceptive brook,' like a dried-up wadi? (15:15–18).

Called to be a prophet in his teens or early 20s, Jeremiah objected that he was too inexperienced. Yahweh promised to give him his words and reasssured him that he had known him since conception. But that day, Jeremiah claimed in the darkest night of his soul, was the one he regretted most.

'The word of the LORD has brought me insult and reproach all day long,' he complained. Yet if he

Jeremiah laments the destruction of Jerusalem, as imagined by Rembrandt.

kept quiet it was like a fire burning within him. 'Cursed be the day I was born! ... Why did I ever come out of the womb to see trouble and sorrow and to end my days in shame?' (20:8–9, 14–18).

Despite his periodic bouts of depression and the often doom-laden content of his prophecies, Jeremiah has been hopeful, expecting Yahweh to restore his people to their homeland. He reveres God as the ultimate ruler, quoting him as asking, 'Am I only a God nearby ... and not a God far away? Can anyone hide in secret places so that I cannot see him? ... Do I not fill heaven and earth?' (23:23,24)

Compared with the man-made gods of other nations, Yahweh 'is the true God; he is the living God, the eternal King. When he is angry, the earth trembles' (10:10). He is the creator who 'made the sand a boundary for the sea ... who gives autumn and spring rains in season' (5:22,24). For him, nothing is too hard (32:27). Indeed, Jeremiah often transmitted messages from Yahweh to other nations (chs 46–51).

Yahweh can be trusted, he claimed. The person who relies on human resources will wither like a tree in a drought, but the person who trusts God will flourish like a tree planted by streams (17:5–8).

His sharpest criticism was reserved for religious leaders whose lies of convenience satisfied their paymasters but disgusted Yahweh. It was religious superficiality which dragged him to Egypt. People who had put down Ishmael's rebellion sought God's blessing on their already-formed plan to flee south.

It took 10 days for Jeremiah to discern Yahweh's answer, and it was not what the enquirers wanted to hear. But they went anyway, taking the prophet as a human insurance policy against an untoward act of God.

Visions of grandeur seem beyond belief

Babylon, c. 580 BC

The eccentric prophet Ezekiel has recently completed his latest series of oracles which continue to baffle and amaze his viewers and listeners. They stretch the imagination as well as faith.

One vision combines the imagery of a dream with the vividness of waking experience. He said he 'visited' a valley full of skeletons. As he walked among them the voice of God told him to call them to life. They rattled together, grew sinews and flesh, and drew in the breath of God to come alive. That, said Ezekiel, is a picture of the Jews' future restoration in Judah (ch 37).

Much of his ministry over the past 13 years has been to convince the exiled Judeans here of the justice of their plight. But behind his outspoken criticisms a majestic view of God hangs like a huge backdrop. Unlike other gods, Yahweh and his realm are beyond representation except by symbols.

Ezekiel's career as a prophet started with a vision of God like a cloud flashing with lightning and surrounded by fantastic creatures each having several faces, wings and eyes; they looked like wheels within wheels, able to turn in all directions. In the centre a man-like figure glowed like molten metal with all the colours of the rainbow (chs 1, 10).

That Yahweh is the Lord of history and the nations is a recurring theme in his work. Like his contemporary in Judah, Jeremiah, Ezekiel devotes several prophecies to nations beyond his own. Egypt (29–32) and Phoenicia (26–28) get the longest treatment as he consigns them to the ashes for their evils and laments the pride which has caused their downfall.

Dried bones of animals in the unforgiving desert is a common sight for the weary traveller.

But God is not vindictive and the prophet stresses his fairness to the point where he introduces a new, or at least unfamiliar, emphasis on personal responsibility. He debunks the popular fatalism caught in the proverb, 'the fathers ate sour grapes but it is the children's teeth which are set on edge'. Nonsense, he cries. People will die for their own sins, not for someone else's. Those who turn back to God will live (chs 18, 33).

Yahweh is also a caring shepherd of his people, he suggests. Unlike the under-shepherds – the prophets and priests who scattered the flock by their selfishness – Yahweh will gather them together again, tend the sick and lead them all to fresh grazing (ch 34).

It is one of Ezekiel's most striking images of the promised return to the homeland. He hints at it everywhere. 'I will bring you back; your stone-hard heart will be softened' (11:17–20); 'you will serve me on my holy hill and know I am Yahweh' (20:39–44); 'I will give you a new heart and a new spirit; you will once again be my people and I shall be your God' (36:24–32). A God who judges and yet who also forgives is truly unique in today's world.

Little is known about Ezekiel as a person. His often extreme or bizarre actions, his uncompromising manner and message, and his apparently high birth, do not make him the most approachable of people. His wife died young and suddenly about the time Nebuchadnezzar finally destroyed Jerusalem and despite his love for her he refused to mourn her. He said it was yet another sign of Yahweh's desecration of the city and temple which were once the delight of his eyes (24:15–24).

Although Ezekiel was a priest, it is unlikely that he ever served in the Jerusalem temple. He was exiled when in his early 20s.

(Ezekiel 1–39)

Fast Facts c. 585–580 BC

Egypt, c. 585 BC: Civil war has broken out between Egyptian soldiers and foreign mercenaries after the combined army returned from assisting Lydia against a Greek invasion, where it had suffered heavy losses. The Egyptians are looking to a general from the Nubian campaign, Amasis (Ahmose), to lead them.

Miletus, c. 585 BC: A Greek philosopher, Thales, predicted accurately this year's solar eclipse. He studied under Egyptian teachers and created 'geometry' by adapting Egyptian land-measurement. He believes that the world comes from and returns to water, which he says is divine.

Delphi, 582 BC: The Pythian Games held in Delphi are to take place in the third year of every Olympiad. Formerly an ancient musical contest held every eighth year, the games will now include athletic and equestrian events. The prize is a crown of bay leaves, and the games will rank second in the world to the Olympics.

Corinth, c. 581 BC: The Isthmian Games are now being held every other year. Athletic events in honour of the god Poseidon are patronised by all Greek states. The winner is given a crown of wild celery. Corinth, the pleasure city of Greece, is a popular venue for spectators who come for more than the games in the arena.

Greece, c. 580 BC: A woman poet, Sappho, has established a school to train upper-class young ladies in music and dance. Her poetry is popular and appeals to the emotions rather than to the intellect. She writes about the intense feelings of love, grief, and jealousy and about the physical beauty of the girls she lives with. She comes from the island of Lesbos and is married with one child.

c. 586–570 BC

'I lived like a wild animal' says king

William Blake, the early nineteenth-century British poet and visionary, was greatly drawn to Nebuchadnezzar's suffering which he depicted in a series of illustrations. Here the king is seen having reverted to an animal state.

Babylon, c. 580 BC
A frank confession issued by Nebuchadnezzar confirms the rumours which have circulated in the city. He admits to having suffered a mental breakdown, but now claims to have recovered fully.

During a period of depression the king believed he was turning into an animal and even began to behave like one.

According to his statement, he was warned of the risk in a dream interpreted by his chief sage Belteshazzar (Daniel). But he did not accept the advice to humble himself before the gods in order to avert the tragedy.

The illness began shortly after a typical outburst of self-congratulation as the king surveyed the city he had planned and paid for, taking little account of the human cost involved. He claims the healing began when he recognised afresh the existence of the Most High God, who Belteshazzar, a Jew, calls Yahweh.

Peacemaker is assassinated

Mizpah, October 586 BC
In a futile gesture of defiance, the governor of Jerusalem has been assassinated and a short-lived but violent civil war has waged among factions left in Judah by the Babylonians.

The pointlessness of it was heightened by the fact that the people had just enjoyed the best harvest for years even though the city and its satellite villages resemble a demolition site. Life had returned to some semblance of normality following the Babylonian orgy of destruction. The invaders were not going out of their way to make things difficult for Gedaliah, the Judean they made governor.

But the fact that he was a peacemaker anxious to restore stability was enough to stir the hot-blooded Ishmael to attack him. A descendant of David and a former officer in Zedekiah's army, he was probably jealous of Gedaliah and

also lusting for revenge against the Babylonians.

Encouraged by the Ammonite king Baalis, Ishmael and ten others accepted Gedaliah's hospitality at a banquet at his regional headquarters in Mizpah some 12 km (8 miles) north of Jerusalem, where they murdered him. The plot had been public knowledge but Gedaliah had remained committed to reconciliation and had refused to authorise a pre-emptive strike against Ishmael.

The assassination was followed by the massacre of 70 pilgrims from the north who had come to mourn the loss of Jerusalem, and by the kidnapping of all the women who had been in Zedekiah's household. Ishmael travelled to Ammon pursued by Johanan, loyal to Gedaliah, who succeeded in persuading all but a handful of the defectors to return.

Ancient stone watchtower in the fields near Mizpah.

However, Johanan was last reported heading towards Egypt, perhaps out of fear of reprisals.
(2 Kings 25:22–26; Jeremiah 40:7–41:18)

200

Grief-stricken poet finds hope in God

Jerusalem, c. 575 BC

Images of suffering become indelibly printed on the memories of those who experience them. Somehow, victims and witnesses have to find ways of expressing their feelings in order to manage their pain.

The remaining residents of Judah and their relatives exiled in Babylon now have been given one such expression which puts into words what many felt during the capital's destruction. A series of five untitled and unsigned poems describe with dignity the emotional traumas of loss and grief.

The five 'Lamentations' recount the horrors of hunger. Some mothers ate their own children (2:20) while babies ebbed away in their mothers' arms (2:12) and the 'skin shrivelled on the bones' of even the wealthy (4:8). The rampaging Babylonians ravished virgins, strung up leaders on gallows and forced young boys into virtual slavery (5:11–13).

The sight of pock-marked walls, the burnt-out shells of buildings, the piles of rubble and above all the desecrated temple, make the tears flood from the poet's eyes (2:7f., 3:48). To the question, 'Why has it happened?' he gives a frank answer: 'We have sinned and rebelzled, and you have not forgiven. ... You have covered yourself with a cloud so that no prayer can get through' (3:42,44).

That does not stop him throwing his grief onto Yahweh whose 'compassions never fail but are new every morning. Great is your faithfulness' (3:22,23). 'It is good to wait for God's salvation,' he adds (3:26) but as all mourners know, waiting is hard. 'Why do you forsake us for so long?' he cries. 'Restore us, O Lord' (5:20f).

The poems are in the classic Near Eastern tradition of laments couched in Hebrew forms with parallel ideas stressing words rather than syllables. The first four are given added dignity by being crafted tightly as acrostics with most stanzas beginning with a different letter of the Hebrew alphabet.

The author is unknown, but there is a strong suspicion that they emanate from the pen of Jeremiah the prophet. He often composed laments within his prophecies, and although the style and language is different in this latest collection there are also allusions reminiscent of the prophet's ministry. There was a fire in his bones (Jeremiah 20:9; Lamentations 1:13) and he recalls a time when he was drowning in a pit (Jeremiah 38:1–13; Lamentations 3:53–60). He is also scathing of the false prophets (2:14; 4:13), a common theme in Jeremiah.

(Lamentations 1–5)

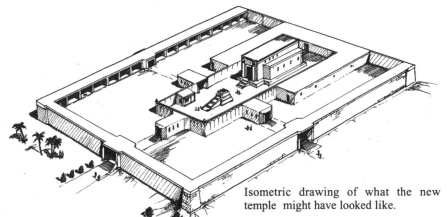

Isometric drawing of what the new temple might have looked like.

Plans laid for new temple

Babylon, April 573 BC

Ambitious plans for a new temple in Jerusalem have been drawn up by the visionary exiled priest Ezekiel. He claims to have received specific instructions from Yahweh on its dimensions and decor.

Although there is much which seems idealistic, the very existence of such plans will give new hope and heart to the thousands of exiles who came here following the destruction of their shrine and capital city. Ezekiel's floor plans are similar to those of Solomon's temple although at 52 m (170 ft) long and 26 m (85 ft) wide it is rather larger. It is also surrounded by an enclosure containing some 30 rooms; there are kitchen areas in the four corners.

The prophet also outlines the jobs of temple staff, the rituals they are to enact, and the apportionment of the former territories of Israel and Judah to the 12 tribes who lived there.

However, as with many of the eccentric's visions, there is more to this than meets the eye at first. In the middle of the technical detail he describes how the visible presence of God returns to the temple just as he saw it leave in an earlier vision. He also pictures a tree-lined river flowing from the temple southwards through the desert to desalinate the Dead Sea.

It is being suggested that behind the practical possibilities there are theological principles which highlight the order and perfection of Yahweh's future new creation. There all human life will be centred on the worship and service of God and his 'living water' will sustain and renew all things. Instead of conflict and chaos, there will be a peaceful orderliness. Ezekiel's visions may be puzzling, but they are not small-minded.

(Ezekiel 40–48; cf. 10)

Babylon rises above the sun

Babylon, c. 565 BC

The Tower of Babel, begun centuries ago, is now probably the world's tallest building. Work on the structure, which Nebuchadnezzar calls 'the house which is the foundation of earth and heaven', has been completed by the construction of a temple on its highest level.

It lies to the north of the temple of Marduk, which is now literally shining like the sun since its walls were covered in gold leaf. An estimated 22 tons of gold were used to build the god's statue. Over two tons of frankincense are burnt at it each day.

Nebuchadnezzar can now look down on the city from the rooftop 'hanging gardens' he has laid for his Median wife, Amyitis, to remind her of the mountains of her homeland. Everywhere there are signs of prodigious building work, some of which was begun by the king's father Nabopolassar.

The triple walls have been greatly strengthened and the city is now surrounded by a wide moat. Set in the walls are eight magnificent pairs of bronze gates hanging from ornate stone entrances. The great Ishtar Gate, decorated with over 150 bulls and dragons (symbols of Adad and Marduk), now also has glazed bricks to create yellow and white animals on a blue background.

The king's southern palace next to the River Euphrates is protected from rising damp by a huge earthwork. It has five courtyards surrounded by suites of offices and apartments. An underground crypt of 14 vaulted rooms serves as a warehouse and administration unit where the ration lists for the Jewish exiles are kept.

Some of the Jews have no eyes for the beauty of the city to which they have been brought. In a deep lament currently circulating, they refuse to sing the songs of Jerusalem (Zion) for their jesting

The Hanging Gardens of Babylon were an extraordinary complex series of irrigated terraces rising high above the king's new palace. Their fame spread far and wide, and they were considered one of the seven wonders of the ancient world.

captors, and mourn the loss of their temple and its sacrifices.

Others, however, have found inspiration here. Ezekiel the prophet seems to have drawn some of his extravagant imagery from the spectacular architecture and sculpture of the city. Priests and lawyers are taking the opportunity of their enforced sabbatical to reformulate their ancient faith and find new forms of religious assembly. Groups gather regularly to hear the Law of Moses read aloud, and scribes are editing these and other religious texts and historical documents.

Secular Jews are meanwhile finding other ways to profit from their exile. Some of them, including Daniel (Belteshazzar) the king's chief of wise men and astrologers, have risen to high office. Others have established trading and other businesses, which are said to be flourishing.

(cf. Psalm 137)

Lunatic trip for lunar god

Babylon, c. 553 BC

The elderly King Nabonidus, a devout worshipper of the lunar god Sin, has left his son Belshazzar in charge of Babylon and taken his army to Taima in north-west Arabia. Some are suggesting that he has taken leave of his senses. The motive for his departure is unclear.

Nabonidus was placed on the throne in 556, replacing Mabashi-Marduk who had been murdered after a brief reign of only three months. Nabonidus is not a member of the royal family but does have a distinguished military and diplomatic record. His mother was the priestess of Sin, the moon god, at Haran.

Babylon has been unsettled since Nebuchadnezzar died 10 years ago. His son and successor, Amel-Marduk, abused his power and was killed in a revolution. An army commander who had served at the siege of Jerusalem, Neriglissar, succeeded him and died mysteriously in 556.

Moral end to fabled animal story-teller's longest tale?

Greece, c. 564 BC

The famous raconteur of fables, Aesop, has died. According to unconfirmed reports, he was executed in Delphi on a false charge of sacrilege. If true, it was a surprising twist of fate he would no doubt have moralised about. Aesop collected and told hundreds of stories, mostly about animals. Each made a moral observation.

Wolves and sheep make a truce by exchanging sheepdogs and wolfcubs as hostages, but the wolves claim it was broken when they hear their cubs crying and attack the defenceless sheep; evil always finds a way. A horse enlists human help to defeat a stag only to find itself permanently tied to human hands; good ideas can have unforeseen consequences.

And a rural mouse lured to the city by his cousin enjoyed the bright lights and high life until the party was smashed up by a dog; he decided that the devils he knew in the sleepy village were better than those he did not know in the city.

More is known about the stories

Heracles fighting the Geryon Triplets. Many of Aesop's fables were based on myths unlike some of the ones we know best today such as the story of the hare and the tortoise.

than the story-teller. Aesop is believed to have been born a slave in Samos but according to some accounts became a freed man and worked as a freelance adviser to state leaders. He is also credited as the author or populariser of numerous aphorisms, including 'it is a virtue not to be vicious' and 'let every man mind his own business'. Few of his sayings and stories have been written down; most are passed on orally.

Heracles and the hydra of Lerne.

'There's a bright new kingdom coming'

Babylon, c. 551 BC

There is a new kingdom coming, according to royal adviser Belteshazzar (Daniel). But even the arch interpreter of dreams confesses himself unable to fathom the mysterious images which have troubled his sleep over the past two years.

One thing he is clear about, however, is that the kingdom which Yahweh's people will enjoy one day will be ruled over by a 'Son of man' who is worshipped by all nations and who carries the authority of God himself.

Daniel describes Yahweh as 'the Ancient of Days', shining white, sitting on a throne of flaming fire, surrounded by countless attendants, and opening the books of judgement. His majestic vision of God as the ruler of history overshadows the details of a dream in which fantastic beasts are said to represent future empires preceding the divine kingdom.

In a second dream he sees strange animals fighting each other. His celestial guide explains that it concerns the future of the Medo-Persian and Greek states. The images were virtually beyond description; Daniel can only say what they resembled rather than what they actually were.

Indeed, he says, it was so appalling that it made him ill for days. Unlike most previous visions given to prophets of Yahweh, these appear to be brief glimpses through the curtain of time into God's eternal present. There is no message or encouragement attached to them, except perhaps the reassurance that when international conflicts arise, Yahweh is not taking a break from his role as sovereign.

(Daniel 7–8)

c. 545 BC

Time to go home?
Fresh hope from prophetic poet

Babylon, c. 545 BC

Jewish exiles in Babylon are taking encouragement from a series of poetic prophecies which suggest that they will be restored to their homeland through the agency of the Persian leader Cyrus, who is currently expanding his spheres of influence.

A budding almond tree.

The messages are associated with Isaiah of Jerusalem, who wrote more than 200 years ago. It is believed that they have been preserved, edited or even written by the descendants of his 'school' of fellow prophets, although detailed predictive prophecy is not unknown in Jewish tradition.

They proclaim the end of Judah's 'hard labour' in exile as retribution for its sin, and promise a restoration of its fortunes in glowing, almost unearthly terms. The poems, often written as if Yahweh himself is speaking, celebrate him as the supreme God of the universe in language unlike anything else in contemporary religious thought.

Yahweh is 'the first and the last' (44:6) who 'created the heavens' and 'fashioned the earth', forming it to be inhabited (45:18). He holds the waters 'in the hollow of his hand' and 'weighs the mountains on the scales' (40:12), having flung the stars into orbit (40:26). He is also the ruler of nations who hands them over to whoever he pleases (41:2). He names Cyrus as his shepherd (44:28) and claims to lead him by the hand to subdue nations and to 'strip kings of their armour' (45:1).

His supremacy is seen most clearly in relation to other gods. Yahweh alone can foresee the future (41:21–24; 46:10). Idols understand nothing (44:18); indeed, they are made from the same tree trunk as the fuel for the cooking oven (44:19). The Babylonian gods are singled out for special scorn. Marduk (Bel) and Nebo are portrayed bowing helplessly in disgrace before Yahweh (46:1)

Babylon itself will be turned to dust by a sudden catastrophe, the prophet claims, which its astrologers and sorcerers will be unable to prevent (47). As a result the Jews will be allowed to return to their home. Here, the writer is at his most lyrical. The language is often tender and reassuring: 'Speak tenderly to Jerusalem' (40:2). 'When you pass through the waters I will be with you' (43:2).

Even though a mother forgets her child, God will not forget his people (49:15,16). The freed captives will 'find pasture on every barren hill and will neither hunger nor thirst' (49:9,10), being satisfied with the richest of foods (55:2). The writer seems vague as to when this might be – soon, or at the end of time – but whenever it is, Yahweh will make an everlasting covenant with his people (55:3).

The latter half of the book (chs 56–66) expands on these themes in a slightly different style, and seems more timeless and less specific. In the same category are the four 'Servant

> **Songs of thankless service**
>
> There are four 'Servant songs' in the manuscript (42:1–7; 49:1–7; 50:4–9; 52:12–53:12) which seem to apply unique qualities to the Israelite nation, to Cyrus, and to some unspecified leader who is perhaps an ideal model or anticipated future deliverer.
>
> The servant is gentle and considerate, careful not to break a bruised reed and concerned to establish justice (42:3,4). He is called and prepared by Yahweh for what appears to be a fruitless task, but is honoured by God for his faithfulness (49:1–7).
>
> Although instructed by God, he is despised by the people (49:7; 50:6; 53:3). Indeed, he suffers greatly and unjustly, carrying his people's sorrows and sins on his own back (53:4,5) but ultimately emerging victorious (53:10–12).

songs' (see box). But poetry is always capable of varying interpretations and the exiled Judeans are no doubt grateful for the sheer wonder and joy of this vision and the hope which it offers them.

(Isaiah 40–66)

The eternal snows symbolise the purity of a new beginning.

204

Sudden death strikes Lydia

Ecbatana, Persia, c. 545 BC

King Cyrus of Persia has conquered the kingdom of Lydia. The campaign was sudden and unexpected. The Lydian king Croesus had called on both Babylon's Nabonidus and the Egyptians for help, but Nabonidus, in Taima, did not even reply. Lydia is now a Persian province.

The Persians are an Indo-European tribe who settled in the territory of ancient Elam in the south of Babylonia. One of their first forts was at Parsua (Fars) from where they take their name.

Cyrus is the son of the Persian prince Cambyses who married the daughter of the Median king Astyages. It is said that Astyages dreamt that his daughter's child would rule the whole of Asia, and he therefore ordered the death of the baby Cyrus. However, a kinsman gave the baby to a shepherd who swapped him with his wife's still-born son.

In 550 Cyrus revolted against Astyages. The Median army also revolted and handed Astyages over to Cyrus, who was welcomed into the capital Ecbatana as the rightful king. Persia is now a major threat as it gains in size and power.

Cyrus and his supporters are flagrant propagandists, encouraging the Babylonians to see Cyrus as the one who will save them from the tyranny of Nabonidus. With many disenchanted with him it may not take much to sway them towards Cyrus who has a reputation for religious tolerance.

The writing's on the wall

Surprise turns to horror at the appearance of the mysterious writing on the wall during Belshazzar's feast. Here graphically captured by Rembrandt, one of the many artists throughout the ages inspired by this story.

Babylon, c. 540 BC

As the Persian propaganda machine continues to blast across the world its promises of a new order under King Cyrus, the Babylonian regent Belshazzar whooped it up with 1,000 friends in a lavish orgy of wine, women and song.

They even used the religious vessels taken from the temple in Jerusalem by his grandfather Nebuchadnezzar instead of the usual royal gold and silver ware.

But as the wine went to his head he suddenly received a sobering vision that called 'time' on his lifespan. Belshazzar claims he saw a divine hand writing 'mene, mene, tekel, parsin' on the wall of the great throne-room.

When no one could interpret the apparently meaningless list of Babylonian weights and measures, the veteran sage and former chief of magicians, Belteshazzar (Daniel), was called out of retirement to help. The Jewish émigré reminded the prince how Nebuchadnezzar had been humbled by Yahweh, the supreme God, through mental illness. Belshazzar had not followed his example, however, and had sacrilegiously praised the work of human hands.

The kingdom, Daniel said, is about to be torn out of Belshazzar's hands and taken over by the Medo-Persian alliance. The regent will be killed. 'You've been weighed in the balance and found short of spiritual capital,' he added.

Despite the grim interpretation, Belshazzar kept his promise of reward and promoted Daniel to third ruler under the absent Nabonidus and himself.

(Daniel 5)

Fast Facts
c. 561–550 BC

Babylon, 561 BC: Evil-Merodach, the new king of Babylon, has released the former Judean king Jehoiachin from prison and made him a member of the Babylonian royal household. Jehoiachin was 18 years old and had reigned for just three months when he was deported by Nebuchadnezzar in 597 (2 Kings 25:27–30; Jeremiah 52:31–34).

Taima, Arabia, c. 550 BC: Unconfirmed reports suggest that the Babylonian king, Nabonidus, has been afflicted with a malignant disease. It is said that he has been given spiritual counsel by an unnamed Jewish prophet. Nabonidus has been campaigning in the region, leaving his son, Belshazzar, in charge of Babylon.

Babylon, c. 550 BC: Inflation is rising fast, adding to the general discontent. Prices have risen by 50 per cent in the past decade. This is due partly to the draining of resources for military campaigns and public building works. The situation is currently made worse by an outbreak of plague.

Egypt, 548 BC: The Egyptian king Ahmose II (Amasis) is developing contact with other nations, and recently funded the rebuilding of the oracular sanctuary of Apollo at Delphi, which had been destroyed by a fire.

Babylon falls from greatness

Babylon, 539 BC

Babylon 'the great' has fallen to the Persians without many of its citizens realising. The music and dancing of the first New Year festival to be celebrated for a decade continued as Cyrus and his troops marched in unopposed.

King Nabonidus had returned only recently from a decade in Arabia to initiate the festival which cannot be held without him present. He fled from the city when the Persians arrived, but was captured and killed.

Cyrus entered with a statue of the god Marduk at his side which encouraged the public acceptance of the man many believe offers the cash-strapped city and its crumbling empire a better future. Cyrus has forbidden his troops to loot Babylon. One report says 'not one spear was brought near to Esagila, nor entered its sanctuary;

not one ceremony was disturbed'. He has promised not to change any of the religious institutions.

He has appointed as local governor, Ugbaru, a Babylonian by birth who went over to Persia some time ago. He was an official when Nebuchadnezzar was king, and now governs a satrapy almost as large as the former Chaldean empire, embracing Mesopotamia, Syria, Phoenicia and Palestine.

Cyrus has left most local officials in place, but each province is governed by a Persian-appointed satrap. Capital cities have a treasurer and garrison commander who are directly responsible to the king. Once a year, there will be an annual visitation by a royal inspector, known as the 'King's Eye'. The satraps are answerable to a small group of administrators, one of whom is Belteshazzar (Daniel) a Jewish émigré who has served

Babylon since the days of Nebuchadnezzar.

Cyrus has been careful to follow Babylonian procedures and customs, calling on the local gods to help and support him. His son Cambyses is to be left in charge while his father is conquering other nations as he seeks to expand his empire. Cambyses has his own capital at Sippar. He is to be known as 'King of Babylon', thus marking him out as Cyrus' successor.

Cyrus has promised compensation to all who have suffered under Nabonidus. He has begun restoring the old temples and returning divine images and cult equipment to their rightful places. The temples of Assyria, Babylonia, Gutium and Elam have all been given back their patron gods. The fall of Babylon has long been predicted by Jewish prophets.

(cf. Daniel 6:1,2)

Trapped by men but released by lions!

Babylon, c. 538 BC

A veteran civil servant who was the victim of a hate campaign has survived certain death after being thrown into the king's lion pit.

The ring leaders of the plot, believed to have been motivated by no more than jealousy, have since been devoured by the same lions which had refused to touch Daniel's kosher flesh.

The Jewish émigré has shone with virtue, wisdom and efficiency through three reigns of varying corruption since he was exiled to Babylon as a youth almost 70 years ago. He may have decided that after a long and distinguished career he had little to lose in ignoring an unnecessary religious law which had been framed specifically to trap him.

Apparently-zealous officials pandered to the ego of Cyrus (who is also locally known as Darius) when they suggested a 30-day ban on all religious worship not directed to the

Lions were kept in Babylon in cages next to a special arena, a large open pit, for the pleasure of the king who was fond of hunting them. This magnificent glazed brick relief comes from the palace in Babylon.

god-king. Caught in the act of worshipping towards his God Yahweh's sanctuary in Jerusalem, Daniel was beyond all but the devastated king's prayers when he was hauled before him.

The city's lion pit housing the

ferocious trophies of the sport of kings was not beyond Yahweh's reach. Daniel's survival was immediately taken as a sign both of his innocence and of his God's greatness.

(Daniel 6; cf. Ezekiel 19:1–9)

Classless religion given royal approval

Persia, c. 550 BC

A new religion has become the official teaching of a small kingdom in north-east Persia, after its king Vishtasp decided to favour it. Founded by 40-year-old Zoroaster, a married priest with several children, it teaches that there is one supreme god, Ahura-mazda, a good and wise friend of human-kind.

Ahura-mazda created everything, including twin spirits, one of which chose truth and light and the other untruth and darkness. This destructive spirit is responsible for the evil in the world, which is the battle-ground between good and evil. God created people to help him win it, says Zoroaster.

Everyone now has to choose between the two and they will be judged accordingly. Their social status is irrelevant. If their good deeds outweigh the bad they will go to heaven. When God finally wins the battle, the world will be restored to perfection.

Zoroaster had a series of visions 10 years ago after which he began to teach his new message. It was generally rejected until the recent conversion of his cousin. King Vishtasp's conversion, however, is more significant.

But the new teaching is not going down well with the established priests and princes who think heaven is their special domain and beyond the reach of peasants. They teach that the world is full of abstract spirits that people must keep appeased by making the right sacrifices, and they object to Zoroaster's teaching of a personal god indifferent to material standing.

Sarcophagus of a rich married couple, also from Cerveteri, c. 550 BC.

Etruscan masters of the fine, erotic arts

Italy, c. 550 BC

Unusual tomb paintings with a mythological theme depict contro-versial erotic images. In one, a bull is shown in sexual activity with two men and a girl and in the other a bull with erect phallus is charging a man having intercourse with a boy. It is unclear if the paintings are a condemnation of homosexuality or relate to an obscure fertility cult.

On the other hand Etruscans also show a degree of civilised practice unseen elsewhere. Contrary to Greek practice, Etruscan wives are welcomed as escorts to their husbands at banquets. They may even recline together on high couches. Food is taken from low three-legged stools, sometimes with secondary shelves for stacking dishes, placed in front of the couches.

Detail of the head of the wife from the sarcophagus illustrated below.

Detail from extensive wall paintings from the Etruscan necropolis of Cerveteri. The figures are 1.25 m (4ft 3in) tall and painted onto the baked earthern wall.

c. 540–535 BC

Cyrus declares general amnesty

Babylon, 537 BC

Tens of thousands of exiled foreign nationals are to be given the option of returning to their conquered territories under the terms of a general amnesty announced by King Cyrus.

For one former top civil servant, the Jewish Belteshazzar, the decree has come as a direct answer to his passionate prayers to Yahweh. Cyrus has especially singled out the Jews, who Nebuchadnezzar took captive in successive raids between 605 and 587. As a religious man who respects all gods, Cyrus claims Yahweh has given him the power

and opportunity to build a temple in Judah's former capital.

He has released all the furnishings and treasures which were taken from the temple, and entrusted them to a senior Jewish elder, Sheshbazzar.

The tomb of Cyrus stands in a desolate, and now isolated, region of Iran.

The so-called Cyrus Cylinder dates from 536 BC. It records how Cyrus conquered Babylon by surprise, without a battle, and documents how he returned the gods taken from various cities to their original homes, along with their servants.

But Belteshazzar. better known to his compatriots as Daniel, will not be among the returnees. An old man, he is content to die knowing that his prayers have been answered. According to his own account, he recently re-read the prophecy of Jeremiah, who foretold Babylon's destruction and predicted an exile lasting for 70 years.

Realising that the time was almost up, Daniel fasted and prayed that Yahweh would keep his promise and demonstrate his forgiveness. He claims to have received a fresh message predicting that after about 500 years a 'messiah' will enter Jerusalem, and that later the city will be destroyed once again. History, for the Jewish prophets, seems to have a habit of repeating itself.

(2 Chronicles 36:21–23; Ezra 1; Daniel 9)

Not in our back yard!

Jerusalem, autumn 537 BC

An ambitious plan to rebuild their temple, by a small group of devout Jews recently returned to Jerusalem, is being opposed by residents who have occupied the area for decades. But despite complaints, the returned exiles have begun sacrificing to Yahweh on a new altar placed on the site of the one desecrated by Nebuchadnezzar in 587.

The task facing them is enormous. At the foundation-laying ceremony some older people wept as they contemplated the work required to complete the structure which King Solomon built from large hewn stones and which now lies in a heap of overgrown rubble.

It would be challenge enough for a prosperous nation, but only a handful of the few thousand returnees are skilled builders and all face the problem of finding or building from scratch family homes and sources of income. Most are staying outside the capital, which is largely a burnt-out shell.

Local residents, many of whom were forcibly settled here from other countries and observing the newcomers with some envy at their wealth, initially offered to help the rebuilding work. But they were rebuffed, largely because although they have worshipped Yahweh as the local god of the land they have also retained allegiance to the gods they brought with them. Fearing a clampdown on their pluralism, their interest turned to opposition.

The fear appears to be mutual. The Jews are reported to be nervous of attack and anxious that their faith should not be compromised. Inspired by senior priest Joshua and civic leader Zerubbabel their initial celebrations included a reinstatement of the Feast of Tabernacles, and regular weekly and monthly sacrifices.

(Ezra 2:64–4:5)

Spiritual war plans in coded message

Babylonia, 536 BC

The myths about warring gods have some basis in fact after all, according to the strict monotheistic visionary, Daniel (Belteshazzar), former head of wise men in the heyday of the Babylonian empire.

In an apparent theophany – a visible divine appearance – which was partially witnessed by his companions, Daniel claims to have been given a further glimpse into the future pages of Yahweh's history books, in which angelic beings (although not gods) vie for supremacy by influencing the conflicts of nations.

His vision on the banks of the Tigris was so powerful that his entourage fled from the scene, leaving the elderly Daniel drained of strength. He was confronted, he says, by a heavenly being – colourful as jewels, bright as lightning – with limbs like polished bronze and sounding like a sports arena crowd in full voice.

The vision which came in answer to his prayers to understand a dream about war, had been delayed because of conflict between the unauthorised angel or demon influencing Persian affairs and Yahweh's official spiritual administration, he was told. As in Daniel's previous clairvoyant insights into future politics, it appears to foreshorten time and combine specific detail about coming empires and rulers with more general truths and principles concerning Yahweh's governance of the world.

He was told that four more kings of Persia will arise, that the empire will be parcelled out, and a 'king of the south' will become strong. After battles between him and the 'king of the north' he will take charge of Daniel's home country, Judah, after which there will be more battles.

God's ultimate plans to renew his creation include raising the dead. At that 'end time' Michael, the protecting angel of Yahweh's people, will flex his spiritual muscles during a period of great trauma and conflict. Daniel's request for further elucidation was refused. The meaning of the vision is apparently only to be discerned with hindsight as an encouragement to Yahweh's people that all along he has been overseeing the

This winged ibex from Persia featured as a decorative handle on a large ceremonial jar, now lost, and dating from c. 500 BC.

---

apparently inexplicable events of evil regimes.

(Daniel 10–12)

Fast Facts
c. 550–535 BC

Samos, Greece, c. 550 BC: The influence of a Greek artist living on Samos is spreading far and wide. Theodorus helped to introduce the art of clay modelling and bronze- and iron-casting. In the past he has made a silver bowl for Croesus of Lydia and an emerald seal for Polycrates. He was called in by the Ephesians when they were building the temple of Artemis (Diana) and advised them to include a layer of charcoal in the foundations. He also designed an assembly hall in Sparta.

Rome, c. 545 BC: A new temple to Diana (Artemis) has been opened, on the Aventine Hill overlooking the Tiber, with the sacrifice of a heifer. King Servius Tullius hopes by it to fulfil prophecies that imperial power will belong to the nation which sacrificed this particular heifer to Diana. The goddess's temple in Ephesus is famed for being a focus of co-operation, and the Romans hope that theirs will have a similar effect.

Cyprus, c. 545 BC: Kings of this Mediterranean island have submitted voluntarily to King Cyrus of Persia. According to the deal, the Cypriots may continue their own culture undisturbed, by paying regular tribute-taxes and keeping their army on standby as reservists for Cyrus' use.

Miletus, c. 540 BC: The first man to draw a map of the earth has died at his home in Miletus at the age of 70. Anaximander made the unprecedented statement that the universe is subject to a rule of law, and he believed in a form of evolution.

Corsica, c. 535 BC: The Greek Phocaeans narrowly won a victory against the combined fleets of the Etruscans and the Carthaginians. But they lost so many ships that they had to abandon their colony at Alalia (Aleria) on the eastern coast of Corsica and they have gone to Velia, an Ionian colony in southern Italy. After the battle the Carthaginians and Etruscans stoned their prisoners to death. They had started the battle because they have been getting increasingly alarmed by the last 40 years of Greek colonisation of the Corsican coast. They were worried that the Greeks might encroach upon Sardinia, which is now in Carthaginian hands. The Etruscans have founded a colony on Corsica.

India, c. 530 BC: Cyrus of Persia has added Gandhara, in the north-west of the Ganges Plain and a rich source of gold, to the Persian empire. Its capital, Taxila, has a reputation as a centre of intellectual excellence. Among its eminent citizens are Panini, who wrote a grammar of the Indian language Sanskrit, and Atreya, a famous botanist and medic.

Babylonia, c. 530 BC: Writing forms are changing due to influences from other nations. Cuneiform (wedge-shaped) script, used for centuries, is being replaced by the Aramaic alphabet with 22 characters. Cuneiform is written by pressing a piece of bone or stone into soft clay or by chiselling into stone, and can go in any direction. The alphabet letters are written horizontally from right to left and top to bottom.

Father is daughter's third victim

Rome, 535 BC

The king of Rome, Servius Tullius, who had reigned for 44 years, has been murdered by order of his daughter Tullia and her husband Tarquin. Tullia had already made Tarquin murder his first wife and her husband so that she could marry him and become queen.

Servius was killed by a group of hired assassins, who left him lying mutilated in the street. Tullia then drove her carriage over her father's body, spattering his blood over her clothes. Blood from the chariot wheels was brought into her house.

Tarquin, known as 'the proud', is now king. An unpopular man, whose claim to the throne is based solely on violence, he rules by fear. Justifiably concerned for his own life, he employs bodyguards and sentences to death anyone of whom he is suspicious. He is the first king to break the established practice of consulting the Senate on matters of public business.

Despot survives allied attack

Samos, c. 526 BC

The Spartans' and Corinthians' joint attack on the Aegean island of Samos has failed after a 40-day siege.

Spartan enmity towards Samos is focussed on the despot, Polycrates, who allegedly stole a Spartan bowl and corslet from a ship at sea. Samos is supporting Persia and has sent a fleet to aid Cambyses' attack on Egypt. The Corinthians also bear grudges against Polycrates.

Polycrates seized the tyranny of Samos in 540, and has built it into a naval power and a place of patronage for poets and artists. He has imported sheep and other farm animals to the island, and has been completing impressive building work, including a temple of Hera and a tunnelled aqueduct.

Fifth-century poets celebrated the victory of Samos over their enemies.

Spartan system controls its young

Sparta, c. 525 BC

The powerful city-state of Sparta, which has exercised considerable influence over the Aegean area for almost 200 years, controls its population rigorously. It has little concept of 'family'.

Sons are regarded as the property of the state rather than of a family, and selective breeding is practised. If a man admires another's wife he may get his permission to have children by her.

When a boy is born his father takes him to the elders for inspection. If they consider him strong and in good health they allow the father to rear him, otherwise the baby must be exposed and left on the hillside. At the age of seven the boy is taken away from his family and educated by the state until he is 21. The state education is headed by the Warden of the Boys, helped by 'whip-bearers' to enforce discipline. Boys learn reading and writing, obedience, bodily fitness and military courage.

The might and determination of the Spartan soldiers of old is clearly visible today.

At the age of 12, life becomes harsher and more military. Athletic contests play a major part and normally have some religious context. Instead of wearing a tunic, each boy is given one cloak to last the whole year. He sleeps on a rush bed, and undergoes harsh endurance tests, such as being left out in the countryside and fending for him-self, stealing food to survive. If he is caught he is whipped. When a young Spartan marries, he lives in the barracks and may only visit his wife in secret.

Girls also undergo physical training, but live at home and do not follow such a strict regime. Unlike other Greek women, they are not expected to stay indoors but can go out in public and, like the boys, are required to dress simply and skimpily. They have a reputation for toughness and for performing gymnastic feats with men.

Despite their harsh regime, Spartans live in fear of the helots, slaves bonded to property. In one treacherous act, 2,000 helots were singled out for honour in battle, and then murdered. Spartan secret police are said to carry out summary executions of helots in rural areas.

Long-term view

China, c. 525 BC

The Wu people, who live in the lower (seaward end) reaches of the great Yangtze River, now dominate the whole of south-east China following their defeat of inland neighbours, Ch'u. Wu's warships fill the region's canal network.

But the long-term views of chief adviser Wu Tze-hsiu cost him his life. A former Ch'u driven by a desire for vengeance, and the real power behind the Wu throne, he had told the king to leave Ch'u alone after the victory and to concentrate on the rising power of of the Yueh (Viet) to the south. He demonstrated his lack of confidence in the king by sending his son north to live in the Ch'i region.

His final request was that a catalpa tree (with heart-shaped leaves and trumpet-shaped flowers) should be planted on his grave. When it was fully grown, he ordered, his body should be exhumed, his eyes plucked out and placed on the gate of the Wu capital 'so that I may see the victorious entry of the king of Yueh'.

King burns in his grave

Memphis, 525 BC

Persia has conquered Egypt religiously as well as militarily. Psammetichus III, who has been king for less than a year, led his army to defeat at Pelusium, the eastern entrance into Egypt. The young king fled to Memphis but has been captured and taken to the Persian capital, Susa.

The Persians, under King Cambyses II, ran like terrorists through Memphis, pulling the embalmed body of the late King Amasis out of his tomb and desecrating it before setting it alight. Cambyses himself stabbed the sacred Apis bull of Memphis and it died. Worship of the Apis bull was initiated by an Egyptian king more than 2,000 years ago, and carried great symbolic value.

The Persians had been advised by a mercenary general named Phanes, who was serving in Halicarnassus, to use the bedouin to guide them across the desert. He paid heavily for his betrayal; his sons, who were still in Egypt, had their throats slit over a large bowl. When they were dead, the Egyptians added water and wine to the blood and guts and made every mercenary soldier drink it.

Cambyses has taken the Egyptian throne name of Mesutire which means 'Offspring of Re'. However, he has no plans to take up residence in Egypt, but will rule it from Susa, leaving a Persian satrap in charge.

Mercenaries recruited for African legion

Carthage, c. 530 BC

The army of this north African city-state is to be made up of mercenaries and troops from neighbouring countries and paid for by the public purse. All generals will be Carthaginians, however.

The largest contingent is of Libyans from Tunisia, who are believed to be able to withstand the heat better than others. With their own preference for swift raids and ambushes they are being used as light infantry.

Mercenaries from as far away as Numidia and Spain are also being recruited. The Spanish are valued especially for guerrilla warfare and their willingness to follow any leader; back home they have no concept of society larger than the clan. Balearic islanders have signed on too, asking for their wages to be paid in women rather than in silver and gold.

Until recently, the Carthaginian army has been conscripted from a citizen levy, but the city is too small to police the widely-scattered Phoenician empire it is now protecting. The use of foreigners releases citizens to concentrate on trade, their main source of income. It is the first known city-state to attempt to rule an empire.

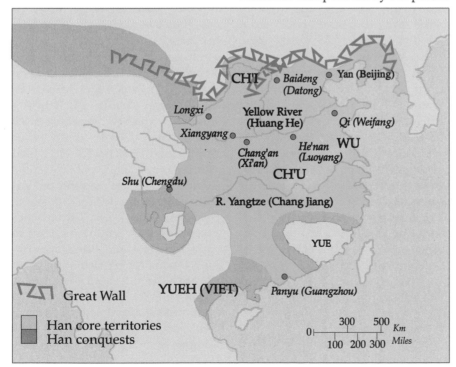

CH'I — Baideng (Datong) — Yan (Beijing) — Longxi — Yellow River (Huang He) — Qi (Weifang) — Xiangyang — He'nan (Luoyang) — WU — Chang'an (Xi'an) — CH'U — Shu (Chengdu) — R. Yangtze (Chang Jiang) — YUE — YUEH (VIET) — Panyu (Guangzhou)

Great Wall
Han core territories
Han conquests

300   500 Km
0
100 200 300 Miles

The Han state is formed of many regions and peoples whose rivalries continue despite a now unified government. Regional identity remains strong.

Darius imposes order across the empire

Babylon, c. 520 BC

Darius the Mede, the fourth king of Babylon in two years, has taken stringent steps to restore order. He has placed his son, Xerxes, in charge of the city, where he himself spends the winter, and has begun to build a new palace.

Darius has established a new Persian capital at Persepolis, and has divided the whole empire into 20 satrapies with a uniform system of law and order. He has also designed a road system across the empire and is digging a canal from the Nile to the Red Sea.

Babylon has been the scene of several coups since Darius took over the Persian empire from Cam-

byses, who died on his way home from conquering Egypt in 521 BC. Nebuchadnezzar II had claimed to be the heir of Nabonidus and took the throne for a few days before being killed in battle.

The yet another keen nationalist, Nebuchadnezzar III, seized the throne, despite Darius' general leniency towards the city. After 10 weeks the Persian forces entered Babylon, impaled the 'king' and his supporters on poles in public places, and then pillaged some royal tombs and sacked the city.

The archers of Darius the Mede in solemn procession are celebrated in the typical glazed brick on the walls of the great palace of Babylon.

'Temple will grow like corn' says Jewish prophet

Jerusalem, December 520 BC

On the very day the winter crops were planted, the latest in the line of Judean prophets, Haggai, has claimed that Yahweh will reverse, not only the recent poor and diseased harvests, but also the blighted rebuilding programme of the Jerusalem temple.

In a barbed message to Jewish

The Menorah, the seven-branched chandelier, has become the symbol of Jewish worship, and even of the nation. This larger-than-life version stands in Jerusalem in front of the Knesset.

leaders, his third in four months, he claims that God will bless them 'from this day on', and that the temple will sprout like corn. But he also rebukes the returned exiles for offering Yahweh 'defiled worship'.

The people here have clearly lost their vision and enthusiasm for rebuilding the city and its temple, a task which first inspired them to make the long trek back from Babylon some 15 years ago. Although they have now established proper settlements, life continues to be harsh and difficult. Some had even rationalised the difficulties as God's guidance that the time was not yet right for the rebuilding work to resume.

But since late August Haggai, recently joined by fellow prophet Zechariah, has been urging them to take up their trowels again. 'This isn't the time to be living in panelled houses while the house of Yahweh lies in ruins,' he says. He suggests that the recent poor harvests were God's warnings that he was being dangerously neglected.

Zechariah, a priest, has brought a similar message but with a stronger urge to repentance. Having considered both messages, Joshua the

high priest and Zerubbabel the Jewish civic leader, initiated a fresh start on the temple.

The task seems as daunting as ever, but Haggai, who is believed to be elderly and may have witnessed the destruction of Solomon's temple by the Babylonians, has added further encouragement. 'It may not seem anything now,' he said, 'but one day God's glory here will be greater than ever.'

His encouragement echoes the theme of a psalm currently used on Jewish feast days which alludes to the Persian habit of stuffing honoured guests' mouths with sweetmeats: 'Open wide your mouth and I will fill it,' God promises.

Once again, the rebuilding has been dogged by local opposition. The Persian governor Tattenai has questioned the right of the Jews to build a temple and has written to King Darius for confirmation of an alleged edict issued by Cyrus authorising the work. Meanwhile, the builders are slowly stretching their plumblines, shifting the overgrown rubble, and setting one good stone upon another.

(Ezra 4:24–5:17; Haggai 1–2; Zechariah 1:1–6; cf. Psalm 81:10)

Horse plays bring sweet smell of success

Jerusalem, February 519 BC

The sweet, but as yet faint, smell of success is wafting over the Jewish community following fresh reassurance that Yahweh will enable them to complete their task of rebuilding the temple. It comes from a series of striking dreams given to the young priest Zechariah who was born in Babylon and was still a child when the first exiles returned to Jerusalem.

He claims that he saw heavenly cavalry, including a man on a red horse who reported that the world was at peace. Standing in a grove of myrtle trees, the message seemed to be that Judah, like the myrtle, was lowly but having been crushed would release the delicate perfume of divine favour into the world.

In seven visions Zechariah saw four destroyers of Judah represented as horns which were themselves destroyed. Jerusalem will be protected and refined by Yahweh as if a wall of fire burned around it, he believes. He saw Joshua, the high priest, being plucked from the fire like a burning stick and clothed in the purity of Yahweh himself, an image which suggests God's forgiveness and renewal.

Joshua and Zerubbabel, the civic leader, were singled out in another dream and warned pointedly of pride, by being told the temple rebuilding would be accomplished, 'not by human power but by God's Spirit'. No one was to despise the small beginnings to the project, the prophet's heavenly guide added.

In his final visions, which pointed to spiritual renewal, Zechariah saw a huge flying scroll, 9 m (30 ft) long and half as wide, covered with curses from God on wrongdoers. A woman representing evil popped out of a measuring basket but was pushed back in and shipped to Babylon. And angelic horses galloped to the ends of the earth with the reassurance that Yahweh controlled all things, that the temple would be rebuilt, and a righteous leader or 'branch' would emerge as a future leader.

(Zechariah 1:7–6:15)

Temple re-opens after 70-year closure

Jerusalem, spring 516 BC

After almost 70 years since its destruction by Nebuchadnezzar in 587, the refurbished temple of Yahweh in Jerusalem is again open for business.

A joyful dedication ceremony has been followed by the Passover celebration, the Jews' chief annual religious festival. There has been a note of relief, too, that a dark chapter in the nation's religious and political history has come to an end.

The scale of the dedication was miniscule compared with former occasions, but for the small and impoverished community the ritual slaughter of 100 bulls, 200 rams and 400 lambs was indeed a sacrifice. When the original temple was opened by Solomon at the peak of Israel's prosperity, 22,000 oxen and 120,000 sheep were given to Yahweh, and the cull barely dented the nation's livestock count.

The work on the temple has taken about 20 years to complete, although there was a 15-year period in which little was attempted. The restart was prompted by the prophets Haggai and Zechariah in 520, and ratified by a personal letter from the Persian king Darius.

Local officials of the king had consulted him concerning the legality of the building, which could have been interpreted as a nationalistic act and a snub to Persian patronage. The original decree of Cyrus authorising the building was unearthed in the royal archives, and Darius sanctioned payment for the work and for worship services from the state treasury. He asked that prayers and sacrifices be offered for his and the empire's well-being.

(Ezra 6)

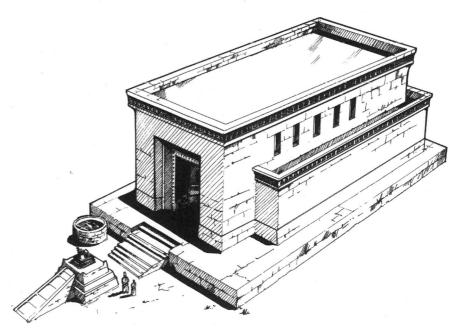

The second temple, completed in 516 BC, 70 years after the destruction of the original.

Brutus avenges rape of Lucretia

Rome, 509 BC

The rape of Roman noblewoman Lucretia which resulted in her needless suicide, has been so thoroughly avenged that 100 years of Etruscan rule in the city has been brought to an end and a new system of government has been inaugurated.

Charismatic leader Brutus who led the revolt, and Lucretia's husband, Collatinus, have been elected as consuls (magistrates) to govern the city in place of King Tarquin who has fled to exile in Caere.

A typical male debate over drinks concerning whose wife was the most virtuous led to a prank which provoked the rape. Sextus Tarquinius, the king's son, was with Collatinus and others who decided to surprise their wives by returning home unexpectedly to see what the women were doing. Most were found partying; Lucretia was at home spinning by lamplight. She celebrated her 'victory' by welcoming her husband and his friends in for dinner.

Sextus returned to the house

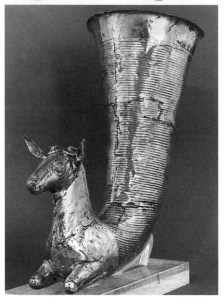

A solid silver rhyton, or ceremonial drinking cup.

some days later and was treated hospitably by Lucretia as a friend of her husband. But he begged to have sex with her, and when she refused he threatened to kill her and her slave, laying their bodies together to create the impression of an adulterous relationship.

After she had been raped, Lucretia wrote to her father and

husband in great distress, and insisted that despite her innocence she should die for having been violated. She then stabbed herself. Brutus, who had accompanied Collatinus to his home, removed the knife from her heart and swore vengeance, urging the people to take up arms against the king and his family.

The army turned to him as a man, and Sextus fled to the Etruscan city of Galbi for asylum. But the people there already hated him for his previous record of robbery and violence, and assassinated him.

The new consuls are to be given equal powers. They command the army, settle disputes and are responsible for the collection of taxes and for public expenditure. They will be advised by the Senate, a council of over 100 patricians (heads of families). The people themselves will elect the consuls, and agree declarations of war or peace, new taxes and laws. Dictatorship will be allowed for a period of no more than six months in the event of a national emergency.

Locust plague shows God is hopping mad

Judah, c. 500 BC

A devastating plague of locusts which have chomped their way through vines and vegetables, figs and cornfields, is being likened to a terrifying 'day of the Lord' when judgement will be executed on the whole earth.

The author of the graphic description is named as Joel, but precisely where and even when he lived remains a mystery. Some observers see a parallel in his phrasing with that of earlier prophets, Isaiah and Amos, and suggest he is foretelling a military invasion such as that by the Assyrians or Babylonians. But he is also rumoured to have been close to the more recent prophets, Haggai and Zechariah.

The short text is being interpreted

as a timeless warning to Yahweh's people to clean up their act, to be ready for the judgement day and hopeful of the restoration which will follow it.

Locust invasions are frequent and unpredictable throughout the Near East. The protein-rich insects are the only 'creeping things' which the Jews are allowed to eat. They are carried on winds, turning the sky dark and filling the air with noise from their beating wings and munching jaws. The wingless infants, often called hoppers, can also do great damage to crops.

Yahweh's day of reckoning will be equally destructive, says Joel. On a day 'of darkness and gloom' God's innumerable angelic army will swarm across the earth. The

only response to such a prospect is heart-felt repentance with prayer and fasting, the rending of contrite hearts rather than the tearing of ritual garments.

But Yahweh is not merely angry at human sins. He is also 'gracious and compassionate' and he will repay his people for 'the years the locusts have eaten' during their spiritual exile.

Leaping ahead to the long-term future, Joel forecasts a spectacular outpouring of God's Spirit causing young and old to prophesy and see visions. The renewal of God's people is figured in the image of a peaceful Jerusalem becoming the source of a stream watering the desert.

(Joel 1–3)

Celtic influence felt throughout Britain

Maiden Castle in Dorset is a typical hill fort occupied for centuries. Its four concentric earthen walls certainly acted as a solid deterrent to any intruder.

England, c. 500 BC

The Celts who have spread into England have introduced a new field system based on terraces dug into hillsides, making previously uncultivated land productive.

Using iron spades and ploughs, farmers dig a metre or two into the slope and throw the soil downhill to produce a level strip. A dozen or so strips are made on each hillside, divided by low walls ridged with stone. Grain produced from the fields is stored in underground pits.

The Celts, who originated in the Upper Danube area of Germany in the thirteenth century BC, have been spreading across Europe since about 900 BC. They have made significant innovations in agriculture and cultivate their fields with ox-drawn ploughs instead of hand implements. They practise animal husbandry and in England breed long-horned sheep, short-horned oxen and pigs.

Another of their less welcome traits is also taking root: tribal warfare. English tribes are separated by forests and their suspicion of each other is leading increasingly to outbreaks of hostility.

Consequently, more hill forts are being built as tribes strengthen their defences. Many forts are simple structures with a single barrier following the line of a hill, but others, such as Hengistbury Head in Hampshire with two banks and ditches, are more complex. They are mostly built to withstand short-term raids rather than the kind of long-term sieges which are employed in the Near East.

English life varies as much as its weather. At Plumpton Plain in the southern area of Sussex, for example, people live in oval enclosures surrounded by banks and connected by roads. Their round wattle and daub huts are thatched, and they cultivate land in square, ridged fields. But a short distance away on the coast near Worthing, however, people use Celtic agricultural methods.

In the Orkney Islands in the far north of Britain, people live in rectangular huts 5 m (18 ft) long built of stone and roofed with animal skins. They have no windows and the entrance is less than a metre high. A square hearth in the centre of the hut is used for cooking, whereas in southern England all cooking is done outside.

The Britons smelt bronze using goat-skin bellows, and cast it using the 'lost wax' method. A clay model is covered with wax and another layer of clay. The molten bronze is poured into the top, melting the wax which runs out through the bottom. When the metal has cooled, the layers of clay are removed.

Beastly statue

Noves, southern France, c. 500 BC

A grotesque statue of a mythical beast, the tarasque, dominates this hilltop town. Its paws are perched on human heads, and a human limb hangs from its mouth.

Another town in the area has a shrine with a pile of human heads sculpted on it, and human skulls nailed to the walls, and yet another has a shrine with hollows for human skulls and a vulture perched over the door.

Although these images are relatively rare, hilltop towns are increasingly common in the area south of the central plateau. Most are small and exist on agriculture, but have developed trade with Greek colonies such as Marseilles on the Mediterranean coast.

Fast Facts c. 530–517 BC

Babylon, 530 BC: King Cyrus has been killed in battle. His body has been carried back to his homeland. He is succeeded by his son, Cambyses II.

Persia, c. 517 BC: The Persian treasury has issued the first-ever imperial currency. It is made of gold, and called the 'daric'. Local currencies continue to be used, and are normally made of silver, but there is no common standard or measure between satrapies. Treasurers will only accept coined silver according to the metallic weight of the pure silver content. In trade, either the coins are weighed or the buyer and vendor simply agree what type of coin will be used.

Delphi, Greece, c. 510 BC: Since fire destroyed the temple at Delphi in 548, a new temple has been designed and built on the same site. The Athenian family of Alcmaeonidae, living in exile at Delphi, has donated considerable funds. The new building includes a polygonal wall below the temple. Delphi is situated about 600 m (2,000 ft) above the Gulf of Corinth on the lower southern slopes of Mt Parnassus.

New religions grow in strength

Several new religions have begun, or have begun to attract, wider attention in recent decades. Among the most significant are two from India and two from China.

Pauper prince sees the light

Nepal, c. 530 BC

A religious teacher in Nepal is sending his followers, who include people from all classes in society, to spread teachings that go against the orthodox, sacrificial and priest-dominated religion of the day.

The teachings of Buddha spread rapidly into China, where, according to tradition, a fat smiling monk called Budai is said to have introduced his teachings to China. Budai has since been venerated in China as a re-incarnation of the Buddha.

Siddharta Gautama's religion has no god. It centres on the law of 'karma' – that is, that we reap in the next life what we sow in this one. He says there are four noble truths: all existence is suffering; the source of suffering is human desire; it is possible for suffering to cease (this state of freedom is called 'nirvana'). The way to achieve nirvana is by an 'eightfold path' including wisdom, ethical conduct, and mental discipline such as meditation.

Siddharta Gautama's followers call him the Buddha, or enlightened one. He was born c. 563 as a prince and sheltered from all outside influences. He was educated in arts and sciences, married and had a harem of beautiful dancing women, but still felt dissatisfied with life. At the age of 29 he left his family and became a homeless wanderer in search for something better.

At first he lived in extremely harsh conditions, studying under a number of religious teachers. But he decided this was futile and turned instead to contemplation. While contemplating underneath a fig tree one day, he became fully 'enlightened', preached his first sermon to a group of five ascetics in the Deer Park near Sarnath, and began to gather a following.

Initially he said women should be excluded from his community because they are dangerous and embody greed for life, but his stepmother and cousin have now persuaded him to admit them. He has done so grudgingly, saying that now his teachings will last only 500 years instead of 1000.

The naked truth

India, c. 500 BC

People in India are confused about what to believe. The traditional structure of society is changing, with tribal divisions in society giving way to regional kingdoms and small republics. None of them have much political influence because they are small, but there is an atmosphere of change afoot.

Another new religion, also with no god, is gaining ground in eastern India under the teaching of its founder, Jina Vardhamana Mahavira, or the 'Great Hero'. He comes from the same martial clan as the Buddha and was a prince in Kundagrama, near Patna in Bihar.

He abandoned his wife and daughter to live as an ascetic for 12 years, before he too became enlightened. He is now teaching by the Ganges, where he walks naked, having discarded the simple loincloth he used to wear because it was too cumbersome.

He has organised his followers into a community of men and women, all of whom are following his discipline of detachment from possessions. Some wear loincloths, others go naked. His teachings, known collectively as Jainism, are not completely new, being based largely on traditions that date back hundreds of years and that have always been disputed by the Brahmins, as they do not accord with the Vedas (Hindu texts).

Like Buddha, Mahavira rejects the traditional sacrificial religion of the day and the caste system. He says every living being has a soul, and that the whole universe is made up of infinite and individual souls. So all life is to be respected, and all sacrifice is condemned.

The goal of Jainism is to enable the soul to escape from the body and thus from the cycle of rebirth and to live in moksha, or eternal joy. The soul's escape is brought about by ascetic discipline and meditation.

Forest reflections

Contemplative and ascetic 'forest teachers' in India are composing treatises on the Vedas, the sacred books of sacred Hindu literature. The Upanishads, or the 'sitting-near', so called because disciples sit near their teachers, are written in Sanskrit and explore the nature of reality. They teach that there is one supreme being, the Brahman, who is the ground of the universe and exists everywhere. Brahman will be found as a person searches for their true self, or atman. The teachers function within the traditional religious heritage and are opposed to Buddhism and Jainism.

Master class for morality

China, c. 500 BC

Two teachers are gaining large followings of disciples in China with different philosophies. One of them, Confucius or 'Kung the Master', gave up his job with the government in the dukedom of Lu to become a full-time itinerant teacher.

He teaches that people should love each other and respect their parents and forebears. One of the supreme goals in life, he says, is the aquisition of humanity, a quality which shows itself in open-mindedness, compassion and unselfishness. It takes self-discipline and contemplation to achieve this, and the person who does so is known as a zhun-zi, or 'person of superior merit'.

Being a zhun-zi is far more important than social status, which he says is immaterial. However, his teaching is generally aimed at members of his own governing class, and he hopes to produce loyal, sincere and honourable men for leading the state.

Confucius is also concerned about maintaining the natural balance and order of the universe by observing customs and rituals. He says everything has its proper place and that past, present and future all exist continuously. Filial piety therefore includes looking after the needs of ancestors in the afterlife.

Confucius is more a moral teacher than a religious one, although the Chinese rarely distinguish between them. He is not opposed to religion – although some of his rivals say that he is – so much as indifferent to it. His concern is with human society rather than with the spiritual world of invisible powers.

Lao Tzu

Mystical way is simplicity

China, c. 500 BC

The other up and coming philosophy is that of Lao Tzu, who is teaching a life of inner contemplation and mystical union with nature. He says everyone should give up the quest for wisdom and learning in favour of absolute simplicity and wu-wei – or letting things take their natural course.

His teaching is known as the Tao Te Ching or 'The Way and its Power'. It is not a practical philosophy, concerned with the mystical rather than the actual.

Whereas Confucius teaches that people should aim to become wise servants of humanity, Lao Tzu says people should aim to become immortal, in perpetual harmony with the Tao (the Way, i.e. the primal, all-controlling force in the universe). There is no other means of attaining peace of mind, happiness or an end to strife, he claims. The Tao itself defies description and the whole philosophy stresses negative attributes such as the value of a bowl being the empty space that it encloses.

Little is known about Lao Tzu himself and many rumours circulate, including one that he was in the womb for over sixty years and was born with snow-white hair and able to speak.

Confucius

Confucius he say...

He who governs by moral excellence may be compared to the pole-star, which abides in its place while all other stars bow towards it.

The higher type of man is not a machine.

He who keeps on reviewing his old and acquiring new knowledge may become a teacher of others.

The wise man is informed in what is right. The inferior man is informed in what will pay.

A man without virtue cannot abide long in adversity, nor can he abide long in happiness.

A gentleman never contends in anything he does – except perhaps in archery.

The wise man desires to be slow to speak but quick to act.

To err and not reform may indeed be called error.

He who demands much from himself and little from others will avoid resentment.

The noble man upholds his dignity without striving for it. He is sociable without entering any clique.

A wise man is not distressed that people do not know him; he is distressed at his own lack of ability.

Plebeians on strike over patrician rule

Rome, 494 BC

The plebs effectively put the future of Rome at stake today when they went on strike in protest at the way they are treated by the patricians. They withdrew from city life and camped on the Sacred Mount, 5 km (3 miles) outside Rome, and refused to return.

The plebs make up 90 per cent of the city's population and Rome depends on them for their fighting skills. They were complaining of being kept from positions of authority. Many have been pushed into slavery by increasingly draconian tax demands. They may be charged 12 per cent interest on money that they borrow and there is no compensation when crops fail, even if the farmer has been called to war by the state.

The plebs were appeased by the magistrate Menenius, who reportedly told the parable of the belly and the limbs in which parts of the body resented the fact that they had to provide everything for the belly, which just sat there doing nothing except receiving food. So they plotted that the hand should carry no food to the mouth and the teeth refuse to chew.

But far from subduing the belly, they found themselves wasting away. They thus discovered that far from doing nothing, the belly was nourishing and sustaining the life of every member of the body. Menenius explained that a nation needs to function together to survive, and that the plebs' revolt would damage not only the state but also themselves.

It was agreed that the plebeians should be allowed to have two elected 'Tribunes of the Plebs' with power to protect them against the magistrates and to prevent the introduction of new anti-plebeian legislation. Rome breathes a sigh of relief.

Runaway victory at battle for Marathon

Marathon, Greece, 492 BC

The Athenians have won a runaway victory over the Persians at Marathon, a city commanding a large fertile plain a few kilometres north of the capital. The Persians lost 6,400 men to the Athenians' 192.

temples and deported the people. They were met at the city by a small but angry and extremely determined army of Athenians who unexpectedly and thoroughly defeated them. Athens now rivals Sparta in military prestige.

The direct route between Marathon and Athens runs through this hilly region. The original messenger's accomplishment was significant and inspiring. His feat is now commemorated in countless marathon races today covering the same distance, though most often over less arduous territory.

According to unconfirmed reports, a runner from Marathon taking the message of victory to Athens collapsed and died as he cried, 'We have been victorious!'

The battle was part of a strategic campaign by the Persians to take the Aegean islands and from them to conquer mainland Greece. The Persians have never forgiven the Athenians for their part in the burning of Sardis in 498. King Darius even has a slave with the special duty of saying to him each day, 'Master, remember the Athenians'.

They arrived at Marathon fresh from the successful sacking of Eretria, where they had burned

Women's luck saves Rome

Rome, 491 BC

The mother, wife and young children of the maverick leader Coriolanus have saved Rome from war by a last-minute intervention in which they pleaded successfully with their man to withdraw his rebel army threatening the city.

The Romans have built a temple to record the women's triumph, called Fortuna Muliebris, the Luck of the Women. Coriolanus, however, has disappeared without trace amid rumours that he has been murdered.

Coriolanus, who was born Marcius Gaius, earned his nickname by what he claimed was a one-man victory over the Volscians at the city of Corioli two years ago. The Roman army, in which he fought, was caught unawares by a Volscian force outside the city. Marcius Gaius took a small group into the city, flung a blazing firebrand into a residential area and caused mayhem. The Roman army then took the city.

But last year the hero turned fugitive and sought refuge among those he had destroyed, when he was condemned by the Senate for his opposition to the distribution of corn to the plebs.

He has been a bitter opponent of the new plebeian tribunes from the moment they were appointed, describing them as 'upstarts from the mob'.

He dismissed a summons against him, and the Senate decided that the risk of sacrificing one of its own members was less than the risk of a popular uprising.

A superb frieze of warriors astride mythical beasts, from Madhya Pradesh, c. 400 BC. King Bambisara recruited a large well-equipped standing army. Its exploits have been celebrated in verse and in stone.

Indian king starved to death

Magadha (Bihar), c. 490 BC
The king of the Lower Ganges region of Magadha, Bimbisara, has been starved to death by his son and heir, Ajatasatra, who is now king.

Bimbisara was an innovative and energetic king. He introduced the concept of a standing army funded from taxation of politically organised territories. He annexed his eastern neighbour, Anga, in order to acquire the trade routes to the Ganges Delta and the sea.

He was sympathetic to the teachings of the Buddha, Siddharta Gautama, but still performed the many sacrifices considered necessary for a king. He leaves 500 wives and will be ceremonially-

buried according to local custom.

The dead often have two funerals in India. At the initial one the body is buried or exposed, and then months later, when the flesh has decayed, the bones are taken to their final resting place. There are various types of grave: large urns buried in small pits; pit circle graves, where the body is exposed on a wooden bier in a large open pit; and cist graves, usually made of slabs of granite with portholes.

The cists may be deeply buried in pits, partly buried or built on the surface of a rock. Grave goods are placed around the cists, and include pottery bowls and waterpots, copper, bronze, stone and sometimes gold objects, carnelian and other beads, and iron weapons. A man was recently buried together with an iron trident that had a wrought-iron buffalo fixed to the shaft. The buffalo is associated with Yama, the god of death, and the buffalo demon was killed with a trident by the wife of the god Siva.

Fast Facts c. 500–480 BC

Babylon, c. 500 BC: Astronomers have calculated the length of the solar year which is 11 days longer than the Mesopotamian lunar year. To synchronise the two calendars, an extra month has to be added every three years, but to spread the effect a cyclic scheme, yet to be implemented, suggests inter-persing seven extra months within a period of 19 years.

Germany, c. 500 BC: The River Mosel has become the main trade route for goods between the Mediterranean and Belgium, Champagne and central Germany. Beaked flagons and two-handled cups are among the more common import items, but more exotic and less common trade goods are silks from Luxembourg and gold from Schwarzenbach. The Mosel area is not very fertile and depends for its wealth on its resources of copper, gold and iron.

Ephesus, c. 500 BC: The Greek philosopher Heraclitus has deposited a treatise in the temple of Artemis (Diana). The nominal head of the Greek throne, who gave the kingship to his brother, says that fire is the origin of all things, that everything changes and that the universe is an unending battle of opposites held in check by an unchanging law. God is a union of opposites.

Ionia, Greece, c. 494 BC: The Persians are claiming victory after nearly five years at war with the Ionian cities. They crushed the Greek ships at Lade and sacked the city of Miletus. The original revolt was led by Aristogoras of Miletus heading an Ionian league which issued coins as a sign of unity. It was supported by the Athenians who donated 20 ships, but who later abandoned the cause. The Persians have also captured Salamis in Cyprus and the cities of the Hellespont. Hatred for them runs deep.

Sparta, Greece, c. 490 BC: King Cleomenes has killed himself amid rumours that he was insane. He made up in adventure what he lacked in foresight, and his reign was peppered with quarrels with his colleague, King Demaratus. Cleomenes even bribed the Delphic oracle to declare Demaratus illegitimate so that he could depose him, but the plot was uncovered and he fled. He is succeeded by his half-brother, Leonidas.

Sicily, c. 485 BC: Aristocrats in Syracuse in south-west Sicily who were overthrown by a democratic revolution a few years ago, have appealed to Gelon, the tyrant of several colonies in the north-east of the island to help them regain power. He met their request without striking a single blow, such is his reputation and influence. He has now moved his seat of power there, making the most of Syracuse's magnificent harbour and easy access to Greece. He now virtually controls the entire island.

Sundried temple

Moche, Peru, c. 490 BC

More than 130 million sundried bricks have been used to construct the 'Pyramid of the Sun' at Moche on the coast of northern Peru. It stands over 40 m (131 ft) high, with a rectangular base 365 m (400 yds)

A sacred gold puma, with a human face depicted on its tongue.

by 137 m (150 yds). The people were commanded to build it by their religious leaders.

Large urban settlements are developing throughout Peru, notably in the valleys of Rimac, Moche, Chancay and Nazca. Many are in centres of maize cultivation. Peruvians have learned metalwork techniques from Colombia and are making golden rings, crowns, spoons and jewellery.

Central Peru has a distinctive art style similar to that of the Olmecs in the Amazon Basin. The Chavin people of Peru, like the Olmecs, worship the sky, earth and water deities which they represent in stone images. The stonework is abstract and minutely executed, and depicts symbols including the harpy eagle, cayman and cats. Priests in Peru have an ever-increasing secular influence.

Africa is plundered in gold rush fever

Carthage, north Africa, c. 485

Two leading members of the ruling Magonid family, Hanno and Himilco, have returned from separate expeditions to explore and enforce control of major trade routes.

Hanno sailed along the 'gold coast' of west Africa, with 60 fifty-oared ships, 30,000 men and women, and a plentiful supply of food. He claims to have founded many colonies and dedicated several sanctuaries.

He encountered savages who 'wore the skins of wild beasts and threw stones at us'. The last island they visited 'was full of women with hairy bodies, called by our interpreters "gorillas" ' (probably pygmies), who 'climbed up steep rocks and pelted us with stones. However, we captured three women who bit and scratched their captors. We killed them and flayed them and brought their skins back to Carthage.'

Himilco, believed to be Hanno's brother, explored the Atlantic coast of Spain, Portugal and France to gain control of the tin routes along the edge of Europe. He reached northern Brittany where his ships were entangled in weeds, shallows, thick mists and sea-monsters.

Carthage is becoming a major city-state and 'Carthaginian' is almost synonymous with 'merchant'. In Morocco the traders have developed a unique system of barter. They lay their goods out on the beach, then return to their ships and send a smoke signal. Seeing the smoke, the Moroccans come to the beach and leave gold in exchange for the goods and then they too go away, without touching the goods.

The Carthaginians return, exam-ine the gold and, if they judge it to be sufficient, they pick it up and sail away. If not, they leave it and wait in their ships until the natives have laid down enough to satisfy them. The gold they collect is usually worth far more than the goods, but the Moroccans have more use for the goods than they do for the gold, lacking the means to exploit it.

A gold pectoral disc, from the later Ahanti tribe from the Gold Coast in West Africa, the traditional source for centuries for African gold.

Black art

India, c. 490 BC

Indian craftsmen from the Punjab to the Lower Ganges are now coating their pottery in polished black gloss. Until now, they have painted it grey.

The high-quality clay is turned into a smooth paste before being worked on turntables. It is then coated with an alkali which acts as a flux when the pot is fired at carefully-controlled temperatures.

The craftsmen, who are famed for their fine work, decorate shallow tray-shaped bowls and deep bowls with a sharp angle between the sides and bottom with rows of dots, spiral chains, concentric circles and criss-cross lines.

Two major fleets sunk by deception

Two Greek ships as seen on a black figure vase, signed by Nicosthenes, potter.

Greece and Sicily, 21 September 480 BC
Superstitious sailors surely will put today's date down in the annals of nautical history as one on which battles should not be attempted. For against the odds, two major powers have been blown out of the water by the much weaker navies they attacked, who employed a mixture of guile and determination.

The Persian fleet, watched by King Xerxes, has been scuppered by the allied Greek navies in the straits between Salamis and Attica in the Aegean. And the huge Carthaginian fleet of mercenaries has been burnt out not by superior sailors but by Sicilian cavalry.

Xerxes had set up his throne on a hilltop near Salamis to watch what he believed was the foregone conclusion of a crushing victory for his ships. However, the battle was precipitated by a cunning message from the Athenian naval commander Themistocles who was afraid that his vital Peloponnesian allies would desert the cause.

He pretended to be a traitor warning Xerxes that the Greeks were about to slip away. The small Persian ships were lured into the narrow strait where they were battered to pieces by the superior Greek seamanship and heavier vessels. The Persians lost 200 ships to Greece's 40, and were further humiliated when a hoplite (slave) force wiped out the Persian foot soldiers on land.

In Sicily, a huge force of Carthaginians, Libyans, Sardinians, Corsicans and Iberians well outnumbered the troops and sailors under the Sicilian tyrant, Gelon. But he intercepted a message summoning Carthaginian cavalry to specific ships, and sent his own cavalry to them first, posing as friends.

After burning the ships, Gelon's forces attacked the Carthaginian camp, which put up little resistance and agreed to a peace treaty. It includes an indemnity payment of over 50 tonnes of silver and funding to build two temples.

Directors bank on inflation

Babylon, c. 485 BC
Directors of the Murashu Bank are laughing all the way to their own account as profits rise. But its customers are increasingly angry at the still-rising rate of inflation which is creating an air of instability. Inflation now stands at 20 per cent a year compared with 10 per cent in Nebuchadnezzar's reign.

Babylonians are also complaining that the level of taxation imposed on the city by the new Persian king Xerxes, successor to Darius, is higher than that elsewhere in the empire. Currently it supplies 30 tons of silver and 500 boys to become eunuchs each year, and provisions for the entire Persian army and court for four months.

Yet private banks are prospering, having cashed in on the fact that the former monopoly of financial and banking services offered by the religious temples has failed to meet demand. The credit system has developed from the earlier method of trading with a borrower's security and now includes direct interest charges.

The Murashu Bank is one of the largest and most diversified. It supplies food and building materials to the temples and manages the lands of Persian dignitaries. It leases land, livestock, farm implements, traction animals and even prostitutes, and it also buys booty from warriors. Recently it equipped one estate with 18 water-lifting machines, and 72 oxen to work them, for an irrigation project.

It controls vast areas of land which it leases to peasants, and is a welcome purchaser of stolen goods – booty brought home by soldiers. The temples continue to own and manage estates and provide jobs and credit, but banks now play a crucial role in the economy.

The guards of King Darius' treasury.

Wisdom literature

The story of Job

A barren tree in the Sinai Desert.

c. 490–480 BC

Jewish reflections on life, the universe and everything have become more popular – and more sophisticated – since the exile, especially with the editing and compiling of what is known as 'wisdom literature'. The category includes Proverbs, Job and Ecclesiastes, but these are not the only such works in world literature or even in Jewish literature.

Wisdom literature is the record of distilled reflection and meditation, but it makes use of literary forms that are different to those of a sermon or historical narrative. Proverbs often shock or amuse the reader into realising a profound truth. Words are put in the mouths of Job's comforters that are almost blasphemous, but the message that refutes them is seen all the more strongly for it.

In Ecclesiastes, a deep pessimism about human affairs seems to make nonsense of godly hope; but the writer shows that in the perspective of God's absolute power and love, human life has great meaning if it is lived out in the fear of God – the abiding theme of the biblical wisdom writers.

Among these writings the book of Job has a special place. Its date and authorship are unknown. It raises many philosophical and theological issues and does not supply specific answers.

Yet the book is marked by a theological sophistication in debate that justifies Job's rejection of the facile comments of his friends who do supply specific – and too easy – answers. Job's sufferings are the means by which he perceives the incomprehensible grandeur of a personal God.

Part of the book's unique role is its clear acknowledgement of the need for a mediator between God and man (e.g. 9:32–35), and the resurrection hope in 19:25–27.

Job is a wealthy and godly man, happy with his possessions and large family. But, unknown to Job, in the courts of heaven God and Satan are discussing him. Satan argues that Job's piety is only due to his good fortune; were that to change, he would certainly curse God. So God permits Satan to test his theory, and Satan proceeds to strip away Job's wealth, his children and his health. Job refuses to curse God in all this adversity.

Three friends arrive to comfort him. Each in turn argues that Job's sufferings must be because of wrong he has done, and that God is therefore punishing him justly. But Job knows that he is innocent and rejects their arguments. He appeals instead to the Almighty, who is able to answer his complaints. Surely someone can argue Job's case before God; one day he will be vindicated; if he could find God, he would argue his own case with confidence.

But a fourth friend, Elihu, now argues that Job has created his own problems by questioning the justice of God. Elihu sees Job's declaration of innocence as self-justification and his rejection of the three friends as a refusal to admit his fault. The Almighty, says Elihu, is remote from the world of human beings, and his power and justice are absolute, detached from local issues of right and wrong. God will not lower himself to answer Job's claim that he is an innocent victim. Job will never get an answer from God.

At which point, God speaks to Job directly. Elihu is wrong; God is almighty and far off, but he is also near. He will not be cross-examined by Job; indeed, he himself has some questions to ask Job. In a series of questions that seem to side-step the problems of Job, God in fact enlarges Job's understanding of God's justice. For example, if human beings cannot tame the hippopotamus and the crocodile, how can they even begin to challenge God?

Job finally realises that he has been on the wrong track. Now that he understands who God really is (instead of accepting his friends' speculations) he abandons his quest for self-justification. Such a God will act fairly even if his ways are incomprehensible to finite humanity. Job repents of his unbelief and bitterness and worships God.

God rebukes Job's 'comforters' for not having Job's integrity and willingness to search for truth. He forgives them – but only after Job has forgiven them. And God restores Job's wealth, friends and family and gives him many more years of life.

Beauty queen foils ugly minister's plot

Susa, c. 473 BC

One man's plot to exterminate the Jews throughout the Persian empire has been thwarted at the last minute by the brave intervention of Queen Esther.

The queen, who won a beauty contest to succeed the disgraced Vashti as King Xerxes' chief consort, revealed her previously secret Jewish nationality in a desperate bid to neutralise an irrevocable law perpetrated by chief minister, Haman. It decreed that all Jews were to be killed on 7 March 473.

The saga began when Xerxes gave a banquet at his capital, Susa, as part of an extravagant exhibition of wealth and power. Queen Vashti refused to be paraded before the guests. As a result she was banished from court and the search began for a suitable successor. Esther, a cousin of Mordecai, a Jew captured by Nebuchadnezzar and now living in Susa and present at

The banquet of Ahasuerus with Haman and Esther, as imagined by Rembrandt.

court, was chosen. Mordecai forbade Esther to reveal her Jewish background.

Two royal officers conspired to assassinate Xerxes. Mordecai discovered the plot, reported it to Esther, who told the king. The conspirators were hanged.

Later, the king honoured his chief minister Haman and commanded that everybody pay homage to him. Mordecai refused, and a furious Haman persuaded the king to issue an edict to kill all the Jews in Susa on the grounds that they refuse to obey the king. Mordecai pleaded with Esther to use her influence. She risked appearing unsummoned before the king (a capital offence), while Mordecai and the Jews fasted and prayed. As a result of her intervention Haman was hanged and Mordecai given his post.

Esther persuaded the king to issue a second decree, permitting the Jews to defend themselves, which effectively revoked the first decree. On the day set for the assassination of the Jews, they in their turn assassinated Haman's sons and others; 300 enemies of the Jews died on that day. Esther and Mordecai decreed that the day should be observed by Jews from henceforward as the Feast of Purim.

The film-maker D.W.Griffiths used the latest archaeological discoveries in his epic portrayal of the Babylonian court in his 1916 film *Intolerance*. The decor was based on German excavations in Babylon from 1905 to 1914, though the dress appears highly imaginative.

Editor's note

c. 460 BC

The story of Esther now being written contains no mention of the name of God, nor of any specific religious observances associated with the worship of Yahweh. The author perhaps deliberately omits reference to God to emphasise and imply Yahweh's sovereignty in what would otherwise be chance coincidence, human wiles and lucky opportunities.

The book's historical content and its description of Persian court life is detailed and authentic. The author probably a Jew living in Persia, as he emphasises the origins of Purim, one of the great Jewish festivals.

(Esther 1–10)

Mathematician to be counted out

Southern Italy, c. 480 BC

The mathematician Pythagoras has died in southern Italy. He discovered the mathematical precepts behind musical intervals and was the first Greek to recognise that the morning and evening stars were identical, something the Babylonians have known for 1,500 years.

Using the knowledge that Egyptian engineers had constructed a right-angled triangle with sides in ratio 3:4:5, he formulated his theory of the square of the hypotenuse equalling the sum of the squares of the other two sides, which enabled him to construct a right-angled triangle of any size.

Born c. 560 in Samos, he emigrated from there in 531, probably to get away from Polycrates. A devotee of Apollo, he founded a religious society, open equally to men and women, involving a strict discipline of purity, silence, self-examination and celibacy.

He said it was possible to reach back in the memory to former existences and he believed that the soul was a fallen divinity trapped inside the body as in a tomb and condemned to a cycle of reincarnation as man, animal or plant. According to him, the soul could only be released from a never-ending cycle of re-incarnation by developing the discipline and study of purity practised in his religious society.

On a firmer scientific basis, students of his school are said to have come to the conclusion that the earth is spherical and are believed to have worked out an astronomical system in which planets circulate around a central fire.

Pythagoras.

Yet, on a more speculative note, they believe that everything, including opinion, injustice and chance, is a number with a cosmic position. The universe was created when the First Unit (heaven) inhaled the infinite (or Void) and formed many groups of units or numbers.

Spartan traitor puts Athens in new League

Greece, c. 475 BC

Pausanius has been recalled to Sparta after leaked letters between him and Xerxes implicated him in a promise to betray the Greeks into Persian hands in return for a royal bride and a Greek tyrantship. He has also been wearing Persian dress and has adopted Persian habits.

The traitor had only recently been acclaimed a hero. In one year, from a base in Thrace, Pausanius had captured the strategic city of Byzantium, and liberated Miletus, Abydos and Cyzicus, as well as the Greek cities in Cyprus and the islands of Khios, Lesbos and Samos.

Because of Pausanius, the Spartans have now lost all credibility with the Ionians. Athens has been made leader of a new Delian League of city-states which does not include Sparta. With headquarters on the sacred island of Delos, the League aims to finish the war with Persia.

Each member-state has an equal vote in policy decisions and joins with a permanently-binding oath of loyalty. All are united in their supreme purpose of riding the area of Persian influence.

The Persians have suffered heavy military losses in recent years, and seem to have turned to bribery and diplomacy in their continued attempt to conquer the world.

Time to run out

Judah, c. 480 BC

Time is going to run out, but human existence will continue, according to an apocalyptic vision currently circulating. It predicts that following the sacking of Jerusalem, Yahweh will fight Israel's enemies and become king of the whole earth.

He will abolish day and night, and his life-giving power will be like a stream of water flowing across the desert from his throne in the city.

The picture is one of a series linked to the prophet Zechariah who encouraged the rebuilding of the Jerusalem temple 40 years ago. The prophecies are written in a poetic style known as a chiasmus, similar to his earlier oracles, in which ideas are repeated in a recognised sequence.

Among the themes covered are God's judgement of the nations (9:1–8; 14:16–21) and the failure of the 'shepherds' of Israel to pastor the people well (11:4–17; 13:7–9).

There are numerous memorable, but somewhat obscure, allusions including one to a great shepherd who renounces his task and is paid off with the slave price of 30 pieces of silver which he then gives away to a potter in the temple (11:8–13). Also striking is the image of a king entering Jerusalem on a donkey.

There is some discussion as to whether Zechariah was responsible for the visions, or if they have been compiled into the present poetic structure from a variety of sources.

(Zechariah 9–14)

Property laws written in stone

Cretan amphora such as these were generally used for transporting wine, oil and other liquids, principally by sea, and also for storing them.

Crete, c. 460 BC
Lawyers in the southern city of Gortyn have compiled what is believed to be one of the first civil law codes in Europe. It deals with such matters as family and property rights, rights of slaves, rape, seduction and adultery, and procedures after death or divorce.

It has been carved on 12 columns of stone which are built into a circular wall some 30 m (100 ft) in diameter. Each column is about 1.5 m (5 ft) high. Most of the 3-cm (1-in)-high letters have been chiselled by one man.

Among its provisions are the entitlement of a divorced wife to her own property. The paternity of children born out of wedlock or after divorce is to be established, although if the father rejects the child it is either brought up by the woman or exposed to die on the hillside.

Property is to pass to the nearest relatives of the deceased, including great-grandchildren. If the heirs of property cannot agree on how it should be divided, it is to be sold and the proceeds shared.

Golden spiral earrings with crested griffin-head terminals, c. 420 BC. Their craftsmanship is typical of the high standard achieved on the island.

Fast Facts
c. 485–465 BC

India, c. 483 BC: Following the death of the Buddha, Siddharta Gautama, a Great Council has been convened at Rajagha to compile a comprehensive doctrine and monastic code of Buddhism.

Cyprus, c. 481 BC: All the cities of Cyprus now have pro-Persian kings, following an abortive revolt. The pro-Persian King Gorgos of Salamis had been ousted by his pro-Greek brother, Onesilos, but after a major battle the Persians regained control and Gorgos was reinstated. Other cities, including Soloi and Palaepaphos, were besieged for several months as punishment for supporting the rebellion.

Babylon, c. 480 BC: King Xerxes of Persia has finally lost patience with Babylon and sacked the city after a siege of several months. He ordered his troops to tear down the fortifications and to burn the temples, including the great temple of Marduk and its statue. The Tower of Babel has also been pulled down. This effectively ends the very existence of the Babylonian kingdom, even within the union of the Persian empire. Xerxes has abolished the Babylonian satrapy and merged it with that of Assyria.

Boetia, Greece, c. 479 BC: The Spartans are claiming a single-handed victory against the Persians. An allied Greek force had confronted the Persians here, with neither side willing to advance, because both had received omens predicting victory to the side which remained on the defensive. Most of the Greeks withdrew to replenish their supplies, and the Persian commander charged the lone but tight Spartan ranks. He failed to break through and the lightly-armed Persians were massacred.

China, c. 476 BC: The kingdom of Yueh is becoming dominant over much of China. Although regarded as a barbarian by the northern states, Yueh is recognised by them as a hegemon because he keeps the Ch'in at bay. Recently the duke of Ch'in asked for peace when Yueh marched against him.

Cyprus, c. 475 BC: A Cypriot king has inaugurated a state health system by agreeing to pay Onasilos, a doctor, a silver talent or a piece of tax-free land in return for treating the wounded in the war against the Medes and Phoenicians.

Cyprus, c. 470 BC: A new sanctuary has been built at Meniko for the gods Tanit and Baal Hamman. A statue of Baal shows him sitting on a throne with a footstool, and with a beard and twisted ram's horns. The walls of the sanctuary are built from large slabs of granite and with mudbricks, and there is a courtyard for sacred trees. Baal Hamman means 'god of the perfumed altar and incense burner'.

Asia Minor, c. 467 BC: Statesman and soldier, Cimon of Athens, has led a fleet of 200 Athenian and allied ships into Pamphylia and Cyprus, utterly destroying a Persian army and fleet at the River Eurymedon. As a result several more Greek cities have joined the Delian League.

Persia, 465 BC: King Xerxes has been assassinated. It is believed that one of his own servants entered his bedroom and killed him. He is succeeded by his son, Artaxerxes.

c. 460–445 BC

No guard but bullion train stays on track

Jerusalem, August 458 BC

A large consignment of gold and silver has safely avoided the attentions of the robber barons during a 4-month, 1,450-km (900-mile)-journey from Babylon to Jerusalem.

The treasure, a gift from King Artaxerxes for the worship of Yahweh, was carried in a human train of more than 1,700 people, the first major migration to Judah for half a century. Many were relatives of people already in the city.

Led by the widely-respected priest and teacher, Ezra, they had refused the king's offer of an armed guard as they walked across the fertile crescent of northern Mesopotamia.

It was a bold act of faith in Yahweh's protection, by a devout group which had spent three days in prayer and fasting before setting out in April from the Ahava Canal where they had gathered.

Ezra carried personal letters from Artaxerxes authorising the expedition and ordering Persian officials in Judah to provide wine, oil, wheat, salt and gold and silver for the temple officers, who were also granted tax exemption.

It is said that Ezra has been personally commanded to teach the law of Yahweh and to mete out traditional punishments on people who do not obey it.

(Ezra 7,8; cf. 2:2–60)

A procession from the royal palace at Persepolis, started by Darius and completed by Artaxerxes, showing delegations from 23 different lands bearing tribute.

Priest presides over mass divorce

Jerusalem, December 458 BC

The divorce courts will be jammed over the next few months as a covenant agreement by Jewish leaders which orders the dissolution of all racially-mixed marriages is put into effect.

Jews have repopulated Jerusalem and its satellite villages over the past 80 years and hundreds have intermarried with people from local tribes and races. Some of the non-Jews are descendants of people brought into the area when Babylonian king Nebuchadnezzar mixed an ethnic cocktail in his conquered territories.

Jewish religious law clearly prohibits such liaisons, largely because of the perceived risk of spiritual compromise with the religious and social customs of partners from other cultures.

The entire population was summoned for an emotional open-air meeting in cold and wet weather in Jerusalem. Ezra, the recently returned priest, taught the Law of Moses before the crowds agreed to the drastic measure. However, unlike some past prophets, Ezra had not pointed out the people's error; their leaders spotted it first and sought the priest's advice.

Ezra prayed to Yahweh in considerable anguish when he heard of the number of mixed marriages that were taking place. The mass divorce was suggested by the leaders as a way of obeying the law and averting Yahweh's wrath.

Local courts appointed by Ezra will decide the cases, a process which is likely to take time. The displaced women and children will probably return to their own families and lands. Most tribes in the region have close kinship ties and few needy relatives are likely to be denied shelter. It is possible that some foreign families might stay on in a relationship of benevolent slavery.

(Ezra 9,10)

Fast Facts
c. 465–445 BC

Sparta, Greece, 464 BC: A massive earthquake has claimed hundreds of lives, and the helots have taken advantage of the chaos to revolt. The Spartans called on Athens for help, but mistrust between the two cities is so deeply entrenched that the Athenians were sent back without reason, and relationships have become even more sour. The helots have set up a guerilla base on Mount Ithome.

Egypt, c. 454 BC: The Egyptians are once more under Persian control after a series of revolts over the past 30 years. Artaxerxes has executed Inaros of Heliopolis, the son of King Psammaetichus III, and the leader of the latest revolt.

Rome, 445 BC: Plebeians and patricians can now marry each other under new laws which mitigate Rome's social divisions. The legislation is limited in that patrician fathers have absolute power over their offspring and so must approve any proposal of marriage. Many patricians still believe that involvement with plebeians is a social pollutant which angers the gods.

Stop – men working!

Jerusalem, c. 455 BC

Rebuilding work in Jerusalem has been halted by the Persian king Artaxerxes following a protest petition delivered to him in Susa.

Persian officials, afraid of a renewed rebellion in a city famed for its antagonism to foreign rulers, had informed the king that the walls were being restored. They claimed that a fortified city would refuse to pay taxes, and asked him to stop the work. The fears may have been evoked by the religious and nationalistic revival inspired by the teaching of the priest Ezra who had returned to the city under the sponsorship of Artaxerxes.

In response, the king ordered the work to cease, but he has left himself the option of authorising repairs at a future date. However, some officials have burned the gates and damaged the walls as a gesture of their disapproval.

The first group to return in 538 began to rebuild the temple, which was dedicated in 516. Some opposition to the subsequent wall repairs was also recorded during the reign of Xerxes, the previous king, in about 486, but nothing was done to stop what appeared to be a sporadic and poorly-organised activity.

(Ezra 4:7–23; Nehemiah 1:3)

Roman censors to keep tabs

Rome, 443 BC

The new office of censor has been created to maintain the official list of Roman citizens (the census). Two censors, who will hold office for 18 months, will have power to take legal proceedings against anyone guilty of withholding information about himself, his family or property. They will also compile lists of those eligible or fit for cavalry service. The state census normally takes place annually in the spring at a building in the Field of Mars.

Rome swallows Law Commission's tablets

The Via Sacra with the Roman Forum beyond.

Rome, c. 450 BC

Romans have opted for a new government in which a commission of 10 leading men will govern the country with justice. The plebeians have agreed to give up their tribunes and the patricians their consuls.

The commission's first task was to draw up a code of law, which has now been published on 12 wooden tablets in the Forum. The code aims to collect together the most important rules of existing law, knowledge of which has so far been confined to the priests, and to reduce patrician privileges. The Twelve Tablets contain laws concerning private, public, criminal and religious behaviour.

The exercise has not been without controversy and scandal. The first commission of 10 men resigned after its chairman, Appius Claudius, was consumed with lust for the daughter of a plebeian. She was killed by her father in order to save her from Claudius' designs. The replacements were hostile to the plebeians and so caused considerable resentment.

The Twelve Tablets recognise a plebeian form of marriage by simple consent of both parties; equal division of inheritance between sons and daughters; easier emancipation of slaves; freedom of association in guilds and colleges as long as they respect the law, and of contract between Romans.

The rate of interest charged by money lenders is limited to 10 per cent (with a penalty fine of four times as much money as has been paid for those who charge more). The death penalty is sanctioned for traitors, judges who accept bribes and anyone convicted of taking part in incantations against a citizen. A fair trial and right of appeal is guaranteed, and the People's Assembly (not the Senate or magistrates) will have the last word in disputes.

c. 445–430 BC

Wine-taster puts fizz into city as walls grow

Jerusalem, October 445 BC

For the past two months Jerusalem has been fizzing like an uncorked flask of new wine, as work parties have turned it into a walled city again after it had lain like a ruined village for 140 years.

Credit for the remarkably quick transformation is being given to the new governor of Jerusalem, former top Persian official Nehemiah, who gave up his job as king's wine-taster in Susa to supervise the reconstruction of his home city.

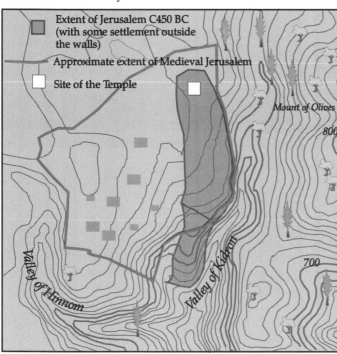

Having rebuilt the walls of Jerusalem following the foundations of the old city walls, it quickly became apparant that the fortified area was too small to contain all those who had returned from Babylon along with those who wanted to live in the renewed capital. Settlements spread rapidly to the west of the fortified town. It must also be remembered that the rebuilding of the wall took years due to opposition from Persian officials.

But despite his royal authority and letters of commendation, he was opposed by several local tribal officials and survived two clumsy assassination plots.

Nehemiah arrived in Jerusalem earlier this year without disclosing the hidden agenda behind his mission. Having made a thorough survey of the perimeter wall, which had been breached in several places, and of the gates which had all been destroyed, he called together the civic and religious leaders who agreed to his plan for the repair work. He organised the community into work gangs, each responsible for a section of the wall.

Opposition from Tobiah and Sanballat, leaders of non-Jewish tribes in the region, began with negative propaganda and accusations of rebellion, later degenerating into threats of violence. To counter the propaganda, Nehemiah has reiterated his belief that the task authorised by Artaxerxes was in fact promoted by the supreme God of heaven.

To counter the violence, he armed half his workforce and posted guards at all strategic points. Because the workers were scattered all around the walls, he also arranged for alarms to be given in the event of attack so that reinforcements could be summoned quickly. The show of defensive strength was sufficient to deter would-be aggressors.

But two attempts were made to lure the governor into secret talks with local tribespeople, to intimi-date and probably kill him. Nehemiah refused to be drawn, however, and also categorically condemned as a lie a document circulated by Sanballat stating that the governor was about to proclaim himself king of Jerusalem and hence leader of a rebellion.

Internal unrest added to his burdens. Workers impoverished by heavy Persian taxes had been forced to sell their children into slave-service with fellow Jews, and others had been reduced to the status of tenant farmers by being forced to sell their ancestral lands.

Nehemiah ordered all interest payments to fellow Jews to cease, as decreed in their religious laws. He also set an example by not using the full quota of food (provided by taxation) to which he was entitled as governor.

(Nehemiah 2:11–7:3)

Jews' new governor is given to prayer and pragmatism

Jerusalem, October 445 BC

'Only the best is good enough for God' seems to be the driving motive behind the work of Jerusalem's new governor, Nehemiah. He has given the same meticulous care to the dedication ceremony for the newly-repaired city wall as he did to the repairs themselves.

And having brought veteran priest Ezra out of the shadows to read the Jewish law to the people, he has collaborated in the revival of the ancient Festival of Booths and a period of national repentance.

The carefully-orchestrated dedication, which included two processions moving in opposite directions around the top of the wall, was led by choirs and bands brought in from surrounding villages. Along the way priests and Levites, having first observed their own cleansing rituals, performed rites of purification and dedication for the people, the wall and its gates.

Nehemiah walked at the head of one procession, and Ezra at the other. Both met at the temple for a final celebration which included animal sacrifices to Yahweh.

It was the culmination of several weeks of religious fervour. Ezra had been reading the law regularly in public. There was a mass confession of sin followed by a prayer of corporate rededication at a major assembly led by Levites who recited Yahweh's great acts and faithfulness in the past. The Festival of Booths, in which the people camp out in temporary shelters for seven days a year as a reminder of their ancestors' desert wanderings, was rediscovered and reinstated during the reading of the law.

Then in a ceremony similar to former renewals of the covenant between Yahweh and his people, over 80 leaders, headed by Nehemiah, signed a solemn declaration to obey Yahweh's laws. It singled out current abuses for special mention, including marrying foreign wives, trading on the Sabbath, and failing to accept financial responsibility for the temple officers and services.

Nehemiah's religious faith is well known as the force behind his administrative flair. He is on record as attributing his appointment by the king as a direct answer to prayer. During conflicts with opponents of the repair work he frequently resorted to prayer at the same time as creating pragmatic solutions to the problems he encountered, including arming some of the workers against threats of violence.

He has also enabled Jerusalem to function commercially as a city again by allocating a tenth of the families of returned exiles to live in it. Most had settled in the villages outside. It is a measure of the respect he has earned that the plan, which involved considerable upheaval, was accepted.

(Nehemiah 8–12)

Star prophet to make a final comeback?

The story of the prophet Elijah being taken up in the chariot of fire rooted itself firmly in the popular imagination. This woodcut from the medieval Nuremberg Bible combines both chariot and whirlwind.

Jerusalem, c. 432 BC

Elijah, the charismatic prophet who withstood evil kings 400 years ago, is to return to earth before the final 'day of the Lord', according to a prophecy now circulating.

Whether it is Elijah in a resurrected form, or a figure exhibiting the same kind of ministry and character as the man who called down fire from heaven, is not stated. Jews do not believe in any form of reincarnation, although a belief in resurrection after death or at the last day is becoming accepted.

The startling prediction is made by an apparently anonymous prophet being dubbed 'Malachi', or 'God's messenger'. It comes in the context of a sweeping condemnation of current religious practice.

Couched in the form of an imaginary dispute between Yahweh and his people, it echoes (or perhaps precipitated) many of the concerns which have been addressed by the Persian-born governor of Jerusalem, Nehemiah.

It claims that imperfect (and thus unacceptable) sacrifices are being offered in the temple, and that the statutory tithes and offerings for the temple services are not being paid. Morality is also criticised; marriages between Jews and people of other tribes or races are said to be against Yahweh's will, as is easy divorce from legitimate partners.

The priests and Levites take the brunt of the criticism, although the prophecy is not without hope. Even though the day of the Lord will be one of judgement, a future messenger (perhaps another reference to Elijah) will come like a refiner's fire. Renewed obedience, it suggests, will be rewarded with Yahweh's bountiful provision.

Those who honour God, it adds, will bask in the warm goodness of 'the sun of righteousness' which will rise 'with healing in its wings'.

(Malachi 1–4)

Olympic poet dies

Boetia, c. 438 BC

Pindar, a lyric poet from Boetia, has died at the age of 80. He had patrons all over Greece, and is particularly famous for his odes celebrating victories at the Olympic Games. Many of his odes are written as choral hymns and have a religious or moral significance. He was skilled in portraying deep emotion, and had a sense of joy and honour.

Common people turned to stone

The Parthenon today is one of the best recognised symbols of the ancient world, as it still dominates the Athenian skyline.

Athens, 432 BC

Ordinary people have been honoured alongside the gods in the temple of Athena Parthenos (the maiden) which has now been completed. Begun in 447, the temple and cult were dedicated in 438, but work on sculptures such as the 'Elgin marbles' has continued until now.

General Pericles paid for the Parthenon out of funds from the Delian League. He commissioned a temple, which incorporated the latest styles in architecture and decoration, to house the great cult statue.

On it, human figures have been depicted for the first time as moving objects, showing anatomi-cal detail, unlike the former stiff, stylized art. The figures are carved onto slabs of marble which are fixed under the eaves of the temple to make a continuous decorative frieze. The marble was brought at great expense from the quarries of Mount Pentelicus a few miles north-east of Athens.

Rather than depicting mythical and religious themes with gods and heroes, the frieze portrays ordinary Athenian people. It shows the procession of the Panathenic festival, when people bring a specially-woven robe to clothe the sacred olive-wood statue of Athena, and includes young men stooping to tie up their sandals and young girls carrying the robe.

The temple itself, measuring 70 by 30 m (228 by 100 ft), was designed by architects Ictinus and Callicrates working under the overall direction of master sculptor Phidias. It has 8 columns instead of the usual 6 at each end and 17 along the sides. The inner structure has a porch with 6 columns at each end.

Phidias, who is in his late 50s, personally sculpted the colossal gold and ivory statue of Athena. He was also responsible, some 20 years ago, for the 9-m (30-ft)-high statue of Athena which is a landmark for sailors at Sunium. He is currently exiled from Athens for political reasons and is working on gold and ivory statue of Zeus at Olympia, which he sees as the crowning acheivement of his career.

Detail from the Parthenon: the 'Elgin marbles' housed in the British Museum. This is Dionysus, from the east pediment of the Parthenon.

Fast Facts c. 432–404 BC

Athens, 432 BC: Metan of Athens has produced a calendar based on a 19-year cycle, having discovered that the solar year is 365 and five-nineteenths of a day long. Each Greek city-state has its own calendar, and at present the Athenians are showing little interest in a new or unified one.

Athens, 430 BC: An outbreak of plague threatens the Athenian defensive strategy in the war against Peloponnesian states headed by Sparta which began last year. Leading Athenian, Pericles, had persuaded the population to move inside the 'long walls' built in 461 to connect Athens with the sea and make the city an isolated fortress. Protected from land assault, the Athenians can focus the war on their more superior naval strength. But the plague is killing many and Pericles has been driven from office.

Rhodes, 408 BC: A town planner from Miletus, Hippodamus, has been chosen to design a new capital. The three city-states on the island of Rhodes have united to build a new capital, to be called Rhodos. Hippodamus believes the ideal population for a city is 10,000 and has designed several other settlements including Piraeus and Thurii.

Athens, April 404 BC: Athens has lost the Peloponnesian war which has lasted almost 30 years. The last Athenian fleet was destroyed at Hellespont. Athens had won several victories during the war but internal political divisions and naval subsidies from Persia for the Peloponnesians weakened the Athenian effort.

Old broom sweeps city clean

Jerusalem, c. 430 BC

Persian-appointed governor of Jerusalem, Nehemiah, a devout Jew, has returned to the city for a second term of office with the same religious zeal he demonstrated when he first arrived in Jerusalem some 15 years ago.

Having been recalled to Susa by Artaxerxes after 12 years in Jerusalem, the king's chief wine-taster found the religious flavour had become unpalatable when he reappeared in the city he had previously skilfully restored to law and order.

In a swift purge, he ordered his former opponent, Tobiah, an Ammonite and a regional governor who was sympathetic to the worship of Yahweh, out of the comfortable suite of rooms he had possessed in the temple with the connivance of the high priest, Eliashib.

Nehemiah then restored the traditional food and money offerings for the temple services and staff, and banned Sabbath-trading. He also rebuked a number of people, including members of priestly families, who had married foreign women and bred children who could not speak the language of Judah.

However, he opted for shaming the miscreants by pulling out their hair rather than initiating a mass divorce as Ezra the priest had done in similar circumstances a couple of decades ago.

His actions seem to have been at least a partial fulfilment of a contemporary prophecy that God's messenger would come to the city 'like a refiner and purifier of silver' to cleanse the Levites and the offerings of the people.

(Nehemiah 13; cf. Malachi 3:1–4)

This old white-washed house, in a village near Elephantine, is typical of the dried-mud houses common to Egypt.

Egyptian Jews want own shrine again

Elephantine, Egypt, c. 407 BC

A century after the Jewish temple in Jerusalem was restored, Jews at this military garrison on the Nile's first cataract are appealing for authority and funding to rebuild theirs.

The temple was destroyed in 410 by the local Egyptian governor Widrang and priests of the god Khnub in an act of political rebellion rather than religious persecution, while Persian governor Arsames was out of the country.

Elephantine is a Persian military town defending the southern borders of Egypt and is staffed by Hebrew mercenaries. There are also Hebrew units at Thebes, Ahydos and Memphis.

The Jews, who were authorised by Darius II to hold the Feast of Unleavened Bread in Egypt for the first time in 419, have written to Bagoas, the Persian governor in Jerusalem who has replaced Nehemiah, and to Persians in Samaria, asking for help.

Earlier requests to the temple leaders in Jerusalem appear to have

Village on the Nile, near Elephantine.

fallen on deaf ears. Jewish law prohibits any sanctuary for the sacrificial worship of Yahweh outside the capital city. The Elephantine Jews, who have been settled in Egypt for perhaps two centuries, are also known to be unorthodox in their theology. They include other divine beings associated with Yahweh, such as Ishumbethel, Anath-bethel and Herembethel, in their worship.

Unlike the Jews who were exiled in Babylon, none of this community appears to have any desire to return to the homeland.

The letter to Bagoas, written in the usual Aramaic language of international diplomacy, recounts how the original temple had five gateways, bronze doors and a cedar roof. The authors claim it was burned down illegally and that its gold artefacts were stolen. They say they have worn sackcloth, the garment of mourning, ever since. Widrang, they report, has been killed.

A memorandum of consent to the rebuilding has been sent by Bagoas, but it is unclear how and when it could be funded.

Halls of fame lose big names

Several well-known writers and patrons of the arts have died over the past half century. But their influence is likely to live on.

Tragic pioneer: Aeschylus

c. 525–456 BC

Poet and tragedian, Aeschylus, who died in Gela in Sicily, will be remembered for his frequent triumphs in the dramatic competitions at the city Dionysia, where he competed for the tragic prize with artists such as Sophocles and Euripides.

Traditionally, Greek theatres, where possible, were carved into the sides of a hill. But none more dramatically than this well-preserved example in Delphi.

monument at Gela records his fighting at the battle of Marathon but makes no mention of his poetry. Some say that he composed the elegy himself.

Greek tragedy developed out of the odes sung by choruses in honour of Dionysus. The scenes of a tragedy consist of set speeches and sometimes a little dialogue, often between actor and the chorus. The scenes are separated by long choral odes of lyric poetry.

Actor and chorus present human beings, or maybe divine beings in human form. In the satyrical plays, the chorus is disguised as satyrs (lusty woodland spirits), mainly human in form but with characteristics of horses and goats and wearing the phallus. The plays represent ancient legends which are grotesque or can easily be made so.

Actors and chorus wear masks to show their changes of identity, but as these preclude the conveying of emotion by changes of expression, all the drama is in the words they speak.

Violence is never shown on stage: murders, battles and sackings of cities are reported by a messenger. Stories are taken from heroic legends already well known to audiences. The poet's skill is judged by the nobility of his moral and metaphysical conclusions and the beauty of his lyrics.

Like theirs, his work is a study in human character and history, but also of the relation of human beings to the powers above that control the universe, and the relations of those powers to human destiny.

He wrote the *Persae*, a history of the Persian wars in 472. In 458 he wrote his most famous trilogy for the competition: the *Oresteia*, consisting of *Agamemnon*, *Choephorae* and *Eumenides*. It tells the story of the murder of Agamemnon by his wife, Clytemnestra, and the ensuing vengeance of their son, Orestes.

Aeschylus broke new ground by introducing a second actor in the performance of plays. Religious and patriotic to the last, his

Comic observer: Aristophanes

c. 450–385 BC

The comedies of dramatist Aristophanes usually centred on topical political themes, and he shamelessly satirized public figures. His favourite targets were politicians, poets, musicians, scientists and intellectuals.

His likeable characters express the feelings of people who object to the cultural changes forced upon them and want to be left in peace to enjoy traditional ways and pleasures, and they are normally ingenious in getting what they want. He had an especially keen eye for the absurd.

His best-known works include *The Birds*, a fantasy about birds being persuaded by an Athenian to build a city in the clouds, from which comes the phrase 'cloud cuckoo land'.

In *The Frogs*, Diony-sus goes to Hades to bring back the recently-dead Euripides, judges a contest for the poetry throne in Hades and brings back Aeschylus instead. In *Lysistrata* all the women of Greece compel the men to make peace by going on a sex strike.

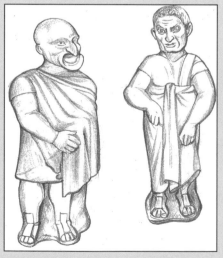

Terracotta models of comic actors, one bald, the other a rustic.

Fact finder: Herodotus

c. 484–420 BC

The Greek historian Herodotus wrote a history and explanation of the Persian Wars and a history of the Persian empire. His work was well respected in Greece, although it was parodied by comic writer Aristophanes. He was the first historian to collect his information logically, and to test its reliability before setting it down in a vivid narrative.

He travelled widely to such places as Samos, southern Italy, Egypt, Gaza, Tyre, Babylon and the north Aegean – all, he said, in order 'to seek more information'. He questioned ceaselessly with a childlike curiosity and fascination. He was more interested in facts than in ideas, having a simple world view in which the gods uphold the righteous and punish wrong-doers, and people are responsible for their own actions.

Herodotus: the father of history.

Arts patron: Pericles

c. 495–429 BC

Athenian statesman and general, Pericles, was driven from office in 430, but was later reinstated. Within six months he succumbed to the plague. He achieved eminence because of his incorruptible nature, his tremendous rhetorical skill and

Pericles, the incorruptible Athenian general.

his generally sound policies.

His public life began as one of the state prosecutors in the ostracism of Cimon in 461. He had an active career in both domestic politics and military affairs. Some of his most significant contributions were the introduction of payment for jurors (so that anyone could be one) and a state allowance enabling poor citizens to go to the theatre.

He introduced cleruchies, Greek colonies where settlers keep their Athenian citizenship rather than becoming independent, which have greatly strengthened the growing Athenian empire. He also commissioned the building of the Parthenon, and was close to leading artists and philosophers such as Sophocles, Anaxagoras and Phidias.

As a person he was reserved and could be arrogant. After a miserable marriage and divorce he cohabited with Aspasia, a highly-intelligent woman who taught rhetoric and was a friend of Socrates. She was often accused of influencing Pericles too much, and was the frequent butt of immorality jokes.

Oedipus complex: Sophocles

c. 496–406 BC

The writer Sophocles was the son of a rich industrialist. He attracted attention because of his good looks and expertise in music and dance. He wrote 123 plays and won 24

victories in contests.

His most famous works are the *Antigone* (441), the *Ajax* (pre-441) and *Oedipus Rex* (430). This last play was about the son of the king of Thebes who, having solved the riddle of the Sphinx, unwittingly killed his father and married his mother. When he realised what he had done he gouged his eyes out and his mother hanged herself.

He introduced a third actor and also scene-painting into dramatic performance. Both developments have made an enormous impact in the range of dramatic possibilities.

Sophocles was well liked as a man for his kindness and easy-going nature; furthermore he played an active role in the life of the state and was imperial treasurer in 443. He was a priest of the healing god Halon, and he founded a literary club.

Comedy plots are usually fantastic but set in the context of contemporary situations. They often follow the formula of hostility, contest and reconciliation. Prominent people are sometimes vilified, ridiculed and parodied, and religion is treated with extreme irreverence. There is no limit to sexual and lavatorial humour. Actors wear grotesque masks.

Antisocial passion: Euripides

c. 486–406 BC

The tragedian Euripides who died at the age of 80 in Macedonia, came from a rich family but had a reputation for being antisocial. He wrote in solitude in a cave at Salamis. He first won the tragedy contest at the Dionysia in 441, and wrote 92 plays. He is best known for *Electra* (417), the *Medea* (431), *Hippolytus*, *Trojan Women* and the *Bacchae*.

He portrayed irrational states of mind with innovative skill and was interested in the pyschology of women as much as men. He was particularly attracted to stories of violent and dissolute passion.

Uneasy peace returns to Greece

Athens, 403 BC

The uneasy peace that has followed the 27-year struggle between city-states Athens and Sparta – the victor after crushing the Athenian fleet and virtually starving Athens into surrender – has been restored.

The victorious Spartan League under Lysander, the gifted admiral/statesman, instituted a system of local tyrannies called decarchies throughout its conquered territories.

The Assembly in Athens was led by the 'Thirty Tyrants', who were installed under Spartan direction and who immediately launched a vicious campaign of terror against the last traces of democracy. For the past year a Spartan garrison in the Acropolis has crushed all resistance; moderate democrats still call for the return of democracy.

Former Athenian democratic leaders have found support in Thebes where Thrasybulus has been in exile. Last winter he led a successful counter-attack against the Thirty Tyrants, defeating them and laying siege to Athens. Lysander responded by blockading Piraeus, which Thrasybulus had conquered.

Lysander, however, has been the victim of a coup at home and has been replaced by Agesilaus, who embarked on a reconciliation programme for Athens. The Thirty and their successors are among the few excluded from a general amnesty.

There has been restraint on both

A typical view in the Peloponnese – olive groves covering the hillsides and reaching down to the deep blue sea, with islands beyond.

sides, the constitution has been revised, and it seems that the moderate voice of democracy has triumphed over the forces of anarchy and repression.

Admiral's plan scuppered as revolt fails

Sparta, 400 BC

Lysander has made what some consider to be a conspicuously misjudged bid to regain power. The admiral-statesman who led Sparta to victory, only to be deposed by his peers has been cultivating the good will of Cyrus the Younger of Persia, satrap of Ionia.

The Spartan admiral encouraged Cyrus to revolt against his brother Artaxerxes II, who has ruled Persia since the death of Darius. Lysander urged Cyrus to hire a large mercenary army and has backed the revolt by supplying extra troops.

Last year, Cyrus moved against his brother, but in the first battle of the campaign, at Cunaxa near the Euphrates, he was defeated and killed. Ten thousand Greek reinforcements escaped through Armenia, led by 33-year-old Xenophon.

The escapers formed a mobile city-state with assemblies and elections. Fighting the Kurds along the way, they greeted the sight of the sea with the victorious cry 'Thalassa!' Some 6,000 made it all the way home.

The consequences have been disastrous for the Greek world. Cyrus' successor, Tissaphernes, is no friend to Greece and has levied punitive taxes on a number of Greek cities. Now these cities have applied to Sparta for help, and an army has been despatched to the region where a deteriorating military situation looks increasingly ominous.

Fast Facts c. 400–380 BC

Thrace, Greece, c. 400 BC: The historian Thucydides has died aged about 60. He regarded Athenian leader Pericles with an almost fanatical respect and reconstructed many of the politician's speeches in his work. Writing in an old-fashioned poetic style he analysed the causes of the Peloponnesian war in painstaking detail. His history of the war filled eight books but was still unfinished when he died.

Veii, 396 BC: The fall of Veii has marked the beginning of the end for Etruscan culture in Italy. As Sparta gains dominance in the Greek world, another power is also rapidly gaining influence in the Mediterranean: Rome.

Vesali, India, c. 383 BC: A second Buddhist council has been held to review decisions passed at the first one.

Larissa, northern Greece, c. 380 BC: The physician Hippocrates has died at an old age. A small man originating from Cos, he will be remembered as the personification of the ideal doctor and the founder of the science of medicine. He taught that nature has its own healing powers and that diseases are closely connected with the environment. He is reported to have said that if food is not digested, air is excreted from the remnants which then invades the body and causes disease.

Socrates acts as his own executioner

Athens, 399 BC

The Greek philosopher Socrates always more interested in questions of moral conduct than in speculation about natural world order, has committed suicide, following a death sentence imposed on him for

A good example of classical Greek art at its height is this life-size bronze statue of Poseidon.

'corrupting morals'. His friends made an elaborate plan to enable him to escape into exile, but he refused to take part and after 30 days drank a fatal dose of hemlock.

One of the brightest sons of a city out of which he rarely travelled, Socrates was also one of the best-known Athenians of his day. A sculptor and soldier before becoming a brilliant thinker–scholar, his mastery of philosophical discourse and logical thought soon made him a sought-after teacher.

He had a number of disciples in Athens, one of the brightest being the up-and-coming Plato.

He was an opponent of the Sophist school of rhetoric, and encouraged his students to question and argue rigorously. His philosophical approach was to make enquiries based on feigned ignorance, a technique known as Socratic irony.

As a person he was well-liked and kindly, known for his good sense of humour as well as for his immense intellectual ability. People came to him from far and wide for help with intellectual problems and questions. He was physically strong, seemingly indifferent to comfort and had a great capacity for endurance which marked his final days.

He followed customary religious observances but is thought to have applied his cross-examining method of criticism to popular religious belief. He is said to have occasionally experienced a divine sign that guided the course of his action, but he never divulged exactly what form the experiences took.

Socrates was considered to be an outstandingly courageous individual, twice opposing the state on moral grounds. His death was by his own hand, in obedience to the sentence of death that had been passed upon him after the court had condemned him both for encouraging young people to abandon worship of the gods and pursue inner enlightenment, and for 'corrupting youth'.

Socrates seems to have had a death wish. He might have avoided the death penalty had he not bravely (if rashly) stood up to the court, and decided to obey the law even when he was its victim, as well as declining the efforts of his friends to secure his escape.

A portrait of the philosopher Socrates, taken from an early Greek bust.

Sparta and Persia redraw the map

Sparta, c. 397 BC

The small but potentially inflammable conflict in the Corinthian region has been settled in a way that is not going to win any of the protagonists much popularity.

After mixed success in war, Sparta has made an alliance with Persia that has resulted in radical changes to the political map.

Under this 'Peace of Antalcidas', the whole west coast of Asia Minor has been given to Persia, and the city-states of Greece have been given autonomy. This arrangement destroys several confederations of city-states and breaks up the coalitions and alliances which Athens had been cultivating as the first steps towards regaining an empire.

It is a politician's peace not supported by decisive victory in battle, and it is a fragile one. Yet it has enabled Sparta to concentrate on extending its control of the Greek peninsula.

Athens in the meantime has been quietly re-establishing alliances and making politically valuable friends throughout Greece and beyond.

Greece and Persia join forces to sink Spartans

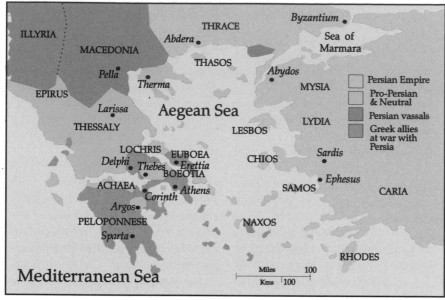

Greece was never a single force to be reckoned with, but a loose federation of city-states – most often at war with each other in ever-shifting alliances. Obviously the fractured, mountainous terrain of the mainland and the countless islands in the Aegean Sea contributed to this spirit of individualism and independance.

Greece, c. 394 BC

The Athenian star is setting, and that of Sparta is in the ascendant. But not all the Greek world is yet prepared to submit to Spartan dominance. Many of the Greek states are looking to their old enemy Persia for help.

Jealousy against Sparta from

Lechaion Way in ancient Corinth.

Thebes, Corinth and Argos has increased the inherent instability of the region, and the Athenians would like revenge for their humiliating defeat. And the wealth of Persia is available to bankroll a major war against the Spartan empire.

What has provoked new hostilities is Sparta's attempt to encircle the Corinthian region by a two-pronged attack from Thessaly and the Peloponesse. The Thebans have reacted by allying with the Athenians.

Only the death of Lysander last year halted the inevitable shift to war, with the Spartans temporarily stopped and the Corinthians boosted by new support from Thessaly, which has decided to back what it regards as the winning side. Spartan commander Agesilaus has been recalled to the Corinthian region, but his arrival has done little to shift the new balance of power, while the Spartan fleet has been decisively destroyed by the Persians who have also made significant gains on land.

Sparta's long winning streak is now broken

Greece, c. 371 BC

Sparta, which so recently looked like ruling the Greek world, is now a shattered and broken force.

Drained by continuous fighting the Spartan army made its last stand at Leuctra against Thebes, and was overwhelmingly beaten. The Theban commander Epaminondas, using ingenious tactics, has ensured that Thebes takes the place of Sparta as dominant power.

Periander, the Corinthian general who opposed Lysander.

This development has been greeted with mixed feelings by other nations. Athens will never submit to being ruled by Thebes and is more likely to cast its lot in with the defeated Sparta, though militarily Sparta has nothing left.

And the grossly unequal society that Sparta has created, in which the rich become ever richer and the poor more and more destitute, is not a good seedbed in which to cultivate the fair and just society to which Athens' history predisposes it. On the other hand, the whole Theban enterprise depends on its brilliant and innovative leader, Epaminondas. It would be a brave person who bet money on the outcome.

Etruscan power now dangerously low

Veii, Italy, 396 BC

After a 10-year siege the Etruscan city of Veii has fallen to Rome. The Roman general Camillus led forces larger than any seen before in Italy. The final victory came after Roman soldiers dug underground overnight, emerging inside the temple of Juno during a premature victory sacrifice being performed by the king of Veii.

The fall of Veii reflects the increasing collapse of Etruscan power. Although the 12 Etruscan cities in Italy have formed a loose federation for religious festivals and games, they do not otherwise act together. When Veii called for help, a few cities merely allowed volunteers to go.

Veii lost popularity in the league recently by reinstating the monarchy; most other cities have abolished theirs. Veii's new king is also said to have behaved arrogantly and aggressively at the last annual meeting.

Left to struggle against the Romans on their own, the Veientines strengthened their natural defences, cutting back cliffs to make them more dangerous and erecting a rampart along the edge. But they stood no chance against the Romans who inflicted massive damage on the city. They have wiped out Veii as an independent city-state, and have taken over its patron goddess Uni and given her

Vases in various shapes were popular with the Etruscans. This bronze vase in the shape of a man's head stands 32 cm tall.

the Roman name of Juno Regina.

Rome now controls the largest territory in Latium, as well as all the traffic up the Tiber and the salt mines at Ostia. Despite the fall of Veii, the Etruscans show no sign of working more closely together.

Two hundred years ago Etruscan power was at its height. Etruscans controlled Italy from the Po Valley to Campania, and had crossed the Apennines to take over Bologna. In 540 they joined with Carthage to push the Greeks out of Corsica. In 509 the Etruscan kings were driven out of Rome during the scandal concerning the rape of Lucretia, and Rome abolished the monarchy in favour of an aristocratic republic.

In 474 an entire Etruscan fleet was destroyed by the Syracusans who then established a garrison on Ischia, cutting off the Etruscans from southern Italy and Sicily.

This delicately painted baked-clay vase is in the shape of a duck.

Goosey, goosey, gotya!

Rome, 387 BC

Rome has been savaged by Gauls but saved by a flock of geese.

Roman consul Marcus Manlius was woken up by the cackling of the sacred geese of Juno in the Capitol as the Gauls made a night-time attack. He roused the garrison and beat off the attackers, although they had managed to sack the city and set it alight.

As a result of this dubiously-achieved victory, Manlius gets a new feather in his cap and is to be surnamed 'Capitolinus'.

The Gauls had previously beaten the Romans at the River Allia. The battle occurred after a Roman soldier, supposed to be mediating between the people of Clusium and the Gauls, fought a duel and killed the Gallic chief.

A child wrestles with a goose!

He had been called in by the Etruscan city-state which had been trading wine and other produce with the Gauls since 400. A nobleman had invited some Gauls to settle in the area, but he was acting without the backing of other Clusines, and a dispute between them and the Gauls broke out. When the arbitration service backfired, the Gauls attacked Rome.

Mausolus' huge tomb could hold an army!

Halicarnassus, c. 353 BC

The dead satrap of Caria, Mausolus, has had his wish for eternal remembrance granted in the building of the world's largest-ever tomb outside of Egypt's pyramids, in the coastal city of Halicarnassus north of the island of Rhodes.

rather than from people's desire to commemorate him. Artemisia commissioned leading architect Pythius, designer of the temple of Athena Polias at Priene, to build the white marble tomb. Pythius has since written a book about both the tomb and the temple.

The Mausoleum at Helicarnassus was one of the seven wonders of the world.

The rectangular foundation stone measures some 30 by 38 m (100 by 127 ft). A colonnade of 36 ionic columns stands on a high base, above which a pyramid-like structure soars up to about 41 m (134 ft). On the very top is a colossal chariot pulled by four horses. Friezes depict scenes from Mausolus' life.

The project has been financed from the immense wealth of the dead man's widow Artemisia

He enlisted several famous sculptors of the day to contribute to the tomb, particularly to the decorative friezes around it, including Scopas, Bryaxis, Timotheus (who took part also in the temple of Asclepius at Epidaurus) and Leochares of Athens, a man described by Plato as 'young and good'. It is said that these men worked without pay, purely for the honour of their art. Pythius himself made the chariot statue on the top.

Philip ends sacred war

Greece, c. 346 BC

Ten years of a so-called sacred war involving almost all the states on the Greek mainland have ended after the intervention of Philip of Macedonia.

Like other sacred wars, it began over a violation of the rules of the Delphic Amphictiony, a league of 12 tribes which are connected to the Delphic Oracle and organise the Pythian Games. Phocian separatist leaders had been fined for cultivating the sacred plain between Delphi and Cirrha, but had refused to pay, and war was declared.

Separatist leader Philomelus called on allies from Sparta, Athens and Achaea to face the coalition of Thessaly, Locris and Boetia. The Thessalians were defeated and withdrew; and then the Phocians invaded Boetia and subdued Doris, Locris and part of Thessaly. In 353 they defeated the Macedonians under Philip.

Several years of heavy sporadic fighting left the Phocians and Thebans exhausted. Last year Thebes and Thessaly called on Philip to intervene, while Phocis invited Athens and Sparta to intervene on its behalf. But Sparta declined and Athens allied with Philip, leaving Phocis isolated.

Phocis has now surrendered and Philip has reconvened the Amphictionic Council. The Phocians have been excluded from the Amphictiony, disarmed and ordered to pay 60 talents a year to repair temple treasures.

Philip of Macedon has taken the place of the Phocians in the Amphictiony, breaking new ground by sitting as an individual member rather than as representative of a state.

Philip's increasing power in Greece is causing some concern. In Athens, the politician Demosthenes is an arch opponent while Isocrates suggests that Philip could be the architect of a united Greece.

'Know thyself' thinker departs for his Ideal

Athens, c. 347

Greek philosopher Plato has died in Athens at the age of 72. He was a disciple of Socrates and founder of the Academy in Athens for training men in state service.

His writings cover metaphysics, politics and ethics and he is perhaps best known for his *Republic* in which he examines the nature of justice and seeks a blueprint for the model state. He proposed a political system which divided people into classes determined by education rather than wealth or birth. He argued against democracy and for constitutionalism or elite oligarchy.

His other works include examinations of the nature of knowledge, virtue and vice, the human soul, communication, falsehood and error, reason and necessity, truth, and law. His educational methods majored on science and philosophy, including mathematics and astronomy.

Plato came from a family of aristocrats and it was expected that he would go into politics. However, as a young man he came under the influence of Socrates and became immersed in philosophy. When Socrates was condemned he left Athens in disgust, abandoning all thought of a political career. He travelled to Egypt, Italy and Sicily before returning to set up what has been described as the first ever university, The Academy, in 385.

Much of his writing takes the form of dialogue, usually between Socrates and another, and it is largely through his work that the world knows about Socrates' own ideas. The use of dialogue in this way was revolutionary; before, the method had only been used for the lower types of entertainment.

The dialogue method encourages the listener to take part in and then continue the argument, instead of learning dogmas by repetition. However, because Plato himself never seems to take part in the dialogues, it is impossible to tell which ideas were fundamental to his own thinking.

In his early work, he stressed the need for individuals to know themselves, and said that it is only when you understand yourself that you can have a proper appreciation of your relation to other people.

Plato, from a contemporary marble bust.

His later work developed the theory that there is an ideal world where eternal truths such as justice, beauty and goodness exist in a state of perfection. He called these truths 'forms'. They act as blueprints for the imperfect entities of this world. People are born with a vague recollection of these perfect forms, even though they may never see them properly worked out. By intellectual and moral study people can truly recollect their early memories of perfection, he claimed.

Socrates had said that 'virtue is knowledge'; Plato expanded this idea by dividing the soul into three parts: rational (where philosophy and knowledge are based), spirited (where honour and ambition are founded) and desirous (or appetitive, from where material gain stems). The direction of a person's desires will depend on which part of the soul is most influential.

In his characterisation of the ideal state in *The Republic* Plato considered that government should be placed in the hands of those most given to philosophy and knowledge, defence in the hands of the spirited types, and the economy in the hands of the appetitive people. Justice occurs when all three parts of the soul co-exist in harmony.

By the end of his life his views had changed slightly. In *The Laws* he proposed a different ideal state, which placed a high premium on law and order. Ironically, his ideal state would not have endured the subversive views of his former master, Socrates.

King killed at wedding

Greece, c. 336 BC

King Philip of Macedon has been assassinated while he was celebrating the marriage of his daughter to King Alexander of Epirus. He was about to lead his troops into Persia.

He was caught off guard by a murderer who claimed to be acting for personal reasons, but who was probably not solely responsible. His death has caused ripples throughout the land.

Some observers claim he was the greatest man the world has ever known, and the orator Isocrates believed him to be a true leader of a potentially united Greece. But he had many opponents, among them Athenian politician Demosthenes, who do not mourn him.

King Philip, who was 46, ascended to the Macedonian throne in 359. He pursued an expansionist policy and early in his reign annexed the kingdoms of Thrace, Chalcidice and Thessaly, which so strengthened his economic power that he was able to support a standing army of considerable size.

In 338 Philip won a decisive victory against the combined forces of Athens and Thebes, after which he formed the Corinthian league which was nominally independent but in effect subservient to Philip.

He is succeeded by his son Alexander, 20, who plans to continue his father's campaign against Persia.

Rural horse farmers ride over the rest of Greece

The mosaic floor of the palace courtyard of Philip of Macedon.

Greece, 338 BC

The unlikeliest of all contenders for supremacy, Macedon is now the most powerful of the Greek city-states. The victory of Philip II over Athens and Thebes in the Battle of Chaeronea in central Greece has made him the ruler of almost the whole of Greece.

A major factor in this latest success was the part played by Philip's 18-year-old son Alexander who commanded the Macedonian cavalry.

The rise to power of Philip of Macedon has redefined Greek politics. Macedon itself was once regarded as little better than a barbarian state, though Hellenic culture has been welcomed there, and cultural and trade links formed with Athens.

But there could not be a greater difference between the elegant sophistication of Periclean and late classical Athens, and the tough rural communities of Macedonia, still peopled by hardy horse-farmers and largely untouched by the Hellenic communities that dot the Macedonian coast.

But these inland Macedonians have provided the core of Philip's infantry and cavalry. When he took the throne in 359, Philip embarked upon a cat-and-mouse game as he planned his attacks on various rivals. He spent the first two years of his reign making his north and east borders safe against barbarian skirmishes, then began to pick off his immediate neighbours one by one. In the process he gained the services, either by war or by diplomacy, of many of Athen's allies.

When he succeeded in conquering Thrace, Athens attempted to raise a confederation against him, but the attempt was thwarted by Philip. When at the same time Greece lost Byzantium as an ally, it was clear that the years of recovery were over and Greece was once again in dire trouble.

The years that followed have seen the rise of Philip and the inevitable decline of Athens. Following the victory Philip has organised a congress at Corinth, at which a league of Hellenic states has been formed, each of which will send delegates to a national assembly at Corinth. Only two major powers are outside the league: Sparta and Macedonia itself, which has exacted a treaty from the League guaranteeing its support in any military confrontation that Macedonia may be involved in.

New king Alex thinks and acts

Macedonia, 336 BC

The 20-year-old King Alexander has already shown outstanding talent as a military commander. Like his recently-assassinated father, his strength of character and fearlessness on the battlefield have earned him the respect and fear of many.

It is in his nature to take huge risks. A more cautious man would hesitate before pursuing Philip's plan to conquer Persia, the success of which depends on the support of the Greek cities which are unsure what to make of this young and politically inexperienced king.

However, Alexander is not a brash fool. As a child, he was taught by the Platonic philosopher Aristotle, and majored in literature, science and politics. His favourite book is said to be Homer's *Iliad* and his favourite sport is hunting. He relaxes at drinking parties with friends, engaging in long hours of philosophical debate in what has become known as the Symposium.

According to some commentators his mother, the Epirote princess Olympias, has a heavy influence on him and her tempestuous, passionate and sometimes irrational nature can be overbearing. She reminds him repeatedly that he is descended from two of the greatest Greek heros, Achilles and Perseus, a belief that no doubt is behind some of Alexander's self-confidence.

Olympias is part of the reason that some Macedonian nobles oppose Alexander's succession, although he has enough support to make his sovereignty secure. Any immediate rivals to the throne have died recently in suspicious rather than fortuitous circumstances.

When the womanising Philip divorced Olympias last year, Alexander openly took her side. Though there were many serious arguments between father and son, it has been suggested that Olympias, unable to bear the insult of divorce, was behind the assassination of Philip.

Massive army stands poised to conquer

Macedonia, c. 335 BC

The people of Thebes have become the latest victims of Alexander's 40,000-strong army which he inherited from his father Philip. Over 6,000 Theban men, women and children were massacred and the rest of the population sold as slaves as a punishment for rebelling against Macedonia.

Alexander the Great.

The city has been razed to the ground. The revolt had begun after an unfounded rumour circulated that Alexander had been killed in action. The savage reprisal has the rest of the Greek states cowering in fear and submitting to the young king.

Alexander's army was built up by his father Philip from the peasant mob which fought with the aristocratic masters. They were unable to arm themselves as well as the Greek hoplites, so Philip gave them each a 4-m (14-ft)-long pike and intensive training. They formed phalanxes to keep enemy infantry at bay with their pikes until the horse riding aristocrats could charge at the enemy line.

The core of Alexander's army is 15,000 Macedonian troops divided into infantry and cavalry. The cavalry are divided into 'companions', mainly aristocrats, who wear helmets, greaves and breastplates and have short thrusting lances and swords. Normally they are led by Alexander himself. The rest of the cavalry are lancers who wear no body armour. They act as reconnaissance outriders.

The infantry are divided into hypaspists, who act as offensive troops after the enemy line has been broken, and phalanxes who act in defence holding down the enemy. They also function as Alexander's own body guard.

In addition, Alexander can call on 15,000 Greek mercenaries and 9,000 light-armed cavalry and infantry recruited from conquered tribes. Among these are 1,000 Agranians armed with javelins who are especially valued for their skill in guerilla warfare.

Philip also introduced a unique modification to siege-warfare. Faced with the major problem that besieging forces could not stop the defending forces attacking them while they built their towers, he devised a long-range catapult to shoot heavy arrows from a distance, keeping the enemy city occupied while the troops erected their siege towers.

Tyre gets blown out

Tyre, Syria, c. 332 BC

The city of Tyre has fallen to the Macedonians after a spectacular siege which lasted over seven months. The end came after Alexander built floating siege towers on ships that sailed round the city battering the walls until they gave way.

In customary style, the city was sacked and its inhabitants massacred or sold as slaves. Tyre was the only Phoenician city to remain loyal to Persia. The city, on an island less than a kilometre (half a mile) from the coast, was surrounded by walls 45 m (150 ft) high, with a strong navy stationed in three harbours. Alexander had no ships and his first tactic was to build a causeway towards the island and place siege-towers on it, but the towers came under constant fire from Tyrian ships and the walls.

He would have failed had not news of the surrender of the other Phoenician cities reached the Phoenician sailors in the Persian fleet, who changed sides, providing Alexander with all their skill, commitment and manpower.

This success severely weakens, if not destroys, the Persian empire. Before the fall of Tyre, Darius of Persia had offered Alexander a peace treaty, but the Macedonian was interested only in conquest.

The city of Tyre seen in the early twentieth century.

Alexander crowned as the king of Egypt

The oasis of Siwa where priests of Ammon recognised Alexander as Pharoah of Egypt.

Memphis, c. 331 BC

Alexander of Greece has been crowned Pharaoh in Egypt, displacing the Persian Darius who had previously been acknowledged as Pharaoh. He marched in triumph through Egypt to Memphis, encountering little opposition along the way. Like the Phoenicians, the Egyptians are only too pleased to be freed from Persian dominance.

To celebrate his conquest, Alexander has founded a new city in Egypt. Situated on the coast where an isthmus forms a natural harbour, Alexandria can accommodate a larger fleet than any of the other harbours along this coast. It is well placed to be the capital of Alexander's Egypt, but it is unclear whether this is his intention.

During his stay in Egypt, Alexander spent a hour alone at the shrine of the Egyptian god Ammon at the oasis of Siwa. It is rumoured that something significant occurred there. He has already been hailed 'Son of Ammon' by the priests, in recognition of his position as Pharaoh.

Son of god is a status Alexander feels quite comfortable with. Those close to him say he is becoming increasingly despotic in his behaviour and relationships with his people are worsening. He is now resting in Memphis and plans to hold some celebratory games.

This bronze head from Cyrene, in Lybia, testifies to the profound and widespread influence of Greek sculpture under Alexander.

'I'm God now,' says king of Greeks

Macedonia and India, c. 327 BC

King Alexander of Macedonia and much of the known world has ordered the Macedonians to treat him as a god.

He is certainly acting more and more like a jealous and superstitious god and is increasingly prone to irrational fits of uncontrolable rage.

He has ordered the execution of the elderly and loyal Parmenion on false evidence of treachery that was extracted from Parmenion's son who was being tortured on a trumped-up charge of treason.

The old man had helped secure Alexander's accession and has been of incalculable help on the battlefield. It is said that Alexander has long wanted to defame and kill the old man and his sons because he resented his debt to him.

In a fit of drunken fury Alexander has also killed his friend Cleitus who saved his life seven years ago at the battle of Granicus.

The king is now said to be filled with deep regret and remorse for what he has done. In addition, Callisthenes, Aristotle's nephew, was sent to prison and then executed for refusing to prostrate himself before him in Persian style.

Meanwhile, Alexander is penetrating deeper into India. He has conquered his way through to the Lower Indus and is heading for the Punjab.

He is reported to have a growing fascination for India's religions and has been engaging in conversations with Hindu and Buddhist teachers. Their reaction to his incarnational claims, to his blood-thirsty campaigns and to his desire to subjugate all he encounters remains unrecorded.

Mutiny over the bounty

Persia, c. 324 BC

Macedonian troops have staged a second mutiny in a year, this time over an unwanted 'reward' of Persian brides. But unlike the first mutiny, the king has forced his troops to back down.

Having marched his men across the impossibly hot Gedrosian Desert, which claimed many lives, from India to Opis on the Tigris north of Babylon, he ordered them to marry Persian women.

They refused, and suggested he discharge them all because he and his father Ammon, the Egyptian god he appeared increasingly obsessed by, could quite easily do without them.

But he fell into a rage and executed the ringleaders before dismissing the army. When the soldiers saw that he was serious, they begged forgiveness. A reconciliatory banquet was held at which Alexander prayed that the gods would grant harmony between the Greeks and Persians.

The first mutiny had occurred earlier in India when exhausted troops simply refused to move on. They had defeated King Porus at Hydaspes, partly by killing the Indian's elephant keepers so that the animals caused chaos by blundering around aimlessly. They refused to go deeper into the sub-continent, however, and Alexander gave in, marching them back to Persia instead.

The command to marry Persians was not the first time the increasingly despotic king has encouraged inter-racial liaisons. About three years ago he held a mass wedding for Greeks and Persians, and gave 10,000 Macedonian soldiers lavish wedding presents as a reward. He increasingly wears oriental dress and organises his court on Persian lines.

Aristotle classified the world with logic

Chalcis, Greece, c. 322 BC

Greek philosopher and scientist Aristotle has died of a digestive disease in Chalcis at the age of 62. He was a disciple of Plato, and tutor to Alexander the Great of Macedonia. He founded a school in Athens and began a collection of manuscripts, maps and objects to illustrate his zoology research using a donation of 800 talents from Alexander who ordered all hunters, fowlers and fishermen to send objects of interest to Aristotle.

His work included analysis of logic, psychology, metaphysics, zoology, ethics, politics and physical science. He established the 'inductive method' of reasoning. Taking an empirical approach, he analysed and described the development of the chick embryo, and of the contents of the stomach.

His very ordered mind produced a series of classifications. He classified existence into actual and potential. Animals were classified by means of a scale at which man is at the top, but he did not imply evolution.

He also divided science into theoretical, practical and productive. The theoretical aims at knowledge and includes mathematics, which studies things which are eternal but not substantial; physics, which studies things which are substantial but not eternal; and theology, which studies things which are both eternal and substantial. The practical side aims at improving conduct and the productive aims to make things beautiful or useful.

Aristotle differed from Plato in that while he believed in the idea of form as the essence of things, he did not believe in the existence of form beyond this world. He believed instead that there is one perfect, pure form, which never changes and never moves. This is God, who spends his whole life in

Aristotle: a Roman copy of the original bust.

self-contemplation. He did not create the world, because it has existed for all eternity, but he is the ultimate cause of all natural development.

As for ethics, he said that 'good' may legitimately vary for different people or in different circumstances. There is no single 'good' transcending all others. His writings on politics were based on a collection of data from 158 different Greek constitutions, collected by himself and his students.

Aristotle was the first person to develop a system of formal logic by using symbols. His logic was based on syllogism, a form of reasoning whereby a conclusion is reached from two assumed propositions such as all animals are mortal; men are animals; therefore men are mortal.

Aristotle was born at Stagira, in northern Greece, and brought up in the court of King Philip of Macedon, where his father was court physician. He believed that no one could attain all truth, but that everyone might contribute a small amount to the world's amassed knowledge of truth.

Alexander the Great has died

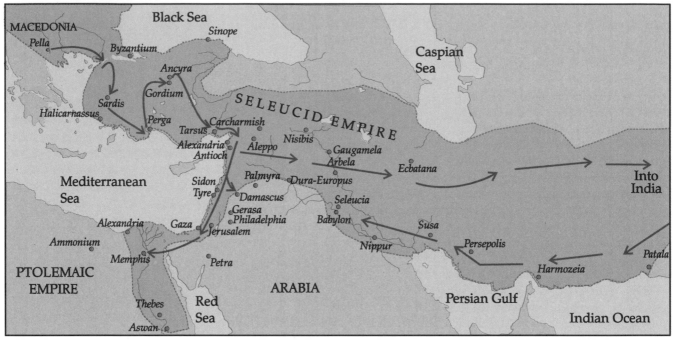

Alexander was the first great conqueror. His lightning campaigns brought him an empire which was to be unmatched, stretching as it did from Macedonia to the Indus (on the Pakistan–India border). It took in Egypt as well. The empire did not however survive his death, but was swiftly parcelled up between rival successors.

Babylon, c. 323 BC

Alexander the Great, who conquered the whole world, has died aged 33. He had caught a fever, although rumours of poisoning are circulating.

Alexander was probably the greatest military genius of all time; the speed of his conquests and the scale of his operations are unique. He had conquered much of the world.

He was the son of Philip II (king from 359–336 BC) who conquered the Greeks in 338 BC and merged the Greeks and Macedonians into a single empire. When Philip was assassinated in suspicious circumstances in 336, Alexander took command of the empire.

Two years after his accession he invaded Asia and at the battle of Granicus conquered the Persian army of 10,000 Greek mercenaries. A year later he defeated the Persian army again. In 332 he took Egypt, and began to build the city that is called after him, Alexandria.

Victory followed victory, until Alexander had extended his father's empire from Egypt as far as India, where he encountered and defeated armies equipped with armoured elephants. Only the fatigue of his soldiers prevented him securing his victory as far as the Ganges itself. In India his admiral Nearchus used Indian labour to build a fleet of 800 ships to bring Alexander's army back down the Indus to Persia and to Babylonia.

He was often ruthless, driven by a brutal and extravagant personality and an insatiable desire to find and conquer new places. But he used ingenious strategies and his personal courage was an inspiration to his troops.

When Darius III of Persia urged Athens and Thebes to rebel against Macedonian rule, he took an army south to Thebes and razed the city to the ground. The shock of this brutal reaction was enough to secure Athenian loyalty for the rest of Alexander's reign.

By inclination a follower of Persian culture, Alexander peopled his empire's cities with Greek settlers and introduced the Greek culture and language into them. He has thus been a major force for Hellenisation and there is no doubt that he leaves one of the great empires of history behind him.

Administratively, he retained the Persian satrapy system but installed Macedonian officers alongside Persian civic governors. Economically, he minted the Persian hoards of gold and silver, injecting great wealth into the markets and creating widespread prosperity.

Of late, some suggested that he may have been mentally unstable – there have been reports of irrational behaviour, perhaps from drink, and he has talked grandly of a global empire. At the end he believed himself to be a god, and ordered his people to worship him.

For his own enigmatic epitaph, he announced that he was leaving his empire 'to the strongest', and political commentators are today assessing just which lucky nation or leader is likely to inherit. It is a legacy that will not be received without bloodshed.

Sculptors strip goddesses bare

Greece, c. 300 BC

Praxiteles of Athens specialises in statues of Aphrodite, but has broken new ground in portraying the goddess naked. He perfects each one a little differently.

One of his most famous stands in naked glory at Cnidos. He had offered this statue to the people of

The Venus of Milo is possibly the most famous classical Greek sculpture.

Cos, along with a clothed one at the same price. The Coans chose the clothed one, thinking it more modest, but later regretted their choice when they saw how famous the naked one had become. The statue at Cnidos is universally desired and acclaimed; the king of Bithynia even offered to cancel the whole national debt of Cnidos if the leaders would sell him the statue, but they refused.

Greek sculpture is taking off again, after the doldrums of the Peloponnesian war. And it is going in a new direction. There is a growing interest in female nudity among artists and sculptors, who everywhere are creating more human and natural figures than the traditional static poses.

Figures stand relaxed in natural poses. There may be less majesty and grandeur, but there is more reality which reflects the increasing dissatisfaction among the Greeks with simpler stylised art. Sculpted clothes drape softly around bodies, quietly suggestive of the shape beneath. Sometimes clothes are shown blowing in the wind, pulled tight and almost transparent across the body. There is more emotion too; grave monuments movingly portray the pain of separation.

Leading sculptor Scopas, from Paros, who was involved in the building of the temple of Athena Alea an Tegea, completed in 350, has been innovative in his treatment of emotion. He portrays it through his figures' facial expressions rather than through their bodily positions. Brows hang heavy over deep-sunk eyes, and faces regard you with unnerving intensity.

Lysippus of Sicyon is probably the most influential sculptor of the day. He has won unique royal approval as the only man Alexander the Great will allow to depict him. His statues encourage spectators to walk all round them – they can be viewed from any position. His lithe figures with long legs and small heads are often seen to be moving in one direction while looking in another.

One of his most popular statues is that of a youth scraping oil off his arm, the Apoxyomenus. Lysippus is also famed for his large groups of sculptures, sometimes as many as 20, and for his portrayal of animals as well as humans.

Generally sculptures are commissioned by the state and officials are appointed to supervise the work. Usually the subjects of the larger works come from mythology – Phidias' frieze on the Parthenon is a remarkable exception to the rule.

Vase painters and potters come from a lower level of society, and are often slaves. Their work is anonymous but reflects modern life in a powerful way. Vases depict scenes from daily life such as schools, dinner parties, bedroom scenes, even the workplace itself, interspersed with scenes from famous legends. While sculptors have the upper hand in their depiction of realistic anatomical forms, painters too are developing this skill. Colours are varied, usually on a white background.

Minor arts flourish in Greece, particularly in Athens. Jewellery using metal and gem stones, and statuettes made out of ivory and gold, are common. Ivory is increasingly used for parts of the colossal statues in the temples. The gemstones show the style of contemporary art in microcosm, with tiny engravings often including portrayals of animals or human heads.

The Apollo Belvedere, a Roman marble copy of the fourth-century Greek original.

Greek gods are just like us!

There are no atheists in Greece. Religion is woven into the fabric of society. But it is not the sort of religion which is bounded by clearly defined doctrines, and it has little effect on personal morality.

The purpose of religion is to establish a two-way relationship with any one or more of the gods who control various aspects of earthly life. This is done through public ceremonies at which sacrifices of animals, cakes or fruit may be offered and where prayers are said and hymns sung. After the ceremony there is usually a feast. The offerings are intended to please or appease the gods and to solicit a favour such as a fertile womb or a fruitful field. Human sacrifice has been almost unknown for the past couple of centuries.

Greek religion is concerned much more with this life than the next. Only the gods are immortal. Even their offspring from unions with mortals do not inherit immortality.

Human beings who die go to the shadowy underworld where there is little to be desired and no real purpose of existence.

There is no professional priesthood. Officiants at the shrines and ceremonies are part-timers who do not need special training or qualifications for their tasks. However, the guardians of the oracles, the prophets or seers, are sometimes full-time professionals and are highly regarded. They are consulted for omens or indications of the gods' wills before all major decisions and battles.

There are 12 chief gods, who congregate on Mount Olympus, but there are many minor gods. The heroes such as Heracles and Perseus, who sometimes have a cult associated with them, are mortals although they may be offspring of the gods. The gods are not in any way exemplary in behaviour, and reflect all the range of human fads and foibles, emotions and excesses.

Mount Olympus.

The twelve Olympians

The senior gods are Zeus and Hera:

ZEUS The chief of the gods and father of several. He is the child of Cronos and Rhea (or Ge) and rules on the advice of Rhea (the mother of earth who was able to foretell the future). He is the god of the sky and the weather, sometimes depicted as a storm god. He gives laws and rules events. He is bad tempered and has had numerous love affairs with both sexes.

HERA Both the sister and wife of Zeus, she is the first among the goddesses and the patron of marriage and childbirth. She is especially associated with the city of Argos, and uses the winds as her messengers. She is eternally jealous of her husband's affairs, and is grumpy as a result.

The rest of the Olympian Pantheon, in alphabetical order:

APHRODITE The daughter of Zeus and Dione (although some say she emerged from Uranus' genitals), she is goddess of love. In one of her manifestations as the goddess of sex she is the patron of prostitutes, but she is also revered as the patron of pure love and her worship is usually restrained.

APOLLO The prince of the gods.

A detail from a stone relief showing Aphrodite's birth from the sea, from the Greek altar commonly known as the Throne of Venus, c. 600 BC.

Apollo, from the Temple of Zeus in Olympia.

Handsome, athletic, just, wise, generous and very desirable. He is the god of light, music, prophecy, healing and of course youth, who cares for flocks and herds. On his adventure to search for the serpent Python, who had tormented his mother Leto (another of Zeus' wives), he killed it at Delphi where he coaxed from Pan the secret of prophecy. His control of the Delphic Oracle made it the chief authority in religious matters.

ARES The god of war and the least worshipped (except in times of battle). He was brutal but also quite a coward. His brother Apollo beat him at boxing. He was the lover of Aphrodite and was publicly humiliated by her husband Hephaestos when he caught them together.

ARTEMIS Twin sister of Apollo, she is the goddess of the wild beasts and she roams about the wild places of the earth including the forests and the hills. She is a virgin but is worshipped in many places as the giver of fertility.

ATHENA The patron goddess of Athens, she is the daughter of Zeus and Metis. Like Ares, her main preoccupation is with war. Her temple, the Parthenon, is probably the most magnificent of all those built by the Greeks.

DEMETER The sorrowful goddess of the earth, responsible for its harvests. The abduction of her daughter Persephone by Hades, the god of the underworld, caused her so much anguish that she neglected her duties and the earth ran wild until Zeus intervened. Persephone was eventually returned to her at Eleusis, where her cult is especially celebrated, but part of the deal was that the girl should return to Hades for a while every year – which is when winter occurs.

DIONYSUS The wild one. He is the god of the forces of nature, of wine, and is also patron of the theatre. He is attended by the satyrs, who are beastly and unprincipled spirits. Some of his worship becomes frenzied as worshippers tear sacrificed animals to pieces and eat them believing that they are eating the god himself. His spring festival is a major event in the religious calendar.

HEPHAESTOS The short, ugly and lame son of Zeus and Hera, he is the laughing stock on Mount Olympus. But he is also very clever, the maker of magical things and the god of fire and craftsmanship. He was thrown out of Olympus because he was so weak, but won his mother's affections when he grew up, by his exquisite jewellery, and was readmitted to the council of the gods. On the orders of Zeus, he married Aphrodite, who didn't love him.

A marble head of Athena: this is a Roman copy of the original bronze head by Phidias.

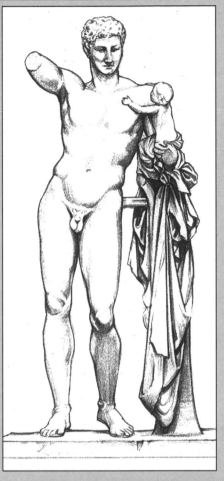

Hermes with a small child: one of the rare Greek originals by Praxiteles, c. 330 BC, not to have been vandalised. This marble statue stands in the Museum at Mount Olympia.

HERMES A jovial, clever and resourceful god who brings good luck and gives sweet dreams. It is well worth keeping on good terms with him because he brings wealth, and so is the patron god of both merchants and thieves. He has wings on his sandals and is frequently portrayed as a messenger of Zeus and a guide for travellers.

POSEIDON The brother of both Zeus and Hades (who is not an Olympian but dwells in the underworld), Poseidon is the god of the seas and earthquakes, and also of horses. He lusted after his sister Demeter so much that she turned herself into a mare to escape his attentions, but he immediately made himself into a stallion and mounted her.

247

All Italian roads lead to Rome

Rome, c. 272 BC

Rome has now conquered the whole Italian peninsular.

The final breakthrough resulted from the army's capture of the Etruscan cities of Caere, Tarquinia and Vulci, all within 80 km (50 miles) north-west of Rome. It completes the reversal of fortunes between the two great powers.

Social unrest in Etruria has brought some cities to virtual collapse. This once great nation of powerful city-state alliances is now making alliances with its old enemy on Rome's own terms.

Carthage rules the waves

Carthage, c. 275 BC

If you want to please a lover or flatter an aristocrat, buy them some of the latest luxuries from Carthage. Nubian slaves are very fashionable, but for that special gift try something really exotic: elephant ivory, for example, or a soft, beautiful leopard-skin. But be careful not to tell too many people who the nation was from whom you bought them. You might find that your generosity rebounds on you.

Carthage, from its location on a small peninsular in the Gulf of Tunis, has been a problem waiting to happen to Rome since it began to gain trading supremacy in the Mediterranean about 300.

The mighty Carthaginian fleet soon challenged both eastern and western seas, and over the past half-century has been using its strength to subdue African, and lately Spanish, tribes. It is now the recognised trade link with the African interior; anybody who wants to trade with Africa has to do so through Carthage.

The Carthaginians have expanded into Spain and Sicily, though problems with Italy have been avoided by Carthage's policy of establishing alliances with the Etruscans and later with Rome.

Carthage lies in ruins today, a pale reflection of its past glory. Seen here is the mosaic floor of the huge freshwater Antonine Baths by the seaside.

Carthage has never succeeded in conquering the whole of Sicily; but the Greeks have held on to their eastern territories centred on Syracuse. But their strong presence on the island represents a threat to Roman control of the northern seas just as their mighty trading interests represent a threat to Rome's plans for future expansion. Relations between the two nations are at an all-time low.

Carthage has a long history of trading strength. Ancient Carthage was a centre of iron smelting as Africa entered the Iron Age. The Nok people of Nigeria were using cylindrical clay-smelting furnaces as long ago as 500.

The use of iron has spread through Africa faster than in almost any other area. It is used for edging weapons and agricultural implements, and iron axes are much in demand for forest clearance. It is thought that Africa may have learned the secret of iron from merchants of the Kush people, who trade widely.

The north African city also has a reputation for barbarity; some of its infants are said to have been sacrificed to the god Molech.

Rome rescues Sicily

Rome, c. 264 BC

Rome today has taken an irrevocable step towards war with former ally Carthage, and Italy is in a state of emergency.

The crisis arose when the Mamertines of Messana in Sicily called on Rome to evict the Carthaginians. The Africans had originally gone to the aid of the Mamertines against Syracuse, but had outstayed their welcome.

Debates in the Senate have been heated, but the final vote was in favour of intervention because the Carthaginians were operating so close to the Roman mainland.

The Romans are in control of Messana tonight, and Carthage has announced that its fleet and army are on a war footing. But despite Rome's initial success, some observers believe that Rome's lack of a navy will swing matters Carthage's way.

The Temple of Concorde in Agrigento, Sicily, belies the fact that the area has always been hotly contested.

Legal symbols go missing

Rome, c. 272 BC

The Twelve Tablets of the Law, inscribed records written about 450 BC and based upon an older oral law code, are missing. The loss was discovered by historians researching the Sack of Rome which occurred in c. 390.

Originally a way of ensuring civil rights by demonstrating that the law was a fixed and recorded code, the Tablets set out the scope of the Roman legal system and described its major penalties.

The loss of the Tablets (which were purely symbolic, as the law was recorded elsewhere) makes no difference to the smooth running of the Roman legal system, nor to the efficiency of government itself. The present-day Republic is politically and legally more sophisticated than the state was under its kings.

Power is ultimately in the hands of the two Consuls, who govern the city and command the army. They have the services of a consultative Senate, and magistrates administer justice in the Quaestor or law-court. A magistracy is often the first step towards higher office such as a provincial governorship.

Because a republic is governed by the will of its people, the principal posts of government are all elected offices.

Huge advances made in ship-building technology

Rome, c. 260 BC

The sound of carpentry and metalworking is to be heard round the clock at Rome's top shipyards. The new Roman fleet is taking shape, and every available skilled workman has been pressed into service.

In the three years of war between capture of a Punic warship has given the Romans the opportunity to examine the enemy strength at their leisure. Construction is now under way of 100 heavy quinqueremes and 20 triremes.

The trireme, probably the fastest warship in the world today, has 85 oarsmen on each side, arranged in a are the key to success, though the Romans will not be able to call on the superbly trained crews who have made other navies great. However, Roman fighting skills and military genius is expected to compensate.

Both ship types are built for speed, and are so light that they can be easily pulled ashore. They are not suitable for long ocean voyages, and are particularly vulnerable to storms at sea. For this reason they are usually sailed close to coasts and beached at nights.

Quinqueremes are larger and the rowing decks are covered to give more space for transporting marines. The quinquereme is the standard warship of today, though the extra space for mar-

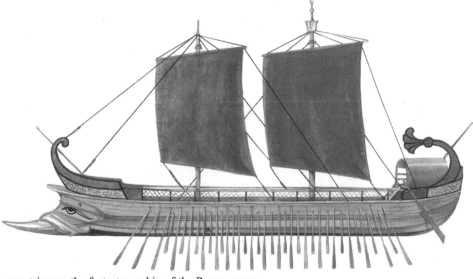

A Roman trireme, the fastest warship of the Roman navy.

Rome and Carthage (now called the Punic War, after the Greek name for Carthage), the woeful Roman lack of adequate sea forces and transport has been all too obvious. But the staggered seating system so that the ship is about 36 m (120 ft) long. Triremes have great speed and manoeuvrability in battle.

Oarsmen, who are highly paid, ines has not added to the overall strength of the ship's structure. The lighter trireme still has a role to play because of its extra manoeuvrability and speed.

Fast Facts 300-262 BC

Ireland, 300 BC: Celtic tribes have arrived in Ireland. Known as Gaels, or Irish, they have also settled the Isle of Man and south-west Scotland, as well as founding colonies in Wales, Devon and Cornwall.

North Africa, c. 300 BC: The first astronomical observatory has been built at Alexandria by Ptolemy Soter. This joins the great library and the harbour as major attractions, and will increase the already great prestige that Alexandria has among scholars and scientists.

Greece, 262 BC: Zeno of Citium has died in Athens. He was the founder of the Stoic school of philosophy. Stoics teach human brotherhood and denounce slavery. The name comes from the porch where Zeno taught. Stoics are known to be involved in a number of Greek and Roman resistance movements.

Mayans build new temples

Guatemala, c. 250 BC

The Maya people in South America are building distinctive and sophisticated temple platforms. They are rubble-filled, with cement added to make the structure firm; the walls are covered with ornate plasterwork.

On the top stand stone temples and palaces with thatched roofs, in a pyramid-like style that has become one of the recognisable characteristics of Mayan design.

The Maya have occupied Guatemala since about 2000 BC, and have always had a complex of state and religious buildings in the centre of their communities.

Mayan temples also contained numerous buried artefacts. This pottery model from Colima is of a hairless dog which was frequently depicted. Dogs were believed to accompany the souls of the dead on their journey into the underworld.

Indians are rounded up

North America, c. 300 BC

Indians in the mid-west and south are building earth tombs designed as symbolic structures, such as the Great Serpent Mound in Ohio. Flat-topped pyramids are also built and serve as foundations for the chief's house and for temples, such as Monk's Mound in Mississippi.

These Indians, known as mound-builders, often work in co-operation between tribes, directed by their leaders, to make even grander projects. Mounds have been built in North America for many centuries, but recently have become sophisticated funerary monuments.

New fleet sinks the enemy

Sicily, c. 256 BC

The new Roman navy has thrashed the Punic fleet in the Battle of Economus.

The battle took place in calm weather near the coast. It was the result of an ambitious attempt by Rome to bypass the Sicilian theatre of war and attempt an invasion of Carthage itself. The Roman fleet included quinqueremes and merchant ships to transport horses and other war necessities.

The Carthaginian fleet intercepted them off Sicily. Regulus, the Roman commander, compensated for Rome's lack of naval skills by taking up a wedge formation, so that their horse-transport ships would be protected in the centre. The Carthaginians drew their quinqueremes up in line formation, intending to encircle the entire Roman fleet and destroy it.

But the Romans put pressure on the Punic centre, which collapsed; and went on to drive their wedge

between the two Punic flanks. The seaward flank fled the battle, and the landward flank, caught between the coast and the Roman fleet, was, given the circumstances, almost entirely destroyed.

Today they are celebrating the victory in the Roman galleys, for the Roman crews are of only average skill, whereas the Carthaginians are the cream of the Mediterranean. Regulus is now heading for the African coast to continue the planned invasion.

This battle, which demonstrates how Rome has neutralised the superior naval skills of Carthage, is perhaps more significant than the first great sea victory of the war by Rome at Mylae four years ago.

Tide of war runs Carthage's way

Mediterranean, c. 249 BC

Rome now stares defeat in the face. Another sea disaster has plunged the war generals even deeper into gloom following the Lucania defeat and the abortive siege of Carthage in 255 BC.

The annihilation of a Roman fleet off the coast of Lucania in 254 was a severe blow to national pride, and now a further defeat at Drepanum has added to the loss of morale, already low because of heavy losses from storms at sea.

In retrospect the failure of Regulus, the Roman war consul who is already famous for his capture of Brindisium in 267 and victory at Economus, was due to all the old Roman shortcomings.

He took Tunis, but the Carthaginians refused to negotiate with him and because his army was badly supplied and equipped he was later defeated by a Carthaginian army equipped with elephants and cavalry, and taken captive.

Many of the Roman soldiers were later evacuated back to Italy.

A marble relief from Carthage showing a man sailing a two-masted coastal vessel. The sails would have been made of cloth, with leather reinforcements at the corners.

King converts all of India to Buddhism

India, c. 250 BC

Asoka, the benevolent Mauryan king of Magadha, has become a zealous evangelist for the Buddhist faith. He has tried assiduously to implement Buddhist principles in every area of national life, and has identified himself with the peasant population. During his reign India has benefited from major social and welfare reforms.

The emblem of King Asoka.

Buddhist shrines are now all over the empire, and Asoka is sending Buddhist missionaries, one of them his own son, to many countries. But, in keeping with Buddhist teachings, Asoka is willing to accept the presence of other religions and to give their followers full civil and human rights.

He inherited a large empire, now even larger, as he now rules over most of the sub-continent. Much of his conquest was by war, and he has publicly expressed his sorrow for the suffering that has brought him to power. Today he is a strong pacifist. A major reason for his conversion from Brahmanism was the attraction of the pacifist teaching of ahimsa, the principle of not harming any living thing.

Carthage surrenders

The ruins of Carthage with the Mediterranean Sea in the background.

Carthage, 241 BC

The Punic War is over. Carthage has agreed to give up its claims to Sicily and to pay war reparations to Rome. Most of Sicily is now the first Roman province.

War-weary soldiers on both sides are counting the cost of this long and exhausting struggle. The Romans for the last 10 years have had to fight for every inch of Sicily against the genius of Hamilcar Barca, a young general of great promise. It was Hamilcar who formally surrendered to Rome.

He has more problems than mere defeat, however, for the Carthaginian mercenaries have not been paid, and are already talking alliances with Carthage's enemies.

The victory that brought the war to an end was the Battle of the Aegates Islands, in which the new Roman fleet, built in 243 BC, finally destroyed the sea power of the Carthaginians.

The war had degenerated into a stalemate. The last major victory before this was the Battle of Palermo 10 years ago, in north-west Sicily. The defeat of a huge Carthaginian force there concentrated the war on to the Sicilian island, where Hamilcar's appointment prevented further large-scale defeats and made the construction of the new fleet essential. Hamilcar, already performing wonders with a poorly-equipped army, would be much less of a threat when Rome blocked the sea supply lines to Carthage.

Hindu epic expands

India, c. 250 BC

A long epic poem begun in India in 300 BC is still growing. The *Mahabharata* is a Sanskrit account of the feud between two aristocratic houses, the Pandavas and the Kauravas, as they struggle for a kingdom in northern India. It contains the *Bhagavad-Gita*, already a profoundly important book for Indian religion.

The *Mahabharata* contains long verse sections separated by short prose segments. Though not specifically a religious poem, the inclusion of the *Bhagavad-Gita* and sections such as a biographical account of the Lord Shiva make it an important contribution to Indian spirituality.

251

Librarian-author dies

Alexandria, 240 BC

The death of the poet Callimachus has shaken the literary world. He was believed to be about 70 years old.

While serving as librarian here he compiled the first catalogue of the library – the main collection is said to hold almost half a million works, and a supplementary collection over 40,000. The catalogue is particularly important because copies of items in the library are made and circulated throughout the world.

Callimachus' chief reputation however was as a poet. An African by birth, he was librarian for 20 years, but his writings and teachings have been widely influential. He is said to have written over 800 items, but his poems are short, elegant pieces in contrast to some of the epics being produced today.

He was strongly critical of Apollonius' epic of the Argonauts, claiming that the storyline was stodgy and the characters lifeless. One of his main works, *Causes*, described how ancient customs began. He will be remembered especially for his witty or cutting epigrams.

The great library of Alexandria in Egypt has the largest collection of books in the world. Founded by Ptolemy I Soter, it is staffed by some of the finest scholars; and some of the greatest writers of the day are the custodians of its treasures.

Rome ends Celtic threat

Europe, c. 225 BC

The Romans have the once-feared Celts firmly under the imperial thumb, and the 'Celtic threat' is a thing of the past.

They have been defeated at the Battle of Telamon. Celts living in Italy have surrendered to Rome.

The Celts, found all over central and north-western Europe, are farmers and skilled workers in pottery and metal, including much elaborate and ornate jewellery. The Celtic calendar is marked by festivals and seasonal rites.

They became a cause of concern to Rome and to Greece when they began to expand south in search of new land in the third century BC.

Chief Brennus, leading 150,000 infantry and 20,000 cavalry, invaded Macedonia; and in 279 he attacked the temple of Apollo at Delphi in central Greece. The attack failed, and a wounded Brennus committed suicide.

Rome is now embarking on an aggressive campaign of conquest in Gaul, a Celtic heartland.

Wonder of the world falls in earthquake

Rhodes, 224 BC

A violent tremor has reduced the great Colossus of Rhodes to rubble. The 30-m (100-ft) statue, built in 304, commemorated the victory of Rhodes in the face of a 12-month siege by the Greek commander Demetrius, who planned to absorb Rhodes into the Greek empire.

The massive structure, depicting the sun god Helios with a flaming torch, straddled the harbour. It was a visible symbol both of the city's endurance and the blessing of the gods. It was considered to be one of the seven wonders of the world.

This theatre is the most significant public building of the period visible in Alexandria.

China is united by its first autocrat

China, c. 221 BC

The powerful emperor Qin Zheng has proclaimed himself 'The first Autocratic Emperor' of a now largely unified China.

He was only 13 when he came to power in 246, following the deposing of the last Zhou emperor in 249. He began an expansionist policy that has annexed new territories and conquered the last outposts of the Zheng territories.

A group of wooden lacquered figures, all servants at the court of Qin Zheng.

The philosopher Meng Zu (Mencius) died in 288 BC without seeing his dream of a unified China fulfilled, but it is doubtful that he would have been pleased to see his hopes made reality by a campaign of conquest.

Mencius, whose major work *The Book of Mencius* is now an established classic, only approved of war in self-defence, and he taught that political power should be used to make the lot of the common people better. Mencius' frequent emphasis on the need for human beings to live in material security is unlikely to be reflected in the new dynasty's agenda.

Hannibal is the rising Carthaginian star

The great Carthaginian general commemorated on a coin of the period.

Carthage, c. 229 BC

Hamilcar Barca, the scourge of Rome, is dead. But his son Hannibal looks like becoming a much greater threat than his gifted father.

Hamilcar's troubles were just beginning when he successfully negotiated peace with Rome. The aggrieved and unpaid Punic mercenaries joined forces with local rebels and almost destroyed Carthage. Only the negotiated peace with Rome allowed Carthage to suppress the danger, in the 'Truceless War' that lasted from 240 to 237. The price was the loss of Corsica and Sicily, which Carthage still regrets.

After winning the Truceless War, Hamilcar devoted all his efforts to the conquest of southern Spain. He hoped to rebuild the might of Carthage, but he was competing against a Roman empire that was growing in size and in resources.

Since the Punic War, Corsica and Sardinia have been pacified by Rome where a rising general, Fabius Maximus, has been leading successful campaigns. Threats from the Gauls and other neighbours are therefore less fearsome because the Roman army has never been out of training since the Punic War and is fully battle-hardened.

But Carthage is determined to avenge its humiliating defeat and the loss of prize territories. Losing Sicily, Sardinia and Corsica destroyed not only the strategic importance of Carthage but also the economic and trading power that had made her great.

Hamilcar's Spanish campaign

Elephants highly trained in the military arts were one of the keys of Carthaginian success.

was probably an attempt to secure a new power base for a fresh attack on Rome. Hamilcar's three sons look competent to continue the attack – Hannibal in particular has done very well in Spain – and there is a rumour that before he died, Hamilcar made each of them swear solemnly never to be a friend of Rome.

The great wall of China at Shanghai Guan.

Chinese are building a great wall

China, c. 221 BC

The Chinese have started work on a massive wall which will run east–west across their territory as a defence against invasion by nomads from Mongolia and Central Asia. The ambitious project has been ordered by Emperor Zheng whose Qin dynasty is now in complete control of the land.

The wall is to be built of earth and stone from 4.6 to 9.1 m (15 to 30 ft) thick at the base (about 6 m / 20 ft on average) and an average 3.7 m (12 ft) at the top. The height will average 7.6 m (25 ft). A system of ramparts and watchtowers will make it possible for the wall to be garrisoned by a strong army force.

Tens of thousands of labourers have been deployed to work on this massive project.

In the struggle for Qin supremacy, hundreds of thousands of people have died. Zheng has forbidden ownership of weapons and has introduced a new system of government, designed to keep him in his new position as the first emperor of China. Standardisation of writing, weights and measures and other systems are all intended to maintain national unity.

Archimedes is hacked down

Archimedes was killed by Romans who came by sea in a surprise attack. This drawing, taken from a Greek amphora, depicts two stylised military ships of the period.

Syracuse, c. 212 BC

Archimedes, the outstanding Greek mathematician and inventor, has died in Syracuse. According to local people, he was killed by one of the invading Roman soldiers who Archimedes had rebuked for walking on a diagram he was drawing in the sand.

Among his inventions were the pulley and an ingenious device for raising water based on a rotating screw. He also discovered the theory of levers, which states that when a lever resting on a pivot near one end of it has pressure applied some distance from the pivot, it can move much greater weights than the pressure put on it. 'Give me somewhere to stand,' he is reputed to have said, 'and I will shift the universe.'

But he was best known for his 'Archimedes' principle' of bodies submerged in fluid. It stated that the weight apparently lost by a body immersed in water equals the weight of the water it displaces, or its 'specific gravity'. He is believed to have discovered it as he got into a bath. His cry of 'Eureka' has become a common exclamation.

Archimedes, who also calculated the value of pi, was a native of Syracuse in Sicily and spent his life in that area. Some of his inventions, such as the military catapult, were used to help defend Syracuse against the Romans. He leaves behind him a number of important mathematical and scientific writings. He is believed to have been about 75 years old.

War breaks out again

Rome, c. 218 BC

A quarrel about the small print in a treaty has ignited hostilities between old enemies Rome and Carthage. Ordinary Romans and Carthaginians may well be reflecting that the quarrel would have been better resolved by lawyers than by the thousands of deaths that are now likely.

The Treaty of Ebro in 226 was intended to reassure Marseilles, a Spanish colony allied to Rome and worried about Hamilcar's Spanish campaign. By signing the treaty Hasdrubal, Hamilcar's son, agreed to remain south of the River Ebro.

But five years later Hannibal became Carthaginian commander and promptly besieged Saguntum, a town actually south of the river but allied to Rome. Rome interpreted this as a treaty violation, and when Saguntum fell to Hannibal in 219 the declaration of the Second Punic War was inevitable.

Hannibal vs Rome

After his mountainous journey, Hannibal quickly reinforced his depleted army by recruiting local Gauls and by conquest. Many of the tribes in northern Italy allied themselves with Hannibal out of fear. This enlarged army, together with Hannibal's gifted leadership, was enough to bring about a series of notable victories, including those at:

- **River Trebbia** (218 BC)
In a winter battle the Romans were lured by Hannibal to attack across a river that was freezing cold and already thawing. When the Romans were exhausted, a concealed Punic force fell upon them. Of the 40,000 men only 10,000 escaped alive.

- **Lake Trasimene** (217 BC)
This was an ambush of the army of Flaminius, who was trying to trap Hannibal in a two-pronged manoeuvre between himself and Servilius. Hannibal attacked the Romans while they were marching and most of the men were either drowned or taken captive. Servilius lost 4,000 cavalry.

- **Cannae** (216 BC)
A classic encirclement strategy was used by Hannibal to annihilate the armies of Varro and Paullis – a total of 80,000 men. The victory, one of Hannibal's greatest, led to some of Rome's southern allies defecting to Hannibal.

- **Tarentum** (213 BC)
The fall of Tarentum was a great prize for Hannibal. It had the best naval port in southern Italy, and had been a wealthy and strategic city for centuries.

Hannibal takes the trunk route through frozen mountain

Europe, 218 BC

Rome intends to take the battle with Carthage to Spain and fight Hannibal on his own ground. The Roman navy is now a sophisticated fighting force and the army is in peak condition.

However it looks as though, yet again, that the Romans have not reacted quickly enough to the threat posed by Carthage.

The Carthaginian leader Hannibal has joined the Gauls against Rome after marching his men and a herd of elephants for hundreds of miles across two mountain ranges in sub-zero temperatures. It was a bold and brilliant strategy which has taken the Roman command completely by surprise.

Hannibal led his small army of 20,000 men plus an additional force of 6,000 attached to a battalion of war elephants across the Pyrenees to the Rhone Valley in France. He then moved away from Roman-held territory, heading north through the freezing snow-bound High Alps to make a mountain crossing in winter which even the locals would consider highly dangerous if not impossible.

He has now arrived in the region of the Po River where he has joined up with a force of Gauls. His army has lost about 15,000 men from the harsh conditions and local skirmishes. But Rome's total army of 600,000 men now seems very vulnerable, especially as the Roman war effort is in complete disarray.

The original plan to invade Spain and seize Hannibal personally has been abandoned as has an invasion of Carthage launched at the same time. The forces involved are reported to be making their way north to meet Hannibal, though disturbing reports are arriving that

Permanent snow covers the high Alps.

the first Carthaginian victory of the war may have been won in a surprise attack on the Romans.

Han dynasty ends wars with Qin

China, 206 BC

The oppressive Qin dynasty of China has ended, leaving behind great achievements and a people weary from years of warfare.

Liu Pang has defeated all rivals and proclaimed himself emperor. He is the first emperor of the Han dynasty and has begun his reign by easing laws and taxes. He is taking a less isolationist attitude to neighbouring countries in the hope that this will stimulate trade.

Confucianism has been officially adopted by the new dynasty, though Liu Pang is not a doctrinaire

Hannibal is running out of supplies!

Europe, c. 207 BC

Hannibal is marching towards Rome, but his army is too small to take the city. He has been demanding reinforcements for some time, but Carthage has been unable to send enough.

His early gains are now largely squandered and Rome, able to conscript a huge local population, is looking to avenge the string of crushing defeats by Hannibal over the past decade.

The latest blow for the African general is the failure of his brother Hasdrubal who brought a reinforcing army across the Alps to join up with him.

The enterprise went wrong when the Romans confronted Hasdrubal in northern Italy, defeated his army, and killed him.

Hannibal is also said to be very alarmed at the activities of Scipio Africanus, who is having great success in his campaign against the Carthaginians in Spain. Unless he can turn the war round in Italy, Hannibal may end up with nowhere to run to.

Confucian and is drawing on other traditions as well.

One Confucian principle he is affirming strongly, however, is that of putting qualified people into leadership rather than choosing them on the basis of nepotism or obligation.

There are plans for a Confucian university to train politicians. Potential state employees already must show that they have the basic skills necessary to do the job – an unpleasant shock after the way lucrative posts were handed out under the Qins.

Africanus defeats African genius on African soil

This amphitheatre still standing today in El-Jem is a lasting memorial to the defeat of Carthage and its subsequent colonisation by the Romans.

North Africa, 202 BC
The Second Punic War is over. Rome has not only crushed Carthage but now has undisputed possession of the island of Sicily.

The Carthaginians in Spain are a beaten and spent force after their defeat by Scipio Africanus. He took his victorious army on to north Africa, threatening Carthage itself, in an attempt to destroy his enemy once and for all.

The Carthaginians, desperate to defend their home base, summoned Hannibal back from Italy to assist them. The war in Italy already was looking a lost cause. The Roman general Fabius Maximus (responsible for the defeat of Hannibal's third brother, Mago, in Liguria) had been recapturing the Italian territories that Hannibal conquered.

It was in Africa that the Carthaginians made their fatal mistake in this long war. Despite the fact that negotiations were in progress for a settlement – Hannibal having decided that defeat was certain – the Carthaginians decided to attack. At Zama, Scipio (who is now a Roman consul) met Hannibal, now joined by his brother Mago, in the final showdown. The Carthaginian rag-tag army of raw recruits was decisively defeated.

Carthage is finished. The Treaty of Tunis that has now been signed by all parties brutally emphasises her departure from the world stage.
• Spain and all Carthage's Mediterranean possessions are given to Rome.
• Carthage must pay Rome 200 talents a year for 50 years.
• All but 10 of Carthage's warships are to be destroyed.

Antiochus restores Seleucid fortunes

Asia Minor, c. 200 BC
Antiochus III (known by his followers as 'Antiochus the Great'), who has been king of Macedonia since 242 and became king of Syria in 223, has expanded his empire into Parthia and Bactria. Both were lost under his father.

He is now engaged in wars with Ptolemy V of Egypt, a nation whose power is on the wane; and he looks set to take possession of Palestine and Lebanon.

Under Antiochus the Seleucid dynasty is rapidly regaining greatness. Antiochus II (known as 'Antiochus the Divine') never fully recovered national prestige after a wearying struggle against Egypt, and though he took back many territories lost by Antiochus I, the empire was badly depleted under his rule.

New media renders papyrus obsolete

Turkey, c. 200 BC
Papyrus stocks running low have prompted Turkish scribes to look for other writing material. They have invented a better quality and longer-lasting product.

'Parchment' takes its name from the Turkish city of Pergamum, where it is said to have been invented by King Eumenes II. It is made from animal skins – usually of sheep, calves or goats.

The skins are not tanned but soaked in water and stretched on frames, then scraped until their surface is smooth. When a good writing surface has been obtained, pumice powder is rubbed on for a final finish.

The best parchment in the world is said to come from Pergamum. An even finer material still, vellum, is made from the skins of unborn calves, and is highly prized for its superb quality and, like parchment, its durability.

The implements remained the same for writing on papyrus or parchment: pen, quills, inkpot and board for mixing inks.

Scythed off

Russia, c. 200 BC

The Scythians, who have occupied the Russian Steppes since conquering them in c. 700, are finally being forced to abandon the rich valleys and fertile fields which they have cultivated for centuries.

Believed to have come originally from Persia, they have been major exporters of grain, wax and slaves to the Greek colonies. Barbarians in Greek eyes, they have nevertheless been partly Hellenised as can be seen by the finely-crafted artefacts which they bury with their dead. The Greek historian Herodotus wrote of them at length in the fifth century BC.

Ironically, the people who are displacing the Scythians from their traditional homeland are also of Persian origin. The Samartians, like the Scythians, are nomads. They comprise a mixture of races, including some slavonic tribes.

Muddied water

Cyprus, 200 BC

Salamis, which was the capital city of the Ptolemies, has been abandoned in favour of Paphos on the south-west of the island. The reason is the silting up of its harbour, ruining it as an economic and naval centre.

The Bay of Salamis was the site of a great sea battle in the Second

Salamis: the east portico of the Palaestra.

Persian War, when in 480 Themistocles rashly engaged the Persians, with the result that his huge fleet was out-manoeuvred and annihilated.

In 318 Macedonia took Salamis, but it was eventually retaken by Athens.

Rosetta stone reveals all

This black basalt stone was to hold the key to deciphering Egyptian hieroglyphics. The first register was written in Egyptian hieroglyphics; the second, also in Egyptian, was written in Egyptian demotic script; the final register was written in Greek.

Egypt, 196 BC

A block of black basalt stone has been inscribed to commemorate the Egyptian king Ptolemy V Epiphanes, with a decree praising him. The inscription is in two languages, but written in three scripts: hieroglyphic, demotic (a later cursive version of hieroglyphic) and Greek.

It has been set up at Rashid near Rosetta, in the Nile delta region of Lower Egypt, following a decree passed by a council of Egyptian priests, assembled in the capital Memphis.

Judea goes crazy for all things Greek

Judea, c. 173 BC

Greek fashions, customs and games are now sweeping Judea off its traditional feet and causing consternation among the religiously orthodox.

A local conflict between the sons of Tobias and the high priest Onias III – who had expelled them from Jerusalem – has escalated into a major confrontation with Antiochus IV, who has ruled Syria for the past two years. The party supporting the sons of Tobias had appealed to him for support.

As a result Onias has been sacked by the king. But Onias' brother Jason has taken the vacant position among rumours that he secured it by bribery. His use of a Greek name is significant, for Jason is a fanatical Helleniser.

He has begun to make Greece and all things Greek the fashion, so that many Jews have adopted Greek versions of their names ('Jason' for 'Joshua', and 'Menelaus' for 'Menahem', for example). The aristocracy has established an arena for Greek games next to the temple, and the streets of Jerusalem are full of people wearing the latest Greek clothes.

Judea still important

While great struggles have dominated the world stage, many people have lost interest in the tiny remnant of the once-great people of Yahweh in Palestine. Throughout the turmoil, Judea has been caught in the crossfire of rival empires. Currently it is being pressured into adopting Greek culture. Here is a brief chronology of significant events (especially in Syria) during the past century.

• 301 BC: The Battle of Ipsus, and the death of Alexander's self-proclaimed successor, Antigonus the one-eyed, resolve the matter of who should inherit Alexander's empire. In the post-battle diplomacy, Syria becomes the possession of two rulers: Seleucus in the north and Ptolemy (who has proclaimed himself king of Egypt) in the south.

• 295 BC: The Seleucid kings temporarily control Palestine.

• 285 BC: Ptolemy abdicates after a reign in which Egypt became a centre of Greek culture.

• 283 BC: In Egypt 70 scholars begin the translation of the Hebrew Scriptures into Greek. The work is called the Septuagint, after the Greek word for 'seventy'.

• 281 BC: Seleucus assassinated and is succeeded by Antiochus I.

• c. 261 BC: Antiochus I dies. During his reign he lost considerable territory to Ptolemy II of Egypt. He is succeeded by Antiochus II.

• 247 BC: Ptolemy III begins to reign in Egypt. He was well-disposed to the Jews and even offered a sacrifice in the temple at Jerusalem. Antiochus II dies, having regained much of what his father lost, but Egypt takes advantage to weaken Seleucid power.

• 223 BC: Antiochus III ('The Great') becomes king of Syria.

• 218 BC: Antiochus begins to attack Judea.

• 217 BC: Antiochus is defeated by Ptolemy IV in the Battle of Raphia. The battle was to resolve the on-going territorial conflict between the two kingdoms, whose only common border is a narrow strip of Mediterranean shore north of Sinai. For Egypt it coincided with the twilight of the Hellenic period and the rise of the meritocracy. For the Seleucids it was the beginning of the end.

• 202 BC: Antiochus III again attacks Egypt. The campaign follows a secret treaty with Macedonia, and succeeds mainly because the new king of Egypt, Ptolemy V, is only a child.

• 200 BC: Battle of Panion (on the Jordan); Antiochus wins a great victory and takes control of Judea and Phoenicia. Judea is now under the control of the Seleucids.

Ruined castles are common throughout Syria, a country which has been the scene of many a battle throughout the centuries. This Arab castle is situated near Palmyra.

Antiochus begins a vigorous programme of Hellenization throughout his empire.

Onias' murder is avenged by king

Antioch, Syria, c. 170 BC

Despite having effectively deposed Onias III as high priest in Jerusalem, Antiochus Ephiphanes has avenged the religious leader's

A Roman acqueduct serving Antioch.

cold-blooded assassination in typically brutal fashion.

Onias had denounced Menelaus, the current title holder, for removing treasures from the temple and selling them. Fearing for his life, Onias sought sanctuary at Daphne, where he was approached by Menelaus and his deputy Andronicus.

Andronicus offered Onias the right hand of fellowship and promised him safe passage. But as soon as the trusting but naive priest emerged from his shelter he was hacked down.

Many Greeks joined the Jews in Antioch in expressing their horror at the death of a man known and respected for his firm opinions and peacemaking role. They appealed to Antiochus for justice, and the king is said to have wept openly when he heard the report. During a visit to Antioch he stripped Andronicus of his purple robe of office and personally killed him on the spot where Onias had fallen.

(2 Maccabees 4:30–38)

No small change at the temple

Jerusalem, c. 171 BC

The job of high priest has been taken by Menelaus, who has outbid the current titleholder Jason during a mission to King Antiochus IV authorised by Jason. He paid 300 talents for the title.

It has left many Jews feeling dangerously resentful. For devout Jews the high priest is the symbol of all that Judaism stands for.

Menelaus is the second in succession who holds the office illegitimately. Onias III was the last legitimate high priest. Menelaus does not even belong to a priestly family.

Jason has fled into exile in Ammon

(2 Maccabees 4:23–29)

Hassidic Jew in Jerusalem today.

Jason seizes chance to become Jewish argonaut

Jerusalem, c. 175 BC

Fortune's smile for one man is Fate's frown on another in the turbulent world of international politics.

In the small but strategic buffer zone of Judea high priest Onias III had just been building bridges of peace in Greece with world ruler Seleucus IV when the monarch was assassinated. Back home Onias' brother Jason (who now parades under his Greek name rather than his Jewish name of Joshua) seized the opportunity to emulate the heroic escapades of his mythical namesake.

He bought himself a place in the history books at Onias' expense by offering the new ruler Antiochus IV (Epiphanes) 440 talents (about 13 tonnes) of silver and the promise of full co-operation with the Seleucid's Hellenization programme. In return he would become high priest.

With everything to gain and nothing to lose from the deal, Antiochus accepted the offer gratefully. The newly-installed Jason is already promoting Greek games and fashion. He has built a gymnasium where youths sport in the nude, to the consternation of the religiously orthodox Judeans, and which is also becoming a centre of alternative Jewish leadership.

Onias, an orthodox and conservative Jew, had been pursuing a damage-limitation exercise to preserve Jewish culture and to restrict the mandatory participation in Greek customs which would offend many of his countrymen.

However, his removal from office has effectively broken the Seleucid pledge made by Antiochus III (198–187 BC) to allow the Jews to retain their distinctiveness. And Jason's brazen purchase of high religious office is regarded by the faithful as a major sin against God.

(2 Maccabees 4:1–17)

A pair of terracotta statuettes of two unmistakably African boxers. The gloves offer little protection and are equipped with balls of lead to give a brutal blow.

Aged defender of Israel dies

Judea, c. 166 BC

Mattathias the father of the Maccabees has died, only months after spearheading a brave resistance to the anti-Jewish forces now occupying Judea. He was a priest at Modein not far from Jerusalem.

When Antiochus' men arrived at Modein demanding that Mattathias obey the Hellenistic decrees, he refused to offer incense to Zeus. When a collaborating Jew offered it instead, he killed him on the spot.

As a result he took to the hills as an outlaw with his five sons and other Jews who joined his cause to engineer a rebellion against Antiochus. They have been raiding towns and villages to harass Syrians and Greek sympathisers.

This task has now been taken up by his son Judas Maccabeus, the surname meaning 'hammer'.

A significant number of other Jews who are called the 'Pious Party' (or Hasidim) have also refused to participate in Hellenistic practices and are accepting martyrdom rather than worship Zeus in the temple.

Mattathias persuaded a pragmatic rather than dogmatic approach to resistance. After some of his supporters were slaughtered because they refused to fight defensively on the Sabbath, he allowed that defence was permitted even on holy days.

(1 Maccabees 2)

Rebellion crushed

Jerusalem, 169 BC

Jason the deposed high priest and his guerilla army of 1,000 men have been evicted from Jerusalem having briefly occupied the city and forced current high priest Menelaus to take refuge in the temple.

The adventurer, who bought the high priesthood from Antiochus IV, had been outbid for the office two years ago. He attacked the city to avenge Antiochus' removal of the sacred furnishings and gold decorations from the temple to finance his war in the Near East.

Jason may have made his strike in response to a rumour that Antiochus had been killed. Although regarded by orthodox Jews as preferable to Menelaus, Jason soon lost popular support by indiscriminately killing a large number of citizens. Menelaus rallied sufficient help to repel the invader, and reassert his loyalty to Antiochus.

(2 Maccabees 5:5–10)

A religion is raped

Jerusalem, 167 BC

The city of Jerusalem is in a state of deep shock. It has experienced what is probably its worst ever violation in its long and chequered history.

Capital of the Jewish nation and centre of the Jewish religion, it has been destroyed several times by invaders in the past. But never before has its sanctuary been so horribly ravished.

A pig has been sacrificed on its holy altar. And pigs, to Jews, are the most unclean of all animals. Further desecration occurred when Greek soldiers had sex in the temple courtyard. It is the religious equivalent of the sordid and brutal rape of a virgin in a manner to cause the greatest humiliation possible.

The rapist was King Antiochus IV, whose vendetta against Jewish resistance to his programme of enforced Hellenization has now reached its nadir. His action was as much a result of hurt pride as hatred of the Jews, however, and Jerusalem happened to be a soft target lying in his way.

Despite his previous successes in Egypt, he had been expelled from Alexandria by the Roman envoy who cut the Greek down to size. He forced Antiochus to promise to retreat before allowing him to step outside a circle the envoy had drawn round him on the ground.

Anxious to stamp his authority on Palestine again, Antiochus attacked Jerusalem on a Sabbath when the majority of orthodox believers refused to fight. Many people were killed in the invasion, including Eleazar, an elderly scribe who became typical of many others by accepting martyrdom rather than eat pig meat at sword-point. Copies of the Scriptures have been burned and all Jewish customs such as circumcision and Sabbath observance are punishable by death.

Antiochus, whose surname Epiphanes (meaning illustrious, as in the sense of divine) has been changed by the locals to Epimanes (madman), then set up an image of Zeus – said to look more like the king than the god – in the temple and ordered the pork sacrifices.

Those orthodox Jews able to reflect on the events point back to a prophecy by Daniel which prefigured the setting up of an 'abominable desolation' in the temple by a Greek king. Abominable it certainly was; desolation is what Jerusalem is now.

(1 Maccabees 1:41–64; 2 Maccabees 6:1–11; cf. Daniel 11:31–32)

South Jerusalem and the Kidron Valley.

Fast Facts
c. 200–175 BC

Greece, c. 175 BC: Seleucus IV has been assassinated and his brother Antiochus IV has seized the throne. Antiochus, who is nicknamed Epiphanes (the illustrious or divine manifestation) has been a hostage in Rome for 12 years. Born in Athens where he served as chief magistrate, he is known to be an ardent Hellenizer determined to force Greek culture on all subject states.

Persia, c. 164 BC: The Seleucid king Antiochus IV, who called himself Epiphanes in a scarcely-veiled claim to divinity, has died during a military campaign in Media. He had ruthlessly opposed foreign cultures and religions which would not accept Greek customs. He is succeeded by his 10 year-old son Antiochus V who will reign through the regency of Lysias, the senior military commander.

South America, c. 200 BC: The alpaca, a domesticated member of the llama family, is being bred in the Andes for its exceptionally fine wool, and for meat. It is thought to have been the product of selective breeding of the guanaco, a wild ruminant.

Mexico City, c. 200 BC: The Zapotec people have rebuilt the centre of their capital, Monte Alban. This thriving city of approximately 20,000 people now boasts a new religious and civic city centre, the hub of a community that lives in a series of terraced dwellings on the surrounding hillsides.

Guerrilla war fares well in Judea

Arad and the South Judean hills provide good pasture-land for most of the year.

Judea, c. 165 BC

Judas Maccabeus is poised to march on Jerusalem following the most outstanding victory in a string of unexpected successes during his two-year campaign against the might of the Seleucid occupiers.

Outnumbered six to one at Beth-zur in Idumea he routed the Syrian troops of Lysias, the commander personally appointed by Antiochus IV to control the rebels.

It was the Syrian's second major reversal at the hands of Judas. The Maccabee (his nickname means the hammer) cheekily ransacked Lysias' camp at Emmaus while part of the Syrian force was roaming the hills looking for him.

Judas had previously inflicted embarrassing defeats on other Seleucid commanders during two years of skirmishing. A mission launched from Samaria by Apollonius was crushed with Judas personally killing the general and then using his dead enemy's sword to inflict further damage on the army. At the Bethshoron Pass he literally chased the general Seron down the valleys after a surprise attack by the Jewish volunteers.

His leadership is reminiscent of great Jewish leaders of the past. Like Joshua, who led the conquest of the 'promised land' a millennium ago, he encourages his troops with faith in Yahweh's providence, power and protection. He is known to pray before battles and any major decisions. Prior to the encounter at Beth-zur the Judeans gathered at Mizpah, an ancient religious centre, to pray, fast and enquire of the Scriptures.

Judas also has the practical advantage of being familiar with the hilly terrain of this strategic strip of land. The steep valleys are more suited to his style of guerilla warfare than to the set-piece battles of professional armies. Since his father Mattathias launched the 'Maccabean revolt' in 167, Judas has harassed numerous Syrian outposts and destroyed many local Hellenistic shrines.

(1 Maccabees 3:1–4:25)

Judas wins Jews a major concession

Jerusalem, 164 BC

Freedom-fighter Judas Maccabeus has scored his biggest victory yet; the Syrians have agreed to recognise the right of the Jewish people to religious liberty.

Menelaus, the usurper high priest, is to be removed from office and replaced by the moderate Hellenizer Eliakim (also known as Alcimus). And Judas is to be granted complete immunity from prosecution.

The concessions were granted by Lysias who had besieged Judas in Jerusalem but was hurriedly called to Antioch where a rival threatened to oust him.

This comes at the end of a series of attacks and counter-attacks that have hurt Syria much more than the Maccabean army.

The Syrians intended to wipe out the resistance army in retaliation for their retaking of the temple, but the Maccabeans have fortified the temple and the city, and have maintained the initiative with the support of the local population.

However, the peace treaty has not been welcomed by Judas, although he has accepted the majority decision of the provisional government in Jerusalem.

Judas Maccabeus is said to regard religious liberty as only part of the goal for which he has been fighting; he wants political freedom as well, and fears that without it the present mood of tolerance will not last for long. He appears keen to achieve his goals whatever the cost.

Antiochus IV, licking his wounds in Babylon, following an abortive attempt to loot the wealthy Persian city of Elymais, was furious to learn that his generals were leading a major retreat from the Maccabees.

(1 Maccabees 5,6)

The Holy City is purified again

Jerusalem, December 164 BC

Many who have been wondering just how far Judas Maccabeus would go in his campaign against the Seleucids now have their answer. After achieving a crushing defeat of Antiochus' general Lysias, who lost 5,000 men in the battle at Beth-zur, he has marched with his brothers at the head of his small army into Jerusalem itself.

There he entered the temple which for three years has been consecrated to the worship of the Greek gods and ceremonially cleansed it amid great rejoicing.

Judas and his men found the temple in rack and ruin. The altar, on which an image of Zeus had been set, was desecrated and defiled. The great gates had been used as firewood, and the courtyards that once had been kept immaculate by the priests were tangled with three years' growth of weeds. They went into the priest's chambers, and found the same story there. To a man, they broke into passionate mourning and abased themselves before God.

Judas has planned the cleansing and rededication of the temple with the same meticulous care with which he plans his battles. Only priests without blemish have been selected to take the sacrilegious objects out of the temple. The defiled altar has been demolished (the parts are being kept in storage until a priest can rule on what to do with them), and a new altar has been built in the pattern of the old. All the soiled furniture and fittings have been replaced, and the courtyards are clean and weeded.

The temple is now back just as it was before the 'abomination of desolation'. The city itself is also being re-fortified and a permanent garrison of loyal Jewish fighters is to be stationed there.

The celebrations to consecrate the new altar took place three years to the day after the desecration of the temple. For eight days, the building

A model of the second temple of Jerusalem.

was alive with the sound of singing, harps, lutes and cymbals, as the people rejoiced that the disgrace inflicted on them and the most holy things of their religion had been erased.

Judas and the people have decided that this is to be an annual festival, called Hanukkah, which means Dedication or the Festival of Lights.

(1 Maccabees 4:34–61)

The Maccabean rulers

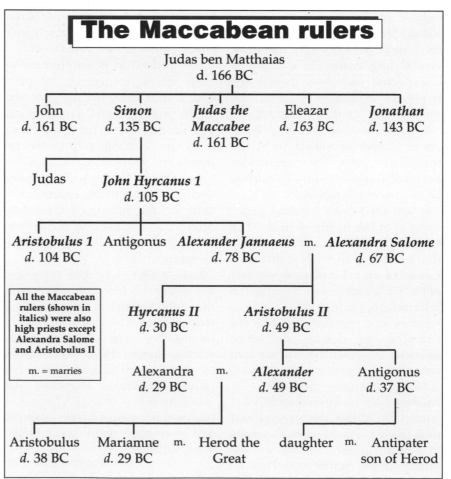

Judas ben Matthaias
d. 166 BC

John	Simon	Judas the Maccabee	Eleazar	Jonathan
d. 161 BC	*d.* 135 BC	*d.* 161 BC	*d.* 163 BC	*d.* 143 BC

Judas   *John Hyrcanus 1*
d. 105 BC

Aristobulus 1   Antigonus   *Alexander Jannaeus*   m.   *Alexandra Salome*
d. 104 BC   *d.* 78 BC   *d.* 67 BC

All the Maccabean rulers (shown in italics) were also high priests except Alexandra Salome and Aristobulus II

m. = marries

Hyrcanus II   *Aristobulus II*
d. 30 BC   *d.* 49 BC

Alexandra   m.   *Alexander*   Antigonus
d. 29 BC   *d.* 49 BC   *d.* 37 BC

Aristobulus   Mariamne   m.   Herod the   daughter   m.   Antipater
d. 38 BC   *d.* 29 BC   Great   son of Herod

Maccabean cause falters after loss

Judea, c. 161 BC

The death of Judas Maccabeus, unquestionably one of the greatest generals that the nation has ever had, leaves the independence struggle in disarray.

His final months lacked the brilliant effectiveness of his earlier campaigns. Having secured religious freedom for the people, Judas decided to fight on for political autonomy.

His own worst fears were confirmed when the puppet high priest Alcimus arrested and executed some of the Hasidim, the orthodox religious patriots who had supported the Maccabeans.

When Antiochus IV died, Judas tried to seize the Syrian fortress in Jerusalem, but failed. Only local problems for the regency of Antiochus V in Syria saved Judas from utter defeat and the loss of his army. Antiochus and Lysias were assassinated in a Syrian army coup and Demetrius I took the throne, appointing a high priest with Syrian sympathies. The Jews were divided over him, but he antagonised the people, giving Judas the initiative.

In the subsequent fighting Judas appealed to Rome for help, who intervened against Syria. At Bethhoron, to the immediate north-west of Jerusalem, he won a major victory, but was killed shortly afterwards in the nearby Battle of Elasa.

Judas has been buried in the family grave at Modein, and the mourning lasted for many days. He was regarded as the champion and saviour of Israel, and his successes in so few years were astonishing.

Following his death, the Syrian governor Bacchides put strong supporters of the Seleucids in control of Jerusalem, who began to root out Maccabean sympathisers. Judas' brothers Simon, Jonathan and Johanan have gone into hiding in the desert.

(1 Maccabees 7:1–9:34)

Many caves in the Judean desert provided the Macabeans with good hiding places.

Diplomatic rebel falls to deceit

Ptolemais, c. 143 BC

Jonathan Maccabeus, the leader of the Jewish resistance forces, has been killed by Trypho, a presumed ally who was seeking to take the throne of Syria.

Trypho lured Jonathan to the small coastal town of Ptolemais south of Tyre with an offer of peace and restitution of settlements previously taken.

Having dismissed most of his forces, Jonathan was hacked down in the city. Trypho was afraid that Jonathan might thwart his plans.

The loss of Jonathan, youngest brother of the great Judas Maccabeus, has not aroused widespread grief so much as fear: it is thought that the Gentiles now regard the Jews as leaderless and vulnerable.

Yet Jonathan leaves the nation in a better state than when he took over. He has led a small rebel army, but his has been a time of rebuilding and consolidation.

His achievements are mainly diplomatic and administrative. He steered a middle line between rival Seleucid kings, and his delaying tactics brokered a degree of peace.

His greatest success was the 157 peace agreement with Syria. Demetrius was anxious to agree because problems in Syria demanded his full attention. He also made treaties with Sparta and Rome, although neither power did much to assist him.

In 153 Alexander Balas, then ruler of Syria, made Jonathan high priest at Jerusalem. That effectively made him leader of Judea.

Simon says – and all obey

Jerusalem, 141 BC

Simon Maccabeus has negotiated a peace deal with Demetrius II of Syria, in which virtually all the demands of this long Maccabean revolt were met.

The Syrians agreed to relinquish Judea and abandon their fortress in Jerusalem. Judea receives some territories, and can now, it is confidently hoped, look forward to many years of peace and prosperity.

Simon has been high priest and unchallenged ruler of Judea as the result of a massive vote of confidence from the people and priests. Many suggest that this remarkable dynasty – Simon is the fourth national deliverer in the family – has proved itself many times over to be God's strategy for the protection of his people.

The decision to make the high priesthood and the civil leadership the hereditary possession of the Maccabeus family has been widely approved.

The new dynasty is to be known as Hasmonean, believed to be named after an ancestor called Hashmon. The Hasidim – the most orthodox Jews – have recognised the line of Onias as true heirs of the priesthood, but as the family has emigrated to Egypt its claims on the title are deemed to have been forfeited.

(1 Maccabees 13)

263

India struggles as Mauryan Buddhist legacy crumbles

India, c. 160 BC

India is in turmoil. The achievements of the recent golden age of art and Buddhist religion during the Maurya dynasty, have been turned upside down. New conquerors are on the horizon.

The last of the Mauryan rulers, murdered by one of his chief ministers in 185, left a dynasty that hardly extended beyond Magadha, its home province. All the other Mauryan lands have been gradually seized by rivals.

India was already a disunited and troubled land, and the new Sunga dynasty is floundering in a period when predatory Greek armies roam India and make uneasy Indo-Greek alliances. It is an sad end to the long years of peace enjoyed by India under benevolent leadership.

The Mauryan dynasty had ruled India since 321 BC, when the kingdom of Magadha in central India was conquered by Chandra-

The head of the Buddha. A typical stone statue from the Gandhara period, second-century BC.

gupta. He became the founder of the dynasty and extended his empire across most of India. It was the might of this empire that led Seleucus I (founder of the Seleucid empire) to make a marriage-treaty with it in 305.

This marked the beginning of increasing Hellenization in India, a time when ambassadors from Greek monarchs lived in the Indian capital, Patilaputra. But the official religion became Buddhism during the life and proselytising of the greatest of all the Mauryan monarchs, the monk Asoka, who died in 232.

It was a period of artistic excellence, often drawing on both Greek and Buddhist themes; under Asoka, characteristic sculptured reliefs began to appear. They reflected the Buddhist doctrine of universal love to all creation and often contained highly realistic representations of nature and animal life.

During this period, however, a split developed within Indian Buddhism, between the purer Hinayana doctrine based in Ceylon and the more mystical Mahayana

whose emphasis on bodhisattvas, or Buddhas of the future, diminished the worship of the original Buddha.

Now Buddhists are being persecuted in India, and Brahmanism is in the ascendant. India is in the process of becoming re-Indianised, and a caste system is beginning to be established which bodes badly for hopes of unification.

But a new threat is facing India which may be more devastating than any internal struggles. Huge migratory movements of peoples in central Asia are impacting on the subcontinent. The Yueh-chi, expelled from Mongolia by the Huns, are moving west and threatening Bactria. Scythian nomads are threatening Parthia. Other tribes are on the move too. It may well be that India's Asoka idyll was the last sustained period of relative tranquillity the subcontinent will be experiencing for some time.

Cato keeps old hatreds well alive

Rome, 160 BC

Two crushing defeats of Carthage in two Punic wars aren't enough to satisfy Roman statesman-writer Cato the Elder.

Cato, who became consul in 195, reserves his greatest hatred for Carthage, which ever since a visit to Africa three years ago he has castigated as a cess-pit of luxury and extravagance and still a threat to Rome. He now ends every one of his speeches with the ringing words, 'Carthage must be destroyed!'

A farmer by upbringing, he hates all foreigners, including the Greeks. He believes Greek culture saps the greatness of the Roman way of life.

The Hindu god Vishna.

Broken truce sparks fears of fresh wars in north Africa

Rome, c. 150 BC

Cato, the scourge of Carthage, has returned to his anti-Carthage rhetoric following the African state's renewed attack on Numidia.

The attack broke a truce which Cato had mediated seven years ago, and confirmed all his warnings about Carthage's untrustworthiness. His predictions that Carthage would be a threat to Rome again are proving true; the aged Numidian king Massinissa is an ally of Rome.

Carthage however is now a shadow of the great power that

Cato, after an eighth-century etching.

once dominated the Mediterranean. Not only is it virtually reduced to being an African vassal state of Rome, crippled with burdensome reparations, but it has been forced to relinquish more and more territory to the growing might of Numidia which is clearly in Rome's interests. It was Numidian cavalry that secured Rome's victory at Zama in 202.

Massinissa himself was once an ally of Carthage, but transferred his loyalty to Rome in 206. He has done well out of the deal and has been paid for his aid at Zama. As part of the victory settlement, Carthage was forced to hand over to Numidia all Carthaginian land that had ever been in Massinissa's or his

family's possession. Though he is an enthusiast for Carthaginian culture, he and his kingdom have prospered on account of Carthage's current plight.

It says much for Carthage's resilience (and accounts for some of Cato's fears) that through its efficient and advanced agriculture, Carthage has managed to regain much of its prosperity. But as more and more of its rich agricultural territory passes into the hands of the ever-competitive Numidians, Carthage's temper is fraying. It is common knowledge that the government there has been re-arming for the past two years in preparation for a possible conflict with Massinissa.

Numidia provoked into new attack

Carthage, 149 BC

Events in Carthage are edging towards another devastating war as two armies face each other across the troubled Punic/Numidian border.

Carthage has finally acted to resolve the growing tension between the two rival states, and in a move that some have seen as reckless has provoked Massinissa, the pro-Roman king of Numidia into attacking her. This has neatly circumvented one of the key terms of the Treaty of Tunis which prohibited Carthage waging war without Rome's permission. Massinissa is demanding that Carthage pay a tribute tax to Numidia.

Rome has responded swiftly; a local war on its southern flank between two client states is certain to be disastrous at a time when stability is all-important. The Roman leadership is also clearly

The sand dunes of the encroaching Sahara desert near Carthage.

wondering whether favouring Numidia as much as it has might have created a potential military threat to itself. Even without Cato's hectoring Romans are irritated that their beaten enemy Carthage seems to be regaining wealth and prosperity even though its trade has been ruined.

Indeed, Carthage has often appealed for help to Rome against the encroachments of the Numidians, but Rome has turned a deaf ear to its pleas. Carthage has been ordered to disband its army and burn its fleet, though for several months now the Roman authorities have seemed content to play a watching game and allow a state of uneasy stand-off to continue.

China returns to harsh rule

China, c. 160 BC

Wu Ti, the Han emperor who inherited a thriving economy has spent most of it on expanding the empire, which now reaches as far as Manchuria and Korea in the north and Kazakhstan in the west. The south below the Yangtze River remains troublesome.

Terracotta figure of a foot soldier, 1.87 m tall (6 ft 2 in) excavated in the mausoleum of the emperor at Lintong, Shaanxi Province.

To pay for this, China has returned to the harsh policies of the Qins, increased taxes and state control, and introduced devaluation. The situation is made much worse by a soaring birth-rate. Already there is discontent and future rebellions are likely.

Rome vows to crush defiant Carthage

North Africa, c. 149 BC

Following its pre-emptive attack on Numidia in defiance of the Treaty of Tunis, Carthage is now deserted by its allies and threatened by both Numidia and Rome.

Its army having been beaten by Massinissa, Carthage rapidly changed policy and tried to negotiate an unconditional peace. Its huge arsenal and war-preparations have been handed over to the Roman consuls, leaving the city helpless and undefended. The neighbouring countries that might have supplied mercenary reinforcements for Carthage are all now siding with Rome.

Roman leader Cato is urging that this is not enough. The Carthaginian threat must be liquidated, he claims. The city must be totally destroyed and its population scattered. The 700,000 residents can only be fed and maintained by the commercial strength of Carthage, and by destroying the city the destruction of everything

A mosaic depicting a large farm and various farming activities near Carthage.

Carthaginian is guaranteed.

The Carthaginians, facing their old enemy for the third time and with nothing to lose, have decided to fight to the death. New weapons and defences have been hastily contrived. Carthaginian cavalry are trying to establish lines of supply through the region, and the people have retreated behind the city walls.

Numidia: Background Note

Numidia lies to the south and west of Carthage. The 'Numidae' – nomads – began to organise themselves into local alliances, and were noted for the quality of their cavalry. The Numidians broke away from Carthaginian domination under their chief Syphax who made an alliance with Rome in 213 BC.

Massinissa, the king of the Massyli people opposed Syphax's move. When Syphax changed his allegiance to Carthage in 206 BC Massinissa was exiled and proclaimed himself an ally of Rome. After a defeat in battle in 203 Syphax was captured and died in prison in Rome in 201 BC.

Massinissa then became ruler of Numidia, and the region entered a period of agricultural and urban expansion. During this period the foundations were laid for what was shortly to become a mighty empire.

Fast Facts 150–140 BC

Rome:, 150 BC The Romans have officially made 1 January the start of their civil calendar. The previous date of 15 March, when consuls traditionally take office, has had to be changed because of rebellion in Spain.

Syria, 150 BC: King Demetrius I, who seized power by killing the 11-year-old Antiochus V, has himself been killed in battle defending his throne against Alexander Balas who is claiming to be the son of Antiochus IV. Alexander has now been made king of Syria, with the recognition and support of Rome.

Syria, 145 BC: Alexander Balas is dead, killed in battle. His young son has acceded to the throne and has the title Antiochus VI.

Syria, 142 BC: Antiochus VI has died. Demetrius II is now king of Syria, in the latest turnaround in this fascinating rivalry between legitimate and illegitimate dynasties. Demetrius has now begun a campaign to conquer Babylonia.

Scipio takes control

Carthage, c. 147 BC

A bleak winter of cold and starvation is all the Carthaginians can look forward to as the new Roman general Scipio the Younger tightens his grip on the beleaguered city.

Scipio, elected Roman consul even though he is technically too young and inexperienced to be normally eligible for the post, has been given sole charge of the Carthage campaign.

This emer-gency resolution brings to an end a period of bungling by the Roman leadership, during which Carthage has been besieged and its field army reduced to skirmishing and foraging in the nearby territory.

Carthaginian hopes revived last year when a new military consul turned out to be a weak leader, preoccupied by the Macedonian conflict and a Spanish rebellion. Carthaginian infiltrators successfully provoked discontent in Numidia and surrounding territories, and morale in the Roman camp was beginning to fail.

The appointment of Scipio, who supervised the peaceful division of Massinissa's Numidian kingdom and earlier rallied the troops gathered round the walls of Carthage, has been seen as a good development.

Already he has instituted tough new disciplinary measures in the Roman camp and sent a number of useless administrators home. Then he began to isolate sectors of the city, clearing them of resistance one by one. The defenders are crowded now into the Old Quarter. Scipio has also taken steps to intercept Punic envoys and infiltrators in the surrounding countryside.

The Carthaginians, under Hasdrubal (who is not the first distinguished general to bear the name) are defending themselves heroically. When Roman prisoners are taken they are tortured to death in full view of both armies; which is hardly the act of a general hoping to negotiate a peaceful surrender. But Scipio's blockades by land and sea are gradually starving the Carthaginians.

Scipio's encirclement strategy has been completed by his closure of the harbour mouth. This has crippled the Punic fleet and ensured its destruction by the Roman ships, and has also secured the Romans a bridgehead.

Now winter has arrived. The last remnants of the Carthaginian field army have been eliminated. Behind the great walls of Carthage, now breached except for the Old Quarter, the starving inhabitants seek shelter and food. But little is to be found.

Roman oratory was highly regarded – and the best public speakers could expect statues to be erected in their honour in public places and at public expense, such as Aurus Metelus, pictured here.

Carthage destroyed

Carthage, c. 146 BC

Scenes of horrific carnage marked the final collapse of Carthage, as flames lit the city and the cries of the wounded and dying rose above the conqueror's shouts of triumph.

The victorious Romans advanced into the Old Quarter, looting and burning each house as they approached the citadel. Fifty thousand Carthaginians surrendered, and in a temple at the city's summit a group of Roman defectors who had joined Hasdrubal made their last stand.

Hasdrubal went to meet the invaders and pleaded for his life. In the temple the defectors, knowing that no mercy would be shown them, set the building alight and died in the flames; Hasdrubal's wife and children died with them.

As he looked out over the devastated city, Scipio quoted a passage from Homer's poem The *Iliad*, predicting the fall of Troy.

The Roman authorities have arrived in Carthage to protect the state's interests in the victory arrangements. The captives – men, women and children – have been sold as slaves. A proportion of the spoils of war and the booty looted from the city has been handed over to the government.

In a brilliant diplomatic gesture Scipio, finding a number of Greek statues in the city that had come to Carthage as trophies of previous Sicilian wars, has returned them to their rightful owners – thus securing links of friendship between several centres of culture in Sicily and Rome.

Carthage's territories are now a Roman province. Land has been given to, or taken from, the neighbouring cities depending on their allegiance during the war. Carthage itself has been levelled and left a wasteland; a curse has been pronounced on the very ground on which it stood.

Rome's century of war in the east

There has not been a single decade in this century when Rome has not been at war. The main theatre of conflict has been north Africa but there have been regular fights in Greece and Asia Minor.

c. 200 BC: Rhodes and Pergamum, allies of Rome, become vulnerable.

Rhodes has taken over Athens' position as trading centre, a role that depends on open sea access. But Philip V of Macedonia has plans to occupy the Hellespont.

Pergamum is apprehensive over Philip's intentions because of the threat to partition Egypt between Macedonia and Syria.

200 BC: Rome declares war against Macedonia.

197 BC: Philip is defeated by Roman consul Flaminius at the Battle of Cynoscephalae. Rome demands the surrender of his fleet, massive reparations, and Macedonian withdrawal from Thessalia and Greece (196 BC: Flaminius, at the Isthmian Games, declares Greek independence). With the threat of Philip removed, Antiochus III of Syria, who wants to be the leader of a united Hellenic world, attacks the Hellespont and a number of Asian cities. Subsequently Pergamum asks Rome to send investigators to assess the situation. Antiochus, convinced that Rome is planning war, now attacks Greece.

192 BC: Greeks in Aetolia, in north-west Greece, unilaterally invite Antiochus to invade Greece, where Rome has become unpopular. The Romans stop Antiochus at the Pass of Thermopylae.

191 BC: Antiochus' fleet is destroyed by the Romans.

189 BC: The Romans defeat Antiochus near Magnesia in Asia. The Seleucid dynasty of Antiochus loses its influence in the Mediterranean. The Roman attack is led by the two Scipios: Lucius Scipio and Scipio Africanus his brother and the father of the conqueror of Carthage.

188 BC: Antiochus is forced to sign the Treaty of Apamea. He loses all Asia west of the Taurus Mountains, which is then divided between Pergamum and Rhodes. The Aetolians and the Galatians are crushed. Booty from this campaign is the foundation of the city of Rome's future luxury, by freeing citizens from direct taxation.

179 BC: Philip V dies. Though he acquiesced in the defeat of Antiochus he has in fact been rearming, intending to punish

The Victory at Samothrace. One of the most famous statues preserved from Greek antiquity is also one of the few sculptures whose original setting we know. This awe-inspiring winged woman standing on a ship's prow was found on the island of Samothrace and was erected to celebrate a naval victory by the men of Rhodes over the Romans.

Rome for his defeat in 197 BC. His son Perseus aggravates friction with Rome. His army is destroyed at Pidna in 168 BC, Macedonia is quartered, and in 148 BC becomes a Roman province.

168 BC: Antiochus' attempt to introduce the worship of Zeus in Jerusalem sparks the Maccabean Revolt, but Syria's internal problems are such that the uprising cannot be suppressed.

Rhodes, which mistrusts Rome's intentions in the region and was only a reluctant ally in the fight against Perseus, loses her Asiatic empire. Delos, her main port, is declared a Free Port and Rhodes' trade is ruined; her ships are now very vulnerable to piracy.

Pergamum, also a reluctant ally of Rome, commences a period of uneasy relations with her.

147 BC: The Achaean League – a confederation of Greek states – is now the major power in the region after the fall of Macedonia. An uneasy relationship with Rome is broken when Rome takes Sparta (a member of the League) and occupies other sites strategically crucial to the League, which decides to fight to regain them.

146 BC: The League is defeated. Revolution in Corinth is brutally put down by Mummius who levels the city. All Rome's enemies are massacred and Greece is reduced to a Roman province.

133 BC: Attalus III of Pergamum dies and bequeaths his property and territories to Rome, and gives freedom to Greek cities within his kingdom. A mass uprising follows in 131 BC.

129 BC: Rome crushes the Pergamum uprising and established a new province of Asia.

Fat cats wallow in their war winnings

Rome, c. 135 BC

In Rome today the rich grow ever richer as the provinces grow ever more numerous. Africa, Greece and Asia are Roman provinces now, and money from them has poured into Rome's coffers.

Most of it has gone into the pockets of the nobiles, the wealthy aristocrats who are the power behind the Senate. They are mainly spending it on land, mostly at the expense of serving soldiers who are finding that the wearisome campaigns of recent years have made it impossible for them to look after their farming interests at home. Once their lands have been taken from them they are not even needed to farm them – there are plenty of slaves available after the recent wars, and slaves don't need paying.

It could all go wrong yet, however. To serve in the Roman army you have to be a landowner. Few of the aristocracy now lounging in their huge estates have realised that there are fewer and fewer fighting males who will be in a position to defend them when the next war starts.

Meanwhile wealthy Romans are enjoying an increasingly luxurious lifestyle. Greek culture is now the height of fashion, and the fine arts are flourishing, all heavily influenced by Hellenic art. Cato, who fought so long for the purity of Roman culture, is now seeing in Rome the very thing he despised in Carthage.

The wealthy Romans have more than Cato's wrath to fear, however. The poor, who have had no benefit from the wars, are becoming extremely restless.

People's champion ambushed

Rome, 133 BC

Rome's Tiber River is full of corpses and is running red with blood tonight. An heroic attempt to bring justice to Rome's poor (made landless by the rich senators) has ended in death for people's hero Tiberius Gracchus, at the hands of an enraged Senate.

Privilege could be bought. Musicians were often hired to perform in public in the streets in honour of whoever paid them. This drawing of street musicians comes from Pompeii.

Tiberius Gracchus, one of the 'Tribunus Plebs' (tribune elected to serve the interests of the people), was planning an ambitious programme of reforms to deal with a burning social injustice.

Many peasants, by serving in the army, have lost their lands. And much of the land that Rome has acquired by the battles the peasants fought is legally common land; peasants have, in theory, grazing and other rights upon it. But large tracts have been taken by the nobiles, quite illegally. Gracchus' suggestion was that all such land – beyond a token holding of around 300 acres, per present holder – should now be confiscated and redistributed among the poor.

Unusually and probably fatally, Gracchus chose not to argue his case before the Senate but to take it to the people's forum, the Concilium, from which senators are excluded. His bill was vehemently opposed by the Senate, not surprisingly in view of the vested interest its members had in the disputed land.

Gracchus, however, outwitted his major opponent in the Senate, by organising popular opposition to him. The result was that his opponent was deposed, the bill was passed by the Senate, and a land commission was created.

Gracchus' fate was sealed when Attalus III of Pergamum bequeathed his territories to the Roman people. Gracchus influenced a popular vote for the income from the new territories to go to the land commission. The Senate is traditionally responsible for overseas matters, but the people, having seen the Senate seize so much public land, were unwilling to entrust them with land actually bequeathed to the people.

For the past few months Gracchus has been campaigning for re-election to the Tribunate, in the face of increasing opposition. His campaign is over now. He died at the hands of an angry Senate mob who ambushed him and several hundred of his followers, and hurled their bodies into the Tiber.

Simon's reign of peace ends in his murder

Jerusalem, 135 BC

Simon, the last of Mattathias' sons, has been assassinated, which almost certainly means the end of what has been an unusually peaceful period in Judea's history.

He was killed by his son-in-law Ptolemy, governor of the Jordan, who hoped by this crime to rule Judea himself. But Simon's son, John Hyrcanus, has acted promptly to prevent Ptolemy profiting from his misdeeds and has gone directly to Jerusalem to claim the succession.

Simon was a wise ruler of the Jews, and while he was high priest (by popular acclamation) and military and civil governor, the nation was firmly established and the people prospered.

He promoted his peoples' prosperity and welfare, and they farmed their land in peace.

He ruled a virtually independent state under the suzerainty of Syria. In his time it was enlarged by the conquest of Gezer, securing the western approach to Judea; Judea now also controls the vital coastal road from Joppa. Gezer was taken after a mighty struggle, and afterwards Jewish colonists were established there. The temple area was also fortified.

He leaves Judea as a strong modern state, though perhaps with a few unpaid bills; not least the simmering resentment of Antiochus VII of Syria, who after first wooing Simon, changed his

Antiochus' death gives Judea's leader hope

Jerusalem, c. 129 BC

Jewish soldiers have marched in the Syrian army against the Parthians, led by their high priest John Hyrcanus. The Syrian monarch Antiochus has been killed in the campaign.

His death brings to an end a period of Jewish history that is all the more ignominious, coming as it does after the reign of John's celebrated father Simon Maccabeus.

John, whose prompt action following his father's assassination secured him the high priesthood and the civil leadership of Judea, has not covered himself with half his father's glory. His reign has been a prolonged attempt to keep Antiochus happy, but at considerable cost.

The Syrian king, who had no intention of seeing Judea slip out of his hands, invaded the country when John became high priest, and besieged Jerusalem. The city fell in 134 BC.

Antiochus now had what Simon had denied him. He extracted a peace indemnity of 500 talents from Judea, disarmed the Jews, and demolished Simon's fortifications around the temple. He also demanded rent for Joppa and Gezer, which Simon's army had denied him previously. Judea remained in John's control, though much more of a subject nation than before.

With Antiochus dead, it remains to be seen whether John Hyrcanus can now finally become the kind of ruler of whom his illustrious forefathers could have been proud.

The waterfront at the old port at Joppa.

policy and demanded that Gezer and Joppa be handed back. When Simon declined, Antiochus demanded heavy tribute payments in lieu. Two years ago Simon's sons Judah and John Maccabeus defeated Antiochus' army, thus ensuring peace for the rest of Simon's reign. Now that Simon is dead, Antiochus may well be looking for revenge.

Secular priest led Judean expansion

Jerusalem, 105 BC

The man who more than any previous ruler took Judea along the road to secular statehood has died. John Hyrcanus was one of the new breed of the Hasmonean House.

Unlike his forefathers, he has decked the state with many of the trappings of secular rule. His insistence on holding on to the title of high priest has become a source of continuous friction between pious Jews and Hyrcanus' regime.

John's title of high priest is relatively meaningless, apart from his discharge of public functions. He has been a soldier ruler, and many who fought in his army were mercenaries rather than people fighting for their families, their nation and above all their God.

Since the death of Antiochus, John Hyrcanus has taken advantage of the independence of Judea to pursue a policy of expanding territorially wherever possible. In the east, he took the major cities of Medeba and Samaga and added the surrounding territory to his possessions.

In the north, he captured Shechem, the capital city of the Samaritans, and on Mount Gerizim he demolished the Samaritan temple – a very popular act among the Jews. In the south he invaded Edom, whose domination of the 'people of God' had been denounced by the prophet Obadiah, and forced them to accept Judaism.

However, his most ambitious project is still going on. The Greek city of Samaria, a key Macedonian stronghold, is currently under siege. This seemingly endless siege began five years ago and is being directed by John's sons Antigonus and Aristobulus. It is certain to be successful.

John Hyrcanus is succeeded by his son Aristobulus.

Aristobulus' year of terror

Jerusalem, 103 BC

Aristobulus is dead, and all Judea is breathing a huge sigh of relief. The son of John Hyrcanus has made the nation run with blood in his mercifully brief reign, and few of his enemies are still alive.

He was the first of the Maccabean rulers to take for himself the title of king, and he ruled with ruthless absolutism. In the past 12 months he has starved his own mother to death, put all his brothers in prison except Antigonus, who he finally killed because he suspected him of treachery.

His major achievement was the seizure and forced Judaisation of the Galilee region, which was mainly populated by Syrians and Greeks. He is succeeded as king by his brother Jonathan, better known by his Greek name Alexander.

Palestine under the Maccabees. The Maccabees revolt succeeded in placing ever-increasing territory under their control.

Map legend:
- Judea at start of the revolt

Additions
- Jonathan 160 - 142 BC
- Simon 142 - 134 BC
- Hyrcanus 1, 134 - 104 BC
- Aristobulus 1, 104 - 103 BC
- Alexander Janneus 103 - 76 BC

Lay theologians in clash over priest-king's pedigree

Judea, c. 100 BC

A powerful group of theological lawyers, the Pharisees, has angered the new ruler of Judea, Alexander Jannaeus, and the political map has shifted as a result.

The Pharisees have been gaining increasing influence, because of their role as interpreters of the Mosaic law, guardians of the work of earlier teachers of the law, and champions of the law as a clear guide to every area of life. This has made them spokesmen on a number of issues on which the religious intelligentsia has not usually pronounced.

Their latest target is Jannaeus. There are reports of long arguments in which the Pharisees have quoted a long-disproved story that his mother was once a captive. This, according to a little-known clause in the law, would have disqualified Jannaeus from being high priest.

Upon this rather flimsy foundation the Pharisees have constructed a demand that he should abdicate as priest and be a secular leader. It seems that the Pharisees, though expert lawyers, are bad diplomats. Jannaeus, once a Pharisee, has now aligned himself with the Sadducees.

The conflict deteriorated sharply when Jannaeus deliberately followed Sadducee practice instead of Pharisaical ritual while presiding at the Feast of Tabernacles. It sparked a riot which had to be put down by Greek mercenaries. It is believed that over 6,000 people died in the temple precincts.

Nobody knows how the name 'Pharisee' came to be applied to a group of religious legal experts. It may mean 'separatists' (an implied insult because they distance themselves from the ruler's secular authority), but other meanings are possible. The Sanhedrin, the religious ruling body, is now divided between the Pharisees and the Sadducees, who are lay and priestly members respectively.

The Pharisees are needed because new situations not covered by the ancient writings require experts, skilled in the Mosaic law, to decide how that law should be interpreted. They are drawn from the people rather than the priesthood, and they have tended over the years to become representatives of the people's interests against the power of the priesthood. Alexander can now include the Pharisees among his more powerful enemies.

Crucifixions end civil war

Judea, 88 BC

Hundreds of Pharisees, Jewish lay theologians, have been crucified in reprisals which have brought a brief civil war to a brutal end.

It began when Alexander Jannaeus returned from a disastrous offensive against the Nabateans in 94 BC. He found the Pharisees organising an uprising against him.

For the next six years Judea was locked in civil war. The Pharisees refused to make peace and demanded that Alexander should be executed, but they seriously miscalculated when they asked the Syrians to help them.

Demetrius III of Syria obligingly invaded and forced the king into exile, but there was an overwhelming reaction in his favour from the Jews. Demetrius prudently withdrew as large numbers of the Jews became fierce defenders of Alexander, who has now returned and wreaked his terrible revenge on the Pharisees. Besides hundreds who have been crucified, many more have fled into exile.

The king's position after this show of strength is now virtually unassailable, and the Pharisees may have been too widely dispersed to ever be a significant political force again.

Maccabees' story joins Jews' anthology

Judea, c. 80 BC

The story of the heroic struggle of the Hasmonean dynasty against Greek attempts to impose Hellenistic culture on the Jews has been added to an anthology of writings which are regarded as inspirational, if not divinely inspired.

The collection of 'apocryphal' works includes fiction titles such as Bel and the Dragon, a legend associated with Daniel. The popular fictional story of Tobit tells how the hero's blindness was cured and his son saved from death.

Other legends include that of Judith, a beautiful Jewess who, like

The blind Tobit at prayer: a detail from an oil by Rembrandt.

Esther, saved her nation from oppressors. She stood alone against the Assyrians and lured the enemy general Holofernes to his death.

Along with the two books of Maccabees, a history of the time of Ezra (1 Esdras) is included. It largely repeats the story of the scribe who led exiles back to Jerusalem in 458 BC. The second book of Esdras is an apocalyptic vision of the future.

Two works of wisdom are included in the anthology. The Wisdom of Solomon owes more to Greek thought than that of the ancient king. Ecclesiasticus collects together wise and pithy sayings such as 'Let us now praise famous men'.

Hebrew Bible is now Greek to the Jews

Alexandria, c. 100 BC

The books of the Hebrew Scriptures and some other religious writings are being read widely by Jews who do not themselves understand Hebrew.

Most of the chief books of the Jewish religion have now been translated into Greek, which is the undisputed language of international communication. However, the style is said to be less koine – common – than eccentric if not archaic. Many Hebraisms are retained in the text which make it obscure for readers not already familiar with Jewish customs and jargon.

But the translation is welcomed because it opens up a rich source of Jewish belief and tradition to the many Jews who have emigrated to Egypt and other parts of the Mediterranean world, or who have been born outside Judea to migrant families.

According to popular belief the thriving Jewish community in Alexandria was responsible for the start of the translation back in the reign of the Greek king in Egypt, Ptolemy II (285–247 BC). He is said to have sponsored personally the initial translation of the Law (the Pentateuch) and to have summoned 70 elders from Jerusalem to travel to Egypt to do it.

The legend suggests that they were accommodated in 70 cells and when they came together they all agreed on the exact words which should be used. The truth is likely to be more prosaic.

Since then others have worked on other books and copyists have added their own revisions, so there is no single agreed Greek text.

For convenience, the Greek copies of Jewish writings are being referred to collectively as the Septuagint (after the 70 original translators).

Rome's most hated man retires from politics

Rome, 82 BC

Lucius Cornelius Sulla, the aristocrat turned soldier-politician who retired today, climbed the army ranks (with the help of extremely good family connections) to become the most hated man in Rome.

A series of military conflicts gave him the chance to show his military prowess, but at a great cost to his popularity. In the Jugurthine Wars of 111–106 BC in Africa, he pulled off a diplomatic coup that ended the war, but his commander Gaius Marius never forgave him for taking the limelight. He also fought under Marius in Germany, and in 93 was appointed a magistrate, the first step to becoming a consul.

In the bitter Social War (90–88 BC), fought between Romans and Italians over the question of citizenship rights, he again distinguished himself and was made consul.

He launched a war against Mithridates, king of Pontus, Asia, but Sulpicius the Tribune had the army placed under the command of Marius. Sulla responded by marching six legions into Rome, taking the army over by force, executing Sulpicius and going to fight Mithridates. Marius, who had been elected consul by popular vote, fled.

Sulla's return in triumph inaugurated a reign of terror, beginning with a savage Civil War (88–86 BC) in which Sulla's Aristocratic Party conquered the Marian Party; though Marius returned in 87 to lead his faction, he died that year. Making himself dictator Sulla executed or banished all Marius' supporters, and set about radically transforming the Roman constitution to put power firmly in the hands of the Senate and the aristocracy.

A ceramic figure of a squatting drummer, 48 cm tall. From Sichuan Province, China.

Emperor of China has humbled the Hans

China, c. 70 BC

The Han empire has now expanded to control much of the eastern side of the profitable 'silk route' to Afghanistan and Iran.

This is due in large measure to Wu Di (140–86 BC) and his successors. They have waged a successful war against the Xiongnu and extended the Great Wall.

As a result the Han's enemies are fighting among themselves, and one of the claimants to their throne has asked Siuan Ti for asylum. The emperor has graciously agreed, has arranged for him to marry a Chinese princess, and is now planning to install this deeply grateful new family member on the Xiongnu throne, where he will no doubt serve China's cause well.

Spartacus' uprising crushed

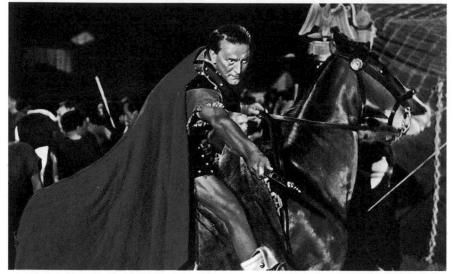

The story of Spartacus was turned into a dramatic film, simply entitled *Spartacus*, with Kirk Douglas in the leading role.

Rome, 71 BC

Anything is better than life as a gladiator. So thought Thracian slave Spartacus, and 90,000 fellow slaves agreed with him.

Two years ago he escaped his Roman master and began to build up a mighty army. For a time his headquarters was in the crater of the extinct volcano, Vesuvius, an accidental symbol that the Roman authorities would have done well to ponder.

For two years his army, at times numbering 70,000–100,000, has threatened Rome. But disagreements among Spartacus' followers led him to abandon his original plan to escape north across the Alps. Instead he embarked on a campaign of terrorising southern Italy. Sicily would probably have fallen to them, if the pirate ships that were to ferry the rebels across had not let them down.

Several Roman attempts at suppressing the revolt failed. Now success has been gained by Crassus, who defeated Spartacus in three battles and finally destroyed him and his army at Lucania. Thousands of captured rebels have been crucified, and Pompey, returning from his victories in Spain to his second triumphal entry into Rome (a rare honour for which many say he is too young) has dealt with the remnants.

Power hungry consuls overturn past

Rome, c. 70 BC

One of the most fragile ruling partnerships in recent Roman history has survived for 12 months; Pompey and Crassus have been consuls for a remarkable year.

Both men are hungry for power and wealth, both recognise each other's formidable talents, and they have united in their consulship to undo many of Sulla's reforms. The tribunes have had their former power restored, for example.

The successful and much-praised Pompey was made consul at the age of 36, despite the fact that at least three of the usual conditions have not been met: he is not legally old enough, he has not first held the post of magistrate or comparable office, and he is not a member of the Senate.

He was a protégé of Sulla, and his rise like Sulla's owed much to good family connections. Under Sulla he achieved military success and was twice given the right to enter Rome in triumph, a rare honour. But he was by no means Sulla's puppet. It seems that he forced Sulla to grant him the Roman triumph, and he is embarking on a programme that threatens to reverse many of the dictator's reforms.

He has an uneasy relationship with his fellow consul Crassus. Crassus resents the fact that after he crushed Spartacus' uprising, Pompey arrived to take some of the credit at the end – after the hard work had been done.

Queen of the Jews

Judea, c. 69 BC

The reign of Judea's first queen is over.

Salome Alexander claimed the throne when her husband, King Alexander Jannaeus, was killed in one of a number of military campaigns he had waged since the Syrians were overthrown by the Armenian king in 83 BC.

It was the kind of death he would have wanted, for Alexander was by inclination an enthusiastic if not always successful soldier, and liked nothing better than the company of fighting men.

Alexander substantially enlarged the Jewish state, and in the process eradicated much of the remaining Greek culture in Palestine – and most of his military conquests were made at the expense of Greek interests.

His widow made peace with the Pharisees, Alexander's implacable foes, and they have now regained much of their former standing. They have been responsible for some initiatives in education, but have also become aggressively opposed to the Sadducees. However the new king Aristobulus is pro-Sadducee; and tension is already growing again.

Pagan general enters temple as Jerusalem falls again

Jerusalem, 63 BC

An estimated 12,000 Jews have been slaughtered by the Roman army in a fierce battle for control of the city of Jerusalem.

Once inside the city, the Roman general Pompey entered the Holy of Holies, the inner sanctuary of the temple, which only priests are allowed to do in Jewish religion. The action has provoked outrage among the religious leaders, and prompted fears of a repeat of the desecration by Antiochus Epiphanes, the Seleucid leader, almost exactly a century ago.

However, Pompey did not loot any of the temple treasures nor enact any pagan ceremonies. He has promised the Jews that they may continue their religious services unhindered, and continue to observe their customs and festivals.

The collapse of Jerusalem came after a three-month siege. Pompey had intervened in the internecine dispute between Hyrcanus II, a supporter of Rome, and his brother Aristobolus II over the leadership of Judea. Aristobolus was rumoured to be plotting against Rome although he was favoured by Scaurus, Pompey's commander of Syrian forces, as the man most likely to have the ready cash to buy Roman support.

First-century bust of Pompey the Great.

In the battle, Aristobolus was defeated and has been extradited to Rome as a prisoner of war. Jerusalem is now a vassal state, contributing to Rome's coffers and controlled by its representatives. It has been made part of the province of Syria and the coastal regions, Samaria and settlements east of the Jordan not occupied by Jews have been removed from its jurisdiction.

Hyrcanus has been appointed ethnarch of Judea and he is to be allowed to continue in the dual role of high priest.

Pompey's invasion was the natural consequence of his relentless march eastwards. Having brought to an end the 20-year conflict with Mithridates of Pontus in Asia and capturing his pickings of the old Seleucid empire, Pompey annexed Syria last year. He was courted by different parties vying for power in Jerusalem as Jewish leaders saw his progress south as inevitable.

As a result of the latest action, the old Hasmonean dynasty which began during the Maccabean revolt 100 years ago has finally come to an end. One person to emerge from it with some credit, but who is regarded by the Jews with grave suspicion, is Antipater (Antipas), the ruler of Idumea.

He had brokered deals with Hyrcanus and was widely regarded as the power behind the throne before the invasion. He retains some influence, and the fact that he rules the territory of Edom, which for centuries was a thorn in ancient Israel's side, sparks fears among orthodox Jews that their distinctiveness is about to be compromised once again.

Jaffa Gate, Jerusalem.

Fast Facts 90–60 BC

India, 90–75 BC: The Scythian tribes-people are on the move, fleeing before the Yueh-Chih who are themselves spreading south from their homelands in central Asia. These Scythians or 'Sakas' come from Baluchistan and Sind, and are settling in the Punjab (the region lying to the south of, and below the curve of, the Himalayas in north-west India), conquering the many small principalities established there in the wake of the Asoka empire by Bactria. Bactria, a creation of Alexander the Great, has been autonomous in recent years and has been beginning an expansion which the Sakas have brought to an end, at least in the Punjab.

China, 87 BC: Wu Ti is dead. Born in 156 BC, he became emperor in 140 BC. He will be remembered for his powerful civil service, who carried out their master's orders. His unremitting campaign against his neighbours gave China its largest territory so far, and trade has flourished under him. There is great rivalry between the great families of China, and Wu Ti's death leaves the prospect of leadership struggles to come.

Greece, 75 BC: It's a new regime of bathing, dieting and exercise for many, following the pronouncements of Doctor Asclepiades of Bithynia that human disease is the result of tissue disharmony. Among those convinced by the new health drive is Mark Antony of Rome.

Rome, 63 BC: Shorthand has been invented by Marcus Tiro, who used to be a slave of Cicero the orator. He has devised a script, based on ordinary handwriting, that enables a competent scribe, using numerous abbreviations and phonetic symbols, to write an exact transcript of what is being said aloud. The speaker does not have to slow down to the usual dictation speed. Only people trained in this new way of writing can read it, but it is proving invaluable for writing down speeches in the Senate and other public oratory – including, of course, the speeches of Cicero.

Third party complicates Rome leadership struggle

Rome, 60 BC

The long stranglehold of Rome's rich senators and landowners could be about to be broken as a new contender enters the uneasy power-struggle between Pompey and Crassus.

A third ambitious and celebrated military genius has succeeded in persuading Pompey and Crassus to make common cause with each other and himself: Gaius Julius Caesar.

The 10 years since he was made consul have been kind to Crassus, who is known as 'Crassus the Rich' because of his immense wealth. It is thought advisable not to ask too many questions about how he gained his fortune; it is rumoured that he was rewarded by Sulla for serving as his strong-arm man.

Pompey's brilliant successes in the eastern part of the empire have also made him a powerful man. He was entrusted with commands against the pirates in 67 and against Mithridates VI in 66; he spent the next four years subduing the eastern provinces and bringing great wealth to Rome. The spectacle of Pompey increasing his personal wealth and influence – he has been compared with Alexander the Great – has worried the Senate and the corrupt ruling classes of modern Rome.

By the time Pompey returned to Rome two years ago, Crassus had already aligned himself with his political opponents. Since then there has been increasing animosity between the two.

Julius Caesar has had a more conventional path to high office than has Pompey. Though born into a noble family he has sympathies with the common people, opposing, for example, the orator Cicero's involvement with ordering capital punishment without trial. Now he

Cicero, the great orator.

has returned from a successful 12 months as governor of Spain and has succeeded in making an informal alliance with Crassus and Pompey.

This 'triumvirate' as it is called (though it has no official status at all) is bound to create an unbeatable force. The nobiles, already bruised from Pompey and Crassus' reversal of Sulla's pro-aristocrat policies, are now looking distinctly vulnerable.

But few who have watched Julius Caesar's rise up the ladder of power doubt that it is all really for the benefit of one man: Julius Caesar.

Britain is invaded by Rome at last

Britain, 56 BC

Julius Caesar has invaded Britain, and in Rome they are treating him as a hero of incalculable courage.

Five years ago the Roman empire reached as far as the Alps; now it extends into the remote island of which only occasional travellers' tales are known.

Britain, with its mineral wealth and air of mystery – it is not even known for sure that it is an island – has always fascinated explorers, and the news of Caesar's invasion has been greeted in Rome with enormous enthusiasm.

It has been an expensive conquest. A large number of ships were lost in the Channel, and the British have proved formidable opponents with their skill in chariot warfare. But there have been major victories. Cassivellaunus in the south-east has surrendered un-conditionally. The Trinovantes, a powerful tribe, have agreed to be 'protected' by the Romans. It is now unlikely that Britain will help the Gauls against the Romans.

Any further plans that Caesar may have for Britain have had to be shelved for the time being. Events in Gaul are demanding all his attention, and the political situation in Rome is unlikely to inspire much more aggression across the Channel. Caesar has secured the south-east of the country, and established appropriate relationships with the inhabitants. With that he will have to be content for now.

Fast Facts: 60–40 BC

India, c. 50 BC: Travellers to Maharashtra State are enthusing over a collection of frescoes that has been building up for years on the walls of caves hewn from a gorge at Ajanta. They portray scenes from the lives of the Buddha and are of superb quality; their vibrancy and colour never fail to astound visitors.

Europe, c. 50 BC: Shepherds and others in Asia and north Africa are to be heard playing the bagpipes, a new reed instrument that accompanies its melody with a drone produced by small bellows often held, and operated, under the player's arm.

Rome, 45 BC: A new calendar came into effect on January 1, ending the centuries-long confusion caused by the 255-day year which required an additional 22-day month to be added every two years. The Julian calendar, named after Julius Ceasar, follows the solar year of 365 days and will need only small adjustments.

Africa, c. 40 BC: The Greek geographer, Turkish-born Strabo, has been exploring the Nile with Aelius Gallius, the prefect of Egypt. He is a prolific author, recording detailed accounts of his discoveries over extensive areas of the world.

Julius Caesar takes charge

Rome, 46 BC

Julius Caesar, the man who looks like an aristocrat but claims to serve the people, has become the sole leader of the Roman empire, after the military defeat and subsequent murder of Pompey.

Caesar, who has been in Egypt for the past year or two where he has fathered a prince by Queen Cleopatra, has now arrived back in Rome as dictator – a post given him for the next 10 years – and is very much in control. He is even finding time to write his own account of his military exploits, which are said be unhampered by any undue modesty.

He has added Gaul (58–50 BC) and Britain (55–54 BC) to his list of conquered nations. It has been a very different matter for the other members of the former triumvirate with whom he shared power for some time.

Crassus the Rich, made governor of Syria in 54 BC, robbed many

Gaius Julius Caesar, the first emperor.

Jewish temples – including the Jerusalem temple – to fund his war against the Parthians, only to be killed in battle against them the following year.

Pompey (known as 'The Great') married Caesar's daughter. For nine years during Caesar's Gallic campaign, Pompey and Caesar saw

little of each other. When Caesar's wife died in 54 BC, and the triumvirate was reduced to two by Crassus' death the following year, Pompey began to side with Caesar's opponents in Rome.

In a confrontation with the Senate, Caesar refused to compromise and in 49 BC led his army across the River Rubicon from Gaul to Italy – an act of explicit defiance of the Senate and of Pompey, now commanding the Senate's armed forces.

When Pompey retreated to Brundisium, Caesar seized com-mand of Italy and then began to pursue his former ally. Defeating Pompey's forces in Spain, he went on to attack Pompey himself, whose army was defeated at Pharsalus in 48 BC and who was later murdered.

Caesar's military campaigns. Caesar's principal campaigns added considerably to the spread of the Roman empire, in particular by conquering Gaul and invading England.

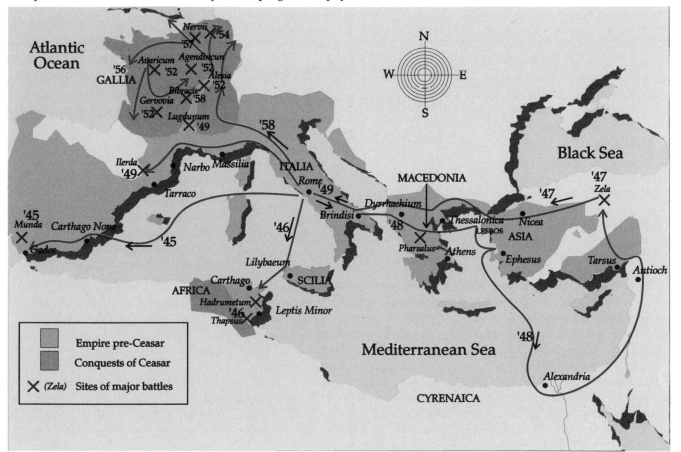

Massed Gallic forces are defeated by Latin strategy

Gaul, 44 BC

Vercingetorix, chief of the Averni tribe in Gaul, who led the 52 BC revolt against Julius Caesar, has been defeated.

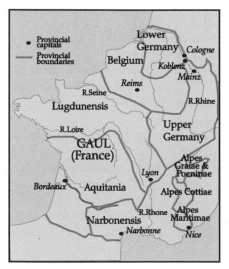

Caesar's campaigns in Gaul.

His campaign ended in a siege at Alesia, a hill fort in Gaul, where he was trapped with 80,000 men after two serious defeats at the hands of the Romans. Caesar's victory in the face of overwhelming odds and a unique tactical problem is a remarkable testimony to his genius as a general.

The problem faced by Caesar was twofold. First, he had to break the siege. Though the Gauls outnumbered Caesar's men, they were less well trained and equipped. All Caesar had to do was to sit and wait.

But he could not afford to do so. Vercingetorix, before entering the fort, had dispatched 15,000 cavalry to muster help from the rest of Gaul. It was only a matter of time before a large relief force would arrive, at which point Caesar would be in danger of being trapped between the large Gallic force in the fort and the relieving force.

His solution was to build two perimeter ramparts encircling the fort, one facing outward, the other inward. They were 26 and 18 km (14 and 11 miles) long respectively.

They provided easy mobility for the Romans, who could now move from point to point round the fort. The perimeters were strongly fortified. When the relief force, arrived, it was 250,000 strong. Caesar was outnumbered 6 to 1.

The Romans benefited from the psychological impact of the fortified ramparts and the poor co-ordination of the Gauls. Much of the fighting was in the dark, with losses on both sides. Parts of the perimeter were taken by the relieving force, but Caesar's preparations meant that cavalry could go round the fort and attack from both sides.

The illusion that enemy forces were coming at them from all directions broke the Gallic morale, and in the ensuing retreat many of the Gauls were struck down by Roman cavalry. Next day Vercingetorix surrendered to save his men from starvation. When Caesar arrived back in Rome in triumph, Vercingetorix was executed at the height of the celebrations.

Et tu, Bruté? Then fall Caesar!

Rome, 44 BC

Brutus, the governor of Gaul and friend and favourite of Julius Caesar, has led a team of conspirators to stab Julius Caesar in a surprise assassination. Earlier this year Caesar had been made dictator for life.

The people of Rome are in mourning, though many of the aristocratic ranks are delighted.

Caesar's death brings to an end a string of military successes and could mean trouble with Egypt, to where Cleopatra and Caesar's illegitimate son have now returned. In the meantime his grand-nephew Octavius, legally adopted by Caesar as his son last year, may well expect

Three way split

Rome, c. 40 BC

Rome now has its second triumvirate this century, the result of three rivals agreeing to settle their differences and carve the Roman empire up between themselves.

They are Gaius Octavius, Caesar's own choice of heir; Marc Antony, who has mustered great popular support; and army general Marcus Lepidus.

They have already dealt with the attempts by Caesar's assassins, Brutus and Cassius, to bring back the republic by force. The armies met at Philippi, and the triumvirate won handsomely – the assassins later committed suicide. However, when Marc Antony attempted to impose his authority on Cleopatra he fell in love with her and went back to Egypt with her.

At this year's conference of the triumvirate in Italy, the three divided the Roman world between themselves.

This coin was minted to mark Caesar's death, during the Ides of March.

(as Caesar's heir-designate) to succeed to the leadership.

The most powerful person in this complicated situation is Caesar's fellow-consul Marc Antony, who by brilliant oratory has swung public opinion firmly against the assassins. Indeed, of all the people contending for the ultimate power, he at the moment is the strongest.

Locally-born king takes complete control

Judea, 31 BC

In Judea, parentage means everything and patronage counts for nothing. So when a man whose forebears were implacable enemies of the Jews is given Judea's titular kingship by a Roman emperor, there is bound to be a protest.

Herod is currently weathering storms of protest from religious and racial purists following his confirmation as king by Octavian.

This unlikely peacemaker, who has been regarded by the Roman Senate as king of Judea for the past two years, has now taken full control and will have to start

reign of Antigonus (40–37 BC), and now they have made him king.

The move has been unpopular with the Hasmonean party, and Herod, in an attempt to win their favour, has married Mariamne, a Hasmonean princess and granddaughter of high priest Hyrcanus II. Whether this will help much in the aftermath of Hasmonean hostility fuelled by Cleopatra, who wanted Judea and Coele-Syria brought back into the kingdom for which she murdered her brother Ptolemy, remains to be seen.

Herod's other main problem is to deal with the bitter enmity between

General view of Petra, the capital city of Herod's father-in-law.

sorting out the tangled rivalries of the province.

His father Antipater had immense influence in the region as a result of his appointment as procurator of Judea in 47 BC by Julius Caesar. He made his son military prefect of Galilee and the Roman governor of Syria made him prefect of Coele-Syria.

He soon came to the attention of the Romans as an efficient administrator, ruthless in his treatment of lawlessness; after Caesar's death he was well thought of by Marc Antony. The Roman Senate gave him the title of 'King of the Jews' as a propaganda device during the

the Sadducees and Pharisees, which is as strong now as ever.

His Edomite descent is as bad a pedigree as any Jewish king could have. The Edomites, against whom both Simon Maccabeus and John Hyrcanus fought, were forcibly Judaised by the latter and have always been hated for the fact that though blood brothers of the Israelites, they have through the centuries despised them and gloated over their misfortunes.

Though a practising Jew himself, Herod is unlikely to quickly overcome the stigma of such a background and the fact that he is Rome's nominee as king.

Octavius claims supremacy with new name and new role

Rome, 27 BC

Octavius, the art-loving, old-fashioned son of a best-selling politician/writer, has finally seized control of the Roman world, assumed the top titles and responsibilities, and has formally announced the birth of the Roman empire and his own accession as Rome's first emperor.

The triumvirate is finished. Peace has returned after years of fighting, in which Octavius' strength has grown ever stronger. His domination of the trio since his conquest of Spain has increased inexorably.

He has imprisoned Lepidus; Marc Antony, after defeat at the Battle of Actium (31 BC), committed suicide on hearing (mistakenly) that Cleopatra had taken her own life; Caesar's illegitimate son Caesarion has been murdered; Lepidus' troops are a broken rabble; and Egypt is now a Roman province.

The stage has been cleared for Julius Caesar's chosen heir, who at 34 years of age is now the uncontested supreme ruler of the Roman world.

The Senate has given him the title Augustus (the holy one) Caesar, and granted him powers far beyond any previous Roman leader's powers. Among his titles is Pontifex Maximus ('chief priest'), which places religion firmly within his authority; and he has proclaimed himself emperor.

An art lover with a special interest in architecture, Augustus is also a patron of poets. Some of the laws he has initiated have shown him to be something of a conservative in ethics and an upholder of strict morals.

Pax works

Rome, c. 23 BC

Augustus is strategically planning the image he wants Rome to have in the eyes of its people and its neighbours. He wants particularly to demonstrate continuity with the old republic.

He has been consul in Rome from 31, but he has now resigned all his 'extraordinary' powers; he has given the state 'to the free disposal of the Senate and the people'. He retains a province of his own, comprising Spain, Gaul and Syria, in which most of Rome's armed forces are stationed, and having conquered Egypt he holds that too.

He nevertheless controls all the other provinces because of his great national standing. Following a recent illness he has been given new powers, but these are framed in constitutional rather than absolute terms.

Among his innovations are reorganisation of the army and the fleet, creation of a full-time imperial bodyguard, a police force for Rome, and a thorough reorganisation of the civil service.

Already the Pax Augusta or 'Augustan Peace' is being felt in Rome, where new buildings of remarkable quality are being erected on the emperor's orders. He has remarkable skills in government, and is also expanding the

This delicate Roman sardonyx cameo is of Augustus wearing the aegis, a goatskin breastplate modelled on that traditionally worn by Athena, and considered to have divine power. The diadem is of later date.

empire by conquest: the frontier now extends to the Danube, though in Germany something of a stalemate has been reached.

Empire spiced

Rome, c. 24 BC

Augustus has won valuable support in Rome and also stamped his authority on the international scene by acting decisively on the price of spice.

Spices have played an important part in world history for centuries; originally controlled by Arabs who dominated the overland trade routes, they have become a major economic currency with the opening up of sea-trade routes in recent times. Two years before he became emperor, Octavius hired Greek sailors to open up the old trade routes between India and Egypt.

Now he has sent Aeilius Gallus, prefect of Egypt, on a military campaign to annexe the South Arabia spice kingdom to the Roman empire, thus securing a domestic source for this valuable commodity.

A spice market in Aswan, Egypt. Free trade meant that all manner of exotic goods circulated freely within the Roman empire.

All roads now lead to Rome

Rome, c. 20 BC

Roads stretching to the horizon in perfectly straight lines are the hallmark of the Roman empire. Facilitating rapid disposition of troops, they are miracles of engineering, far outclassing the roads of the Etruscans and other earlier cultures.

These well-preserved remains of a Roman road are of the Via Sacra approaching the Forum in Rome.

A Roman road is straight, unless a bend is unavoidable. A simple surveying system ensures accuracy. A foundation of large stones is given solidity by a top layer of smaller stones, and the two are often bonded with cement. Then a surface is laid of gravel, cobbles or paving slabs.

Drainage ditches run alongside, and the surface is curved to allow water to drain. Where the road crosses bogland or uneven surface a special raised causeway is built to carry the new road. Milestones are incorporated into the road network.

Although the primary use of the road system is to maximise troop mobility, the roads also form the basis of trading networks and social infrastructures.

Herod's building to get support

Judea, 19 BC

Herod has been investing in major public-relations exercises involving huge expenditure on public works in order to win support from the Jews and to further his own reputation within the empire.

In an attempt to win the dissident Jews over, he has embarked on the building of a new temple in Jerusalem. His intentions are suspect, not least because he is also building a temple to Augustus in Sebaste – his new name for Samaria. Nevertheless, he has invested huge amounts of money in the Jerusalem temple.

He has built theatres and stadiums at Jerusalem, Jericho and Caesarea, though it is doubtful whether these will win him support from the nationalist or the religious parties in his kingdom, as they are intended for the Greek games held in honour of Augustus.

Indeed the name Caesarea is controversial; it is Herod's choice of name for the refurbished Tower of Strato which he has equipped with a splendid harbour and named in honour of the emperor. He has rebuilt Samaria, also renamed in honour of the emperor; and he has built fortresses and strongholds throughout the kingdom. In Jerusalem, he has built himself a splendid palace.

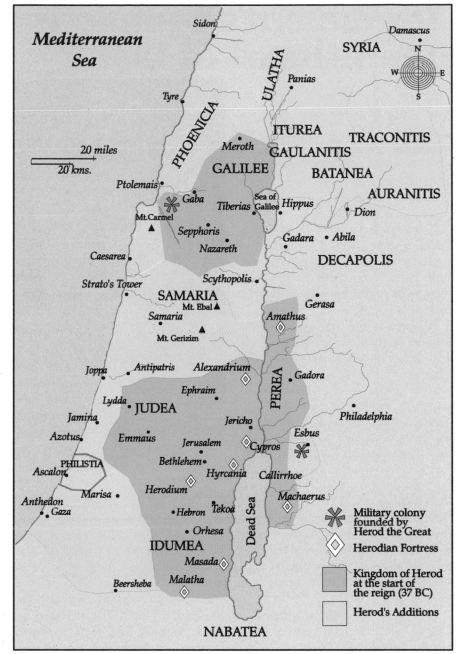

Palestine under King Herod. The 'kingdom' of Herod, in reality a Roman province under his jurisdiction, covered more or less the same area as that controlled by the Maccabees some 75 years earlier.

Fast Facts 31–7 BC

Qumran, 31 BC: An earthquake at the ancient Jewish settlement of Qumran on the Dead Sea has forced the local cave-dwellers to abandon the site. They are believed to be Essenes – members of a Jewish sect who have been harshly treated by the Hasmonean rulers and now seek out desert dwelling places. Those who have visited the site in the past report that the caves have been adapted as simple refectories, bathing places and workshops for the copying of scrolls.

Rome, 27 BC: Even more prolific than Strabo is Marcus Varro, the elderly librarian who has died in Rome. A supporter of Pompey, he was given an amnesty by Caesar who wanted the great scholar's gifts for the new public library in Rome. He wrote over 600 works, and was competent in every academic discipline.

Africa (Kush), c. 24 BC: The Roman empire extends as far as Aswan in southern Egypt, where there is a border – currently very vulnerable – between the Roman province and the African nation Kush. There have been a number of attacks by Kushites against Roman strongholds. One, against Philae, was led by a woman, Queen Candace. Her skill in battle has caused enough consternation in Rome to prompt immediate negotiations for an agreed frontier between the two territories.

Jerusalem, c. 15 BC: A Jewish rabbi called Hillel has for the first time put the interpretation of the Mosaic law onto a systematic basis. Born in Babylonia in 70 BC, he has risen to become a senior Jewish leader and scholar. A liberal rather than a conservative in theology, he is having a wide influence, especially for his emphasis on personal piety and love for one's fellow human beings.

Jerusalem's temple is operational at last

Jerusalem, 9 BC

Herod's new temple towers 15 stories above the holy city. The king has given enormous attention to making sure that the Jews' sensitivities are respected. 1,000 masons are actually priests who have been retrained for the job.

A large area about 265 m x 300 m (290 yd x 328 yd) was cleared as a building site, which includes the location of the previous temples built by Solomon and Zerubbabel, over which the new sanctuary is built.

The structure is encompassed by a massive rubble-filled wall, which in places looks down into the Kidron Valley. Prominent in the temple area is the Fortress of Antonia, which is designed to ensure order and civil obedience in the temple. Herod apparently has not forgotten that the temple, fortified by the Maccabeans, was able to hold out against Pompey for three months in 63 BC.

The temple will be a place for theological debate, facilities for market stalls and moneychangers to offer a service to people needing sacrifice animals and birds are provided.

There is a Women's Court and a Court of Israel, and of course a holy place, called the Priest's Court. Within this court is the inner sanctuary.

The plans follow the pattern of Solomon's temple closely; there is a massive porch, the doorway opens into the Holy Place, and a curtain separates the Holy Place from the Most Holy Place. Above the sanctu-

A colossal bust of Hercules. This Roman copy of an earlier Greek original would have been prominently placed in some public arena.

ary is another room, and the north, south and west sides contain three stories of rooms. There will be golden spikes on the roof to deter birds from roosting.

The whole building will be finished off by being covered in valuable gold leaf. This splendid structure will eclipse the former glory of Solomon's temple and of the second temple, the remains of which lie buried beneath the new building site. Now basically completed, the final touches are likely to take some time. Great celebrations surround the official opening.

Rome's poet of destiny leaves before end

Brindisium, 19 BC

The death of Mantuan poet Virgil at Brundisium at the early age of 50 has shocked poetry-lovers everywhere. He died on a research trip, intending to revise his great poem the *Aeneid*, but died before the work was finished. The emperor has overruled his dying request that the poem be destroyed.

He was the author of a collection of pastoral poems called the *Eclogues*, which incorporate references to real people and prophesy the birth of a child who is to usher in a new golden age.

His *Georgics* reflect Virgil's farming family background, and are of superb literary quality. They celebrate rural values in an almost nationalistic way.

The 12 books of the *Aeneid* describe the adventures of Aeneas following the fall of Troy and during the seven subsequent years leading to his victorious arrival in Italy. The poem argues that the Romans are an ancient people linked, through Aeneas, with legendary Troy.

Though the *Aeneid* has much in common with other epics, it is common knowledge that Augustus wanted it written to enhance the Roman people's origins.

But though written to order, it is one of the most perfect literary creations produced by any Roman, and has become deservedly popular throughout the educated world.

Fast Facts 63–1 BC

Astronomical Events, 11 BC: Halley's Comet has returned to the vicinity of the earth after an orbit of two centuries. It is visible as a faint moving light among the stars.

7 BC: Saturn, Jupiter and Venus are in conjunction in the constellation of Pisces; from Earth the two appear as one large celestial body. Jewish astrologers have predicted that the Messiah will be born at the time of such a conjunction.

5 BC: Chinese and Korean astronomers have recorded a nova – the explosion of a star – lasting 70 days. Throughout the ancient world such phenomena are universally considered to herald events of great historical significance.

4 BC: Another comet is visible from earth, though it is not easily seen by the naked eye.

World, 7 BC: The population of the world has been estimated at 250 million.

Japan, 1 BC: Rice has been imported from China for the first time and is being cultivated for food. This has necessitaed considerable irrigation and terracing works to be undertaken in a short time.

'I'm dumbfounded!' says father priest

Judea, c. 6 BC

An elderly priest who has become a father for the first time was literally dumbfounded at the prospect.

Zechariah has been unable to speak since the child was conceived. But now that his wife Elizabeth has just given birth to their son John, he has found his tongue again.

As the happy family relaxed at home in the Judean hills with their incredulous neighbours and friends, Zechariah recounted the extraordinary tale of how an encounter with an angel forced him into nine months' silence.

Zechariah writes John's name on a tablet after his birth, as seen by Rembrandt.

He had been on a week's rotation of duty in the temple at Jerusalem. Although sharing the responsibility with many others, his name was pulled out of the hat for the once-in-a-lifetime experience of offering incense in the temple.

While performing the sacred ceremony, Zechariah suddenly realised that he was not alone in the building. To the right of the altar was a majestic figure who claimed to be Gabriel, one of only two angels named in Jewish tradition. Trembling with fear, the old priest was told that his post-menopause and hitherto childless wife would have a son.

When he dared to question it, he was struck dumb. When he eventually emerged, having been in the temple much longer than protocol allowed, he was unable to pronounce the traditional blessing on the waiting crowds.

Since then, he has been communicating with his family in sign language and occasional written notes, and has become withdrawn from the village community.

It was only when he confirmed – in writing – that the child was to be called John, a name not previously used in his family but the one commanded by the angel, that he found he could speak again. Among his first words was a prophetic hymn of blessing predicting that his son would 'prepare the way for the Lord' and 'bring knowledge of salvation to Israel'.

(Luke 1:5–25, 57–80)

King Herod executes rival sons

Judea, c. 7 BC

King Herod has tried to put an end to the rivalry and intrigue which have plagued his family for years – by killing his two sons Alexander and Aristobulus.

Born to Mariamne, of the Hasmonean dynasty, the second of Herod's five wives, the two men were earmarked as the king's heirs to his extensive territory.

But their privileged position had attracted the envy of other members of the family, especially their half-brothers, and Herod's eldest son Antipater is said to have spread rumours that the two were plotting against the king. They were tried, found guilty, and strangled.

Herod has named Antipater as his sole heir. Antipater himself is believed to have been involved in a plot against Herod which backfired when his uncle Pheroras accidentally took the poison Antipater had intended for his father.

Herod's kingdom is split among three sons

Jericho, spring 4 BC

King Herod of Judea has died. Following a dispute over his sixth and final will, written only five days before his death, the emperor has divided the kingdom among his three sons Antipas, Archelaus and Philip.

His reign of 33 years, preceded by a decade as governor, was marked by extremes of generosity and violence. A half-Jew, the son of the Idumean Antipater II, Herod 'the Great' as he is being called, became governor of Galilee in 47 BC when he was only 25. He won immediate approval from the Romans for ridding the region of the rebel Ezekias.

He was the subject and perpetrator of numerous murder plots, and on frequent visits to the Roman court ingratiated himself with successive rulers. When the Parthian capture of Judea in 40 BC forced him into exile, the senate appointed him king and he returned to recapture Jerusalem in 37 BC.

He rode out opposition from the Pharisees, the Hasmoneans and Queen Cleopatra until in 31 BC his kingdom was extended after he sided with Octavius against Antony. He embarked on a large building programme of fortresses, theatres and stadia, rebuilding the Tower of Strabo and renaming it Caesarea. To the Jews, however, he will be remembered and honoured for starting the still-unfinished temple in Jerusalem.

Intrigue and violence again dominated his final years. He ruthlessly executed those whom he perceived as enemies and having married many times, his considerable dynasty was torn with jealousy and rivalry as relatives jockeyed for position and power.

Virgin's child prompts visions

Bethlehem, Judea, c. 5 BC

A wave of religious and political fervour has swept this small village near Jerusalem following the birth of a child to a teenage girl who claims to be a virgin.

Shepherds in the nearby fields say that the night the child was born the sky lit up and they heard

The Annunciation by Fra Angelico (1387–1455). This fresco (230x321cm) is situated in the Convent of San Marco, Florence, Italy.

fanfares of angels heralding the long-awaited Jewish Messiah. They abandoned their flocks and discovered the mother and baby huddled in the decidedly un-messianic setting of an outhouse with a cow's feeding-trough serving as a makeshift cot.

The young mother, Mary, is one of many people herded into Bethlehem in the latest round of Caesar Augustus' apparently unending game of organisational tag. Military governor Quirinius of Syria is fulfilling his master's wishes to the bureaucratic letter by compiling an accurate count of citizens according to their family origins. To do it, he ordered heads of houses to return to their ancestors' birthplaces. It is one of many censuses provoked by the emperor's obsession with administration.

Technically Mary did not need to

undertake the hazardous journey from Nazareth in the north. But her husband Joseph, believed to be somewhat older, preferred to take his heavily pregnant partner riding uncomfortably on a donkey rather than leave her to ride out the gossip at home by herself.

She had become pregnant during

The Shepherds' Fields, Bethlehem.

Elizabeth's unborn child 'leaped in the womb' when it sensed the presence of its younger cousin in Mary's womb.

Jewish hopes for a Messiah, a god-like figure who will re-create national identity and freedom, have been riding high in recent years. All portents are seized upon eagerly by a people who have never welcomed Roman civilisation.

(Matthew 1:18–25; Luke 2:1–20)

her engagement. She claimed that the angel Gabriel had visited her in a vision and told her that she would give birth to 'the Son of the Most High' before she had sex with her husband-to-be.

Joseph, a pragmatic carpenter-builder, is said to have found her story far-fetched and assumed that she had been unfaithful. However, he too claims to have had an angelic vision in which he was told that the child had been conceived through the Holy Spirit and was to be called Jesus (which means 'the Lord saves') because 'he will save his people from their sins'. Even more remarkably, he believed it.

Strange births seem to run in this obscure family. Mary's elderly aunt Elizabeth also gave birth recently following visions of angels. They claim that when the two women met up a few months ago,

Madonna and child. Mosaic from the Church of the Annunciation, Nazareth.

Man-eating Julia sent to Pandateria

Rome, 2 BC

Julia, the adulterous daughter of the emperor Augustus, has been banished to the island of Pandateria and forbidden wine and men. Her latest paramour, Iullus Antonius, grandson of Mark Antony, has been sentenced to death, allegedly for having eyes both for her and for imperial power.

Julia was widowed at 16, when Marcellus died. She then married Agrippa 24 years her senior, and they had five children. When Agrippa died Augustus ordered Tiberius, his heir apparent, to divorce his own wife and marry Julia in order to ensure the succession.

Her pleasure-loving lifestyle had become increasingly profligate and coarse as the years wore on. She took part in orgies in the Forum, and solicited passers-by. Despairing of her, Tiberius went into self-imposed exile in Rhodes four years ago, although that was also partly precipitated by his anger at Augustus' appointment of him as tribune (vice-regent) for only a five-year period.

Star-struck priests keep Herod in the dark

The three wise men: camels and riders in the Sinai Desert today.

Jerusalem, c. 4 BC

Three high-ranking visitors from Babylonia have slipped out of Judea without saying goodbye to King Herod. He is not amused.

They had travelled to find the newly-born 'king of the Jews' who, they claimed, was announced in the stars. But their horoscope sounded like a horror story to Herod; the old king has not had a child for years and has already bequeathed the kingdom to his youngest son, Antipas, in his fifth will.

The men, believed to be members of the priestly class of Magi, said they had seen an unusual astral conjunction usually associated with the birth of royalty. They had brought appropriate gifts of gold, frankincense and myrrh for the child.

When the king failed to illuminate them, they turned back to their heavenly charts. They reportedly ended up paying homage to a toddler belonging to a refugee family from Galilee staying in Bethlehem, a village just outside the city. Then, trusting their lucky stars more than Herod, they slipped out of the back door without revealing to the king the child's whereabouts.

Herod, furious at their diplomatic snub, is taking no chances. Paranoid as ever about potential rivals, the man who once murdered his wife, mother-in-law and three sons, as well as numerous others, has ordered all children under the age of two in the area to be killed. It is not known if his wishes are being carried out, but the family concerned is believed to have sought asylum in Egypt.

(Matthew 2:1–12)

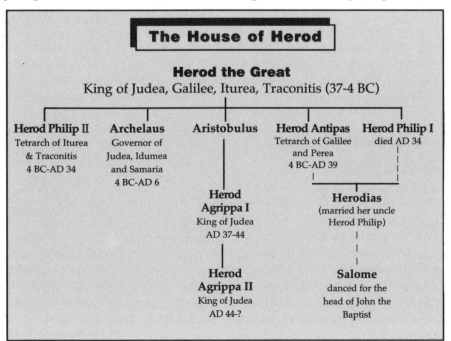

The House of Herod

Herod the Great
King of Judea, Galilee, Iturea, Traconitis (37-4 BC)

Herod Philip II
Tetrarch of Iturea & Traconitis
4 BC-AD 34

Archelaus
Governor of Judea, Idumea and Samaria
4 BC-AD 6

Aristobulus

Herod Antipas
Tetrarch of Galilee and Perea
4 BC-AD 39

Herod Philip I
died AD 34

Herod Agrippa I
King of Judea
AD 37-44

Herodias
(married her uncle Herod Philip)

Herod Agrippa II
King of Judea
AD 44-?

Salome
danced for the head of John the Baptist

Boy prodigy astounds teachers

Jerusalem, c. AD 7

A 12-year-old boy from Nazareth in Galilee has astounded religious teachers here by his knowledge and perception. But he got a stern lecture from his parents for staying too long in the discussions and not letting them know where he was for four days.

Jesus, son of Joseph, a village carpenter and builder, has travelled south to Jerusalem for the Passover festival on several occasions. He was born nearby in Bethlehem, but his family emigrated to Egypt for a while before moving back to Joseph's northern home area.

This year, fresh from his bar mitzvah, the Jewish rite of attaining adulthood, he spent most of the time on his own in the temple precincts listening to and taking part in the endless theological debates, where his questions and answers attracted scholarly attention.

His family party left for home without him, everyone assuming he was with someone else. He was discovered missing only after they had travelled for a day, and it took another three days to locate him. The resourceful lad had fended for himself and seemed surprised when his anxious parents told him off. 'Didn't you know I had to be in my Father's house?' he protested with wide-eyed innocence.

It is not the first time he has been the centre of attraction in the temple. Family members today were recounting how, when he was a baby brought in for the traditional after-birth religious offerings, they were accosted by two elderly eccentrics.

Simeon, who claimed that God had told him he would not die until he had seen the Messiah, seized the baby and said that he could now go to the next life in peace. The child, he claimed, would be 'a light to

Jesus in the Temple by William Holman Hunt.

open the eyes of the Gentiles and for the glory of Israel'. Then the 84-year-old Anna praised God for him and pointed him out to her friends who were hoping for a God-sent deliverer.

Mary, the mother of Jesus, says she always believed her son was special. But she refuses to reveal what she thinks of his religious knowledge and interest.

(Luke 2:22–52)

Judean ruler banished to France

Rome, AD 6

The ethnarch (ruler) of Judea, Samaria and Idumea, Archelaus, has been banished to Vienne in southern France and his kingdom has been designated a Roman province to be governed by imperial prefects.

Archelaus received his territory when the region was parcelled out after the death of his father Herod the Great. His brothers' territories (Antipas in Galilee and Perea, and Philip in the north-west districts), which were granted by Augustus at the same time, are unaffected.

The disgraced ruler was deposed by an unusual alliance of Jews and Samaritans, tired of his brutality. He had killed 3,000 pilgrims in Jerusalem during an uprising almost as soon as his father was buried. He further angered religious sentiment by divorcing his wife and marrying the widow of his half-brother (which is against Jewish law), and by deposing high priests with whom he disagreed.

Such was his reputation that some refugees returning to their homeland from Egypt, refused to settle in Judea but instead went farther north to Galilee.

(cf. Matthew 2:19–23)

Germans wipe out three legions

Koblenz, AD 9

Three legions of Roman soldiers have been massacred by German tribespeople and the land to the north-east of the Rhine has been lost. All hopes of expanding the empire north to the river Elbe have been abandoned.

The Rhine frontier has been saved following a brave dash there by Tiberius. The emperor Augustus has divided what land remains in Roman hands into Upper and Lower districts, with their boundary near Koblenz.

Blame for the disaster has been laid on the commander of the Roman troops in Germany, P. Quinctilius Varus, who is related to the emperor by marriage. He has committed suicide.

Varus had been enticed by a report from Arminius, a Romanised chieftain of the Cherusci tribe, claiming that an uprising was taking place in the Teutoberg Forest, between the Osnabruck and Detmold regions in Lower Germany, north of Munster. But the three legions – XVII, XVIII and XIX – were caught in an ambush and massacred. Arminius is being celebrated as a German hero.

The legions will not be replaced due to lack of manpower, and their numbers, now considered omens of bad luck, will never be used again. Rome has lost over one-tenth of its entire forces in this one fell swoop, and eight of the remaining 25 legions will guard the new districts.

Clubs will be licensed

Rome, c. AD 7

All working mens' clubs are to be licensed by the state. Some had begun to exert political opposition and had to be suppressed.

The clubs, which unite men working in the same trade, exist mainly for friendship and social activity. They may also have strong religious affiliations, but generally do not attempt to influence wages or working conditions.

The new licences are not likely to be difficult to obtain.

This detail of Trajan's column in the Roman Forum depicts Roman troops at battle with Germanic warriors.

Fast Facts AD 1–9

Halicarnassus, c. AD 1: The people of this eastern province of the empire have honoured Augustus as a god. His policy is to allow such deification only if temples and cults established in his honour are associated with local deities. In an inscription, he is described as 'the father, god and saviour of all mankind.whose providence has not only fulfilled but even surpassed the prayers of all'.

Rome, AD 6: Pensions are to be paid to discharged soldiers by decree of the emperor. He has provided 170m sesterces from his own funds, to be supplemented by a 1 per cent sales tax and 5 per cent inheritance tax. New terms of service for soldiers now require legionaries to remain with the colours for 20 years; they will be paid 10 asses a day (less than a third of the Praetorians' pay); and will be discharged with a gratuity of 3,000 denarii. The new system will save generals the political task of seeking land-grants for their men at the end of every campaign.

Black Sea, AD 8: The leading Roman poet Ovid has been banished to Tomis (Constanza) on the Black Sea for unspecified reasons described as 'notorious'. The poet insists he has committed no crimes but does admit to an 'indiscretion'. Some of his work has been deemed pornographic and has gone against the emperor's moral reforms. Tomis, on the extreme edge of the empire, is superficially cultivated, culturally isolated and subject to attacks from fierce tribes, as well as having a miserable climate.

Rome, AD 6: About 320,00 people in the capital are receiving free grain handouts, up from 150,000 some 40 years ago. About 14m bushels of grain are imported each year to feed the city. A third of it comes from Egypt, the rest from north African countries farther west.

Rome, AD 6: After another serious fire in the capital, the emperor Augustus has created a corps of 7,000 freedmen to act as firefighters and police. They are organised into seven centuries (100s) in seven cohorts (1,000s). Each cohort is responsible for two districts, and the troops are quartered in private houses.

China, AD 9: Lin Ying, the young prince and heir apparent of the Han dynasty founded in 206 BC, has been usurped by Wang Mang who is calling his dynasty the Xin, or New dynasty. There is much unrest in the country and rebellions continue to break out sporadically. The Yellow Turban rebellion and the revolt of the Five Pecks of Rice group have devastated large areas.

New marriage law to benefit freed women

Rome, AD 9

In an attempt to stimulate Rome's flagging upper-class birth rate, new marriage laws have been passed which reward women for having large families. Freeborn women (born Roman citizens) will become

Neo and his wife. A rich Roman couple, depicted on the wall of their house in Pompeii.

independent of their guardians when they have three children, and freedwomen (slaves who buy or receive citizenship) when they have four.

Freedwomen are the greatest beneficiaries of the law *Lex Papia Poppaea*. They are now permitted to marry anyone except a senator and their children will be regarded as legitimate. Before, they were not allowed to marry freeborn men, who outnumbered freeborn women and were not always able to find suitable wives. Freedwomen may

now also pass on some of their property at death to their children. Before, their former owner received it all.

The new law mitigates some aspects of the unpopular *Lex Julia* law (promulgated by Augustus in 18 BC) which made marriage almost compulsory. Under it, unmarried people were barred from inheriting wealth or legacies. Now, a widow does not forfeit her inheritance if she marries within two years of her husband's death, and a divorcee within 18 months of the separation. Previously, the limits were 12 and 6 months respectively.

However, what has not changed is the long-term trend for the state to interfere in family life in its attempt to restore old Roman values. That started as a result of the social chaos of the civil wars last century during which paternal power over family fortunes was loosened and the aristocracy became more interested in pleasure and autonomy than in duty and community.

The law for men remains the same. They cease to become wards of their guardians once they reach puberty. The law also still prohibits the remarriage of adulteresses, and marriages between freedmen and 'women of ill repute'.

Divorce remains common in Rome, and is granted when one or both partners wish to dissolve a marriage for whatever reason. Their wish must be expressed publicly before seven witnesses. A divorced wife can reclaim her dowry in full unless her former husband is granted some of it by a judge for the maintenance of children in his care, or as compensation for damage caused by his wife's misconduct or extravagance.

Eastern Britain becomes united kingdom

Colchester, c. AD 9

Cunobelinus, king of the Catuvellauni tribe, has formed a united kingdom in the Essex region of Britain by annexing the neighbouring Trinovantes tribe. He is now minting his own coins at his capital Camulodunum near Colchester and also at St Albans a large centre in the west of his territory. They bear Latin inscriptions and depict various mythological scenes.

Camulodunum has become an export centre of goods to Rome which include gold, silver, slaves and hunting dogs for field sports and arena games. The occupying Roman army is also a major consumer of British grain, beef, leather and iron. Profits from the trade enable local leaders to indulge in a lavish lifestyle, and the Catuvellauni have other tribes at their trading mercy.

Their influence stops at the river Cherwell in Oxfordshire, beyond which is a Belgic tribe acting as a buffer between them and the powerful Dobunni centred at Bagendon in Gloucestershire who also mint their own coins.

Augustus bows out of life's comedy

Rome, 19 August AD 14

The emperor Augustus has died at Nola, aged 77. Almost his last words were, 'How have I played my part in the comedy of life?'

Most observers would reply, 'Very well'. His loss is being deeply mourned. Even in his old age he had a calm beauty, reflecting perhaps the peace which he had brought to the world by expanding the empire and reuniting Italy, and by supporting Roman traditions

A wall mural, from the house of Livia, wife of Augustus, showing her seated in front of a victory column, crowned with a statue of her husband.

and virtue. He tried to establish a government in which there was an accurate balance of classes and countries.

Born in 63 BC and named Octavius after his father (who died when he was four) he was brought up by his mother, Atia, the niece of Julius Caesar. He was introduced to Roman life by Caesar himself and despite delicate health joined him in Spain when he was only 18. After Caesar's assassination it was revealed that Octavius had been nominated by him as chief heir.

He was cautious and superstitious, but also exceptionally clever, mature and decisive. He restored more than 80 temples and reformed moral and religious life. His superstitions never affected his strength of will. He was accorded the title 'Augustus' (venerable) in 27 BC and while many hailed him as divine he never openly encouraged the association, although there were many shrines to him. The poet Horace described him as Mercury.

His lifestyle was simple. He slept on a camp bed in the same room for 40 years, wore clothes made by his wife or daughter, drank little alcohol and often refreshed himself between meals with a sour apple or piece of cucumber. Although he gave formal dinners, he preferred coarse bread, whitebait, pecorino cheese and green figs; he often lived on snacks.

A handsome man, he cared little about his appearance. He worked hard and used simple methods of relaxation: conversation, walking, running and playing handball. His health improved as he grew older, and as a friend he was faithful to all who were faithful to him.

He and Livia had no children, but he had a daughter Julia by his first wife Scribona in 39 BC. In his will he has named Tiberius and Livia as his heirs. He left 43.5m sesterces to the nation and people of Rome and 1,000 to every guardsman, 500 to each of the troops in the capital and 300 to every citizen soldier.

Reluctant emperor assumes office

Rome, AD 14

Tiberius has accepted the office of emperor but with considerable reluctance. He pleaded with the Senate that the burden shouldered by Augustus was too great and should be divided, but it decided that the empire was one and indivisible.

He accepted the role 'until such time as you judge it fair to grant me some rest in my old age'. Tiberius is remote and awkward as a person, and seems to possess few political skills. He has ascended to power through inheritance rather than achievement, and thus lacks the authority as well as the affability of Augustus. He is also out of touch with the Senate, having attended irregularly since he became a praetor in 16 BC.

The Forum of Augustus, constructed adjacent to the old Forum in central Rome.

German conquest finally abandoned by emperor

Rome, AD 16

The emperor Tiberius has refused his commander-in-chief in Germany, Germanicus, permission to make one final assault on the country's rebellious tribes. Instead, the beleaguered commander has been transferred to Armenia, where trouble has recently flared.

The decision brings to an end almost three years of conflict in the Roman garrison, in which campaigns against the German tribespeople have been conducted against a background of internal strife and intrigue. The trouble began shortly after Tiberius assumed power on the death of Augustus in AD 14. The commanders of the legions of Lower Germany mutinied and offered the empire to Germanicus, who has always been seen as a rival to Tiberius.

In an equally theatrical gesture he refused and claimed that the soldiers had insulted him. He then made unauthorised and lavish promises in the name of the emperor and sent away his wife Agrippina and their son Gaius (nicknamed 'Baby Boots' and something of a mascot to the army). The soldiers, distressed by an action they interpreted as lack of trust in them, were then ordered to punish the mutineers. Germanicus kept face, but Tiberius was not amused by his commander's devious manoeuvres.

In the corridors of power, observers are suggesting that Tiberius has either lost interest in expanding the empire, or is prudently cutting the expense and danger of another campaign for an already overstretched army. Germanicus' supporters, who compare him to Alexander, are complaining that Tiberius has acted out of jealousy.

Tiberius has appointed Calpurnius Piso as legate of Syria to subdue the popular commander. He will have control over four legions in the east and will act as a restraining influence on Germanicus, who it is feared could engage the army in an untimely Parthian War.

Historian of morals writes no more

Padua, AD 17

The historian Titus Livius has died at the age of 76. His seminal history of Rome from its inception until 9 BC filled 142 books, 100 of which covered merely the last eventful 150 years.

He grew up in Padua under the influence of a stern Italian morality which was to dominate all his writing. He often lamented the decay of discipline and looked back affectionately to the social morale.

In his preface, he asked his readers to address the early life and morals of Romans and then to 'note how, with the gradual relaxation of discipline, morals first then sank lower and lower, and finally began the downward plunge' to the present day.

He added that, in his opinion, the less men's wealth was, the less was their greed. More recently wealth has imported avarice and excessive pleasures with the longing to carry wantonness and licence to the point of ruin for oneself and of universal destruction.

A frieze from the walls of a Roman villa in Pompeii, depicting Silenius playing the lyre while the lady of the house eats a meal.

Piso cleared of murder, then kills himself

Rome, c. AD 19

The Roman commander in Syria has committed suicide after a protracted trial in which he was accused of murdering the army commander Germanicus. The charges were not proven, but Piso was unable to clear himself of other charges of bribing troops, inciting mutiny, and failing to regain his province.

It is widely believed that Piso, who had been a personal friend of Tiberius, as he had of Augustus, may have misunderstood or misinterpreted secret instructions to restrain Germanicus. If they could have been produced at the trial, they might have implicated the emperor in the murder, but despite dark hints they never came to light.

Germanicus died mysteriously at Antioch, possibly by being poisoned, after ordering Piso to leave. The enmity between the two men had come to a head when Germanicus, returning from a visit to Egypt, discovered that Piso had countermanded some of his orders. Agrippina, wife of Germanicus, and local people supported the poison claim, and suspicion fell heavily on Piso who publicly rejoiced at Germanicus' death.

Agrippina had returned to Brindisi with her husband's body, and had been feted all the way to Rome. However, although the city was packed with mourners, the emperor and his wife were noticably absent from the funeral. Germanicus' ashes were deposited at the mausoleum of Augustus.

Meanwhile, Piso had been charged and sent for trial by the Senate. There, Tiberius declared that if Piso had merely rejoiced at Germanicus' death, he would simply end the friendship. If he was guilty of murder, he should be punished accordingly. The emperor urged a fair trial, but although the murder charge was not proven the case has dented the emperor's already failing popularity.

The extensive ruins of the once proud city of Palmyra, former Roman centre in Syria.

Fast Facts AD 14–28

Asia, c. AD 14–27: Spices from Asia are being used increasingly in medicine as well as in cooking, according to the new encyclopaedia of medicine by Celsus. For example, the drug Mithradatium has 36 ingredients including pepper, saffron, ginger, cinnamon, frankincense and myrrh. It was named after Mithradates of Pontus (120–63 BC) who, when surrounded by ambitious relations, noticed peculiar tastes in his food. The drug proved so powerful an antidote to poison that when defeated and deposed he was immune to the poison with which he tried to kill himself.

Lower Danube, AD 19: One of the two client kings in the divided kingdom of Thrace has murdered the other. The survivor has been captured and sent to Rome for trial. The region had been divided by Augustus to control it.

Gaul, AD 21: Another rebellion has broken out in Gaul, initially because of demands by Roman financiers, but fanned into something greater by the Druids, tribal priest-leaders. However, Gallic resistance to Rome is usually token and never united; the total Roman garrison numbers only about 1,200 men. The legions of the Upper Rhine under Gaius Silius were eventually called in to help crush the local leader Julius Sacrovir, a Roman citizen and Druid.

Rome, AD 23: Drusus, son of the emperor Tiberius, has died, apparently of natural causes. However, it is rumoured that his wife Lavilla, sister of Germanicus, instigated it while having an affair with Aelius Sejanus, the prefect of the Praetorian Guard. Sejanus had already divorced his wife, and it is said that Livilla wishes to marry him. Drusus had been nominated as Tiberius' successor, following successful campaigns in Illyricum in AD 17–20. The emperor is said to be deeply depressed, and according to the Jewish Herod Agrippa, 'he cannot bear to see people about the court who remind him of his son'.

Rome, c. AD 25: The historian Cremutius Cordus has begun a hunger strike after the Senate decreed that his books should be burned and the author prosecuted for treason. He had refused to glorify Augustus and had praised Brutus, the murderer of Julius Caesar. His daughter is believed to have hidden some of his works for safe keeping.

Rome, c. AD 28: The interest rate for safe investments still stands between 6% and 10%, as it has since 100 BC. Unregulated loans in kind can attract interest of up to 50%, however.

Rome, c. AD 28: The art of glass blowing is flourishing in the city. The skill is said to have come either from Sidon or Alexandria. Romans are still importing expensive Murrhine glass vases however.

Less sex, more freedom among German tribes

Koblenz, AD 19

King Maroboduus, the autocratic former Roman soldier who ruled the Marcomanni tribe with an iron fist, has been deposed and has fled to an outpost of the empire. His German subjects felt he had used too much power, and their Roman overlords are pleased at his departure too. The country is now likely to remain a collection of small and easily-contained tribes fighting each other.

The occupying forces have discovered that the Germans are more puritannical than Romans. Homosexuals are drowned in swamps when convicted. Marriage ties are observed strictly and proven cases of (female) adultery are punished severely. The woman's head is shaved, she is driven from her village, and sometimes executed. People do not marry until their late teens or early twenties, and warriors do not marry until they have proved their valour in battle.

Slaves, however, are treated more leniently than in Rome. They have accommodation separate from their masters, and pay rent in the form of grain, cloth or cattle. They are more like Roman tenant farmers except they are not free. But the number of slaves is low. Women, children and the elderly do much of the menial work and there is no large-scale industry for which cheap labour is required.

The people are big-built, with powerful limbs, blue eyes and red or blond hair. According to Roman soldiers, German fighters have a fierce and terrible look in their eyes. They exert immense strength in the first rush of battle, but lack staying power if they do not win quickly.

Sarmartians take big steppe

Central Europe, c. AD 25

The Roman empire is now confronted by a formidable array of tribespeople gathered along the length of the river Danube across central Europe following the move of the Sarmartian tribe of the Iazyges into the Hungarian Plain.

A Sarmartian arm-bracelet, from Hungary.

This is the last outlier of the Eurasian steppe before it gives way to the woodland and hill country of Austria and Slovakia. Their former territory on the lower Danube has been taken by another Sarmartian tribe, the Roxolani.

Potential enemies strung along the river include the Germans on its upper reaches. They give way eastwards to the Iazyges, then come the Dacians in the Transylvanian mountains of Romania, and finally the Roxolani towards the Black Sea.

Each could contribute something different to an anti-Roman coalition. The Germans have the greatest physical strength and courage. The Dacians have the greatest political cohesion; the Iazyges have the best light horsemen and the Roxolani have heavily-armoured knights.

MARE GERMANICUM

CHAUCI
SAXONES
FRISII
R. Weser
R. Elbe
SEMNONES
BATAVI BRUCTERI
TUBANTES
LANGOBARDI
CHERUSCI
R. Rhine
SUGAMBRI
Vetera
Germania Inferior
CHATTI
Colonia
Belgica
Germania
Mogoniacum
HERMUNDURI
Augusta Trever
MARCOMANI
Germania Superior
R. Danube
Lugdunensis
Augusta Vind
Vesontia
Raetia
Noricum
Lugdunum
Aventicum
Curia

Tiberius retires to Isle of Capri

Rome, AD 26

The emperor Tiberius has left Rome and is now living as a recluse on the island of Capri.

He travelled to the coastal area south of Naples on the pretext of dedicating the temple of Jupiter at Capua and the temple of Augustus at Nola. But on his arrival he issued an order forbidding disturbance of his privacy. Troops were posted to keep the crowds away.

He disliked the towns and crossed the three miles to the island. It is harbourless, enjoys a mild winter climate and delightful views across the Bay of Naples to Mount Vesuvius. Tiberius is living in 12 separate villas. His absorption in state affairs seems to have ended and he apparently divides his time between secret orgies and malevolent thought.

Commentators are suggesting that his withdrawal is due partly to the intrigues of Sejanus, his close

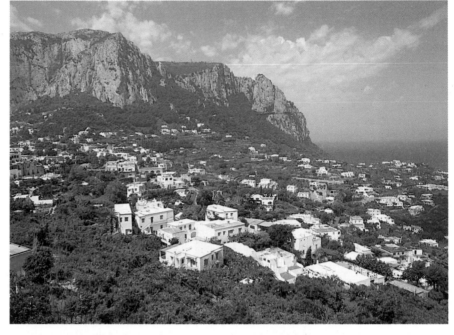

Enjoying a delightful climate, Capri has always been a popular resort.

aide and confidante who may be leading a double life. Others believe that the emperor was driven away by his mother's continual bullying, to whom he owes his seat of power. Tiberius has been unable to share control with her and cannot dislodge her.

Passionate poet dies in exile

Tomis, AD 17

Publius Ovidius Naso, the one-time leading poet of Rome, has died in exile at the age of 60. Despite repeated appeals to Augustus and latterly to Tiberius, he was never allowed to leave the inclement and culturally isolated Tomis.

Ovid came from the small town of Sulmo, 90 miles from Rome. He was born into an equestrian family and was intended by his father for an official career. Sent to Rome for education, his public speaking was described by the elder Seneca as more like free verse than prose.

Ovid held some minor judicial posts and was chosen by Augustus as a candidate for senatorial rank, but, saying that public life would take up too much of his time, he abandoned it all for poetry.

His poetry books were instant bestsellers. His subject was always human emotion, and his fans like his lightness of style and the wit with which he explored even the deepest passion. He will be remembered particularly for his *Metamorphoses*, an epic poem which tells stories from classical and near-eastern legend, progressing chronologically from the Big Bang (the first ever metamorphosis) to the turning of Julius Caesar into a god (the culmination of all metamorphosis).

He also wrote the noted *Fasti*, a poetical calendar of the roman year, with a book for each month, and the wittily didactic *Art of Loving* which critics said was a direct incitement to adultery and offensive to Augustan morality.

He was banished, he said, because of a poem and a mistake. The poem was *The Art of Loving*; the mistake was never revealed. It is believed that he was the eye-witness to a serious offence that directly concerned the emperor.

He was married three times and had one daughter.

Poet's musings

'I see and approve better things, but I follow worse.'
Metamorphoses

'God send my enemies a moral life, single sleep and limbs relaxed in mid-mattress ...'

'Let soldiers impale their hearts on a pike and pay down blood for glory ...'

'But when *I* die let me faint in the to and fro of love and fade out of its climax.'

'I can just imagine the mourner's comment: "Death was the consummation of his life." '
Amores (Love Poems)

'When evil overtakes the good, to disbelieve in God can be forgiven.'

Theatre tragedy claims 50,000 victims

The Colosseum, completed in AD 80, was Rome's grandest amphitheatre. Built to last, it is still one of ancient Rome's most potent symbols. It could seat over 100,000 and had a removable canvas roof – so that the spectators could enjoy the games in the shade during the hot Roman summer. It was also capable of being flooded so that naval battles could be re-enacted, in addition to the more usual gladiatorial games.

Fidenae, Rome, AD 27

A jerry-built amphitheatre has collapsed, killing or trapping the 50,000 spectators inside. The builder has been banished from the empire and new laws governing the safety of public buildings have been enacted.

The theatre was built by a former slave, Atilius, motivated more by profit than by municipal benevolence. The people of Rome had been starved of gladiatorial shows while the austere emperor Tiberius was living in the city, and they flocked to the spectacle.

The building literally bulged at the seams, collapsed under the weight, burying people under tons of rubble. Many died instantly while others lay trapped and mangled by the wreckage. Relatives rushed to embrace the corpses, quarrelling over the identification of those most mutilated.

Leading Romans threw open their homes to provide medical attention and supplies for the injured. The Senate has decreed that in future no one with capital of less than 400,000 sesterces should stage shows, and theatres should only be built on land of proven solidity.

Seried ranks of seats rose high above the floor of the arena.of the Colosseum. This floor is no longer: what can be seen are the myriad passages and rooms below it in which wild beasts and prisoners were kept.

Conspiracy theories prompt treason trials

Rome, c. AD 27–28

As the struggle for a successor to Tiberius rages between the houses of Germanicus and Claudius, treason trials have become rife, suspicion runs riot and professional informers are growing rich through the rule that a convicted man's property is divided among his accusers.

Agrippina, the widow of Germanicus, is determined that her children should have the title, while equally determined on behalf of her children is Livilla, widow of Tiberius' son Drusus, who has enlisted the support of Sejanus, a trusted aide of Tiberius and a sworn enemy of Germanicus. That support may be a double-edged sword, however, as Sejanus' subtle power is adding to Tiberius' sense of paranoia.

Relations poisoned in court feud

Capri, c. AD 27–28

Agrippina, widow of Germanicus and daughter-in-law of the emperor Tiberius, has slipped further from imperial grace and favour after pleading unsuccessfully for mercy for her accused second cousin Claudia Pulchra, who has been condemned for attempting to poison the emperor.

She enraged Tiberius by claiming that she, and not the statues to which he sacrificed, embodied the spirit of his adoptive father Augustus. The emperor sealed Pulchra's fate, who was also accused of using sorcery and of immorality. In another incident, Agrippina refused to eat with Tiberius who she believed was poisoning her.

The emperor recently moved from Rome to live as a recluse on the island of Capri.

The Roman empire in Jesus' day

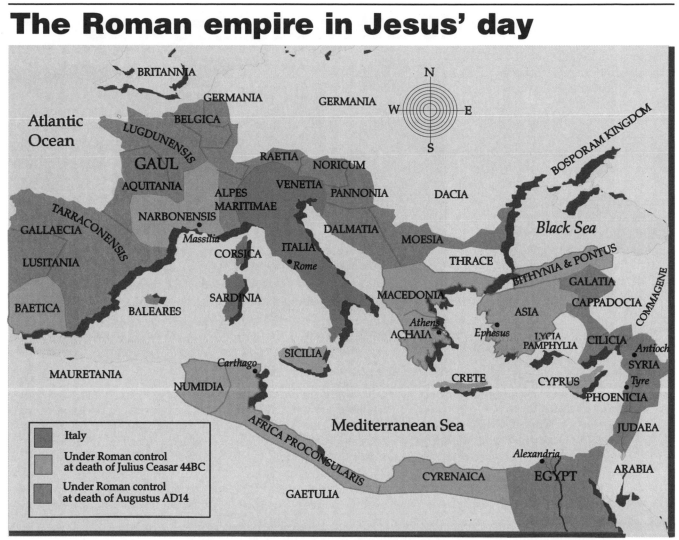

After the rapid expansion of the empire, due to the campaigns, treaties and annexations carried out actively throughout the reign of Augustus, a period of consolidation followed. The infrastructure of the empire was established through the collection of taxes; the establishment of the legal system; the positioning of numerous garrisons and massive road building and civil engineering projects. An era of prosperity and stability followed, ushering in a period in which travel and commerce increased greatly.

Earth is a single land mass, claims Strabo

Amaseia, Pontus, c. AD 25

The historian Strabo has died here recently. He was believed to have been aged at least 85. Contemptuous of religion and no great traveller himself, he stayed in Rome for many years collecting geographical material. He wrote 47 books of history and 17 of geography. He described the earth as a single land mass surrounded by ocean. He had lived at Amaseia for at least 30 years.

Building on the theories and discoveries of Strabo, Ptolemy, some 80 years later, produced an uncannily complete and accurate map of the world. This picture shows a medieval reproduction based on the earlier, now lost, Roman original.

Fiery hermit attracts crowds

Bethany, east of Jordan, c. AD 29

A charismatic hermit who chooses as his pulpit the desolated east bank of the river Jordan is drawing crowds of people from the towns of Judea miles away.

They cross the shallow fords to hear a message of repentance and renewal that is as stark as the preacher's lifestyle. John the Baptist, as he is known, wears a crude camel-hair smock with a thick leather belt and appears to live on the only food you can gather in the wasteland hereabouts – locusts and wild honey.

This is an area of contrasts which provides a fitting backdrop for such an enigmatic figure. As the river, never very wide and often sluggish, meanders through its steep valley, a thin band of dense forest where lions are said to prowl gives way to a hill country of ash-grey marl which is either dry as dust or slippery as mud and always impossible to cultivate. On the west bank are patches of fields like oases where water and soil in fertile combination allow the peasants to grow numerous grain and fruit crops.

On the east side, however, nothing grows that's worth eating, and no one lives here who can avoid it. It's a place for passing through, not for visiting, but since John began preaching to the travellers it's become a mecca for the tourists. Indeed, curiosity must be partly what draws them, because his message is not exactly light entertainment.

The baptism, as seen in the film *Jesus of Nazareth*, by Zefferelli.

At least, it was fun when he pointed his bony finger at the pompous Pharisees and Sadducees who came to see what all the fuss was about and stood at the back taking notes. 'You brood of vipers!' he cried, 'Who warned you to flee from the coming wrath?' But then everyone realised that his finger was sweeping across the whole crowd.

He got cheers for his answer to both hecklers and the conscience-stricken who asked what they were supposed to do about the terrible state of the world. Ever specific, he told tax collectors to cut their profits and soldiers to give up their favourite pastime of rape, pillage and extortion. Ordinary people, however, had to give away half their goods to the poor. They became quiet after that.

For those who take him seriously, John offers a ritual washing in the none-too-clear waters of the Jordan to signify their change of heart and determination to put God first in their lives. He has a small band of followers who believe he's the best thing since Elijah, the Israelite prophet who resisted kings and conquerors 900 years ago. Some are even saying he is Elijah, back from the grave.

Only one thing seems to have shaken his bullish confidence and aggressive manner. When he was approached for baptism by his cousin Jesus recently, he went uncharacteristically quiet for him. According to those who were close by, John refused at first to baptise Jesus.

'I'm not worthy to untie your shoelaces,' John said to him. 'I can't baptise you; you ought to baptise me.' Jesus persuaded him, however, and as he emerged from the water a dove landed on Jesus' head and some said they heard a voice saying that he is the Son of God.

Turning to some of his closer followers, John said: 'Look! There's the Lamb of God who takes away the sin of the world!' As John has been claiming for some time that he is only the forerunner of a spiritual leader 'who will baptise you with fire', eyes are beginning to observe this Jesus with more than passing interest. If he is right, John himself takes on a new significance; it's not every popular star at the height of his fame who tells the crowds to leave him and follow someone else.

(Matthew 3:1–17; Mark 1:1–11; Luke 3:1–18; John 1:19–34)

One of the possible baptism sites in the Jordan River, as seen today at Degany.

Preacher pulled back from the cliff edge

Nazareth, c. AD 29

A young preacher has escaped certain death here after being chased by an angry crowd to a cliff edge outside the town. He had been the focus of a religious dispute in the synagogue.

Jesus of Nazareth had been invited to read and comment on the Scriptures during a worship service, and chose a passage from Isaiah in which the prophet claimed that God's Spirit had anointed him to preach good news to the poor.

Claiming that the passage was now being fulfilled in a new way, the man known locally as Joseph the Carpenter's son first met with approval and then disbelief. The young 30-something speaker with no formal rabbinic training is rumoured to have performed healings in Capernaum. He had been met in Nazareth with the cynical request to prove it and so rebuked his hearers for having no faith. As he was chased out, he managed to slip through the throng and escape with his life.

It was the second time in recent weeks that he is reported to have been taken to the edge. According to his friends, while in the southern desert preparing for his teaching ministry he thought about jumping off the pinnacle of the temple in a spectacular stunt to demonstrate his unusual powers. It was one of three spiritual temptations to misuse his powers which he overcame more successfully than today's human opposition. The others were to turn stones into bread and to gain world power by underhanded methods.

(Luke 4:1–30)

Precipitous cliffs such as these were not to be found in Nazareth itself, but nearby.

Smyrna lands temple prize for services to the Empire

The columns of the Roman Agora, Smyrna.

Rome, AD 26

The city of Smyrna (Izmir) has beaten ten other candidates to win the privilege of erecting Asia's only temple of Tiberius. The decision was reached after the emperor spent several days listening to submissions from all the candidates.

The Senate voted for Smyrna, a prosperous port on the Aegean Sea famed for its magnificent buildings and fertile hinterland, because of its services to Rome in the past. It has often sent naval forces to support Roman troops, and it founded a temple of Rome in 195 BC before the empire's power had reached its present height.

Its chief claim to fame came during the first war against Mithradates VI of Pontus, about 88 BC, when Sulla's army was freezing in an exceptionally cold winter because of inadequate clothing. A public announcement of the fact caused the audience in Smyrna to strip naked and send their clothes to the Roman soldiers.

Among the other candidates, Hypaepa, Tralles, Laodicea and Magnesia were dismissed as being of lesser importance. Illium, despite Troy being the mother city of Rome, was considered a has-been. A stronger contender was Hali-carnassus, which has stood firm on its rock foundations for 1,200 years. Pergamum, which already has a temple of Augustus, Ephesus with its cult of Diana, and Miletus focussing on Apollo, were considered to have sufficient temples already. Sardis was runner-up.

(cf. Revelation 2:1–17; 3:1–6, 14–22)

Children are great, says man of God

Judea, c. AD 30

Children not only should be seen and heard, they should also be looked up to as role models, says the religious teacher Jesus of Nazareth in his latest reversal of normal values.

'If people really want to enter God's kingdom then they've got to become like little children,' he is telling his followers. 'No one's greater than a child there.'

He made his comments as he arbitrated in two disputes which had broken out among them. In

inclusion of children in the front row of the crowds that mob him everywhere. His aides had been turning away parents and children who had approached him for a prayer of blessing. 'Don't stop them,' he ordered. 'The kingdom belongs to people like them.'

They were anxious that such children would waste Jesus' time and that the parents were treating him like a lucky charm. The only Jewish precedent for blessing children is one given annually by an elder on the Day of Atonement.

contain nothing of substance.

Despite having no children of his own (he is unmarried, itself unusual), he has always taken an interest in them. Children and teenagers have been among the people he has healed, and he has told stories about children's games to illustrate his views.

(Matthew 18:1–5; 19:13–15; Mark 9:33–37; 10:13–15; Luke 9:46–48; 18:15–17)

Many births make light work for Jews

Judea, first century AD

Jewish families see children as valuable workers and earners as soon as they are old enough to go into the fields or workshops. As a result Jews tend to have a higher birth rate than Romans, although the survival rate of infants is similarly low.

A terracotta group of two girls playing knucklebones, from Taranto, southern Italy.

one, they were arguing over which of them would have the main positions of power in the coming 'kingdom', presumably as ministers of state.

In a devastating blow to their egos he implied that the only people who could be called truly great were those who were prepared to forgo human status, even to become despised by others and to accept an apparently inferior and insignificant role like that occupied by children.

And on another occasion, speaking at a meeting on the east side of the Jordan, he reversed normal adult values by encouraging the

In a further enhancement of the value of children, Jesus has also said that anyone who leads a child into sin will be judged severely by God. 'He would be better off strapping himself to a heavy millstone and jumping into a deep lake,' he asserted, emphasising the guilt accredited to, if not felt by, the offender.

Jesus of Nazareth has made similar statements before. The Jewish leader Nicodemus was once told he had to be 'born again' as a child if he would enter God's kingdom. Jesus has consistently pricked the bubbles of human pride which attract public attention but which

Boys are preferred to girls because they continue the family line, but children of either sex are not generally abandoned. Child sacrifice is prohibited in their religious scriptures.

Patterns of upbringing here vary little from elsewhere in the empire. Newborn babies are rubbed with salt to toughen their skins and then wrapped tightly in cloth strips to keep them straight. The bandaging is loosened several times daily and the skin treated with olive oil. Babies are generally breast-fed for up to three years, sometimes by a wet nurse.

Abortion is not widely practised and there is a popular belief that the unborn child can be the object of God's care and even calling. The prophet Jeremiah was called in the womb, and it is said that Jesus of Nazareth and his cousin John the Baptist recognised each other in their respective wombs. Boys are circumcised when they are eight days old, as in several cultures, but the ceremony is endowed with religious significance as marking the child's entry into God's 'covenant' community.

Wine, wisdom and sanity flow from teacher's common touch

Ruins of the first-century synagogue in Capernaum in which Jesus would have taught.

Capernaum, c. AD 29

He speaks the people's language. He addresses the people's needs. He even heals them when they're ill. And the people of Capernaum and surrounding villages nestling near the Sea of Galilee love him.

'He's got real authority and power,' said one local. 'The regular teachers haven't.'

The self-effacing Jesus of Nazareth, first hit the local headlines at a family wedding in Cana when the wine ran out during the extended festivities. Without a touch of the histrionics associated with quack magicians, he just filled up – of all things – the foot-washing jars with water from the well.

He then got the head waiter to take a cupful of the liquid to the best man, which must have been a miracle of persuasion in itself. But the biggest miracle was that the contaminated water had become a superb vintage wine. 'It was a sign of what Jesus is all about,' said John Zebedee, one of his associates. 'He brings new life into bad situations.'

Further evidence of that was provided a few days later with two notable healings in Capernaum, the chief town of this densely-populated region which Jesus appears to be making his base. The first was in the synagogue, when a demented man suddenly shouted at Jesus, 'You're the Holy One of God! Have you come here to torture us?'

With an authoritative word, Jesus commanded the hellish spirit which controlled the man to leave him. He fell heavily to the ground, but was uninjured and, more remarkably, was suddenly sane.

The second incident was at the home of Simon Peter whose mother-in-law was seriously ill with a fever. When Jesus healed her, her recovery was so sudden that she cooked for the visitors afterwards.

(Luke 4:31–41; John 2:1–11)

Fishermen sink all to net converts

Sea of Galilee, c. AD 30

Two fishing families have beached their boats and sunk their assets in an extraordinary decision to net converts for Jesus of Nazareth instead of trawling a living out of the deep waters of Galilee.

Their decision came after Jesus had borrowed Simon's boat to use as a floating pulpit from which to teach the crowds who had followed him to the stony beach.

When the sermon was over, he ordered Simon's tired crew to row out from the shallows in full daylight despite the fact that they had caught nothing all night, when the fish are normally near the surface.

However, when the large nets had been cast from the small boat they immediately trapped a huge shoal. The Zebedee brothers came to their assistance and the catch put both boats dangerously low in the water.

Awestruck by the fact that a carpenter's son had taught experienced fishermen their job, the four men agreed that following Jesus was likely to be more rewarding. But the defection of these two families to an itinerant teacher will make no difference to the economy of this prosperous area nor to the supply of fish elsewhere.

Galilee, some 21 km (13 miles) north to south and 11 km (seven miles) broad, lies 210 m (700 feet) below sea level and is the chief source of fish for the province of Judea. Nine towns, each with a population of 15,000 or more, circle the lake to harvest and process its abundant stocks.

(Luke 5:1–11)

Upon hearing Jesus, fishermen left their boats to follow him.

John the Baptist jailed for judging court

The Roman road to the rock-hewn city of Petra, from which Herod Antipas' wife came.

Machaerus, Perea, c. AD 30

John the Baptist, the fiery prophet who set alight people's hopes for the long-expected Messiah, has had his ministry extinguished by Herod Antipas. King Herod, as the tetrarch of Galilee and Perea is known locally and unofficially, had been incensed by John's public criticism of his many marriages, and jailed him for contempt of the court.

Herod Antipas is the most able of Herod the Great's sons and has inherited his father's passion for building. He completed the city of Tiberias, named in honour of the emperor Tiberius, four years ago. He also inherited his father's penchant for political intrigue and frequent marriages, adding to the already complex inter-relationships in the Herodian dynasty.

Antipas' first wife was the daughter of Arepa, king of Petra in Arabia, but he divorced her in order to marry his niece Herodias, daughter of his half-brother Aristobolus. The cost of the wedding was inflated by the subsequent war of revenge started by Arepa.

Herodias was already married to another of her uncles, Herod Philip, who is also a half-brother of Antipas. During a visit to their Rome residence, Antipas had persuaded her to get a divorce and marry him instead. Both the divorce and the remarriage to his living half-brother's wife are contrary to Jewish law to which the Herods still pay lip-service. John was put into prison for pointing out this illegality.

Machaerus is a bleak outpost on the eastern side of the Dead Sea. John is not held in solitary confinement, however, and his disciples are allowed to visit him.

(Matthew 4:12; 14:3–5; Mark 1:14; 6:17f; Luke 3:19f)

Tax man works for prophet

Capernaum, c. AD 30

A customs official has sold off his lucrative securities to become the latest full-time disciple of Jesus of Nazareth. Levi Alphaeus, or Matthew as he has become known, collected tolls assigned to Herod Antipas, tetrarch of Galilee. But putting a higher value on religious interest, he walked out of his job with an arrogant final gesture.

He threw a banquet for his former colleagues and invited Jesus and his friends as guests of honour. Whatever credit that may have added to Matthew's spiritual account, it finally bankrupted Jesus' already-failing reputation among the brokers of religious orthodoxy. The Pharisees regard tax collectors and all who associate with them as unfit dining companions on a level with prostitutes.

But the prophet-like teacher who always has a fund of quips, justified his expenditure of time on such people with cast-iron logic. It's precisely the unfit who need a doctor, he said, enjoying the food while his critics chewed over the thought.

(Matthew 9:9–13; Mark 2:13–17)

Galilee in the time of Jesus

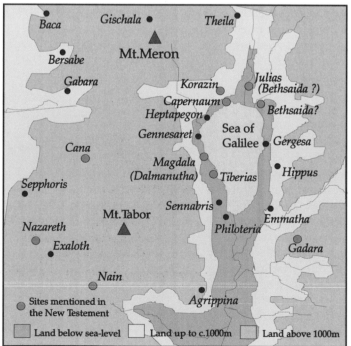

The Lake of Galilee lies at the head of the great rift valley, below sea level, which extends all the way to the Dead Sea following the Jordan valley. The land around the lake is a verdant, fertile area, surrounded by high, rolling hills. Jesus travelled repeatedly throughout the area during his ministry.

Cousins still stay friends

Galilee c. AD 30

John the Baptist and his cousin Jesus of Nazareth, sometimes regarded as rival prophets, are still the best of friends according to recent communiques between them. However, both are in no-win situations, with their different lifestyles and messages attracting widespread criticism.

John, imprisoned in Machaerus by Herod Antipas, has been tugging at his chains with frustration and uncertainty. Having declared that his younger cousin is the expected Messiah, or deliverer of Israel, the patience and credulity of this forthright man of action have been stretched by Jesus' apparent lack of dynamic national leadership.

According to two of his prison visitors, John sent a terse message urging Jesus to prove if indeed he is the once and future leader. In response Jesus quoted from the ancient prophet Isaiah. He claimed that through his work blind people see, the lame walk, lepers are healed, dead people are brought to life and the poor hear good news. Scribes say that these activities are normally associated with the Messiah.

'Don't cause me any bother,' Jesus added, adapting a colourful local phrase which implied that trying to force his hand would be like an animal springing a baited trap.

Having sent the couriers back with his cryptic reply, Jesus continued in his customary riddle-ridden style. John, he said, 'was the greatest man who ever lived'. He was neither ordinary, like a reed waving in the wind, nor a rich and unmotivated man bored with life. Rather, he was a true prophet.

On the other hand, Jesus said, everyone who belongs to God's kingdom is greater even than John. His disciples explained that he probably meant that John had prepared the way for the new order of

Machaerus, the Herodian stronghold in which John the Baptist was imprisoned.

life to which they claim to belong.

But Jesus was clear on one thing. The crowds, especially the religious leaders, had complained that John was a madman because of his severe message and austere lifestyle. They had also criticised Jesus for being ungodly because of his acceptance of outcasts and his love of food and wine.

'We can't win,' he claimed. 'It's like kids in the street trying to get their friends to play. One lot sings and the others tell them to clear off. So they play something serious and they still get rejected. But the wise person will see through the different externals to find the truth behind them both,' he added.

(Luke 7:18–35; cf. Matthew 11:2–19; Isaiah 35:5f; 61:1)

Disciples given own mission

Galilee, c. AD 30

The 12 closest associates of Jesus of Nazareth have been sent out in pairs to carry his message far and wide. They have been forbidden to take food, money or supplies, and are not to carry the beggar's bag sometimes used by itinerant preachers.

However, Jesus is said to have given them the same power to heal and cast out evil spirits which has drawn the crowds to him. Having been with him for about a year, the disciples are used to periodic preaching tours when they do not know where their next meal is coming from or where they will spend the night. This time, however, they are denied the comforting presence of their master.

(Luke 9:1–6; cf. Mark 6:7–13)

Miracle-worker raises the roof

Capernaum, c. AD 30

A householder at this customs post and fishing centre is counting the toll of importing Jesus of Nazareth after some of the teacher's zealous fans stripped the roof off his house.

The lakeshore at Capernaum.

His patience was taxed to the limit as, trapped inside by a huge crowd, he watched helplessly while four men pulled away the mud and branch roof over his main living room, where Jesus was teaching. They had climbed the outside staircase of this large block basalt home of several families.

Then, without a word, they lowered a paralysed man on a stretcher through the hole into the room. The crowd watched spellbound as Jesus turned to the man and pronounced that his sins were forgiven. A murmur of disapproval rippled through the house because Jews believe that only God can forgive sins.

But the master of miracles proved himself also a master of suspense. Asking 'Which is easier, to say he's forgiven or to tell him to walk?' he audaciously laid claim to divine power and authority. When no reply was forthcoming, he did both. The man got up and pushed his way to the exit.

A first-century mosaic of boats and the Capernaum lakeshore.

That really raised the roof as people exclaimed their amazement. But while the paralytic had his unspecified debt to the Almighty remitted, the householder was left to mend the gaping hole in his earthly assets.
(Matthew 9:2–8; Mark 2:3–12; Luke 5:12–26)

Madam's sin smells sweet at banquet

Galilee, c. AD 30

A prostitute put a Pharisee into a potentially embarrassing position when she gatecrashed his dinner party. But she bestowed her favours on his guest of honour, Jesus of Nazareth, by washing his feet with her tears and sweetening them with her perfume.

The other guests, reclining on couches in the open courtyard of Simon the Pharisee's sumptuous dwelling, were even more outraged by Jesus' reaction. He forgave the sinner her sin.

Explaining his unorthodox acceptance of someone who would be regarded as an abomination by polite religious society, Jesus pointed out that Simon had overlooked the normal courtesies for honoured guests: a foot-wash and general freshen-up usually administered by a servant girl.

The prostitute, believed by some to be called Mary Magdalene, had done both for him. She emptied the entire contents of the phial of perfume over his feetbefore then washing them with her long hair.

'Who has the most love and gratitude?' Jesus asked the bemused guests. 'The person who's been let off a big debt or the person who's been let off a small debt?' When he got the obvious answer, Jesus pointedly remarked that in present company, the one let off the biggest debt to God had shown the most love in response.

The implied criticism of the host did not go unnoticed by the guests. Nor did Jesus' audacity in taking over, not for the first time, God's traditional role of absolution. Unlike the perfume, that left an unpleasant odour hanging over the rest of the evening's conversation.
(Luke 7:36–50)

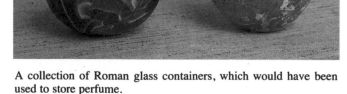

A collection of Roman glass containers, which would have been used to store perfume.

John loses head to royal dancing girl

Judea, c. AD 30

John the Baptist finally lost his fight against corruption in high places when executioners presented his head on a plate at Herod's birthday party. Guests looked on in stunned silence as the grisly object was paraded through the ballroom and given to Salome, daughter of Herodias the wife of Herod Antipas.

The episode started after Heriodias performed a seductive dance in front of the assembled courtiers. This dance so enthralled the titular king, who in one of his more extravagant moments had publicly promised her anything she asked. After consulting her mother, the teenager requested the popular preacher's head.

Antipas could not rescind his offer in front of his guests, who included top military and civilian leaders and Roman officials. He was also unable to persuade Salome to choose something of greater value, but less politically embarrassing.

He signed the execution order, which was carried out immediately without trial, contrary to Jewish law. Beheading is also contrary to local custom; execution is normally stoning for religious offences or crucifixion for political crimes.

Although off-ended by John's condemnation of his marriage to Herodias, Antipas had often listened to the preacher. Court officials say he is now sleeping uneasily and is expressing the belief that Jesus of Nazareth, whose riveting teaching, fearless controversies and miraculous healings have been widely reported, is in fact John the Baptist raised from the dead.

Following the execution, John's dismembered remains were collected by his friends and given a proper burial. Jesus, who is his cousin, is said to have gone into private mourning.

(Mark 6:14–29; cf. Matthew 14:1–12; Luke 9:7–9)

The beheading of John the Baptist. This dramatic scene has captured the imagination of artists throughout the ages, such as Aretino Spinelli (c. 1340-1410).

Cowboy farmers round up professional soldiers

North Sea coast, c. AD 29

A herd of cowboys has inflicted a series of embarrassing defeats on the professional Roman army on the North European lowlands.

A revolt by the Frisians, a poor tribe whose main livelihood comes from beef and dairy cattle raising, resulted in successive waves of Roman soldiers being scattered or slaughtered.

The Frisians had been paying taxes in ox-hides, to be used for military equipment, for some time without complaint. But when senior staff officer Olennius chose to interpret that the tax meant that larger buffalo hides should be provided instead, the demand became a massive burden which the Frisians were unable to pay with their relatively small animals.

They lost their cattle, their lands and even sold their dependents into slavery before finally losing their patience and executing the tax collectors.

The imperial governor of Germany, Lucius Apronius, sent in both infantry and cavalry, but his forces were separated by space and time, giving the poorly-armed Frisians the opportunity to rout them. Some 900 Romans were slaughtered in the Baduhenna Woods, and another 400, who had occupied a villa, killed each other in fear of treachery.

The other German tribes have glorified the Frisians. Olennius has taken refuge in Flevum, a fort on the North Sea coast.

Storm-trooper restores peace

Gadara, c. AD 30

People in this area south-east of the Sea of Galilee are still shaking with fear after witnessing some of the most sensational exploits yet performed by the travelling teacher Jesus of Nazareth.

First, the forces of nature appeared to bow to his command. He had been caught in a squall while crossing the lake notorious for sudden storms as cold air rushes down to it through narrow ravines. Tired after a day's teaching, he slept through the noise until the crew woke him to help bail out the sinking boat.

But instead of bailing out, he bawled out: 'Quiet! Be still!' According to his disciples, the storm subsided at once and even the sea became calm, something which the seasoned fishermen among them had never seen happen before. Normally, the water remains choppy for some hours after a storm has blown itself out.

'I don't know which was more frightening,' one of them said later. 'The power of the storm or the authority of the Master over it.'

As if that were not enough, on landing they were confronted by a naked cave-dwelling lunatic with superhuman strength. Notoriously unpredictable, mutilating himself with stones and completely unrestrainable (he has reportedly bro-

Early morning, Lake Galilee.

ken every chain that has ever been put on him) he fell at Jesus' feet, called him 'Son of the Most High God' and begged not to be tortured.

While the disciples cowered away from him, Jesus conversed with him. Calling himself Legion, the deranged man spoke and acted as if gangs of rival warlords were fighting inside his body and mind. With different voices they squealed and grunted for fresh bodies to inhabit should they be evicted.

Also squealing and grunting on the hillside was an illicit herd of pigs owned by local people whose adherence to Jewish meat laws seems determined more by market forces than religious

scruples. At a word of command from Jesus the man fell quiet while the pigs suddenly stampeded over the cliff top and into the waters below, as if the 'spirits' had transferred to them in a short-lived bid for freedom.

The significance of unclean spirits taking over unclean animals and then drowning hurt the locals' consciences as well as damaging their economy. When they discovered the loss of their prize porkers and the recovery of the man's sanity, they decided they preferred the devil they knew to the stranger they didn't, and hustled Jesus and his friends out of town.

Jesus rejected Legion's pleas to accompany him, but sent him back to his suspicious fellow-countrymen to act as a permanent reminder that a spiritual storm-trooper had once invaded their territory.

(Luke 8:22–39; cf. Matthew 8:18–34; Mark 4:35–5:20)

The Storm on the Lake of Galilee by Rembrandt (1606–1669).

Delayed action restores dead child to life

Galilee, c. AD 30

A dead girl has been restored to life after a mercy mission to save her was delayed by sightseers.

The 12-year-old, who may have been suffering from a form of meningitis, was the only child of Jairus, the official responsible for sought anonymous healing.

When a woman who had had a haemorrhage for many years came forward to recount her tale of woe, he reassured her that her faith had made her whole again. He seemed not to notice that he was made technically 'unclean' by the contact.

The waking of Jairus' daughter, as seen in the film *Jesus of Nazareth* by Franco Zefferelli.

synagogue services. He threw theological orthodoxy to the wind by throwing himself at the feet of the controversial healer and teacher, Jesus of Nazareth, begging for help.

News of his plea spread quickly through the close-knit community and crowds converged from all directions, blocking Jesus' progress through the narrow streets. At one point, jostled by hundreds of people, Jesus refused to fight his way any further until someone owned up to deliberately touching him.

Despite protests from the anxious family and incredulity from his associates, he insisted that he knew that someone in the crowd had

Wonder turned to weeping as the news spread that he was now too late for the little girl, who had died already. And weeping turned to ridicule as Jesus insisted on going to the house 'to wake her from sleep'. Evicting the village mourners who had already started up their wailing dirges, he forced them to change their tune when he emerged later holding the girl by the hand and ordering that she should be fed.

Only her parents and three of his associates were present during the 'raising'. Despite pressure from neighbours and others, they have refused to divulge how the miracle was achieved.

(Luke 8:40–56; cf. Matthew 9:18–26; Mark 5:21–43)

Disaster victims not to blame

Jerusalem, c. AD 30

People who are hurt or killed in disasters are not worse sinners than those who escape, says Jesus of Nazareth, who also claims that everyone is in danger of sudden divine judgement.

He was speaking after news broke of Pontius Pilate's latest barbarity against the Jews. The procurator had sent soldiers to the temple precincts to butcher a number of worshippers who were offering sacrifices. Officially, they had infringed unspecified Roman regulations.

Eighteen people were also killed recently when a tower in the southwestern wall of the city collapsed on them.

In popular Jewish thought the victims of accident or massacres are said to have received their just deserts for sins they have committed. The issue is debated in the biblical book of Job. The conclusion is that sin and suffering are not always linked in a simple chain of cause and effect, not least because often the wicked seem to escape lightly and the righteous seem to suffer unjustly.

In his comments, Jesus supported the view that suffering is indiscriminate and claimed that the victims were no worse than anyone else. However, he added that unless everyone 'repents' by turning back to God they would one day 'perish' under his judgement.

He made similar comments in a test-case brought by critics who presented him with a man born blind. They asked for a definitive ruling as to whose guilt he was being punished for, his own or his parents'. Jesus simply replied, 'Neither,' then spoke of God being glorified through the defect, and healed it.

(Luke 13:1–9; cf. John 9:1–3)

King of storytellers sows seeds of doubt

Galilee, c. AD 30

Jesus of Nazareth is the undisputed king of storytellers. No other Jewish rabbi can match his skill in weaving religious threads into homespun yarns.

But, as he acknowledges himself, his stories are so deceptively simple that listeners can miss their point completely. He even suggests that his real meanings are hidden from those who lack a positive attitude

The hills above Galilee where Jesus taught are still windswept and open today.

towards him. Some religious leaders are now suggesting that the subliminal message beneath his tales may be seditious or even blasphemous.

Drawing on familiar images of farmers sowing seed or fishermen casting nets, he speaks frequently about the kingdom of God (or kingdom of heaven as he more usually calls it, observing the traditional Jewish reticence to pronounce the name of God). By this he seems to

mean the rule or reign of God present in the world.

This reign is not yet complete but grows like a seed co-existing with less than worthy weeds until a future harvest. At the same time, perhaps to dispel passive interpretations, Jesus also portrays the kingdom as something precious which only certain people find, and that at the cost of everything.

He claims to be personally at the centre of this kingdom, which some interpret as verging on blasphemy. When he is present, he seems to suggest, so too is the rule of God; when he performs miracles, the supreme power of God's kingdom is demonstrated.

He admits that some people will never be able to understand the message in his stories. In a vicious

Kingly claims

- 'Repent because the kingdom of heaven is near.'

- 'How happy are those who know their spiritual poverty; the kingdom of heaven is theirs.'

- 'Seek God's kingdom before anything else and he will give you all you could need as well.'

- 'If I am exorcising demons by God's Spirit, then God's kingdom has arrived among you.'

- 'Unless you are completely changed and become like a small child, you will never get into the kingdom of heaven.'

- 'It's easier for a camel to get through a needle's eye than it is for someone who's tied to their wealth to get into the kingdom of heaven.'
  (Matthew 4:17; 5:3; 6:33; 12:28; 18:13; 19:24)

spiritual circle, they harden their hearts to the message because they do not wish to face its challenge, and as a result become even harder to it, he claims. In a blistering attack on his opponents, he uses the words of the prophet Isaiah to accuse them of being calloused, with their eyes closed to God's truth.

Some observers predict that he will go the way of previous messianic pretenders, and that it will not be long before this popular and likable young man stakes his claim to be king of the Jews. Others, more charitably, take his words as prophetic confirmation that the Messiah, the long-awaited deliverer of the Jewish nation, will be revealed shortly. Both are claims which the Roman garrison takes less seriously than the religious hopefuls.

(Matthew 13:10–17, 34f)

A sting in the tale

Many of Jesus' stories about the kingdom of God contain an implicit challenge to his listeners to respond in a personal way. Here are some – and their apparent morals.

The sower and the seed

A farmer hand-sowed a field. As he threw the seed from his bag some of it fell on the path and was eaten by the birds. Some fell on shallow, stony soil; it grew at first but then withered. Some fell in thorn patches which soon choked the young shoots. But some fell on deep fertile soil, germinated and developed grain – between 30 and 100 times what was sown.

The sower is God, the seed is his word. The soils are those who hear it. And only some understand it enough to become fruitful disciples who put the teaching into practice.

Moral: Listen carefully or else you'll miss God's word to you.

(Matthew 13:1–9, 18–23)

The weeds in the field

Once upon a time a farmer sowed good quality seed corn in his field. But an enemy sowed poisonous darnel in it too, contrary to the law. The farmer told his workers not to pull up the darnel because its strong roots would dislodge the weaker roots of the wheat. They could be pulled up just before harvest when there could be no mistaking the plants and no damage to the crop.

The farmer is the 'Son of Man', a title Jesus uses for himself. The seed is the people who follow him, among whom the devil sows his minions who are often indistinguishable from believers at first. The harvest is the end of the world when evil is weeded out for ever.

Moral: The kingdom will grow quietly, and the wicked will get their come-uppance – so watch out!

(Matthew 13:24–30, 36–43)

Small beginnings

God's kingdom is like a small mustard seed. From insignificant beginnings it becomes a huge shrub, home to numerous birds. If Jesus is thinking of the bird's-nest tree in Nebuchadnezzar's dream in Daniel, he means the nations of the world will be incorporated into God's kingdom. It is also like a tiny pinch of yeast which makes a whole batch of dough rise sufficiently to feed about 100 people.

Moral: Be patient!

(Matthew 13:31–33; cf. Daniel 4:10–12, 20–22)

Worth a fortune

There was this farm worker who dug up a pot of coins in his employer's field. So he sold everything he had to buy the field at market rates – with its forgotten added value! He was overjoyed. So too was the merchant who saw the biggest pearl ever. He sold all he had to buy it, because its value was incalculable.

Moral: If you want real happiness, you've got to give the kingdom all you've got.

(Matthew 13:44–46)

Sorting the catch

The real work in large-scale fishing comes when the catch is landed. The dragnet pulled between two boats trawls up many inedible creatures which have to be sorted out and thrown away.

Moral: Don't think you're acceptable to God just because you are caught up in kingdom activity.

(Matthew 13:47–50)

Most fields in Israel were small and rocky like this one.

Rulers come up short

The Damascus Gate, Jerusalem. Travellers from the north in Jesus' day would have entered the town through this gate, which was rebuilt in the Middle Ages.

Jerusalem, c. AD 30

Two of Israel's top rulers were cut short when they tried to measure themselves up against Jesus of Nazareth. But unlike many of his high-ranking opponents, they had not attempted to cut him down to size first.

During one of his journeys to the capital, Jesus was approached by a young and wealthy aristocrat who asked the 'good teacher' how he could inherit eternal life.

Jesus, pointing out that no one was good except God, referred him to commandments such as not committing adultery and not stealing. When the ruler claimed to have kept on the straight and narrow all his life, Jesus told him that he could only find what he was lacking by giving away his possessions.

Despite the obvious bond of mutual sympathy between the two men who come from opposite ends of the social and religious scale, the young ruler felt unable to go to such lengths and left dejectedly.

The second ruler, Nicodemus, one of the top 70 Jews who make up the Sanhedrin, the supreme court, confessed that he had been unable to figure out the equation between Jesus' 'acts of God' and his flagrant breaking of the rules of God.

In a private interview one evening, Jesus gave the wealthy leader an equally disproportionate solution. Grown men must be born again, he said, not by shrinking back into the maternal womb but by expanding into the realms of God's Spirit. Only then would they discover a workable formula for God-centred living, he claimed.

The northern-bred preacher seems to delight in confounding his southern-based questioners and potential patrons with fanciful images. Following the rich young ruler's departure, Jesus quipped that a camel could be threaded through the eye of a needle more easily than a rich man could enter the kingdom of heaven. Those who gave everything for it, he said, would discover ample compensation.

(Matthew 19:16–30; Mark 10:17–21; Luke 18:18–30; John 3:1–21)

Five-times wife is talk of the town

Sychar, Samaria, c. AD 30

A woman co-habiting with her sixth man has become the talk of the town for different reasons after she fell for the teaching of Jesus of Nazareth. She says he claimed to be the promised Messiah and that he gave her a new outlook on life.

Generally shunned by the respectable people of this small hill-country town near Shechem, she encountered the travelling preacher while she was alone drawing water at midday. He was taking the direct route from Jerusalem to Galilee, unlike many orthodox Jews who avoid on theological grounds the territory they despise. He added acceptance to tolerance by initiating a conversation with her.

The Samaritans are a people of mixed race who adhere to the pentateuch (the first five books of Moses in the Jewish Bible). They are descendants of people left behind when Assyria conquered and decimated the ten northern tribes of Israel in 721 BC, who then intermarried with non-Jewish immigrants. They have built a rival temple on Mount Gerizim, not far from Sychar.

The woman's previous five husbands had all died or divorced her, leaving her destitute and vulnerable to lusty men, and earning her the reputation of being difficult to live with. Although Jesus had asked for a drink, he offered her running water which would satisfy her needs permanently. Only slowly did she realise that he meant a spiritual spring of life which would quench her thirst for acceptance and security.

He then astounded her by recounting her marital misfortunes, despite being a stranger to the area. Recognising him as a prophet, she asked for a clear answer to the top question: which is God's chosen site for worship, Mount Zion (Jerusalem) or Mount Gerizim?

'The time is coming when people won't worship at either place,' he replied. 'Instead, they'll worship God in spirit and truth anywhere and everywhere.'

Disappointed, she asserted that the Messiah would give them an answer even if Jesus couldn't. 'I am the Messiah,' he replied. Dropping her bucket, she ran to the town and called people to come and see Jesus. Jesus and his disciples stayed for a couple of days explaining their message.

(John 4:1-42)

Sychar and the surrounding area today, seen from Mount Gerizim.

How did he feed so many?

Bethsaida, Galilee, c. AD 30
Magicians can pull rabbits out of empty baskets but Jesus of Nazareth brings enough loaves and fish out of thin air to feed an army and to fill a dozen baskets with the leftovers.

A crowd estimated to exceed 5,000 men, besides women and children, could not believe their eyes when the free handout was distributed by Jesus' associates. Some even began plotting to make

The feeding of the five thousand, from *Jesus of Nazareth* by Franco Zefferelli.

the miracle-worker king of the Jews.

Jesus had made a private retreat to the isolated hills above this fishing village on the north-east side of the Sea of Galilee, home of Philip, one of his 12 closest disciples. As usual, crowds followed him to seek healing and to listen in to his teaching, spread out on the lush spring grass under a warm sun. At the

end of the day, visibly moved by the hunger of the people who had travelled far from home, he suggested that the disciples buy them all a simple meal in the town. The bill, however, would have amounted to eight months' wages for a working man, far beyond their means.

All they had between them was a teenager's lunchbox containing five cheap barley rolls and a couple of bony fish. It was nothing for the crowd, but it was enough for Jesus. Pronouncing the traditional blessing over food ('Blessed art thou O God for this fruit of the earth') he broke the rolls and gave the pieces to the disciples to pass round.

To their amazement each time they gave a piece to someone, there was more in the basket. And even more left over which no one had the appetite for.

If this was one of Jesus' famous kinetic pictures of God ('signs', his disciple John calls them), as some are suggesting, it revealed the extraordinary and overflowing generosity of a caring Father. Others, however, are still trying to work out what sleight of hand could have concealed so much food for so long. And for what reason.

(Matthew 14:13–21; Mark 6:30-44; Luke 9:10–17; John 6:1–15)

Half-baked teaching or wholesome doctrines?

Capernaum, c. AD 30

Last week's miracle bread has stuck in the throats of religious leaders here who find Jesus' teaching hard to swallow. Controversy is rising as surely as a batch of yeasted dough.

Not content with one square meal, they asked him during a synagogue service to emulate Moses, through whose prayers the Israelites were fed by manna for 40 years in the Sinai desert. It is said that such a sign would confirm that he is a prophet from God, perhaps the Messiah himself.

But he turned the conversation away from physical to spiritual hunger, echoing the prophet Isaiah who scolded the people of his day for spending on 'bread that cannot satisfy' (55:2). 'Don't work for food that goes off,' Jesus said. 'Instead work for the food that lasts for ever.'

In the course of his argument he made several extravagant claims, which his hearers noted with a mixture of alarm and amazement:

• 'The true bread of God is the Son of Man who came from heaven to bring life to the world.

• 'I am the bread of life. Whoever comes to me will never be hungry again, and whoever trusts me fully will never be thirsty again.'

• 'My Father has given me followers and I will never, ever turn away anyone who comes to me.'

• 'I came to earth from heaven to do my Father's will and to give eternal life to everyone who trusts me.'

• 'Only one person has ever seen God the Father – the one who has come from him. And if you trust me, the bread who has come from heaven, you will live forever.'

• 'The bread that I offer is my body and the drink I offer is my blood. Eat it and drink it, and you'll live for ever.'

Jesus' local parentage is well known, so his claim to 'come from heaven' was met with derision. His other claims were met with hostility or confusion. The logical conclusion of his teaching is at least that he

Loaves piled high in a Jerusalem bakery.

believes himself to be a special messenger from God conscious of the stamp of divine approval on all that he says and does.

This is proving too indigestible for some people who have remained loyal to him so far. It is reported that some of his former followers are now distancing themselves from him. There is no dissension among his inner circle of 12, however, despite his cryptic announcement that one of them 'is a devil'.

According to Simon Peter, 'Jesus has the words of eternal life. He's the holy messenger from God. Who else should we follow? If it's tough – it's tough!'

In private conversation, Jesus is warning the 12 to beware of the yeast, or teaching, of the Pharisees which causes the whole loaf of God's truth to go mouldy. His teaching, he claims, is more wholesome and will never go stale.

It is one of those loaded comments of Jesus of Nazareth which has more than one level of meaning. Leaven – a piece of dough left over from one batch of dough until it begins to ferment, and then mixed into the next batch to make it rise – is often seen by Jews as a symbol of evil and corruption. Bread for religious offerings has to be unleavened.

To have their teachings likened to heaven would leave a bitter taste in the Pharisees' mouths. However, Jesus is not beneath applying the picture to his own activity. In one parable he likens 'the kingdom of God' to a small piece of leaven affecting a much larger batch, the world itself.

(John 6:25–71; cf. Matthew 13:13; 16:5–12; Mark 8:14–21; Luke 12:1)

Stones seem to grow in the desert today where the Israelites were fed by manna from heaven during the 40 years they wandered in the desert.

Wave breaker!

Bethsaida, Galilee, c. AD 30

Twelve men in a boat got the fright of their lives last night when 5 km (3 miles) from the shore they ran into their boss – walking over the waves. But when one of them tried to follow in his footsteps, he got cold feet.

The disciples of Jesus were crossing the Sea of Galilee, having left their teacher to pray alone in the hills above Bethsaida, where he had miraculously fed a huge crowd.

Navigating by moonlight and the stars, they were making slow progress rowing against the strong wind and high waves.

Suddenly they saw a figure approaching them out of the gloom, walking as if the choppy water was

The Sea of Galilee.

merely boulder-strewn desert rock.

'We thought it was a ghost,' they said when they landed. 'We've seen demon-crazed lunatics and we've had death threats from fanatics, but we've never been so scared as when we saw a man on the sea. When you're in a small boat, you're trapped – there's absolutely nowhere to run.'

But their cries of fear received a response of reassurance as a familiar voice called out, 'It's me! Jesus! Don't be afraid.'

Their impulsive spokesman Simon Peter, with unusual presence of mind, asked for proof of the stranger's identity. If it really was Jesus, then he should command Peter to walk on the water too. 'Come on then,' said he.

Tension in the boat rose as for a few steps the water supported the big fisherman. But as he lost sight of Jesus in the swell and began to sink, the teacher grabbed him and hauled him into the boat. 'You started doubting the reality of God's power, didn't you?' Jesus said light-heartedly as the shivering surf rider towelled his legs. 'What happened to your faith, then?'

For once, the spokesman was lost for words. Although everyone else was quietly saying, 'My God!'

(Matthew 14:22–33; Mark 6:45–52; John 6: 16–24)

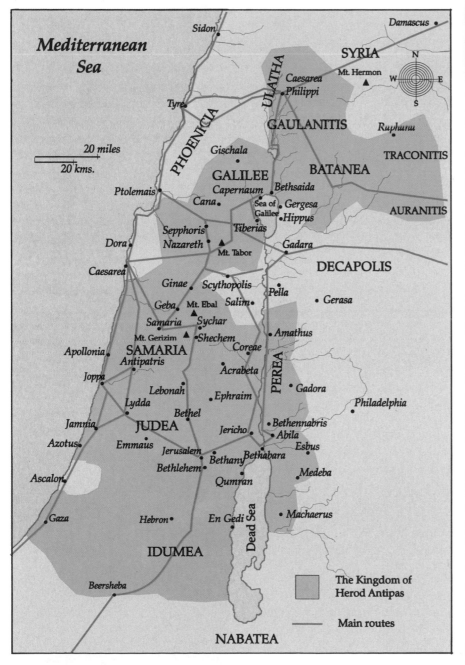

Under Herod Antipas, very much the puppet king under Roman rule, travel was safe. Though not always easy due to the mainly hilly terrain, people were able to move freely – as testified by Jesus' 'frequent travelling', mainly within the traditional boundaries of Israel, but also beyond.

Man of the people brings God down to earth with catchphrases

Western Galilee, c. AD 30

Wild flowers in a meadow in the spring, Galilee.

They come from miles around: men, women and children trekking up the hillside to where Jesus sits with his closest followers. It is only the middle of the day, but some carry bread to stave off the pre-supper hunger pangs, and others carry a cloak to guard against the evening chill; they know from experience that they could be here a long time.

But most come as they are, eager to eavesdrop on the earnest discourse of Jesus and the animated discussion of his 12 closest disciples, and they don't care what time it is. For this teacher offers no dry theological ideas, no bookish moralising; he's a man of the people who the fishermen and farmers, boat-builders and tanners of this bustling northern part of Judea can identify with.

The air is still and his strong voice carries into the crowd. Sometimes he points to the scenery around him, and brings God down to earth. The poppies and daisies gaily splashing colour over the lush grass

on these fertile hills: 'Look at the flowers of the field. They're not fashion-conscious, yet not even Solomon in his state robes looked so splendid! The God who clothes the fields will take care of you.'

The flocks of swallows and swifts circling and swooping overhead: 'Look at the birds of the air. They don't labour from morn till night but your heavenly Father feeds them. He'll look after you, too.'

And in the distance the Sea of Galilee sparkling in the sun, a blue diamond-studded cloth patterned with the random white and brown triangles of fishing-boat sails, covering a rich fishing ground: 'If your children ask you for fish, will you give them a snake instead? So why do you think your heavenly Father won't give you good things too?'

The eavesdroppers savour the familiar allusions, and mutter about them in small groups. Their conversation creates a continuous hum like the steady note from a distant

flute, over which the easy-to-distinguish voice of the teacher floats like that of a singer. The crowd quietens when it senses a fresh tone of speech, then lapses back into holiday mood as Jesus expounds his theme to the 12. Many have heard it all before; he teaches by repetition. But they like what they hear, and come back for more.

The traditional site of the Sermon on the Mount, high above the Lake of Galilee.

A revolutionary message

The core of Jesus' message is almost revolutionary. He challenges the accepted mores of everyday life. 'Don't hit back. Do twice as much as you're asked. Be kind to your enemies.' He turns familiar laws inside out, like he's prying the flesh out of a shellfish. Angry? Then there is really no difference between you and a murderer, even if the deed exists only in your head. Second look at your neighbour's wife? Then you're sleeping with her in your imagination and there's no real difference between that and adultery in the flesh.

And he's the master of aphorisms. His memorable turns of phrase cling to the mind like burrs to the shirt. Once heard, never forgotten, and even if the meaning isn't clear, the phrase remains to remind you that it must mean something. 'You're the light of the world. So let your light shine. If your hand causes you to sin, cut it off! You can't be a slave to God and to money.'

Wheat ripe for the harvest.

If he weren't so affable and sincere, he would sound arrogant and opinionated. As it is, he speaks with an authority that is at once breathtaking yet plausible. 'You've heard it said in the past ... but I say to you' is a catchphrase often on his lips.

At times he seems to be writing off the traditions which have held the Jewish community together for the two millennia since Abraham. But if he is challenged on the point he replies with the same self-assurance, 'I didn't come to destroy the law; I came to fulfil it.'

Rather like a farmer at harvest time, Jesus seems to be tossing a forkful of religious belief into the air; the human traditions blow away in the breeze like chaff while the divine seed inside drops to the floor. That is something which the official teachers, the Pharisees and their scribes, find hard to follow. Their Torah, the written law, has 365 negative prohibitions and 248 positive commands designed to cover every imaginable contingency of life. To them, seed and chaff are one.

The crowds on the hillside listen to him with delight. The lawyers frown and shake their heads. You don't have to be a prophet to see storms gathering on the horizon, as the public continues to flock to his lectures.

Sermon notes

What Jesus the teacher says

- Only the poor in spirit, who know their unworthiness before God, will inherit God's kingdom.
- If you're really hungry for God's truth and goodness, you'll get really fulfilled.
- No one sticks a light under a cover; so let the light of God shine through you so others can see it.
- You'll have to do better than the Pharisees if you want to get to heaven.
- Tell a man he's a fool and you'll end up in hell.
- Don't boost your image by high-sounding oaths; just say 'yes' or 'no' and keep your word.
- What's the use of only loving those who love you? Love your enemies, too – because God does.
- Don't go public over what you do for charity; do it for God, not for your reputation.
- If someone hits you once, let them hit you again; don't strike back.
- Don't store up goods for the thieves and rust; store up godly living for long-lasting effect.
- Seek God's kingdom before everything else and you'll always be content with what you have.
- Don't be judgemental; that's like flicking a speck out of someone's eye while you've got a floorboard stuck in yours!
- Ask your heavenly Father for what you really need; you'll always get an answer.
- Behave towards others in the way you want them to behave towards you.
- The way to God is like a narrow track; most people are on a wide road going straight to their doom.
- You can tell real prophets from false ones only by seeing if they practise what they preach and by the effect they have on others; if they sound sweet, look for the grapes and let go if you find thorns!
- You'll only get to heaven if you do what my Father says.
- Once upon a time, a man built his house on a sandbank. It crumbled in the storm. Another man built on a rock, and his house stood firm. Build your life on my words, and you'll stand firm too.

(Sermon on the Mount, Matthew 5–7;
Sermon on the Plain, Luke 6:17–49)

313

No arrest while the 'Son' shines

Jerusalem, c. AD 31

The temple guards have failed to arrest Jesus of Nazareth despite being supplied with an official warrant. They returned empty-handed saying they had never heard anyone teach with such authority and sincerity.

Rumours are spreading through the city packed with pilgrims for the week-long Festival of Tabernacles that there is a high-level conspiracy to kill the popular teacher who now is claiming to be God's Son.

To the man on the street Jesus is anything from deceiver to good man, from prophet to Christ. The authorities' failure to act or speak decisively has fuelled speculation that, despite their public opposition, they also suspect he may be genuine. One member of the Sanhedrin, Nicodemus, has spoken up for him and insisted that if Jesus is to be accused of anything he must be given a fair hearing and trial.

Part of the controversy surrounds Jesus' birthplace, which to the genealogically-sensitive Jews is crucial to the identity of the Messiah. Some allege that the Saviour will appear out of the blue; some point to a biblical prophecy saying that he will be born in Bethlehem (Matthew 2:4–6).

Jesus is believed to come from Nazareth in northern Galilee, supposedly a wasteland as far as prophets are concerned, despite the fact that it was home to Jonah. There are also persistent rumours that he was conceived out of wedlock, which jeopardizes any chance of his being accepted by theological purists. However, Jesus' associates allege that he was born in Bethlehem while his parents were visiting there.

The teacher has fuelled the mystery because although he has responded to his critics he has done so ambiguously. 'You think you know my human origins but I'm not here on my own authority,' he told an impromptu audience in the temple. 'I was sent here by the One who is true.' He followed this with a threat – or a promise – to go where no one can follow. He could mean the Gentiles, with whom he has flirted on several occasions, but whom Jews normally avoid like the plague.

Jesus has made two startling statements during this festival week – which doubles as a harvest celebration and a memorial of Israel's 40-year wandering in the Sinai desert – during which people camp out in temporary shelters made of branches and thatch.

Herod's Temple
20 BC to AD 70

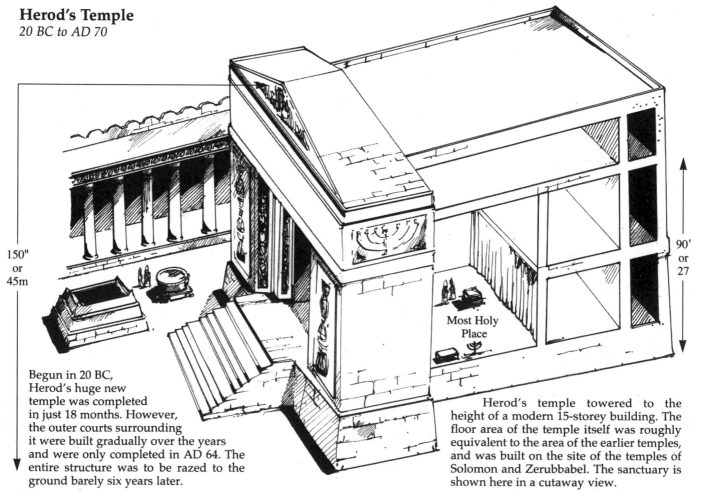

150" or 45m

90' or 27

Most Holy Place

Begun in 20 BC, Herod's huge new temple was completed in just 18 months. However, the outer courts surrounding it were built gradually over the years and were only completed in AD 64. The entire structure was to be razed to the ground barely six years later.

Herod's temple towered to the height of a modern 15-storey building. The floor area of the temple itself was roughly equivalent to the area of the earlier temples, and was built on the site of the temples of Solomon and Zerubbabel. The sanctuary is shown here in a cutaway view.

First-century oil lamp.

Perhaps referring to the festival's daily ceremonial libation of water drawn from the Pool of Siloam and the streams of water produced from the desert rock by Moses, he said, 'If anyone comes to me who is spiritually thirsty, I'll make streams of living water flow from inside them.' According to John Zebedee, one of his associates, he means God's life will bubble up in people and spill out in love towards others.

His second statement picked up on the great candelabra-lighting ceremony in the temple. 'I am the light of the world,' he declared. 'Whoever does what I say will never be in the dark about God but will walk in the light of God.'

Far from seeing the light, however, many of his opponents saw red. 'I am' is a technical term for God which no Jew normally utters even in casual conversation. He also calls God his father and his critics children of the devil, he promises to give people freedom from sin, and despite being only thirty-something claims to have seen Abraham, the founder of the Jewish race.

That was the last straw for some. Claiming Jesus had said, 'Before Abraham was, I am', making himself identical to God, they tried to stone him for blasphemy. The dense crowd made such action impossible and he escaped through it. Rarely has one teacher stirred such intense passion.

(John 7:1–52; 8:12–59)

He's testing their patience

Jerusalem, c. AD 31

Law-abiding Pharisees are worse off in God's account book than despised Judeans who collect taxes on behalf of the Romans. In fact, they are in danger of being taken out of his reckoning altogether.

That is the thrust of some of the stories which Jesus of Nazareth has been telling recently. They back up his overt claim that the religious elite have missed the point of religion completely.

One story tells of a Pharisee and a tax collector who each stood to pray in the temple. Following a familiar liturgical pattern, the Pharisee

Jews at the Wailing Wall today, some stones of which are all that remains of Herod's temple.

thanked God that he had more than obeyed the fasting and tithing requirements of the law, had not committed sin, and had not been disloyal to Judea.

The 'traitorous' tax collector asked God only for forgiveness of his sins, pleading for God's mercy and not seeking to justify himself. 'It was this man who went home right with God,' declares Jesus. 'You can't boast about anything before the Holy One.'

In another story Jesus is suggesting that those who consider themselves to be the rightful heirs of God could be rejected by him. Speaking of people who turned down an invitation to a wedding feast by making feeble excuses, he said that the party of God's kingdom would be thrown open to the weakest and most needy. No one on the original guest list would get in, he added, implying that their rejection of his message was a feeble excuse.

He put a further dent in their egos in a yarn about a vineyard let out to tenants who killed the rent collectors and finally the owner's son in their bid to take control of the land. They would not get away with it, he said. Again referring to himself, he quoted Psalm 118:22 which describes a stone that is initially rejected by the builders as unsuitable but ultimately ends up as the key stone binding the walls together in a true right angle.

The Pharisees are well aware that these stories, which delight the crowds, are directed at them. They, unlike the crowds, are not amused.

(Matthew 21:33–46; Mark 12:1–12;
Luke 14:15–24; 18:9–14)

Ever on a sabbath?

Pop preacher gives rules a welcome break

Jerusalem, c. AD 30–31
Current Jewish law on Sabbath observance is an ass, according to Jesus of Nazareth.

It says you can rescue a donkey which has fallen into a ditch but you cannot heal a man who keeps falling over. You can untie an ass to take it to water but you cannot loosen the spine of a woman who has been knotted up for years.

The popular preacher with a healing touch has been confronted on several occasions by people offended by his refusal to stop his 'work' on the day of rest. He admits that he is breaking the original law of Moses as well as stricter interpretations placed on it by latter-day scribes.

But he claims a higher authority for doing so. 'The Son of Man is Lord of the Sabbath' is one of his more audacious comments when

'It seems to be a clash of interpretations,' some observers are saying. 'On the one hand there's a strict instruction not to work on the Sabbath. But on the other hand there's also encouragement in the law of Moses to help the needy and to do good whenever the opportunity arises. Religion wasn't meant to foster hard hearts and insensitive behaviour; Jesus seems to be majoring on compassion.'

The controversy has sparked some of his memorable statements. 'The Sabbath was made for man, not man for the Sabbath' is one of them. And as the controversy flared over his Sabbath healing of a man born blind, he said, 'I came into the world so that the spiritually blind could see, making the so-called religiously-sighted blind to God's work. While I'm here, I'm the light of the world.'

expanded by the official commentary, the Talmud. The scribes themselves regularly debate the precise application of the laws. Ordinary people regard them as guidelines which can be dispensed with when necessary.

The law of Moses explicitly forbids work on the Sabbath (Exodus 20:8). It rules out ploughing and reaping (34:21), travel (35:2, applied specifically to food-gathering) and lighting fires (35:3). The penalty for Sabbath-breaking was fixed as death (35:2).

Trading on the Sabbath was one of the evils singled out by the prophets as a cause of the downfall of northern Israel in 721 BC (Amos 8:5–6) and of southern Judah in 587 BC (Jeremiah 17:19–27). This fuels the controversy over whether or not Jesus is a true prophet.

Originally the Sabbath was provided to give everyone a break, including hired servants and animals, and to focus attention on God the creator and provider. Taking one day off in seven was also seen as a sign of the Israelites' continued adherence to the covenant between them and God (Exodus 31:12–17). National insistence on it has been so strong that Jews are now exempt service in the Roman army because they refuse to fight or carry arms on the Sabbath.

Jews holding up the Torah at the Wailing Wall, in Jerusalem.

challenged on the subject. He points out that his 'father' God is constantly working to sustain the universe whatever day of the week it is, and therefore he can do similar work too.

This only stirs up more anger because he appears to be making himself equal to the Almighty. He also refers back to the prophets who showed that God 'desires mercy and not sacrifice'. He appeals to the spirit of compassion as his rule of life.

He is not the first person to challenge the string of Sabbath regulations which tie up the fourth commandment like a captured bear. Under them, no one can cook anything, walk little more than 900 m (half a mile) or lift anything heavier than a dried fig. For obscure reasons connected with their reproductive habits, you may kill a louse but not a flea on the Sabbath.

The scribes' book of laws (the Mishnah) has a 24-chapter section on the Sabbath which is further

The supporters of Jesus point out that he does not break the law wholesale. He attends synagogue worship regularly. On one such occasion he left his critics speechless with a deft piece of logic.

'Does the law of Moses allow you to heal on the Sabbath or not?' he asked them. Their silence was eloquent; the law never mentions healing. The preacher notched up another moral victory; a man with frequent blackouts got the Sabbath first-aid normally restricted to fallen donkeys; and the Pharisees got a flea in their ear.

Sabbath breaks for needy people

Among the actions said to have been performed by Jesus on Sabbath days

Food for thought

When he was accused of 'working' one Sabbath by gleaning his breakfast cereal from a field he was passing through, Jesus cited the famished King David who illegally ate the consecrated bread reserved for the priests. Compassion and human need take precedence over religious laws, he seemed to be saying (Matthew 12:1–8; Mark 2:23–28; Luke 6:1–5).

The Pool of Bethesda in the Old City of Jerusalem.

Right hand man

The man with a withered hand was probably planted in the front row as a test case to see if the guest speaker in the synagogue would heal him. Jesus, with his uncanny second sight, clearly knew as much. He asked: 'Which is in accordance with Moses' law; to do good or bad on the Sabbath?' He answered his own question by healing him in the silence which followed (Matthew 12:9-14; Mark 3:1–6; Luke 6:6–11).

Straightened out

At another synagogue service was a woman with curvature of the spine who had been unable to stand upright for 18 years. The synagogue moderator chastised the congrega-tion for coming to church to get healed. They could come any other day of the week, he suggested. Jesus straightened out his views by responding that if animals can be set free so can people. Then he healed the woman (Luke 13:10–17).

Drop out to dinner

A man with probable kidney failure whose accumulation of fluid caused him to pass out regularly literally dropped in – or out – at a Pharisee's Sabbath supper party. Once again Jesus asked what the law said, received no response and healed him. Then he started telling after-dinner stories about inviting the needy to meals with pure motives (Luke 14:1–6).

Pool cue

The sick and disabled people who gather at the Pool of Bethesda in Jerusalem believe an angel agitates the water occasionally. The first person in will be healed. But many are too ill to get in unaided, like one disabled man who had been there for 38 years. He seemed resigned to his fate and could not even say he wished to be healed. Jesus took the cue and issued a stern warning about his attitudes after healing him. Berated by the Pharisees for carrying his bed on a Sabbath, the bewildered man let them take a pot shot at Jesus for telling him to do it (John 5:1–15).

Neighbourhood watch

A man born blind had watchful neighbours. When they saw him walking unaided they took him to explain his cure to the Pharisees. They even doubted he was the same man, so they called his parents in for an identity check. Told that Jesus was a law breaker, the man said he had no views about his healer's character and knew only that 'yesterday I was blind and today I'm not!' He added that as God only listens to people who love him, Jesus must come from God. The teachers did not like being taught, and threw him out. Later, when Jesus told him to believe 'in the Son of Man', he fell down and worshipped him. The Lord of the Sabbath had another grateful follower (John 9:1–41).

The healing of the blind man, as seen in *Jesus of Nazareth* by Franco Zefferelli.

Stay faithful or stay single!

Perea, c. AD 31

In an unprecedented attack on contemporary divorce laws, Jesus of Nazareth has sided with conservative Jewish factions and called on the nation to adopt a stricter approach to marriage.

He has also encouraged people to consider singleness as a valid option and not as a sign of failure or weakness.

The controversial but pastorally sensitive teacher is not normally known for his support of traditional views. It is generally accepted that one of his chief concerns seems to be for the raw deal which women get from both Jewish and Roman current practice.

He was responding to one of the now regular confrontations with Jewish lawyers who have turned Jesus-baiting into a fine art. They had crossed the Jordan to this eastern region to quiz him, but as so often, fell into their own trap.

Asked if it was lawful for a man to divorce his wife for any reason at all, Jesus referred back to the ancient scriptural view that marriage creates a unique bond between two people which should not be broken. Subsequent Jewish law, allegedly given to Moses by God, had allowed divorce as a concession to human weakness and sinfulness, he suggested.

Divorce, he said, is allowable but far from ideal and should only be practised for serious reasons such as adultery. In such situations the original marriage bond had already been broken. The view is close to that held by the rigorist Jewish teacher Shammai, whereas popular attitudes reflect the more liberal views of Rabbi Hillel.

But he gave a new twist to the debate by saying that anyone divorcing his wife for trivial reasons was himself committing adultery if he married again. His views thus ruled out the easy-come, easy-go serial polygamy which some

stratas of Jewish society condone.

Even Jesus' disciples found this position hard to accept and suggested that it made marriage impossible. Jesus denied this, but added that singleness was itself an honourable estate and should not be despised. However, only those born with a low libido, or those who have voluntarily renounced marriage as part of their sacrificial service of God should consider it, he added.

His answer still leaves his followers with unanswered questions and difficult decisions to make in the complex field of human relationships. Having asserted the ideal, he has left them to work out how and when to apply the concessions. He is not the sort of teacher who replaces one kind of 'Pharisaism' with another.

(Matthew 5:31–32; 19:1–12; Mark 10:1–12; Luke 16:18)

Till death us do part?

Jerusalem, c. AD 30

Jewish teachers differ widely on their interpretation of the biblical laws concerning marriage and divorce, but all hinge on the meaning of a loose phrase in Deuteronomy 24:1–4 which sanctions divorce on the grounds of the woman becoming 'displeasing' to the man. There are two schools of thought.

The followers of Hillel (c. 60 BC–AD 20) advocate a liberal approach which allows a man to divorce his wife without appeal or compensation for a wide range of causes. This gives the man an almost free hand to change wives at will. Some rabbis have condoned

A modern Jewish wedding, from the film *Fiddler on the Roof*.

divorce in cases where the man has simply found someone more attractive than his wife.

A despised wife has only to spoil a meal to earn the formal certificate of divorce, which does not require legal or community ratification. Divorce is regarded as essential if she commits adultery or is discovered to have been unfaithful before her marriage. Women do not have reciprocal rights to divorce unreasonable or unfaithful husbands.

The followers of Shammai take a tougher line. They interpret the biblical texts as referring only to sexual unfaithfulness, and normally require witnesses to attest to it before a divorce is granted. They refer back to the wider biblical teaching in which God declares that he hates divorce (Malachi 2:16). They also appeal to the traditional Jewish virtue of marital fidelity which, while broken in every generation, has never been abandoned wholesale.

Marriage is seen by Jews as a duty to God and to the community, and is primarily for the procreation of children. Very few people remain single voluntarily, and the Hebrew language has no noun to describe a single man. Marriages are generally arranged and money is paid by the groom or his family to compensate for the bride's family's loss.

Engagement or betrothal is regarded as binding as marriage itself and 'divorce' before marriage is possible on the grounds of adultery. Wedding ceremonies are largely civil rather than religious occasions, when the groom collects the bride from her house and takes her to his. The partying can continue for up to a week.

Adultery by a woman is punishable by death, although this is not always applied and does require witnesses. Men are not usually penalised for their affairs. Prostitution has been denounced in every generation. It was sometimes used by the ancient prophets as a picture of Israel's unfaithfulness to God. But that has not stopped the world's oldest profession being peddled in the back streets of Jerusalem.

Tempers flare

Samaria, c. AD 31

Tempers flared when a Samaritan village banned Jesus of Nazareth and his entourage from staying there. The teacher may be no ordinary person to his own countrymen but to the Samaritans he is just another tiresome Jew begging bed and board on the way to Jerusalem for a festival. They have a reputation for ignoring or even abusing

Amorous Romans prefer mistresses to their wives

'Music is the food of love,' said Shakespeare, but it appears to have been true much earlier. *The Music Lesson*, a Roman wall-painting from Herculaneum, first century AD.

Rome, first century AD

Roman wives get a raw deal from their philandering husbands but public opinion in the capital is against changes in the law.

According to the man in the street, wives are for child-bearing, mistresses are for co-habitation, and casual relationships are for sheer pleasure. One popular joke suggests that the two happiest days of a man's life are when he first has sex with his wife and when he buries her.

The empire which was built on a strong family foundation has now left it in search for more and more intense sexual pleasure. Couples rarely share a bedroom but within the larger households every slave is a potential partner for the free men. Consequently, many children are born out of wedlock and there is confusion over precise blood relationships. A man's mistress could be his servant's daughter and he could be the father of both.

Current practice began 200 years ago as lax Greek attitudes began to filter into Roman life. The Greeks also encouraged a close link between sex and religion, employing temple prostitutes, a practice still popular in cities such as Corinth.

Double standards prevailed then as now. Greek wives, like their Roman counterparts, were expected to remain secluded in the house and were forbidden to have extramarital relationships. Women are not accepted in the community until they have borne at least three children.

The high divorce rate, which in the circumstances hardly seems necessary, is probably encouraged by the fact that Romans marry at an early age most often before they reach puberty. Girls can legally be married when they are 12, and boys when they are 14. Lengthy engagements are sometimes spent cohabiting.

people bound for the rival temple.

'We wanted Jesus to call down fire from heaven, just to show them who's really on God's side,' said the Zebedee firebrands James and John. 'But he wouldn't let us.'

According to the other disciples what he actually did was to douse thoroughly the brothers' hot tempers. If he is Elijah reincarnated, as some suggest, his personality has changed over the centuries.

(Luke 9:51–55)

Who does this man think he is?

Caesarea Philippi, c. AD 31

Mystery surrounds the assumed or real identity of Jesus of Nazareth following unconfirmed reports that he accepted the attribution of the divine 'Christ' or Messiah from one of his closest followers. His inner circle of 12 disciples has been sworn to complete and utter secrecy following a private retreat to Caesarea Philippi.

However, sources close to the group suggest that Jesus had quizzed his friends about his reputation. Speculation ranges from being in the line of Jewish prophets to being a reincarnation of people such as Elijah, Jeremiah or John the Baptist.

Asking them for their own opinion, Jesus is said to have received a characteristically forthright response from Simon Peter, who often acts as the group's spokesman.

'You are the Christ, the Son of the living God,' he is alleged to have said. Peter was not rebuked by the others and his opinion was confirmed by Jesus who claimed that he had given it as a result of a direct revelation from God.

Jesus also confirmed Simon

A fourth-century stone cross, in Ephesus.

Peter's hitherto unofficial role of group spokesman. Having previously nicknamed him 'Petros' (stone), an almost unheard-of first name in Judea, Jesus appointed him to be the human 'rock' or foundation on which the messianic community would be built. He also asserted that this 'church' would never die out.

The bustling activist is well suited to the role of fixer and organiser. He is not the most rock-like and stable member of the 12, however. The volatile former fisherman tends to speak his mind before thinking, and does not always perform well in delicate or pressurised situations.

Some cynical commentators here are suggesting that Jesus has imbibed more of the spirit of Pan, the god to whom this pleasant city at the foot of Mount Hermon is dedicated, than the spirit of the true God he claims to serve. Pan the flautist played a very individual tune, was a backwoodsman who loved mountains, was ascribed as a universal god, and had the habit of giving people nightmares.

Jesus the 'Christ', who comes from an obscure background and frequently retreats to the mountains to pray, certainly gave his followers a nightmare to think about after Peter's 'confession'. He predicted that he would be rejected by the religious leaders of Jerusalem, be killed and then resurrected.

This is not the normal understanding of 'messiahship' among Jews, and throws more heat than light onto the current controversy surrounding the Nazarene. The 12 are said to be equally mystified by his latest prediction.

(Matthew 16:13–23; Mark 8:27–33;
Luke 9:18–22)

The spring at Banyas (former Caesarea Philippi) was dedicated to Pan and was the focus of his cult.

Shekinah! He's whiter than light

Caesarea Philippi, c. AD 31

Three of Jesus of Nazareth's closest associates returned here visibly shaken by what they describe as an out-of-this-world experience in the nearby mountains.

Simon Peter, and James and John Zebedee, along with Jesus, had climbed one of the high peaks, possibly Hermon, the highest (2700 m/ 9,000 ft), to pray through the night. As they began to doze off they saw Jesus suddenly transformed into an angel-like being.

His face and clothes shone with an intense unearthly light, bright as the sun and dazzling white. As they shaded their eyes against the glare, they saw two other figures, who were identified to them as Moses and Elijah, who talked with Jesus about an 'exodus' he was shortly to experience in Jerusalem.

Bewildered yet also enthralled by this glimpse through a gap in the curtain covering the heavenly realms, Peter offered to build temporary shelters of the kind used by Jews during the festival of Tabernacles to accommodate Jesus and his guests.

But his enthusiasm was cut short as the figures were shrouded in a radiant cloud. From its 'shekinah glory', like that of the cloud of God's presence which accompanied the Israelites through the exodus from Egypt led by Moses, came a commanding voice identifying Jesus as God's chosen Son and telling them to listen to him.

Awestruck, they hid their eyes. When they dared look again, they saw no one except Jesus, and the glow had gone. When they descended the mountain they confronted another parallel to Moses' experience on the Mount Sinai. Moses had to deal with a golden calf; Jesus with a failed exorcism

Snow covers Mount Hermon for a few months each winter.

attempt by his remaining nine associates who were surrounded by an impatient crowd.

The father of a demonised child pleaded with Jesus to help and explained that the boy had often been thrown into fires or pools by the convulsions. 'Everything's possible to those who believe,' Jesus told him.

'I believe! Just help me to believe more!' cried the desperate man. As the boy convulsed again, Jesus healed him. If everything is possible, Peter, James and John may not have been dreaming on the mountain when the darkness of the night fled like a guilty thief before the glory of the Almighty.

(Matthew 17:1–21; Mark 9:2–29; Luke 9:28–43)

Fast Facts AD 31

Some of Jesus' many reported miracles:

Galilee region: A man covered with a skin disease begged Jesus to make him 'clean' because his ailment barred him from social and religious activity (Matthew 8:2–4; Mark 1:40–42; Luke 5:12–14)

Capernaum: A Roman centurion who asked Jesus to heal his servant recognised that he had authority over illnesses as if they were lower ranks, so asked Jesus to give the order rather than make the trek to his house. Jesus said he had never come across such faith. (Matthew 8:5–13; Luke 7:1–10)

Nain: A widow's only son had died, leaving her destitute. Jesus was deeply moved by the many mourners who attended the funeral. He went to the coffin and told the corpse to get up. He did, and began talking at once. (Luke 7:11–17)

Tyre: A Greek woman asked Jesus to release her daughter from an evil spirit. Testing her faith by referring to the normal Jewish attitude to Gentiles, he first said that it was wrong to take the children's bread and give it to the 'dogs' (non-Jews). 'But the dogs eat crumbs that fall from the table,' she said at once. He liked that and healed the child. (Matthew 15:21–28; Mark 7:24–30)

The Decapolis: A deaf man who could barely talk was brought to Jesus, who took him aside privately. He placed his fingers in the man's ears, prayed intensely, commanded the ears to open, and the man began to talk. (Mark 7:31–35)

Galilee region: A crowd of about 4,000 men, plus families, had been with Jesus for several days with little food. He took the seven remaining loaves and a few fish and once again fed them all from it, with plenty left over. (Matthew 15:32–38; Mark 8:1–10)

Bethsaida: Jesus took a blind man away from the crowd and spat on his eyes. This restored his sight only partially; people looked like trees. Jesus prayed a second time and healed him. (Mark 8:22-26).

Brought back from the grave!

Bethany, c. AD 31

It was the stuff of which nightmares are made. In an eerie silence broken only by the sound of birdsong, a dead man tightly bound in grave-clothes walked unsteadily out of a tomb. Bystanders held their breath and looked on with a mixture of horror and disbelief, too petrified even to scream.

But it was no nightmare. It took place in the cold light of day. And there is a village of confused and bewildered people pinching themselves – and the once-dead man – to prove it, their traditional week of mourning cut short when the impossible became real and the unthinkable forced itself upon them.

If ever anyone needed a further reason to mark out Jesus of Nazareth as a man unlike all others, it was this. In the latest and most bizarre of all his miraculous signs, he called his friend Lazarus back from the grave. But in doing it he may have signed his own death warrant. For the religious leadership in nearby Jerusalem, Jesus' helping hand across death's chasm was a bridge too far.

Lazarus, a wealthy man who lives with his unmarried sisters, Mary and Martha, in this dormitory village half an hour's walk from the city gates, had befriended Jesus in the early days of the teacher's ministry. The spacious home was thrown open to him and his aides as a private retreat, and the residents became almost a second family to Jesus.

Certainly they were on terms close enough to be argumentative without falling out. Once, when Lazarus had thrown a dinner party for friends and neighbours to meet Jesus, Martha had complained bitterly that her sister had been too preoccupied with Jesus' teaching to take her fair share of the cooking and preparation.

'You're anxious about too many things,' Jesus had chided her. 'Mary has chosen the best thing of all, which is something that'll remain with her for ever – unlike your food!'

Yet ironically, when Lazarus was taken seriously ill it was the activist Martha who sent for Jesus, while the inconsolable Mary fell to pieces. The teacher was far away, and as his associates later revealed, he waited inexplicably for two further days before setting out to see his

The village of Bethany today.

friends. By the time he arrived, Lazarus had already been buried for four days.

He had missed the opportunity of healing him. He had even missed the funeral. And Martha did not miss the opportunity of reminding him of the fact. Jesus poured out his own grief and frustration mixed, it seemed, with anger at the obscenity of death itself, in heaving sobs at the graveside.

After recovering his composure, he then took the bystanders completely by surprise. He ordered the rock across the tomb entrance to be removed, ignoring the fetid air which escaped from it. Then he commanded: 'Lazarus! Come out!' When the mummified figure

emerged, he was unbound and welcomed back into the land of the living by his awestruck family.

As news of the restoration spread, the supreme council of the Jews, the Sanhedrin, met in emergency session to consider the implications. Some fear that the delicate peace in this strategic bridgehead between east and west will be shattered by an uprising prompted by Jesus, and that the religious privileges granted by the Romans will be withdrawn.

Uttering a veiled threat, high priest Caiaphas told the assembly that it would be expedient for one man to die to save the nation being crushed again. 'Expedient' is the operative word; it will take some legal juggling to make capital charges stick on this man of exemplary virtue, despite his close contacts with prostitutes and criminals. But he is taking no chances. He has reportedly left Bethany and is holed up in a safe house about a day's journey north of Jerusalem.

(John 11:1–54; cf. Luke 10:38–42)

'What Jesus said to me'

Martha, the grieving sister of Lazarus, gave Jesus a piece of her mind when he eventually turned up after the funeral. 'If you had been here, you could have healed him,' she said. 'So why weren't you?' The answer gave her more than she bargained for. 'Jesus told me about life after death, and I said I believed my brother would rise at the last day. Then he said, "I am the resurrection and the life. Whoever trusts in me will die on earth but will live in heaven for ever. So in that sense, whoever lives by trusting me will never really die."

'All I could say to that was that I believed Jesus was – is – the chosen Messiah, the Son of God sent into the world. He accepted that. Then I went and got Mary.'

(John 11:17–28)

Babies culled by parental choice

Rome, first century AD

Children born to Roman parents are being dumped on the streets, sold into slavery, starved to death or even suffocated if they do not meet with the father's approval.

The common practice of choosing whether or not to recognise a legitimate child after it has been born is adding to the already high infant mortality rate. Only one third of all babies born survive their first year, and only half of these reach puberty.

Weak, deformed and apparently retarded infants are the prime targets of parental fiat. Girls are less likely to be accepted than boys, and illegitimate children have no chance of survival unless the mother's family takes them in. Normal babies are also abandoned if the father has too many to feed or if the new arrival will force him to divide his estate too thinly.

Some unwanted children are aborted before birth, but the practice is dangerous, even fatal, for the

A swaddled infant.

mother and therefore avoided by all but the most desperate. It also offends some Romans. The poet Ovid once wrote that even lions and tigers do not destroy their own young yet some women do so merely to avoid the unsightly stretch marks which pregnancy would give them.

Once born, even desired children are subjected to harsh treatment. Boys are considered soft and are toughened up by being wrapped tightly in swaddling clothes for several months. Their legs are placed in splints to straighten them. Later the right hand is freed from the cocoon so that the child learns to use it.

Wet nurses, employed by well-to-do families until the child is about three, are changed periodically to avoid the risk of any emotional bonding. They sometimes knead a child's head to make it round in the ideal Roman fashion, and attempt to mould the jaw, nose and buttocks into pleasing shapes, considered socially desirable. They are chosen for their character, which the child is believed to imitate.

Unfortunately good weaning does not seem to eliminate bad breeding or violent sibling rivalry, both of which are apparent in the intrigues of the highest families in the land.

Schooldays are not happy days

The journey to school in modern Rome is fraught with danger, the routine is rigorous, and character building is low on the curriculum. Children are being seduced in the streets or by their tutors.

Following the Greek pattern, many Roman schools focus on one subject, forcing students to travel to different sites for lessons. Literacy and numeracy, followed by law, rhetoric and philosophy are the main subjects, combined with athletics which includes running, throwing, swimming and boxing.

By contrast, Jewish boys are educated almost entirely in religious matters and not all learn basic reading and writing skills. The Jews are suspicious of athletics, partly because of the Greek tradition of competing naked and in honour of the gods. Schools became widespread only in the last century and

are held in the synagogues. As in Rome there is little discussion and much learning by rote.

Jews prize education for life more

than the learning of many facts. Their scriptures extol the virtue of wisdom, which is right action in complex circumstances based on biblical principles.

Women gymnasts, as depicted on a Roman mosaic.

Mission reaches cloud nine

Judea, c. AD 31

Seventy evangelists sent out on a faith mission with no visible means of support have returned to base amazed at seeing sick people healed and demons exorcised as the results of their work.

The mission was launched some weeks ago by Jesus of Nazareth. The 70 (or 72; reports from the area vary) were handpicked from the hundreds of devoted followers who have boosted his rise to fame and were sent into the villages and towns of Judea which he intends to visit personally.

They were on cloud nine as they gathered for a joyful debriefing with their leader. But while sharing their delight he warned them to keep their sights on the reason for the mission and not on its results.

'Don't get excited because the demons do what you say in my name,' he said, 'but get excited by the fact that your names are permanently recorded in God's heavenly account books. That's what counts most.' As he brought them down to earth, he said that as a result of their

Cape Blanco, on the Mediterranean coast, south of Tyre.

ministry he had seen Satan fall like a shooting star from his evil orbit.

The evangelists had taken off with only the most basic of survival kits. They were even forbidden to carry the excess baggage of spare shoes and clothes, and were also denied the luxury of a pilgrim's bag for holding offerings of food or money.

'You're going to be like a flock of lambs among a pack of wolves,' Jesus had warned them at the start

of what to many must have seemed a daunting enterprise. Having given them the spiritual power to soar over the forces of evil without being knocked off course by them, he told them not to indulge in social niceties, not to beg from house to house, and not to linger where they were not welcomed.

They were to speed past the spiritual black holes which repelled his message, but he himself gave such places a rocket. He especially singled out for criticism the Galilean towns of Korazin and Bethsaida, which had been so unresponsive that the disciples had almost forgotten that they had ever been there, and his home town of Capernaum. Had the Gentile cities of Tyre and Sidon on the coast heard his message, they would have embraced it, he declared.

Observers differ over the significance of Jesus' choice of 70 associate preachers in addition to the 12 who remain his inner circle. Some suggest that they parallel the 70 nations of the world mentioned in Genesis 10, or the elders appointed by Moses in Numbers 11:16,17 (both rendered 72 in the Greek translation). Others suggest they parallel the members of the Sanhedrin, the Jewish supreme court. But any obscure significance is currently eclipsed by their success.

(Luke 10:1–24)

Good news: quotes from the teacher

Good food: 'People cannot live on physical bread alone.' (Luke 4:4)

Good people: 'It's the sick who need medicine, not the healthy. I've come to call sinful people back to God, not to win the applause of the upright.' (Luke 5:31,32)

Good wine: 'My teaching is like new wine. It needs new wineskins to contain it – renewed people to practise it. If you put new wine into already-stretched old skins, the wine will go on fermenting and burst them.' (Luke 5:37–38)

Good fruit: 'Each tree has its own fruit. You don't get figs off thorn bushes. People with pure hearts produce pure words and deeds; people with evil hearts do bad things.' (Luke 6:43–45)

Good shepherd: 'I am a good shepherd who will lay down his life for the sake of the sheep, unlike the casual labourer who leaves the flock and runs away as soon as he sees a wolf. I know my sheep and they know me.' (John 10:14–15)

Good deeds: 'The two greatest commandments in God's law are these. First, love God with all your heart, mind, soul and strength – that is, completely. Then secondly, on this basis go out and show as much practical love to your neighbour as you would to yourself.' (Mark 12:29–31)

Good faith: 'If your faith was even as small as a mustard seed you could tell a tree to jump in the lake and it would!' (Luke 17:6)

Caught in the act!

Jerusalem, c. AD 31

Smirking lawyers had the smiles wiped from their faces when they brought their prize exhibit to Jesus for judgement.

A woman who had been caught in bed with a man who was not her husband had been dragged off to the teacher. They explained that the Jewish law insisted that she be stoned to death, but the Romans do not allow Jews to carry out the death penalty for such offences.

'What do you say we should do?' they asked, and then waited to see how the man reputed to love and forgive sinners would wriggle out of this legal teaser. Sources close to the lawyers say they hoped to gather evidence of heresy or sedition which could be used against him.

For a while he was silent, then Jesus began doodling in the sand with his finger. What he wrote is unknown, although some suggest he began cataloguing their sins using his second sight.

Pressed for an answer Jesus looked up and said simply, 'If any of you has not committed sins, then he is entitled to throw the first stone.' The smiles turned to scowls. He had upheld the letter of the law and caught the lawyers in an act of hypocrisy.

Stoning is the Jews' preferred method of execution. There must be at least two witnesses to secure a guilty verdict, and they must throw the first stones. If they do not kill the offender, bystanders are then allowed to throw stones also.

The woman's accusers melted away into the surrounding streets without pressing charges. Then Jesus reassured her that he did not condemn her either, but told her to stop sinning. In the presence of this remarkable man even his critics see themselves in a new light. Whether they will now regard him more favourably is doubtful, however.

(John 8:1–11)

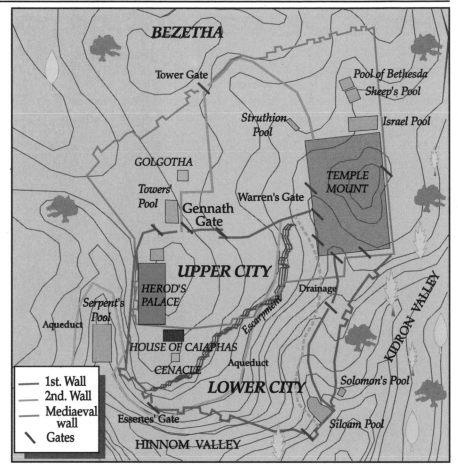

Jerusalem was a thriving city, which had grown steadily through the years. Whilst the first and second walls would have been standing, the city roughly covered the area later enclosed by the medieval wall. This still stands today and defines the area of the old town. The most significant feature of the town then was the temple, dominating it by its size and area covered.

The devil of a row

Judea, c. AD 31

The Pharisees who raise a buzz at the activities of Jesus of Nazareth have been well and truly swatted by the man they say works for the 'lord of the flies', Beelzebub, rather than for the Lord of heaven.

He told them that by deliberately ascribing the work of God's Spirit to the devil they were guilty of committing the only sin God could never forgive, because they are completely hard and wilfully refuse to listen to him.

Having evicted an evil spirit which apparently had sealed a man's lips, he turned the accusation of being the devil's agent back on the Pharisees. 'If Satan is destroying his own soldiers, then his empire is collapsing', he said. 'And if I drive out evil spirits by the power of Beelzebub, who do your exorcists drive them out by? But if I do it by God's power, then the kingdom of God has truly come to you.' He described the devil as a 'strong man' who has been overcome by someone stronger still. 'If you're not on my side then you're against God and for the devil,' he added.

Beelzebub (Beel-zebub, the lord of the flies) is a Hebrew nickname for Baalzebul (prince Baal), an ancient Canaanite god. Over the centuries Jews have used the name as a synonym for the devil who they believe is a fallen angel.

(Matthew 12:22–33; Mark 3:19–30; Luke 11:14–23; 12:10)

Don't be caught napping!

Jerusalem c. AD 31

Two men are reaping together in a field; their wives are grinding the grain down at the mill. Suddenly, without warning, the sun goes out. The sky falls in. The earth heaves.

Women grinding flour in the time-honoured manner, drawn from life in 1880.

And one man finds himself catapulted into the warmth and light of God's eternal presence. So does his colleague's wife. The others are plunged into the cold chaotic darkness of the underworld. They never meet again.

Gloom and doomsters over the past couple of centuries in Judea have made a fine art out of decorating the darkest of futuristic backgrounds with the most vivid special effects. Hardly anyone takes them very seriously, even if they do feed a popular interest in the 'day of the Lord'. But now Jesus of Nazareth has joined their ranks, and true to form he raises more questions than he answers.

Most of his teaching is couched in stories which have one common theme: always remain alert, don't be caught napping. The full stop at the end of life's sentence will come abruptly, at any time, and you need to be ready and alert. Privately, to those of his disciples who ask, he forecasts a series of horror stories before the final curtain falls on the drama of history. (See box opposite).

His most graphic story is of a rich man in his castle and a poor man begging at his gate. Both die; the rich man sinks into the vacuous underworld where he burns with unfulfilled desire, intense frustration and deep anxiety. The poor man, named Lazarus, relaxes secure in the comforts of heaven.

Looking across the huge void between them, the rich man calls for Lazarus to serve him a drink of water to cool his boiling blood. When that is denied he asks if Lazarus can go back to life in order to warn the rich man's family to avoid the hellish pit. 'If they won't believe what God has already revealed, why should they believe someone who's risen from death? Besides, it's too late. There's enough time in this life to sort out your spiritual affairs,' he is told.

The notes of wasted earthly opportunity and the absolute finality of 'the end' sound continuously through Jesus' stories of God's judgement. There are the bridesmaids waiting for the groom to arrive to claim his bride at her father's house and to accompany them both back to his. Five are ready for a torchlight procession should the groom come at night; five are unprepared. By the time the oil-less girls have found some supplies, they are too late; the door is shut and the party has begun.

Then there are the estate managers who are put in charge of resources by a landowner to boost his profits. Two, with differing amounts, do all that can be expected of them and on the landowner's return are suitably rewarded. The third just stores his resources, without even loaning them out on interest. For his carelessness he gets evicted from the master's presence to languish 'where there are the tears of grief and the rages of anger'.

Similarly, there is a manager of another absentee landlord who keeps the estate in good order and pays the labourers on time. He contrasts with a neighbouring tenant who takes his landlord's absence as licence to do what he likes and to mistreat his labourers. Guess who gets the push and who gets the rise?

Finally, there is a story of a shepherd separating sheep and goats. The 'sheep' are those who have

It is not uncommon to find mixed herds of sheep and goats grazing together in the Middle East today.

'I will come again' claims Jesus

Jesus' futuristic predictions given to his disciples at a private meeting on the Mount of Olives

- The Jerusalem temple will be completely destroyed.
- There will be false messiahs and false prophets.
- There will be wars, earthquakes and famines.
- There will be betrayal and personal wickedness.
- A 'desolating sacrilege' will be set up in a holy place.
- There will be great suffering across the world.
- All these things are likely to occur in most generations.
- But one day, the Son of Man will return to earth.
- There will be no mistake, he will be seen by everyone.
- It will be a cataclysmic event and the universe itself will be shaken.
- His people will be gathered from every corner of the earth.
- No one – not even he – knows when this will be; so be ready for it!

(Matthew 24:1–36; Mark 13:1–37; Luke 17:26,27,34,35; 21:5–33)

served God in small ways often without realising they were doing so. The 'goats' are those who had similar opportunities to serve God by serving others, but who failed to take them. These are thrown into eternal punishment; the selfless ones are taken to eternal life.

What makes these pictures of the future different to many others, apart from their stark simplicity, is the implication that Jesus himself is to be identified with 'the master' or 'bridegroom'. He foresees a role for himself which implies that he expects 'the end' to happen soon. Or else he believes his own fantastic scenarios and expects to come back from the grave to orchestrate them.

(Matthew 24:37–51; 25:1–46; Luke 12:35–48; 16:19–31; 19:12–27)

Angry teacher whips up traders in temple market

Jerusalem, c. AD 31
Traders in the Jerusalem temple have had their stalls overturned by a whip-waving rabbi who objected to their commercial presence in 'God's house'. In an extraordinary outburst of indignation, the teacher Jesus of Nazareth sent animals stampeding and coins flying around the open Court of the Gentiles. He used a whip to crack on the tables but did not threaten anyone with it.

The traders, who are entering their busiest week of the year leading up to the Passover Festival, supply pilgrims with approved sacrificial animals and change all currency into Tyrian coinage which is the only legal tender in the religious market.

prophets predicted that there would come a time when traders would not operate in the temple and the Messiah would renew the worship there. There is also a suggestion, prompted by his assertion that he is 'greater than the temple', that he rejects the whole sacrificial system of Judaism as a suitable way to find God. Much of his teaching focuses on personal devotion rather than public ritual.

The Court of the Gentiles is a wide space surrounding the relatively small shrine. The magnificent white and gilt buildings are surrounded by porticos and offices and are perched on a massive platform some 450 m (1,500 ft) long and 300 m (1,000 ft) wide. It was started by Herod the Great in 19 BC and is

A model of Fort Antonia as it would have stood in Jesus' day.

While on his rampage, the preacher quoted the prophet Isaiah who designated the temple as a 'house of prayer for all nations'. The banter of stall holders, the bleating of sheep, and the bustle of the crowds all contribute to make the wide courtyard an impossible place for quiet prayer. Gentiles are not allowed further into the Temple complex where more hushed tones prevail.

Some observers suggest that Jesus was reinforcing his apparent claim to be the Jewish Messiah. Other

still incomplete. The chief garrison for Roman soldiers in the city, Fort Antonia, is built into a corner of the Temple Mount.

The soldiers were not needed to quell the minor skirmish in the market, however. Having made his point Jesus left to continue his teaching elsewhere, and the traders reassembled. It is believed that he made a similar gesture some three years ago when he was relatively unknown.

(Matthew 21:12–16; Mark 11:12–18; Luke 19:45–48; 14:21; John 2:12–17)

Jesus and lawyers in head-on clash

Jerusalem, c. AD 32

Traditionalist religious teachers have drawn ordinary people into a poisonous snake pit, shut the door and thrown away the key, claims Jesus of Nazareth.

In a heated clash with his critics, the normally considerate prophet, to whom the sick and weak turn for comfort, displayed another side to his character. He traded insults with academic lawyers and pious Pharisees. They are now said to be baying for his blood like hunters on the trail of a wild boar.

He accused the scribes, whose legal interpretation of Moses' law is said to carry as much authority as the law itself, of setting double standards. Instead of helping ordinary people bear the burdens of the law, they have driven loopholes through it so the scribes themselves can wriggle out of its demands.

Jesus raised a laugh when he suggested that their teaching was like straining a gnat out of a drink while they swallowed a whole camel, playing on the similar Aramaic words for two 'unclean' creatures.

And he poured cold water on those who had disapproved of his practice of eating without the prescribed finger-washing ritual, a ceremonial rather than hygienic requirement. They were like people who washed the outside of cups but left the inside stained, he declared, returning to his own obsession for purity of inner thoughts, feelings and motives.

The Pharisees are like people who decorated beautiful marble and lime plaster jars and filled them with dead men's bones (which are classified as ceremonially defiling), he added; their teaching looks good but is spiritually contaminating.

The itinerant teacher with a simple lifestyle has attacked ceremoni-

Jesus faces up to the Pharisees in the temple courtyard. From the film *Jesus of Nazareth*.

al scruples before. He stresses that, contrary to orthodox opinion, it is not what people eat which 'defiles' them, but what they spew out in terms of language and behaviour. And that comes, he says, from 'the heart', the inner self, which is more like a can of worms than a pure cocktail.

He cannot resist mocking the ostentation of some Pharisees. They tie small leather boxes (phylacteries) containing extracts of the law to their foreheads all day instead of only at the prescribed prayer times – implying a steady state of continuous prayer; they make the symbolic tassles on their robes (worn by all Jews and signifying God's commandments) extra long and colourful; and they arrive at the synagogue early in order to get the platform seats facing the congregation.

'That's not how you're to behave,' Jesus has told his own large open-air congregation. 'Don't encourage people to defer to you by using respectful titles like "teacher" or "rabbi". You're to be servants of each other.' Using an unusual allusion to the elders of Israel he added that his followers were not to be called 'father' either. It may refer to his own habit of addressing God as Father.

Jesus spoke in a manner reminiscent of the ancient prophets, prefacing each denunciation with the phrase 'how sad'. It contrasted with some of his earlier speeches to the crowds when he spoke of 'how happy' are those who acknowledge their spiritual needs and bear with each other's failings.

'You can learn from the professors but you're not to live like them,' he warned. They are hypocrites, acting a part but more out of blindness than wilful insincerity. They are so spiritually blind, he argued, that they cannot see the wood for the trees. Their intense focus on trifling details such as correct tithing of garden herbs obscured their view of much greater things such as justice and neighbourly goodness. As Jews pride themselves on being God's chosen guides for a blind world, their anger was understandable.

(Matthew 23:1–36; Luke 11:37–54; cf. Matthew 15:1–20; Mark 7:1–23; Isaiah 5:8–25)

Devout Jews still wear phylacteries today.

Godliness yes; cleanliness no

Judea, c. AD 32

Roman visitors to Judea are appalled that while the Jewish state of godliness is admirable their state of cleanliness is literally the pits.

Travellers from major Roman cities who normally enjoy daily baths and latrines flushed by underground conduits find that the sanitation in this outpost of the empire is primitive at best and obnoxious at worst. Even in places where self-emptying latrines are not available, Romans are used to human waste in domestic cess pits being carted away by the authorities each night.

It is not so here. Animal droppings and human sewage mixed with general household refuse carpet the unpaved streets with an unspeakable and foul-smelling gunk which turns to slimy ooze after rain. Yet most people wear only open sandals, and children often go barefoot, oblivious to the filth. The best lavatories are shallow holes dug in waste ground.

There are virtually no public baths in Judea, largely because the Jews object to open displays of nakedness. Expatriot households have built some luxury homes with their own bathrooms and piped water in Jerusalem and Caesarea. Visitors staying elsewhere must forgo their daily pleasure of steam rooms, warm and cool baths and sunbathing terraces which they take for granted at home.

Fortunately, perfumes are widely available in the markets. And visitors to Jewish homes are normally offered the courtesy and relief of a foot-washing given to them by domestic servants. The locals seem to limit their washing to douses in streams or rinses with water collected in jars from wells by women.

Despite their apparent attachment to their own dirt, religious Judeans are scrupulous about ceremonial cleansing, which is one thing Roman visitors can identify with. The pious will wash their hands meticulously in a prescribed manner before each meal, and food is prepared in accordance with strict religious rules.

Our poet Ovid, who died just a decade ago, would not have been at home here. His instructions in *The Art of Love* to keep oneself pleasantly clean, not to go around with shaggy hair and to have clean, neat nails, would fall on deaf ears. But he would find plenty of examples to justify his heartfelt plea that 'your breath should not be sour and unpleasant, and your body should not stink like that of a he-goat'.

Roman comunal latrines, such as these in the ruins of a bath house in Ephesus, were routinely provided for public use throughout the empire.

Spies left in the cold after clash

Jerusalem, c. AD 32

In a new development in the bitter relationship between Jesus and the religious leadership, undercover agents are now being employed to keep Jesus of Nazareth and his supporters under constant surveillance. They are planted in the crowds to ask apparently innocent questions and to collect evidence of Jesus' controversial views.

Roman silver denarius depicting Tiberius.

They asked him if it was lawful for Jews to pay taxes to the occupying Romans.

Taking a Roman coin, which Judeans use for many daily transactions, he pointed to the image of Tiberius on it and said simply, 'Give back to Caesar what belongs to Caesar, and to God what belongs to God.' Few would have missed the deliberate irony mixed with the diplomatic logic. Jews believe that human beings bear the image of their Creator God, whom they are to serve and obey.

On a previous occasion when the penniless teacher with no fixed address was asked to pay the Jewish temple tax, he did so by sending his right-hand man Simon Peter fishing. He caught a fish with a coin wedged in its mouth, sufficient to pay the dues both owed. 'God doesn't require it,' he said, 'but it's best not to offend the authorities.'

(Matthew 17:24–27; 22:15–22; Mark 12:13–17; Luke 20:20–26)

Check out for hidden costs

The teaching of Jesus sounds like a tempting offer. But now even he is telling potential followers to read the small print before they commit themselves to him and his ways.

Some people find out the hard way. One man so taken by what he heard said he would follow Jesus anywhere and everywhere. Then he discovered that the teacher was sleeping directly under the stars. 'No fixed abode' was not to him a desirable address, so security triumphed over adventure.

Others have asked leave of absence to settle their domestic affairs before joining the travelling teacher. But they have been told in no uncertain terms that the dead can make their own funeral arrangements, and that there is no going back to any former activities. It is all or nothing.

High charges

'Anyone who puts even his closest relatives before the demands of God's kingdom cannot be a disciple of mine.' (Luke:14:26)

'Anyone who wants to come my way must first of all deny his or her own ambitions, then take up the cross of self-denial every day. If you want to preserve your life for ever you've got to lose it in God first. If you hand your life over to me, you'll find it in a new way.' (Luke 9:23,24)

'What's the use of possessing everything this world has on offer if in the process of getting it you lose your true self?' (Luke 9:25)

Those are just some of his hard sayings (see box above). Unlike many who desire to get a following, Jesus does not attract the crowds by offering them easy terms. He goes so far as to warn them to do their sums first to check that they can afford the full price he is asking – which is lifelong and total commit-ment to all that he stands for.

'If you're going to build a house you don't start laying the stones until you've worked out if you can pay for all the materials, not least

Ploughing methods have changed little in many parts of the Middle East.

because everyone will think you a fool if you can't finish it,' he says. 'And no ruler on earth would send an army of 10,000 against one of 20,000; he couldn't win so he wouldn't start – he'd negotiate.'

At times he describes his way as being equivalent to a convicted criminal under a Roman execution order shouldering his own cross to the graveyard. He calls for a life of self-denial which is normally associated with hermits in the desert. Unlike theirs, his asceticism is not concerned with food, drink and social gathering (he frequently attends dinner parties) but with a rejection of the values generally placed on material gain and social status.

At the same time Jesus does make a number of special offers which some say are unrefusable and which more than make up for any losses they may experience (see right). They are not loss-leaders to entice unwary customers, nor are they offered on a *quid pro quo* basis – buy this, get that free.

But they do represent 'added value' which is only available to those who pay the full price he demands. Among his offers are 'eternal life', by which he seems to mean a quality of relationship with God in this life which lasts for ever and expands after death. Another is the promise of a continuous experience of God's care and provision through unavoidable hardship and even persecution.

God, he says, is not a hard taskmaster as the Pharisees portray him, but a caring Father who loves to give good gifts to his children, and to hear them out when they pray both in joy and in distress. The real issue is not what God demands in terms of sacrifice, but what comforts human beings wrongly expect as their right.

(Matthew 8:19–22; Mark 8:34–38; Luke 9:57–62; 14:25–34)

Special offers

'Come to me when you're tired and weighed down, and I'll give you rest. Take my harness on your shoulders instead of pulling your own burdens by yourself, and learn from me. I'll treat you gently and kindly, and you'll get a deep-seated peace. My harness is much easier than you think, and the burdens I give you are lighter than you realise.' (Matthew 11:28–30)

'If you hold fast to my teaching you'll be my true disciples. Then you'll know what's true and right, and that truth will set you free. If the Son of Man releases you from the slavery of your sins, you'll be as free as ever you could be.' (John 8:32,36)

The bottom line

Stories and images used by Jesus to put a price on discipleship

Give indiscriminately

Everyone accepts the duty to care for one's neighbour, but just who is the neighbour? When a lawyer asked that, he was told the story of an injured victim of a highway mugging who lay helpless on the ground. He was ignored by a passing priest and a Levite, who perhaps feared becoming ceremonially defiled or of being drawn into a trap. But a passing Samaritan, someone most Jews despise, stopped, attended to the man, put him up at a hotel and paid the bill. That's being a neighbour.

(Luke 10:25–37)

Pray persistently

God doesn't always answer prayers immediately, or in the way we hope. That doesn't mean he never will. Think of when a friend turns up unexpectedly late at night and you've no bread in the house. You call next door, even though they're in bed. They'll get up and give you something just for being bold! God isn't a miser and you'll find him and his answers if you seek sincerely.

(Luke 11:5–13)

Barren hillsides between Jerusalem and Jericho, through which the only road passes.

Save wisely

What sort of savings have you got? There was once a rich landowner with surplus crops who decided to demolish his barns and build bigger ones so that he could take it easy, and eat, drink and be merry for the rest of his life. But he died suddenly. What good were his savings to him then? He couldn't take them with him to the next life. But if you are rich in faith, that'll earn you interest for ever.

(Luke 12:13–21)

Forgive completely

Once upon a time there was a king who called in his loans. One of his debtors owed him thousands of dollars but could not pay it back. The king threatened to bankrupt him, but when he begged for more time the king cancelled the debt. The former debtor then went out and found someone who owed him a few hundred dollars, who was in the position he had just been in and couldn't pay. And the mean old Scrooge sent in the bailiffs. The king was angry when he found out and punished the man. God has forgiven you completely, so you should forgive others – even when they sin against you many times.

(Matthew 18:21–35)

Old store rooms at Masada, first century AD.

331

Hundreds hit jackpot as corrupt tax man says, 'I'll pay it back'

Roman stone relief dating from the first century of tax collectors counting their booty.

Jericho, c. AD 32

A corrupt tax inspector who defrauded hundreds of people has promised to pay back what he overcharged them, with compensation. He has also made a substantial donation to charity.

The chief inspector of taxes for the Jericho district, Zacchaeus, had his change of heart after sharing a meal with Jesus of Nazareth. Like a Mafia godfather, he controlled a team of junior collectors who coerced inordinate sums from hapless merchants who had to pay up or have their goods seized.

Born a Jew, Zacchaeus contracted to supply a fixed sum to the Romans from Jericho's strategic customs post. He and his minions wrested every penny they could get from their victims and pocketed the profits. That, and the fact that any Jew working for the Romans is regarded as a traitor by his fellow-countrymen, made Zacchaeus' name stink in the balsam-scented air of this 'palm city'.

His change of heart came after he sneaked into the pre-publicised visit to Jericho of the teacher and healer. A small man easily elbowed out of the way by a bustling and unsympathetic crowd, he climbed the short trunk of a sycamore-fig tree along the route and hid in its spreading foliage.

As Jesus and his entourage proceeded down the tree-lined avenue, they made an unscheduled stop beneath Zacchaeus' hideout. Peering into the branches, Jesus called the tax collector by name and invited himself to Zacchaeus' home for an evening meal.

In this culture eating with a stranger implies acceptance, friendship and trust, a fact not lost on the surprised tax man who had been excommunicated by the religious establishment for his professional activities. The followers of Jesus were equally surprised; none of them can recall any previous occasion when their leader has invited himself to someone's home.

During the meal Zacchaeus announced his decision to repay fourfold those he had defrauded, the Jewish legal penalty for robbery with violence. Technically, he needed only to repay double, the fine for ordinary robbery. In addition he also pledged to give away half his goods to the poor.

Clearly delighted by this spontaneous act of repentance and gratitude, Jesus declared, 'salvation has come to this house. Zacchaeus is a child of God, and I have come to find those of God's children who have lost their way.' Meanwhile, citizens in Jericho were working out how to spend their unexpected windfall.

(Luke 19:1–10)

No sex in heaven

Jerusalem, c. AD 32

There is to be no marriage in heaven, according to Jesus of Nazareth. All bodily functions as we know them will cease and there will be no more death or decay.

He was replying to the Sadducees who, unlike the Pharisees, do not believe in life after death. They had tested him with a typical scholar's question concerning a woman whose seven husbands had all died, and wanted to know who her husband would be in heaven.

Jesus affirmed his belief in 'the resurrection', citing Moses' description of 'the God of Abraham, Isaac and Jacob' as witness that 'God is not God of the dead but of the living'. He added that the dead would be like angels, released from earthly desire and decay.

(Matthew 22:23–33;
Mark 12:18–27; Luke 20:27–40)

Losers find God

Judea, c. AD 32

God does not keep polite company and the 'losers' in this life are the ones who are most likely to find him. Indeed, he goes out of his way to search for them, rather than waiting for them to seek him, Jesus of Nazareth has told a gathering of lawyers.

He was responding to criticism that according to the Pharisees' rule book no religious teacher should associate with people who are religiously and socially beneath God's dignity. Jesus has repeatedly rejected this exclusivity and has eaten with and taught the so-called 'ungodly' who include professional 'sinners' such as prostitutes and people who work for the occupying forces.

In a strong rejection of religious exclusivism, he has told a series of parables illustrating God's intense desire to comfort and welcome such people. For example, a shepherd who loses a sheep will pen up the remainder and go and look for it. It may be only one in a hundred, but it is still important to him. Or, if a woman drops a day's wages on the earthen floor of her dark cottage, she will light a lamp and go on hands and knees until she finds the lost coin.

People like that who find what they have lost give a big shout and the whole world knows. So God searches out the lost and rejoices when he finds them and they recognise him, says Jesus. This is a big development of current Jewish

Welcome home the wanderer!

In one of his more elaborate stories, Jesus describes how two people with very different attitudes to life can both risk throwing away their spiritual privileges.

The younger son of a family asked for his share of the estate in advance of his father's death. He then lost the lot, playboy style, on wine, women and song. Destitute, he was reduced to the lowest possible level of life, sharing food with a herd of 'unclean' pigs on a Gentile's farm. Remembering that even his father's servants had a bed, clothes and food, he decided to go back home, say he was sorry, and ask to join the slave gang.

Meanwhile his brother was doing all the right things at home, being a good son and heir and living a clean life. And dad, every day, went off for a walk to the edge of his land just to see if, by any chance, his younger boy was coming home. He knew he would return, one day.

And so he did. His father saw him from a distance, and hurried down the road to greet him and welcome him. The starving, ragged boy began bleating out his apologies but his father brushed them aside. He gave him a new set of clothes and ordered a banquet to celebrate his homecoming. But the older brother was not amused. What was there to celebrate? The kid had blown half the family fortune!

The father told the sullen man that his younger son had been as good as dead, but now he was alive. He had been lost, but now he was found. He was not to be rejected. The older son had stayed safe in the family house, which was good, but so was the prodigal's return. So too, of course, was the father's amazing grace.

(Luke 15:11–32)

Basalt archways are all that remain today of substantial early dwellings in Chorazim.

thought, which acknowledges that God welcomes the penitent but does not conceive of him taking the initiative in contacting them.

Jesus has also spoken of God 'drawing' people to himself, creating in them a hunger which only he can satisfy.

(Matthew 18:12–14; Luke 15:1–10;
John 6:44)

Rift widens in Jesus' camp

Bethany, c. AD 33

Discontent among followers of Jesus boiled over here for the third time in as many weeks when they complained about a money-wasting gesture bestowed on their teacher by a grateful supporter.

Mary, the sister of Lazarus who Jesus brought back to life recently, anointed the miracle-worker with a flask full of expensive perfume. It was probably a thank-you gesture

ding figure of their mother.

Jesus ruled that there will be no pre-appointed successor to him, and that places in his leadership team will not be allocated in advance. He is therefore discounting the possibility that he will set up an alternative 'kingdom' organised on imperial lines. He repeated his standard – and seemingly impractical – assertion that in his group it is a matter of 'first come,

first servant'; the most ambitious member of his team must serve rather than direct the others.

He cited his own example of having served them, and warned them that they might have to 'drink the cup that I shall drink'. He appears to imply that they are called to suffer human and perhaps even divine wrath.

Other rumblings of discontent are occurring in the Jesus camp among followers who are openly sceptical about the wisdom of going to Jerusalem at this time of year. The jealous and jittery religious authorities are said to be looking to arrest Jesus on any charges they can make stick. Jesus has added to their fears by speaking repeatedly about the inevitability of being betrayed and condemned. He adds mysteriously thet he will 'rise again', and without understanding him his close followers seem at present prepared to trust his judgement – just.

(Matthew 20:17–28; Mark 10:32–45; Luke 18:31–34; 22:24–27.)

Jericho is still today a city surrounded by palm groves.

for the safe return of her brother.

'It was a total waste of money,' said an exasperated Judas Iscariot, who acts as treasurer for the inner circle of 12 disciples. 'If she didn't want the ointment we could have sold it and given the proceeds to the poor.'

Jesus defused the outburst by pointing out that there will always be poor people who need help, but he will not always be with them. 'She did it for my burial,' he added, 'so leave her alone.'

Rifts among the formerly close-knit group had widened earlier in Jericho, on the journey here. There was a strong argument after James and John, two of Jesus' closest aides, had pressed him to appoint them as his chief advisors and ministers. They were encouraged to seek clarification of the future shape of Jesus' work by the forbid-

More stories and surprises from Jesus

Plan for the future: An estate manager who was laid off was told to clear his desk. He decided to cut the interest and profits which clients owed his boss. That way he made friends who might give him work in the future. You, too, should prepare for your (eternal) future. (Luke 16:1–9)

Pray for justice: A widow who needed her affairs sorted out went to see the local judge, a heartless man. She wouldn't take no for an answer and eventually the judge did what she asked just to get some peace! God isn't heartless and will give you justice. Pray and believe. (Luke 18:1–8)

Prepare to work: You've been at it all day. When you come in, do you tell your housemaid to put her feet up while you get your own supper? Of course not. You are paying her to get it for you, and you prob-

ably won't thank her because it's her job. So when you do what God tells you, you've only done your job. In fact, you haven't done anything extra at all. (Luke 17:7–10)

Pleading his cause: A blind man, Bartimaeus, heard that Jesus was in Jericho. So he called out, 'Jesus! Son of David! Have mercy on me!' Everyone around told him to shut up, but he carried on calling. Jesus heard him and healed him. 'Your faith has made you whole,' he said. (Mark 10:46–52)

Please say thank you: A colony of ten lepers on the Galilee–Samaria border asked Jesus for healing. He told them to go to the priest for official clearance from the disease. They went, and were healed. But only one came back to say thank you, and he got complete wholeness through his faith. (Luke 17:11–19)

Royal welcome for Jewish 'king'

Jerusalem, c. AD 33

Jesus of Nazareth was today feted like a victorious king as he entered the ancient capital city of the Jewish nation. Although peaceful and without a ceremonial sword in sight, the demonstration sent shock waves throughout the corridors of religious if not political power where jittery leaders strive to maintain an uneasy truce with the Roman occupiers.

The spontaneous expression of popular support for this outstanding teacher and healer was charged with nationalistic symbolism. Crowds who lined the route were chanting victory psalms (religious hymns) and waving palm branches, which here are often viewed as emblems of military conquest. Hailed as the 'King of Israel', Jesus mounted a donkey commandeered for the occasion by his disciples, and rode from the Mount of Olives, outside the city, over a carpet of cloaks and branches laid on the dirt track by the spectators.

King David, the hero of all Jewish

The old city of Jerusalem, seen from the Mount of Olives.

Scale model of first-century Jerusalem, erected recently to convey the likely extent of the city.

leaders, once rode in victory into Jerusalem on a donkey provided by a well-wisher. The prophet Zechariah foretold that a future king in David's line of succession would enter the city on a donkey, after which God would take from it the 'chariots and war horses' and set the prisoners free.

The crowd's chant of 'Hosanna!' (Save us!) is both an acclamation of praise and a petition for deliverance. It comes from a psalm which thanks God for military victory, speaks of besieging enemies being 'cut off', and calls for the people to parade in the streets 'with tree boughs in their hands'.

It all launched the city into holiday mood earlier than normal. Hundreds of thousands are already flocking to this compact city for the annual Passover Festival in a week's time. Most, in accord with ancient Jewish practice, make the pilgrimage on foot as a symbol of the 40 years of foot-slogging in the desert by their ancestors which the festival celebrates.

Jesus accepted the fanfares gracefully, even though in the past he has forbidden his followers to proclaim their belief that he is the Messiah. When asked why he did not try to silence them this time, he replied that if they did not shout it, the stones of the city would.

There was just one sobering moment in the triumphant parade. Looking across the Kidron Valley from the Mount of Olives at the city spread out before him, Jesus paused and wept. He prophesied that 'what makes for peace' would be rejected by the people, that siege earthworks would be built against it again, and that people would be killed 'because you didn't recognise the day God came to you'.

But for the moment at least, the day Jesus came to the city has been marked. High-level talks about how to avoid a possible insurrection are taking place. But the Roman presence here can contain any trouble these disorganised crowds could bring if the praises of Jesus ever turn to curses of Caesar.

(Matthew 21:1–9; Mark 11:1–10; Luke 19:28–44; John 12:12–19; cf. 2 Samuel 6:2,11; Psalm 118; Zechariah 9:9–11)

Minority groups with majority influence

On the surface, Judea is a monochrome culture held together by centuries-old Jewish traditions. But beneath the surface factions vie for power and influence. Some are purely religious, others overtly political. It all makes for a province difficult to govern and difficult for the visitor to understand. Even a messianic pretender like Jesus of Nazareth has little likelihood of creating unity among the people, unless he succeeds in uniting them against himself. These are the main groupings, in alphabetical order.

Elders

Councils of seven elders oversee and administer such civil matters as the Romans allow through the Jewish synagogues, where religion and civic life are closely entwined. They do not detérmine matters of worship but they adjudicate in matters relating to their law and can punish offenders by flogging or excommunication. They are represented on the Sanhedrin.

The Dead Sea Scroll Caves, Qumran.

Essenes

The largest of several monastic orders who have withdrawn into communities to preserve what they consider to be authentic Jewish lifestyle. Essenes have numerous communities around Judea where they work hard on their land and offer hospitality to visitors. Their day is punctuated by regular liturgical services.

They are scrupulous concerning ceremonial purity, encourage celibacy, and avoid commercial or military operations. They await a great war when they will emerge as victors over both Jews and Gentiles who do not share their lifestyle. They believe in two messiahs, representing kingship and priesthood, and that in a heavenly war God will overthrow foreign influence and restore true worship and faith.

A major community at Qumran, north-west of the inhospitable Dead Sea, is said to be run by Essenes although it appears to be more isolationist and idiosyncratic in its teachings. The community has a large library of biblical texts and scrolls relating to its life and worship.

Herodians

A relatively small group of influential people who are joining with others in hostility towards Jesus of Nazareth, perhaps because he threatens to spark off an uprising against Rome. Herodians are supporters of the Herods' much-weakened dynasty which is strongly pro-Roman. They tend to be Sadducean in outlook.

Pharisees

The largest of the sects, it only numbers about 6,000 people, and originated some 200 years ago as a minority group of the Hasidim who advocated strict observance of Jewish food and ceremonial laws. The name derives from a term meaning 'separated ones'.

They are gaining influence in the Sanhedrin and many, but not all, tend to be anti-Roman in politics. Most of them come from lower-middle-class backgrounds. Conscious of a general failure to comply with the ritual laws, especially those relating to food, they have developed a fence of sub-laws which defines what can and cannot be done.

Pharisees are generally sincere, if also rather austere and inflexible, and intend to help people to be good Jews. However, while their rigidity may have attracted admiration, it has not won support. As a result, Pharisees tend to be dismissive of others. They have the most vociferous public relations machinery of all the groups, and the strength of their voice is out of proportion to their influence.

Priests

The religious ministers of the temple trace their lifeline from Aaron, and are closely associated with the Levites who are also descended from Levi but not through Aaron. There is a pecking order differentiating ordinary priests who perform ceremonial functions from the chief priests who are members of the high-priestly and other leading families in Jerusalem. The chief priests control the temple finances and currently dominate the Sanhedrin.

Annas, who was high priest between AD 6 and 15, still wields considerable influence. His son-in-law Caiaphas is the current title holder; he is reputed to be a highly-skilled diplomat.

Revolutionaries

Judea is a hotbed of unrest, and numerous small groups are dedicated to the violent overthrow of the Romans. Generally, their attempts are local and minor. Among them are the **Zealots**, who are believed to have been formed by Judas the Galilean about AD 6 when he staged an attempted coup. They claim to be the political descendants of Judas Maccabeus, who recaptured Jerusalem from the Greeks 150 years ago.

They are not well organised at present, but as a determined guerilla force they have growing influence among the younger Jews frustrated by their official leaders. One of Jesus' closest aides, Simon nicknamed 'the Zealot' (not Peter) may have been a member of the group – or just a zealous person.

The **Sicarii** are so called because of the small curved daggers they conceal to assassinate individuals in cold blood and often in broad daylight. They frequently escape detection simply by melting into the crowds. There are also common-or-garden bandits who roam the country picking off unwary travellers, motivated more by greed than ideology.

Sadducees

Boorish, rude and argumentative is about the best that can be said about this upper-class party low in numbers but high in political influence. Most are priests and many belong to high-priestly families (although not all priests are Sadducees). They control the temple worship and regard ordinary people with scorn; the sentiment is returned.

Some suggest that they were founded by one Zadok in the mists of history, but this is not verifiable. They supported the Hasmonean priest-kings about 150 years ago, which gave them entrance into the corridors of power. They currently dominate the Sanhedrin but their power is on the wane.

Theologically they are at odds with the Pharisees. They accept only the five books of Moses and deny the possibility of resurrection. But they are forced to ally with the Pharisees on matters of national importance in order to gain popular support.

The Sanhedrin

The Supreme Court of the Jews given authority by the Romans over religious and certain civil and criminal matters. It consists of some 70 people appointed rather than elected, and is currently dominated by the Sadducee party. It has its own police force and can judge all cases which do not carry a death penalty. Most capital cases have to be brought to the Roman procurator, although in some religious matters this requirement is waived.

It meets on set dates with councillors sitting in a semi-circle and employing clerks to record their votes. Evidence for the defence is heard first. Capital offences require a two-thirds majority to secure a conviction; other offences are decided on a simple majority vote.

The Sanhedrin is said to date from the time of Moses, who appointed 70 elders to assist him, but there is no record of the council until it was cast into its present shape by Ezra the scribe sometime

after 500 BC. Its fortunes have waxed and waned over the years. Herod the Great clipped its wings when it indicted him on capital charges, but it is now enjoying the power it once had under Julius Caesar.

Herodium, seen from Bethlehem.

Scribes (lawyers)

Often closely associated with the Pharisees because of their common interest in the ceremonial law, scribes were never a sect or party. They originated as writers and teachers during the Babylonian exile (sixth century BC). They were largely responsible for the development of synagogue worship and government which provided a substitute meeting-point for Jews unable to visit the temple. They have also become the recognised teachers of children. Many continue with their secular jobs, and also undertake the mundane but time consuming copying of the Scriptures.

Sober meal on festive night

Jerusalem, April c. AD 33

An estimated two million pilgrims are tonight crammed into rented lodgings and relatives' houses in Jerusalem to carve into the quarter of a million lambs whose freshly-shed blood literally ran through the streets this afternoon.

This is the Jews' most holy night of the year, the Passover Festival. It commemorates the hurried exodus of Israelite slaves from Egypt after the sudden death of their captors' firstborn sons. The story claims that the Israelites were spared the plague, and passed over by the angel of death, because of the symbol of the blood of slaughtered lambs daubed on their doorposts.

In a small hired upstairs room, thick with the smell of burning oil lamps and spit-roast lamb, the scene is much like that everywhere else. Yet it is also different. Here Jesus of Nazareth, the headline-grabbing teacher and healer, has gathered with his friends. They wear outdoor clothes in a re-enactment of the drama of that long-past but never-forgotten ready-steady-go night.

They follow the familiar rituals of the meal: sharing wine, bread made without yeast, and bitter herbs, punctuated by ritual washings and time-honoured liturgies. There had been a tense start to the evening because in this ad hoc gathering there had been no domestic servant appointed to wash the guests' feet – a customary welcome gesture. So Jesus himself had got up from the table and performed the duty despite loud protests (but no offers of help).

'I'm among you as one who serves,' he reminded them as he has so often, although never before with such a dramatic gesture. 'You are to serve one another as I have served you.'

He is in a sober mood. Dark thoughts seem to preoccupy him; he has spoken mysteriously of being betrayed by one of his inner

This fresco, painted by Leonardo da Vinci in 1497 and situated in Milan, is the best-known portrayal of this fateful meal.

circle. They press for detail, but he remains secretive. He offers herbs sandwiched in bread to Judas Iscariot, the group treasurer, and says almost in an undertone, 'Get on quickly with what you have to do.' Judas hesitates, then leaves the room.

'What's the scatterbrain forgotten to buy now?' muses Simon Peter.

Jesus sighs, and turns to Peter. 'You're all going to forget me soon,' he says. 'You're going to be scattered like sheep with no shepherd.' The big fisherman responds with a vehement denial, and a murmur of approval ripples round the room. 'Peter, before the night's out you'll have denied you know me three times,' Jesus continues. 'Now, let's have the main course.'

The whole lamb is brought in and carved. The conversation lightens and as spirits rise Jesus begins teaching his followers again (see box opposite). Even on a festive night, his thoughts are serious and profound. Later, as the meal draws to a close, he diverges from normal practice and adds his own personal touch to the rituals.

As the last piece of bread is shared with the remains of the lamb, he breaks it and says simply, without explanation, 'This is my body which is broken for you.' Then he takes the evening's third cup of wine and says over it, 'This is my blood of the new covenant, which is shed for you and for many others. Whenever you drink, do this simple thing in remembrance of me.'

They pass the cup one to another in silence; none knows what to say, how to respond. 'Come on,' he says. 'Let's go out. I need some fresh air.' The outdoor clothes turn from liturgical robes into practical necessities, and someone sheaths a couple of swords in case of trouble when all law-abiding people are safely indoors. Elsewhere in the city there is laughter and song as the wine proves its presence.

(Matthew 26:17–29; Mark 14:12–25; Luke 22:7–38; John 13:1–38)

Table talk: Jesus' mealtime teaching

'Don't worry. I'm going to prepare a place for each of you in my Father's house. I'll come back to take you there later.'

'I am the way, the truth and the life. There's no other way you can find the Father, except through me.'

'If you trust me, you'll do greater things than even I have done. Ask for anything that's in accordance with my will, and I'll do it for you.'

'When I've gone, I'll send you another comforter to be with you for ever. He's the Holy Spirit of God, the Spirit of truth who will teach you all you need to know. He will point to me always, as you must too. He will convince people of their sin and of God's right judgement on it.'

'If you love me, you'll do what I tell you.'

'I am the real vine. You are my branches. You can't be fruitful unless you stay firmly attached to me. You can do nothing without me. I chose you to go and to be fruitful.'

'My Father has loved me, and I love you. Now hear a new commandment: you are to love each other in the same way as I have loved you. There's no greater way of showing you love someone than to count your life as nothing compared with theirs.'

'People will hate you sometimes. Just remember that they hated me first. The servant can't expect any better treatment than the master.'

'Now I'm going where you can't come. But you'll see me again after a while. I'm giving you my peace, which is different to anything you'll get from what the world offers. Don't worry; I'll help you overcome all that's troublesome in the world.'

(John 14–16)

Togas are no-goes say Romans

Rome, c. AD 33

Togas are uncomfortable and impractical according to a growing number of city dwellers who are rejecting the traditional uniform in favour of more casual clothes imported from other countries.

The folded woollen rectangle which drapes over the left shoulder and is supported by the left arm is too cold in winter and too hot in summer, gives no protection against rain, and is a positive hindrance to free movement, says its

linen undergarment and a longer outer tunic which itself can be covered by a cloak in cold or wet conditions. Some more expensive garments, such as the robe worn by Jesus of Nazareth, probably a gift from an admirer, are woven without a seam. The style is almost sack-like, but clothes can be colourfully dyed for formal occasions while remaining practical at all times.

Traditionalists argue that the toga symbolises peace and wearers clearly pose no threat to other

Well-to-do Romans always wore the toga, consisting of numerous folds of material, most often worn over a T-shirt-like vest and a tunic covering the lower body.
White was the only colour to be worn by men. Women's togas progressively became more and more coloured, and were increasingly made of finer and finer cloth.

critics. A man cannot run or fight while wearing one, and most men now ignore the custom of wearing little under it for the sake of added comfort from under-tunics.

Toga-wearers are looking enviously at the fashions of other cultures. The Jews, for example, wear much simpler robes; a waist-length

pedestrians. It provides a modest covering and different colours give public awareness of a person's rank. They are not likely to win the argument. Dress at banquets is now becoming so exotic that there is a good trade in imported fashion, and some party-goers even turn up in nothing but their jewellery.

Secret arrest for public figure

Jerusalem, April c. AD 33

A large force of heavily-armed temple guards and Roman soldiers has arrested Jesus of Nazareth on suspicion of sedition under cover of darkness.

The arrest took place at Gethsemane, a private and secluded olive grove on the edge of the Mount of Olives, which Jesus frequently uses as a prayer garden.

The Garden of Gethsemane contains ancient olive trees, some of which might even have witnessed the arrest of Jesus.

The arrest, as pictured by Zefferelli in the film *Jesus of Nazareth*.

The guards were accompanied by religious leaders and were led to the spot by Judas Iscariot, one of Jesus' inner circle of 12 disciples. He identified the teacher in the shadows by embracing him.

Jesus went with the guards without resistance. There was one minor scuffle when his lieutenant Simon Peter lashed out with a sword, severing the ear of Malchus, a senior servant to the high priest. But Jesus immediately ordered Peter to stop and he healed the victim. He did complain, however, at his captors' unnecessary weapons and their covert action; he had not been on the run and could have been taken openly in daylight.

After the arrest Jesus' followers melted into the night. One, believed to be the teenage John Mark whose family own the garden where he was sleeping as nightwatchman, lost his tunic in the melee and ran away naked.

According to sources close to the group, it was not the first drama of the evening prayer meeting. Jesus had commended them to God, asking that they might be united in love and truth and protected from evil in the world. He also prayed that they would see the glory he had enjoyed with God since creation.

But then he grew anxious and distressed as he contemplated his own future. His friends awoke from sleep to find him agonising over 'the cup' he was about to drink. Despite the cool temperature, he was pouring sweat and bursting blood vessels. Three times he pleaded with God to release him from what lay ahead, but concluded that he would do God's will if it would achieve his purposes. His disciples could not recall ever having seen him in such a state before.

(Matthew 26:36–56; Mark 14:32–52; Luke 22:40–53; John 17:1–18:11)

Personal failure adds to grief

Jerusalem, c. AD 33

There were no dry eyes among Jesus' supporters as they watched the events following his arrest unfold (see next story). But the wettest eyes belonged to Simon Peter who unwittingly fulfilled Jesus' prediction that he would disown his master.

The right-hand man fell to pieces when, skulking in a corner of the high priests' courtyard around a hastily-lit charcoal fire, he was asked by servants kept awake by the frenetic activity if he was a supporter of the Galilean prisoner. One of his interrogators was a relative of Malchus, whose ear he had cut off in the skirmish.

Unable to hide his Galilean accent but gripped by paralysing fear and panic, three times he vehemently denied any association with him. At 3.00 a.m. a cock crowed heralding the dawn, and Jesus' prediction was fulfilled to the second. The strong man of the team had thrown in the towel.

(Matthew 26:57–58, 69–75; Mark 14:53–54, 66–72; Luke 22:54–62; John 18:15–18, 25–27)

Doubts raised over legality of hurried night-time trials

Jerusalem, c. AD 33

At least one member of the Jewish Sanhedrin, Joseph of Arimathea, has protested against the hasty trials of Jesus of Nazareth which resulted in him being sentenced to death by the Roman procurator.

Doubts are being raised in the city about the legality of the night-time court hearings which resulted in a verdict being reached in barely 12 hours, despite conflicting evidence from prosecution witnesses in three separate examinations.

Following his arrest Jesus was first examined by Annas, the former high priest and father-in-law of the present incumbent. When asked about his teaching Jesus suggested questioning those who had heard him, a remark which earned him a thrashing for insolence. He was transferred to Caiaphas who presided over a full emergency session of the Sanhedrin, ignoring its rules prohibiting night trials.

Here, as at all other times during this bizarre night, witnesses failed to agree with each other and gave every impression of being little more than hired actors. Jesus treated their evidence with silent contempt. He had promised, they alleged, to destroy the temple and rebuild it in three days.

But after a final desperate attempt by Caiaphas to make some charges stick by asking Jesus directly if he was the Son of God, the teacher signed his own death warrant by answering simply, 'I am'. The assembly dissolved into uproar as outraged councillors arraigned him for blasphemy. After an adjournment, during which Jesus had a taste of the rough justice of power-crazed soldiers, the court reconvened at first light to pronounce sentence and to refer the case to Pontius Pilate.

The procurator, despite his well-earned reputation for hardness, faced an unenviable dilemma not made any easier by a warning from his superstitious wife that the prisoner had given her bad dreams. He recognised that the core issue was religious, but it had been presented to him as political. The charge of blasphemy was equivalent, it was alleged, to sedition, because Jesus made himself out as a king.

Pilate shuttled between private meetings with Jesus, who maintained a regal silence for much of the time, and public discussion with the religious authorities and, ultimately, with the ever-growing crowd of onlookers.

At one point he used a legal loophole to transfer Jesus to Herod Antipas, tetrarch of Galilee, because Jesus came from his territory. The outcome of that brief trial was as indecisive as the others. Herod sent Jesus back dressed in royal robes which Pilate interpreted, rightly, as a verdict of not guilty of anything except madness. The joke had one positive result; it repaired his strained relationship with Herod.

In a final attempt to release a man who was unusual but clearly not dangerous, Pilate offered the waiting crowd a traditional Roman opportunity to utter a verdict and give an amnesty. He suggested releasing either Jesus, to whom they had given a hero's welcome only a week before, or the convicted murderer Barabbas, who was awaiting execution. They voted to crucify Jesus. And anything else, the prosecution alleged, would be disloyalty to Caesar.

Publicly and literally washing his hands of the affair, Pilate took his

---

The cardo (a colonaded street) is all that remains of Roman military and judicial rule in Jerusalem.

---

formal seat at The Pavement, near his palace, delivered the verdict, passed the death sentence, and let the system take over. Jesus was scourged with a bone-studded leather whip, a punishment so severe that it could take a man to the point of death.

Too weak to carry his cross to the place of execution on Golgotha, a small hill to the north-west of the city, Jesus staggered through crowds of jeering and weeping pilgrims. The cross was forced on a bystander, an African named Simon of Cyrene, who discovered what it felt like to be a condemned man. But unlike Jesus, he was allowed to walk away from the cross at the critical moment.

(Matthew 26:57–67; 27:1,2,11–31; Mark 14:53–65; 15:1–20; Luke 22:54–70; 23:1–25; John 18:12–40; 19:1–16)

Dark night of the soul as Jewish 'Messiah' is executed on cross

Jerusalem, c. AD 33

Jesus of Nazareth has been executed on charges of sedition by order of the Roman procurator of Judea and by popular acclaim. His death dashes the widespread hope that he was the 'Messiah' or special divine deliverer of Israel.

The crucifixion, the most universal of Christian images, by Rembrandt.

As the emaciated figure, now looking much older than his 30-odd years, almost crawled to the execution site, the weather turned unseasonally dark and foreboding. It was like the twilight of a solar eclipse as he and two other criminals were nailed to their crosses. It was a strangely appropriate symbol for what many here regard as a dark day for the nation in which the causes of truth and justice seemed also to be eclipsed by the unseemly hurry of the untidy trials.

Jesus of Nazareth had stripped the establishment of the robes of tradition and exposed the nakedness of official ritualism. In its place he had offered spiritual comfort and hope to thousands of ordinary people in terms they could understand. He combined his common touch as a teacher with a compassion for the outcast and an unprecedented gift as a healer of all kinds of ailments.

He hung beneath the inscription, 'The King of the Jews', put up at Pilate's orders despite local protests, implying, perhaps, some secret admiration for the man the procurator had been unable to fathom. Jesus retained a regal dignity to the very end, which led one of the normally cynical Roman executioners to exclaim, 'Truly this man was the Son of God!'

Subjected to the intense physical pain and slow death from crucifixion, he proved in his extremity the depths of his sincerity. He who had offered forgiveness of sins to many prayed that his captors might be forgiven. Having refused a mild anaesthetic to ease the agony, he had the presence of mind to give spiritual encouragement to one of his fellow victims, and as a dutiful elder son to authorise his close friend John Zebedee to take care of his widowed mother Mary.

But the man who had walked on water, calmed the storm, healed the sick and raised the dead was unable – or unwilling – to respond to the taunts of some bystanders and prove his divine origins by saving himself from this ignoble end. As the darkness drew in he died surprisingly quickly, uttering in his last moments the spine-chilling cry to God, 'Why have you left me alone?'

Later in the day anxious religious leaders petitioned for a speedy death; their laws forbid burial on the Sabbath which was due to begin at 6:00 p.m. A seasoned soldier sent to break the victims' legs – thus preventing them supporting themselves and making breathing virtually impossible – believed Jesus to be already dead but made doubly sure by thrusting a spear into his side. The tell-tale flow of separated blood and plasma confirmed death had already occurred.

Following a hasty burial of the body in a nearby tomb owned by wealthy Sanhedrin member Joseph of Arimathea, a supporter of Jesus who had tried to mediate in the legal proceedings, the rest of his disciples went into hiding. They fear a crackdown by the authorities and face an uncertain future without the teacher for whom they gave up everything for three years.

(Matthew 27:33–61; Mark 15:22–47; Luke 23:26–50; John 19:17–42)

The hill of the skull, just outside Jerusalem, is one of the two sites identified as Golgotha.

Betrayer found dead in field

Jerusalem, April c. AD 33

Judas Iscariot, the follower of Jesus who led the authorities to arrest him at his secret garden, has been found hanging in a field. There were no suspicious circumstances and it is assumed that he committed suicide.

Shortly before he was found he had returned the money he had been paid for his information and protested that Jesus was innocent of any crime. Yet he had taken the initiative about a week before the arrest, offering to help the authorities to take Jesus into custody away from the crowds.

There is much speculation among the followers of Jesus as to why someone so close to him should have acted as Judas did. It is believed that as the only southerner of the 12 he may have been out of sympathy with the rest. However, he was included in all the group's activities of teaching and healing.

As group treasurer he is known to have misused funds, but the scale of his betrayal seems small. He was paid the normal price for a slave, 120 denarii (about four months' wages for a labourer) for his information, hardly a fortune and unlikely to have been the main

Judas returns the thirty pieces of silver to the high priests by Rembrandt (1606 –1669).

motive for such an extreme action.

There have been suggestions that he was an 'agent in place'. It is rumoured that he had once been a student in training for the priesthood, and therefore had natural sympathies for the establishment. But there is no evidence that he had ever traded information before, and no one could have anticipated Jesus' meteoric rise to fame in which such a double agent might have been useful to the authorities.

It is possible, especially in the light of his return of the money, that he was genuinely anxious for Jesus'

welfare and felt obliged to arrange the arrest for his master's own safety, only to discover that safety was not what the chief priests had in mind. More likely, he was frustrated by Jesus' persistent refusal to show his hand as Messiah, and hoped that by being catapulted into the corridors of power Jesus would inaugurate the new kingdom quickly.

So bemused are the other disciples that they are attributing the inexplicable deed to Satan. They suggest that Judas Iscariot became infected by a demonic agent which blinded his perception, clouded his judgement, and drove him into precipitate action.

What is beyond question is that the outcome was not what he intended. His hasty suicide bore the marks of bitter frustration over events outside of his power, and of the inability of a complex personality to face his former colleagues with explanations they would not understand. The Jesus drama has ended not with one tragedy but with two.

(Matthew 26:14–16; 27:3–10; Mark 14:10–11; Luke 22:3–6; John 12:6; Acts 1:18–19)

Words that pierced the gloom

'I am a king, but my kingdom is not the sort which currently reigns in the world. Otherwise my friends would fight.' (Jesus; John 18:36,37)

'I came into the world to bear witness to truth. Everyone who is on truth's side will listen to me.' (Jesus; John 18:37)

'What is truth?' (Pilate; John 18:38)

'I find no legal basis on which to charge Jesus. Look – here is the man.' (Pilate; John 19:4,5)

'This man has done nothing wrong. Jesus, remember me when you come into your kingly realm.' (The thief on the cross; Luke 23:41,42)

'You would have no authority to kill me unless God had given it to you.' (Jesus; John 19:11)

'I tell you the truth: you'll be with me in paradise before the day's out.' (Jesus; Luke 23:43)

'If you're really the Son of God, get off the cross and prove it!' (The bystanders; Matthew 27:40)

'Father God, I hand over my spirit into your safe hands.'

(Jesus; Luke 23:46)

c. AD 33

Missing body 'seen alive'

Jerusalem, c. AD 33

The Jesus enigma will not lie down. Crucified, certified dead, buried in tight bandages under even tighter security in a locked cave, his corpse is now missing amid claims that it has gone walking. People in increasing numbers are saying they have seen him, spoken to him, even eaten with him. Extensive enquiries have not revealed the whereabouts of the body.

According to official sources the body was stolen by Jesus' followers who are now claiming that he has risen from the dead. The chief priests were aware that Jesus had apparently predicted his own resurrection; his followers, surprisingly, had been more reluctant to take his words at face value. A guard had been mounted at the tomb as a precaution against a carefully-mounted hoax.

Soldiers guarding the rock-hewn tomb just outside the city's northern defences have admitted falling asleep on duty. But they have not been punished and are likely only to be repeating the official line. Privately they are saying that they witnessed some supernatural event which caused the stone door to move open and gave them the

The sun rising over the Lake of Galilee symbolises the resurrection.

fright of their lives.

The tomb was discovered to be empty by several women early on the Sunday morning following the crucifixion. They had gone there to complete the mummification of the corpse and included Mary Magdalene and the mothers of three of Jesus' inner circle, Salome Zebedee and Mary Alphaeus. They reported the matter to the disciples, and later in the day Mary Magdalene had what is believed to have been the first encounter with the re-living Jesus (see opposite).

It is difficult to see what anyone could hope to gain either from a simple theft or from a complex hoax. The authorities need only to

produce the body, if they have it, to end all speculation. The disciples, if they have it, are unlikely to be able to keep it secret for long. One of their number, Judas Iscariot, has already defected and there could be others with a faith weaker than the desire for fame or fortune.

It is also conceivable that one of those who now live in fear of arrest and possible execution will spill the beans under interrogation or torture. Indeed the panic attack they collectively experienced after the execution seems itself to rule out the likelihood that they could perpetuate a lie.

Another possibility is that Jesus himself moved the stone, having been placed in the tomb unconscious but not dead. Against this, it is evident that he was half-dead even before the execution and the Roman soldiers on duty that day are convinced he showed no sign of breath or heartbeat. Indeed, even the temporary graveclothes would have been suffocating.

According to John Zebedee, who examined the tomb, the graveclothes were intact with headpiece laid to one side, implying a resurrection to a new form of life. Either it is all in the imagination, or it happened. Either way, the arguments among baffled people here look set to continue.

(Matthew 27:62–28:15; Mark 16:1–8; Luke 23:50–24:12; John 20:1–9)

The Garden Tomb, just outside the walls of Jerusalem; one probable site of the burial.

Strange encounters of a very personal kind with 'risen' Jesus

'There were angels in the garden'

The women who discovered the empty tomb claim to have encountered angels there. The shining figures explained that Jesus had risen from the dead and was going ahead of his disciples into Galilee. They ran back to their friends trembling with fear. (Matthew 28:2–8; Mark 16:5–8; Luke 24:2–9)

'I thought he was a gardener'

After Peter and John had examined the tomb, Mary Magdalene stayed behind, alone in her grief. Suddenly she saw someone who she assumed was the gardener, and asked him if he knew where the body was. He spoke her name gently: 'Mary!' She recognised Jesus' familiar voice. (John 20:10–18)

'We thought he was a ghost'

The disciples were huddled together behind locked doors fearing it would be their turn for the gallows next. Without warning, Jesus was standing among them. Startled, they thought he was a ghost; he had not used the door. 'Peace!' he said.

The meal at Emmaus by Rembrandt (1606–1669).

'A ghost doesn't have flesh and bones! Got any food I can have?' And he ate some fish in front of them, and began teaching again. (Luke 24:36–49; John 20:19–22)

'We met him on the road'

Two of Jesus' followers set off for home after the Passover festivities along the road to Emmaus about 11 km (7 miles) out of Jerusalem. A stranger joined them and they walked together discussing the death of Jesus. He explained that the Scriptures had predicted such things. At an inn, they invited him to join them for a meal. He gave thanks over some bread and broke it. They recognised the unmistakeable action; it was Jesus himself. But he left at once. (Luke 24: 13–35)

'I didn't believe a word of it'

Thomas, one of the 12, was missing when Jesus entered the locked house in Jerusalem. He thought the others were mad when they told him their news. 'Let me put my fingers into the nail holes, then I'll believe!' he said. A week later Jesus appeared again to them all and Thomas got his chance to prove the reality. But one sight was enough. 'My Lord and my God!' he gasped. (John 20:24–29)

'He showed us where to fish'

After a while, the disciples went back to their home base of Galilee. Peter went off to fish with the Zebedee brothers and two others. They caught nothing all night. As they were heading for the shore in the morning, a figure called to them and told them to put their nets down. They tried it – and netted a huge catch. Suddenly John realised the figure was Jesus; Peter, still impulsive, left the others to haul in the fish while he swam ashore. (John 21:1–14)

'He put me back together'

Simon Peter, the spokesman of the group of 12 disciples, had denied knowing Jesus three times while his leader was on trial. It made no difference to the outcome, but it made a big difference to Peter. He seemed ready to go back to his old way of life.

On the shores of Galilee, Jesus recommissioned him. Three times he told him to 'feed my sheep', hav-

A fire burns at dawn by the Lake of Galilee.

ing drawn from Peter a confession of love and commitment. Jesus also warned Peter that he too would die for his faith. (John 21:15–19)

'My brother came home'

James, the brother of Jesus and one of the family of at least five children who had considered the teacher to be out of his mind in the early days of his ministry, received a personal visit from the risen Jesus. No details of the content of their discussion are available. (Mark 3:21; 6.3; 1 Corinthians 15:7)

'We all saw him at once'

A crowd of 500 people claim Jesus addressed them at a meeting. (1 Corinthians 15:6)

Is this the end of Jesus' story?

Jerusalem, c. AD 33

Jesus of Nazareth has disappeared. No more sightings are being reported of the man who was crucified and who his followers claim came back to life again.

The latest appearance of Jesus to his disciples also seems to have been the most dramatic. At a pre-arranged meeting on the Mount of Olives, south-east of Jerusalem, he left them in a manner which they interpret as being his final farewell.

Having taught them for a while, he disappeared from view slowly, rather than suddenly as he has before. According to the witnesses, it was as if he were being carried out of this world into the next. A cloud hid him from sight, and reminded them of the shining cloud they had seen at the transfiguration.

'We'd asked him whether the time had come for him to restore the kingdom at last,' one of them reported later. 'He told us yet again

The Mount of Olives, just outside the old city of Jerusalem.

These spring fields in Galilee provide a reminder of Jesus' ascension.

that it was none of our business to know when God would act decisively in history. All we were to do was to go to Jerusalem, wait for something to happen – he didn't tell us exactly what but he said we'd

know when it did – and then we were to be his witnesses in every part of the world. Our travelling days aren't over yet, it seems!'

Some of them also reported a vision of angels who told them that Jesus would one day return to earth in a similar manner to his departure. That would seem to rule out any possibility that his future followers could claim to be reincarnations of him, or indeed to claim further 'appearances' of the kind they have experienced over the past six weeks or so.

(Luke 24:50–53; Acts 1:6–11)

Get ready to go!

Jerusalem, c. AD 33

In terms reminiscent of the ancient Israelites' departure from Egypt, for which they had to be prepared in advance and ready to travel light, Jesus of Nazareth has spent the past few weeks of his post-death appearances preparing his closest followers for their continuation of his ministry on his behalf.

In a formal commissioning, he ordered them to go into every part of the world, to make disciples of others by teaching them all they had themselves learned from Jesus. They were also told to perform a rit-

ual washing or baptism on converts as a sign of their commitment to 'the Father, Son and Holy Spirit'.

Their journey was not to start until they received a definite and unmistakeable signal, however, which he said would be like 'being dressed in God's power'. He declined to give further explanation, preferring to spend his time explaining the Scriptures and the references in them to himself as Messiah.

He did promise, however, that in some different way he would be with them at all times and in all places. That is being taken as a reference to 'another comforter, God's Spirit' who he spoke of during his final supper with them before the execution. On one occasion he breathed over them in a kind of acted parable, saying 'Receive the Holy Spirit', implying that the Spirit is God's breath of life.

He also promised them that they would receive divine protection from the troubles they would encounter, and would have the power to heal as well as to teach. The message was clearly 'business as usual' after the traumas of the past couple of months.

(Matthew 28:16–20; Mark 16:14–20;
Luke 24:44–49; Acts 1:3–8)

Hard life for hard men

Rome and Judea, c. AD 33

Had Roman soldiers allegedly fallen asleep during the night that Jesus of Nazareth's body disappeared from his tomb, they would have been punished severely by their comrades. Each man whose life had been endangered would strike or stone the culprit, often until he died, in a camp beating.

Soldiers who do well are praised and rewarded publicly. If a general is miserly with his praise, he can expect mutiny. But to the consternation of subject peoples such as the Judeans, Roman soldiers also enjoy another perk of the job – rape and pillage. They are usually let loose on a town they occupy and are allowed to keep any valuables they find. However, the resident garrison in Judea is relatively restrained and acts as a peace-keeping force.

Only Roman citizens, or freemen, can join the army. They must be taxpayers and householders, and aged between 17 and 46. Those who have fought 16 infantry campaigns, or 10 cavalry, are automatically retired. There is no conscription except when Rome is officially at war. Once selected, the would-be warrior cannot fight until he has sworn an oath called the sacramentum. It binds him to the power of the general and releases him from the prohibitions of civilian life.

A soldier's life is hard, but it could be worse. He never sleeps under the stars, a practice which Romans consider is fit only for barbarians. However, when arriving at a new place after a long march, the tired soldiers must pitch their leather tents and build a camp before earning their sleep.

Camps are usually surrounded by a ditch, and the excavated earth is piled into an embankment on which a stake fence is set. They are always built on the same plan. Two axes, one running north-south the other east-west, divide it into quadrants with gates at the four cardinal points. The general's tent is at the centre, and doubles as a temple.

Soldiers wear dark red tunics (to hide the blood stains) as well as their armour and insignia.

Weapons include short and long swords and spears up to 2 m (2 yd) long. Rations are adequate but not lavish and when on a campaign soldiers eat little but wheat bread.

Their secret weapon is discipline. Whereas the Gauls and other tribes use magical rituals to put soldiers into trances and to make them bloodthirsty, the Romans remain stoical and efficient. They are unmoved by emotion and submit passively to both the insults of enemies and the loss of comrades. For that, they are greatly feared.

officers helmet

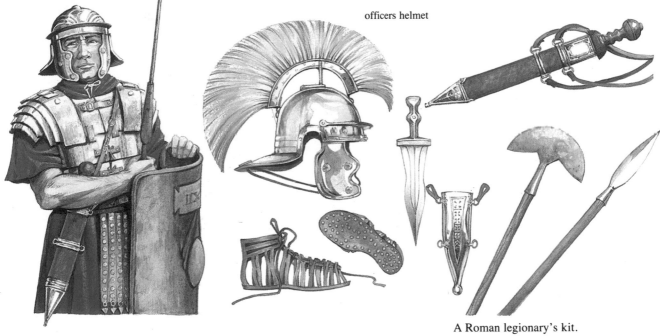

A Roman legionary's kit.

Fast Facts AD 30–35

Rome. Books on agriculture, medicine, military science and rhetoric have been combined into an encyclopaedia called *Artes* by Aulus Cornelius Celsus. It is the first major encyclopaedia to be published for 50 years since Varro's *Disciplinae*. In the medical section, Celsus has formulated four cardinal signs of inflammation: pain, redness, heat and swelling.

China. Ginseng 'invigorates the five organs, calms the mind and prolongs life' according to the newly-published classic of herbal medicine. It lists 365 drugs from plant, mineral and animal origins and classifies them as superior, average or inferior. The 120 superior drugs are non-toxic and have an invigorating effect. The 120 average drugs, some of which are toxic, are used as tonics to resist illness and include Chinese angelica and the stalwart ephedra. Among the other drugs described are sage, asparagus, magnolia, licorice, lily, peony, rhubarb and Japanese plum. The book describes the source of each medicinal plant, and how to prepare it for use.

Mass baptism of new converts

Jerusalem, c. AD 33

A mass baptism of some 3,000 people has taken place as leaders of a new cult focusing on the recently crucified Jesus of Nazareth converted pilgrims with a display of spiritual phenomena and persuasive preaching.

Some three months after his public execution for sedition, followers of Jesus are still claiming that he has risen from the dead. No sightings of him have been reported for six weeks, but they are now suggesting that his 'Spirit', who they seem to equate with him and with God, has inaugurated what they call 'the last days'.

The cult suddenly sprang into new life as Jews celebrated the wheat harvest in their annual Feast of Pentecost. Early in the morning some 120 followers of Jesus were meeting in a large house for prayer when they were corporately struck by what they claim was a manifestation of God's power. Along with an inner sense of God's love and presence, they also experienced sensory phenomena like a wind and visual phenomena like flames.

They spontaneously broke into worship in languages they say they had never learned but which were given them by God. This outburst drew a crowd of curious onlookers, some of whom recognised some of the languages. (The population of Jerusalem, estimated between 55,000 and 90,000, is swollen at least 10 times at festivals by pilgrims who trek in from all quarters of the empire.)

According to their spokesman, Simon Peter, the outburst was not that of early-morning drinkers as some bystanders suggested (Jews tend to eat – and drink – later in the day). Rather, it had been forecast in the biblical prophets. He quoted Joel, probably written some 400 years ago, who foretold that the heavens would fall and people would prophesy before God's final judgement. As the heavens have

The immersion of the pilgrims in the River Jordan, as observed in 1839 by David Roberts.

not yet fallen, the Jesus followers are claiming that this is the beginning of the last days.

In explaining the phenomena, Peter claimed that Jesus of Nazareth was God's promised Messiah, a deliverer who would set up a new order. But despite his perfect life, his miracles and teaching, he was wrongly executed. God had vindicated him by raising him from the dead, Peter claimed. His speech caused widespread concern, and 3,000 brokenhearted people were baptised in water as a sign of their sorrow and their desire to follow the risen Jesus.

The disciples, as they are called, are said to have an unusual common life. Like cult communes elsewhere, they share their possessions freely with each other, but they do not generally live together. Nor have they so far been accused of deviant behaviour. They meet regularly to receive instruction in their faith, and to eat a memorial meal recalling the death of Jesus.

(Acts 2:1–47)

Man eats bed and dies

Rome, AD 33

Drusus, the son of Germanicus and grandson of the emperor Tiberius, has starved to death in a palace cellar. In a desperate attempt to stay alive, he ate his mattress, but to no avail. He had been declared a public enemy of the state and imprisoned. His brother Nero, also a declared a public enemy, committed suicide two years ago on the island of Pontia.

Tiberius had recommended both to the Senate, but when he discovered that senators were offering prayers for their safety as well as for his own, he became displeased. He arranged for false charges to be brought against them. The bodies of both were chopped into so many pieces that it proved difficult to collect them for burial.

It is believed that Nero's suicide was forced on him by an executioner who threatened him with a noose and hooks to drag him to the Tiber.

Beggar is cured while asking preachers for cash

Jerusalem, c. AD 33

A crippled beggar got more than he bargained for when he asked two men for money. Instead of cash, he got a cure. And his healers got a night in jail as their reward.

Peter healing the cripple as seen by Masolino (1383–1447).

Previously unable to walk properly, the unnamed beggar was a familiar sight at the somewhat inappropriately-named Beautiful Gate, a popular entrance to the temple and a haunt of beggars. When the two men, Peter and John, leaders of the sect following Jesus of Nazareth, spoke to him, the 40-year-old sprang to his feet and began leaping around like a 2-year-old.

They had told him they had no money to give, but could offer him something more valuable, and by pronouncing the name of Christ apparently effected an instant cure. The catch is that he will now have to work for a living.

The incident did not meet with official approval. As crowds gathered to hear Peter explain the story of Jesus, and his death and resurrection, Jewish leaders includ-ing Sadducees who deny any resurrection arrested the two men for creating a public disturbance. In their trial the following day, the two men stated that Jesus was the Christ who had been rejected by the people but raised from death by God.

In accordance with Jewish law, Peter and John were bound over to keep the peace and warned not to speak in the name of Jesus again. They could not be imprisoned for a first offence of this nature. However, future incarceration looks more than likely; they refused point-blank to accept the conditions of their discharge.

The sect is now said to number some 5,000 people and appears to be growing rapidly. Its members exhibit a strong care for the poor and needy among them, and are frequently seen preaching in the streets.

(Acts 3:1–4:36)

'Drop dead!' And she did!

Jerusalem, c. AD 34

A husband and wife have both dropped dead, apparently as a direct result of lying to their God, leaving bystanders in a state of shock.

Although the man's death could possibly be explained as the result of a sudden heart attack, his wife's demise a few hours later had been predicted, if not commanded, by the leader of the sect of which they had been members.

Ananias and Sapphira had, like others of the followers of Jesus Christ, sold land for the common purse. They had retained some of the proceeds for themselves, which they were entitled to do but which they hid from their leaders, pretending that they had given everything away.

According to Simon Peter, their leader, they had therefore lied to God. Sapphira, unaware of her husband's death, was cross-examined and when she corroborated his story was told that she would be carried out feet first. She is said to have immediately dropped dead at Peter's feet.

Members of the sect are said to be in a state of shock. Ordinary people who have contact with the group tend to regard it with a mixture of awe and fear. It seems to have stumbled upon a terrifying spiritual power and to have converted to an unusually active God whose hand of judgement can squash people like flies.

However, he also appears to be benevolent towards some people. Since the incident, there have been reports of numerous healings in the name of Jesus Christ. People are even laying their sick relatives out in the streets in the superstitious hope of a miracle cure if the shadow of one of the leaders crosses them in passing.

(Acts 5:1–16)

Colonnade in the temple precinct.

Stephen stoned for blasphemy

Jerusalem, AD 35

A senior official of the new sect of Christians has been stoned to death for blasphemy by a crowd of orthodox Jews, with the approval of their leaders.

Following the execution, the religious authorities launched a major attack on Christians. Saul of Tarsus, who supervised the execution, has begun arresting Christians in their homes and imprisoning them.

Stephen was accused of blaspheming the Law of Moses, largely because he denounced scribal additions to the Scriptures and asserted that the real presence of God is not confined to the temple. He also proclaimed Christ's superiority over both law and temple.

Arguments over Stephen's assertions had been strong for some time in the synagogues, where Christians continue to meet for worship in addition to holding their own sectarian meetings. His opponents at the trial came mostly from synagogues formed by freed Roman slaves, immigrants from Cyrenia, Alexandria, Cilicia and Asia.

West Temple Mount. There was no lack of stones – or suitable places for a ritual stoning just outside the temple walls, Jerusalem.

In denying the charges, Stephen conducted his own defence before the high priest. He outlined the familiar story of God's choice of the Israelites, his provision of leaders for them, and their subsequent rejection of both God and their leaders.

Among his examples were Joseph, sold off by his brothers, and Moses, rejected in his absence on Mount Sinai. Finally, claimed Stephen, the people of his own day had rejected Jesus Christ, the long-expected Messiah.

Quoting from Isaiah 66 he also argued that God himself had claimed not to be restricted to buildings such as the temple: 'Heaven is my throne, and the earth my footstool. What kind of house will you build for me?'

During the trial, observers were struck by Stephen's appearance. Despite facing charges which if proven carried the death penalty, his face was radiant – like that of an angel, said some who were present.

But his speech outraged the court. His claims were answered only by anger, not by arguments. The last straw came when he claimed to see a vision of heaven with Christ standing at God's right hand. In what was in effect a riot, the deacon was dragged from the city and summarily executed by stoning.

Even then, Stephen prayed, as Jesus had prayed, for the forgiveness of his captors and that his spirit would be received in heaven.

Stephen, recently appointed as one of the seven 'deacons' ministering to Greek-speaking Christian groups in Jerusalem, is believed to be the first of the sect to be officially executed for their beliefs since the crucifixion of Jesus about four years ago.   (Acts 6:8–8:3)

Deacons avoid a racial rift

Jerusalem, c. AD 34

A threatened rift between Greek-speaking and Hebrew-speaking Jews who have joined the Christian church has been avoided by the appointment of 'deacons'.

All bear Greek names and were chosen by the dissenters themselves. They had complained that they were being discriminated against in the church's charity handouts.

The appointment was proposed by the apostles, the senior leaders, who accepted that there was a problem. They felt their role of teaching and preaching was being hindered by the administrative burden of overseeing food distribution to the poorer church members, a task which others could take over.

The seven 'deacons', as they are called, are Stephen, Philip, Procorus, Nicanor, Timon, Parmenas and Nicolas (the latter being a Gentile convert rather than a born-Jew). The appointment was ratified by the apostles in a ceremony which included prayer and the laying-on of hands.

(Acts 6:1–7)

The key points of Stephen's speech

- Abraham was chosen by God to be Israel's ancestor.
- The patriarchs sold Joseph through jealousy.
- God used Joseph to save his family.
- Moses grew up in Egypt and was initially rejected as a leader.
- After 40 years, he was called to lead Israel to freedom.
- The people refused to obey him in the desert.
- The tabernacle was the meeting place until the temple.
- The Israelites killed prophets who foretold Jesus Christ.
- He too has been rejected in the same way.

Good Samaritan response to gospel

Sebaste, c. AD 35

People of Sebaste (Samaria) are becoming Christians following the visit of Philip the deacon and the apostles Peter and John.

But local celebrity magician Simon Magus has been refused access to the apostles' secrets, despite offering them a large cash donation.

Philip, one of the seven Greek-speaking Christians appointed to handle food distribution, turned from table-serving to preaching, healing and exorcism as he travelled among the Samaritans,

boldness to preach and power to do miracles.

Such was the effect that the crowds deserted Simon Magus, a magician with spectacular powers who is almost worshipped here as a heavenly being. He offered money to be taught how to pass on the Christians' powers.

But instead of accepting it, Peter literally told the magician to go to hell. He accused him of being bitter and sinful, and called on him to repent and seek God's forgiveness. Although chastened, Simon's full reaction – and that of his consort

Ruins of the Temple of Augustus, built in Samaria by King Herod.

who traditional Jews regard as heretics.

His message of Christ fell on open ears. Samaritans have long believed in a coming 'rescuer'.

Following numerous baptisms, the apostles Peter and John visited Sebaste to confirm the new believers in their faith. After they laid hands on them, the Christians experienced a further spiritual awakening which the apostles explained as the Holy Spirit coming on them. They too received

Helen, a former slave said to be an incarnation of the divine power 'Thought' – is unknown.

Samaritan communities had not encountered this form of Christianity before. The sect's founder, Jesus Christ, had visited the village of Sychar and won some followers. Other villages, however, had rejected him. He had also made a Samaritan the hero of one of his famous stories.

(Acts 8:4–25; cf. Luke 9:51–55; John 4:1–42)

Jail birds mystery flight

Jerusalem, c. AD 34

The sect of Christians have demonstrated yet again the remarkable powers with which they appear to have been endowed. Not content with healing cripples, they have added jail-breaking to their repertoire.

Several of the senior leaders had been arrested following further disturbances in the city. The charges are unclear, and some commentators are suggesting that jealousy of success rather than breach of the law lies behind the action. Certainly the architects of the arrest were religious leaders whose theology is incompatible with the claims being made for Jesus of Nazareth.

With the charismatic preachers and healers safely locked up for the night, the Sadducees retired to consider their next action. But the next day it wasn't their eyes that were red from lack of sleep but their faces. The jail was empty and the 'prisoners' were back in the market-place preaching

How they escaped is unknown. According to them, they were released by an angel. Whether this was a supernatural being or a friendly locksmith depends on one's beliefs. What is not in doubt is that the timing of the incident was nothing but providential for them.

They did however stand trial later in the day, and their defence caused some members of the Sanhedrin, the highest Jewish court, to demand their deaths for blasphemy. They were saved by an influential moderate, Gamaliel, who suggested that the sect could be a nine-day wonder. If it was not of God it would die out quickly; if it was of God they had no right to stop it.

Once again the Christians were let off with yet another order to stop preaching about forgiveness and salvation in the name of Jesus. Which, of course, they promptly ignored. (Acts 5:17–42)

Saul stopped by light on road

Damascus, c. AD 35

Saul of Tarsus, self-styled persecutor of the sect of Christians, has stunned the Jewish community here by joining those he had come to arrest.

According to his own account, he was thrown to the ground not far from Damascus by a light more dazzling than the noonday sun. It left him blind for several days. He claims it was a vision of the resurrected Jesus Christ, who told Saul to stop trying to destroy him and instead to begin serving him.

His companions also experienced the phenomenon, some seeing a light and others hearing a thundering noise. There have been no reports of unusual electric storms in the area.

Saul of Tarsus was an outstandingly bright young Pharisee who stood head and shoulders intellectually, but not physically, above his contemporaries. A man noticeably shorter than average, he has an impeccable Jewish pedigree traceable back to the tribe of Benjamin.

He pursued Christians who had fled Jerusalem following the crackdown on the sect by the temple authorities. He carried papers authorising the fugitives' arrest, although technically Jerusalem has no jurisdiction over synagogue affairs or members in Damascus.

After his experience, Saul was taken into Damascus. He recovered his sight after a Christian named Ananias laid hands on him and prayed for him.

Ananias was apparently prompted to overcome his fear of Saul's intentions by a vision in which Christ reassured him that the persecutor had himself been arrested by God.

Following their meeting, Saul was baptised into the Christian faith and spent time discussing it with the church members. The church in Damascus is thought to have been formed by Christians from the Galilee area shortly after Christ's

Saul's escape in a basket over the city walls, from a mural in a church in Damascus.

death, before the Jerusalem persecution began.

The Jewish community in this Hellenistic city is sizeable, and Saul, his youthful zeal as strong as ever, launched straight into the synagogues in an attempt to prove to the shocked and sceptical worshippers that Jesus of Nazareth was the expected Messiah.

(Acts 9:1–22; 22:3–16; 26:9–18; Galatians 1:13–17; Philippians 3:3–7;)

Acacia tree, Red Canyon, near Eilat.

Saul gets into some hot spots

Jerusalem, c. AD 37

Saul of Tarsus, who for the past three years since his sudden conversion to Christianity has been living obscurely in Arabia, has emerged from the arid desert and begun preaching again in Damascus. However, such was the heat of opposition that he was smuggled like contraband from the city by being lowered down the wall in a basket at night.

Hoping for a cooler reception at Jerusalem, he found the church here cold-shouldered him, believing that he meant to do them more harm. However, Barnabas warmed to him and introduced him favourably to the leadership.

But the intolerance level rose to fever pitch when he began debating with Greek Jews, and after two weeks he received a death threat. Christians escorted the fire-brand back to his native Tarsus.

(Acts 9:23–30; Galatians 1:17–23)

Great Day! Emperor Tiberius is dead!

The Emperor Tiberius.

Rome, 16 March AD 37
Scenes of celebration have accompanied the news that the emperor Tiberius is dead. Crowds ran through the streets shouting 'To the Tiber with Tiberius!' and praying for his eternal damnation. The circumstances surrounding his death are unclear. He had been ill, and it is rumoured that he was refused food. Other reports suggest he was poisoned.

The tyrannical and sadistic 77-year-old had ruled for 23 years, succeeding his stepfather Augustus. Before his accession he had had a brilliant military career. However, for the past 11 years he has lived in fear of assassination away from Rome on the island of Capri. It is rumoured his mental health has been unstable and his speech full of sinister language.

He was a cruel man who enjoyed watching people suffer. For much of his reign, hardly a day passed without an execution. In Capri, he watched victims thrown from a cliff after several hours of torture. He also had a private sex parlour in which boys and girls copulated in front of him in groups of three. A miserly emperor, he leaves over 2,000 million sesterces in the treasury due to rigid controls; he paid for no public games.

He is succeeded by his great-nephew Gaius, 25, son of Germanicus and Agrippina. Gaius was nicknamed Caligula ('Baby Boots')

Nahal Argot, En Gedi waterfall, Judean desert near the Dead Sea.

as a toddler by his father's soldiers on the Rhine because he dressed up in uniform. He has had little training in public life but promises to spend lavishly on chariot races.

Chancellor exchanges religion

Ethiopia, c. AD 35
A senior adviser to the Ethiopian queen mother has exchanged his adopted Jewish religion for Christianity after a chance meeting with an evangelist.

The queen mother's chancellor of the exchequer was travelling home along the Gaza road from a pilgrimage to worship God in Jerusalem. Philip, one of the seven deacons of the church in Jerusalem, joined the official's caravan in the desert, claiming he had been prompted by God to do so.

The chancellor invited the Greek-speaking evangelist to explain a portion of Hebrew prophecy he was reading at the time. Philip told him that the passage, from Isaiah 53, referred to the recently-crucified and resurrected Messiah, Jesus Christ. He went on to explain what Christians believed.

The chancellor bought the new currency of ideas on the spot, and sank his personal assets into them by being immediately baptised in a nearby river.

(Acts 8:26–40)

Fast Facts AD 35–39

Armenia, AD 35–36: Tiridates III has been crowned king at Ctesiphon, on the Tigris River some 100 km (60 miles) north of Babylon. He was sent there by the emperor Tiberius with the military support of the governor of Syria to expel Artabanus III. Artabanus, king of Parthia since AD 12, has accepted Roman sovereignty in Armenia in return for power in Parthia.

Rome, AD 36: Pontius Pilate, prefect of Judea for the past decade, has been summoned to Rome and is to be removed from office. It is believed complaints were laid against him by Samaritans. On his arrival in Judea he offended Jews by bringing images of the emperor into Jerusalem. He has been described as inflexible, merciless, and obstinate. He did concede to the Jews the crucifixion of Jesus of Nazareth on a charge of sedition.

Rome, AD 37: The emperor Caligula has suffered from what appear to be a nervous breakdown. On his recovery, he declared himself an absolute monarch. The emperor also suffers from epileptic fits.

Rome, August AD 37: The temple of Augustus has been dedicated by Caligula. It was begun by Tiberius, one of only two public works which he undertook. The other was the restoration of Pompey's theatre, which he also failed to complete before his death

Italy, May AD 38: Tiberius Gemellus, the emperor's adopted son, has been executed, and Caligula is now seeking out aristocratic partisans of the whole Claudius family and executing them under newly-revived laws of treason.

Prison food, AD 39: When wild animals had been collected for a circus, Caligula objected to the price being asked for butcher's meat to feed to them. He ordered that they be fed with criminals instead. A prison spokesman said that without looking at the charge sheets, the emperor ordered a random group to be killed.

Caligula reverses himself over temple statue

Rome, c. AD 40
In a major reversal, the emperor Caligula (Gaius) has revoked his own order to erect a statue of himself as Jupiter in the Jewish temple at Jerusalem.

He had made the order in a fit of rage after Jews in Jamnia, in western Palestine, had allegedly insulted him. The Jews, who coexist uneasily there with a substantial Greek population, had objected to Greek plans to erect the emperor's statue in common with most other cities in the empire.

Their objection was reported back to Caligula as an insulting treason, and he dispatched the legate of Syria, Petronius, and two legions of soldiers, to erect the statue in the central shrine of the Jewish religion.

In a mass demonstration of civil disobedience, thousands of Jews refused to work the fields, and some lay down in front of the soldiers, preferring to be killed rather than see the statue erected. They do not have the arms or organisation to pose a military challenge to Roman forces.

While Petronius was in corres-pondence with Caligula over the impasse, King Agrippa of the Jews, was dining with the emperor. Court sources say that during the party Agrippa was offered the imperial equivalent of a fairy godmother's three wishes, and he asked for the order to be revoked out of respect for all gods.

As a result, the tolerance of the unique Jewish belief in only one God and their refusal to engage in any form of ceremonial honouring the emperor continues as official policy for the time being.

Caligula on horseback, Pompeii.

Civil disturbances in Mauretania follow murder of King Ptolemy

Mauretania, c. AD 40–41
Civil disturbances have been put down by Roman general Suetonius Paulinus in this province on the Mediterranean coast of North Africa. Paulinus has used the opportunity to extend Roman influence southwards into the Sahara Desert.

The disturbances followed the execution of the local king Ptolemy who had been summoned to Rome and executed by his cousin, the emperor Caligula. It is unclear exactly what crime he had commit-ted. Some suggest Caligula killed him for wearing a purple cloak in public; or that he was too wealthy; or that it was a high-level decision to annex Mauretania.

Ptolemy, son of Juba II and Cleopatra Selene (and thus a grandson of Antony), had been king of Mauretania since AD 23.

Fast Facts AD 40-43

France, AD 40: Speculation mounted over Caligula's mental health as he prepared for the long-awaited invasion of Britain. As the army drew up on the Channel coast, he ordered them to gather sea shells. He considered them 'plunder from the ocean'. His 'victory' is to be commemorat-ed by the erection of a tall lighthouse. The invas-ion did not take place.

Rome, AD 40: Caligula's palace has been extended all the way to the Forum, turning the shrine of Castor and Pollux into his vestibule. A new shrine to Caligula as god has been built, at which flaming-goes, peacocks, grouse, guinea hens and pheasants are offered. A life-size golden image of the emperor will be dressed every day in clothes identical to those he is wearing.

Central America, c. AD 40: The Arawak people have canoed the length of the Orinoco River and have settled in Iguana Island (San Salvador). They are skilled farmers and irrigate the land. They are also settling on many of the West Indian islands, including Jamaica and Cuba. They use their dug-out canoes for fishing, hunting and travel-ling.

Corsica, AD 41: The writer and orator, Lucius Annaeus Seneca, has been banished here by Caligula. It is alleged that Seneca had an affair with the emperor's sister, Julia Livilla.

North Africa, AD 42: Romans advance deep into the Sahara Desert, seemingly searching for fabled gold treasure.

Britain, c. AD 43: The commander Vespasian has captured the Isle of Wight (Vectis), fought 30 battles, captured 20 native centres and subjugated two tribes, the Durotriges and the Artebates of Dorset.

Italy, AD 43: The geograph-er Pomponius Mela has written a new book which divides the entire world into hot and temperate zones. The book, *De Situ Orbis*, presents a fresh view of the world based on the first-hand observations of explorers.

Britain, AD 43: The emperor Claudius has authorised the building of a new city at Colchester to replace the old tribal capital. It is intended to become the headquarters of the Roman occupation. At the same time the settlement at Verulamium (St Albans) has been granted the status of a self-governing municipality, and a new bridge-head has been established called London.

Tonkin, Vietnam, AD 43: Chinese troops have finally crushed a four-year revolt by Tonkin noblewomen. The aristocratic Trung sisters had not gained popular support for their revolt. China has occupied Vietnam for a century, and although at times ruthless, its stabilising influence has been welcomed generally by the ordinary people because it curtailed the power of landowners.

Woman restored to life in Joppa

Joppa, c. AD 39

A highly regarded woman has been brought back to life here after dying from a sudden illness.

Tabitha (or Dorcas, her names mean 'Gazelle') was a much-loved member of the Christian group in this coastal city. After her death, fellow believers placed her body in an upper room, and summoned the chief spokesman of the Christians, Simon Peter, who was in Lydda 19 km (12 miles) away.

He followed the example of his mentor, Jesus of Nazareth: after praying, he ordered her to get up, which she did, to the amazement of everyone. As a result, a number of people have joined the church.

The incident followed an earlier

Buildings on the waterfront, Joppa.

healing by the apostle in Lydda. Aeneas, a church member, had been paralysed for some eight years. At Peter's command, he got off his bed and returned to normal life.

(Acts 9:32–42)

'New Pentecost' as Gentiles join church

The remains of the aqueduct bringing water to Caesarea, founded by King Herod.

Caesarea, c. AD 40

People of non-Jewish descent have been admitted as full members of the Christian church for the first time following a dramatic incident in the Roman garrison here. A centurion, Cornelius, had called friends together at his home to hear the chief Christian apostle, Peter, when they suddenly broke into spontaneous worship in unknown languages.

This Gentile Pentecost, so called because it was similar to the incident which launched the church among Jews in Jerusalem at the Pentecost festival some seven years ago, took everyone by surprise. The apostle immediately concluded that it was God's sign of acceptance of Gentiles, and he allowed them to be baptised into full church membership. He also gave them a new catchphrase: 'God has no favourites.'

Peter is himself no purist when it comes to religious scruples. While at Joppa, some 48 km (30 miles) south of Caesarea, he lodged with Simon the tanner, whose trade rendered him and those under his roof ritually unclean in orthodox eyes.

But his views were challenged by a dream in which he saw a sheet full of animals. He heard a voice, which he believed was God's, telling him to eat the flesh, but he refused on the grounds that it was 'unclean'. The voice then warned him not to regard as unclean what God had declared clean.

When messengers from Cornelius called for Peter, he obeyed his dream and disobeyed his tradition by going with them to the Gentile's house and eating there. He was accompanied by six other Christians. Cornelius is a centurion with the Italian cohort which performs garrison duties in Caesarea, Herod's new town which has become the centre of Roman regional government in Judea. He had been following the Jewish religion for some time, and claims that through a dream he had been given full instructions on how to contact Peter.

When the two men compared notes, they agreed that the coincidences of their dreams were signs of God's activity.

As Peter explained the purpose of the death and resurrection of Jesus Christ and the promise of forgiveness of sins in Christ's name, the phenomena took place. They were explained by Christians on the scene as the work of the Holy Spirit. The baptisms, a ritual immersion in water, took place shortly afterwards.

(Acts 10; 11:12)

Church leader sprung from jail

Jerusalem, AD 43-44

Simon Peter, one of the leaders of the Christians in Jerusalem, has been rescued from prison despite being under heavy guard.

Following the summary execution by Herod, of James Zebedee, one of Jesus Christ's earliest and closest followers, Peter had been arrested on vague charges which are believed to have been put to Herod by the Sanhedrin. The trial was postponed for several days until both the Festivals of Passover and Unleavened Bread were completed.

The night before the trial was due to take place, an intruder entered the prison, evaded the sentries, and released the handcuffs which secured Peter to two guards. The intruder then guided Peter through three sets of doors which he opened with ease, before apparently disappearing into the night once they reached the street.

According to Christian sources, Peter was then denied admission to the church prayer meeting being held for him at the home of Mary, mother of John Mark, for some time. The 'believers' who had been praying for his release were unable to believe their ears when he knocked at the door. He is now staying at a secret address.

The identity of Peter's rescuer is unknown. The Christians claim it was an angel of God, partly because Peter was aware of an unusually bright light in his cell. He said later that he thought he was dreaming.

The guards, who were apparently asleep during the whole episode, have all been executed for allowing this major breach of security.

(Acts 12:1–19)

The medieval Jaffa Gate and Citadel in Jerusalem were built on earlier foundations.

Caligula falls to assassin

Rome, 24 January AD 41

The emperor Caligula was assassinated in his palace today by a conspiracy of centurions led by Chaerea and Cornelius Sabinus. He was 29. His fourth wife, Milonia Caesonia, and his only daughter were also murdered.

A deeply hated emperor, he had governed for only four years, and will be remembered mainly for his cruelty. His reign was characterised by Accius' famous phrase, 'Let them hate so long as they fear'.

This applied just as much to his diplomatic relations with rulers from other countries. In AD 40 the king of Mauretania was killed by Caligula's specific orders whilst on a diplomatic visit to Rome.

Caligula's accession was initially welcomed but power seemed to turn his head. He thought himself a god and preferred to be addressed as one. He was openly incestuous with his sister Drusilla and after her death claimed she was divine.

Unpredictable, unstable and tyrannical, his military achievements were negligible and his control of the economy disastrous. His lavish spending caused many new taxes to be imposed on the people. He murdered one of his wives and one of his sisters, as well as a number of aristocrats.

First reports of his assassination were disbelieved. People thought Caligula himself may have invented the rumour to discover what people thought of him. Caligula's uncle Claudius, handicapped from birth, has been made emperor: the army and Praetorians see him as a convenient tool. He suffers from a tic, a speech impediment and a mouth which always dribbles.

Freedmen threaten Rome's elite

Rome, c. AD 40

Members of the upper classes are objecting to the rise in power of some freedmen who are being given government positions. Freedmen are either children of, or are themselves, born slaves and later manumitted.

The emperor Claudius' financial secretary Pallas and his private secretary Narcissus are both such men and they invite hostility because while their talents are undisputed, they are arrogant and pushy, driven by the desire to succeed despite their roots. There is therefore pressure for more power to go to the elite of society.

Roman army sweeps through southern Britain's tribes

Richborough, AD 43

Four legions under the command of veteran general Aulus Plautius have swept through southern Britain to establish Roman rule.

The emperor Claudius has arrived and is now commanding the army personally as it presses north of the River Thames.

Some 40,000 men – 20,000 legionaries and a similar number of auxiliaries – landed at Richborough in Thanet, which they have made their base, and at two other south coast locations. They met only token resistance from the British, whose soldiers are mostly ill-equipped part-timers except for a few professional charioteers and cavalrymen.

There was a two-day pitched battle, however, at a crossing of the River Medway. The young Second Legion commander Vespasian succeeded in a surprise attack and routed the Britons. Some defenders retreated southwards under the leadership of Caractacus, while others fled north of the Thames.

The invasion is intended to consolidate the Roman hold on the island which is inhabited by numerous small tribes. Since Julius Caesar's invasion in 55 BC, Roman merchants have gained access to much of the country south of a line from the Humber to the Severn, but Roman rule is not enforced.

Political analysts have long debated the cost-effectiveness of such a large campaign at such a distance from Rome. The country is not rich, only producing a few metals such as copper and iron, and some inferior

Claudius' physical disabilities were not portrayed on official busts.

pearls, although it is fertile.

It also holds few charms for Roman soldiers. Folklore stories of witches and druids were in part to blame for a rare and temporary mutiny by troops who refused to embark on ships to cross the Channel, thus delaying the mission for some two months.

The decision to invade was made partly because of continued British incursions into Gaul (France). Either the British had to be subdued, or the Gaullish defences strengthened considerably. It was seen to be more expedient to subdue the nations right to the Atlantic coast.

It is also being seen in Rome as a politically astute move by Claudius to establish his reputation and power base. There have been few conquests of note in recent years, but as the poet Virgil wrote around the turn of the century, the Roman genius is to 'rule the peoples to impose the ways of peace, to spare the defeated, and to crush those proud men who will not submit'. No emperor can sleep securely if he has not fulfilled that noble ambition.

World survey

Tingentera, between AD 37–44

Pomponius Mela of Tingentera near Gibraltar has written a geographical survey in Latin of the whole inhabited world. *De Chorographia* fills three books.

The author claims the earth is divided into northern and southern hemispheres and five zones, two of which are habitable. He describes the relative positions and boundaries of the three continents, surrounded by ocean which indents it by four seas: Caspian, Persian Gulf, Red Sea and the Mediterranean.

He also describes all the known countries: Gibraltar Straits, Egypt, Palestine, Euxine, Scythia, Thrace, Macedonia, Greece, Italy, South Gaul, Spain, all the Mediterranean islands, outer coasts of Spain, Gaul, Germany, unknown North Europe, East Asia, British Isles, Thule, India, Persian Gulf, Red Sea, Ethiopia, West Africa.

The work includes no mathematical details or distances, although it includes details of physical nature, climate and customs.

Richborough Fort still marks the Roman landing.

Herod Agrippa is dead

Caesarea, AD 44

Herod Agrippa, king under Roman direction of much of Israel's ancient land, has died after a brief and sudden illness.

He had travelled to Caesarea for

Herod's family tomb outside Jerusalem.

peace talks with the people of nearby Tyre and Sidon, who had quarrelled with him but who depended on Judea for grain supplies. After giving a much-acclaimed speech at a public festival in honour of the emperor Claudius, Herod was taken ill with a severe intestinal disorder and died five days later.

Herod Agrippa was a colourful and volatile character, the grandson of Herod the Great. Brought up in Rome after his father Aristobolus was executed in 7 BC, Agrippa was forced to leave the capital in AD 23 because of his mounting debts. He lived in Tiberius with his uncle Antipas (who had married Agrippa's sister Herodias), returning to Rome in 36.

He was imprisoned by the emperor Tiberius after a quarrel, but released by his successor Gaius (Caligula) who made Agrippa king of the territories to the northeast of Palestine. When Antipas was banished in 39 Agrippa took control of Galilee and Perea, and later received Judea and Samaria from Claudius in 41.

Distantly related to the Hasmonean dynasty, he retained a warm relationship with the Jewish community. He had recently launched a strong attack on the Christian church.

The Christians are claiming that his death was a direct result of the acclaim he received from the crowds in Caesarea. In their enthusiasm they called him a spokesman of the gods, a title he did not repudiate and which allegedly brought a swift and final retribution from God Almighty.

Herod Agrippa leaves his wife and three children, Agrippa Jr (b. 27), Bernice (b. 28) and Drusilla (b. 38).

(Acts 12:19b–23)

Teacher of 'the Word' has died

Alexandria, c. AD 45

The unique Jewish philosopher Philo of Alexandria has died aged about 65. A statesman who represented the Egyptian Jews to the Roman emperor in a petition in AD 39, he wrote allegorical expositions of Genesis, Exodus and other biblical books.

He drew heavily on Stoic philosophy from which he introduced the concept of the Logos (the Word) to Jews, which he described as the means by which God operates in the world. He also drew on the works of Plato and Pythagorus, but his emphasis on mystical experience prevented his writings from being aridly intellectual.

It is believed that he spent his formative years in a Jewish religious community before taking up the public service which occupied much of his working life.

Fast Facts AD 44–45

Italy, AD 44/45: The Roman palate is being tickled by new fads. The capon, a cock castrated to make it grow fatter, is now being farmed for the table. And the emperor is popularising the vomitarium, in which slaves tickle diners' throats after a meal to enable them to empty their stomachs and return to the banqueting table to gorge themselves yet again.

China, AD 45: A severe drought in the Hsuing area has been followed by a devastating plague of locusts which consumed what little vegetation had grown, causing great hardship for the people.

Wessex, AD 43–44: The Roman legion commander Vespasian has consolidated the empire's hold on southern and western Britain by capturing Vectis (the Isle of Wight) and the strategic hill fort of Maiden Castle in Dorset. Having taken 400 years to complete, the castle was effortlessly razed by the Romans. Heavy fighting resulted in large casualties among the British. Two other legions have successfully moved northwards into the Midlands.

Judea, AD 44: The troublesome outpost of Judea has been declared a procuratorial province after the death of King Herod Agrippa. The new procurator is to be Cuspius Fadus. The dead king's son, Agrippa Jr, is at 17 too young to succeed his father and is still studying at the Roman court. Meanwhile, statues of Agrippa's virgin daughters in Caesarea have been toppled.

Thrace, AD 46: The ancient kingdom of Thrace has been reunited and made into a Roman province following the murder of King Rhoemetalces who ruled the coastal area. It had been divided since a king of the same name died in AD 12, when Augustus partitioned it among the king's relatives.

Rome, AD 47: 'Secular games' are being organised to mark the 800th anniversary of the founding of Rome. It is 64 years since such games were held, then organised by Augustus. The games include the spectacular Troy Pageant performed by young horsemen, including the emperor's son Britannicus and Nero, son of Germanicus.

Rome, AD 47: Claudius has ordered the construction of an aqueduct to convey streams from the Simbruine Hills into Rome. Its lofty arches will channel the water into a number of ornamental reservoirs situated throughout the town.

Famine relieved by Syrians

Antioch, Syria c. AD 43–44

Christians in Antioch have responded to the famine in Jerusalem by sending a delegation with relief aid to the church there. The food shortage is one of several which have occurred in recent years in different parts of the empire.

In a parallel gesture, Queen Helena of Adiabene has ordered consignments of corn from Egypt

Amphora from the first century, used for grain storage and in transport.

and figs from Cyprus to assist the poorer people of Jerusalem. Helena has embraced the Jewish religion for some time, and was visiting Jerusalem to worship God. Her son Izates has also sent a cash donation for relief work.

The church in Antioch had been collecting money for this purpose for some time, having been alerted to the likelihood of a famine by the prophet Agabas who had travelled from Jerusalem.

The delegation from Antioch was headed by two of the church's leaders, Barnabas and Saul of Tarsus. Saul was previously a notorious Pharisee and persecutor of Christians in Jerusalem. During the 15-day visit Saul met with the leadership of the Jerusalem church, including the apostle Simon Peter

and the brother of Jesus, James.

He explained the message he has been preaching for the past decade in the churches of Syria and Cilicia. His activities there had been heard of only at second hand by the Jerusalem leaders, who after the meeting gave him the formal handshake of fellowship.

Saul had only visited Jerusalem once before since his dramatic conversion about 14 years ago. Then he met briefly with the leaders and preached the Christian gospel boldly, before a death threat from Jewish extremists forced him to leave the city hurriedly.

Among the topics of conversation during the latest visit was the inclusion of Gentile Christians into the church. The leaders in Jerusalem declared themselves open to such inclusion without pre-conditions, and Titus, a member of the Antioch delegation and a Greek, was not compelled to be circumcised in addition to the baptism he has already received.

The church in Antioch grew initially from Christian Jews who fled there from persecution in Judea. Some Gentiles had since joined the church and Barnabas had been sent to check them out.

(Acts 11:19–30; Galatians 1:21–2:5; cf. Acts 9:26–30)

Cripple leaps for joy

Lystra, Lycaonia, c. AD 47

It was carnival time in this small Roman colony as villagers got out the garlands after a lifelong cripple was healed from his affliction.

The men responsible for the healing, Christian preachers Paul and Barnabas, were feted as Zeus (chief of gods in popular thought) and Hermes (the messenger of the gods) in human disguise. The local priest of Zeus hurriedly arranged a special bull-sacrifice for the visitors, but they refused the honour.

In an equally extravagant gesture, the Christians tore their cloaks to shreds to demonstrate their rejection of the sacrifice and their repudiation of the titles.

Paul (Hermes) and Barnabas (Zeus) were probably unaware of the legend that said Zeus (then called Jupiter) and Hermes (Mercury) had been unknowingly entertained by an elderly couple Philemon and Baucis, as described in one of Ovid's poems.

While the villagers thought that history had repeated itself, Paul and Barnabas pleaded with them to stop. They said that they were mere mortals and that the miracle had been evidence of the power of the one true God, whom they had come to the village to talk about.

The party came to a swift end when religious Jews arrived from Iconium and played on the villagers' disappointment by stirring up a riot in which Paul was stoned unconscious. His body was dragged outside the village, but he later recovered and continued his journey.

(Acts 14:8–20)

The hills above Lystra, Lycaonia, Turkey.

Romans force rout at March

Colchester, c. AD 47/48

The Roman army has routed the Iceni tribespeople and their neighbours in Britain's East Anglia after a short insurrection.

Auxiliary troops won a fierce battle at Stonea Camp, a small island near March in the Cambridgeshire fens. It was a notable achievement because the Roman preference for a pitched battle was made impossible by the flat fields divided by many ditches and small lakes.

But the revolt raises questions about the tactics of the new commander-in-chief of the occupying forces, Ostorius Scapula.

His arrival in Britain in late autumn, when the battle season was almost over, was greeted with several surprise attacks by British rebels operating from outside the area controlled by Rome. These were swiftly put down by lightly armed cohorts headed personally by Scapula.

He then reversed the policy of his predecessor Aulus Paulinus by declaring his intention to disarm all tribespeople south of the Severn and Trent rivers. This huge triangle is the breadbasket of Britain, producing most of the corn on which the Roman soldiers depend.

Previously, the native people had been allowed to keep their simple weapons so long as they remained peaceful. Scapula seems to have fallen foul of the Roman tendency to create resentment among subject peoples which makes battles almost inevitable.

Meanwhile trouble is brewing for the new commander on the western front. The rebel leader Caractacus has retreated into Wales following his defeat at the battle of Medway, and has gathered a guerrilla force from the Silures tribe which is making lightning attacks from the narrow Welsh valleys.

Opposition overcome

Iconium, Phrygia, c. AD 46–47

Despite opposition, slander and a death threat from the religious hierarchy, Paul and Barnabas have established a new Christian church at Iconium.

The city, 145 km (90 miles) east of Antioch-towards-Pisidia, has seen a large number of its inhabitants embrace the new teaching. The travelling preachers have demonstrated many of what they call 'signs and wonders', which include healings and other physical manifestations, people being changed suddenly for the better, and spontaneous prophecies and worship in strange languages.

The apostles weathered the storms of opposition for some time until they learned of the death threat. Fearing for their safety, they travelled to Lystra, about 50 km (30 miles) away, to continue their mission.

(Acts 14:1–7)

Roman underfloor heating ensured that the wealthy stayed warm – whatever the weather.

Fast Facts AD 47–48

Rome, AD 47: The Senate is considering establishing an official Board of Soothsayers. According to the emperor, whose idea it was, 'this oldest Italian art' is about to die of neglect and public indifference. 'The advice of soothsayers has often been the cause of the revival of religious ceremonies,' he said. 'Gratitude to divine favour must be shown by ensuring that rites observed in bad times are not forgotten in periods of prosperity.'

Rome, AD 47: The citizen population of the empire has been put at 5,984,072 following a census. There have been debates in the Senate over whether conquered peoples given citizen status should be allowed to become senators. The emperor Claudius believes they should, so as to ensure that excellence is brought in to the ruling class 'from whatever source'.

Ephesus, AD 47/48: John Zebedee, the 'beloved disciple', who with his now-martyred brother James and with the apostle Peter was one of the inner triumvirate of Jesus' disciples, is believed to have travelled to Ephesus from Jerusalem to assist the fledgling church.

Judea, AD 47/48: The rebels James and Simon have been crucified by the procurator of Judea, Tiberius Alexander. They had continued the fierce resistance, both to Rome and to those Jews believed to be collaborating with the occupying forces, which was started by their father Judas the Galilean in the early years of this century.

China, AD 48: The people of Inner Mongolia have once again been subdued by the might of China under its Han dynasty emperor Guang Wudi, keen to extend his empire.

Civil servant blinded by preacher

Cyprus, c. AD 46

One of the senior advisers to Proconsul Quintus Sergius Paulus has been struck blind during a confrontation with a group of Christian missionaries.

Acting against the advice of Bar-Jesus (also known as Elymas), a religious expert attached to the court, the proconsul invited the missionaries to explain their beliefs to him. This is believed to be the first time that a leader of the sect has been given an audience by a senior Roman official.

The group led by Barnabas (formerly Joseph), a Cypriot Levite by birth, and Paul of Tarsus (also known as Saul) had arrived in the island's capital New Paphos after an uneventful preaching tour of

Attalya harbour today, where Paul landed after leaving Cyprus.

Jewish synagogues.

During the interview, Elymas – who practises black magic and sorcery – repeatedly interrupted and contradicted the visitors. Paul confronted him, calling him a 'child of the devil' and accusing him of 'deceit and trickery' and of 'perverting the ways of the Lord'.

Paul then pronounced a curse on Elymas, who became blind immediately, taking the proconsul and his other advisers by surprise. Sergius Paulus, impressed by this display of divine power, declared that Paul must be teaching God's truth.

After the confrontation, the missionaries left the senatorial province for the (Turkish) mainland, sailing from Paphos to Attalya in Pamphylia.

(Acts 13:4–13)

Mixed fortunes on mission

Antioch-towards-Pisidia, c. AD 47

The civil authorities of Antioch have quickly expelled Christian missionaries Paul and Barnabas despite a volcanic-like eruption of enthusiasm for their message.

The preachers had trekked for 160 km (100 miles) through the rugged Taurus mountains to reach Antioch from the southern plains city of Perga. Their journey had been dogged by Paul's ill health, the attention of brigands, and the unexpected desertion of one of their party, John Mark of Jerusalem.

On arrival at the synagogue Paul was invited to speak after the second Scripture reading. What he said was so popular that the following week huge crowds came. But there was a strong backlash when he said that non-Jews were as free to encounter the Jewish Messiah Jesus Christ as were Jews themselves.

The synagogue rulers encouraged the wives of leading citizens – who had joined with the Jews to worship God – to persuade their husbands to have the preachers expelled from the city. Their anger at the preach-

ers' success was matched by the derisory gesture of Paul and Barnabas. As they left Antioch they symbolically emptied their sandals of the city's dust.

The troubled journey had begun when the company landed at Attalia from Cyprus. John Mark, a cousin of co-leader Barnabas, caught the next ship home, probably because he was tired of the austere and dangerous lifestyle. It was the second time he had defected from Christians; he had previously fled the scene when Christ was betrayed.

Injury was added to insult when Paul contracted a mystery disease in the malarial lowlands near Perga. The group decided that the arduous trek to the healthier Antioch, 1,100 m (3,600 ft) above sea level near the Pamphylian border with Pisidia, was essential to his recovery. Despite the preachers' short stay in the city, the Christians they left behind continued to praise God joyfully for their new understanding and faith.

(Acts 13:13–52; cf. Galatians 4:13; Mark 14:51–52)

What Paul said in Antioch

Basing his talk loosely on 2 Samuel 7:6–16, which promises to the house of David an everlasting kingdom, and quoting from elsewhere in the Jewish Scriptures, Paul stressed:

- God's faithfulness to Israel in the desert
- The descent of Christ from David
- The unlawful execution, and later resurrection, of Christ
- Christ is God's unique Son
- Through faith in Christ people have a new access to God. This was not possible by observing the Law of Moses alone.

Galatian churches appoint leaders

South Galatia, c. AD 48

Official leaders have been appointed to the new Christian churches in the southern part of the Roman province of Galatia.

Following their church-planting tour in the region over the past 12 months or so, Paul and Barnabas have retraced their steps from Derbe – the latest addition to the growing number of churches – through Lystra, Iconium and Antioch-towards-Pisidia, to appoint leaders who will teach and maintain discipline. The 'elders' were appointed in ceremonies which included prayer and fasting.

In their final address to each church, the apostles stressed that being a Christian inevitably involved hardship and persecution.

They urged believers to stand firm on the basic truths they had been taught.

On their return to the south coast the group stopped at Perga, which they had hurried through before. Surrounded by the splendour of the temple to Artemis, the theatre and stadium, they turned once again to pioneer evangelism before setting sail for Seleucia, the port of their Syrian home base Antioch-on-Orontes.

There they reported their experiences of seeing non-Jews receiving the message of Christ. They had travelled some 1,930 laborious kilometres (1,200 miles) on foot and by sailing ship over the space of 18 months.

(Acts 14:2–28)

An old stone wall and archway are about all that remains of Perga today.

Britannicus won't rule the waves

Rome, AD 48/49

The emperor's natural son, Britannicus, has been passed over for succession in favour of Nero, the son of Claudius' third wife Agrippina.

Claudius recently married the powerful Agrippina, who is his niece, the daughter of Germanicus who was murdered in 41 and the sister of Gaius Caligula.

The emperor's second marriage, to Messalina, broke down following the latest in a series of scandals: a mock wedding with her lover Gaius Silius. Claudius decided enough was enough, and had her executed.

Following the adoption of Nero, Claudius has recalled the philosopher Seneca from exile and appointed him as the boy's tutor, possibly at Agrippina's request. Britannicus (the name was added to his others in honour of Claudius' campaign in Britain) will not lose his other privileges as a son of the court.

Port to be enlarged

Ostia, Italy, c. AD 50

Work has begun to enlarge the port of Ostia, which lies at the mouth of the Tiber River some 25 km (16 miles) from Rome. For many years the river mouth itself has provided sufficient anchorage, but marine experts have discovered that silt carried downstream by the river is now posing a danger to shipping as sandbanks threaten the harbour.

The new development will be built about 3 km (2 miles) north of Ostia. Part of the new harbour will

be dug out of the shoreline, and two breakwaters will be built out into the sea. The harbour is expected to cover an area of some 647,500 sq m (160 acres). A giant lighthouse or pharos is to be built on one of the breakwaters.

According to tradition, Ostia was the first Roman colony founded by King Ancus Marcius 600 years ago. The new harbour is a vivid testimony to the recent growth of trade between Rome and the Mediterranean area.

Roman warehouses lining the Via dei Molini are still standing in Ostia today.

Act of God leaves rulers trembling

Philippi, Greece. A general view of the Roman Forum, agora and 6th-century basilica.

Philippi, c. AD 50

An earthquake hit the centre of Philippi during the night causing minor structural damage.

Among the buildings affected was the city jail where the pioneer Christian preachers Paul and Silas were being held. They had been arrested, flogged and imprisoned without a trial after a riot in the market place.

Unsubdued, the pair were praying and singing hymns when the earthquake shook them and the other prisoners free. The force of the tremor also burst the locks on the doors.

In the confusion which followed, Paul kept all the other prisoners together and prevented the jailer from committing suicide. (According to Roman law, he would have paid with his life for any prisoner who escaped.)

But when the magistrates offered to set Paul and Silas free the next morning, they refused to go and revealed that they were full Roman citizens to whom the normal courtesies of a proper trial had been denied. Alarmed by their own illegal actions, the magistrates gave the preachers a public apology and allowed them to visit their new converts before finally leaving the city quietly.

Among their converts was the jailer whose life they had saved. He had asked them to explain the Christian way of salvation, and had requested initiation into the new church by water baptism for himself and his family.

The riot had begun when Paul exorcised a fortune-telling slave girl. When her spirit-guide departed, so too did the livelihood of her owner. He stirred up the crowds, claiming that Paul's monotheism was contrary to Roman custom.

(Acts 16:16–40)

More riots in Greek cities

Thessalonica, c. AD 50

An angry mob brought the first visit of the apostle Paul to the Macedonian capital Thessalonica to an abrupt end as they rioted outside the house where he was staying.

And when he and his companions moved to Berea, 80 km (50 miles) to the west, trouble erupted again.

Paul had begun his visit to Thessalonica by preaching in the Jewish synagogue. For three Sabbath-days in succession he was given a hearing, and numerous Jews and Gentile sympathisers joined the new Christian church.

He argued that the Scriptures predicted that the expected Messiah would suffer and then rise from the dead. Jesus of Nazareth fulfilled those qualifications, he claimed.

But a minority of Jews are said to have recruited local troublemakers to cause a disturbance. The crowd stormed Jason's house, where Paul was staying, but the apostle was not in. So the crowd dragged Jason and other Christians to the city rulers claiming that they were 'defying Caesar's decrees by saying that there is another king, one called Jesus'.

The rulers made the Christians post bail and Paul and Silas slipped out of the city to Berea. Jason, however, was imprisoned for sheltering the strangers.

In Berea they were given a warm reception by studious Jews who wanted to hear their message. But agitators from Thessalonica once again organised a demonstration against them. Paul was quickly despatched to the coast while Silas and Timothy remained in Berea to assist the church.

(Acts 17:1–15)

Remains of the triumphal arch of Galerius in the old forum of Thessalonica, now surrounded by appartment blocks.

First-ever council of Christian leaders reaches verdict on Gentiles

A major conference of Christian leaders from Judea and Syria has issued a directive stating that most Jewish customs are not to be imposed on Gentile converts. It appears to have resolved an issue which threatened to split the church.

How the crisis began

Jerusalem, c. AD 49

Following the dispersion of believers after the martyrdom of Stephen almost 15 years ago, the church has expanded far more rapidly than most Christians dreamed possible.

The remains of the Roman aqueduct in Antioch in Pisidia, Turkey.

Christians believe that Christ is the expected Jewish Messiah – God's final messenger sent to rescue his people from all that oppresses them. Those converted from an orthodox Jewish background believe that as the Messiah fulfils Jewish hopes, Jewish customs are a correct expression of faith in him. They therefore require

insisted on all Christians submitting to Jewish practices.

It came to a head in Paul's home church of Antioch in Syria, which has a high proportion of Gentile members. Delegates claiming the authority of Jerusalem church leader, James the Just, travelled to Antioch in order to attempt to enforce Jewish practices.

After fierce debate, the elders in Antioch agreed to send a delegation to Jerusalem to talk with the senior leaders. The group was headed by Paul and Barnabas, whose successful missionary trip to Cyprus and Galatia had resulted in many Gentile converts.

Apostles clash in public

During the visit of the Jerusalem delegation to Antioch the apostles Paul and Peter clashed publicly over Jewish–Gentile relations. Peter had been staying in Antioch and fraternising openly with Gentiles when the delegation arrived. Then he suddenly withdrew from the Gentiles and refused to eat with them, aligning himself firmly with the strict views of the visitors. Others, including Barnabas, followed his example.

Paul publicly accused him of hypocrisy: 'You don't normally live like a Jew, so why are you now supporting the enforcement of Jewish practices onto Gentiles?' A right relationship with God did not depend on outward observation of Moses' law but on inward faith in Christ's death, he stressed. That applied to all people from whatever ethnic background (Galatians 2:11f).

At the Council in Jerusalem Peter defended the Gentile case. He had become the first apostle to lead Gentiles to faith in Christ; in

It has brought into sharp focus the differences between peoples who, in religious if not political terms, have been arch-enemies for generations but who are now worshipping the same Christ.

It has also created the probability that Gentiles will soon outnumber Jews in the worldwide church – if, indeed, they do not already. This has fuelled fears among Jewish Christians that moral standards, if not doctrinal beliefs, will be watered down. Unlike most Jews, few Gentiles come from backgrounds where strict moral purity and religious certainty are prized.

Gentile converts to be circumcised as well as baptised, and to observe Jewish dietary and other laws.

Gentiles, on the other hand, point to the basic Christian belief that a relationship with God can be founded only on faith – which they interpret as personal trust – in Christ. This faith does not require particular forms of religious expression other than adopting a lifestyle which obeys God's moral laws.

The controversy has been brewing for some while. Paul has written recently to the churches in Galatia rebuking them for what they called a return to slavery, after they

Caesarea, the centurion Cornelius had responded to his message.

It is likely that the visitors to Antioch had frightened him with suggestions that his behaviour was causing something of a scandal in Jerusalem.

It is not the first time that Peter, the rock-hard fisherman, has proved to have feet of clay. The story of his denial of Christ at the crucifixion and his subsequent reinstatement to leadership is widely told.

Taking on the role of a judge, James, the Lord's brother, declared that on the basis of all the evidence

A scroll of the Torah, seen at the Western Wall, Jerusalem. This segment of the wall is all that remains from the temple rebuilt by Herod and that Jesus would have known.

no extra burden should be placed on Gentiles.

'It seemed good to us and to the Holy Spirit,' he declared in an official communiqué, 'that we should not make it difficult for the Gentiles who are trusting God.'

He went on to refer explicitly to the testimony of Simon Peter, Christ's former right-hand man, who had seen 'the grace of God' poured out on Gentiles.

Light burden

Quoting from the prophet Isaiah, who foresaw the day when Gentiles would be grafted into the family of God's people, James decided that such believers should, as a token gesture of solidarity with the Jewish believers, abstain from meat tainted spiritually by pagan ceremonies or butchered in ways which are abhorrent to Jews. James also insists that Christians must be free from sexual immorality.

The first and last are restrictions already commonly accepted throughout the churches. The rule about butchery arises from the Christian belief that church members should not cause unnecessary offence to others' scruples, even if those scruples are of secondary importance to doctrinal issues.

James reminded the remaining sceptics on the Jewish side that the Gentiles could still hear the law of Moses read in the synagogues throughout the Roman empire every sabbath.

As a result of his verdict, which was accepted unanimously, a letter setting out the position was drafted. A delegation including Judas (known as Barsabbas) and Silas from Jerusalem joined with Paul, Barnabas and the other Christians from Antioch, to deliver the letter
(Acts 15:1–30)

Happy ending

Antioch, AD 49
The Christians in Antioch have received the verdict from Jerusalem with joy and relief.

The official letter was read publicly at a worship meeting. Judas and Silas, the Jerusalem couriers who are also gifted speakers and prophets, encouraged the Christians and strengthened their faith.

They stayed for some time before returning to Jerusalem. Paul and Barnabas remained with their friends in Antioch.

(Acts 15:30–35)

The participants:

JAMES – Jesus' brother – Chair Has been the undisputed leader of the Jerusalem church for some years. Has recently written a hard-hitting letter to believers urging them to match their beliefs by their actions. Reputed to be a man of personal discipline and public fairness.

PHARISEE-CHRISTIANS – Pro-circumcision A representative group of orthodox Jews who embraced Christ as Messiah. Already believed in resurrection, so the Christ-event fitted naturally into their doctrinal framework. Insist on Gentile converts being circumcised and observing fully the Law of Moses.

SIMON PETER – Apostle, first missionary to Gentiles Led the Gentile God-fearer Cornelius to Christ in Caesarea. But most of his ministry has been to Jewish communities. Told the Council of his vision from God which challenged him not to call people unclean, even Gentiles.

PAUL AND BARNABAS – Pioneer church planters Told of their recent journey through Cyprus and Galatia, and of the spread of the gospel around Antioch. Also spoke of miracles which they suggested implied God's acceptance of Gentiles without ceremonial or legal requirements.

APOSTLES AND ELDERS – Jerusalem leadership team Acknowledged as the authoritative governing body of the church. Have stayed firm in their faith under great pressure from religious and secular sources. Are mostly Jewish in origin and outlook.

The first circular letters

Don't be so stupid!

Antioch-on-Orontes, c. AD 49

The apostle Paul, still recovering from his recent gruelling 18-month mission tour of Cyprus and south Galatia, has sent a strongly-worded rebuke to errant believers in the churches he founded.

Using the modern Roman provincial title of Galatia to embrace the churches of Antioch-towards-Pisidia, Iconium, Lystra and Derbe (although the title properly belongs to the ancient kingdom of Galatia north towards the Caspian Sea), he calls the Christians there fools who have been bewitched by false teachers.

Paul begins by asserting his authority as a true apostle against those who questioned his right to teach them. In a lengthy introduction outlining his life so far, he stresses that he received his gospel by revelation from Christ.

Referring to his own Jewish pedigree, he reminds his readers that Jewish customs could never be necessary for an authentic Christian faith. Those who had persuaded the Galatians to return to those customs are perverting the faith, he writes.

He goes so far as to consign them to eternal condemnation.

The true children of Abraham, Paul argues, are those who have faith in Christ and take God at his word – which is what made Abraham acceptable to God. Therefore there is no need to join Abraham's 'family' physically through circumcision in order to be a true child of God. The Law of Moses was designed to show us our need of Christ, not to provide an alternative way of salvation.

He reminds his readers of the illness he contracted in Perga, and the marks on his body received in the stoning in Lystra. Then, the Galatians cared about him so much that they would have given their eyes as a transplant for him, if it was possible, he says. 'So why have you abandoned my teaching?' he cries.

The tone of the letter changes towards the end, as Paul turns to practicalities of Christian living. Freedom, he says, is not licence to indulge but responsibility to care. 'Serve each other in love,' he commands, spelling out love's nature by picturing nine 'fruits of the Spirit' which stand in stark contrast to the gross works of raw human nature.

He adds a personal postscript in his own ungainly handwriting, having dictated the letter to an unnamed assistant.

(Galatians 1-6)

Points from the post

1:1–10 Greetings; there is only one gospel.

1:11–24 Christ revealed the gospel to me; I didn't learn it from men.

2:1–10 On my relief-aid visit to Jerusalem, non-Jews didn't have to observe Jewish customs.

2:11–21 But Peter and Barnabas were inconsistent. We are crucified to the law!

3:1–25 The law cannot get you to God. Christ saved us from it; believers are Abraham's heirs.

3:26–4:7 We're children of God, not slaves of sin. And we're all equal in God's sight.

4:8–20 Leave the slavery you're falling back into!

4:21–31 An allegory using Abraham's wives Sarah and Hagar.

5:1–15 Freedom is not indulgence; hold firm to it.

5:16–26 Live by God's Spirit, not by your desires.

6:1–18 Do good at all times; final personal greetings.

Paul's first missionary journey.

Paul's first journey took him from Antioch to Cyprus and then on to a number of key towns in Asia Minor, never far from each other.

This was a ground-breaking journey. Though travel was relatively easy and safe within the Roman empire, Paul was the first documented Christian leader to undertake such a lengthy journey, with the specific object of evangelizing Jews and Gentiles.

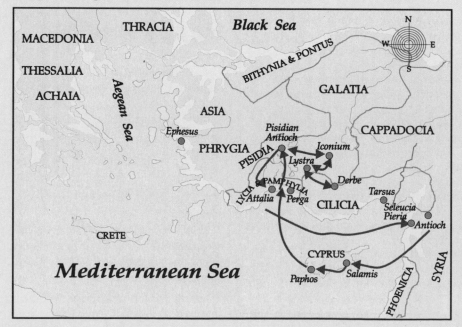

Jerusalem – at this early stage of the church, it is probable that worship was still centred on the temple, or at least on the complex of colonnades and old houses forming part of the Temple Mount (centre).

James urges Christians to live out their beliefs

Jerusalem, c. AD 49

In a circular letter addressed to Jewish Christians scattered by persecution across the Roman empire, the apostle James has called for a faith that is visibly demonstrated by good works, controlled language and steadiness under pressure. Writing in forthright terms, James warns rich landowners that they will pay dearly for hoarding their wealth and refusing to pay labourers.

He begins by encouraging faithfulness in the face of difficulty. He reminds his readers that the unchangeable God who gives wisdom to all is never the source of temptation. 'The crown of life' awaits all who press on, he asserts.

Every Christian should listen carefully to, and consider, God's truth – and then put it into practice, he says. Such practice includes treating people equally whatever their economic situation.

Wishing someone well who needs practical help is no help at all, he claims. Abraham was commended not just for believing God's promise but for doing what God asked, and preparing to sacrifice his son Isaac.

A person's speech is also a test of their faithfulness to God, says James. The tongue can be like a spark that sets a forest ablaze; one word out of place can do immense damage. And curses on people have no place in the mouths of those who praise God.

The root cause of all sin is selfishness and greed, he argues. Humility before God is the only safe way to live. God will judge others, and he will determine the number of someone's days. So he urges his readers to bear in mind that Christ will return soon and not to boast, argue, or slander each other.

James concludes his letter with some practical instructions on praying for the sick and turning people back to God.

(James 1-5)

James – just the man

Jerusalem, c. AD 49

One of the four brothers (or as some say, half-brothers) of Jesus, James has been the undisputed leader of the Jerusalem church ever since Peter embarked on a wider, travelling ministry.

Nicknamed 'The Just', he remains true at heart to his Jewish roots while at the same time being a man of broad mind and fair principle. He is known to take a conciliatory view on the acceptance of Gentile Christians into the church.

As a young man, James, together with the rest of his household, was sceptical of the ministry and claims of Jesus. However, he received a personal visit by Jesus after he had risen from the dead, which seems to have convinced him and qualified him to be called an apostle.

According to some sources, he was personally appointed by Jesus as the chief elder of the Jerusalem church. He leads a highly disciplined ascetic lifestyle and is respected by Roman and Jewish leaders as well as by the Christians.

Tribal gods have no temples

Europe, c. AD 50

Romans now occupying Britain are discovering that most religious worship by the native tribespeople takes place in circular clearings in woodland, or beside springs or river banks which are believed to be the borders of the Otherworld. One major water shrine in the west country settlement of Bath is dedicated to Sulis, a healing god which Romans identify with Minerva.

Deep well shafts are also used for rituals, especially in the south of the country. The bones of sacrificed animals, and votive offerings of coins, jewellery and other items are thrown down the shafts, perhaps to the spirits believed to dwell there.

Mythology concerning the gods is not unified. On the Welsh fringes and in Ireland there are well-developed myths of gods such as

The neolithic standing stone circle in Avebury was also a centre for Druidic rites in Roman Britain.

Lug, a powerful craftsman, warrior, poet, musician and magician rather like the Roman Mercury. He is also patron of travellers, and has a magic spear which can kill or cure. But most of the British gods are local deities, often without names and with all-purpose powers to influence human affairs.

The clan of priests called Druids, the object of Roman censure in Gaul because of their political influence, were said by Julius Caesar to have originated in Britain. Their influence seems to have waned at the present time.

The Roman practice of cremation has not spread here, and most bodies are buried in the earth. They are often laid in a crouched, almost foetal position on their right side, surrounded by household artefacts. Local people apparently believe that the soul of a dead person lives on in another body.

According to central European tribespeople, the dead are ferried across the English Channel from Gaul in an hour, compared with the usual 18 hours. The Germans also believe that people's souls can leave their bodies temporarily in this life.

The chief god of northern European tribespeople, Odin, is both a powerful warrior and a wise counsellor. Known elsewhere in Europe as Woden and by Romans as Mercury, he is said to be handsome and able to assume the form of man, fish, beast or bird. When he appears to humans, it is usually as a humble traveller.

He usually dwells in the glittering hall of Valhalla. His speeches are made with such eloquence that none can doubt the truth of his words, and are often in verse because he once stole the mead of the poets from some giants. He knows the magic secrets to cure illness and battle-wounds. He is married to Frigg (or Friga), a fertility goddess.

Also dwelling in Valhalla are the Valkyries, females who wait on the heroes at their feasts and who also attend earthly battles to determine which warriors shall fall. Other gods worshipped in Germany and northern Europe include Tiw (regarded as the same as the Roman Mars, the god of battles); and Thor, a storm god like Jupiter.

Woodlands are thick with elves and sprites

The dense woodlands of central and northern Europe are said to be thick with non-human creatures. Chief among them are the elves, more attractive but generally smaller than humans. They are wise and able to divine the future, and their main occupation is dancing.

Related to them are the dwarves, who are said to quarry gold and precious stones from mines deep in the earth. Dwarves are far better blacksmiths than humans, and they also fashion jewellery, some of which is said to have magical powers.

Watersprites are believed to enjoy drawing men to their deaths, while household spirits often take on domestic tasks and are said to bring good luck.

Quite different are the giants, or trolls as they are called in Scandinavia. They are believed to be descendants of the gods and their bad-temperedness results in storms and landslides.

Satirist's tale ends

Rome, AD 50

The satirist, fablist and poet Phaedrus has died. Born a slave, he was educated in Italy and became a freedman under Augustus.

He compiled the first Latin collection of fables, many of which are translations of the sixth-century BC Aesop. Phaedrus is quoted as saying that the fable was a useful literary device for when one dare not be outspoken for fear of the consequences.

He will be remembered particularly for his great wit and skill in telling anecdotes, and for the freshness and simplicity of all his work.

Romans not very religious

Rome, c. AD 50

The ordinary people of Rome are pragmatic and have little interest in things mystical. The gods are believed to control all that happens; a mortal's main concern is to get the rituals right so that the gods do what they are supposed to.

Roman gods offer no comfort for broken hearts nor any encouragement to a more moral life. They cannot change a person's character.

Each Roman family has its own protector or 'genius', with a shrine

The Roman baths still survive today in the English city of Bath, named after them.

like a small cupboard with a statue inside. Family members pray to their gods each day and sometimes offer a gift of wine or food. There are special rituals for significant stages of life. At birth, for example, if the child is a girl, they spread a couch for Juno for eight days; if it is a boy, a table is laid for Hercules.

There are numerous ways of getting in touch with the gods, including the interpretation of dreams and calling up the spirits of the dead. A medium might act as a prophet of the spirit which inhabits him. Augurs specialise in observing and interpreting the habits of birds or the entrails of sacrificial animals as signs of things to come.

People seeking to know the will of the gods may cast lots or throw

dice, or consult the supposedly divinely-inspired books of the great poets. Astrology is becoming more widespread, but it is forbidden to prophesy the date of a person's death.

Few people attend temple worship; for a city of an estimated million people, there are only 100 temples. Temples also house the state treasury and trophies of war, and act as private banks and public meeting halls. However, in times of crisis, people may spend a whole night praying in a temple.

Prayer is said standing up, with the palms upturned. Worshippers often burn incense and kiss the feet of images. There are no formal worship services, although there may be formal intercessions made by priests.

The Roman year begins in March when the Vestal Virgins relight the fire in Vesta's hearth. There are annual games for several of the gods including Apollo and Jupiter, and in December the whole city has a week's public holiday for the Saturnalia festival in which religious ceremony is followed by unbridled feasting.

Not everyone approves. Three schools of philosophy have little time for popular religion. The Stoics believe that rationalism gives people courage. The Epicureans reckon that people should pursue pleasure of the soul, while the Cynics reject all conventions and practice shamelessly.

A major issue for Christians in the next few years is likely to be that of emperor worship. As the empire spread, the need for a more unified religion grew. Octavian tried to restore the gods to pre-eminence in public life, repaired over 80 temples, and reinstated traditional rites and ceremonies.

He also declared Julius Caesar to have been a god and regarded himself as a son of the gods. He called himself 'Augustus', or 'reverend', and many Romans

The gods of the empire

Among the most popular gods today are:

Jupiter (Zeus). The god of light and weather, manifested in thunderbolts, rain and holy trees. According to Cicero 'he makes us healthy and rich and prosperous'. He has a temple in the Capitol.

Mars (Ares). More popular than Jupiter, the god of war began his mythological life as god of the soil. The third month is named after him. He was the father of Romulus, who founded Rome, and has a shrine on Palatine Hill.

Juno (Hera). Goddess of childbirth and the state, and associated with the moon, she is the sister and consort of Jupiter and shares a temple with him.

Minerva (Athena). A newcomer to the Roman pantheon, she is the goddess of handicrafts. She shares a temple with Jupiter and Juno and governs the fortune of industries.

Apollo. The great Greek god honoured by Augustus who built a temple to him on the Palatine Hill. He represents youthful, manly beauty, and is especially concerned with music, prophecy, archery, medicine, domesticated animals and religious principles. His oracles are regarded as having supreme authority, his chief shrine being at Delphi.

Vesta (Hestia). A beautiful goddess who personifies the earth and domestic fire. Her shrine is the symbolic hearth of Rome. The fire at her temple near the Forum is cared for by the six Vestal Virgins, women chosen between ages six and ten for a lifetime ministry.

wanted to go the whole way and call him divine. He was deified after his death, as was Claudius. Emperor worship has given back to Roman religion the life and soul it had lacked.

New teaching puzzles thinkers

The Acropolis dominates the old town of Athens.

Athens, c. AD 51

Many philosophers who teach in Athens remain sceptical about recent claims made by Paul of Tarsus that Jesus Christ rose from the dead.

Stoic and Epicurean thinkers had invited the apostle to address the Areopagus Court after hearing him preach in the market place. The Court, meeting in the Royal Portico, a corner of the market area, has jurisdiction over religion and morals in the city.

The ruins of the Temple of Apollo.

Paul began his address by referring to the common practice of erecting altars to 'the unknown god' and claimed that it was this God that he would speak of. He described him as the creator and sustainer of all things, and quoted the poets Epimenedes and Aratus in support.

He also condemned multi-god worship as 'ignorance', using arguments common in some strands of Greek thought since the days of Xenophanes 500 years earlier.

'In the past God overlooked such ignorance,' he declared, 'but now he commands all people everywhere to repent.'

The general approval of his audience gave way to ridicule and even anger, however, as he added that God would judge the world through Christ, and that 'he has given proof of this by raising him from the dead'.

One member of the Areopagus, Dionysius, is reported to have believed the message and to have joined the church, along with a small number of Athenians.

(Acts 17:16–34)

Rebel leader finally defeated

Rome, AD 51

The emperor Claudius and the entire Roman Senate are celebrating the defeat and capture of Caratacus, one of the most powerful rebel leaders of the Britons. He has been a thorn in the flesh of the Roman forces in Britain for several years, recently commanding a guerrilla force among the Silures tribe of Monmouthshire and mounting repeated attacks on Roman positions.

The final battle took place in central Wales, in the territory of the Ordivices.

The Emperor Claudius, from a golden Roman coin.

Caratacus drew together a large army from several tribes, all of which were violently opposed to the *pax Romana*. 'They call it peace,' said one rebel soldier defiantly, 'but it is desolation.'

The British tribes were in a highly advantageous position. They dug in on a range of steep hills above the River Severn, and fortified the places where the gradient was easiest with crude stone ramparts. Behind them lay dificult terrain, so their chances of being surrounded were minimal.

The Roman governor Ostorius Scapula, whose tactics have been criticised in previous battles with the British, admits that he was dismayed at first when he saw what his troops were up against. However, Roman discipline prevailed and the governor commended his troups for their eagerness and superior expertise in achieving an outsanding victory.

Members of Caratacus' family were captured in the battle, but the leader himself escaped and sought refuge among the Brigantes tribe. However, their queen Cartimandua is a supporter of Rome, and she handed him over. He and other captives were promptly deported to Rome to face trial.

Senators are comparing the capture of Caratacus with the famous captures of kings in ancient days. Claudius even staged a public parade of the captives before the Praetorian Camp in Rome.

But when Caratacus delivered a powerful speech, the emperor was moved to pardon him and his family, thus 'showing mercy to the defeated', as the poet Virgil prophesied Rome would do.

In the wake of the victory, Ostorius Scapula has been awarded military honours, but his troubles in Britain are unlikely to be over. Although their troops are far less advanced than Rome's, the British are vowing to seek revenge.

A decorative scabbard slide, from Han dynasty China.

Han's up for China trips

China, c. AD 50

Following the restoration of the Han dynasty by Emperor Kuang-Wu a generation ago, travel and trade in the Far East is becoming more popular. Visitors will discover that most Chinese cities are laid out on a grid system like Roman ones, although there has been little cultural contact between the empires. The rationale is quite different; the Chinese believe that cities are like miniature worlds, should imitate the plan of nature and be aligned with the five

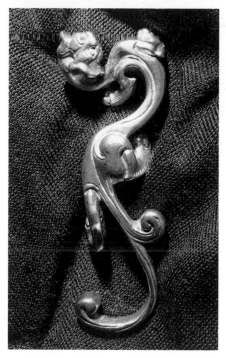

cardinal points of north, south, east, west and centre.

All Chinese cities are walled for defence and security, sometimes with both external and internal fortifications dividing them into wards. At night, the gates between wards are locked. Cities and towns are linked by a network of roads as comprehensive as anything found in the Roman empire. Roads there are built more sparingly and therefore more cheaply. China also has an efficient postal service.

Other surprises for travellers to see include the use of iron to make castings in moulds like bronze, requiring furnace temperatures in excess of anything so far achieved in the West. The Chinese have also learned to drill deeply into the earth to extract brine which lies beneath oil in underground caverns.

More familiar to Romans are the luxury goods which come from the Far East. The greatly prized jade is worked by highly skilled craftsmen who grind it into shape. Silk, the origins of which Romans still argue over but will none the less pay handsomely for, is the cocoon of a worm which the Chinese weave into cloth. The country also specialises in lacquer work, decorating and waterproofing objects from hats to swords with the coloured sap of the lac tree.

Fast Facts AD 50–51

Rome, c. AD 50: People of the republic now have soap for use in their baths. Invented by the Gauls for giving a reddish tint to the hair, it is said to also be a remedy against sores. Made from tallow and ashes, soap is now available in solid or liquid form and is reported to be very expensive.

Rome, c. AD 50: The Christian teacher Aquila and his wife Priscilla were among hundreds of Jews ordered to leave Rome. The crackdown by the emperor Claudius was prompted by continued disturbances within the Jewish community concerning the god Chrestus, who the sect of Christians worship. Aquila and Priscilla have moved to Corinth in Greece, where they practise tent-making.

Ceylon, c. AD 50: A freedman of Annius Plocamus has been blown in a ship from Arabia to Ceylon in a record 15 days by monsoon winds. He was received by the king of Ceylon, who sent an embassy to Rome.

France, c AD 50: It is said that Lazarus, who was raised from the dead by Jesus of Nazareth about 20 years ago, has gone to France to preach Christianity. He and his sisters Mary and Martha were said to have been placed in a boat without oars or rudder and they landed near Marseilles, where they made many converts.

Germany, AD 50: The emperor Claudius has founded a colony in honour of his wife Agrippina on the left bank of the Rhine at the site of Oppidum Ubiorum, the chief town of the German Ubii tribe. It is called Colonia Agrippina (Cologne) and has been laid out in regular form. A naval base intended as the headquarters of the Rhine fleet, is to be built a little further upstream.

Achaia, c. AD 51: Marcus Annaeus Novatus, son of a Spanish orator and brother of the famous Stoic philosopher Seneca, has been appointed pro-consul of the Greek province of Achaia. More usually known by the name of his adoptive family Gallio, he is known as an amenable and pleasant man who suffers from poor health.

Rome, AD 51: The commander Vespasian has received triumphal insignia from the emperor. Furthermore, he has been elected to two priesthoods and has now advanced to the consulship as a result of his triumphs in Britain. His family is now included among leading senatorial houses.

New church steady under pressure

Thessalonica in Paul's day was the capital of the Roman province of Macedonia. Named after the half-sister of Alexander the Great, it was sited near the hot springs of Therma and on two major trade routes, the East–West Egnatian Way and the North–South route from the Aegean to the Danube. It was a free city, and Luke's description in Acts of its rulers as politarchs has been confirmed by inscriptions found there. Today, Thessaloniki is Greece's second largest city.

Points from the post

Paul's first letter to the Thessalonians includes:

* *Thanksgiving* for people's first response to Paul's preaching, the demonstration of God's power, and for the missionary work emanating from them (ch 1).

* *An account* of Paul's ministry there, which was not a failure. He and his associates had earned their own living and taught the gospel free of charge (2:1–16).

* Paul's *concern* for them, so that he sent a delegation to find out how they were. The report has delighted him and he prays that they may grow (2:17–3:13).

* *Instruction* Christians are to live in ways which please God, free from immorality and over-indulgence, and marked by 'brotherly love' (4:1–12).

* *Reassurance* People who died before Christ's return will be re-united with those alive and will be with him for ever (4:13–18).

* A *reminder* Christ's return will be unexpected, so Christians are to be constantly ready (5:1–11).

* A call for *respect and support* for church leaders and people in need; and to keep the fires of the Holy Spirit burning (5:12–28).

Corinth, c. AD 51

The church in Thessalonica, founded some six months ago, has remained steady despite opposition and a lack of apostolic leadership, according to a report from a fact-finding delegation just returned to Corinth.

Led by Timothy and Silas, associates of Paul the apostle, the delegation had taken the 724-km (450-mile) round trip from south to north Greece at Paul's request. He is barred from the city; a major riot had led to his hasty departure after only a few weeks' ministry there.

However, despite a widespread reputation in the surrounding area for Christian love and mutual support, the Thessalonian Christians are confused over the mode and timing of Jesus Christ's expected 'second coming', and the destiny of people who have died before that event, according to the delegation.

Paul immediately penned a letter to encourage the church and to explain his teaching about Christ's return. After time for recuperation, the footsore delegation was despatched back to the Macedonian capital with the letter, while Paul continues his work in the morally lax and religiously pluralistic city of Corinth.

(1 Thessalonians 1:1; 2:17–3:10; 4:9–10,13)

Apollos replaces Paul

Corinth, c. AD 52

A new leader has joined the Corinthian church following the departure of Paul. Apollos, an Alexandrian by birth is, like his predecessor, well-versed in the Jewish Scriptures. Since his arrival he has argued powerfully in the synagogue that Jesus was the Messiah, and he has strengthened the faith of the Christians.

Apollos (his full name is Apollonius) came to faith in Alexandria following the dispersion of Christians in the 30s, but his understanding of Christ's ministry was defective. Although familiar with the life of Jesus, and endowed with spiritual passion, his experience of Christian faith was limited to the baptism preached by John as a sign of a new start with God.

During a visit to Ephesus he met with Priscilla and Aquila, Paul's companions who had moved on from Corinth. They explained the distinctive Christian belief in 'the atonement' by which people are said to be forgiven for their sins through Christ's death on the cross, in their place.

(Acts 18:24–28; cf. 1 Corinthians 3:6,9)

Gallio ignores religious riot

Corinth, c. AD 51

The newly-appointed proconsul of Achaia, Gallio, has resisted strong pressure from the Jewish community to bring the Christian leader Paul to court. In doing so he has maintained his reputation for absolute fairness and his independance from special interest groups.

A delegation of Jews in Corinth, reputed to be the red-light capital of Greece because of its lax moral standards, had alleged that Paul was activelly inciting illegal religious activity. But Gallio refused even to allow Paul to defend himself by ruling that the charge was purely a question of Jewish law and that he had no jurisdiction over it.

Incensed, the agitators beat up Sosthenes, the ruler of the synagogue, in full view of the proconsul. But as the victim was thought to be a Christian sympathiser, Gallio took no action on the assumption that the incident was a religious punishment for heresy rather than a civil crime of assault.

Paul is one of three senior Christian leaders now working in Corinth. A tent-maker by trade, he is devoting all his time to the church following the arrival in the city of his colleagues Silas and Timothy, who brought funds from elsewhere to support Paul.

This was their second major confrontation with Jewish leaders in Corinth.

Not long after their arrival about a year ago they left the synagogue after being subject to continuous abuse. A recent convert, Gaius Titius Justus, then offered his home as a base for the preachers. As it was next door to the synagogue, further clashes were almost inevitable.

(Acts 18:1–17; cf. Romans 16:23; 1.Corinthians 1:14)

Keep up the good work!

Corinth, c. AD 52

Paul the apostle has written a second letter to Christians in Thessalonica telling them to keep up their good work for God. However, he has also warned them not to give up their work in the world because they expect Christ to return again soon.

The letter was written when Timothy and Silas returned to Corinth after their second fact-finding trip to the Macedonian capital, during which they had

Pools at Pamikkale (Hierapolis) in the sunset.

delivered Paul's first letter to the church there. They had reported that the Christians' faith was growing steadily but that some church members had given up their jobs and were living off the gifts of others.

In his letter, Paul rebuked those who, instead of keeping busy, had become busybodies. He cited his own example of having worked for a living while he was with them. In a typically uncompromising statement, he ruled that, 'If a man will not work, he shall not eat.'

The main reason for the idleness is the continuing speculation in Thessalonica, as indeed in churches elsewhere, that Jesus Christ is to return to earth and set up the kingdom of God in the very near future.

Paul also warns against false teachers who claim Christ has already come; pointing out that Christ's return will be an unmistakeable cataclysmic event.

Paul adds that a certain 'man of lawlessness' has to be unmasked before Christ returns. He gives no clue as to the person's identity, but Caligula's attempt to set up his image in the Jerusalem temple a decade ago may have given Paul a model for his belief. The man, who could be some time in appearing, Paul implies, will be a miracle-worker able to deceive believers despite being evil.

In the face of continuing opposition, the Thessalonians are encouraged to stand firm for God and to be assured that God 'will pay back trouble to those who trouble you' on the final day of judgement.

(2 Thessalonians 1-3)

Apostles go back to base

Antioch, Syria, c. AD 52

The apostle Paul has returned to his home base of Antioch after an absence of almost two years, much of it spent in Corinth.

Unusually, for one who does not advocate strict adherence to his former Jewish traditions, he had his head shaved as a sign of the conclusion of a temporary Nazirite vow he had taken, which also involved abstinence from alcohol.

The vow was probably connected with his safe return from what was always going to have been an arduous missionary tour into the unknown.

But true to form, he could not resist the opportunity to preach Christianity in Ephesus on the journey home. Priscilla and Aquila remained there to help the few believers who converted to Christ.

(Acts 18:18–22)

373

Battling for their minds:
Paul's Corinthian correspondence

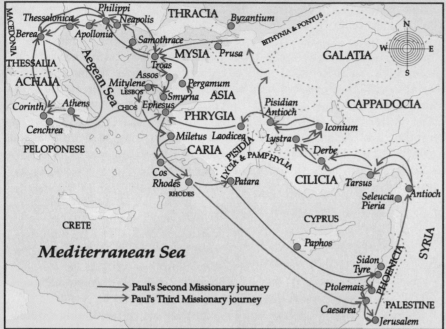

Paul's second and third missionary journeys. Paul's second journey started overland through Asia Minor until he heard God calling him to visit Macedonia. He then visited the principal towns of mainland Greece before going on to Jerusalem. In his third journey Paul called upon many towns he had previously visited, to strengthen the Christian converts and add to the growing church.

The church in Corinth has proved to be yet another thorn in the flesh for the apostle Paul. Despite a stay of 18 months in the city after founding the church there, it has proved to be the most emotionally and spiritually draining of all young churches.

Divided by factions, the church has opposed Paul and stumbled into scandals. Its worship meetings have sometimes resembled Bacchanalian orgies with unbridled feasting and rowdy services.

Since leaving the city, Paul has been in constant communication with the church. His first letter (not preserved) took the Christians to task for tolerating sexual immorality (1.5:9). They responded by writing to Paul asking his opinion on matters such as celibacy (1.7:1), eating meat that had been slaughtered in a pagan ritual (1.8:1), and the use of spiritual gifts such as speaking in tongues (1.12:1).

Members of Chloe's household had brought him news of growing

factions (1.1:11). More news came from a visit to Paul by Corinthian

Corinth. The remains of the Temple of Apollo (sixth century BC).

Christians (1.16:17). In response to the letter and the visits, Paul sent what is now called 1 Corinthians. It was delivered by Timothy who found himself unable to enforce

Paul's authority. On hearing this, Paul interrupted his ministry in Ephesus (Acts 19) to make what he called a painful visit to Corinth (2.2:1, 12:14, 13:1).

This seemed to have been ineffective, and he followed it up with a stinging letter (also not preserved) sent via Titus (2.2:4, 7:8). Anxious for news, he made his way to northern Greece where he met Titus on his way back from Corinth in the south (2.2:12f, 7:5–7). This time, the news was good. The church was sorrowful for its excesses, and held Paul in high esteem.

From Macedonia, Paul immediately wrote his fourth letter (now known as 2 Corinthians), full of encouragement. He then received further bad news of 'false apostles' usurping his authority once again, which caused him either to change tone suddenly or to send a fifth letter which was later clipped to the previous one (I2.10-14).

Finally, he followed that up with his third personal visit to the city

towards the end of his third missionary journey (2.13:1; Acts 20:2–3). He stayed three months, but no details are available of events during that time.

Points from the post

The wisdom of God

Perhaps because of some so-called Gnostic or mystical influences, some Christians are claiming to have received a superior or secret wisdom about God. Paul says that true wisdom comes through God's Spirit. God has turned on its head

Vegetable market in the old city of Jerusalem.

human wisdom by calling insignificant people to him and by sending his Son to die on a cross (1:1–2).

Divisions in church

Factions with people following human leaders such as Paul or Apollos are a contradiction in terms. There is one foundation, Christ, on which all build. The apostles have given themselves utterly for the church and should not be criticised (1:3–4).

Problems of morality

Some Christians believe that 'freedom in Christ' – release from the Jewish law and from the eternal consequences of wrong doing – means they are free to do anything, especially sexually. One man is sleeping with his stepmother, others are consorting with prostitutes. The body is God's; he dwells in it. Immorality is therefore a sin against 'God's temple' (1:5-6).

Celibacy or marriage?

Reacting to the immoral extremes, some people are advocating total abstention from sex even within marriage. Paul cites his own current single state (perhaps as a widower or as someone deserted by an unbelieving spouse) as ideal for serving God, but recognises that marriage is legitimate and probably essential for many. Husbands and wives ought not to abstain from sexual relations except for short periods of prayer (1:7).

Food, drink and idols

Idols are not real, but some believe they are. So while there is nothing wrong with eating meat that has been slaughtered in a pagan ritual, if a fellow Christian is offended, then don't. However, you should not allow someone else's scruples to become binding on you – but you can't take part in pagan rituals which invoke demons (1:8,10).

Apostolic authority

Paul did not use all his rights as an apostle, and he worked hard for his living. His example is to use freedom to become a slave to Christ in order to win others to the faith. His ministry has been full of suffering, which is his mark of commitment.

Worship matters

Local customs, such as women who are not prostitutes keeping their heads covered, should be observed. The agape fellowship meal and communion service should be treated with reverence and not as an opportunity for selfish indulgence. Spiritual gifts are distributed by God to individuals for everyone's benefit. Each Christian has a different gift; none are to be despised and love is to bind them all together (1:11–14).

Life after death

Christ is risen – which proves that those who say there is no such thing as resurrection after death are wrong. Everyone who has died will be raised when Christ returns. To the sceptics who ask what they'll look like, Paul uses analogies from nature to stress that the same thing can have different kinds of body at different stages in its development. If Christ is not raised, then faith is futile: death is not conquered. But it is! (1:15).

New beginnings

The gospel of Christ is the new covenant of God by which people are brought into a fresh relationship with him. It is more glorious than the old covenant with Moses. Of course, we have that glory in decaying, weak bodies, but don't lose heart, says Paul. There is a heavenly dwelling awaiting us.

View through a Roman aqueduct – there is life beyond.

Meanwhile, the old has passed away and the new has arrived in our experience of Christ (2:.2–5).

Give generously

The collection in Macedonia has been very generous. Now the Corinthians can be generous too, as the believers in Jerusalem need help. God loves a cheerful giver, says Paul, so use this to show how much you love him (2:8–9).

Claudius poisoned by spiked mushroom

Rome, AD 54

The emperor Claudius has died at the age of 64, by poisoning. His wife Agrippina had ordered the notorious poisoner Locusta to prepare a lethal dose which was sprinkled on

Claudius and his wife, from the arch celebrating his victory over Caratacus.

a mushroom by the emperor's food taster Halotus.

When Claudius' drunkenness made it hard to tell if the poison was working, Agrippina asked Dr Xenophon, the emperor's physician, to tickle Claudius' throat with a feather dipped in fast-acting poison, under the guise of helping him to vomit. Agrippina has been anxious to secure her 16-year-old son Nero's succession to the title and to increase, through him, her hold on the empire.

At his enthronement ceremony, Nero delivered a polished speech prepared by his tutor Seneca. It recounted his stepfather's military and literary triumphs, and caused mirth at the mention of Claudius' 'foresight and wisdom'.

Claudius has been declared a god, the first emperor since Augustus to be so honoured. However, some senators including Seneca have described this as a 'cheapening of godhead'. His will has not been published. It is rumoured that his preference for Nero over his natural son Britannicus would have created a public impression of injustice.

Magic spells go up in smoke

Ephesus, c. AD 55–56

Magicians here have watched their spells disappear in a pall of blue smoke in the certain knowledge that they will not be able to conjure them back again.

The wizards claim that they have discovered a superior wisdom and even greater power which requires no trickery or incantations. But in order to avail themselves of it they first had to build a bonfire of books to destroy their old spells. According to local estimates, they sent material worth about 50,000 drachmas up in flames – enough to pay about 700 workers for a year.

In a city famous for treating people to tricks, the Christian

preacher, Paul of Tarsus, has been doing wonders no one can explain by traditional means. A tent-maker by trade, even his aprons and cleaning cloths are said to have healing powers.

He heals, exorcises demons and preaches in the name of Jesus Christ. He claims that the name of Christ, who was crucified over two decades ago but is said to have been raised from the dead, can heal people and bring them eternal forgiveness of their sins.

In one extraordinary scene, some Jewish exorcists of the Sceva family attempted to exorcise a demon in the name of Christ. The man they were trying to cure overpowered them and stripped them naked, claiming that he knew Paul and Jesus but not them. Local magicians realised that the power and name of Christ was to be respected as more than a mantra. Paul and his companions have been in Ephesus

The Library of Celsus in Ephesus.

Fast Facts AD 54–57

Rome AD 54/5 : Seneca has exchanged his role as Nero's tutor for that of his chief political adviser and minister. He has also published a satire written in a mixture of verse and prose which is a witty skit about the deification of Claudius. It contains some serious political criticism and

bitter personal malice and is bound to stir up some controversy.

China AD 57: The king of Nu, in Japan, has sent an envoy to the court of the emperor Guang Wudi in Loyang, the capital of Han China. Like many other autonomous tribes in Japan, the Japanese king was seeking Chinese recognition of his authority. Guang Wudi has given the king of Nu a seal

confirming his kingship in the name of the Han emperor.

Anatolia c. AD 54: The Greek botanist and army physician, Pedanius Dioscordis, has published a major work on drugs and drug treatments. Dioscordis, who comes from Anazarbus, north east of Tarsus in Cilicia (southern Turkey) has travelled widely in his research. His book, *De Materia Medica* (Medical Matters) lists the

properties of some 600 medicinal plants and 1,000 drugs. Unlike previous pharmacological works, his provides a systematic study of drugs according to their use rather than a mere alphabetical list.

Rome AD 57: The Roman governors of Cilicia and Asia have been recalled on the grounds of misgovernment. The action demonstrates the efficiency of Rome's central administration.

for about two years. When they first arrived they preached in the synagogues for three months. They then transferred to Tyrannus' lecture hall, using it in the 11.00 a.m. – 4.00 p.m. siesta slot when lectures are normally suspended.

On their arrival, they found a dozen Christians already in the city who had not heard about the power of what they call the Holy Spirit. After a prayer meeting and baptism in the name of Christ, they began to speak in new languages and exhibit new powers.

(Acts 19:1–20)

Flying visit 'painful'

Ephesus, c. AD 56

Paul the apostle has returned from a brief and painful visit to Corinth. No details are available about the precise cause of the dispute, but it is understood that a few church members have opposed both his teaching and authority. It seems that in seeking to address the problem personally, Paul found himself isolated from those he expected to support him.

News of the continuing unrest was brought to him by Timothy, who had delivered the second of Paul's letters from Ephesus to Corinth.* The letter challenged the church's fragmentation, spiritual excess, and moral laxity.

Paul had expected to visit Corinth later this year during a trip through Greece and on to Jerusalem next spring. The news that Timothy had been unable to enforce Paul's authority in Corinth caused him to make the special trip at once, but he failed to convince his opponents. On his return to Ephesus Paul sent another stinging letter 'out of great distress and anguish of heart and with many tears', he said. Its text is currently unavailable.

(2 Corinthians 2:1–4; 7:8; 12:14; 13:1)

*See article on the Corinthian correspondence (pp 374–375).

March for Artemis ends in chaos

Ephesus, c. AD 57

A mass demonstration on behalf of the goddess Artemis has ended in a near riot. It was dispersed after several hours by the chief magistrate.

The disturbance followed a trade union meeting in which silversmiths making souvenir models of Artemis' temple alleged that their business was under threat from Christianity. Their fiery convener Demetrius alleged that the missionary preacher Paul taught that man-made gods were impotent. He added that such teaching robbed Artemis of due honour.

The meeting spilled over into the streets as the protesters chanted 'Great is Artemis of the Ephesians'. People downed tools and joined the march, without knowing what it was about, and crowded into the 25,000-seat theatre cut into Mount Pion, taking Paul's companions Gaius and Aristarchus with them.

Paul himself escaped capture, but was dissuaded by some of the Asiarchs, provincial officials responsible for the emperor cult, from going voluntarily to the demonstration to explain his views. When a Jewish spokesman, Alexander, tried to reason with the crowd, perhaps fearing the rally would become anti-semitic, he was shouted down.

The chief magistrate eventually calmed the demonstrators by telling them that the only illegal offence committed was their unlawful assembly. Christians had neither robbed temples nor blasphemed Artemis. Despite the interregnum between proconsuls in Ephesus, with equestrians Publius Celer and Helius holding the reins, any legitimate complaint could be taken to the courts, he added.

Artemis, the Greek goddess of hunting, is identified with the Asian fertility goddess and is represented as a many-breasted figure. Her image has a block of stone instead of legs, and is alleged to have fallen from the sky. She is known to the Romans as Diana.

Her temple in Ephesus, built on the site of a meteorite landing, is reckoned to be one of the great wonders of the world. It boasts over 100 white marble columns, and is some 130 m (425 ft) long and 67 m (220 ft) wide. It was four times the size of the Parthenon in Athens.

Following the demonstration, Paul left the city. Ironically, he had already stated his intention to depart for a tour of Greece before the riot began.

(Acts 19:21–41)

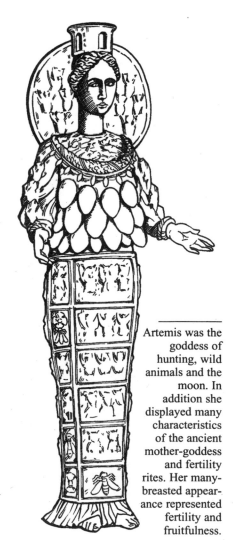

Artemis was the goddess of hunting, wild animals and the moon. In addition she displayed many characteristics of the ancient mother-goddess and fertility rites. Her many-breasted appearance represented fertility and fruitfulness.

Claudius' son poisoned

Rome, AD 55

Thirteen-year-old Britannicus, the son of Claudius, has been poisoned in front of his family during a banquet. The young emperor Nero watched impassively.

The boy was given a poisoned drink, which caused him to convulse and stop breathing. Some of his companions fled in terror while others seemed rooted to the spot.

Britannicus' sister Octavia, the wife of Nero, who knew nothing of the plot, remained expressionless. Nero lay back unconcernedly and said such things often happened to epileptics and that the boy would soon recover. After a short silence, the banquet continued.

It is believed that Nero had ordered Britannicus' murder out of hatred and fear of the boy's popularity. His mother Agrippina, angry at her weakening control over Nero, had switched her support to Britannicus as the true heir of Claudius. He had also gained popular support from the Roman people.

As his remains were buried in the Field of Mars there was a violent storm, leading to speculation that the gods were furious at the murder. Nero's cold-bloodedness has caused terror among his household.

Detail, from Trajan's column, of a coastal trading vessel, of the type Paul would have taken.

Sermon sleeper gets shock awakening

Troas, April AD 57

Teenager Eutychus, attending the apostle Paul's long sermon on Sunday night, got an unexpected awakening – but not the spiritual sort.

His body was tired after a long day, and his mind dulled by oil-lamp fumes in the stuffy downtown tenement. So he did what comes naturally and fell asleep – and promptly fell backwards out of a third-floor* window.

He was believed to be dead, but after prayer by Paul, regained consciousness and was found not to be seriously harmed. The meeting continued after the incident with the 'breaking of bread', a fellowship meal which recalls Christ's death.

Paul had followed several colleagues to Troas, arriving after a five-day voyage from Neapolis, the port of Philippi 200 km (125 miles) away, where he had joined in Passover celebrations. For the past 18 months he has been touring much of Greece to encourage the faithful and to raise money for the church in Jerusalem. He plans to arrive there by late May for the Pentecost festival. Details of his recent travels, which may have taken him as far west as the Adriatic coast, have not been released.

Apart from bringing valuable help to impoverished believers, the collection is also being seen as a token gesture to promote the unity of Christians in 'the body of Christ' which Paul has been emphasising recently. Gentile Christians are known to be impatient with the more conservative mother church, while its leaders have remained uncomfortable with the independent spirit of the mission churches.

(Acts 20:1–12, 16; cf. Romans 15:19)

*Second floor in British reckoning.

'We'll never meet again'

Miletus, May AD 57

There was an emotional farewell on the dockside here as Paul told the elders of the Ephesian church that he expected never to see them again. He had spent the best part of the years 52 to 55 in the city.

On his coast-hugging voyage from Troas to Jerusalem he had sailed on past Ephesus. But then during a few days' stopover at Miletus, on the mouth of the Maeander some 48 km (30 miles) south of Ephesus, he called for the elders who were able to reach him before the small merchant ship sailed again.

In his address, Paul reminded them of his exemplary conduct during his stay with them. He withheld none of God's truths, he claimed, and he took no financial remuneration from them. The church would face opposition from outside and false teachers from inside, he warned, and they were therefore to guard their faith carefully.

There were no dry eyes in the group as Paul declared categorically that none would see him again. Already prematurely aged by his stress-packed lifestyle, he believes he must take his pioneer church-planting ministry where no one else has gone before.

He has Spain firmly in his sights, once he has visited Jerusalem and then Rome.

(Acts 20:13–38, cf. Romans 15:23–29)

Christians' worst fears realised

Miletus with Ephesus in the background.

Jerusalem, May/June AD 57

Paul the apostle has been arrested and taken into custody, having narrowly escaped a lynching during a riot against him.

And while few Christians would publicly chide the man who has travelled further and planted more churches than any other, they are saying privately, 'We told him this would happen but he wouldn't listen.'

Paul and a number of others had travelled to Jerusalem from Greece at the conclusion of his so-called third missionary journey to bring financial aid to Christians here. At the request of James, the brother of Jesus and leader of the church, Paul accepted the Jewish discipline of purifying himself for seven days before entering the temple. He also paid for four Christians to complete their temporary Nazirite vows which included making sacrifices of pigeons and lambs.

But this gesture of solidarity with the Jews was not enough to satisfy some extremists. Seeing Paul accompanied by Trophimus of Ephesus, they assumed that he had taken the Gentile into the temple area. They immediately attacked Paul. Roman peace-keepers were quickly on the scene and carried Paul away for his own safety.

Later, the commander allowed Paul to address the crowd, when he related his experience of conversion to Christ. But his reference to a calling to preach to the Gentiles stirred their fury once again. In a further attempt to explain himself to the Sanhedrin the next day, his belief in the resurrection of Christ divided the Pharisees (who accept resurrection) and the Sadducees (who do not), and the meeting broke up in disorder.

Twice on the journey to Jerusalem, at Troas and again at Caesarea, he was warned by prophets that certain imprisonment awaited him if he continued to Jerusalem. His travelling companions, who include his personal physician and biographer Luke, had begged him to turn back, but he had refused. He is still in Roman custody.

(Acts 21:1–23:11)

Blown by the monsoon to the Orient

Arabian Sea

The Greek merchant Hippalus has confirmed the existence of regular monsoon winds blowing across the Arabian Sea in the North Indian Ocean. He successfully sailed from Ras Fartak, a cape on the south Arabian coast, to the mouth of the Indus in the north-east of the Indian peninsular.

His discovery will improve trade between the Roman empire and the Orient, which hitherto has largely been confined to overland routes. Imports of spices, perfumes, gems and ivory, and exports of linen, glass and precious metals are likely to increase.

Fast Facts AD 55–60

Britain, c. AD 55: Foundations have been laid by Vespasian for a new permanent port on the Cornish coast at Nanstallon, near Bodmin.

Britain, AD 57: Queen Cartimandua of the Brigantes, and a supporter of Rome, has quarrelled with her husband Venutius and captured all his relatives. Venutius is rallying support for an invasion as his wife calls for Roman forces to restore order.

Germany, AD 58: The Hermunduri tribe from Thuringia in southern Germany has defeated its northern neighbour the Chatti tribe which lives the other side of the River Main. After a fierce battle the victors sacrificed their enemies to the gods Tiw (Mars) and Woden (Mercury).

China, AD 58: A new emperor, Ming, has been enthroned. He is known to be a devotee of Buddhism, a religion of the Indian highlands which is growing in China.

North Europe c. AD 60: The tribe of Goths have set up a kingdom on the Baltic coast, on the banks of the lower Vitsula River. They have migrated from their homeland in Gotaland in southern Sweden.

Northern Italy c. AD 60: The Fucine Lake is to be drained by order of Claudius. It is being paid for by businessmen in return for the reclaimed land. The three-mile outlet is likely to take a decade to build, despite having over 30,000 workmen assigned to it.

Apostle sets out basic beliefs

Corinth, AD 57

In a thoughtful letter addressed to Christians in Rome who he has never met, the apostle Paul has set down his basic teaching about how people can get right with God.

Unlike most of his writings so far, the letter has not been prompted by a local dispute. Instead, Paul is reflecting on the false emphases and misunderstandings he has encountered elsewhere and is in effect sending his visiting card and brochure prior to his planned visit to Rome.

The letter to the Romans, dictated to Tertius the scribe, begins by describing the folly of idolatry and selfish living. People who should know better have been corrupted by the idols they made (chapter 1).

Paul's phrasing will find echoes of approval in both his Jewish and Gentile readers. 'The invention of [idols] was the corruption of life,' the Jewish author of the Wisdom of Solomon bemoaned a couple of centuries ago.

Even Seneca, current adviser to Nero, says those who live for the body have predeceased their death.

Both Jew and Gentile have sinned against God, Paul claims. Observance of neither the moral nor the ceremonial law is adequate to overcome the consequent alienation from God. So, in a detailed exposition of the prophet Habakkuk's statement that 'the righteous shall live by faith', Paul suggests that even Abraham was counted righteous by God not because of what he did but because of who he believed (chapters 2–5).

Christ's death has saved the believer from the ineffectiveness of the law and also from the tyranny of sin itself, he says. He has met people who say that if God's undeserved love is poured out on sinners, then they ought to have a sin-filled time in order to get more of God's love. Nonsense, he responds; sin is to be banished from the believer's life. As Christ died for

The Roman Forum at dawn, with the Temple of Castor and Pollux, the Arch of Titus and the Colosseum beyond. This was the hub of imperial Rome.

sin, Christians have died to it (chapter 6).

Unfortunately, life's not that easy, he confesses. It's a battleground as the old nature rears its head. But there's a free pardon for all who believe, which results in God's Spirit being released into their lives. God is in charge of their circumstances, however difficult they are (chapters 7, 8).

Then Paul turns to the Jews, who some Gentile Christians reckon have been written out of God's script for good. Not so, he asserts. There is, as there has always been, a remnant of Jewish believers (he is one himself), and one day there will be many more, he predicts (chapters 9–11).

Having nailed his theological colours to the mast, Paul anticipates the impatient church member's question, 'So what?' He suggests numerous practical applications for his beliefs. Total commitment to the God who gave all is one. Active love for others is another, and good citizenship is a third; Paul encourages obedience to the state which has protected his liberty on several occasions. Finally, he encourages meat-eaters and vegetarians not to pass judgement on each other.

He also greets by name some 30 people who now live in Rome and who he has met on his travels. They, of course, will vouch for him prior to his arrival. After sending the letter, Paul prepared to leave for Jerusalem, where he is to deliver financial aid to the church.

(Romans 1-16)

Seneca promoted

Rome, AD 56

Seneca, the political adviser of Nero, has been promoted to suffect consul, the senior civil and military magistrate of Rome. With Burrus, the prefect of the Praetorian Guard, he is effectively co-ruler of the empire.

The two men's unstated policy is to direct the excessive deviations of the young emperor into legitimate channels of indulgence. They also act as a buffer between Nero and Agrippina; it is believed that his mother wants more power for herself.

Seneca is described as a man of amiable high principles, while Burrus is said to be of serious character and soldierly efficiency.

Murder plot foiled

Caesarea, Syria, c. AD 57

A plot to kill Paul has been foiled by the bravery of his nephew and the quick thinking of Claudius Lysias, the Roman garrison commander in Jerusalem.

The hastily-conceived plot was hatched by an extremist group of 40 men who swore not to eat until Paul was dead. Members of the Sanhedrin, the Jewish ruling council which had already heard Paul's defence, were also implicated. They were to seek Paul's release on the pretext of hearing him again, thus exposing him to ambush.

But in the small city of Jerusalem the narrow lanes are full of whispers. Paul's nephew, barely beyond his bar mitzvah, had his streetwise ears tuned to them. As a relative he had easy access to the prisoner, who relayed the intelligence to the commander.

Lysias ordered Paul to be transferred to Caesarea at night. He sent 200 soldiers, 70 horsemen and 200 spearmen as guards, temporarily halving the Jerusalem garrison. The foot soldiers escorted him to Antipatris, 48 km (30 miles) north of the city, before turning back. The conspirators did not pursue them.

Paul was handed with a letter of explanation to the regional governor, Tiberius Claudius Felix, and kept under guard in Herod's palace.

(Acts 23:12–35)

The springs at Caesarea Philippi.

Governor adjourns trial

Caesarea, Syria, c. AD 57

The governor of Judea and Samaria has adjourned the trial of the Christian leader Paul after hearing evidence from both sides.

Tiberius Claudius Felix, listened to a top-level delegation from Jerusalem, headed by the high priest, accuse Paul of stirring up riots. Their spokesman, Jewish lawyer Tertullus, also alleged that Paul had attempted to desecrate the temple.

In his defence Paul denied all charges of sedition and public disorder. He explained the belief he shares with others of 'The Way', as the Christians are often called.

Felix is already familiar with both Judaism and Christianity. He is a freed slave who rose through the ranks and married Drusilla, the daughter of Herod Agrippa I.

After adjourning the case he and Drusilla heard Paul speak privately about Christian belief and behaviour. It is unlikely that he will find the preacher guilty but despite following Roman jurisprudence carefully he is currently keeping Paul locked up in order, it seems, not to offend the Jews.

(Acts 24)

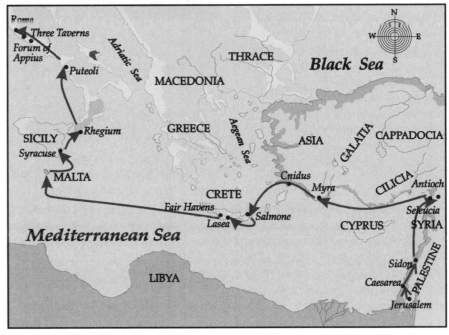

Paul's journey to Rome under armed escort was mainly by sea during the autumn winds.

Paul appeals to Roman court

Caesarea, c. AD 59

Paul has used his rights as a Roman citizen to ask for trial before the emperor Nero. He had been held in prison by the previous governor Felix, now recalled to Rome.

The case against him was immediately re-opened by Jewish leaders in Jerusalem when the new governor Porcius Festus paid them a courtesy call. They added charges against imperial law to their original religious objections.

During a new trial before Festus, no evidence for these charges was submitted. However Paul, fearing the governor was inclined to favour the Jewish leaders, appealed to Caesar, a right which has existed since Augustus' reign about 30 BC.

While waiting for a suitable ship to take him to Rome, Paul was also arraigned before Herod Agrippa II. Reactions to his description of his conversion from Pharisaism to Christianity were mixed. Festus called him mad but Agrippa seemed impressed by Paul's logic that Jesus fulfilled the Scriptures predicting the Messiah. They agreed that Paul could have been released if he had not appealed to Caesar.

(Acts 25-26)

Saved from shipwreck in Malta

Malta, November c. AD 59

The ship taking the Christian leader Paul and his companions Luke and Aristarchus to Rome has been lost. All 276 passengers and crew are safe, but the cargo has gone down with the ship.

The vessel, belonging to the Alexandrian merchant fleet carrying grain from Egypt to Rome, was wrecked off the coast of Malta after a 14-day battering by hurricane-force winds.

Paul, along with other prisoners being escorted to Rome by an Augustan cohort auxiliary officer, Julius, had transferred to the ship at Myra, on the southern coast of Lycia, from one which was returning to its home port of Adramyttium, near Troas. Had they stayed on board, they could have taken the safer overland route from Troas for the remainder of the winter journey.

The grain ship ran into difficulties almost from the start of its voyage. Progress westwards along the Asiatic coast was slow against the continuous north-west wind, so the captain sailed south with it hoping to turn west later along the sheltered southern coast of Crete. But by the time they reached Fair Havens it was already October. Sea travel is considered unsafe by Romans after 14 September, and suicidal after 11 November.

They made a final attempt to reach the more suitable winter port of Phoenix in south-west Crete when a favourable southerly wind blew up. But this soon backed into a howling north-easter, the notorious 'euroquito' (or gregale). Despite deploying anchors, the ship was driven helplessly out to sea.

The storm robbed the crew of all navigational and time-keeping aids from the sun and stars. They abandoned tackle and cargo to keep the ship afloat. Shortly after Paul had a vision in which he claimed God had promised to protect everyone on board, they hit land.

St Paul's Bay, Malta from a nineteenth-century print.

The bow stuck fast on a submerged mud bar and the stern broke up under the pounding waves. Passengers and crew swam ashore or clung to driftwood carried in by the surf.

But the drama continued. Once ashore, the shipwrecked mariners built a fire, assisted by local people who brought food and drink. A snake, rigid with cold and mistaken for a stick, dug its fangs into Paul's wrist. According to local legend, the sea god Nemesis pursues offenders who escape drowning, and the bystanders assumed that Paul was indeed about to meet his nemesis.

However, when he failed to die, he himself was treated as a god. While on the island, he healed a number of local people, including the father of the island's governor who was ill with dysentery.

(Acts 27:1–28:10)

Apostle remanded in comfortable jail

Rome, c. AD 60

Pending his trial before Caesar or senior members of the Senate, the Christian pioneer church planter Paul is putting down roots in his own rented home in the city.

Although constantly guarded, he has been allowed to stay in a house rather than a public prison, and to receive unlimited visitors.

The final lap of his journey here was a leisurely affair compared with the traumas of the earlier stages. Christians at the grain import centre of Puteoli played host to the party for a week while the officer in charge, Julius, completed business there. Then others came from Rome itself to provide a friendly escort from the Forum of Appius 69 km (43 miles) south of the capital. More joined the procession 16 km (10 miles) further on at Three Taverns.

One of Paul's first actions on arrival was to contact the local Jewish community and to explain his beliefs to them. Since Claudius expelled Jews from Rome in 49 for riots about Christ, other Jews have drifted back to the metropolis. They seem to have had little contact with the local Christians who are largely Gentiles. Like their compatriots elsewhere, they were divided among themselves by Paul's assertions.

(Acts 28:11–30)

Essex woman falls to Rome

Queen Boudicca, as traditionally drawn.

Colchester, Britain, AD 60
Eighty-thousand Britons have been slaughtered by Roman troops. The rebels' leader, Queen Boudicca (Boadicea), committed suicide.

The Britons had been so confident of victory, having recently routed the Romans at Colchester, that they brought their wives and children to watch the battle.

Relationships between the Romans and the people of Essex had soured when, after the death of King Prasutagus, soldiers and slaves plundered the wealth he had left jointly to his daughters and the emperor. He had hoped that way to ensure protection of his household. His wife Boudicca was flogged and his daughters raped. His relatives were treated as slaves and East Anglian chiefs were deprived of their hereditary estates.

In response, Boudicca rounded up troops from East Anglia and destroyed the Roman settlement at Colchester. When the Statue of Victory there fell with its back turned, the Britons took this as a good omen. Other strange omens were also reported; a phantom settlement in ruins was seen at the mouth of the Thames, the sea turned blood red, and shapes like corpses were left by the tide.

The Colchester garrison with barely 200 men fell after a two-day siege. The Britons then marched on to St Albans and London, and plundered both. An estimated 70,000 Roman soldiers and sympathisers were hanged, burnt or crucified by Boudicca's mob.

Suetonius Paulinus, the imperial governor in Britain, ordered a final attack. A hail of javelins was followed by infantry with shield bosses and swords. Despite their smaller numbers, the skill and discipline of the Romans was utterly superior to the disorderly Britons, who had even blocked their own escape routes with wagons and baggage animals. The Romans suffered only 400 casualties compared with the 80,000 Britons. Boudicca poisoned herself in defeat.

Agrippina stabbed

Baiae, AD 59
Agrippina, mother of Nero, has been stabbed to death after escaping an attempt to drown her. Nero had put her on board a ship designed to sink but she swam ashore. Later, two sailors visited her home: she apparently recognised them and let them in. They then stabbed her, apparently on the emperor's orders.

Nero is said to have inspected the corpse and commented on her figure. He is staying in Naples but has no need to fear returning to Rome. Seneca's story that Nero himself narrowly escaped Agrippina's plot to kill him has resulted in the Senate passing a vote of thanks to the gods for his safe deliverance.

Battle scene, from Trajan's column, showing Roman troups in the 'tortoise formation.

Soldiers paralysed by frenzied women

Anglesey, Wales, AD 60
A mass of natives which included black-robed women with dishevelled hair like Furies brandishing torches, and Druid priests screaming curses, brought the Roman army to an abrupt halt as it tried to conquer this island off the north coast of Wales.

The soldiers, some of whom had swum with their horses across the narrow strait from the mainland, were briefly paralysed by fear. When they gathered their wits and strength, however, they quickly defeated the hordes which were enveloped in the flames of their own torches.

The ambitious Roman governor of Britain, Suetonius Paulinus, garrisoned the island, which is a centre of Druidism. It is said to be the religion's custom to drench altars in the blood of prisoners and to consult the gods by means of human entrails.

Paul fills mailbag in jail

Rome, c. AD 61–62

Although chained to an ever-present Roman guard, Paul the apostle has been using his enforced leisure to turn from preaching to letter-writing.

While under house arrest, the man who has travelled thousands of miles over the past 15 years can now only travel in his mind. But his influence can still be felt far away through his lucid and sometimes impassioned writing.

At least four letters have been dispatched recently from Rome in the trusty hands of Tychicus, Paul's personal courier and news-gatherer who these days is doing nothing but travel between Rome and the churches of Greece and Asia.

It is believed that many other letters have been written and delivered by Tychicus or others. Unfortunately they have not become public knowledge – maybe simply because the people they were addressed to have chosen to keep their contents private.

Mosaic of a Roman slave. Third-century mosaic from Paphos, Greece.

'Christ is above everything in the whole of creation'

Christians in Colossae have been told to abandon the subtle but false slants on Christianity which are creeping into their community.

According to Epaphras, who planted the church in this small town on the Lycus Valley while Paul was working in Ephesus about eight years ago, some people now regard Christ as less than divine. Epaphras, who is currently visiting Paul in Rome, also reports that angels are worshipped, special spiritual knowledge is claimed, and strict rules of abstention from legitimate food and sex are imposed by some leaders.

In response Paul, who has never visited Colossae, has written a kind but firm letter playing down the world of spirits, which he calls the 'basic principles of the world' and to which Christians 'died' when they believed in Christ. Indeed, Christ effectively paraded them like disgraced prisoners of war in a victory march when he defeated them on the cross, he writes.

To those who delight in mysteries and secrets, Paul says that Christianity does unveil some of the mysteries of God but there is no extra special knowledge for the enlightened few. As for the ascetics who impose mostly Jewish disciplines as a framework for holy living, he adds that their rules are humanly motivated, not divinely inspired. Their 'humility' could even be inverted pride.

Paul describes the ascended Jesus Christ as the supreme agent of creation who still holds the world firmly in his hands. He is the embodiment of the fullness of God's character, he claims. In a series of practical instructions, he tells Christians to submit to each other, to work hard at their jobs as if Christ were their employer, and to devote themselves to prayer and worship.

(Colossians 1-4)

Lycus Valley looking towards Colossae.

'Give slave a second chance'

In an impassioned plea, Paul has asked his friend Philemon not to apply the letter of the law and have his slave Onesimus executed for theft and desertion.

The slave had fled to Rome where he became a Christian under Paul's influence, and has already started to show signs of being a gifted church leader. Paul asks that Philemon, who himself was converted under Paul, possibly in Ephesus, receive Onesimus as a brother, and then release him to serve with Paul in the church.

The personal letter was taken by Tychicus to Philemon in Colossae along with Paul's open letter to the church. In a bold act of faith, Onesimus accompanied him, clearly anticipating a prodigal's welcome rather than a prisoner's gallows.

(Philemon)

Carried away by his own enthusiasm

Having tried to set the church in Colossae to rights, Paul seems to have been carried away by his own enthusiasm for some of the themes he majored on.

In a written sermon now being circulated around the churches of Ephesus, Laodicea and Hieropolis, Paul repeats over half the sentences or phrases he used in Colossians. But he omits all local details and references, instead focusing on universal truths.

Four especially capture his imagination and make his pen flow with purple prose. He begins with the supremecy of Christ, in whom every believer is a chosen child of God and through whom the mysteries of God's plans will be revealed. Christ now sits as a king 'far above all rule and authority, power and dominion', with every created thing subject to him.

By comparison, human beings are effectively dead to God, separated from his unending life by their sinfulness. However, Christians are given new life, raising them from spiritual death so they can live in ways which please God. Because all Christians have this new life, there is a unity between them whatever their cultural background; separation between Jew and Gentile has ended.

This leads Paul to his third theme, which has been much on his mind recently, that of unity of Christians in 'the body of Christ'. The church has one Lord who has distributed gifts to his people so that all should grow to mature faith and live harmoniously with each other, he says.

Finally, in a long section of practical instruction, he calls on his readers to imitate God in holy living and speaking. That means being vigilant, and all are to submit to each other, even in the family. He concludes with a description of a Roman soldier armed for battle, using it as a picture of the Christian's defences against the enemies of God.

(Ephesians 1–6; cf. Colossians 4:17)

Ruins of the Roman aqueduct bringing fresh water to the city of Laodicea.

'Thanks for the gift – beware of the dogs!'

Referring to Christian joy no less than 16 times in a short but fulsome letter, Paul has thanked the Philippian Christians for yet another substantial gift of money sent for his support in Rome. It had been delivered by Epaphroditus, who had fallen ill while helping Paul in Rome, and who was now being sent back to his anxious friends with Paul's reply.

In what must be one of the greatest poetic contributions to Christian thought to date, Paul eulogises the sacrificial death of Christ. He laid aside his majesty as the second Person of the Trinity and the privileges he enjoyed in order to live and die as a suffering servant. As a result, he claims, 'at the name of Jesus every knee should bow ... and every tongue confess that Jesus Christ is Lord.'

Not all is well with the church in Philippi, however. Paul issues a passionate plea for two of his former associates, Euodia and Syntyche, to end their quarrel. What made the two women fall out is unclear, but the church was being disrupted by their argument.

He also warns the Philippians to have nothing to do with a legalistic sect pressuring Gentiles to adopt Jewish practices. He charges them sternly to 'watch out for those dogs' who wish to force circumcision on all believers. He catalogues his own spiritual pedigree as a Hebrew-speaking child of a devout Jewish family and a member of the Pharisee party.

All this, however, was just garbage compared to the supreme privilege of knowing Jesus Christ as his Lord, he says. 'For his sake, I've lost everything.'

Finally, Paul says that his sufferings over the years had taught him 'the secret of being content' in any situation.

He reminds them that despite his achievements he has not attained perfection and like an athlete on the track drives himself on towards the finish line. He also introduces his associate Timothy to them, who is currently in Rome and who may visit Philippi shortly.

(Philippians 1–4)

Paul free to roam

Rome c. AD 62

The apostle Paul is said to have been freed from house arrest here and is now undertaking what some are calling his fourth missionary journey.

The details surrounding his whereabouts are obscure, but Paul has often stated his desire to visit Spain. Sources close to him also suggest he has been revisiting some of the churches which he helped to establish, including Ephesus and Philippi, and has also planted a new church in Crete, possibly on his way to Spain.

It seems that at the preliminary hearing of Paul's case before the imperial court the charges against him were not proved, and he was remanded pending further investigations. Surprisingly, his associates in Rome deserted him during the trial, perhaps fearing a form of religious genocide in the wake of the emperor Nero's increasingly random waves of killing.

(Romans 15:24; 1 Timothy 1:3; 3:14; 2 Timothy 1:15; 4:13, 16f, 20; Titus 1:5; 3:12.)

Be prepared for trouble

Rome, c. AD 63

Simon Peter, the first leader of the Christian church after Jesus Christ's death, has told Christians in five provinces in Asia Minor to get ready for the antagonism and persecution which is already hitting the church in Rome and could spread across the empire.

In a circular letter, he tells his readers not to be surprised if they suffer, because Christ himself also suffered. They are to prepare for the worst by living in holiness towards God and in submission to each other.

Peter, who calls Rome 'Babylon' as a symbol of a godless pagan city, may have been invited to the capital by Paul, who is believed to have left the city, to deal with a split between Jewish and Gentile believers. His letter states that 'the chosen people' are all who have put their trust in Christ.

Although the two apostles have always avoided working in the same area, the animosity which flared between them at Antioch in Syria about 12 years ago has never recurred.

It has been Paul's declared policy not to work in someone else's mission field but to plough his own furrow. Peter has also travelled widely, and it was possibly his presence in Asia which prevented Paul moving in there during his second missionary journey.

Peter's letter, in fact, bears close similarities to Paul's teaching, as well as including several quotes from Jesus. This, and the polished literary style which would be unusual even in a bi-lingual fisherman, may be partly due to the influence of Silas (Silvanus), Paul's travelling companion, who Peter acknowledges as his co-writer.

(1 Peter; cf. Acts 16:6–10; Romans 15:20; 1 Corinthians 9:5; Galatians 2:11–21.)

Points from the post

Peter's first letter says:

- God has given his people a new hope which outweighs all suffering (1:1–12).

- Christians are to prepare themselves by being like God in holiness, and to put aside all deceit (1:13–2:3).

- Christ is a cornerstone on which the people of God are built (2:4–12).

- Holiness includes submission to secular authorities and within families, and harmony in the church (2:13–3:12).

- Believers must be ready to answer their accusers, be self-controlled, and ensure they suffer for their faith, not for criminal activity (3:13–4:19).

- Church elders are to set a good example; all are to cast their cares on God (5:1–14).

Innocent wife loses head

Rome, AD 62

The head of Nero's 20-year-old ex-wife Octavia has been cut off and presented to his mistress Poppaea. To kill her, Octavia had been bound, and her veins opened, but fear had retarded her flow of blood, so she was put in a hot vapour bath where she suffocated.

The Roman people have never been so sure of a woman's innocence. She had been divorced by Nero who first said she was sterile and then that she had committed adultery. He later claimed she had had an abortion having been made pregnant by her lover. Octavia's maids, who swore to her innocence, have been tortured for their loyalty.

Two former slaves of the emperor have also been murdered. Doryphorus had opposed Nero's marriage to Poppaea, and Pallas apparently offended by living for so long that he had spent his wealth on himself instead of leaving it to Nero.

Nero, from a contemporary bust.

Private lives exposed

Ephesus, c. AD 64–65

Two confidential letters sent by Paul to his assistant Timothy have been released here. The most recent one, written from Rome shortly before Paul's execution, contains the apostle's last known instructions concerning church life and Christian conduct.

The first letter to Timothy, probably written from Greece during Paul's travels between his two trials, shows that the false teachings he had rebutted in Colossae have spread to other churches in Asia. They include attention to genealogies, speculative myths, enforced celibacy and strict dieting. Arrogant claims to special knowledge, and human desire for wealth, lead to division, he says.

Church leaders are to have exemplary personal and family lives. Bowing to the social mores of the area and the Jewish community, Paul warns women not to disrupt worship meetings nor to assume the role of teachers.

The second letter depicts a more lonely figure. Back in prison, Paul has been disowned by some former associates while others have been sent on foreign missions – Titus to Yugoslavia, Crescens to Galatia, and Tychicus to relieve Timothy in Ephesus. 'Only Luke is with me,' he complains, suggesting perhaps that he had taken up the scribe's pen as the language and style is more like Luke's than Paul's other letters.

Timothy, he says in both letters, is to guard the gospel against false teachers and overbearing leaders. He is also to guard himself against the weakness of the flesh by being bold rather than timid and by drinking wine to prevent his frequent illnesses – a prescription, perhaps, directly from doctor Luke.

Shut up, you Cretans!

Crete, c. AD 64–65

Maybe an angel could tolerate Cretans, but a mere apostle can't. Paul has become the latest Mediterranean traveller to fall foul of the islanders' unenviable reputation for surliness, madness and downright hostility.

In a sharply-worded letter to his associate Titus, who Paul left on the island after a visit there during his parole from prison, the apostle says that deceptive teachers 'must be silenced'. Titus is to 'rebuke them sharply' to prevent myths, controversies over the law, and errors spreading. Leaders are to be 'straightened out' and offenders given two warnings only – but he fails to say what happens next.

Church members, he adds, are to be self-controlled, sober, and abstaining from the Cretan pastime of slandering each other. Paul obviously believes in miracles. But he is also a realist and gives Titus a get-out clause. They are to meet up on the mainland at Nicopolis. Titus has probably bought his ticket already.

Olive groves near Iraklion, Crete.

Ambassadors' hard tasks

Timothy and Titus are among several ambassadors sent by Paul to assist new churches. Although carrying his authority, they act as advisers rather than leaders.

Timothy was to many observers an unusual choice for a hard job. Quiet, subject to depression and illness, he was thrown like a Daniel into a den of roaring opponents ready to maul his theology and savage his tactics. He was born of a Jewish mother and Greek father in Lystra, where he probably became a Christian through Paul. Set apart for service by prophecies, he has travelled widely with Paul.

Titus is a more robust person and a good organiser. Like Timothy he is Greek, but unlike Timothy has never been compelled to be circumcised as a token gesture to Jewish Christians. Before going to Crete he had already smoothed ruffled feathers in Corinth. He is said to be Luke's brother.

(1 & 2 Timothy; Titus; cf. Acts 16:1f; 20:4f)

387

Fire sweeps through much of Rome

Rome, July AD 64

Flames still rage through the streets of Rome several days after the great fire began in the night of 18–19 July. Over two-thirds of the city has been affected; three divisions have been destroyed, seven severely damaged, and only four are unaffected.

The emperor Nero has arranged emergency accommodation for people in the Field of Mars, including Agrippina's public buildings and his own Gardens. Food has been brought in from Ostia and other neighbouring towns and the price of corn has been cut.

The fire began in the north-east corner of the Circus Maximus, and quickly spread through nearby shops. It is calculated that it was exactly 418 years, 418 months and 418 days since the last fire of Rome, started by the Gauls in 390 BC.

The hunt is now on for the alleged fire-raisers, even though it appears that the cause is likely to have been accidental. Wild rumours are already circulating that Nero himself instigated the fire in order

The great fire in Rome, as seen in the film *Quo Vadis*.

to rebuild the city according to his own plans, although he was away at Antium at the time.

Power of Roman senator Piso leans too far

Rome, AD 65

A conspiracy of some senators to replace Nero with Calpurnius Piso has failed the night before it was due to take place. Among the plotters were Rufus, who with Tigellinus had replaced Burrus as praetorian prefect three years ago.

Also implicated in the conspiracy was Seneca, Nero's tutor who had resigned when Tigellinus and Rufus were appointed. He was almost certainly innocent, but along with 19 others has been forced to commit suicide.

It took the 69-year-old rhetorician four attempts to die. His wife wished to die with him, and they

slashed their wrists, but Seneca bled too slowly so he also slashed veins in his legs. In severe pain he asked for hemlock, and drank it without effect. Finally he was carried into a vapour bath and suffocated. His wife was saved on the emperor's orders.

Nero appears shaken by the conspiracy and is fearful for his own safety. He is ordering the execution of numerous people on flimsy pretexts. Salvidienus Orfitus has been killed for leasing part of his premises to representatives of allied states, and Thrasea Paetus allegedly for looking like a cross schoolmaster.

Christians get the blame

Rome, AD 64

The sect of Christians has been officially blamed for the fire of Rome and are being rounded up for public execution in Nero's Gardens.

Some are dressed in the skins of wild animals and thrown to dogs while others have been dipped in pitch, impaled on stakes, and set alight to become living torches. Others have been crucified.

Privately, few people believe the Christians guilty but allege their anti-social tendencies and depravity is worthy of punishment. However, the savagery of their execution is being seen as excessive by many. A Jewish sect, they take their name from Jesus Christ who was crucified in Judea during the reign of Tiberius.

Top leaders executed

Rome, c. AD 65

Peter and Paul, probably the two greatest leaders of the Christian church to date, are reported to have been executed in separate incidents during the persecution in Rome. Both will be greatly missed.

Although details are sketchy, it is believed that Peter had been intending to flee the capital but in a vision saw Jesus entering the city, so he turned back. It is said that he was crucified upside down.

Paul, who had already been subject to a preliminary trial under Nero, is believed to have returned to the city for the second hearing and found guilty of the charges. He is believed to have been beheaded outside the city on the road to Ostia. He began his public ministry some 15 years after Peter, and planted churches across the empire. His thought and teaching have become normative for churches everywhere.

Chinese take a way to Buddhism

Peking, AD 65

The Han dynasty, in power almost continuously since about 200 BC, has given official recognition to Buddhism, a religion which has filtered through the silk-trade routes from central Asia for several decades.

The new emperor Ming has been sympathetic to it for some time. It

The Shakyamuni Buddha with two attendant Bodhisattvas. A first-century sandstone carving from the Han dynasty.

has been rumoured that he once had a vision of a divine being like a golden man, and on being told it must have been the god Buddha he sent envoys to India to find out about it.

The new recognition is surprising in that Confucianism has become the official state religion and is considered responsible, controlled and temperate. Folk religions and local cults have been stamped out and wayside temples to gods destroyed. Although Confucius accepted a variety of gods, he taught respect for ancient values and customs with the main religious observance focused on ancestors.

However, while government scribes have been consolidating and standardizing ancient beliefs, some of the aristocracy have been attracted to Taoism. They reject the priestly hierarchy of state Confucianism and instead preserve a more intimate relationship with the gods. The aim of Taoism is to conform to the tao (way, or path) of nature and create a new immortal body fit for paradise.

According to philosopher Wang Ch'ung, Taoists 'dose themselves with the germ of gold and jade, and eat the finest fruit of the purple

Earthenware figure of a male dancer.

polypore fungus' to gain spiritual enlightenment.

This has opened the way for Buddhism in China, and some of its devotees consider the new religion to be an exotic form of Taoism. Buddhism, founded by Siddharta Gautama on the Indian–Nepal border about 500 BC, teaches a form of enlightenment which liberates people from 'karma', the cycle of cause and effect which imprisons the soul on earth in endless reincarnations and sufferings.

Through an eightfold path of enlightenment, which embraces wisdom, strict ethics and mental discipline, the goal of nirvana, the eternal realm, can be reached, it is claimed.

Fast Facts AD 60–63

Rome, AD 60: A brilliant comet has appeared, causing speculation that the emperor is about to fall. It was further fuelled by a bolt of lightning which struck and broke the table at which Nero was eating in his mansion near the Simbruine Lakes.

Rome, AD 60: A new competition, the Neronia, based on a Greek model, will take place every five years. In the inaugural games, the emperor was declared winner in poetry and oratory, although prizes were not awarded. There were also contests in athletics, chariot-racing and music. Opponents of foreign influences suggest that the latest import is bringing more corruption and perversity into the capital at a time when traditional morals are already deteriorating.

Qumran, c. AD 60: The Essene sect, a monastic order which has communities scattered across Judea emphasising strict discipline and sharing of property, has recently published its war scroll giving detailed instructions for fighting the enemies of Judaism. Weapons and military tactics described are copied from the Romans. The scroll reveals the extent of fear and tension among the Jews.

Caesarea, c. AD 62: Porcius Festus, governor of Judea and Samaria for the past four years, has died suddenly. He has been succeeded by Albinus, who has begun to free criminals from prison for money. Albinus is also suppressing free speech, imposing high taxes and creating an atmosphere of fear.

Jerusalem, c. AD 62: James the brother of Jesus has been stoned to death for breaking Jewish law by order of the high priest Ananus. He had been the undisputed leader of the Jerusalem church since Peter embarked on an itinerant ministry. Ananus, a rigid Sadducee, has been reported to King Herod Agrippa II and the incoming procurator Albinus for what is regarded by many as an extreme act. He has been deprived of his office, but continues to influence affairs with bribes and force.

Rome, AD 63: The sudden death of Augusta, the four-month-old daughter of Nero and Poppaea, has plunged the emperor into extreme grief. The baby has been declared a goddess. At her birth Nero had erected a temple of Fertility.

Nero's suicide ends six months of unrest

Rome, June AD 68

The emperor Nero has committed suicide at the villa of freedman Phaon, near Rome. When the news was announced, citizens ran through the streets wearing liberty caps. It brings to an end six months of intrigue and rebellion when the tyrant king finally reaped the fruits of destruction he had sown all his short life.

The final chapter in the brutal saga of his reign began in January when famine hit Rome while Nero was in Greece. He was recalled by freedman Helius, his appointed deputy, to discover the city in turmoil over the exercise of rule by freedmen.

In March, Julius Vindex, governor of the province of Lyons in Gaul, rebelled against Nero with the battlecry 'Freedom from the tyrant!' He may have hoped for some political independence similar to that granted to Greece. Several Gallic tribes joined him and he had 100,000 armed men.

However, not all the Gauls supported him and his force was overwhelmed in the spring at Besancon by the legions commanded by the governor of upper Germany, Vindex committed suicide.

Meanwhile, Sulpicius Galba, governor of Hispania, had sided with Vindex. He believed that Nero was plotting his death, declared Vindex 'Legate of the Senate and Roman people' and announced his intention to overthrow Nero. His soldiers saluted him as emperor. He had only one legion at first, but Nero did not respond with the prompt military action which would have defeated Galba.

Instead, the emperor lost his nerve when first Tigellinus, the prefect of the Praetorian Guard, deserted him, and then a provincial governor in Africa, Clodius Macer, revolted against Nero 'in the name of the republic'.

In early June, all the provincial armies renounced their allegiance to Nero, who fled from Rome. The Senate, which had previously pronounced against Galba, now recognised him as emperor. All that remained was for Nero to respond, which he did by asking Epaphroditus, his secretary, to cut his throat for him.

He was 31 and had ruled since his teens. His last words were that the world was losing a great artist. He was buried on the Pincian Hill.

Family feud gives Cerealis food for thought

York, AD 69

Cerealis, the Roman commander in Britain, is leading a difficult and complex campaign against the Brigantes of northern Britain following a husband–wife feud in the tribe. Queen Cartimandua, who is loyal to Rome, had divorced her husband Venutius and assumed command of the tribe in 67, but he has rallied anti-Roman forces and recaptured his former territory.

The Brigantes are the largest tribe in Britain and their territory includes the bleak Pennine mountains where warfare is difficult. However, their forces are widely scattered and socially fragmented; many tribespeople are semi-nomadic shepherds. Some of their hill forts are undefended and their eastern flank is exposed to the Parisi in eastern Yorkshire and Humberside who are friendly to Rome and whose dry territory provides an obvious route to the main Brigantian stronghold at Stanwick.

In preparation for the necessary assault, Cerealis is building a line of forts from Brough on Humber to Malton in Yorkshire.

A first-century mummy case of a Roman citizen, from Egypt.

Fast Facts AD 65–68

Rome, AD 65: Poppaea, the pregnant wife of Nero, has died after being kicked by the emperor in a fit of rage. Her body has been stuffed with spices and embalmed, according to foreign customs.

Achaia, November AD 67: Freedom for Greece has been declared by Nero, emancipating Achaia from the control of the governor of Macedonia. The whole of Greece is now autonomous and immune from taxation. Nero has been touring Greece this year and taking part in artistic and athletic competitions. The Greeks have celebrated all their national games in one year and awarded Nero 1,808 first prizes.

Dead Sea, AD 68: The Roman commander Vespasian, having captured Jericho from rebel forces, has visited the mysterious Dead Sea. He ordered non-swimmers to be thrown into deep water with their hands tied behind their backs, and found that they bobbed to the surface as if blown upwards by a strong wind. The sea also regularly throws up black lumps of bitumen which is collected by the local people. It is used for caulking ships to keep them watertight. Bitumen is also included in many medical prescriptions.

Madras, AD 68: It is reported that Thomas, one of the original twelve apostles of Christ and the one who initially doubted the resurrection stories, has been martyred in Mylapore near Madras. He had travelled to India and is believed to have founded a flourishing Christian church in Kerala, on the western coast.

Jews put knives into Masada

Dead Sea, AD 66

The Jewish rebel group the Sicarii, or daggermen, so called because of the long knives they conceal in their garments, have captured Masada from the Romans.

An isolated plateau 400 m (1,300 ft) above the western shore of the Dead Sea, Masada was founded by the Jewish defender Judas Maccabeus about 160 BC. It was used as a family refuge by Herod the Great during the Parthian invasion and was later developed into a sumptuous residence.

The summit is 1,200 m (1,300 yd) round, enclosed with a limestone wall 5.5 m (18 ft) high and 3.5 m (12 ft) thick. There are 37 towers inside, each 23 m (75 ft) high. The soil on the summit is rich for food production, and there are deep water tanks cut into the rock. The Sicarii found enough provisions inside to last several years. There were also enough weapons for 10,000 men, which had been horded over the years by Herod.

The Jewish revolt.

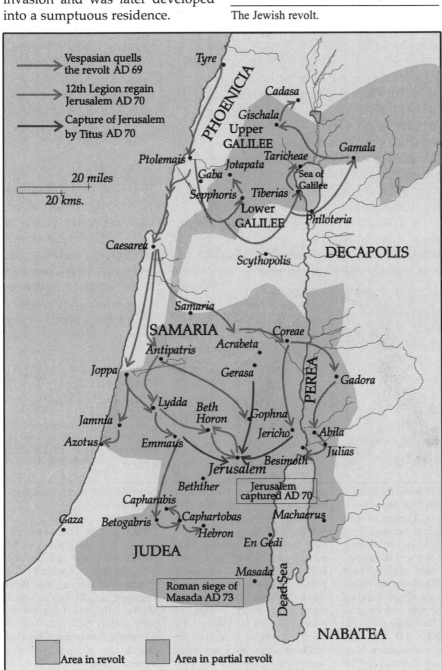

Vespasian quells the revolt AD 69

12th Legion regain Jerusalem AD 70

Capture of Jerusalem by Titus AD 70

20 miles

20 kms.

Tyre
PHOENICIA
Cadasa
Gischala
Upper GALILEE
Gamala
Ptolemais
Taricheae
Jotapata
Gaba
Sea of Galilee
Sepphoris
Tiberias
Lower GALILEE
Philoteria
Caesarea
Scythopolis
DECAPOLIS
Samaria
SAMARIA
Coreae
Antipatris
Acrabeta
Joppa
Gerasa
PEREA
Gadora
Lydda
Beth Horon
Gophna
Jamnia
Jericho
Abila
Azotus
Emmaus
Julias
Besimoth
Jerusalem
Bethther
Jerusalem captured AD 70
Capharabis
Betogabris
Caphartobas
Machaerus
Gaza
Hebron
En Gedi
JUDEA
Masada
Dead Sea
Roman siege of Masada AD 73
NABATEA

Area in revolt   Area in partial revolt

War continues in Judea

Jerusalem, AD 68

The sporadic fighting between Rome and Jewish rebels in Judea continues despite the efforts of Vespasian and the Fifth, Tenth and Fifteenth Legions. So far, Jerusalem, the religious and political capital of the Jews, has proved to be a final point of resistance.

The Northern Palace, in Masada.

While the area has always proved volatile, the troubles began in earnest four years ago during the governorship of Florus, who succeeded Albinus. A long-running dispute in Caesarea, claimed as a Greek city by the Gentiles despite its historic associations with the Jews, was declared Greek by Nero. One Sabbath, a Greek placed a chamber pot at the entrance to the synagogue and sacrificed birds on it, violating Jewish law and desecrating the site. Fighting broke out.

Florus then ordered the Jerusalem temple authorities to pay 17 talents to Caesar. When riots of protest broke out, Florus sent in the troops who sacked the Upper Market Place and killed 3,600 men, women and children. Outright war was avoided by the intervention of King Agrippa II, but when he urged the people to obey Florus they banished him from the city.

Then in AD 66 Eleazar, son of the high priest and also a temple captain, persuaded the temple authorities not to accept gifts or offerings from foreigners. This effectively outlawed offerings to Rome and made war inevitable.

Boom in Christian literature

Life of Christ still good news

Four written accounts of the life and teachings of Jesus Christ are now being circulated under the corporate title of 'Gospels', or good news, after the opening phrase of the one by Mark. They differ in detail and emphasis, but they also contain much common material drawn from earlier sources.

From the start of their religion around AD 30, Christians have collected stories and sayings of Christ, repeating them verbally in their meetings and sometimes writing them down. Among the earliest writings were lists of ancient biblical texts pointing to Christ as the Messiah, or promised messenger, similar to those composed by esoteric groups such as the Essenes of Qumran.

The apostles, especially Paul, have written numerous letters to churches, but these assume

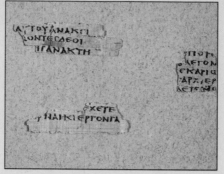

This fragment of Mark's Gospel has been identified as the earliest existing copy of any of the New Testament writings. It is dated to the midddle of the first century AD, putting the authorship of Mark's Gospel to around AD 50.

knowledge of the life of Christ. With many people joining the churches who have never before heard of the Nazarene, the need for systematic instruction about his life and teaching has increased.

According to Luke, one of the four authors, many attempts have been made to write such accounts. His Gospel, and that named after Matthew, draw heavily on Mark's work which itself probably records words and incidents taught by rote in many churches. Matthew and Luke also appear to draw on a common source or tradition.

The fourth document, by John, complements the others by adding detail about Jesus' visits to Jerusalem not recorded elsewhere. Typically for its author, once nicknamed 'son of thunder' by his cousin Jesus, it emphasises more directly the meaning of Jesus' words and calls for a response to them.

All four give disproportionate space to the final week of Jesus' life. Christians place great importance on his death and resurrection, claiming that through it people are reconciled to God. None of the accounts contains more than cursory detail about Christ's early life, and each sets out to be a teaching manual rather than a standard biography.

Four Gospels to choose from

'MARK'

Written by John Mark who was a teenager in Jerusalem during Christ's ministry. He became a travelling companion of Paul until he pulled out of a mission and was taken on instead by his uncle Barnabas. He also teamed up with Peter, who he had known in Jerusalem, and the book depends largely on Peter's teaching and reminiscences. It is written in poor Greek with appalling grammar, and has a jerky style, breathlessly lurching from one incident to the next.

'LUKE'

Penned by Paul's physician and companion for a believer called Theophilus who wants a historical basis for his new faith. A Gentile, Luke probably comes from Antioch in Syria. He has pieced together information from numerous sources, probably including the mother of Jesus, to show that Jesus is Messiah for all nations.

The work is marked by attention to factual detail and an absence of polemic. He portrays Jesus as kind and sympathetic to outcasts, women and the poor. Luke is also writing a companion volume, 'The Acts of the Apostles', describing the growth of the church and the activity of Paul.

'MATTHEW'

More thematic than the first two, this book focuses on such teachings as discipleship, the kingdom of God, and judgment, although it follows the same chronological sequence. Named after the tax collector associate of Jesus, it may be the work of someone close to him because it seems to rely more heavily on Mark than one would expect of an eyewitness. It is written especially to convince Jews that Jesus is the Messiah, and to instruct new converts in his basic teachings.

'JOHN'

With an almost meditative style, John the apostle betrays his Palestinian fisherman's origins by writing Greek according to Aramaic rules of grammar, and by inserting minute eye-witness details of Jerusalem as it was during Jesus' lifetime.

He also picks up images such as darkness and light which are of interest to some Jewish mystical sects. John, who describes himself as 'the disciple who Jesus loved', is now believed to be working in Ephesus.

'Christ is all you need'

Rome, c. AD 68

An unsigned letter, from an unspecified address, urging Jewish Christians to endure hardship and not to compromise Christ by reverting to Hebrew traditions has been received here. Among the candidates as author, who says he was not an eyewitness of Christ, are Barnabas, Paul's former associate, and Apollos, one of Paul's converts. 'The letter to the Hebrews' describes in considerable detail the difference between the work of Christ as High Priest and the ministry of Jewish priests. Its readers, who may belong to an isolated house church or who share a common background such as the priesthood, are taught Christian truth with Hebrew imagery.

The author is aware of their sufferings (10:32–34), although whether these refer to persecution in Jerusalem or more recent events under Nero in Rome is unclear. They are encouraged to persevere by recalling the greater sufferings of Christ (12:3–4). He is superior to angels, to Moses and to the traditional priesthood, he claims. Christ's divinity is stated, but the letter focuses on his humanity.

Christ's sacrifice for sin remains effective for ever, he asserts, whereas 'it is impossible for the blood of bulls and goats to take away sins' (10:4). As a result of Christ's death, a new covenant with God has been enacted which supersedes all previous covenants.

The letter contains numerous warnings against drifting from God (2:1), falling into unbelief (3:12, 6:4–6), isolationism and habitual sin (10:25–27), bitterness, immorality and greed (chs 12–13). But it is also peppered with encouragements. God can be approached confidently because Christ understands human weakness (4:14–16), giving hope as secure as a ship's anchor (7–19) and an assurance that God will keep his word (10:36).

Even if persecution seems hard, it can be seen as God's discipline of love (12:4–11). A summary of the endurance of the saints of the past includes such unlikely characters as the prostitute Rahab and Samson, the womaniser, as well as Moses, Abraham and David. The author says they remained faithful even though they knew less of God's purposes than his readers do now.

(Hebrews 1-13)

Beasts of Balaam savage young flock

Rome, c. AD 64

Serious divisions in the Christian church have prompted two vitriolic memos to be circulated warning believers of the dangers of false teachers who act 'like brute beasts'.

The memos, which are very similar, are said to come from the

The prophet Balaam is remembered for his overwhelming desire for personal gain, which led him into trouble with God who, in the end, had to send his angel to communicate with him through his ass, as portrayed here by Rembrandt.

desks of the apostle Peter, now in Rome, and Jude (or Judas), the brother of Jesus Christ whose current location is uncertain. Indeed, this second letter from Peter includes over half of Jude's verses, and his future tense may indicate that he believes in the probable spread of the heresies which Jude is witnessing elsewhere.

Certainly Jude has been written in a hurry, and Peter's style lacks the more studied influence of the scribe Silas who assisted with his first letter.

The contention of both is that people behaving like brute beasts are denying Christ's humanity, divinity or both, slandering celestial beings, and appear to be hungry for personal gain and sensual satisfaction like the ancient anti-prophet Balaam. They are 'springs without water' according to Peter, and 'clouds without rain' according to Jude. Both conclude that 'blackest darkness is reserved for them'.

In the face of the attack, Christians are to remain firm in their faith, consistent in their behaviour and patient in their attitudes. Above all, they are to watch out that they are not led astray, say the authors.

(2 Peter, Jude)

Vespasian is fourth emperor in twelve bitter months

Rome, 22 December AD 69

Vespasian, the veteran campaigner who led Roman forces to victory in Britain and Judea, has been declared emperor. His appointment brings to an end the bitter civil war and the succession of inept leaders appointed since Nero.

The first to go had been Galba, the 73-year-old widower appointed in October last year without military support for his old fashioned strictness. Claiming to be a descendant of the god Jupiter, he had been commander of troops in Germany and a proconsul in Africa and then Spain where he seemed to do little more than sunbathe.

Troops in upper Germany revolted against him in January when he withheld payment for their services against the Gauls and Vindex. Others joined them when he refused to pay a promised bonus. He appointed Piso – who had conspired against Nero – as his successor, and five days later was murdered. His head was paraded scornfully around the Praetorian camp.

His replacement was Otho, because Piso was also murdered. The 37-year-old, who was completely devoid of body hair, claimed to be the legitimate successor of Nero who had banished him to Lusitania. He was doomed from the start. The military had already declared Vitellius, governor of lower Germany, emperor. With the support of troops in Gaul, Raetia, Britain and Spain, he began marching towards Rome.

Vitellius lost three battles against Otho, but won a decisive victory at Betriacum despite being short of supplies. Otho, who still controlled the sea, appears to have lost heart when he could have continued the war with a good chance of overall success. He is said to have had an abhorrence of civil war. Otho then committed suicide on 16 April with a single well directed stab, which caused considerable displays of public grief.

Vitellius then declared himself the undisputed master of the Roman world, but it was two months before he entered Rome itself, accompanied by 60,000 troops carrying drawn swords. While the troops ran amock, Vitellius sat down to a banquet where 7,000 game birds and 2,000 fish were served.

Shortly afterwards he declared himself chief priest, made himself consul for life, and declared elections for ten years' time. He sacrificed to the ghost of Nero. He had spent his childhood among the male prostitutes on the isle of Capri, and was notorious for every kind of vice. He was a glutton who always had an alcoholic flush.

Meanwhile, in the far-flung outpost of Judea, Vespasian was hailed as emperor in early July by legions in Egypt, Judea itself, and then Syria. He was also supported by eastern client kings and, after initial hesitation, by the Danubian provinces. With 14 legions behind him, he sent an expeditionary force to threaten Italy while he himself went to Egypt to cut off Rome's grain supply.

Despite a premature attack on Italy which Vitellius' commanders could easily have repulsed, the Flavians (supporters of Vespasian) faced comparatively little opposition. At the crucial and bloody battle of Cremona in October the Flavians accepted surrender but then killed 50,000 inhabitants. After that, Britain, Gaul and Spain switched allegiance to Vespasian, as did troops on the Rhine.

On 18 December, Vitellius agreed to abdicate, but was prevented by soldiers loyal to him. Two days later he was found hiding in the palace, and was dragged by the hair through the streets before being

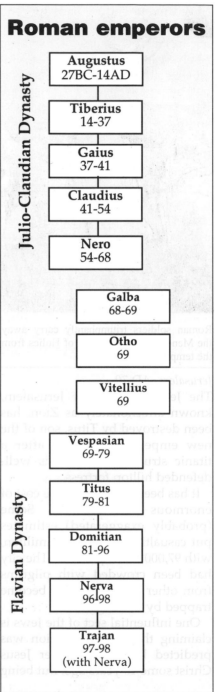

Roman emperors

Julio-Claudian Dynasty

| Augustus 27BC-14AD |
| Tiberius 14-37 |
| Gaius 37-41 |
| Claudius 41-54 |
| Nero 54-68 |

| Galba 68-69 |
| Otho 69 |
| Vitellius 69 |

Flavian Dynasty

| Vespasian 69-79 |
| Titus 79-81 |
| Domitian 81-96 |
| Nerva 96-98 |
| Trajan 97-98 (with Nerva) |

killed near the Stairs of Mourning. He was 56. With his victorious and seemingly uncontrollable soldiers again rampaging through the streets, Vespasian was recognised as emperor by the Senate today. For the first time, all imperial powers have been bestowed on an emperor en bloc.

Titan Titus topples Zion

Roman soldiers triumphantly carry away the Menorah from the Holy of Holies from the temple in Jerusalem.

Jerusalem, AD 70

The Jewish capital of Jerusalem, known affectionately as Zion, has been destroyed by Titus, son of the new emperor Vespasian, after a titanic struggle against this well-defended hilltop fortress.

It has been achieved at the cost of enormous loss of life. Some (probably exaggerated) estimates put casualties as high as a million, with 97,000 taken prisoner. The city had been crowded with pilgrims from other areas who had become trapped by the siege.

One influential sect of the Jews is claiming that the destruction was predicted by their founder Jesus Christ some 40 years ago. But being forewarned did not protect the Christians and there was no discrimination between religious groups in the massacre.

The city had been under siege for some months, and it was the soldiers' impatience and desire for battle which precipitated the final attack. Morale was already at rock-bottom in the famine-stricken city, and many people had already died from thirst and hunger. One soldier reported that he saw a woman kill her baby and roast it in order to feed herself.

Jerusalem, a compact city with a labyrinth of narrow streets and dominated by a magnificent temple, has now been flattened. Only three towers and a stretch of wall to the west remain, possibly as a base for a future garrison. The Tenth Legion, with some additional cavalry and foot soldiers, has been left to guard it.

The ultimate humiliation for the Jews was the destruction of the temple, built by King Herod at the turn of the century. Corpses were burned by the altar – a sacrilege to the Jews – and temple treasures, including a heavy golden table and a unique seven-branched candelabra, were removed to Rome.

Judah has always posed problems for Rome. The independent-minded Jews, with their stubborn monotheism, have proved impossible to assimilate into the empire. In the past, they were given considerable local autonomy, and their religious practices were generally tolerated.

But relationships worsened during the 60s as sporadic rebellions broke out whenever Roman rule seemed to weaken. Rioting in Caesarea a few years ago, which began after a high priest refused to sacrifice on behalf of the emperor, sparked a chain reaction of rebellion.

Jerusalem was then fortified, and the Jewish scholar and historian Josephus raised an illegal army of 60,000 men in Galilee. Sectarian killings throughout the country prompted by disputes between moderates and extremists led to further unrest.

Some Christians claim that the destruction is a sign of God's judgement on the Jews for having rejected Jesus Christ as the promised Messiah. Others within the group point out that Jesus' prediction of the event was always couched in terms of sadness, not vengeance. In his prophecy he promised eternal peace and salvation to those who trusted him, however troubled the times.

The Arch of Titus was built by the emperor to commemorate his acheivements, his victory over the Jews in particular. This relief shows him on his chariot.

Fast Facts AD 70–73

Rome, AD 70: Vespasian has resorted to a small tax in his attempt to raise 40 billion sesterces for state projects. Users of Rome's urinals will now have to pay for the convenience. Former free cities such as Rhodes and Byzantium are now also expected to contribute to the imperial cause.

Rome, AD 71: The two parties of the Stoics and the Cynics have been expelled from Rome for their continued opposition to Vespasian's autocratic rule supported by the military.

Black Forest, AD 73: The first moves are being made by Roman forces to annex this triangle of land between the upper Rhine and upper Danube to facilitate communication between the Rhine and Danube camps.

Spain, AD 73: Full Latin rights have been granted to all native communities here. Leaders of such municipalities automatically receive Roman citizenship and can advance to high imperial office.

Rome, AD 73: Work has begun on the Flavian Amphitheatre, commonly called the Colosseum, between the Caelian and Esquiline hills. It is designed to hold more than 80,000 people.

Cult leader orders mass murder

The virtually impregnable fortress of Masada was the centre of Jewish resistance to the Romans and the scene of a most horrific mass suicide.

Masada, Dead Sea, AD 73

The famous cliff-top fortress of Masada in the arid southern desert of Judea has fallen to the Romans without an imperial sword being drawn.

Only an elderly woman and five children survived as the rebel Jewish Daggermen (or Sicarii) led by the charismatic Eleazar chose mass suicide rather than accept defeat. Soldiers who entered the eerily-silent fortress were moved to tears as they found the bodies huddled together.

Roman forces had besieged Masada for six months. Some 7,000 legionaries and auxiliaries built eight siege camps, then erected an earth ramp to the lower walls. When a battering ram breached the wall, the Romans discovered that the inhabitants had created an inner double-skinned wall with an earth-filled cavity which was too hard to breach but was eventually destroyed by fire.

When the soldiers assembled for the final attack the next day their battle-cries were answered only by silence and a smell of burning. Eventually, the old woman emerged and told the sad tale of how Eleazar had preached his counsel of despair.

He believed that God had deserted the Jewish community, because he had already allowed Jerusalem to be destroyed. Instead of protecting them he was wreaking vengeance on them for their wrongs. Eleazar called on them to commit suicide, and when they hesitated he warned them of the atrocities the Romans would commit if they broke in.

But instead of suicide, they elected for murder. Men killed their own families and torched their belongings, then drew lots to choose 10 executioners. The last man alive set fire to the palace and then killed himself. The Sicarii had believed they were the people most faithful to the Jewish cause. Soldiers who viewed the scene were humbled by their nobility and resolve; it was a hollow victory.

German revolt crushed

Cologne, AD 70

The city of Cologne, along with Treves, Vetera and the Rhine island home of the Batavians finally have been wrested from the grip of German rebels and restored to Roman sovereignty.

The Roman commander-in-chief Petilius Cerealis who has previously suppressed rebels in Britain, has been rewarded for the victory by being made governor of Britain.

The rebellion began during the 68–69 civil war. Julius Civilis, a brave Batavian, saw an opportunity to seize independence while the Roman forces on the Rhine were depleted. He had the added advantage that the Roman auxiliaries left behind were mostly recruited local men only too willing to change sides and fight for their own people.

Most German tribes, except the Cimbri and Cherusci, joined him, together with three tribes from Gaul (the Treveri, Lingones and Nervii). The rebels cleared the island of Romans, besieged the legionary camp at Casta Vectia, and when the Gauls joined them destroyed all but two of the Roman camps in the whole of Gaul and Germany.

Against these huge odds, legions from Italy, Spain and Britain under Cerealis have recovered many of the lands and forts. Meanwhile in upper Germany Annius Gallus has led four legions to defeat the Lingones. Central Europe is once more under Roman protection.

Unique reference book is 'too wordy'

Italy, AD 77

Pliny the Elder has published an encyclopaedia of natural history in 37 books. The author claims in his preface that the work contains 20,000 important facts, histories and observations obtained from 100 main sources.

The index, which takes up the whole of the first book, actually contains quite a lot more than that number. The encyclopaedia is the first of its kind; critics say it is too wordy to be useful, but it is still unique in its comprehensiveness. There are entries on medicine, zoology, botany, geography, mineralogy, the

A mosaic of wild beasts being hunted. Was this the first safari?

arts, customs and religion.

The medical section includes some bizarre remedies for sickness. For example, he offers the swallowing of earthworms in wine as a cure

for asthma, and kissing a mule's nostrils for catarrh. Urinary problems might be solved by eating the dung of ringdoves with beans.

Pliny also gives his own philosophical or moral views on the subjects he discusses. He repeatedly refers to the weaknesses of humankind. We are the only creatures that have to be taught all we know, the only ones who fight with their own kind, and the only ones to be guilty of excesses and seeking after luxury, he says. We are responsible for our misfortunes and he recommends a simple lifestyle.

Vespasian, from a contemporary bust.

Emperor dies of the cold

Rome, AD 79

The emperor Vespasian has died at his summer retreat near Reate, aged 69. He had caught a cold on a visit to Campania, which he made worse by taking a cold bath, and then continued his imperial duties until almost fainting after a bout of diarrhoea. He struggled to rise, saying an emperor should die on his feet, and collapsed into the arms

of his attendants. He joked, 'I must be turning into a god!'

Vespasian had a distinguished military career in Britain, Africa and Judea, before being made emperor in AD 70. He is succeeded by his son Titus, 40, .

His succession is uncontested, but despite his own military prowess Titus is said to be profligate and greedy.

Fast Facts
AD 74–80

Wales, AD 74–78: The chief tribespeople of Wales, the swarthy and curly-haired Silures, have been subdued by Rome. They lived in well-defended cliff-top sites and small walled farmsteads on the edge of the Black Mountains and the River Usk. A new legionary fortress has been established at Caerlon in the Usk Valley, and building works for a major fort in the north near Chester have begun.

Rome, AD 75: The celebrated Quintillian has become the first-ever professor to be paid from the public purse. All teachers of Latin and Greek rhetoric are now to receive an

annual salary of 1,000 gold pieces from the state.

North Wales, AD 78: The warlike tribe of the Ordovices has been virtually annihilated by the new Roman commander in Britain, Agricola. To do so, he used surprise attacks outside the normal campaigning season. He has also fully annexed the island of Anglesey.

Britain, AD 79: Tax abuse is said to be rife. Some people are being forced to buy back at inflated prices grain they have given as taxes, in order to give it a second time to pay further taxes. But meanwhile, the masses have taken to wearing the toga and Agricola is encouraging them to build temples, public squares and private houses in the

Roman style. The children of leading Britons are being given a Roman education.

Bay of Naples, AD 79: A major volcanic eruption from Mt Vesuvius has buried the cities of Herculaneum, Pompeii and Stabiae. The mountain, 48 km (30 miles) round and 1,280 m (4,200 ft) high poured molten rock, ash and mud without warning. The emperor has designated public funds to assist with relief work. Pliny the Elder was among those killed by the eruption. He had sailed from Misenum to watch the eruption from Stabiae, but was overcome by the fumes.

Ireland, c. AD 80: A Roman camp has been established at Drumanagh on the east coast of Ireland north of Dublin. It is the

first time the empire has had a permanent presence on this large land mass which marks the western fringe of Europe. The beach-head consists of a heavily-fortified compound surrounded by earth mounds and ditches as well as a wall. Inside are tightly-packed mud dwellings linked by mud and gravel roads and housing several hundred people. From Drumanagh, Rome can make exploratory forays into the hinterland which is home to scattered Celtic tribespeople who are unlikely to be conquered easily, if at all. Campaigns elsewhere and the logistical difficulties of transport across the wide and often wild Irish Sea may limit Rome's influence in the country.

The Roman Empire in AD 90

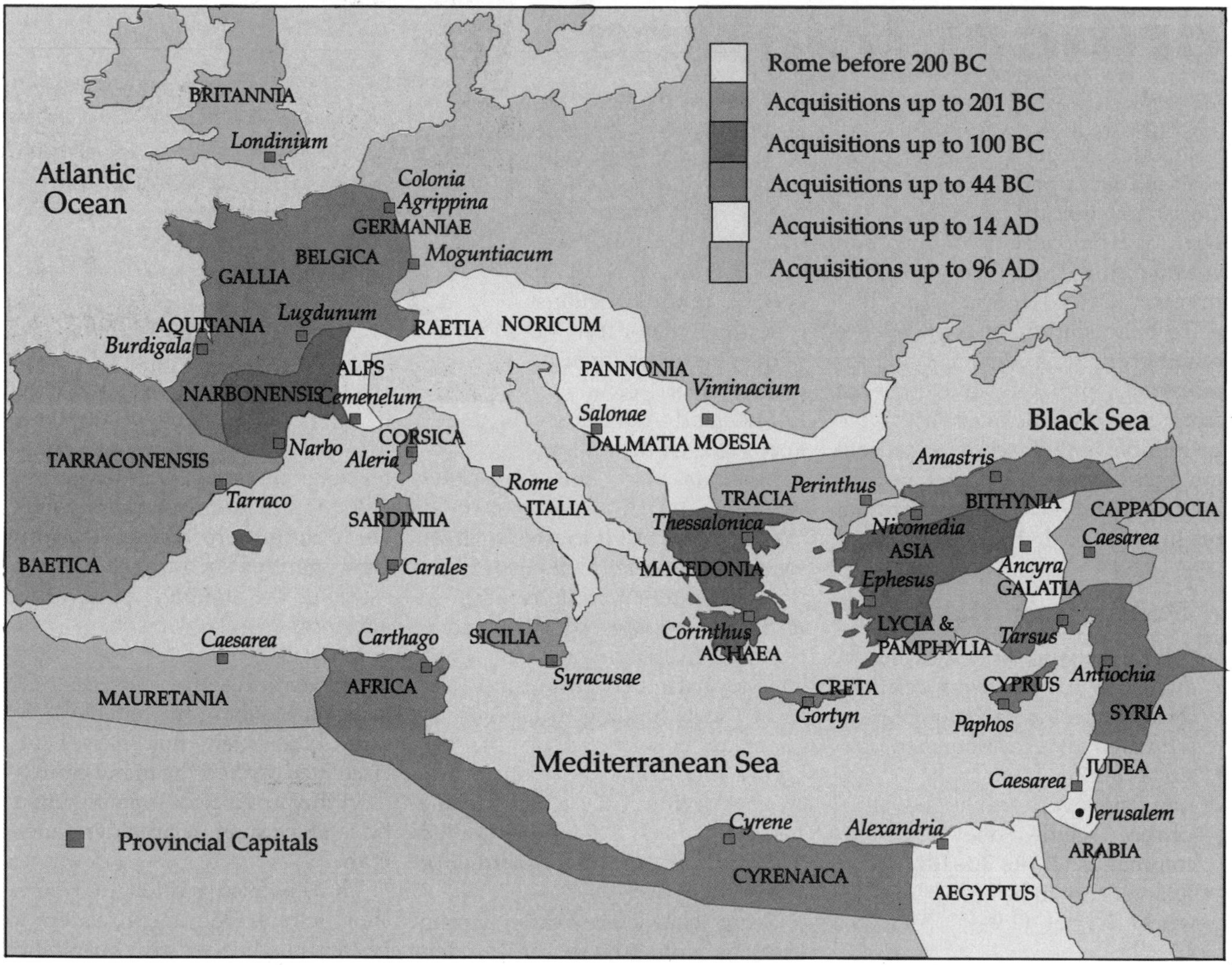

Legend:
- Rome before 200 BC
- Acquisitions up to 201 BC
- Acquisitions up to 100 BC
- Acquisitions up to 44 BC
- Acquisitions up to 14 AD
- Acquisitions up to 96 AD
- ■ Provincial Capitals

The Roman Empire. The inexorable expansion of the number of territories and nations under Roman control can easily be plotted on this map. Their military and administrative genius enabled those under Roman control to lead relatively safe and prosperous lives.

Scotland the brave thrown out of kilter

Carpow on Tay, Scotland, AD 84
Thirty-thousand Caledonian clans people have been thrown into disarray by Roman forces after a four-year struggle for domination in the wild mountains of this northern outpost.

The pitched battle near Inverurie in Aberdeenshire was launched by Agricola from his camp at Carpow following an invasion by marines from the Roman fleet.

The red-haired Caledonians, who are the dominant tribe of northern Scotland, were urged on by their leader Calgacus who insulted the Roman empire by calling it 'a rag-

bag of races united by success and sure to collapse if repulsed'. They had the advantage of the slope on a battle-site of their own choosing and the numerically evenly-matched armies began by exchanging missiles and fighting hand-to-hand.

Then the Roman cavalry routed Scottish chariots, and four reserve squadrons broke through the Caledonian ranks and surrounded them. Some 10,000 Scots were killed; Rome, ever meticulous in their statistics, lost only 360 men. Following the battle, the remaining Scots melted into the night.

Agricola, the commander of Roman forces in Britain, had begun his advance into Scotland four years ago. He encountered impressive fortifications, including the hill-fort at Traprian Law 150 m (500 ft) high and enclosing some 160,000 sq m (40 acres).

The southern parts of Scotland have fortified settlements including some built on the edges of lochs and approachable only by boat or narrow causeway. Agricola is now said to be considering an invasion of Ireland, a large land mass west of Britain where there is little Roman influence.

Apostle calls for critical thinking

Ephesus, c. AD 85

The apostle John, cousin and close associate of Jesus Christ, has released an open letter warning Christians not to be taken in by attractive but false teachings, and commanding them to use their minds.

'Test the spirits,' he says, 'to see whether they are from God, for many false prophets have gone out from the world.' Believers are not to be gullible but to check that preachers' messages agree with the truths of Christianity which were taught originally, and that their lives match up to the message.

The letter does not flow logically from start to finish, but meanders like a river around the subjects. However, the author, who is now quite elderly, returns regularly to three major tests of faith. One is obedience; people who claim to know God but don't keep his unchanging commands are liars, he says bluntly.

The second test is love; Christians who hate their fellow believers are not enlightened but remain in darkness, he says, turning catch-phrases from the new mystical heresies back on their authors. The third test is holding to established Christian beliefs such as the full bodily life, death and resurrection of the divine Christ, which the new teachings, sometimes called 'gnostic' (from the word for knowledge) deny.

Using characteristically strong language, John 'the son of thunder' claims that 'many antichrists have now come', heralding 'the last hour'. They were never true Christians, he asserts. To counter them he recalls his own personal experience of the presence and teaching of Jesus. But the stormy elder has not lost his pastoral touch. He combines forthright teaching with gentle encouragement, re-assuring the doubtful of the love and forgiveness of God.

The apostle, who has been based in Ephesus for some years, does not indicate to whom the letter is to be sent. It is likely that it is being circulated around the many churches in the province of Asia, to whom he is something of an elder statesman.

John has also written two other short letters. One urges readers to be careful who they give hospitality to; not all strangers who come in the name of Christ are angels in disguise. The other is a personal message of encouragement to John's friend Gaius.

(1,2,3 John)

The great theatre at Ephesus.

Points from the Post

- Full forgiveness and cleansing is available for all who confess their sins sincerely to Christ, who died to make atonement for sin (1:5–2:2).
- True believers must be like Christ, and obey God's commands (2:3–6; 3:1–10).
- Believers are to be loved, but the world is not (2:9–17; 3:11–20; 4:7–21).
- People who deny that the human Jesus is the divine Christ are deceivers (2:18–27; 4:1–6).
- Anyone who trusts Jesus is assured of eternal life (3:21–24) 5:1–12).

Fast Facts AD 80–90

Rome, AD 80: A huge fire has destroyed the new Capitol, the Parthenon and Agrippa's baths. There has also been the worst outbreak of plague known in the city.

Rome, AD 81: The emperor Titus has died after reigning for only two years. He was greatly loved, and built luxurious baths which he sometimes used alongside the common people. He had been in poor health and died of natural causes. He has been deified, and succeeded by Domitian.

Vietnam, c. AD 80–90: This tropical coastline is once again under Chinese rule. It was reclaimed by the septuagenarian Ma Yuan ('Wave Tamer') for the Hua people. He erected two bronze pillars to mark the southern limits of the civilised world.

Germany, AD 83–85: A two-year campaign has succeeded in defeating the Chatti tribe and completing the Roman line of defence from Main to Neckar. The territory of the Mattiaci, in the Odenwald, and the land between the Rhine and the Danube have been added to the empire, and a full imperial legate has been appointed to Germany.

Rome, AD 85: The emperor Domitian has become priest and king. As Pontifex Maximus he is undertaking a considerable building program, building new temples to Jupiter, rebuilding old temples to Janus, Castor and Apollo, and has founded a college of priests for Minerva, his protector. He has also appointed himself Censor Perpetua, which means he is effectively sole ruler of the empire and the Senate has been stripped of real authority.

Yugoslavia, AD 88: Rome has made an honourable peace with the defeated Dacians at Tapae. Decebalus has been recognised as king of Dacians in return for the release of Roman prisoners of war. The king has also been given money and engineers to build new defences. The suggestion that Rome has been humiliated by the Dacians is being strongly denied by the emperor.

Nightmare vision of aging apostle throws light on life

Patmos, c. AD 95

The aging apostle John, last-known survivor of the original 12 close associates of Jesus Christ, has published a vision of world events which reads like a nightmare with a happy ending.

His 'Revelation' is being circulated among seven churches in Asia Minor, each of which is also addressed in a prophetic letter which John claims comes from Christ himself. The book offers encouragement to all beleaguered Christians that God is in charge of world affairs despite hardship and persecution, and that ultimately his purposes will triumph over evil.

by a gorgeously-dressed woman dripping with jewels. She is called Babylon, probably a cryptic name for Rome, leading commentators to conclude that the beast represents the empire, or world government generally, as oppressor. However, some are suggesting that the beast symbolises a specific individual the 'Anti-Christ' who they believe will appear close to the end of time.

John has issued no explanations of his book, and even he finds parts of the vision difficult to understand. He is conducted through parts of the vision by an angelic helper who gives some elucidation, but on one occasion John sees or hears

divides and subdivides the book's sections (see box opposite).

There is no Christian precedent for this kind of writing. The ancient book of Daniel with its dream-imagery is tame by comparison. The closest parallels are Jewish apocalypses, which have proliferated over the past 200 years. These, however, tend to be anonymous and far more fanciful and wild than John's Revelation, which though complex is sober by comparison.

John has been exiled to the penal colony on the volcanic island of Patmos in the Aegean Sea as a result of the emperor Domitian's crackdown on religious groups which refuse to honour him as a god. John is clearly aware of the hardships faced by his readers, and he portrays the forces of evil as rampant in the world.

But he also sees God's hand controlling and even restraining their full impact. In one vision of destruction only one-third of the target is destroyed. This is reminiscent of the author of the Jewish book of Job who saw Satan under God's ultimate control, like a wild animal on a trainer's rope.

Interspersed throughout the vision are images of the worshipping and victorious community of heaven, made up of supernatural beings and humans who have remained faithful to Christ.

These images reach their climax in a series of spectacular word-pictures which turn the nightmare into a futuristic fantasy as glass and gold geometric shapes dominate the supernaturally-lit landscape of the new and incorruptible creation. Significantly for Jewish readers, the sea, which they have always feared and hated ever since their escape from Egypt about 1,300 years ago, is banished from the perfect world to come, together with all godless people.

Christ separates the sheep from the goats. A sixth-century mosaic from Ravenna.

Much of its message is couched in complex symbols with at times a nightmarish quality. Among the more bizarre is a beast with ten horns and seven heads, looking like a leopard but having a lion's mouth and a bear's feet. It emerges from the sea, joins forces with a dragon and has a client two-horned beast working on its behalf.

In a later scene the beast re-appears covered with blasphemous names and coloured scarlet, ridden

something which he is forbidden to reveal, leaving the reader frustrated and none the wiser.

Support for the view that the vision is a general overview of the whole of history, rather than a tight timetable focusing only on the grim twilight years of a planet, is given by the fact that the book appears to be a series of parallel visions and not as a narrative moving from A to Z. The number seven, which Jews believe signifies completeness,

John's sevenfold vision

The main body of John's vision appears to have seven parallel sections, each of which has seven elements. It conveys a timeless picture of God's supremacy over human degradation in every generation and points forward to the final judgement day when justice will be seen to have been done. Several similar sevenfold analyses with minor variations are possible; this is one.

1. SEVEN SEALS (6:1–8:1)
Christ, a slain lamb, opens seals on a scroll which release sufferings, in four cases conveyed by coloured horses. The church remains undefeated.

2. SEVEN TRUMPETS (8:2–11:19)
As each sounds, earth, sea, rivers and sky are partially afflicted; the ungodly are tortured and a third of humanity is killed. Before the final fanfare, there is bitter persecution, but the church is again shown to be victorious.

3. SEVEN VISIONS OF THE DRAGON'S KINGDOM (12:1–13:18)
God snatches a newborn child from the dragon's jaws, after which there is war in heaven and Satan falls to pursue (vainly) the child's mother. The beasts emerge with limited time to persecute the saints who are told to be patient.

4. SEVEN VISIONS OF CHRIST (14:1–20)
The scene opens in heaven, flashes back to the proclamation of Christ's message on earth, and ends with the final harvest of people to their destinies.

5. SEVEN BOWLS OF ANGER (15:1–16:21)
Again, the worship of heaven provides a backcloth of reassurance as bowls of God's anger afflict the people who worshipped the beast. The environment is also hit, and the scene ends with a cataclysmic earthquake.

6. SEVEN VISIONS OF 'BABYLON'S' FALL (17:1–19:10)
The woman and beast are likened to Roman emperors (although which ones is still unclear). Babylon falls, God's people are called out of it, and merchants mourn their losses. Finally, the victory of the church is celebrated.

7. SEVEN PICTURES OF CHRIST'S TRIUMPH (19:11–21:4)
Christ rides out on a white horse to destroy the forces of evil. The bound dragon is temporarily released and those who remain faithful to God during its reign are taken to heaven. Satan is destroyed, the dead judged, and the new creation is established for ever.

The Four Horsemen have always preyed heavily on the imagination. This sixteenth century woodcut by Albrecht Durer is one of the most powerful.

Seven desperate churches

Seven churches in the Roman province of Asia are addressed at the start of Revelation, real yet also perhaps symbolic of the whole church. All are clearly facing difficulty. Most are commended for some virtue and condemned for some vice. John's own church, Ephesus, where he worked for many years, is said to have lost its first love. Sardis is pictured as having dozed off.

Smyrna is told not to be afraid of suffering, and Philadelphia is reassured in its weakness. Pergamum and Thyatira are told to repent of harbouring heretics. Laodicea gets the worst assessment; the great Judge says it makes him feel sick.

Fast Facts AD 90–97

Hierapolis, c. AD 90: Two virgin daughters of Philip the apostle have been buried here alongside their father. A third daughter has been laid to rest in Ephesus. They had lived to a ripe old age and had been valued as first-hand informants on the people and events of the pioneer church. Their father had been one of the original six 'deacons' who later developed his own evangelistic ministry.

Rome, AD 96: The emperor Domitian has been murdered despite elaborate precautions to protect himself. He was stabbed by his niece's steward, Stephanus, who had hidden a dagger in an arm bandage he had worn for several days after a feigned injury. He was 44, and had reigned for almost 15 years, but was carried out by public undertakers like a pauper. His old nurse Phyllis cremated his body and secretly took his ashes to the Temple of the Flavians. Senators have denounced him. He will be remembered as a cruel and sadistic person, who liked to be called lord and god, although he governed efficiently and provided Rome with many splendid libraries.

Caspian Sea, AD 97: The Chinese General Pan Chao has reached this inland sea overland from the east with an army of 70,000 men. He has already established Chinese overlordship of central Asia but has not had major contact or conflict with the Roman empire which is now his next-door neighbour.

Globetrotters new guide

One of the most sought-after items in the Roman world were spices from the East, which formed the most common commodity imported by traders.

Arabia, c. AD 90

A new guidebook for world travellers has been written by an anonymous Arabian sea captain, charting courses and describing the peoples and products of Arabia, Africa and India.

Among his discoveries in the eastern side of Africa is the city of Auxume (Axum), the capital of Abyssinia (Ethiopia). It is eight days' trek inland from the port of Aulis. The ruler of the Abyssinians, Zoscales, is described as 'mean in his way of life and with an eye on the main chance, but otherwise high-minded and skilled in Greek letters'.

Further south he describes ports in the horn of Africa, where the 'Cape of spices' acts as a transit port for cinnamon from south-east Asia. Traders apparently conceal the origin of the spice from customers, who believe it comes from Africa.

The author warns readers of the 'scoundrelly people', nomads who speak two languages, along the south Arabian coast. Mariners who fall into their hands are either plundered or carried into slavery. There are no harbours on this rocky and hazardous shoreline.

At the southern end of the Red Sea he encounters two kings who he calls the Myrrh King and the Frankincense King. The latter, Eleazus, runs the port of Cana where 'the incense is handled by royal slaves sent there as a punishment. The place is fearfully unhealthy, and pestilential even to those who sail past it. To those who work there it is always fatal; and in addition they are killed off by sheer lack of food.'

Off the tip of India lies what the author believes to be the biggest island in the world, Ceylon (Sri Lanka). It is troubled by frequent wars between Tamils and Ceylonese Buddhists who claim to possess one of the Buddha's teeth. In India the captain's eye was caught by ships from the Far East much larger than Roman vessels. They were powered by four sails instead of one, and according to what might be the captain's over-excited imagination, could be over 610 m (2,000 ft) long carrying 600–700 passengers and 900 tons (914 tonnes) of cargo.

Christians caught in wave of killings

Rome, AD 95

The emperor Domitian has executed his cousin Flavius Clemens, and exiled his niece Flavia Domitilla (Flavius' wife) for alleged atheism by converting to a foreign religion, believed to be Christianity. It is the latest and most extreme act in the emperor's crackdown on religions, not least because the couple had been nominated as his heirs.

Christians elsewhere are said to have been caught up in the persecution, partly because they are seen as a sect of the Jews, who are bearing the brunt of the emperor's anger. A devotee of Isis, Domitian has been antagonistic to Judaism for a decade, but his crackdown began in earnest five years ago when he reintroduced the dreaded trials for treason last used by Tiberius.

Several senior senators, including Frontinus and Agricola who had led successful campaigns in Britain, took early retirement rather than risk the emperor's ire. Among his more bizarre executions have been a beardless boy, killed because he looked like his teacher, the actor Paris; Senator Salvius Cocceianus because he celebrated the birthday of his paternal uncle, the former emperor Otho; Sallustius Lucullus, governor of Britain, because he allowed a new lance to be named after himself; and Junius Rusticus because he had described two Stoic philosophers as 'saintly'.

Domitian is known to have used torture to elicit confessions, including scorching prisoners' genitals or cutting off their hands. However, he has also cracked down on immorality, and has executed three offending Vestal Virgins. He worships Minerva, is building temples to Jupiter and restricting the spread of religions such as Judaism.

Church split by leadership row

Corinth, c. AD 96

The church in Corinth has been split by the election of a new group of leaders and the enforced resignation of their predecessors, although no charges of misconduct have been laid against them.

On hearing the news, one of the senior leaders in Rome, Clement, wrote a long letter exhorting the Corinthians to put aside jealousy and strife, ordering them to reinstate the previous leaders, and pleading with them to respect order and authority in the church.

The causes of the dispute are unclear. It may stem partly from the Jewish practice of electing administrative officials for a fixed term of office, which some Christians, who regard church leaders chiefly as administrators, believe should be continued. The dispute may also represent a clash of generations and theologies. The new leaders are younger and seem to prize the spontaneous charismatic ministries of preaching and prophecy above the regularand less flamboyant service of teaching and administering.

The letter, signed by Clement but apparently carrying the approval of the Roman congregations generally, appeals strongly to the ancient Scriptures, to the words of Jesus and the writings of Paul, and also draws on the liturgy, or service order, of the Roman church.

Christ, he says, appointed apostles, who in turn appointed presbyters and elders (he uses the titles interchangeably) and deacons in the churches they formed. They did so because they knew there would be arguments in the future over leadership roles. Leaders appointed by the apostles should only be replaced after they had died, he suggests.

'It will be no small sin on our part, if we depose from the episcopal

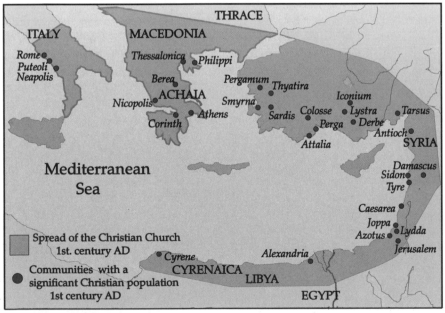

Christ Triumphant. This early Christian mosaic was found in a pre-Constantine necropolis excavated beneath the Basilica of St Peter in the Vatican, Rome. It shows Christ in classical pose on a victors chariot: his halo takes the form of the sun's rays.

office those who have in blameless and holy ways offered the gifts (i.e. led the communion service),' he writes.

Clement points to the 'Old Testament' as the basis of divine revelation. It looks forward to the life and teaching of Christ, who died for the redemption of those who believe in him. He adds that personal works for God are also an important element in the salvation process.

This is not the first time the Corinthian church has been rebuked for schism. There were sharp divisions, again largely over personalities, some 40 years ago. They caused the apostle Paul to write four letters and make several visits. The Corinthian church's response to Clement's letter is so far unknown.

What is sure, is that the church, despite persecution, is growing throughout the Roman world.

The spread of Christianity

THRACE

ITALY

MACEDONIA

Rome
Puteoli
Neapolis

Thessalonica
Philippi

Berea
Pergamum
Thyatira

ACHAIA
Nicopolis
Smyrna
Iconium

Athens
Sardis
Colosse
Lystra
Tarsus

Corinth
Perga
Derbe

Antioch

Attalia
SYRIA

Mediterranean
Sea

Damascus
Sidon
Tyre

Caesarea
Joppa
Azotus
Lydda

Jerusalem

Spread of the Christian Church
1st. century AD

Cyrene
Alexandria

Communities with a
significant Christian population
1st century AD

CYRENAICA
LIBYA

EGYPT

The spread of the Christian Faith.

By the end of the century Christianity had spread widely throughout the Roman empire. This map shows the areas and towns where incontrovertible evidence points to the establishment of significant communities of Christians. In some towns they would have been counted in their thousands. In some places persecution was severe; in others less so. Legend also attributes a much greater spread of the gospel: for instance, Thomas the disciple, is said to have evangelised coastal towns in India.

403

Index

412

Picture Credits

ALINARI-GIRAUDON: 11 ml, 16 – ANCIENT ART & ARCHITECTURE: Cover Ftl, 219, 220 mr, 248 br, 252 bl, 338, 354, 371, 376 tl, 389 – ARCHIV FÜR KUNST UND GESCHICHTE, BERLIN: 58 tl – JON ARNOLD: cover: Bt, Bbr, S, Ftcl, Ftcr, 6-7, 8-9, 10, 21 tr, 22 bc, 23, 27 bl, 31 bl, 35, 36, 38 tr, 38 bl, 39 mr, 40, 42, 43, 47, 52, 55, 56 tr, 56 ml, 63 mr, 64 ml, 68 bl, 69 t, 69 bc, 71 bc, 71 tr, 74 tc, 76 tl, 77, 78 ml, 80, 81, 82, 84 bl, 87, 88, 89, 97, 98 tc, 100, 102 br, 103 mr, 104 br, 106, 107, 108 ml, 108 mc, 109 tc, 109 br, 111 , 112 tc, 114 ml, 114 t, 115, 117, 118, 119, 126, 128 bc, 129, 131, 132 bc, 136 cr, 136 bc, 138, 142, 146 tl, 147 tc, 147 br, 150 ml, 150 tr, 153, 156, 158, 162, 171 tr, 171 ml, 172 mc, 174 tl, 175 ml, 176 tr, 179 tr, 180 tl, 188, 191 tl, 196 br, 199, 204 tl, 204 br, 210 tr, 212 bl, 218, 222, 227, 231 tr, 231 bc, 232 ml, 234, 236 bl, 240, 242 tl, 246 tr, 248 ml, 251 tr, 253 br, 255, 256 tl, 259 tc, 260, 261, 262 tr, 263, 265 tr, 266 tr, 270, 275 mr, 279, 280 mr, 280 bl, 284 tr, 284 br, 285 tr, 287, 289 ml, 289 br, 294 tl, 294 bc, 296 bl, 297 tr, 297 bc, 299 tl, 299 bc, 300 tl, 301, 302 ml, 302 tr, 304 tl, 306, 307, 308, 309 tr, 310 br, 310 tc, 311 tr, 312 br, 312 t, 313, 315 mr, 316, 317 ml, 320 tc, 320 b, 321, 322, 324, 326 br, 327, 329 bl, 331 tr, 331 bl, 333, 334, 335 tr, 335 bl, 336, 337, 341 tr, 341, 342 br, 344 bl, 344 tr, 345 mr, 346 ml, 346 tr, 349 bc, 350, 351, 352 bc, 353 tl, 353 mc, 355 tr, 355 ml, 356, 358, 359 ml, 359 br, 360, 361, 362tr, 364, 365, 367, 368, 370 tl, 370 bl, 372, 373, 375 tl, 375 mr, 376 mr, 378, 379, 381 bl, 384 bl, 385, 391 tr, 395 tl, 395 mr, 396, 399, 402 – ASHMOLEAN MUSEUM: 179 ml – AUSTRIAN ARCHEOLOGICAL INSITUTE/M. BIETAK: 62 mr – BIBLE SCENE SLIDES: Cover Bbc, 352 tr, 363 bc – BIBLE SOCIETY: 296 tr, 305, 309 ml, 317 br, 328 mr, 341 ml – BIRMINGHAM CITY ART GALLERY: 286 – LEE BOLTIN: 60 bl – BPK: 116 – BRIDGEMAN ART LIBRARY: 288, 290, 323 br, 389 – BRITISH FILM INSTITUTE:223 ml – THE BRITISH MUSEUM, PHOTOGRAPHIC DEPARTMENT: 93 br, 130, 143, 175 tr, 176 bl, 180 br, 183, 184 bc, 242 – BRITISH MUSEUM, LONDON/BRIDGEMAN ART LIBRARY, LONDON: 33 – BROOKLYN MUSEUM: 20 tc – HOWARD BIRCHMORE/BRUSHMARKS: 72, 122, 201 bl, 213, 314 – CHINA CULTURAL RELICS PROMOTION CENTER: 98 ml, 252 mr, 266 ml, 273 – MUSEE COGNACQ-JAY: 393 – COMSTOCK: 178 ml, 195 – DA VINCI MUSEUM: 15 mr – DRESDEN MUSEUM: 11 br – ALISTAIR DUNCAN - MIDDLE EAST ARCHIVE: 12 bc – TOR EIGELAND/SUSAN GRIGGS AGENCY: 140 – JOHN FULLEYLOVE: 41 tr, 44 lr, 78 tr, 79, 90, 148 ml, 161, 163 mc, 326 ml – GIRAUDON/BRIDGEMEN ART LIBRARY: 13 tl – RONALD GRANT ARCHIVE: 66, 68 tr, 73, 274, 318, 388 – SONIA HALLIDAY:13 bc, 65 tr, 169, 200 br, 257 ml, 258 mc, 258 tr, 291, 293, 302 bc, 330, 363 tl, 374br, 380, 384 tr, 387, 403 tr – PAUL HAMLYN PHOTOGRAPHIC ARCHIVES: 157 – ROBERT HARDING PICTURE LIBRARY: 18, 19 ml, 123 tl, 135 tl, 208 tl, 215, 357 bc, 362 bl, 369 – THE HERMITAGE MUSEUM: 41 bl – MICHAEL HOLFORD: 137 tr, 196 mc, 220 tl, 251 ml – DAVID HUGGETT: 102 tc, 144 tr – HUGHES-GILBEY: 230 tl – ISABELLA STEWART GARDNER MUSEUM: 304 br – MUSEE JACQUEMART-ANDRE: 345 bl – AUSTIN H. LAYARD: 152 bl, 166 bc, 187, 197 tr – MAGDALEN COLLEGE: 392 – SALLY MALTBY: 17, 19 tc, 22 tc, 27 tl, 34 m, 46, 63 tl, 74, 75 b, 83, 84 tl, 93 tl, 113, 114 br, 120, 124, 127 tl, 166 ml, tr, 184 ml, 193 br, 197 bl, 211, 228, 236 tl, 244, 271, 277 b, 278 tl, 281, 292 bl, 295 t, 300 br, 311 ml, 325, 366, 374 tl, 381 mr, 391 ml, 398, 403 – MANSELL COLLECTION: 382 – MAROON/ZEFA: 226 – LE MAS D'AGENAIS:342ml – MUSEE DU LOUVRE: 25 mr, 31 tc, 34 br, 39 bl, 44 tl, 45, 49 ml, 49 bc, 51, 53, 58 mr, 59, 60 tl, 61 tr, 62 bl, 67, 85 tr, 134, 145 bl, 160 ml, 160 tr, 165 tr, 165 ml, 168 tr, 172 tr, 181 mr, 203 tc, 203 bl, 207 tr, 207 bc, 207 mc, 209, 212 tc, 214, 221 tl, 237 tc, 237 mr, bl, 245 tl, 256 bc, 268, 283, 397 tc – MUSEUM OF FINE ARTS, BUDAPEST/BRIDGEMAN ART LIBRARY, LONDON: 303 – THE NATIONAL GALLERY: 94, 174 bc, 205 – OFFENTLICHE KUNSTSAMMLUNG: 105 mr – O'SHEA GALLERY, LONDON/BRIDGEMAN ART LIBRARY, LONDON: 14 t – PALESTINE INSTITUTE, PACIFIC SCHOOL OF RELIGION: 103 tl – PLANET EARTH PICTURES: – JOSEPHINE POWELL: 264 bl – PRIVATE COLLECTION: 25 tl, 57 ml, 125 mc, 295 bl, 343 – PRIVATE COLLECTION/BRIDGEMAN ART LIBRARY, LONDON: 229 – PUSHKIN MUSEUM: 223 – RIJKSMUSEUM: 198 – DAVID ROBERTS: 96, 348 – ROYAL COLLECTION ENTERPRISES: 12 tc – SAN MARCO CONVENT: 284 ml – SANT'APOLLINARE, RAVENNA/BRIDGEMAN ART LIBRARY, LONDON: 400 – SCALA:164 – STAEDELSCHES KUNSTINSTITUT: 95 – SOURCE UNKNOWN: 132 ml, 159, 401 – TATE GALLERY: 200 tl – TRUSTEES OF THE BRITISH MUSEUM: Cover: Bbl, Fbl, Fbc, Ftl, 24, 26, 28, 29, 32, 50, 54, 60 mr, 61 bl, 64 mr, 76 bc, 104 ml, 104 mr, 112 mr, 128 tl, 135 mc, 137 bc, 141, 144 mc, 148 tr, 154, 167, 168 bl, 170, 182, 186, 189, 193 bl, 225 mr, 230 mr, 257 tc, 280 tc, 282, 298, 319, 390 – JANE TAYLOR: Cover Fbr, 19 bc, 20 br, 21 mc, 58 bl, 65 ml, 85 bc, 86, 92, 97, 99, 101, 105 bl, 110, 127 tr, 133 tr, 133 ml, 139, 146 br, 149, 159, 163 ml, 173 ml, 191 mr, 194, 202, 217 bl, 217 tr, 224, 225 tl, 232 br, 233 tc, 233 ml, 235 br, 235 tl, 238, 239, 241 ml, 243, 245 br, 246 br, 247 tl, 247 bc, 247 tr, 249, 253 tl, 253 mc, 254, 259 bl, 264 tc, 265 ml, 267, 269, 275 tc, 276, 277 tc, 278 mr, 292 mr, 315 tl, 323 tc, 328 bl, 329 mr, 332, 339, 347, 357 tc, 370 mr, 377, 382 tl, 383 mc, 386, 397 ml – VICTORIA AND ALBERT MUSEUM: 121 – THE WALLACE COLLECTION: 48 – DAVID WAVRE: 57 br, 70, 98 br, 145 tl, 152 mr, 173 br, 181 tc, 192 ml, 192 br, 193 tr, 206, 208 bl, 210 bc, 216, 221 bl, 236 mr, 250 tc, 250 bl – MICHAEL & LUZZI WOLGENSINGER: 77, 155, 185, 241 br – YORK CITY ART GALLERY/BRIDGEMAN: 123 mr – ZEFA: 93, 177, 178 tr.

416